Conflict and Consensus in American Politics

Conflict and Consensus in American Politics

Stephen J. Wayne
Georgetown University

G. Calvin Mackenzie
Colby College

Richard L. Cole
University of Texas at Arlington

THOMSON ™

WADSWORTH

Australia · Brazil · Canada · Mexico · Singapore · Spain · United Kingdom · United States

Conflict and Consensus in American Politics
2006-2007 Election Update
Stephen J. Wayne, G. Calvin Mackenzie, Richard L. Cole

Executive Editor: Carolyn Merrill
Development Editor: Stacey Sims
Editorial Assistant: Patrick Rheaume
Senior Marketing Manager: Janise Fry
Marketing Assistant: Kathleen Tosiello
Marketing Communications Manager:
   Tami Strang
Senior Content Project Manager:
   Josh Allen

Print Buyer: Betsy Donaghey
Production Service: Newgen–Austin
Cover Designer: Brian Salisbury
Cover Image: Todd Gipstein/National Geographic/
   Getty Images
Compositor: Newgen–Austin
Printer: Transcontinental Printing/Interglobe
Design Background Art: age fotostock/Superstock;
   Stephanie Dalton Cowan/Getty Images

Thomson Higher Education
10 Davis Drive
Belmont, CA 94002-3098
USA

Printed in Canada
1 2 3 4 5 6 7 10 09 08 07 06

Library of Congress Control Number: 2006937839

ISBN 0-495-10443-4

Brief Contents

Contents

3 Federalism in Theory and in Practice   66

4 Issues of Freedom, Equity, and Justice   108

7 Political Parties 236

10 Congress   368

13 The Judiciary   496

14 Domestic Policy   532

15 International and National Security Policy 578

The Politics of American Democracy: An Introduction

Conflict and Consensus

The public response to Hurricane Katrina was overwhelming. Americans contributed their money and voluntary efforts to help those displaced by the storm and the flood in New Orleans that followed it. In the aftermath of the terrorist attacks of September 11, 2001, they did the same. In a crisis, people come together. They unify to meet the challenge. Partisan politics is suspended.

As people adjust to the new situation or revert to the old one and resume their daily lives, disagreements begin to surface. Most Americans believed that the response of local and national government to the September 11 attacks was appropriate, even heroic. Trust in government increased. However, the consensus of opinion to the Katrina response was just the opposite: most Americans believed that the federal, state, and local governments did too little, too late.[1] Almost immediately, the blame game, a favorite sport in Washington and one covered extensively by the news media, began. Democrats and some Republicans blamed the administration of President George W. Bush; the Bush administration blamed state and local governments; state and local government blamed the Federal Emergency Management Agency. Politics as usual had reemerged. So what's new?

Consensus and conflict are constant companions in American democracy. They are bedfellows. They coexist, sometimes easily and sometimes uneasily, with each other.

If you follow the news daily, you would think that conflict is the more dominant condition. The press thrives on reporting it—in elections, in government, among people, between politicians. On almost any subject, from the war in Iraq to U.S. policy in the Middle East, from the partial privatization of Social Security to the adequacy of the health care system, from the "No Child Left Behind" educational reforms of the Bush administration to its automobile and factory emission standards and its support for drilling for gas and oil in the Arctic National Wildlife Refuge, people disagree. Some would argue that conflict is precisely what politics is all about.

If politics is a struggle among people in their pursuit of differing beliefs and interests, it is also a struggle conducted on the basis of certain rules to which most agree. In other words, we agree to disagree but to do so according to the Constitution, law, and commonly accepted norms of behavior.

Conflict drives U.S. politics, but consensus underlies the system in which those politics occur. Conflict stems from social diversity; consensus from a shared experience. Conflict results from the differing priorities people place on their values, differing beliefs they have about what government should do, and differing economic, social, and political interests. Consensus stems from similar values, common beliefs, and overlapping interests people have to which American culture and history contribute.

This book is about how conflict and consensus coexist and interact in the politics of American democracy. It is about how and on what issues Americans differ and how and on what issues they agree. It is also about how that disagreement and agreement naturally and thankfully find their way into politics. We say *naturally* because people naturally differ in their goals, desires, and beliefs; we say *thankfully* because if conflict were not resolved by political decisions and actions, it might have to be settled by force. Thus, our title, *Conflict and Consensus in American Politics,* is also the basic theme of this book.

Theory and Practice

The coexistence of conflict and consensus also explains why American democracy differs in theory and in practice. In theory, democracy is guided by several fundamental principles, the most basic of which is the right of people to determine the purpose of their government, the form it takes, the people who run it, and the policy decisions they make.

The principles of American democracy are enunciated in the Declaration of Independence, the Constitution of 1787, and the Amendments to it. There are few Americans, if any, who oppose "Life, Liberty, and the pursuit of Happiness"; few, if any, who do not support the purposes of government as set forth in the preamble to the Constitution, "to form a more perfect Union, establish Justice, ensure domestic Tranquility; provide for the common defense, promote the general Welfare, and secure the Blessings of Liberty"; and few, if any, who object to the freedoms protected by the First Amendment: speech, press, religion, and the right of people to assemble and petition their government for grievances. The system of separate institutions, the division and sharing of powers, and the internal checks and balances are also supported by the vast majority and have been over the years, as evidenced by the absence of amendments to change the constitutional framework, modify its power arrangement, or eliminate or adjust the checks and balances.

But theory is also a goal, an ideal. Even if most Americans strive for the same or similar ideals, they may disagree about how to reach them: what power should be exercised, what policy decisions should be made, how those decisions should be made, and by whom.

It is important to be aware of the differences between the theory and the practice of American democracy. That is why we begin this book with a chapter on the theory of American democracy and devote most of the remaining chapters to its practice. To remind readers of the theory–practice connection to practically every aspect of American democracy, we also provide a short boxed discussion in every chapter on the theoretical roots of the democratic practices we discuss.

Although the gap between theory and practice is persistent, the system has undergone change, significant change. Politics and government have become more democratic. Whether that change is beneficial or harmful we leave to our readers to decide. Case studies at the beginning and the end of each chapter illustrate the theme of the chapter and provide a framework for judging how well the political system is functioning, whether practices conform to theory, and equally important, the extent to which these practices contribute to or detract from an efficient and effective political system today.

Democracy in the Twenty-First Century

The revolution in communications and other inventions and scientific discoveries have had a profound effect on the operation of politics and government. They have affected the information people receive, the impressions they form, the knowledge they retain, and the behavior in which they engage. There are new issues such as stem cell research and cloning, new diseases such as severe acute respiratory syndrome (SARS) and avian flu, and new threats such as international terrorism and nuclear proliferation—plus the older problems—all with more extensive consequences in an ever-shrinking world.

The relationship between the people and their government has undergone significant change, from when and how we vote, demonstrate, lobby, and communicate with those in power to how they communicate with us. The policy focus has changed as well. Fighting terrorism, protecting the environment, maintaining adequate energy resources, treating new diseases, and coping with what seems like an increasing number of major natural disasters, such as earthquakes, volcanoes, tsunamis, and violent hurricanes, are today's front-page stories. The weather has become a major item in the news.

We highlight some of these changes and their consequences for American democracy with boxes in each chapter. The boxes are intended to provide insight into how the politics of the twenty-first century is being affected by new communications technologies and by conditions and events that threaten the well-being of society and force those in positions of authority to act more quickly and decisively and to think outside the box.

The Challenge of American Democracy

Maintaining a vibrant democratic system, connecting practice to theory, and responding to the needs and potentialities of the twenty-first century requires an active and civic-minded population and a government responsive to that population's needs and hopes. That is where you come in. That is also where the authors of this book and you come together and engage in what we hope will be a common and exciting learning experience.

To put our cards on the table, we believe that politics is good, not bad. As the fuel that drives our system of government, politics is necessary. It doesn't create divisions within society as much as it reflects them. It is a vehicle for resolving conflict and doing so in a way that does not undercut the fabric of society and the bonds that unite us. That is why we stress the importance and legitimacy of politics under law throughout this book.

Our second belief follows from the first. If politics is the manner in which disagreements over competing values, beliefs, or limited resources are resolved, then *it is in everyone's interest to understand the way the system works and try to affect what is does.*

Just think for a moment about how government affects you today. The pills you take in the morning, even the vitamins, have been approved by the Food and Drug Administration (FDA); the food you eat has been inspected or grown according to rules specified by the Department of Agriculture; the water you drink has to meet minimum standards established by the Environmental Protection Agency (EPA); whether you are permitted to smoke in a café or restaurant has been decided by the relevant state or local authority. If you attend a state college, your tuition has been subsidized by taxpayer funds; the interest you pay on a student loan may also be supplemented by some government program. If you earn money as part of a work-study program, that, too, is supported by federal funds. Your living conditions are regulated by some government authority. If you have a disability, the school has an obligation to help you under the Americans with Disabilities Act, and your institution of higher learning could not and did not discriminate against your admission on the basis of your race or ethnicity.

We could go on, but you undoubtedly get the drift of our argument. Government *does* matter. It matters to you. So here's our challenge: Get involved. Make a difference. Make yours a better community and ours a stronger, more vibrant democracy. The truth is that people can and do influence who governs, when and how they make public policy decisions, and on what issues. You can be one of those people. Our objective in writing this book is to provide you with the information and incentive to do so.

Democracy works best when citizens take their responsibilities seriously. The torch of government is inevitably passed from generation to generation, but you can hasten that passage. You can make a difference and do so now.

Stephen J. Wayne
G. Calvin Mackenzie
Richard L. Cole

| Notes |

[1]David W. Moore, "Public Skeptical New Orleans Will Recover," Gallup Poll, September 7, 2005, http://www.gallup.com/poll/ default.aspx?ci=18412. "Two-In-Three Critical of Bush's Relief Efforts," Pew Research Center for the People and the Press, September 8, 2005, http://people-press.org/reports/display.php3?ReportID=255.

About the Authors

Stephen J. Wayne (Ph.D., Columbia University) is a professor of government at Georgetown University. A Washington, D.C.–based "insider" for almost 40 years, Wayne has written or edited 10 books, many in multiple editions, and has authored more than 100 articles, chapters, and reviews that have appeared in professional journals. His best known works include *The Road to the White House*, soon to be published in its eighth edition; *Presidential Leadership* (with George C. Edwards); and *The Legislative Presidency*. Professor Wayne lectures widely at home and abroad to international visitors, college students, federal executives, and business leaders. He has testified before Congress on the subject of presidential elections and governance and before the Democratic Party and Republican Party advisory committees on the presidential nomination processes. Professor Wayne has been a past president of the National Capital Area Political Science Association and a founder and president of the Presidency Research Group.

G. Calvin Mackenzie is the Goldfarb Family Distinguished Professor of Government at Colby College. He is a graduate of Bowdoin College and has a Ph.D. in government from Harvard. Mackenzie is the author or editor of more than a dozen books on American government, including *The Politics of Presidential Appointments, The House at Work, America's Unelected Government, The In-and-Outers, The Irony of Reform and Bucking the Deficit, Innocent until Nominated,* and *Scandal Proof: Can Ethics Laws Make Government Ethical?* Mackenzie has been a consultant to Congress and to several federal departments and has been a participant in the work of many national reform commissions. His own public service includes stints as chairperson of Maine's Board of Arbitration and Conciliation, as chairperson of Maine's Commission on Governmental Ethics and Election Practices, and as a soldier with the First Cavalry Division in Vietnam. In 1999 and 2000 he was the John Adams Fellow at the Institute of United States Studies at the University of London, and in 2005 he was a Fulbright professor in the People's Republic of China.

Richard L. Cole (Ph.D., Purdue University) is Dean of the School of Urban and Public Affairs at the University of Texas, Arlington, where he is also a professor specializing in American government, public policy, and federalism. A former Fulbright scholar in Great Britain, he has lectured widely in the United States and abroad on issues of American government and federal relations. He is a former president of the Southwest Political Science Association and has served terms as an executive council member for the Federalism and Intergovernmental Relations Section of the American Political Science Association. He serves on the editorial board of several journals, including *Publius: The Journal of Federalism.* Dr. Cole's numerous published articles have appeared in the *American Political Science Review,* as well as most regional journals in political science. Dr. Cole has been recognized as a "distinguished graduate" by the School of Liberal Arts, Purdue University, and by the College of Arts and Sciences, the University of North Texas.

Reviewers

1

Conflict and Consensus in American Politics: An Introductory Discussion

Introduction

THERE IS NOT A DAY that goes by without some disagreement being reported in the news. The president suggests a plan to partially privatize the Social Security system; the American Association of Retired Persons (AARP), organized labor, and most members of the opposition party object. Congress considers limits on medical malpractice suits; the insurance industry supports the limits, but trial lawyers and public interest groups oppose them. Florida courts refuse to intervene in the case of a brain-damaged woman who has been in a vegetative state for 15 years; Congress enacts legislation that requests federal courts to intervene, the president rushes back to the White House from his home in Texas to sign the law, but the judiciary refuses to get involved. Oregon voters support a ballot initiative to permit doctor-assisted suicide. The Attorney General of the United States, John Ashcroft, threatens to prosecute Oregon doctors who prescribe a lethal dosage of a controlled substance. The Supreme Court rules in 2006 that the Attorney General does not have the authority to carry out his threat.

President Lawrence Summers listens to Harvard faculty debate his remarks about women scientists.

It would seem that Americans disagree about practically everything. But they don't. Most Americans agree to disagree, as long as that disagreement occurs within the framework of the law. There is also agreement on the need for a government to make and enforce the law, on the need for a government that rests on popular consent, on the right of citizens to choose their public officials, and even on the processes for choosing them.

In other words, **conflict** and **consensus** are constant bedfellows in a democratic society. They coexist, sometimes easily and sometimes uneasily with one another. Each justifies the need for the other. Conflict sharpens differences; consensus clouds them. Conflict reflects and stems from social diversity; consensus provides bonds that hold people together. For example, Americans value individualism and personal freedom even though conflict often results from the exercise of that freedom.

Here is another example. Americans believe that they have a right to express their own beliefs and opinions, but when Harvard President Lawrence Summers speculated that women do not pursue careers in the math and sciences as frequently as men do because of "intrinsic aptitude" differences, he unleashed a torrent of criticism and a no-confidence vote by the Harvard Arts and Sciences faculty. Should Summers have expressed in a public forum such a controversial view that men may be naturally superior to women in math and science? What if he used race or ethnicity as a criterion for distinguishing people's innate abilities? Would he have been called a bigot?

Summers was not fired—nor was Colorado professor Ward Churchill, who compared the victims of the September 11 terrorist attacks to Nazis who blindly followed an ideology that justified inequality and contributed to human suffering. Should Summers and

Churchill have been fired for speaking their minds, for expressing unpopular, and what many would regard as untrue, beliefs? Their respective Boards of Trustees said "no," although Summers subsequently resigned.

Where do conflict and consensus play out in America's democratic political system? The answer is in politics. This book, *Conflict and Consensus in American Politics*, is all about politics: how it works within a democratic system, how politics affects government, how government makes policy, how that policy affects people in their daily lives, and how that effect generates additional conflict (and perhaps consensus) within the political system.

In this chapter we examine the theory of the politics of American democracy; in subsequent chapters we look at its practice. A gap naturally exists between theory and practice, between the ideal and the actual. People tend to agree more on basic principles than they do on the application of those principles, particularly when that application adversely affects them.

Questions to Ponder

- What is politics, and why does it naturally occur?
- What role does government play in structuring political activity and resolving political disputes?
- How does a democratic political system differ from a nondemocratic one?
- What are the basic components of a democratic government, and how do they work?
- Does the Constitution contribute to or detract from American democracy?

American Political Beliefs

America is a diverse society and proud of it. It is a country of about 300 million people who have come from every continent over a period of more than 400 years to live, work, and enjoy the political and economic benefits of a free and democratic society. That enjoyment has not been equally shared by everyone who came to America. Slaves did not travel to the American colonies and states of their own free will, and most remained in bondage until the Civil War. Inequalities still exist. Throughout this book we will discuss these inequities, how and why they developed, and what can and should be done about them.

Diversity is a source of strength, but it is also a source of conflict. The strength comes from the differing intellectual, economic, and cultural heritage that people have brought with them to the United States, which becomes assimilated into the society and, in the process, produces a shared American experience. Conflict springs from differences in backgrounds, lifestyles, and aspirations. In a society in which there are limited resources and competing values and goals, conflict is inevitable. However, the greater the diversity of the society, the more likely conflict will occur within it. Table 1.1 indicates how diverse the United States is today. Table 1.2 gives some idea, based on immigration trends, of how diverse it will be in future years.

Table 1.1 United States: Vital Statistics

	Yesterday (1990) (%)	Today (2005) (%)	Tomorrow (2010) (%)
GENDER			
Male	52.2	49.0	49.1
Female	47.8	51.0	50.9
RACE			
White	87.9	76.7	79.3
Black	11.6	12.1	13.1
Other	.5	11.2	7.6
Two or More		2.0	
Some Other Race		1.0	
Asian/Pacific Islander		4.4	
American Indian/Alaska Native		.9	
AGE			
Under 15	34.5	21.0	20.1
15–24	19.6	13.5	13.9
25–44	28.1	28.4	26.8
45–64	13.7	25.0	26.2
65+	4.1	12.1	13.0
SIZE OF AVERAGE HOUSEHOLD	4.6	2.4	

Source: "Demographic Trends in the 20th Century," United States Census Bureau, November 2002. http://www.census.gov/prod/2002pubs/censr-4.pdf (accessed April 15, 2005). Data for 2005 from the 2005 American Community Survey conducted by the Census Bureau. http://www.factfinder.census.gov/survlet/ADPTable?_bm=y&_geo_id=01000US&ds_name=ACS_2005 (accessed October 25, 2006).

Table 1.2 A Nation of Immigrants

	1990	2005
FOREIGN-BORN POPULATION	19.8 million (7.9%)	35.8 million (12.44%)
Naturalized Citizens	8.0 million (40.5%)	13.9 million (47.3%)
World Regions of Birth		
Latin America		53.3%
South and East Asia		23.4%
Middle East		3.4%
Other		19.9%

continued

Table 1.2   *continued*

	1990	2005
PERCENTAGE OF FOREIGN BORN FROM TOP FIVE COUNTRIES		
Mexico		30.7%
China		3.4%
Philippines		4.5%
India		3.9%
Vietnam		3.0%

Source: Per Hispanic Center Tabulations of 2000 and 2005 American Community Survey. October 17, 2006. www.pewresearch.org/reports/?ReportID=61 (accessed October 25, 2006).

consensus

An agreement on values, norms, and goals; developed on the basis of shared background and experience.

conflict

A disagreement over values, norms, and goals; results from struggle to pursue one's interests.

The next section of this chapter illustrates the political **consensus** and **conflict** that exist in the United States today. The consensus stems from a common set of values and beliefs. The conflict results from the priorities attached to them, the means of pursuing them, and the unequal political, economic, and social consequences that result from that pursuit.

Basic Values and Beliefs

Political Rights   For Thomas Jefferson and other signers of the Declaration of Independence, "Life, Liberty and the Pursuit of Happiness" were considered basic human rights that could not be taken or even given away. The purpose of government was to protect these rights. When it failed to do so—the claim the American colonists directed at King and Parliament—the people who supported the American Revolution contended that they had the right to establish a new government that would serve their needs, respond to their interests, and uphold their values. In making this argument, Jefferson and his colleagues were restating the philosophic argument of John Locke, an eminent British philosopher, and using it to support their rights as Englishmen.

personal liberty

The freedom to pursue one's values and interests; doing what one wants when one wants to.

Let's explore those rights. Life is obviously a prerequisite for all else. The right to **personal liberty** is the freedom to pursue one's desires. Slaves were not free to do so. They lacked personal liberty. Although liberty is a necessary condition for achieving happiness, the exercise of freedom—doing what you want when you want to—is not absolute because one person's freedom can directly or indirectly impinge on another's. Your freedom to smoke interferes with your neighbor's desire to breathe smoke-free air; your freedom to listen to music loudly interferes with someone's desire for quiet.

The exercise of liberty results in unequal consequences: someone gains, someone loses. Take the proposal to limit medical malpractice suits. The insurance industry and health-care providers would benefit under such an arrangement, but those who suffer from medical malpractice, the victims, and those who represent them, the trial lawyers, would lose. President George W. Bush and his Republican backers see such limits on suits as necessary to reduce the high cost of health care; Democratic opponents see them as unfair because they deny patients their right to fair and just compensation if they are poorly treated by a physician. Another example concerns campaign contributions. Should wealthy people have the right to spend their own resources as they see fit in a political campaign? Congress says no. It has enacted legislation that limits the amount of money that Americans can contribute to candidates for national office, but the Supreme Court has declared that individuals and groups can spend as much as they desire so long as they do so independently of the candidates and their parties. But doesn't the Supreme Court's decision also reduce the control that candidates and parties can exercise over their own campaigns? Is that right?

The expenditure of personal wealth can conflict with a second basic democratic value, that of **political equality.** When Jefferson wrote that "all men are created equal," he was expressing the belief that all human lives must be considered of equal worth, although in practice most people in the colonies at that time (women, slaves, Native Americans, and non-Christians) were not treated as equals. His words, which were designed to support the claim that the American colonists had been unjustly denied the rights of Englishmen, have subsequently been used by many groups that allege that their rights have also been denied.

political equality
A principle based on the belief that everyone in society has equal worth, should have equal voting power, and is equal under law.

Although Jefferson presented a theoretical argument in the Declaration of Independence, the principle of political equality has become an operative norm in American society, incorporated into the law of the land through the Fifth and Fourteenth Amendments to the Constitution. Due process of law, equal protection of the laws, and equal opportunity under law are now recognized as legal principles, derived from the concept of political equality and firmly embedded in America's living Constitution. The principle of political equality does not stipulate that everyone has equal abilities or resources; obviously, they don't. What it does prescribe is that everyone's abilities and resources, whatever they may be, are equally valuable and, therefore, must be considered in the making of public policy.

People's abilities and resources vary, putting the exercise of liberty (doing what you want with your resources) and the maintenance of equality (exerting equal influence on public policy) in conflict with each other. That conflict cannot be eliminated without destroying liberty or perpetuating inequality, but it can and must be resolved on an issue-by-issue basis for the benefit of society. President George W. Bush and some of his Republican backers want to eliminate the taxes on the estates of people who die. They argue that income and investments that contribute to the estate have already been taxed. Why do it again? That's unfair! Eliminating the estate tax, however, not only reduces income the government receives, thereby representing an additional burden on all of society, but also perpetuates inequality over generations. Is that fair? Do those born to low-income families have the same opportunities in education and business as those born to the wealthy? In theory they may, but in practice most do not. What is in the best interest of the entire society? How can and should individual freedom and political equality be balanced?

common good
That which benefits society as a whole.

This brings us to a third basic democratic value: the **common good.** In addition to the rights people have as individuals, there is a collective right, one that pertains to the well-being of society. Were we all hermits, there might not be a collective good except that of being left alone. But we live with others within a **community.** In a democracy, the community has value.

community
The collectivity of people living within a specified area; people who share a common history and culture.

How can individual and collective values be protected and preserved? Here is where **government** comes in. The purpose of government is to make **authoritative decisions** on public policy, decisions that it has the power to make and enforce. But government needs to do so in a way that balances individual values with common good and continually resolves the tension between them.

government
The formal institutions that have the authority to make, implement, and adjudicate public policy.

Consider admission to college. In a country that protects individual liberty, every person should be able to apply and potentially be admitted to whatever school that individual wishes to attend. But should colleges and universities also have the freedom to admit whomever they want and on the basis of whatever criteria they wish to establish? Should they be able to give sons and daughters of their alumni an advantage in the admissions process, even if those alumni children are less qualified academically than others who may be rejected? Should colleges and universities be able to give special preference to minority or international students in the interests of creating a diverse student body? The Supreme Court has said that they may do so. However, they cannot do so by establishing quotas for minorities.[1] Nor can they reject applicants on the basis of race, religion, ethnicity, or, in some states, sexual orientation; that would constitute discrimination, which in turn violates the principle of equal protection of the laws.

authoritative decisions
Decisions made by public officials that have the force of law.

Although Americans believe in both personal liberty and political equality in theory, they argue over them in practice. They support the idea that everyone should have equal opportunity to succeed, but some people do not want opportunities for others to come at their own expense. Affirmative action programs provide specific opportunities for people whose race, ethnicity, or gender has been subject to past discrimination. These programs have generated considerable controversy because they represent a fundamental clash between the priorities attached to the two basic values of liberty and equality. Which of the two is more important? The answer depends on personal philosophy and personal economic and social conditions. Those who support affirmative action programs in hiring, promotion, and university admissions argue that the achievement of genuine equality of opportunity requires policies designed to compensate for past discriminatory practices. Others, however, contend that giving women and minorities an advantage discriminates against people who do not fall into these categories.[2]

economic liberty
The freedom to purpose one's financial self-interests.

Economic Rights   Americans believe not only in political liberty but also in **economic liberty,** the right of individuals to pursue their self-interest. For many, the pursuit of happiness involves the possession, protection, and preservation of **private property.** John Locke, the English political philosopher whose ideas shaped the Declaration of Independence, argued that the protection of property was a fundamental obligation of government. Without a rule of law in which life and property could be protected, people would have to be constantly on guard to protect themselves, their families, and their possessions from those who threaten them. Although Jefferson's use of the phrase "Pursuit of Happiness" broadens the ends to which government serves, it does not diminish the right to own private property or the government's duty to protect it.

Taken to its extreme, however, a person's pursuit of private property could lead to a situation in which a relatively small number of people reap a relatively large portion of the economic benefits. Such a system, in which wealth is concentrated in the hands of a few, could become uncompetitive, unproductive, and unstable over time. Therefore, the government may need to regulate economic activity to prevent individuals and groups from monopolizing the means of production and distribution within a society. The ownership of the mass media is a case in point. If one corporation were to dominate the media outlets in a particular region, then people might be exposed to only one source of news—hardly a desirable outcome for a nation that prides itself on its free and competitive press and a thorough discussion of the issues.

Competition is the fuel that drives the **free enterprise system.** It is the principal motivation for improving goods and services so that someone can profit from them. That improvement benefits society, according to Adam Smith, an eighteenth-century British economist. In his classic study, *The Wealth of Nations,* Smith contended that "an invisible hand" guides the self-interested behavior of people in a way that promotes the general welfare of society as a whole. Thus, according to Smith's theory, individual initiative in the pursuit of private interests invigorates and improves the economy for the entire community. Those at the lower end of the socioeconomic scale, however, often have difficulty seeing how their interests are enhanced when the rich grow richer and are able to use their wealth to maintain their economic, social, or political advantages. The tax cuts proposed by President Bush and enacted by Congress in 2001 are a case in point. People in the upper-income brackets received the largest benefits, thereby prompting critics of the law to raise the equity issue.[3] The administration also used the fairness argument in its response to these critics: Shouldn't people who pay the most taxes be entitled to the largest cuts? Government constantly has to balance the demands of individuals with the needs of society.

The principle of equality is difficult to apply in a free-enterprise, private-ownership economic system. It does not require everyone to possess equal material resources, but it does require people to have a realistic chance of pursuing and achieving their economic goals. They must have **equal opportunity** to do so. "No child left behind," the slogan and rationale of President George W. Bush's educational initiative, was based on the principle that everyone should have an equal opportunity to succeed. To do so, elementary and secondary schools, particularly in low-income areas, had to be improved. But because most school funding

private property
The right to own land and other commodities of value.

free enterprise system
A competitive economic system in which people are encouraged to pursue material self-interests and the market determines their success or failure.

equal opportunity
The principle that all people should have an equal chance to pursue their goals and achieve them in the political, economic, and social systems.

comes from property taxes, how can schools in low-income districts compete with those in higher-income areas unless they receive additional financial aid? It was this dilemma that prompted the Bush administration to use financial incentives to motivate all public schools to improve their performance. But if all students improve their performance, the gap between the best and the worse might persist and could even widen.

The ideal of equality of opportunity and the reality in which people find themselves often vary significantly. For years discriminatory practices prevented certain people from achieving their full economic potential. As a consequence, laws have been enacted to end discrimination on the basis of race, ethnicity, gender, age, disability, and sexual orientation. However, in practice it is often difficult for people to prove that they have suffered discrimination because of their race, ethnicity, or gender. Some people simply work harder and are more talented than others.

And what about the advantages that inheritance, family and social contacts, and income give some and not others? Should they continue to exist? The debate over the taxation of estates relates partly to how these questions are answered.

In short, the tension between economic liberty and economic equality is similar to the tension that exists between political liberty and political equality. People value both economic liberty and economic equality but prioritize them differently. Sometimes that prioritization is based on the economic situation in which people find themselves, such as when poor people tend to favor a greater sharing of wealth. At other times, it is based on a structure of beliefs formed over the years, such as the belief that individual initiative and effort should be rewarded, not discouraged, by economic incentives and the companion belief that those initiatives and efforts have benefited society.

Consensus, Conflict, and Apathy

People tend to agree on basic values, be they political or economic, but disagree on the priorities attached to each, the best ways to achieve each, and the role of government in promoting and protecting these values. As noted previously, political consensus in the United States embraces the desire for a government, based on popular consent, in which the people choose public officials and hold them accountable for their decisions and actions in office. That consensus extends to a body of established rules and procedures by which politics and government operate, the so-called rules of the game, framed by the Constitution, enumerated by law, and stabilized and hallowed by the American political tradition. It also extends to the capitalist economic system, including the value of competition, opportunities for exercising individual initiative, and the desirability of private ownership. President George W. Bush often uses the words "ownership society" and "personal investment accounts" to characterize the desire of most Americans to own their businesses, houses, and savings and pass them on to their spouse and children.

The pursuit of individual goals and the beliefs that underlie them, however, often lead to conflict in public policy, conflict on such issues as abortion, doctor-assisted suicide, teaching evolution in public schools, the use of public property to display religious symbols and or permit religious practices, and even whether states should permit much less recognize marriages between two people of the same sex.

On many of these issues, people who feel most strongly become the most involved. They actively campaign for certain candidates and are more likely to turn out and vote for them; they lobby public officials, communicating to them by writing a letter or sending an e-mail, making a telephone call, or attending a public forum or town meeting. They participate in or are attentive to the public debate.

Those who do not feel as strongly, who do not see the difference it will make to them in how the issue is resolved, or who believe that whatever they do or say will make no difference tend to sit on the sidelines. On most issues for most of the time, the general public is not involved. Occasionally, however, an issue will capture people's attention. Threats to the nation's security, such as domestic terrorism; to its prosperity, such as a recessed economy; or to its social fabric, such as changing social mores on marriage, will energize more people because the issue hits home. But these are exceptions to the rule that for most issues only a small portion of the population is knowledgeable and becomes involved. Tort reform, bankruptcy rules, telecommunications policy, intelligence integration, and nuclear waste affect different professions and industries and the groups that represent them but not most people most of the time. Even in elections, a large portion of the population does not follow the campaign, does not inform itself on the major issues, and does not vote.

Is it unhealthy for a democracy to have relatively few people involved on most issues? Those who answer "yes" point out that apathy increases the likelihood that a well-organized, well-financed interest group can get its way. The plight of consumers in the United States before the government instituted and enforced health and safety standards, such as warning labels for cigarettes or certification for drugs, is an example of how even a majority can suffer when it is unorganized or uninvolved. A silent or inattentive majority can pose a threat to the democratic character of the political process.

However, if most issues excited most people most of the time, society would be in constant turmoil. Compromise would be even more difficult to achieve than it already is, and public officials would be pushed and pulled in almost every direction and, perhaps, unable to act or able to make only minor changes in existing policy. In all likelihood, overall public support for government and law would be weakened because many people who feel strongly about issues would not get their way.

A vibrant and stable democracy needs both consensus and conflict. Some people, preferably not the same ones on every issue, must be well informed and actively involved. Most people must support the system and abide by the decisions that government officials make and the policies that emanate from those decisions, even though they may not benefit directly from them or perceive their effects in the course of their daily lives.

The strength of the American system is that it permits those who are interested to participate and to pursue their own interests and support their own beliefs. It also gives the general citizenry many opportunities to do so, through periodic elections and ongoing efforts to influence public officials on issues of public policy. The maintenance of a free and critical press alerts the public to contemporary controversies and provides information about what government is doing about them.

In the next section we explain how that system works in theory and how the various pieces fit together to form a democratic government.

The Theory of American Democracy

The Role of Politics

Despite the consensus in America on the need for government in general and on the democracy in particular, differences of opinion persist over what government should do, how it should do it, and for whose benefit and at whose expense it should be done. These differences constitute the sources of and motivation for political activity; they are the basis of politics. If **politics** consists of struggles by individuals and groups in pursuit of their own interests and goals, then practically everything government does, every action it takes, is the result of political activity of one kind or another.

Today, the word *politics,* like **politician,** is often used disparagingly. Candidates for public office who accuse their opponents of "playing politics" imply that they are acting primarily to promote themselves or the special interests of a particular group, not the public good. In every election campaign, the promises that candidates make to their constituents to garner votes—to improve government by reducing its costs and increasing its benefits—make them sound like "typical politicians People believe that politicians will tell voters what they want to hear, not what they actually will do in office.[4]

Originally, however, the term *politics* had a positive meaning. The modern word is derived from the Greek word *polis,* roughly translated as "city-state." In ancient Greece the polis, an independent city and the land that surrounded it, formed the basic unit of political organization. Early Greek philosophers such as Plato and Aristotle believed that loyalty to a polis was part and parcel of being human; Aristotle referred to the citizens of a city-state as "political animals." In these small communities, citizens engaged in face-to-face discussions of issues; they deliberated and then made decisions on the basis of their discussion.

In the ancient world, politics was the process by which the community decided what to do. Politics involves that same process today. Even though contemporary society has become larger and more complex, so has politics. But politics is still the means through which "who gets what, when, and how" is determined.[5] It is still fundamental to the operation of government.

Politics occurs in many forms: the selection of public officials, the pressures by outside groups on those in government, the compromises among policymakers in government, the way in which the laws are implemented, and even the

politics
A struggle by individuals and groups to achieve certain ends; "who gets what, when, and how."

politician
A person who views the struggle for power within the political system as a profession or calling; one who seeks elective office.

Gathering of the Areopagus, a deliberative court that met in the open air, in ancient Athens.

judiciary's interpretation of those laws. Although politics sometimes leads to excesses and abuses, it is neither pernicious nor dangerous in and of itself. Insofar as politics facilitates the expression and resolution of disagreement, it is essential to the health and well-being of a democratic society.

Politics is both a means to an end and an end in itself. It is a means in that it gives people opportunity and methods to advance their own interests in a manner that is not harmful to society. They do so by influencing the election of people to office and the actions the officeholders take while they are there. It is an end in that it links citizens to their government and guides that government as it goes about its business.

Politics can occur within all types of political systems. It is not unique to a democratic form of government, but it does flourish in such a system. It structures and encourages political activities. As we said at the beginning of this chapter, it is the fuel that fires the democratic system and that keeps it running. So that you understand the relationship of politics to democratic government, we must first explain what a democracy is and how it is designed to work.

The Relationship Between the People and Their Government

democracy

A system of government in which the people rule directly or indirectly.

direct democracy

A system in which the people as a collectivity decide on public policy; examples include town meetings and ballot initiatives.

A **democracy** is a political system in which the people rule. If they were to do so directly, as in the Greek city-states, every adult would be able participate in all public policy decisions. The democracy would be direct. The people would be the decision makers.

In a country of about 300 million people, a system of **direct democracy** is neither feasible nor desirable on a national level. It is not feasible because there are too many people to deliberate on policy matters; it would take them too long to do so; and it would turn decision making into such an arduous process that few decisions would be made and fewer still would be made in a deliberative manner.[6] It is also not desirable because most people lack the time, interest, and knowledge to participate effectively in public policy decision making. As we noted previously, people tend to be indifferent to issues that do not directly concern them. Most lack the incentive to become involved, to inform themselves, to stay focused on the issues, to understand the complexities of policy, to take a long-term perspective, and to profit from the deliberation and compromises that result in wise policy judgments.

There are some examples of direct democracy in America, but they occur at the state or local level. In some states, certain policy issues may be put to a vote in the form of initiatives or referenda on a general ballot. In 2004, people in eleven states were asked to vote on the issue of marriage, specifically, whether it should only involve a man and a woman.[7] In two states, the medical use of marijuana was put to a vote.[8]

Cities also hold elections on public projects, such as whether to levy a tax or provide public funds for a sports stadium. George W. Bush participated in a form of direct democracy when he was a managing partner of the Texas Rangers baseball team. He and his supporters mounted a successful drive to convince voters in Arlington, Texas, to support a tax that would pay two-thirds of the cost of a new baseball stadium.

Another form of direct democracy is the town meeting. Some local towns, especially those concentrated in New England, have a long tradition of conducting their business in meetings in which any resident can participate.

representative democracy

A system of government in which citizens choose others to represent them in the formulation and execution of public policy.

The larger the scale, the more difficult it is to practice direct democracy. That is one reason **representative democracy** exists. In this form of government, the people choose public officials to represent them. Representative democracy is preferable to direct democracy partly because it results in the selection of people who have an interest in public policy and service and who presumably have the skills and will have the incentive for acquiring the knowledge and spending the time they will need to make informed policy judgments.

The idea of representation is based on the belief that people in government can adequately and fairly reflect the views of those outside it. But representation is not easy. Opinion is usually divided. When there is not a consensus, to whom should representatives look for guidance—the majority, a plurality, or those most affected by the issue? Should the intensity with which a group supports a particular policy, such as the National Rifle Association on gun ownership or the American Medical Association on smoking, be considered? And to what extent should people in government rely on their professional judgment, personal values, or partisan political position in making policy decisions? Should they act as delegates of the people or trustees for them?

In theory, the more the government reflects the composition of a society, the better able it will be to make, implement, and adjudicate policy in a manner that meets the desires and needs of that society. Can a legislative body with only a handful of women be responsive to the needs of a society in which more than 50 percent of the population are women? If African Americans, Hispanics, or another racial or ethnic group are underrepresented in government, can they receive fair treatment from that government? Take the 109th Congress, for example. Table 1.3 compares its demographic breakdown to the United States as a whole.

A related representational issue stems from unequal resources. Some groups, by virtue of their size, wealth, leadership, or organization, may exercise, or at least appear to exercise, a disproportionate degree of influence. After the collapse of the Enron Corporation, for example, it was revealed that company officials had used their connections with top government officials over the years to gain special favors from the government, such as tax breaks, access to new markets, and regulatory exemptions. And Enron was not alone. Most major corporations, labor unions, trade and professional associations, and issue-oriented groups spend large sums of money trying to influence the outcome of elections and the scope and content of government decisions and the product of those decisions—public policy. And they are not alone. Foreign governments and multinational corporations spend millions hiring American lobbyists to represent their interests and American public relations firms to present their policy positions and goals in the most favorable light. Do such actions cross the line? Should U.S. laws permit such activity by foreigners? Does the United States try to exert similar influence on other countries, such as Iraq or China?

Table 1.3 **Demography of the Voting-Age Population and Elected Officials at the Turn of the Century, 2000 and 2006**

	Country (%)	Congress (%)		State Legislatures (%)
GENDER		House	Senate	
Male	47.9	86.1 (84.6)*	87.0 (86)	78.0 (77)
Female	52.1	13.5 (15.4)	13.0 (14)	22.0 (23)
RACE				
White	83.3	91.0 (85.5)	100.00 (97.0)	89.0 (80.3)
Black	11.9	8.9 (9.2)	0 (1.0)	8.0 (19.7)
Hispanic	10.6	5.0 (5.3)	0 (2.0)	3.0 NA

*Parentheses indicate actual percentages in 2006.

Source: *Statistical Abstract of the United States: 2004–2005*. United States Census Bureau, November 2004, pp. 250, 254, 255. Updated by authors.

The allegation that special interests exercise undue influence over election outcomes and government decisions is one of the most persistent public complaints about the way American government works. But what is the alternative? Restricting the use of private resources flies in the face of political liberty, and putting no limits on the use of economic resources gives advantage to the wealthy.

Review Questions

1. Political conflict in the United States exists primarily because American society is

   A. Middle class
   B. Diverse
   C. Homogeneous
   D. Large

2. To which of the following basic rights do most Americans subscribe?

   A. Individual liberty
   B. Economic equality
   C. American exceptionalism
   D. Religious fundamentalism

3. Conflict over public policy is usually resolved by

   A. Elections
   B. Governmental decisions
   C. Political parties
   D. The private sector

4. The vitality of a democratic society hinges on

   A. The ability of people to participate in the political process
   B. A well-educated and well-informed public
   C. An unbiased news media
   D. Civility in political discourse

Answers:

   1. B
   2. A
   3. B
   4. A

Conflict and Consensus in Review

In short, the theory of American democracy is not particularly controversial for most Americans. People want the opportunity to affect politics and government even though they do not exercise this opportunity much of the time. According to a survey conducted by the Pew Research Center

continued

for the People and the Press, Americans also believe that politics has become more partisan and that politicians lose touch with people pretty quickly.[9] On values such as the importance of religion, the power of personal initiative, and the need to protect the environment, people agree. On how to achieve these values, on what role the government should play in this effort, and on what policies should be formulated and implemented, they disagree.[10] Interestingly, this disagreement was not primarily partisan in nature but rather different views on the merits of different policies.

The consensus-conflict dichotomy extends to the structure and operation of government itself. It is to that subject that we now turn.

Components of Democratic Government

A democratic government functions within a political system. It receives inputs, directly and indirectly from the people, parties, and the groups that reflect and represent their interests. It converts those inputs within an operating mechanism composed of rules, structures, and procedures into outputs that take the form of public policy. That policy, in turn, affects society, generating new inputs for government, pressures on it, and evaluations of it. (See Figure 1.1.)

Figure 1.1 **The Politics of American Democrary**

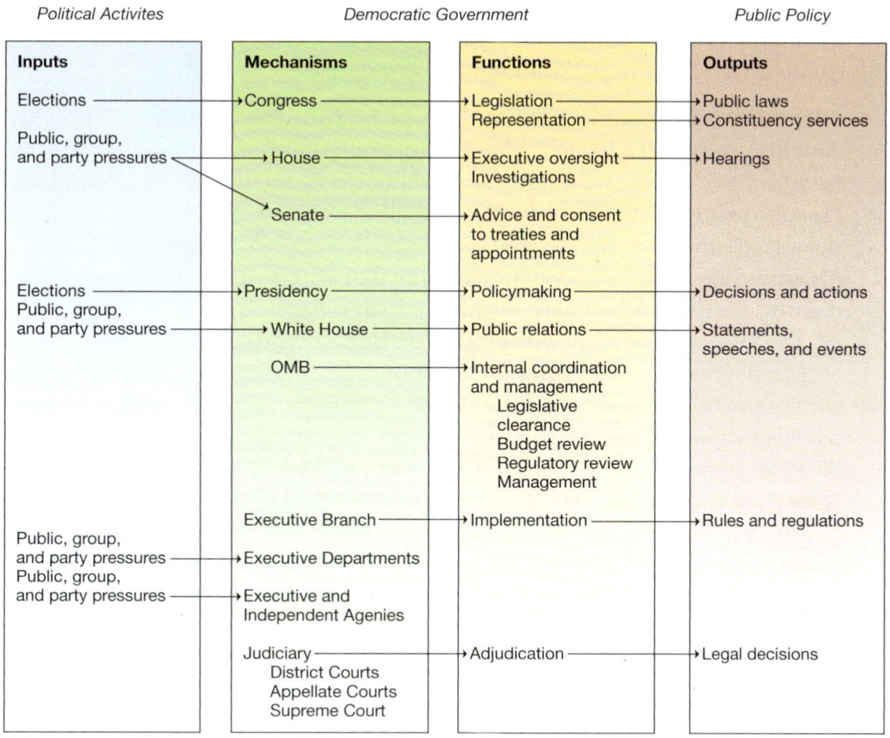

Political Activites		Democratic Government		Public Policy
Inputs	**Mechanisms**	**Functions**		**Outputs**
Elections	Congress	Legislation		Public laws
		Representation		Constituency services
Public, group, and party pressures	House	Executive oversight Investigations		Hearings
	Senate	Advice and consent to treaties and appointments		
Elections	Presidency	Policymaking		Decisions and actions
Public, group, and party pressures	White House	Public relations		Statements, speeches, and events
	OMB	Internal coordination and management Legislative clearance Budget review Regulatory review Management		
	Executive Branch	Implementation		Rules and regulations
Public, group, and party pressures	Executive Departments			
Public, group, and party pressures	Executive and Independent Agenies			
	Judiciary District Courts Appellate Courts Supreme Court	Adjudication		Legal decisions

Public Inputs

Choosing Public Officials If the key to representative democracy is the link between the people and their representatives, then elections are a vital component for a democratic government. Elections give citizens the opportunity to express their opinions, choose their leaders, and hold those in elective office accountable for their actions. They also give candidates an opportunity to educate the electorate, demonstrate why they should be elected, and build the foundation for the coalitions that make governing possible. President George W. Bush called on the business community to back his Social Security reforms; he and Republican congressional leaders turned to the same groups to support the Central American Free Trade Agreement (CAFTA).

Coalitions between those inside and those outside government help keep public officials responsive to the people who elected them. When they are not responsive and make decisions that adversely affect their constituents, then theoretically they face a greater likelihood of being defeated the next time they stand for reelection. We said theoretically because in practice those in elective office have great advantages that they use to win reelection most of the time. In the last decade, well over 90 percent of House incumbents and over 80 percent of Senate incumbents who ran for reelection won, and yet, the American people evaluated the Congress poorly during most of this period.[11]

Although the playing field may not be even for all candidates, especially for challengers, the election system may be considered democratic if it meets three criteria. The first pertains to suffrage, the right to vote; the second concerns the choices people have when they vote; and the third relates to the availability of information necessary to make an informed judgment.

universal suffrage
The principle that every adult citizen should be able to vote.

1. **Universal suffrage.** Elections must be based on the principle of political equality. All adult citizens who are mentally competent should have the right to vote[12]; the election must be conducted in such a way that people can exercise this right without duress; and all votes must count equally—hence the adage "one person, one vote."

meaningful choice
An electoral decision in which voters have the ability to select from among different candidates, parties, and sometimes policy positions, generally within the political mainstream.

2. **Meaningful choice.** Free elections imply that voters can choose among candidates, parties, and sometimes policy issues. An election in which there is no choice (e.g., only one candidate) or one in which the choice is not an acceptable one for most voters would not meet this criterion. An example of the latter would be an election in which a mainstream party candidate is pitted against a person who subscribes to an unpopular ideology such as Nazism, Socialism, or Communism.

informed judgment
A rational decision made on the basis of knowledge of choices and consequences.

3. **Informed judgment.** The electorate must be able to obtain the knowledge required to make an informed judgment. Ignorance is not bliss in a democratic electoral process. Rather, it is recipe for choosing unwisely, haphazardly, and irrationally, not necessarily in the voter's best interests or those of the country.

A free, fair, and critical press would seem to be a prerequisite to an informed electorate but certainly no guarantee of one. After all, people may not expose themselves to the information they need to make an intelligent voting decision. Nevertheless, without a free press that gives adequate attention to candidates and issues, public knowledge would be limited to infrequent contact with candidates or their parties and more frequent, but self-promoting, advertising read, heard, or seen by voters.

Influencing Government Decisions Once the election is over, people need access to public officials to continue to voice their interests and make demands on those in government. For this condition to occur, there must be channels of communication to and from public officials, as well as a political climate that encourages people to express their views on the issues that are most salient to them. But how accessible must government officials be to every individual or group that wants something from them?

Public policy decisions made on the basis of public opinion polls or strong group pressures may not be the best possible solution to a specific problem or be in most people's interests. On the other hand, policy that does not adequately reflect the will of the people is also deficient from a democratic perspective. Former President Bill Clinton was accused of governing by public opinion polls because he consulted them regularly. Although George W. Bush indicated that he would do what he believed to be right, not necessarily most popular, he and his

© AP/Wide World Photos

Senator Hillary Clinton, D-N.Y., left, listens intently to a question from a constituent at a luncheon held in Buffalo, New York.

aides regularly discern the public mood when making and selling the administration's policy priorities.[13]

In addition to public opinion, interest groups and political parties seek to influence the formulation, implementation, and adjudication of public policy. They do so by lobbying government officials and actively becoming involved in election campaigns. The resources that they expend in these activities provide them with the access necessary to make their case but do not guarantee favorable results—although those resources probably increase the odds that they will be successful, or so groups believe. Why else would they spend the time, effort, and money?

Similarly, political parties exert political influence through the label they provide, the funds they raise, and the capacity they have to organize the government. Partisan candidates do try to redeem their campaign promises and their party's platform. The more heterogeneous the party, however, the more difficult it may be to reach a partisan consensus on policy issues. For years, Democrats were divided over social issues such as civil rights; more recently, Republicans have been beset by internal differences over health and welfare programs for the elderly, government support for stem cell research, and immigration policies.

The Mechanism of Government

Operational Rules   The relationship between the people and their elected representatives is only one dimension of the democratic governing cycle. The rules by which those in government convert public opinions into policy outputs are another. Decisional rules are important because they contribute to or detract from support for government in general and the policies that emerge from it in particular. For policy to be perceived as legitimate by the public, there must be agreement that fair and proper procedures were followed in making the policy decision. When the Republican leadership in the House of Representatives extended the time for voting on a bill to reform the Medicare system in 2003, Democrats cried foul because the extension violated voting practices in that legislative body. Yet in the Senate, the Democratic minority has used the tradition of unlimited debate to prevent votes on several of President Bush's judicial nominees whom they opposed but did not have the votes to defeat. Are such actions justified because they protect minority rights or unjustified because they prevent the majority from getting its way?

Sometimes government appears to overstep its constitutional authority and intrudes in state or private matters. Such an intrusion generates criticism and often questions the legality of the action. A case in point—the bill enacted in March 2005 that asked the federal courts to take over jurisdiction and force Florida medical authorities to restore a feeding tube in a brain-damaged women. Three out of four Americans surveyed after the legislation was enacted opposed Congress's involvement in the matter.[14]

Today, the national government may not require states to implement federal law without providing the funds to do so. The Supreme Court invalidated part of a

Democratic Minority Leader Harry Reid questions the President's use of intelligence prior to the war in Iraq.

gun control law on such grounds. The law required state law enforcement officials to conduct background checks on individuals before they could purchase firearms, but did not reimburse states for the costs of these activities.[15]

In theory, decisions in policymaking bodies should also be based on the principle of equality—one person, one vote—with all votes counting equally. Those in the majority, defined as more than half, should prevail. However, there are several problems with imposing a **majority rule** principle on institutions such as the U.S. Congress. What happens if there is no majority—a likely scenario in a heterogeneous society? Building a majority takes time and resources, which in turn gives an advantage to those with organizational support and a grassroots base, thereby undercutting the principle of equality.

To make it easier to reach decisions, the majority rule principle is often relaxed to allow a plurality, the side with the most votes, to win. **Plurality rule** still incorporates the equality principle, but it lessens the consensus requirement. Because for many, perhaps most, issues a sizable proportion of the population may have no opinion, little interest, or not much concern, a relaxation of majority rule makes sense. However, it also makes those who oppose the decision or action more vulnerable, a reason those in the minority tend to oppose rule changes that reduce their right to object and to prevent the dominant group from imposing its will on others.

Institutional Structures The **separation of powers,** in which the legislative, executive, and judicial authority is vested primarily in one of the three branches

majority rule
A principle based on the proposition that everyone is equal, all votes should be equal, and decisions should be made on the basis of the judgment of more than half of those involved.

plurality rule
A decision made on the basis of the side that has the greatest number of people but not necessarily more than half of those participating.

separation of powers
A system of government in which separate institutions representing different constituencies over different time frames share the authority to govern.

1.1 In Theory . . .

How Democratic Is the U.S. Constitution?

The U.S. Constitution was designed to prevent a majority from easily, quickly, and permanently dominating the government. That is why power was divided between the national government and the states and why within the national government it was divided among the three branches: Congress, the presidency, and the judiciary. That is also why the Constitution imposed an internal system of checks and balances to maintain the division of power.

The framers of the Constitution, themselves an economic and social minority, were fearful that minorities could not adequately protect their rights and successfully pursue their interests if political and policy decisions were determined solely on the basis of plurality rule. So they excluded some basic rights from the reach of government.[16] Later, they added significantly to this list by attaching the Bill of Rights, which prohibited government from making laws that abridge freedom of speech, religion, press, and assembly. The reasoning behind these prohibitions on government was that minorities would have little, if any, recourse if the majority were to deny them these fundamental rights through legislative action; hence, the Constitution had to protect them.

The framers also created overlapping constituencies that operated on different electoral timetables to restrain the momentary impulses of the people. They did so to ensure that there would be a variety of perspectives on most policy issues.

Today, the American constitutional system reinforces and responds to social diversity more than it generates policy consensus. In the United States, the various constituencies within the country are represented more effectively than the country as a whole. The principal exception to this rule occurs during and after national crises, such as the Japanese attack on Pearl Harbor in December 1941 or the terrorist attacks in New York and Washington in September 2001, when unity is generated by a common threat and the need for a national response. In more normal times, division over policy, not consensus on it, is the order of the day. To move from the status quo and change public policy, at the least, a plurality has to persist over time and across institutions.

---

checks and balances
An internal system of constraints on the exercise of power designed to prevent any one unit of government from becoming dominant.

of government, and the internal **checks and balances** were designed primarily to protect minority rights. (See Chapter 2.) They have done so, but at the cost of requiring pluralities, majorities, or even—in the case of the Senate—supermajorities, at each step of the legislative policymaking process. Put another way, the absence of a majority on a committee considering the legislation, establishing the rules for debating and voting on it, or reconciling the differences between House and Senate bills is usually sufficient to kill the legislation. The U.S. constitutional system purposefully places the burden on those who want to change policy, not to maintain it. (See Box 1.1.)

Policy Processes The processes for making public policy should incorporate the components of wise policymaking: information, expertise, and the time necessary for reflection, deliberation, and sound judgment. A perpetual issue is choosing between what the public thinks it wants and what policymakers think would be best. Such choices may require that those in power restrain their democratic impulse to respond to public pressures directly and quickly. Tax legislation provides a good illustration. Cutting taxes is usually popular but not necessarily wise economic policy. Much depends on the conditions and needs of the economy. Nonetheless, the electoral pressures are to do what is popular; more painful, short-term solutions are harder to sell to the American people.

A second issue involves the desire for deliberation and the need for decisive action. Moving too quickly, limiting inputs, or circumventing or shortening debate can lead to poor decisions. Clinton found this out the hard way when his administration's health-care task forces, which were charged with designing a plan to reform the health-care system, failed to consult with a range of executive branch officials, members of Congress, and health-industry groups. Their failure to touch all relevant bases increased opposition to the proposed plan and reduced the coalition on which the president could rely in trying to convince Congress and the American people of the merits of his reform proposal.[17] Similarly, the administration of George W. Bush was accused of adopting a "group think mentality" in its rush to war with Iraq. External views were not encouraged; the president and his advisers seemed to have their minds made up.[18]

Outputs: Public Policy

The output of government is **public policy.** It is the product of active representation and the operational rules, structures, and processes for decision making. The adequacy of the representation and the fairness and efficiency of the decision-making process should be reflected in how the policy is perceived by the people. Do they approve of it? Do they think it is fair? Do they believe that it will solve the problem for which it was intended and, if so, for how long?

According to democratic theory, public policy should enhance society, in addition to any benefit it conveys to specific groups. Public perceptions are important here. If the policy is perceived as wise and just, then support for it, for those who made and implemented it, and for the way government works will be enhanced. If the policy is viewed less favorably, if it does not seem to meet the needs or satisfy the demands of those most affected by it, or if the same groups seem to be perpetual beneficiaries or losers, then discontent with the policy, the policymakers, and possibly even the governmental system is more likely to occur.

Public reaction is a necessary ingredient for judging policy choices and evaluating policy outcomes. That is why public officials keep their ears to the ground. They are concerned with whether an issue will fade quickly, slowly, or not at all and whether it will spill into the next election cycle and become part of a future government agenda. Timing is critical. Most members of Congress do not want to vote on controversial issues that divide their electoral constituencies during an election campaign. They would rather deal with them well before the election or right after it. Thus, the 108th Congress put off consideration of a bill to close military bases in the United States until after the 2004 elections. The 109th Congress wanted to deal with it as far as possible before the 2006 midterm elections and did.

An additional consideration is the public's reaction to policy after it has been put into effect. Did it solve the problem? Did it generate other conse-

public policy
The decisions and actions of government that establish rules for collecting and distributing economic costs and benefits and permitting and prohibiting certain behaviors in society.

quences, intended or unintended, beneficial or harmful, and if so, for whom and with what effect? Take the case of the 1979 amendments to the Federal Election Campaign Act. Designed to provide political parties with additional funds to enhance their organizational and grassroots activities at the state and local levels, the legislation created a huge "soft money" loophole in the contribution limits for individuals and groups and a way around the expenditure ceilings imposed on presidential candidates. It took Congress 13 years to try to correct the problem. The new law enacted in 2002, the Bipartisan Campaign Reform Act (also known as the McCain-Feingold bill), banned the parties from raising soft money, but that did not prevent wealthy people from giving large sums to nonparty groups that used the money to supplement the major parties' electoral campaigns and to advocate their own interests and support candidates favorable to them.

Another persistent allegation about American national policy is that it is usually incremental in character, policy that is minimally feasible rather than maximally optimal. The implication of this criticism is that political compromise somehow undercuts the best policy solutions. But compromise also contributes to the political support necessary for achieving that policy. Besides, what is the alternative? If those in power always got their way, better public policy would not necessarily result, nor would public support for that policy be ensured.

Another criticism of public policy in a democracy is that it is oriented toward the here and now, that short-term factors take precedence over long-term planning. Not only does the public demand a quick fix, but the electorate also rewards those who "bring home the bacon." The prevalence of this view, combined with the motivation to seek reelection, encourages elected officials to make policies that provide concrete and immediate benefits for their constituents (and indirectly for themselves) rather than longer-term solutions. The persistence of large federal budget deficits is an example of short-term benefits outweighing future considerations.

The public places a premium on the efficiency with which government deals with a problem, not on the deliberation that may be required to produce a viable policy solution. Congress as an institution tends to be evaluated more on the basis of its productivity—how many laws it enacts—than on how well it represents diverse interests or resolves contentious issues.

Similarly, presidents are usually assessed more favorably for their decisiveness, confidence, and consistency than for their thoughtfulness, nuance, or hesitation in rushing to judgment. If the policy does not meet its goals, however, the public judgment may change, as it did with President George W. Bush and the war in Iraq. The courts are normally praised when their decisions coincide with the popular view, not for their adherence to legal doctrine. Yet, government officials who act to satisfy these public propensities may not be exercising good judgment, much less producing good policy.

Governing in a democratic manner is not easy. It is not usually efficient. It produces perceptions of inequality. It often encourages a rush to judgment. The emphasis is on satisfying the loudest voices, most persistent pressures, and best organized interests, not necessarily the voiceless majority.

Review Questions

1. Which of the following statements about politics is true?

   A. Politics requires political parties
   B. Politics is a twentieth-century phenomenon
   C. Politics reconciles ideological differences
   D. Politics determines public policy winners and loses

2. The Constitution was designed to facilitate which of the following:

   A. The application of majority rule
   B. The protection of minority rights
   C. The promotion of political equality
   D. The spirit of American nationalism

3. Elections are important for a democratic society primarily for which reason?

   A. They provide people with a way to vent their emotions and act on their beliefs
   B. They provide people with an opportunity to choose public officials who will represent them in government
   C. They provide people with an opportunity to select the most qualified people for office and the news media with an opportunity to write about a subject that people find informative and important
   D. They energize the society and stimulate the economy through campaign spending

4. In making government decisions, lawmakers will usually

   A. Decide on the basis of their personal beliefs
   B. Follow the president's lead
   C. Do what is in the national interest
   D. Represent their constituencies' views and interests

Answers:

   1. D
   2. B
   3. B
   4. D

Conflict and Consensus in Review

The Constitution is a revered document that most Americans believe has served their country well over the years. As such, they tend to approve of the system of government it established, with its separation of powers and checks and balances, even though they become frustrated and voice disapproval when Congress and the President cannot seem to find common ground to make policy decisions.

Although people may laud the constitutional structure, they do not follow the rules by which it operates that closely. A case in point was the 2005 debate in the Senate over the

continued

Democratic minority's use of the filibuster to prevent votes on controversial presidential nominations. Although 37 percent opposed the elimination of filibusters on nominations, 35 percent had no opinion.[19] Controversy does ensue over public policy decisions, but it is a controversy among those who stand to gain or lose the most from the decision, not the entire population. Very few policy decisions divide, much less arouse, the whole country.

Politics in Action

Illegal Immigration and American Democracy

America is a land of immigrants, yet Americans have always been ambivalent about immigration. They have welcomed new immigrants, yet have viewed them with suspicion. They have taken pride in the assimilation of members of their diverse society, yet have also discriminated against religious, racial, and ethnic minorities. They view their country as a land of opportunity, yet resent it when newly arrived immigrants take American jobs and avail themselves of "free" public services.

The ambivalence of Americans can be seen in recent attitudes toward illegal immigration and immigrants, whose population is currently estimated at about 12 million and growing.[20] Most Americans agree that immigration in general is good but illegal immigration is bad. They agree on the need for secure borders. There is also a consensus that the number of immigrants entering the United States should not be increased, but there is disagreement over whether it should be decreased. Two out of three Americans believe that illegal immigrants cost the taxpayers too much by using government services like public education and medical care; they also believe that these immigrants take jobs Americans do not want. A majority oppose granting amnesty to illegal aliens, yet two out of three also believe that people living in the United States illegally should be given the opportunity to stay in the country and become citizens. The public is critical of President Bush's handling of the immigration issue, yet supports his plan for a temporary guest worker program and a way in which illegal immigrants could become legal residents and even citizens.[21]

Clearly immigration is an issue upon which there is considerable conflict but also much underlying consensus. The conflict divides Americans along familiar partisan and ideological lines. Republicans and conservatives tend to favor limited immigration, tougher laws, stricter enforcement, and tighter border security. They are sensitive to the economic costs of illegal immigration, the drain on state and federal social services, and the development of non–English-speaking communities within American society. They have also expressed national security concerns in the light of the terrorist attacks of 9/11, concerns that have led to calls for tamper- and counterfeit-proof government-issued drivers' licenses and other official documents for identification. Republicans have had a political problem with the issue: Hispanics, the most rapidly growing immigrant group in America, tend to vote Democratic.

Democrats and liberals in general, and the Hispanic community in particular, see the immigration issue differently. They are more willing than most Republicans to give immigrants, legal or illegal, the social services they need; they are sensitive to the situation of illegal workers—their low salaries, long hours, poor working conditions, and even the criminal exploitation they face; and they would like to give them the opportunity to work legally and become citizens.

Ironically, certain business groups, which have been supportive of the Republican Party, now seek a national policy under which immigrants can gain status as guest workers. The agricultural, restaurant, and other service industries claim that they need guest workers to fill jobs that Americans won't take, such as picking crops, packaging meat, cleaning rooms and offices, even working at fast-food restaurants. Labor unions, on the other hand, which have traditionally opposed Republican policies, reject this claim, contending

continued

Politics in Action *continued*

that if the jobs paid better and had more benefits, Americans would take them. The business community in turn says that higher wages would lead to higher prices and ultimately lower the standard of living for most Americans.

The issue is a difficult one for a diverse country such as the United States, where most people can trace their ancestry back to another country yet also prize and wish to maintain America's unique culture, language, and values in addition to the economic and political benefits they enjoy as U.S. citizens. It is a difficult issue for a federal system in which the interests of regions in which most immigrants settle—the South, Southwest, and California—may be different from those of the nation as a whole. It is also a difficult issue for a constitutional system that provides liberties and opportunities for *all* and for an administration whose foreign policy trumpets human rights and democracy around the world.

What should be done? Responding to the problem and to its constituency base, the Republican-controlled House of Representatives enacted a bill to improve border security by building a fence along the 700 miles of the U.S.-Mexican border, to penalize employers who hire illegal workers, and to make it a felony to work in the U.S. without proper documentation. The House bill was designed to make illegal immigration less attractive by reducing or eliminating the economic incentive for people to come to the United States.

Democrats and some Republicans believe that this approach was mean-spirited, impractical, and unenforceable. They also saw it as inconsistent with an America

that has prided itself on welcoming "the tired, the poor, the huddled masses yearning to breathe free" and insensitive to the economic hardships people face in many parts of the world.

President Bush's proposed immigration policy, in turn, included beefed-up security at the borders (more border guards, including assistance from the National Guard; better technology to detect crossings; and more detention facilities). The president also advocated a guest worker program and a path to citizenship for illegal immigrants who pay a fine, learn English, and have no criminal record. Deporting millions of illegal aliens would not work, according to the president.[22]

For its part, the Senate enacted bipartisan legislation in August 2006, sponsored by Senators John McCain and Ted Kennedy, which provided for increased border security, a temporary workers' program, and a plan by which illegal workers could become American citizens. But the House of Representatives refused to go along. Responding to the concerns of its conservative constituents, opposed to any legislation that rewarded illegal behavior, and to its members who feared that compromise on immigration could jeopardize their reelections in 2006, House Republican leaders stuck to their initial bill that would enhance border security. The Senate reluctantly followed suit, and the president signed the Secure Fence Act on October 26, 2006. But the issues of the status of illegal immigrants already in the United States, the need for temporary workers, the number of new immigrants to be legally admitted, and the paths to future citizenship remained unresolved.

What Do You Think?

1. Does immigration strengthen or weaken the basic fabric of American society? Do its costs outweigh its benefits or vice versa?
2. Is there a contradiction between promoting human rights, personal liberties, and economic opportunities abroad and enacting legislation that prevents illegal immigrants from working in the U.S. even if they are offered jobs?
3. Should people who break the law by entering the United States illegally be protected by the law while they are here? Should they receive minimum wages, health benefits, and other rights that Americans enjoy?
4. Should employers of illegal immigrants be subject to criminal prosecution? Should individuals who hire illegal immigrants to clean their houses, cut their lawns, or take care of their children also be prosecuted?

Summary

We began this chapter by considering how the diverse nature of society affects politics. Then we discussed how politics affects government; how government responds to political pressures in its formulation, execution, and adjudication of public policy; and how that policy in turn generates new issues within society and pressures on government. We referred to this process as the politics of American democracy, a process that relies on an underlying consensus on the nature of the system and the democratic principles that sustain it. As part of this consensus, there is an agreement to disagree and to do so in accordance with the law.

Society in the United States consists of many ethnic, racial, and religious groups. That diversity contributes to the vitality of America. But it has also led to continuous struggles that pit individuals and groups against one another as they pursue their own interests, act on the basis of their values and beliefs, and defend their basic rights, protected by the Constitution. These struggles occur within the political system. They provide the rationale for having such a system. They are the fuel that drives American politics.

The governmental part of that system is designed to protect and promote basic values as set forth in the Declaration of Independence and enumerated in the Constitution: political values such as personal liberty, political equality, and common good and economic values such as individual initiative, equal opportunity, and private ownership within a competitive, free enterprise system.

Although the constitutional system is founded on the principle of popular consent, it is also designed to provide protection for minorities so that their rights and interests will not be subject to the tyranny of the majority. This protection is accomplished by dividing power within the national government and between it and the states. That division of powers is maintained by an internal system of checks and balances that makes it difficult for a majority, or even a plurality, to get its way easily, quickly, and consistently. In other words, the constitutional design puts the brakes on democratic tendencies in order to protect minority rights.

The government operates according to decisional rules in each of its institutions. Those rules, themselves a product of historical practice and contemporary consent, are intended to facilitate public input into the policymaking process and to increase efficiency in government decision making. The decisions and actions of government shape public policy, which is codified by law and enforced by the authority vested in government. In most instances, the policy is a product of deliberation and compromise among varying interests that promote differing beliefs and compete for limited resources and goals. Because policy decisions result from a confluence of forces, public policy tends to be incremental—what is feasible under the circumstances rather than what may be an optimal solution. In times of crisis, such as during the Great Depression of the 1930s or the terrorist attacks of September 11, 2001, greater policy change may occur.

The public reacts to policies on the basis of perceived self-interest and individual perceptions of national interest. These reactions contribute to an ongoing political debate in elections and over the course of governing. Elections are referenda on how those in government are performing and a constant reminder for those in power to keep in touch with their constituents and take their interests into account when making public policy decisions. If most adult citizens are able to participate in elections, have a reasonable choice when voting, and are capable of making an informed judgment, then the electoral system is said to be democratic. Similarly, if people have access to those in power and can affect public policy decisions, then government may be said to be operating in a democratic manner, even though its particular decisional rules do not always allow the majority or plurality to prevail.

The tension between majority and minority, between the many and the few, is perpetual. As long as there are no permanent winners and losers, the system is probably handling that tension fairly well. The danger arises when one group, because of its size, superior resources, or the current popularity of its beliefs, is able to dominate. The framers intended the constitutional structure to prevent such domination.

The remainder of this book will explore how the political and governing systems operate. To what extent does theory accord with practice? To what extent does the political system promote, protect, and preserve the society's fundamental values? To what extent do those in government represent and respond to the views, needs, and interests of those outside of it? To what extent does government accurately translate public preferences into policy outcomes and do so in a timely fashion? To what extent do those outcomes solve the problems, and to what extent do they create new ones? You be the judge.

Key Terms

conflict
consensus
personal liberty
political equality
common good
community
government
authoritative decisions
economic liberty

private property
free enterprise system
equal opportunity
politics
politician
democracy
direct democracy
representative democracy
universal suffrage

meaningful choice
informed judgment
majority rule
plurality rule
separation of powers
checks and balances
public policy

Discussion Questions

1. Explain the connection between politics and government, government and public policy, and public policy and politics.
2. What are the principal pros and cons of a democratic political system?
3. Why are elections so critical for a democracy?
4. List three democratic principles on which most Americans agree and three practices that follow from these principles on which there is considerable disagreement.
5. To what extent is the U.S. Constitution a democratic document? Indicate its most democratic and nondemocratic features.

Topics for Debate

Debate each side of the following propositions:

1. Liberty and equality are incompatible in a democratic society.
2. Universal suffrage is neither necessary nor desirable.
3. A press that is free, fair, and balanced is a contradiction in terms.
4. To promote national security in an age of terrorism, it is necessary to limit some basic rights for all Americans.
5. If the majority rules, then the minority is always in jeopardy.

Where on the Web?

American Civil Liberties Union **www.aclu.org**
Census Bureau www.census.gov

National Archives and Records Administration
www.archives.gov

Statistical Abstract of the United States
www.census.gov/stat_abstract

Go to **www.thomsonedu.com/thomsonnow** to learn about a powerful online study tool. You will get a personalized study plan based on your responses to a diagnostic Pre-Test. Once you have mastered the materials with the help of interactive learning tools, activities, timelines, video case studies, simulations, and an integrated E-Book, you can take a Post-Test to confirm you are ready to move to the next chapter.

Selected Readings

Bok, Derek. *The Trouble with Government.* Cambridge, Mass: Harvard University Press, 2001.

Dahl, Robert A. *Democracy and Its Critics.* New Haven, Conn.: Yale University Press, 1989.

_____. *How Democratic is the American Constitution?* New Haven, Conn.: Yale University Press, 2001.

_____. *On Democracy.* New Haven: Conn.: Yale University Press, 1998.

Delaet, Debra L. *U.S. Immigration Policy in an Age of Rights.* Westport, Conn.: Praeger Publishers, 2000.

DeSipio, Louis, and Rodolfo O. de la Garza. *Making Americans, Remaking America: Immigration and Immigrant Policy.* Boulder, Colo.: Westview Press, 1998.

Dionne, E. J. *Why Americans Hate Politics.* New York: Simon and Schuster, 1992.

Ellis, Richard J. *American Political Cultures.* New York: Oxford University Press, 1993.

Greider, William. *Who Will Tell the People? The Betrayal of American Democracy.* New York: Simon and Schuster, 1993.

Held, David. *Models of Democracy.* Cambridge, Mass.: Polity Press, 1996.

Lasswell, Harold. *Politics: Who Gets What, When, How.* New York: Meridian Books, 1971.

Lipset, Seymour Martin. *American Exceptionalism: A Double-Edged Sword.* New York: W. W. Norton & Co., 1996.

Orwell, George. *Animal Farm.* New York: Alfred A. Knopf, 1993 [1946].

Schuck, Peter H. *Diversity in America: Keeping Government at a Safe Distance.* Cambridge, Mass.: Belnap Press of Harvard, 2003.

Smith, Hedrick. *The Power Game: How Washington Works.* New York: Random House, 1989.

Stout, Jeffrey. *Democracy and Tradition.* Princeton, N.J.: Princeton University Press, 2004.

Tocqueville, Alexis de. *Democracy in America.* Edited by J. P. Mayer. New York: HarperCollins Publishers, 1988.

Notes

[1] In a landmark decision upholding the principle of affirmative action, the Supreme Court ruled in the case of *Grutter v. Bollinger* (2 U.S. 241) that universities can consider race and ethnicity in their admissions decisions to create a diverse student body. However, the Court rejected an undergraduate admissions plan at the University of Michigan that used a point system based partly on race (*Gratz v. Bollinger*, 2 U.S. 516).

[2] A case in point—the Army instructed its promotion boards to consider "past personal or institutional discrimination" when they made promotion decisions. Sued by a white, male lieutenant colonel who felt that he was unfairly passed over for promotion because of preferences given women and minorities, the Army defended its policy on the basis of fairness to those who have had fewer opportunities to move ahead. A federal judge

disagreed. Siding with the officer who felt that the preferences given to women and minorities were unfair to him, the judge ruled that promotional preferences that gave advantage to a race or gender were unconstitutional because they violated the equal protection that the Constitution gives all citizens. Yet how can a legacy of discrimination and racial and gender preference be overcome if review boards continue to use criteria that have traditionally favored the majority or a powerful group within it?

[3]According to a study by the *New York Times,* those in the top 0.1 percent (about 145,000 people) received 15.2 percent of the tax cut (averaging $195,762 per year) over 15 years, and those in the bottom 20 percent (28 million people) received 0.3 percent of the tax cut (averaging $23 per year). David Cay Johnston, "Richest Are Leaving Even the Rich Far Behind," *New York Times, June 5, 2005,* A1, 17.

[4]Pew Research Center for the People and the Press, *Deconstructing Distrust,* 1998, 27.

[5]Harold Lasswell, *Politics: Who Gets What, When, How* (New York: Meridian Books, 1971).

[6]Technologically, however, direct democracy is probably more feasible today then it would have been in 1776 when independence was declared or in 1787 when the Constitution was designed. A system in which it is possible to communicate almost instantaneously and securely would make a national plebiscite possible, although it is probably not the best or even a good way to make public policy.

[7]Heterosexual marriage was the overwhelming choice of voters in each state.

[8]Voters in Oregon and Montana approved the use of marijuana for certain medical conditions. A ballot initiative in Alaska to legalize all uses of marijuana failed; that state had already approved marijuana's use for medical purposes. However, the Supreme Court ruled that such state laws violated the federal government's authority to establish national health standards and, in the process, ban the use of marijuana.

[9]"Politics and Values in a 51%–48% Nation," The Pew Research Center for the People and the Press, January 24, 2005, http://www.people-press.org (accessed September, 16, 2005).

[10]Ibid.

[11]According to Gallup Polls, public opinion remained below 50 percent for most of this period. "Congress and the Public," Gallup Poll, http://www.gallup.com/content/default.aspx?ci=1600

[12]Whether those who are incarcerated for committing a crime, had been convicted of a felony, or received a dishonorable discharge from the military should be allowed to vote is a controversial issue, one on which states disagree. All states but two, Maine and Vermont, do not permit people in jail to vote; some states permanently bar felons or those receiving dishonorable discharges from ever voting. Such restrictions disproportionately affect African American men, disfranchising one out of seven.

[13]Katie Dunn Tenpas, "Words vs. Deeds: President George W. Bush and Polling," *Brookings Review* (Summer 2003).

[14]*CNN/USA Today/*Gallup Poll conducted April 1–2, 2005, as reported on the Polling Report website: http://www.pollingreport.com/news.htm (accessed April 4, 2005).

[15]*Printz v. United States,* 521 U.S. 898 (1997).

[16]These included titles of nobility, taxes on imports, bills of attainder, and ex post facto law.

[17]Haynes Johnson and David Broder, *The System* (Boston: Little, Brown & Co., 1996).

[18]Bob Woodward, *Plan of Attack* (New York: Simon and Schuster, 2004).

[19]"Disengaged Public Leans Against Changing Filibuster Rules" Pew Research Center for the People and the Press, May 16, 2005.

[20]Ester Pan, "The U.S. Immigration Debate," Council of Foreign Relations, March 22, 2006. http://www.cfr.org/publications/11149.htm (accessed November 4, 2006).

[21]"Gallup Poll Topics: Immigration," Gallup Poll. http://www.galluppoll.com/content/default.aspx?ci=1633 (accessed November 4, 2006). See also Pollingreport.com. http://www.pollingreport.com/immigration.htm (accessed August 30, 2006).

[22]President George W. Bush speech, "President Bush Discusses Comprehensive Immigration Reform in Texas," August 3, 2006. http://www.whitehouse.gov/news/releases/2006/08/20060803-8.html (accessed August 29, 2006).

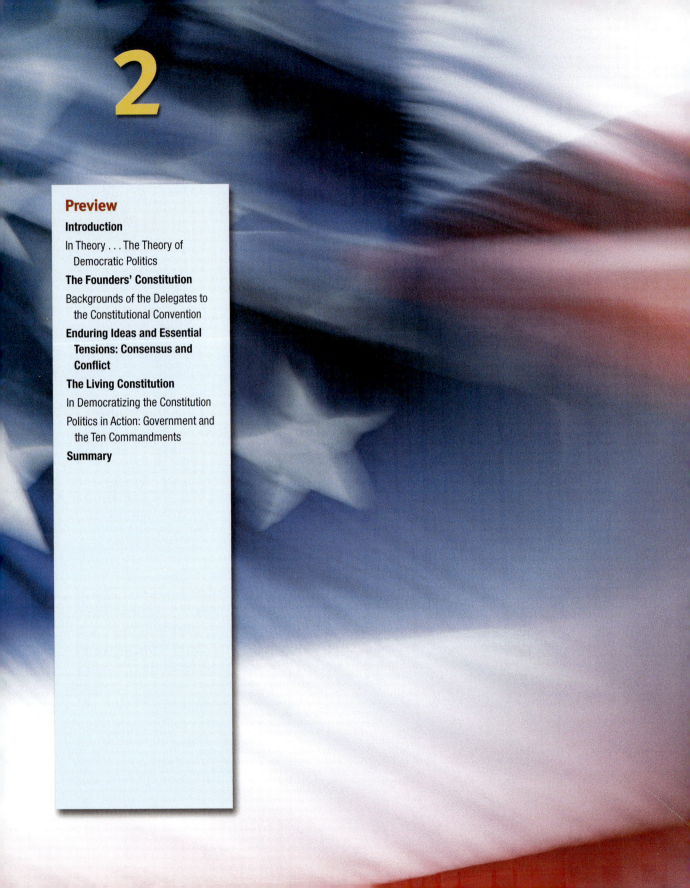

2

The Constitution: A Framework for Conflict Resolution

Introduction

NO EVENT IN U.S. HISTORY better illustrates the dynamics of conflict and consensus in American politics than the drafting of the Constitution. Although the delegates to the Constitutional Convention of 1787 agreed on many issues, especially the need to fix the problems that stemmed from the Articles of Confederation, they also disagreed on many fundamental points. Nonetheless, they were able to overcome their differences and through a series of compromises eventually were able to reach consensus on the important dimensions that shaped the new government. In so doing, the delegates created a document that would serve as the political framework for the resolution of conflict from its ratification in 1788 until today.

Often, issues arise in the American system that can be said to pit the wishes of those holding a majority opinion against the rights of those whose opinions might be in the minority. The framers created a constitutional system based on the consent of the governed, one in which the majority (or at least the plurality) rules, but they also created a system respectful of the

Phyllis Lyon (L) and Del Martin, who have been together for 51 years, embrace after their marriage at City Hall. They are the first legally married same-sex couple in San Francisco. Witnessing the ceremony are (L-R): Kate Kendell, Executive Director of the National Center for Lesbian Rights, Roberta Achtenberg, Senior Vice President of the San Francisco Chamber of Commerce, members of Mayor Gavin Newsom's staff including Steve Kawa, Chief of Staff, and Joyce Newstat, Director of Policy.

rights of the minority, even when the causes protected by those rights might be unpopular. As James Madison, probably the most influential delegate at the Constitutional Convention, put it, "In a free government the security for civil rights must be the same as that for religious rights. . . . In a society under the forms of which the stronger faction can readily unite and oppress the weaker, anarchy may as truly be said to reign as in a state of nature, where the weaker individual is not secured against the violence of the stronger."[1] But precisely what rights, and precisely which behaviors, are secured by the Constitution? How far must we go to protect the activities of those in the minority, especially when those activities may be very unpopular?

The issue concerning same-sex marriages, or as some say "gay marriages," is a case in point. The Fourteenth Amendment of the Constitution (ratified in 1868) provides that no state shall deny to any person "equal protection" of the laws. In essence, this means that the rights and privileges extended to one person must be extended to everyone; a certain activity permitted to one group of individuals must not be denied to another group. However, the amendment is unclear about just which activities fall into this protected category. In the 2003 case of *Lawrence v. Texas,* the Supreme Court ruled that intimate noncommercial sexual conduct between consenting adults, including those of the same sex, is part of the set of constitutionally protected activities.

But what about same-sex marriages? Should homosexual couples have the same privileges, including the right to legally marry, as those extended to heterosexual couples? Further, since Article IV of the Constitution holds that every state must give "full faith and credit" to the public acts, records, and judicial decisions of every other state, does this mean that if one state decides to grant marital privileges to same-sex couples that such marriages would have to be recognized as valid in all other states?

Public debate over the same-sex marriage issue dates to 1993 when in that year the Hawaii Supreme Court ruled that laws denying gay couples the right to marry violated equal protection rights of citizens in that state. Although the matter in that state was resolved in 1998 when Hawaii voters approved an amendment giving the legislature power to restrict marriage to heterosexual couples, the gay marriage question has remained a potent, divisive, and many would say "firestorm" issue in American politics ever since.

In 2000 the Vermont legislature approved legislation recognizing civil unions between same-sex couples, action that granted them virtually all protections available to married couples. Connecticut followed suit in 2005. (Earlier, in 2004, Massachusetts had become the first state to issue marriage licenses to same-sex couples.) In some other areas, such as in San Francisco and in a few jurisdictions in New York, Oregon, and other states, officials began performing same-sex marriage ceremonies in violation of state law.

Congress first entered the fray in 1996 when it approved the Defense of Marriage Act, action that bars federal recognition of gay marriages and permits states to ignore gay marriages performed elsewhere. This act was passed in large part out of the concern that gay couples might marry in a state permitting such marriage and then return to their home state demanding recognition of their marriage. Following passage of this act a number of states passed legislation explicitly prohibiting same-sex marriages or recognition of same-sex marriages approved in other states.

Several attempts to amend the U.S. Constitution to bar same-sex marriages have been made since 1996. In the 2004 presidential campaign, President Bush indicated his support of such an amendment. And in his 2006 State of the Union address the President called for a "national dialogue" on the subject, further signaling his support of a constitutional amendment by observing that "If judges insist on forcing their arbitrary will upon the people, the only alternative left to the people would be the constitutional process."[2] In June 2006 the U.S. Senate rejected by a vote of 49 to 48 continued debate on such an amendment, ending its chances for ratification in the 109th Congress; the vote fell far short of the 67 that would have been needed to approve a constitutional amendment.

For the last decade, public opinion polls have consistently shown that the American public opposes legalizing same-sex marriages while at the same time also opposing amending the Constitution to preclude such marriages. Under the circumstances, it has been left to the state governments to act.

As of 2006 some forty-eight states have passed Defense of Marriage acts, defining marriage in those states as between a man and a woman. Of the other states, two (Connecticut and Vermont) have allowed civil unions providing spousal rights to same-sex couples, one state (California) has passed legislation providing nearly full spousal rights to "unmarried" couples, two states (Hawaii and Maine) have passed legislation providing some spousal rights to "unmarried" couples, and one state (Massachusetts) has approved the issuing of marriage licenses to same-sex couples.

However this issue is ultimately resolved, the debate illustrates a basic principle of American constitutional democracy: Certain rights, even if they are unpopular, are so basic that government cannot take them away. But what are these rights, and which activities fall under such protection? Unless the Constitution is amended to specifi-cally eliminate same-sex marriages from such protection, it ultimately will fall to the Supreme Court to decide if such marital arrangements are protect-ed by the Constitution.

The Constitution as interpreted by the federal judiciary is both a prescrip-tion for political struggle and a frame-work for resolving that struggle. It establishes the blueprint for govern-ment, a blueprint for a dynamic political process in which individuals and inter-est groups compete for influence and power.

Politics in America differs from poli-tics in other countries partly because of the nature of the Constitution. The U.S. Constitution, the oldest written consti-tution in the world, is unique because it combines the idea of the rule of law with the idea that government is based on the consent of the governed. This chapter examines the basic principles and structure of the Constitution. We discuss the historical context in which the document was drafted and ratified, the original Constitution of 1787, and how the Constitution has changed over the years, as well as the ways in which constitutional change may occur.

Questions to Ponder

1. How does the Constitution reflect consensus on fundamental issues, and in what ways does it set up a process to resolve conflict?
2. How democratic is the Constitution today, and how democratic was it intended to be?
3. Does the Constitution provide an effective framework for resolving political conflicts of the twenty-first century?
4. In what ways might the Constitution be made more democratic? Should it be made more democratic?

2.1 In Theory . . .

The Theory of Democratic Politics

In this book, we define democracy as "a system of government in which the people rule directly or indirectly." Judged by this criteria, just how democratic is the American Constitution? In *How Democratic Is the American Constitution?*, Robert Dahl argues that the framers were forced to make numerous compromises to secure agreement on the new Constitution. Dahl says that although the framers were "men of exceptional talent and public virtue," they also were "limited by their profound ignorance." Their limitations arose because no "relevant models of representative government on the scale the United States had already been attained." The framers simply had no comparative models to choose from; in essence, they were

creating a national government "from scratch." For the Constitution to be accepted and ratified, many compromises had to be reached. Some of these compromises are squarely at odds with our understanding of democracy today. Among the more important democratic shortcomings of the 1787 Constitution, according to Dahl, are the following:

1. *Slavery.* The Constitution neither forbade slavery nor empowered Congress to do so.
2. *Suffrage.* The Constitution left the question of suffrage—who is eligible to vote—to the states. At the time, this had the effect of excluding women, African Americans, and Native Americans.

3. *Election of the president.* The electoral college, created by the framers, insulated the selection of the president both from popular majorities and from Congress.
4. *Selection of senators.* The framers ensured that senators would be chosen not by popular election but by state legislatures.
5. *Equal representation in the Senate.* The framers awarded each state the same number of senators (two), regardless of population.
6. *Judicial power.* The framers failed to limit the powers of the judiciary to declare unconstitutional any laws that had been passed by Congress and signed by the president.
7. *Congressional power.* The framers limited the powers of Congress, thus preventing the federal government from regulating the economy in various ways.

The Founders' Constitution

The founders' Constitution, as the historian Max Farrand observed, was a "bundle of compromises."[3] It was forged by a group of pragmatic statesmen who had to overlook, if not reconcile, their conflicting views about the politics of government. How did the Constitution come about? (Key events relating to the creation of the Constitution are listed in Table 2.1.)

The Revolutionary Background

In 1774 twelve of the original thirteen British colonies sent delegates to the First Continental Congress. This gathering had no official status; rather, it was convened to pass resolutions denouncing the British Parliament and Crown (king). The colonies had unsuccessfully demanded the right to have their own representatives in Parliament, arguing that this was the only way they could defend their economic interests. When Britain imposed taxes on goods imported into the

Table 2.1 Key Events in the Creation of the Constitution

Date	Event
April 1775	American Revolution begins in Massachusetts, at Lexington and Concord.
July 1776	Declaration of Independence in proclaimed.
November 1777	Articles of Confederation are adopted by the Continental Congress.
March 1781	Articles of Confederation are ratified by the states.
September 1783	Treaty ending the Revolutionary War is signed in Paris.
April 1784	Congress ratifies the Treaty of Paris.
August 1786–February 1787	Shays's Rebellion takes place.
May–September 1787	Constitutional Convention drafts and adopts the U.S. Constitution.
June 1788	U.S. Constitution is ratified.
March 1789	Congress meets for the first time, in New York.
April 1789	George Washington is inaugurated as president, in New York.
September 1789	John Jay becomes the first chief justice of the Supreme Court.
September 1789	Congress proposes the Bill of Rights.
December 1791	The Bill of Rights is ratified.

colonies, the demand for political representation intensified and the slogan "No taxation without representation" became a popular rallying cry. In addition, the colonists opposed the use of judges appointed by King George III to enforce laws that they deemed unjust.

In response to growing opposition to the Crown, the First Continental Congress recommended economic sanctions against Britain and boycotts of its goods. It also declared some acts of Parliament null and void and urged colonists to arm themselves and form their own militias. In April 1775, fighting broke out between colonial and British troops, and in May, a Second Continental Congress passed a resolution putting the colonies in a state of defense. Hostilities spread, and pressure grew for complete separation from Britain.

A committee of the Continental Congress began work on a resolution proclaiming the colonies free and independent in the spring of 1776. Committee members decided that Thomas Jefferson would draft the resolution, now known as the Declaration of Independence. Drawing on the eighteenth-century (commonly known as the Age of Enlightenment) notions that advances in

Benjamin Franklin was an instrumental figure in early American politics, signing the Declaration of Independence, negotiating peace with Great Britain, and being a member of the Constitutional Convention.

Articles of Confederation
The first constitution of the United States, approved by the Second Continental Congress in 1777 but not ratified by all thirteen former colonies until 1781. It provided for a unicameral legislature, the Continental Congress, which had extremely limited powers.

scientific knowledge could be applied with equally positive results to the understanding of human affairs and on the belief expressed by John Locke that individuals had certain rights that could not be given or taken away, Jefferson compiled a long list of despotic "abuses and usurpations" of power by King George. On July 1, 1776, the Continental Congress began debating Jefferson's draft and making changes in the wording. Three days later, on July 4, it approved the Declaration of Independence. (See Appendix A.) The members of the Continental Congress had agreed on a basic document, although the people they represented were still divided on the wisdom of severing ties to Parliament and the Crown.

Later in 1776, the Continental Congress considered a proposed set of "Articles of Confederation and Perpetual Union." The **Articles of Confederation,** the United States' first constitution, was approved in 1777, but not until 1781 was it ratified by all thirteen of the former colonies. In order to gain approval, the architects of the Articles were careful not to intrude on the authority of the separate states, each of which had drafted its own constitution.

The Articles of Confederation

The Articles of Confederation provided for a unicameral, or one-house, legislature known as the Continental Congress composed of delegates from the states. But this Congress had no effective power to regulate interstate commerce or collect taxes; tariffs, weights and measures, and currency varied from state to state. There was no separate executive or national judiciary; neither was there a national army. Instead, each of the original thirteen colonies was an independent and sovereign state that could conduct its own foreign policy.

This lack of a central governing authority presented grave problems. For example, when several states refused to repay debts they had incurred during the Revolutionary War, the Continental Congress had no power to compel them to do so. It had no enforcement powers at all. It could only ask each state to comply with and enforce its laws and policies voluntarily. Economic problems facing the country became a growing concern, and in the summer of 1786 delegates from five states met in Annapolis, Maryland, to discuss issues of trade and commerce. One of the results of the Annapolis Convention was a call by attendees for a larger conference to meet in Philadelphia the following year to consider revisions to the Articles of Confederation.

Also of growing concern were mounting tensions between creditors and debtors. In the aftermath of the Revolutionary War, imports and exports declined sharply, wages fell by as much as 20 percent, and money was in short supply. In 1786 and 1787 these tensions came to a head in economically depressed western Massachusetts. The state legislature refused to respond to petitions from debt-ridden farmers demanding the issuance of paper money and legislation to stop banks from foreclosing on their homes and farms. The angry farmers, led by Daniel Shays, formerly a captain in the Revolutionary army, rebelled against the state government and eventually marched on the federal arsenal at Springfield. It took a militia appointed by the Massachusetts governor to put down Shays's Rebellion.

Shays's Rebellion dramatically underscored the weakness of the national government under the Articles of Confederation. It also coincided with the states' selection of delegates to the Constitutional Convention, which opened in Philadelphia in May 1787. And it was fresh in the minds of convention delegates, who planned to revise the Articles of Confederation but ended up drafting an entirely new Constitution, one that greatly strengthened the powers of the national government.[4]

The Constitutional Convention

Despite their diverse interests and conflicting views of government, the delegates to the Constitutional Convention agreed that the Articles of Confederation were defective. The Continental Congress lacked three important powers: to regulate commerce, to raise funds to support a national army, and to compel compliance by the states. Within five days after the convention convened, on May 25, 1787, the delegates had decided that "a national Government ought to be established consisting of a supreme legislative, executive, and judiciary."[5]

Although they agreed on the principle that government must be based on the consent of the governed, the delegates shared a distrust of direct democracy. They feared a tyranny of the majority as much as they feared the tyranny of a minority—the concentration of power in too few hands. From the outset, therefore, the convention was inclined toward creating a **republic** (one in which power is exercised by elected representatives) rather than a government in which the people could rule directly. The republican government would have considerable power to make and enforce laws and would derive its authority directly or indirectly from the citizens through popular elections. The objective, in the words of James Madison, a delegate from Virginia, was a "mixed" form of government, one that combined democratic and representative elements to minimize the possibility of tyranny by either the majority or a minority.[6]

For information about the makeup of the Constitutional Convention, see Box 2.2.

republic

A government whose powers are exercised by elected representatives directly or indirectly accountable to the people governed.

Basic Compromises

Large State—Small State Compromise: Representation Although they agreed on the broad outlines of the new republic, the delegates were sharply divided over the precise form that government should take. Conflicts between large and small states over their representation in Congress and between states in the

In this rendition of the Constitutional Convention by Howard Chandler Christie, George Washington is pictured presiding over the session.

Box 2.2 Backgrounds of the Delegates to the Constitutional Convention

State legislatures and governors appointed seventy-four men to go to the Constitutional Convention, but nineteen of the appointees declined to attend. Rhode Island was not represented. Of the fifty-five who attended, fourteen left before the convention closed, thirty-nine signed the final draft of the Constitution (that number includes the signature of one absentee that was added later), and three refused to sign the document. Of these fifty-five men,

- Forty-six had been members of colonial or state legislatures
- Seven had been governors
- Forty-two had been delegates to the Continental Congress
- Eight had signed the Declaration of Independence
- Forty-seven had been born in America
- Thirty-one had attended college—some in Britain; some in America: Princeton (ten), William and Mary (four), Yale (three), Harvard (two), Columbia (two)
- Twenty-one had seen military service—eighteen as officers in the Continental Army
- Thirty-four had studied law
- Thirteen were in business
- Ten were planters
- Twenty-one were younger than forty years old (the youngest was twenty-six)
- Fourteen were over fifty years old (Benjamin Franklin, the oldest, was eighty-one; the average age was forty-three)

North and in the South over taxation and representation proved to be the major problems.

During the first few weeks, the Convention focused on the **Virginia Plan,** which was drafted by James Madison and presented by Edmund Randolph, the governor of Virginia. It called for a strong central government with a bicameral legislature—that is, a legislature with two houses. Members of the lower house would be elected by voters in the states, and members of the upper house would be chosen by those in the lower house from nominees submitted by the state legislatures. Representation of states in the national legislature would be based on wealth and population; thus giving the large states—Virginia, Massachusetts, and Pennsylvania—more influence. In addition, the Virginia Plan called for an executive chosen by the legislature, for a judiciary with considerable power, and for a council of revision (composed of members of the executive branch and the judiciary) with the power to veto legislation.

Delegates from small states objected to this plan and supported the **New Jersey Plan** drafted by delegates from Connecticut, New York, New Jersey, and Delaware and introduced by William Paterson of New Jersey on June 15. It called for a unicameral legislature with considerable regulatory and taxing power in which all states would be represented equally. Executive powers would be exercised by a group that would not have the power to veto legislation.

Roger Sherman of Connecticut emerged as the chief spokesperson for the opposition to Madison and the Virginia Plan. As described by David Robertson,

Virginia Plan

One of the main proposals for the overall structure of government presented at the Constitutional Convention in 1787. It was drafted by James Madison and called for a strong central government, including a bicameral legislature with representation of states based on their wealth and population, a chief executive chosen by the legislature, and a powerful judiciary. This plan was favored by larger states.

"Sherman slashed at Madison's abstractions with Ockham's Razor, incisively questioning the need for such proposals as the national veto proportional representation in both houses of Congress, and special ratifying conventions for the new Constitution. Sherman used his adversaries' own claims to frame issues in a way that weakened their resolve and united Madison's opponents."[7]

By the end of June, the Convention had reached an impasse, and a committee known as the Committee of Eleven was given the task of hammering out a compromise. On July 5, it presented the solution that became known as the **Large State–Small State Compromise:** a bicameral legislature in which representation in the lower house (the House of Representatives) would be based on population and representation in the upper house (the Senate) would be equal for every state. House members were to be chosen by popular election, whereas senators were to be chosen by their state legislatures.

North–South Compromise: Slavery Slavery was another divisive issue. Delegates from southern states wanted slaves to be counted as part of a state's population, which would increase the South's representation in the House of Representatives (because most slaves lived in the South). Delegates from northern states insisted on the principle of equal representation of all citizens, which discounted slaves because they were not considered citizens. The delegates finally agreed to the **North–South Compromise** on slavery, which stated that "three-fifths of all other Persons [that is, slaves]" would be counted for purposes of representation but that the same standard would apply for any taxes assessed on the basis of a state's population. As a concession to the southern states, the larger issue of slavery and trading in slaves was put off for two decades by Article I, Section 9, which prohibited Congress from outlawing the slave trade before 1808.

After negotiating the three-fifths compromise, the Convention spent more than a month debating issues involving the powers of Congress and those of the president. But the major conflicts over state representation and the structure of government had been resolved. On September 17, 1787, thirty-nine of the remaining delegates signed the document; only three refused to do so.[8] The politics of the Convention were over; the politics of ratification loomed ahead.

Ratification

Although the delegates had approved the Constitution, they still had to secure its ratification by the states. To outmaneuver the opposition, which was considerable, they recommended (in Article VII) a novel method of ratification. Amendments to the Articles of Confederation were supposed to be ratified by all state legislatures; but instead of submitting the Constitution to all the state legislatures, the delegates at the Constitutional Convention recommended that the document be ratified by special conventions of the people within the states. In this way they hoped to avoid opposition that might be engendered by state legislatures unhappy with some of the limitations the Constitution placed on their authority. Moreover, they provided that the Constitution would be ratified if at least nine of the thirteen states gave their approval, not the unanimous consent that the Articles required. Congress and the thirteen states eventually agreed to this plan.

Ratification by special state conventions was politically significant because, in James Madison's words, it meant that the Constitution was not a mere treaty "among the Governments and Independent States" but the expression of "the supreme authority of the people themselves."[9]

The erosion of the states' power and the repudiation of their sovereignty under the new Constitution did not escape the attention of those who were opposed to it. Known as the Anti-Federalists, they saw the document as concentrating too much power in a national government and retaining too little authority for the states, both individually and collectively. In the words of Patrick Henry of Virginia, "What right had they [the delegates] to say, We, the People? . . . Who authorized them to speak the language of, We, the People, instead of We, the States? States are the characteristics and the soul of the confederation. If the States are not the agents of this compact, it must be one great consolidated National Government of the people of all the States."[10] But Henry lost, not only in Virginia, but eventually in all other states.

Delaware ratified the Constitution first on December 7, 1787. Within weeks Pennsylvania, New Jersey, Georgia, and Connecticut followed suit. Massachusetts approved the Constitution in February 1788, but it did so only after supporters promised to amend the Constitution to add a bill of rights. In the spring of 1788, Maryland and South Carolina gave their overwhelming endorsements. Then, in June, close votes in New Hampshire and Virginia secured the nine states needed for ratification. But the battle was not over. New York's ratification convention was bitterly divided; New York's approval, however, was crucial for the success of the union because of its geographic position between New England and the rest of the states. Opponents feared that the national government was being granted too much power and that representatives from small states might conspire in Congress against New York's commercial interests. It was largely because of the leadership of Alexander Hamilton and the threat of New York City to secede from the state that New York finally voted in favor of ratification.[11] (North Carolina did not ratify until November 1789, and Rhode Island held out until May 1790.)

In addition to Massachusetts, New York, and several other states the price of ratification was an agreement that the First Congress would adopt a **bill of rights** that specifically guaranteed individuals' civil rights and liberties. The framers had not done so because they thought that individual rights were adequately protected by the constitutional prohibitions placed on the federal government and by the bills of rights in the state constitutions.

In 1789 the First Congress adopted twelve amendments to the Constitution and promptly submitted them to the states. Ten of the amendments, now known as the Bill of Rights, were ratified by the states December 15, 1791. The protections contained in the Bill of Rights are listed in Table 2.2.

With the ratification of the Constitution and the Bill of Rights, the framework for a dynamic but safe political process was in place. It remained for

Bill of Rights

The first ten amendments to the U.S. Constitution, which guarantee specific civil rights and liberties. Introduced in the First Congress, the amendments were ratified by the states in 1791.

Table 2.2 The Bill of Rights

Amendment	Rights
First	Freedom of religion, speech, the press, and assembly
Second	The right to bear arms
Third	Protection against the quartering of soldiers in one's home
Fourth	The right to be secure against unreasonable searches and seizures
Fifth	The right to "due process of law," protection against double jeopardy, and the privilege against self-incrimination
Sixth	The right to counsel for one's defense and to a speedy and public trial by an impartial jury
Seventh	The right to a jury trial in civil law cases
Eighth	Prohibition of excessive bail and fines and of "cruel and unusual punishment"
Ninth	The retention by the people of rights that are not enumerated in the Constitution
Tenth	The retention by the states or by the people of powers not delegated to the national government

succeeding generations to work out how that system would operate. Maryland delegate John Mercer observed toward the end of the Constitutional Convention, "It is a great mistake to suppose that the paper we are to propose will govern the United States. It is the men whom it will bring into the government and interest in maintaining it that is to govern them. The paper will only mark out the mode and the form. Men are the substance and must do the business."[12] Mercer was right.

The Constitution: Democratic or Reactionary?

During much of the nineteenth century, the nation's founders and the Constitution they created were revered. But early in the twentieth century Charles A. Beard, along with historians of what is called the Progressive School, advanced a critical economic interpretation of the Constitution, arguing that it was a reactionary and antidemocratic document. They contended that the founders had thwarted majority rule and created a strong national government to protect the interests of an economic elite.[13] And in a recent study, Robert Dahl points out that because of the compromises the framers had to make to secure agreement, the Constitution included many antidemocratic provisions that future generations of Americans would find unacceptable.[14] (See Box 2.1 earlier in this chapter and the case study at the end of this chapter.)

Others, however, such as historians Bernard Bailyn, Forrest McDonald, and Gordon S. Wood, claim that the real struggle was not over protection of certain economic interests but over differing political views of government power.[15] They point out that in late-eighteenth-century America there was no great mass of people without property and that all founders had an interest in promoting economic prosperity. The deeper political conflict was over republicanism and how to promote civic order yet preserve individual liberty.

Indeed, political scientist Martin Diamond argues that the Constitution, far from being reactionary, was revolutionary.[16] It carried forth the revolutionary principles of the Declaration of Independence, respecting individuals' equal freedoms and popular sovereignty as the foundational values on which the government was based. Thus by creating a system of ordered liberty and limited government based on the consent of the governed, the Constitution brought to completion the revolution that had begun with the Declaration of Independence.

In certain respects, the Constitution was both reactionary and revolutionary: reactionary in addressing the defects of the Articles of Confederation and revolutionary in creating what became a strong central, representative republic.

The Constitution and the Bill of Rights reflected the political conflict of the founding period as well as an underlying consensus about the nature of government and the rights that Americans desired to exercise. The conflict was over the division of authority between the states and a central government, specifically over how much power individual states would have to pursue their own economic, social, and political interests. The consensus related to the need to revise the Articles of Confederation, to maintain a representative form of government based directly or indirectly on popular consent, and to be responsive to the majority while at the same time protecting the rights of the minority. The Constitution embodied this consensus and tried to resolve the conflict in the major compromises that were agreed to at the Convention.

Review Questions

1. Among the characteristics of the government under the Articles of Confederation were

    A. Congress could not regulate commerce
    B. There was no separate executive
    C. Each state could conduct its own foreign policy
    D. All of these

2. The Virginia Plan introduced to the Constitutional Convention by James Madison favored

    A. A strong national government
    B. A continuation of the Articles of Confederation
    C. A monarchy
    D. A perpetuation of the states as the central feature of the new government

continued

3. Probably the most important individual delegate to the Constitutional Convention in opposition to Madison's proposals was

   A. George Washington
   B. Benjamin Franklin
   C. Roger Sherman
   D. Alexander Hamilton

4. To secure ratification by several states, supporters of the new Constitution promised that the First Congress would amend the Constitution to provide

   A. A bill of rights
   B. Power of judicial review
   C. Congressional war powers
   D. Presidential impeachment provisions

Answers:

   1. D
   2. A
   3. C
   4. A

Enduring Ideas and Essential Tensions: Consensus and Conflict

In just 4,300 words, the Constitution provides a blueprint for self-government, institutions and processes by which conflict could be resolved through the formulation and implementation of public policy. Moreover, it provided an agreement that the policy would be accepted by the people even if they did not like it.

The Constitution not only structures conflict and builds consent but also provides for continuity and change. The principles of popular sovereignty, limited government, and unalienable rights led the founders to establish a system of checks and balances by distributing power among the branches of the national government, dividing power between the national and the state governments, and creating the basis for judicial review.

Popular Sovereignty

popular sovereignty
The idea that government is based on the consent of the people and is accountable to the people for its actions.

In rejecting the British monarchical model of government, in which sovereignty rested with a hereditary monarch, the Crown, the colonists proposed the revolutionary idea of **popular sovereignty,** the idea that government is based on the consent of the people and is accountable to the people for its actions.[17] This principle is expressed in the opening lines of the Preamble to the Constitution: "We, the People of the United States, . . . do ordain and establish this Constitution for the

United States of America." The framers believed that popular consent could and should be achieved through representative government, not direct democracy.

Limited Government

The idea of **limited government** follows from the notion of popular sovereignty. Fearful that the alternative to a constitutionally limited government was a tyrannical one, the founders sought to ensure that the authority of government, its ability to make and enforce laws that limit individual freedom, would be restricted to **expressed powers**—that is, powers specified and delegated to the national government by the Constitution.[18] These expressed powers, listed in the first three articles of the document, detail the legislative powers of Congress (Article I), the executive branch (Article II), and the federal judiciary (Article III).

But the framers knew that they could not possibly anticipate all the issues upon which Congress would need to legislate. As a consequence, they conferred **implied powers** on Congress, powers that might be logically inferred from those that were expressly delegated. The basis for implied powers is the "necessary and proper" clause (Article I, Section 8), which gives Congress the power "to make all laws which shall be necessary and proper for carrying into execution the foregoing powers, and all other powers vested by this Constitution in the government of the United States." Because this clause gives Congress flexibility in the exercise of its legislative authority, it is often referred to as the "elastic clause."

How far Congress may go in exercising its implied powers has often generated political controversy. Indeed, the scope of Congress's legislative powers became the focus of an enduring struggle almost immediately after the ratification of the Constitution. In December 1790, Secretary of the Treasury Alexander Hamilton proposed that Congress charter a national bank. A debate over the constitutionality of creating a national bank followed it, pitting Hamilton and the Federalists (who favored a strong national government) against Madison and who desired a more limited role for the national government.

Hamilton contended that a national bank would strengthen the national government by aiding in tax collection, administering public finances, and securing loans to the government. The Senate, half of whose members had been delegates to the Constitutional Convention, unanimously endorsed Hamilton's proposal. But in the House of Representatives, Madison maintained that creation of the bank was beyond the scope of Congress's delegated powers. Despite Madison's opposition, the House adopted a bill chartering the bank. On February 25, 1791, President George Washington signed the act incorporating the first Bank of the United States and granting it a twenty-year charter.

When the bank's charter expired in 1811, its renewal was defeated in Congress by just one vote; but four years later Congress established the second Bank of the United States with another twenty-year charter. Economic hardship brought by the War of 1812 and the national government's reliance on state banks for loans were the overriding considerations in Congress. Opposition to a national bank remained strong in the states, however, and eventually it led to the Supreme Court's landmark decision in *McCulloch v. Maryland* (1819).[19] In that

limited government
The idea that government powers are limited and specified or are traceable to enumerated powers in a written constitution.

expressed powers
Powers enumerated in a constitution. Article I, Section 8, of the U.S. Constitution, for example, enumerates seventeen specific powers of Congress, including the powers to tax, coin money, regulate commerce, and provide for the national defense.

implied powers
Government powers inferred from the powers expressly enumerated in a written constitution. The "necessary and proper" clause of Article I, Section 8, of the U.S. Constitution has been interpreted to give Congress broad implied powers.

decision, Chief Justice John Marshall, writing for a unanimous Court, upheld the constitutionality of the national bank with a broad reading of Congress's implied powers: "Let the end be legitimate, let it be within the scope of the Constitution, and all means which are appropriate, which are plainly adapted to that end, which are not prohibited, but consistent with the letter and spirit of the Constitution, are constitutional."[20]

Although Madison agreed with the *McCulloch* decision, he continued to bristle at the Court's expansive interpretation Congress's power. Opposition to the bank persisted, even though Congress extended its charter in 1832. President Andrew Jackson vetoed that extension and in doing so again challenged the Court's interpretation of and authority over the Constitution. But the precedent had been set for future Congresses to benefit from broad interpretation of congressional powers.

In addition to expressed and implied powers, the national government has **inherent powers** not specifically enumerated in the Constitution, but required to conduct relations with other countries. In the 1936 case *United States v. Curtiss-Wright Export Corp.*,[21] the Court stated, "The power to declare and wage war; to conclude peace, to make treaties, to maintain diplomatic relations with other sovereignties, if they had never been mentioned in the Constitution, would have vested in the federal government as necessary concomitants of nationality." The states may make no claims in this area. But conflict over which institution has the authority to exercise this power has persisted over the years. A recent example occurred in 2006 when members of Congress challenged the president's order to monitor some telephone calls to people in the United States without first obtaining a court order to do so.

Individual Rights

One of the founders' main objectives in constraining the powers of government was to ensure the protection of **unalienable rights** of individuals to "Life, Liberty and the Pursuit of Happiness." Because these rights precede the creation of government, they were not granted by government nor can they be taken away by government. Moreover, it is the duty of government to protect its citizens against any encroachment on these rights.[22]

By limiting the national government's power to that which is specifically granted in the Constitution, the founders hoped to safeguard individuals' unalienable rights. As Hamilton wrote in *Federalist paper,* 84, one of a series of newspaper essays defending the new Constitution, "The Constitution itself, in every rational sense, and to every useful purpose, is a bill of rights." Hamilton's argument that a government with limited and delegated powers would not expand to usurp individuals' rights, did not persuade opponents of the Constitution who distrusted distant, central authority. They therefore urged the adoption of a separate bill of rights, which was ratified in December 1791.

James Madison, the principal drafter of the Bill of Rights, had sought to include protection for individuals, "rights of conscience," and limitations on the powers of the states to deny civil rights and liberties, but Congress rejected those proposals.

---

inherent powers

Powers possessed by a national government that are not enumerated in a constitution. In the conduct of foreign affairs, presidents have often claimed that they possess inherent powers.

unalienable rights

In the social theory of John Locke, certain natural rights of individuals that are believed to precede the creation of government and that government may not deny. The Declaration of Independence proclaimed that individuals have the unalienable right to "Life, Liberty and the Pursuit of Happiness."

Separation of Powers

Because the founders were wary of the concentration of government power, they distributed power among the three branches of the national government (see Figure 2.1). This separation of powers was designed to create a delicate structure in which the legislative, executive, and judicial branches would check and balance one another in various ways. (See Chapter 1.) "Ambition must be made to counteract ambition," Madison argued in *The Federalist,* No. 51.

The principle of separation of powers is embodied in the Constitution's grant of legislative power to Congress, executive and other powers to the president, and judicial power to the Supreme Court and other federal courts. This system stands in contrast to unitary systems such as that of Britain, in which the majority party in Parliament (the legislative branch) appoints the prime minister and cabinet (the executive branch), and cabinet members retain their seats in the Parliament. Nevertheless, the powers given to the three branches are not entirely or completely separate; the branches are actually separate institutions that share political power. For instance, Congress passes legislation that the president must approve or veto; a two-thirds vote by both the House of Representatives and the Senate may override a presidential veto. The president makes treaties with foreign governments and appoints members of the federal executive and judiciary branches, but presidential treaty making and most executive and judicial appointments are subject to ratification or confirmation by the Senate.

Congress, the president, and the judiciary share other powers. In the process of sharing, they check and balance one another, thereby making political change slower and more difficult. In the words of Justice Louis D. Brandeis,

> The doctrine of the separation of powers was adopted by the Convention of 1787, not to promote efficiency but to preclude the exercise of arbitrary power. The purpose was not to avoid friction, but, by means of the inevitable friction incident to the distribution of the governmental powers among three departments, to save the people from having one institution dominate the government.[23]

The effects of power sharing by separate institutions are evident in the operation of constitutional checks and balances through the years. From the beginning of the federal government in 1789 through 2005, presidents had vetoed more than 2,550 bills and Congress had overridden only 106 of them. Moreover, during the same period, the Supreme Court had that ruled more than 150 congressional acts or parts of acts were unconstitutional.

Five federal judges have been impeached by the House and convicted by the Senate; two others were impeached; and another nine resigned to avoid impeachment. Presidents Andrew Johnson (in 1868) and Bill Clinton (in 1998) were impeached but not removed from office. Richard Nixon probably would have been impeached had he not resigned.

Congress has passed, and the states have ratified, five amendments to the Constitution, overturning decisions of the Supreme Court in the process. In short, separation of powers is often a prescription for political struggle. The conflict is reflected in President Andrew Jackson's irate response to a Supreme Court decision with which he disagreed: "John Marshall has made his decision, now let him enforce it." Each branch of government at different times and in various ways checks and thwarts the actions of another.

On the other hand, power sharing also encourages cooperation, compromise, and consensus. For example, Congress and the president must work together to enact legislation and appropriate funds for the operation of government, and the Supreme Court sometimes depends on the other two branches to enforce its rulings. In 1954, when the Court handed down its landmark rulings mandating school desegregation in *Brown v. Board of Education*,[24] both presidential action and congressional action were required to overcome opposition to the decision in the South.

Federalism

By dividing power not only among the branches of the national government but also between the national and the state governments, the Constitution created a system known as **federalism**.[25] The framers of the Constitution had no real alternative to establishing a federal system, one in which certain powers

federalism

A system of government in which powers are shared between central or national government and state or regional governments. The U.S. Constitution establishes a federal system.

Figure 2.1 Separate Institutions Sharing Power

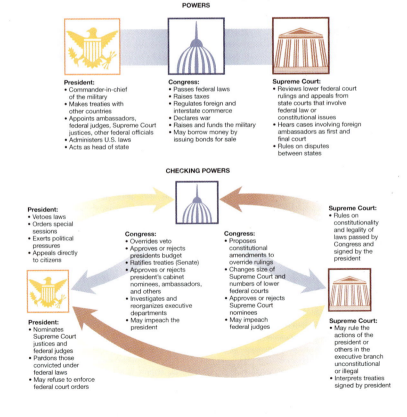

POWERS

President:
- Commander-in-chief of the military
- Makes treaties with other countries
- Appoints ambassadors, federal judges, Supreme Court justices, other federal officials
- Administers U.S. laws
- Acts as head of state

Congress:
- Passes federal laws
- Raises taxes
- Regulates foreign and interstate commerce
- Declares war
- Raises and funds the military
- May borrow money by issuing bonds for sale

Supreme Court:
- Reviews lower federal court rulings and appeals from state courts that involve federal law or constitutional issues
- Hears cases involving foreign ambassadors as first and final court
- Rules on disputes between states

CHECKING POWERS

President:
- Vetoes laws
- Orders special sessions
- Exerts political pressures
- Appeals directly to citizens

President:
- Nominates Supreme Court justices and federal judges
- Pardons those convicted under federal laws
- May refuse to enforce federal court orders

Congress:
- Overrides veto
- Approves or rejects presidents budget
- Ratifies treaties (Senate)
- Approves or rejects president's cabinet nominees, ambassadors, and others
- Investigates and reorganizes executive departments
- May impeach the president

Congress:
- Proposes constitutional amendments to override rulings
- Changes size of Supreme Court and numbers of lower federal courts
- Approves or rejects Supreme Court nominees
- May impeach federal judges

Supreme Court:
- Rules on constitutionality and legality of laws passed by Congress and signed by the president

Supreme Court:
- May rule the actions of the president or others in the executive branch unconstitutional or illegal
- Interprets treaties signed by president

are granted to the national government and the rest are retained by the states. They could not abolish the thirteen original states or deny them most of their governing powers, but they could and did establish a national government with independent powers and leave intact state powers that were not exclusively delegated to the national government. Thus, each state retained its own government based on its own constitution. Individuals were to be subject to both state and national laws. This division between the national government and the states has decentralized much of the politics of American democracy so that those politics remain responsive to the growing heterogeneity of the United States.

The Constitution reserved to the states all powers not granted to the national government and not expressly denied to the states. These **reserved powers** are supplemented by other powers not given exclusively to the national government. Known as **concurrent powers** because they are exercised by both the national government and the states, they include the powers to tax citizens, regulate commerce, and make and enforce criminal laws.

Because the national and state governments share certain powers, conflicts may arise between them. The Constitution requires that federal law prevail in such conflicts. The **supremacy clause** in Article VI stipulates that "this Constitution, and the Laws of the United States which shall be made in Pursuance thereof; and all Treaties made . . . under the Authority of the United States, shall be the supreme Law of the Land; and the Judges in every State shall be bound thereby, any Thing in the Constitution or Laws of any State to the Contrary notwithstanding." Every government official, state and national, is bound to support the Constitution.

Rarely do state laws directly contradict federal law. More common—and more troubling—are cases involving the concurrent powers of the national and state governments, such as the powers to tax and regulate commerce. Conflicts between the national and the state governments are ultimately decided by the Supreme Court. For instance, when state and federal laws governing highway safety or telecommunications come into conflict, the Court must decide whether Congress has preempted state regulations or whether the existence of a variety of different state laws interferes with the need for uniform national regulations.

Throughout the nation's history, the Court has generally supported the authority of the national government to regulate interstate commerce and has increasingly interpreted that authority broadly. But within the last two decades, it has also issued several rulings acknowledging the powers and authorities of states at the expense of the national government. These cases and their implications for American federalism are examined more carefully in Chapter 3.

Judicial Review

Article III, Section 1, of the Constitution states, "The judicial power of the United States shall be vested in one Supreme Court, and in such inferior courts as the Congress may from time to time ordain and establish." Nowhere does the

reserved powers
Powers that have not been delegated to a government body. The Tenth Amendment to the U.S. Constitution provides that powers not delegated to the national government are reserved to state governments or the people of the states.

concurrent powers
Powers shared by both the national government and the state governments, such as the power to tax.

supremacy clause
A clause of Article VI of the U.S. Constitution, providing that the Constitution and other national laws are "the supreme law of the land." National laws thus supersede state or local laws when there is a conflict between them.

judicial review

Power and authority of a court to determine whether acts of a legislature or an executive violate a constitution. The U.S. Supreme Court, for instance, has the power to strike down any congressional or state legislation, as well as any other official government action, that it deems to violate the U.S. Constitution.

Constitution give the federal courts the power to strike down any congressional or state legislation or any other government action because it violates a provision of the Constitution. Yet the courts have assumed this power of **judicial review,** a power that makes them the final arbitrator of major political conflicts and places them in the role of guardian of the Constitution.[26]

The power of judicial review was a distinctive American contribution to the practice of government and remains so today. For example, there is no such power in Britain, which does not have a written constitution. In other European democracies, only in the last fifty years have special courts been created to decide constitutional questions.

Both Alexander Hamilton and James Madison argued that judges should exercise some checking power over state legislatures, but they did not agree on whether the Supreme Court should have the power to strike down acts of Congress and the president. Hamilton contended in *The Federalist,* No. 78, that "independent judges" would prove "an essential safeguard against the effects of occasional ill humors in society" and deemed the judiciary to be "the least dangerous branch" of government. In *The Federalist,* No. 51, Madison called the judicial power an "auxiliary precaution" against the possible dominance of one branch over another. Yet during a debate in the First Congress, he observed that "nothing has been offered to invalidate the [view] that the meaning of the Constitution may as well be ascertained by the legislative as by the judicial authority."[27]

Despite the absence of a specific constitutional provision, the Supreme Court assumed the power to interpret the Constitution in the 1803 case of *Marbury v. Madison.*[28] This case grew out of one of the most fascinating episodes of early American politics. Shortly after the ratification of the Constitution, two rival political parties emerged with widely different views of the Constitution and government power. The Federalists supported a strong national government in which the federal courts would have the power to interpret the Constitution. Their opponents, the Anti-Federalists and later the Jeffersonian Republicans, favored the states and state courts.

The struggle came to a head with the election of Thomas Jefferson as president in 1800. In that election the Jeffersonian Republicans defeated the Federalists, who had held office since the creation of the republic. Fearful of what the Jeffersonian Republicans might do once they assumed office in March 1801, President John Adams and the Federalist-dominated Congress created several new judgeships in January and appointed Federalists to fill them all. Appointed as Chief Justice was Adams's acting secretary of state, John Marshall. Even after his appointment, Marshall continued to work as secretary of state because the Court was not in session. One of the jobs of the secretary was to deliver commissions for the newly-appointed judges. Marshall delivered some but not all of them in the final days of the Adams's presidency.

The Federalists' attempt to "pack" the courts with their own partisans infuriated the Jeffersonian Republicans, and President Jefferson instructed his secretary of state, James Madison, not to deliver the rest of the commissions. William Marbury, one of the newly appointed judges whose commission was not delivered, decided to sue to force Madison to deliver the commission. In his suit,

Marbury went directly to the Supreme Court for a writ of mandamus, a court order directing a government official (Madison) to perform a certain act (hand over the commission) in accordance with Section 13 of the Judiciary Act of 1789, which authorized the Supreme Court to issue such writs. He saw this strategy not only as a way of obtaining his commission but also as a means by which the Court could take a stand against the Jeffersonians.

The Supreme Court faced a major dilemma. On the one hand, if it ordered Madison to deliver Marbury's commission, President Jefferson would likely refuse and the Court's prestige would suffer. On the other hand, if it refused to issue the writ, it could appear to be confirming the Jeffersonian argument that the courts had no power to intrude on the executive branch.

Chief Justice John Marshall handed down the Court's decision February 24, 1803. He said that Marbury had a right to his commission but that the Court had no power to issue it. The reason was that the Judiciary Act's authorization for the Supreme Court to issue such a writ was unconstitutional because it expanded the Court's original jurisdiction beyond that provided in the Constitution. According to Marshall, Article III of the Constitution granted the Court original jurisdiction only in cases involving ambassadors, foreign ministers, and those in which the state was a party. William Marbury did not fit any of these categories. Thus the Court declared Section 13 of the Judiciary Act unconstitutional and simultaneously established the Court's power to declare any act of Congress unconstitutional. Marshall's brilliant opinion not only asserted the power of judicial review but defused the political controversy surrounding the case. Because the Court's decision went against Marbury on the immediate point at issue, it gave President Jefferson no opportunity to retaliate. The Jeffersonians fervently disagreed with the reasoning behind the decision, but there was little they could do about it.

During the first half of the nineteenth century, the Court struck down several state laws, thereby reaffirming the power of the national government over the states. But it was not until 1857, in *Dred Scott v. Sandford,*[29] that the Court declared another act of Congress unconstitutional. In that case, the Court struck down the Missouri Compromise, which had excluded slavery from the nation's territories. The decision badly damaged the Court's reputation and helped precipitate the Civil War. However, it confirmed the precedent and practice of judicial review established in *Marbury v. Madison* and reaffirmed the Supreme Court's position as a coequal branch of government with considerable influence on the politics of government and the direction of public policy.

The Living Constitution

The Constitution is a flexible document. Indeed, the major conflicts of American politics—between the national government and the states and between majority rule and minority rights—are fueled by conflicting interpretations of the meaning of the Constitution. The amendments added to the Constitution along with these interpretations have made it more democratic, expanding the personal liberties and civil rights for most Americans.

Amending the Constitution

Thousands of proposed constitutional amendments have been introduced in Congress. Two such proposals in 2006 received considerable attention. One of these would have prohibited desecration (such as burning) of the American flag; the other would have prohibited same-sex marriages. Both proposals failed, though, as has virtually every proposed amendment since the Constitution was ratified. In fact, over the entire history of the country, attempts to amend the Constitution have succeeded only twenty-seven times. These figures give some indication of how difficult the amendment process (spelled out in Article V) was designed to be and how adaptable the Constitution has become. Two-thirds of the members of each chamber of Congress (or a national constitutional convention called for by two-thirds of the states) must pass an amendment, and then three-fourths of the states must ratify it (see Figure 2.2). To date, only Congress has initiated amendments. The idea of a national constitutional convention worries many political observers, who fear that such a gathering might seek to revise the Constitution itself, much as the Constitutional Convention of 1787 "revised" the Articles of Confederation. Among recent proposals that have failed to win approval were the Equal Rights Amendment, which would have outlawed discrimination on the basis of gender, a proposal to grant home rule (self-government) and voting representation to residents of the District of Columbia, and a requirement that the government maintain a balanced budget.

As noted earlier, the first ten amendments—the Bill of Rights—were ratified just four years after the adoption of the Constitution. They were necessary to quell fears about the coercive power of the national government and to secure the rights of individuals. Five later amendments overturned rulings by the Supreme Court—a remarkably small number, given the thousands of decisions handed down by the Court. The Eleventh Amendment (1798) granted the states immunity from suits by citizens of other states. The Thirteenth (1865) and Fourteenth (1868) Amendments (known as the Civil War Amendments) abolished slavery and made African Americans citizens of the United States. The Sixteenth Amendment (1913) gave Congress the power to enact a federal income tax, and the Twenty-Sixth Amendment (1971) extended the right to vote in all federal and state elections to citizens age 18 or older.

The majority of the remaining amendments to the Constitution have made government processes more democratic (see Box 2.3). The Seventeenth Amendment (1913) provided for popular election of senators. Voting rights were extended to African Americans by the Fifteenth Amendment (1870), to women by the Nineteenth Amendment (1920), to residents of the District of Columbia by the Twenty-Third Amendment (1961), and to indigents (through the ban on poll taxes) by the Twenty-Fourth Amendment (1964). Together with the Supreme Court's rulings promoting the principle of one person, one vote (i.e., all electoral districts within the same state must be approximately equal in population), these amendments have made the Constitution a more democratic document and the political process more open, accessible, and responsive to the people.

Box 2.3 In Democratizing the Constitution

Earlier, we noted that the framers had to reach numerous compromises to secure adoption of the Constitution. Many of these compromises resulted in a document that was "less democratic" than several framers actually wished and future generations of Americans would accept. Earlier (in Box 2.1) we also reviewed the various aspects of the U.S. Constitution that political scientist Robert Dahl finds most "undemocratic." What are the prospects for significant change? For most of these issues, the probability of change is not great, according to Dahl. He says, "The likelihood of reducing the extreme inequality of

representation in the Senate is virtually zero. The chances of altering our constitutional system to make it . . . more clearly consensual . . . are also quite low. The likelihood is very low that the Supreme Court will refrain from legislating public policies." Despite this, the Constitution has been amended several times to expand the electorate, thus making it a more democratic document. These amendments are as follows:

1. Amendment 14, 1868. Gives citizenship to all people born or naturalized in the United States (including former slaves), prevents states

from depriving any person of "life, liberty, or property without due process of law," and declares that no state shall deprive any person of "equal protection of the laws."
2. Amendment 15, 1870. Guarantees that citizens' right to vote cannot be denied "on account of race, color, or previous condition of servitude."
3. Amendment 19, 1920. Extends voting rights to women.
4. Amendment 23, 1961. Extends to residents of Washington, D.C., the right to vote for president.
5. Amendment 24, 1964. Prohibits charging a tax to vote in presidential or congressional elections.
6. Amendment 26, 1971. Lowers voting age to eighteen years.

Figure 2.2 The Amendment Process

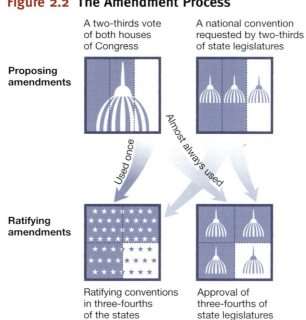

Interpreting the Constitution

Chief Justice Charles Evans Hughes once declared, "We are under a Constitution, but the Constitution is what the judges say it is."[30] Through judicial review, the Supreme Court gives authoritative meaning to the Constitution in light of new claims and changing conditions. It does so by bringing new claims, such as a right to privacy, within the language, structure, and spirit of the Constitution.

Through its interpretation of the Constitution, therefore, the Court legitimates and occasionally initiates constitutional change. Perhaps the most significant change judicial interpretation achieved was the nationalization of the Bill of Rights. Initially, the Bill of Rights was viewed as limiting the federal government not on the states. After all, the First Amendment begins, "Congress shall make no law . . . .

The Supreme Court confirmed this understanding in the 1833 case of *Barron v. Baltimore*.[31] That case involved a person whose wharf had been made unusable when the City of Baltimore graded some streets and diverted some streams, producing soil deposits on the wharf. Barron therefore sued the city for depriving him of his property without "just compensation" and "due process of law" as stated in the Fifth Amendment. But the suit was invalid unless the Fifth Amendment was found to apply to states and localities, not just to the federal government. In ruling that the Fifth Amendment did not apply to the states and localities, Chief Justice John Marshall pointed out the language of the First Amendment and the history of the adoption of the Bill of Rights demonstrated that the purpose of the entire Bill of Rights was to guard against, as he put it, "encroachments of the general government—not against those of the local governments."[32]

With the adoption of the Fourteenth Amendment in 1868, however, there was a new basis for applying the Bill of Rights to the states. Indeed, one of the motives of Congress at that time was to overturn Marshall's decision in the *Barron* case.[33] Like the Fifth Amendment, the Fourteenth Amendment contains a due process clause, but the clause specifically limits the power of the states: "No State shall make or enforce any law which shall abridge the privileges of immunities of citizens of the United States; nor shall any State deprive any person of life, liberty, or property, without due process of law; nor deny to any person within its jurisdiction the equal protection of the laws."

Immediately after the adoption of the Fourteenth Amendment, lawyers tried to convince the Supreme Court that the Fourteenth Amendment "incorporated" or "absorbed" the guarantees of the Bill of Rights and applied them to the states. Yet with one exception, that of eminent domain (the taking of private property for public use), the Court refused to go along with that argument in the nineteenth century.

In the twentieth century, however, it reached a different conclusion. In the case of *Gitlow v. New York*,[34] which involved a man who had been convicted under a New York State law that made it a crime to preach or advocate the overthrow of the government by force, the Court ruled that the guarantee of the freedoms of speech and press in the First Amendment apples to the states. In the 1930s and 1940s, the Court applied the remaining First Amendment guarantees, those dealing with religion and the right of assembly, to the states on a case-by-case basis, but it was reluctant to apply the rest of the Bill of Rights to the states, particularly the rights of the accused contained in the Fourth through Eighth Amendments.

Table 2.3 The Nationalization of the Bill of Rights

Year	Guarantee, Amendment, Case
1897	Eminent domain, Fifth, *Chicago, Burlington & Quincy Railroad v. Chicago*
1925	Freedom of speech, First, *Gitlow v. New York*
1931	Freedom of press, First, *Near v. Minnesota*
1932	Right to counsel in capital cases, Sixth, *Powell v. Alabama*
1934	Free exercise of religion, First, *Hamilton v. Regents of the University of California*
1937	Assembly and petition, First, *DeJonge v. Oregon*
1947	Establishment of church and state, First, *Everson v. Board of Education of Ewing Township*
1948	Public trial, Sixth, In re Oliver
1949	Unreasonable searches and seizures, Fourth, *Wolf v. Colorado*
1961	Exclusionary rule, Fourth, *Mapp v. Ohio*
1962	Cruel and unusual punishment, Eighth, *Robinson v. California*
1963	Right to counsel in all criminal cases, Sixth, *Gideon v. Wainwright*
1964	Compulsory self-incrimination, Fifth, *Malloy v. Hogan*
1965	Confrontation of witnesses, Sixth, *Pointer v. Texas*
1965	Right of privacy, Fourth, *Griswold v. Connecticut*
1966	Trial by impartial jury, Sixth, *Parker v. Gladden*
1967	Right to a speedy trial, Sixth, *Klopfer v. North Carolina*
1968	Jury trial in nonpetty criminal cases, Sixth, *Duncan v. Louisiana*
1969	Double jeopardy, Fifth, *Benton v. Maryland*
1972	Right to counsel in all cases involving a jail term, Sixth, *Argersinger v. Hamlin*

During the 1960s, however, when the Court was headed by Chief Justice Earl Warren, it selectively incorporated the other principal guarantees of the Bill of Rights into the Fourteenth Amendment's due process clause and made them applicable to the states (see Table 2.3).[35] In addition, in the 1965 case, *Griswold v. Connecticut*,[36] it found a "right of privacy" (which was not specifically mentioned in the Constitution) and applied it to the states under the Fourteenth Amendment. By the 1970s, all major provisions of the Bill of Rights had been applied to the states. The only ones that do not apply are the right to keep and bear arms (Second Amendment); the provision against quartering of troops in private homes (Third); the provision for grand jury indictments (Fifth); the right to a jury trial in civil cases (Seventh); and the provision that the other enumerated rights "shall not be construed to deny or disparage others retained by the people" (Ninth).

nationalization of the Bill of Rights
The interpretation of the Supreme Court over time that expanded the guarantees of the Bill of Rights to apply to states.

The **nationalization of the Bill of Rights** has involved the Court in continuous political controversy because it expanded the judiciary's supervision over state legislation and made the Court a powerful arbitrator in the struggle for civil rights and liberties. Particularly in the area of criminal justice, the Court's decisions have pitted the proponents of law and order against the advocates for personal liberties and civil rights. This ongoing confrontation is an integral part of the politics of American democracy.

Frequently, the justices have disagreed among themselves on how to interpret the Constitution. That disagreement may be based on judicial philosophy or on the substance of the case. Some justices have subscribed to a philosophy of **strict construction.** They believe that the Constitution should be interpreted literally, supplemented by historical precedent and whatever can be learned about the historical context of specific provisions. Others believe in a **broader reading** of the text, structure, and spirit of the Constitution, an approach that permits judges to formulate a general principle applicable to different cases in light of changing circumstances.

strict construction
The idea that the U.S. Constitution can and should be interpreted in a narrowly literal sense, as it was written and understood by its framers.

The debate on the meaning of the Constitution began with the early Court decisions, has continued over the years, and is likely to do so in the future because as Justice Felix Frankfurter wisely observed, "Constitutional law is not at all a science, but applied politics."[37]

broad reading
An approach to interpreting the U.S. Constitution that allows its general principles to be widely applied to different cases in light of changing circumstances.

Think of the interpretation of the Constitution as a constantly evolving dialogue between the Supreme Court and the American people over the resolution of the political controversies that those cases represent. The Court can resolve the individual cases, but putting the political issues to rest is more difficult. Thus, in *Marbury v. Madison* (discussed earlier), Chief Justice Marshall may have resolved the dispute over whether the "midnight judges" were entitled to their commissions, but he could not end the partisan bickering that gave rise to the dispute and the attempt by an outgoing party to try to preserve its influence through judicial appointments; nor could he provide a constitutional interpretation that would direct Congress in making its future legislative judgments. Similarly in the *Roe v. Wade*, the case in which the Court acknowledged a woman's right to privacy included the right to obtain an abortion, controversy was not ended by the Court's decision; in fact, it may have been stimulated by it.

In addition, the Court cannot move too far ahead of the public in its legal decisions. In the words of Chief Justice Edward White, the Court's power to interpret the Constitution "rests solely on the approval of a free people."[38] The major confrontations that the Court attempts to resolve—such as controversies over school desegregation, school prayer, and abortion—are determined as much by the possibility of developing consensus in a pluralistic society as by what the Court says about the meaning of the Constitution.

Resolution of conflict is the role of the judiciary. But that role must be exercised within the constraints of the constitutional system, not outside it. That system was designed to protect against abusive government as it concentrated power in that government; it was designed to protect minorities as it reflected consensus of the majority; it was designed to protect specific rights and liberties because it provided flexibility in interpreting those rights and liberties as conditions changed and societies evolved.

Review Questions

1. Charles A. Beard is among those who argue that the Constitution is largely

   A. A racist document
   B. An economic document
   C. A states' rights document
   D. A democratic document

2. Powers that may not be specifically mentioned in the Constitution, but may reasonably be inferred from those that are, are known as

   A. Implied powers
   B. Expressed powers
   C. Reserved powers
   D. Inherent powers

3. The constitutional principle that distributes power among the three branches of government and provides checks and balances on each is known as

   A. Federalism
   B. Separation of powers
   C. Limited government
   D. Popular sovereignty

4. The principle that makes the courts the final arbitrator of political conflicts and places them in the role of guardian of the Constitution is known as

   A. Federalism
   B. Limited government
   C. Popular sovereignty
   D. Judicial review

Answers:

   1. B
   2. A
   3. B
   4. D

Conflict and Consensus in Review

The framers knew that political conflict was inevitable. What they tried to do was to keep it from getting out of hand by prescribing a set of rules within which democratic politics could function, a mechanism that could resolve policy disputes, at least temporarily, and a process by which over time a consensus could be forged. The chapters that follow examine how well their constitutional system has met these challenges.

Politics in Action

Government and the Ten Commandments

Earlier, we noted that the framers of the Constitution considered the rights of all individuals to be equally important. Although the majority (or plurality) rules, the minority's rights must be protected. Consider the right to adhere to your own beliefs. The First Amendment of the Constitution bars government from ever making a law that establishes religion. But does such a provision bar certain religious symbols from being displayed in public buildings or on public grounds?

A case in point involves public display of the Ten Commandments. In 2005 the Supreme Court agreed to hear two cases contesting the display of the Ten Commandments on government land and buildings. One of these arose from a situation in Texas *(Van Orden v. Perry)* where a six-foot-tall granite monument depicting the Ten Commandments had been erected on the state Capitol

grounds in 1961; the other arose from a situation in Kentucky *(McCreary County v. ACLU of Kentucky)* in which the Ten Commandments were posted in courthouses. The Kentucky case was initiated by the American Civil Liberties Union, which argued that the Commandments represented an endorsement of a particular religion. The Texas case had been initiated by a homeless man in that state who felt that the Capitol monument had no valid secular purpose and that it in essence represented the endorsement of a particular religion. Although a suspended lawyer, Thomas Van Orden compiled his case while living in a tent in a wooded park area in Austin, obtaining food stamps to eat, and using the facilities at the library of the University of Texas law school. It is said that at times "he lacked the 10 cents to print out even one page of his briefs and did

Workers struggle to remove monument of the Ten Commandments from an Alabama Court.

continued

Politics in Action *continued*

not have the money to mail his appeal to the federal court in New Orleans."[39]

In both Kentucky and Texas, the displays had been donated by private groups, and in both cases, they were included with other American documents and monuments. In Kentucky, the Ten Commandments were included in a display depicting the Declaration of Independence, the Mayflower Compact, and the Magna Carta; the grounds of the Texas State House also included monuments as tributes to various veterans, firefighters, and children's groups. In the Kentucky case, the appeals court ordered removal of the Ten Commandments; in the Texas case lower courts declined to order the monument's removal.

In both cases, supporters of the monuments argued that the Ten Commandments contained both secular (prohibitions on stealing, killing, and adultery) and religious directives and that the Ten Commandments have had a significant role in the development of American law. Supporters also pointed to the context of each display—each containing numerous other memorials to significant historical events. As with the "Pledge" case discussed earlier in this chapter, public opinion polls showed that the American public overwhelmingly supported maintaining the Ten Commandments displays.[40]

Opponents, however, contended that the primary purpose of the displays were to advance and endorse a particular religious view, that they lacked any legitimate secular purpose, and that both discriminated in favor of some religions and against others.

The Supreme Court resolved the issue in 2005 by rendering a mixed judgment. It upheld the constitutionality of the Ten Commandment monument in Texas, declaring that it was a religious display, but one with historical meaning, reflective of a cultural heritage. The Court also noted that the monument was one of 17 and 21 historical markers that had been on the grounds of the Texas capitol for 40 years without dispute. On the other hand the Court ruled that the framed copies of the Commandments in Kentucky were unconstitutional because they were placed there, initially alone, for the expressed purpose of conveying a certain moral and ethical belief. Other displays were added after litigation began. Advocates for both sides of this issue expressed disappointment and frustration with what they saw as a split decision and it is certain that similar cases soon will follow.

The Ten Commandments issue presents a classic example of the interplay of conflict, politics, democracy, and resolution in the context of the American political system. The case also illustrates the nature of consensus and conflict that often characterizes the American system. Although there is broad consensus in America for religious freedom and for the lack of government interference in the exercise of religious belief, there is often sharp conflict when it comes to the specific exercise of those beliefs. In the Ten Commandment cases, both sides presented clear and (at least to their supporters) reasonably convincing arguments. Still, one side sees the displays as unwarranted and unconstitutional government infringement on their religious freedoms; the other sees it as permissible government activity. Disputes over the specific exercise of religious rights within the overall context of broad approval of religious freedom have from the outset been a defining feature of the consensus and conflict existing within the American system, and they certainly will continue to be so.

What Do You Think?

1. Should a religious expression be part of the Pledge of Allegiance to the country?
2. Should the words "In God We Trust" be removed from U.S. currency?
3. Should Congress be allowed to open each day's session with a prayer? What about the president taking the oath of office with his hand on a Bible?
4. If the Ten Commandments are allowed to be displayed in a public setting, what about phrases from the Koran or the New Testament?

Summary

Earlier we noted that the framers had to reach numerous compromises to secure adoption of the Constitution and that these compromises resulted in a document that was "less democratic" than some of them wished and future generations of Americans would accept. These compromises occurred because the Constitution was, and remains a political document, one revered by most Americans but also one that has been subject to varying interpretations.

The Constitution established a framework within which political struggles occur and are resolved. It does so by proclaiming popular sovereignty and limiting government simultaneously. It concentrates authority but separates institutions and powers within the national government and between that government and the states. In this way it uses conflict as a vehicle for limiting excess and forcing compromise, and it builds consensus as it resolves issues.

The First Continental Congress met in 1774 to pass resolutions denouncing the English Parliament and Crown. In 1776, the Second Continental Congress drafted a resolution—the Declaration of Independence—that proclaimed the American colonies to be free and independent states. In 1777, it approved the Articles of Confederation, the nation's first constitution. Under the Articles, Congress lacked the power to regulate commerce, collect taxes, or enforce its legislation. After the Revolutionary War, the nation's economic problems worsened, coming to a head with Shays's Rebellion.

In 1787, delegates from the states met in Philadelphia to revise the Articles of Confederation but soon decided to establish a national government with separate legislative, executive, and judiciary branches. They resolved the two most contentious issues, representation and slavery by compromises that established a bicameral legislature, counted three-fifths of a state's slave population for purposes of taxation and representation, and prohibited Congress from eliminating the slave trade for another twenty years.

The Constitutional Convention recommended that the new Constitution be sent to the states for ratification by special conventions. Only nine states needed to concur before the Constitution went into effect. The primary objection to the new document came during the ratification debates from those who feared that it gave the national government too much power. To allay those fears, proponents agreed to a group of amendments that guaranteed the civil rights and liberties of individuals; this became known as the Bill of Rights.

During the last 200-plus years, constitutional change has occurred in three ways: through applications of the Constitution to the day-to-day operation of government, through formal amendments, and through judicial review. Changes in government institutions, scientific and technological advances, and social forces have brought about modifications of the constitutional structure of government. In addition, the Constitution has been amended twenty-seven times, and the Supreme Court also initiated change through its continuing interpretation of its meaning.

The Court's role in constitutional change has been controversial. Some justices and scholars have argued for a strict construction, or literal reading, of the text of the Constitution. Others have urged a broad reading of the text, structure, and spirit of the Constitution. Although American may disagree over how the Court interprets the Constitution, they agree on the merits of the constitutional design and the right of the Supreme Court to be its final arbiter.

Key Terms

Articles of Confederation
republic
Virginia Plan
New Jersey Plan
Large State–Small State
Compromise
Slavery
North–South Compromise

Bill of Rights
popular sovereignty
limited government
expressed powers
implied powers
inherent authority
unalienable rights
federalism

reserved powers
concurrent powers
supremacy clause
judicial review
nationalization of the Bill
  of Rights
strict construction
broader reading

Discussion Questions

1. The Constitution often is called a "bundle of compromises." Discuss those important compromises that had to be reached for the delegates to the Constitutional Convention to reach agreement and what you believe are the motives behind those advocating each set of compromises.
2. In what ways does the Constitution as drafted in 1787 provide a framework for resolving important political conflicts today?
3. The framers of the Constitution were concerned with creating a system based on majority rule but also one respectful of minority rights. Have they succeeded in achieving this dual objective?
4. If a constitutional convention were called today, what do you believe would be some of the important issues that those drafting an American Constitution for the twenty-first century would want to consider? Explain your reasoning.
5. Discuss the ways in which the Constitution, over the years, has become a more democratic document. Are there other changes that you would recommend?

Topics for Debate

Debate each side of the following propositions:

1. The Constitution was and remains a reactionary document designed primarily to maintain power of the economic elite.
2. The Articles of Confederation, with just a few modifications, would satisfactorily serve the needs of the United States today.
3. In furthering democracy in America, the process of amending the Constitution should be made easier.
4. It doesn't matter whether the justices of the Supreme Court read the Constitution literally or liberally.

Where on the Web?

GPO Access Home Page **www.gpoaccess.gov**

The National Archives Experience **www.archives.gov/national_archives_experience/ charters/constitution.html**

Federalist Papers **www.foundingfathers.info/ federalistpapers/**

Go to **www.thomsonedu.com/thomsonnow** to learn about a powerful online study tool. You will get a personalized study plan based on your responses to a diagnostic Pre-Test. Once you have mastered the materials with the help of interactive learning tools, activities, timelines, video case studies, simulations, and an integrated E-Book, you can take a Post-Test to confirm you are ready to move to the next chapter.

Selected Readings

Alley, Robert S. *The Constitution & Religion: Leading Supreme Court Cases on Church and State.* Amherst, N.Y.: Prometheus Books, 1999.

Beard, Charles. *An Economic Interpretation of the Constitution of the United States.* New York: Macmillan Publishers, 1913.

Beer, Samuel H. *To Make a Nation.* Cambridge, Mass.: Harvard University Press, 1993.

Berkin, Carol. *A Brilliant Solution: Inventing the American Constitution.* New York: Harcourt, 2002.

Dreisbach, Daniel L. *Thomas Jefferson and the Wall of Separation between Church and State.* New York: New York University Press, 2002.

Ellis, Joseph J. *Founding Brothers.* New York: Alfred A. Knopf, 2000.

Farrand, Max. *The Framing of the Constitution,* New Haven, Conn.: Yale University Press, 1913.

Kramnick, Isaac, and R. Laurence Moore. *The Godless Constitution: The Case Against Religious Correctness.* New York: W. W. Norton & Co., 1997.

Nord, Warren A. *Religion and American Education: Rethinking a National Dilemma.* Chapel Hill: University of North Carolina Press, 1995.

O'Connor, Sandra Day. *The Majesty of the Law.* New York: Random House Publishers, 2003.

Peltason, J. W., and Sue Davis. *Understanding the Constitution,* New York: Harcourt Brace, 2000.

Roberts, Cokie. *Founding Mothers.* New York: HarperCollins Publishers, 2004.

Wood, Gordon S. *The Creation of the American Republic.* Chapel Hill: University of North Carolina Press, 1969.

Notes

[1] James Madison, The Federalist, No. 51, in *The Federalist Papers,* ed. Clinton Rossiter (New York: New American Library, 1961), 320–325.

[2] President George W. Bush, State of the Union Address, January 21, 2006, cited in David Morris and Gary Langer, "Same Sex Marriage: Most Oppose It, but Balk at Amending the Constitution." http://www.abcnews.go.com (accessed August 11, 2006).

[3] See Max Farrand, *The Framing of the Constitution* (New Haven, Conn.: Yale University Press, 1913), and John P. Roche, "The Founding Fathers: A Reform Caucus in Action," *American Political Science Review* (December 1961): 799.

[4] For further discussion, see Gordon S. Wood, *The Creation of the American Republic, 1776–1787* (Chapel Hill: University of North Carolina Press, 1969).

[5] "Resolution of Federal Convention (May 30, 1787)," in *The Records of the Federal Convention of 1787,* vol. 1, ed. Max Farrand (New Haven, Conn.: Yale University Press, 1913), 30.

[6] "James Madison," in *The Federalist Papers,* No. 39, ed. Clinton Rossiter (New York: New American Library, 1961), 240–246.

[7] David Brian Robertson, "Madison's Opponents and Constitutional Design," *American Political Science Review,* 99 (May 2005), 234–235.

[8] Forrest McDonald, *Novus Ordo Seclorum: The Intellectual Origins of the Constitution* (Lawrence: University of Kansas Press, 1985).

[9] "James Madison," in Farrand, *The Records of the Federal Convention of 1787,* vol. 1, 122–123.

[10] "Patrick Henry," in *The Complete Anti-Federalist,* vol. 5, ed. Herbert J. Storing (Chicago: University of Chicago Press, 1981), 211.

[11] For studies of the debates in the various state ratification conventions, see *Ratifying the Constitution,* ed. Michael Gillespie and Michael Lienesch (Lawrence: University of Kansas Press, 1989).

[12]Quoted and discussed in David O'Brien, "The Framers' Muse on Republicanism, the Supreme Court, and Pragmatic Constitutional Interpretivism," *The Review of Politics* 53 (1991): 251.

[13]Charles A. Beard, *An Economic Interpretation of the Constitution* (New York: Macmillan, 1913).

[14]Robert Dahl, *How Democratic is the American Constitution?* (New Haven, Conn.: Yale University Press, 2001).

[15]See Bernard Bailyn, *The Ideological Origins of the American Revolution* (Cambridge, Mass.: Harvard University Press, 1967); Forrest McDonald, *We the People: The Economic Origins of the Constitution* (Chicago: University of Chicago Press, 1958); Gordon S. Wood, *The Creation of the American Republic, 1776–1787;* and Gordon S. Wood, *The Radicalism of the American Revolution* (New York: Knopf, 1992).

[16]Martin Diamond, "The Declaration and the Constitution: Liberty, Democracy, and the Founders," *The Public Interest* 41 (Fall 1975): 40.

[17]Peter Onuf, "State Sovereignty and the Making of the Constitution," in *Conceptual Change and the Constitution,* ed. Terence Ball and J. G. A. Pocock (Lawrence: University of Kansas Press, 1988).

[18]John Reid, *The Concept of Liberty in the Age of the American Revolution* (Chicago: University of Chicago Press, 1988).

[19]*McCulloch v. Maryland,* 17 U.S. 316 (1819).

[20]Ibid.

[21]*United States v. Curtiss-Wright Export Corp.,* 299 U.S. 304 (1936).

[22]Ellis Sandoz, *A Government of Laws: Political Theory, Religion, and the American Founding* (Baton Rouge: Louisiana State University Press, 1990).

[23]*Meyers v. United States,* 272 U.S. 52 (1926).

[24]*Brown v. Board of Education of Topeka, Kansas,* 347 U.S. 483 (1954).

[25]This discussion draws on David O'Brien, "Federalism as a Metaphor in the Constitutional Politics of Public Administration," *Public Administration Review* 49 (1989): 411.

[26]For two studies of judicial review and the founding of the United States, see Robert Clinton, *Marbury v. Madison and Judicial Review* (Lawrence: University of Kansas Press, 1989), and Sylvia Snowiss, *Judicial Review and the Law of the Constitution* (New Haven, Conn.: Yale University Press, 1990).

[27]James Madison, speech in the House of Representatives, in *Annals of the First Congress,* vol. 1 (Washington, D.C.: Gales and Seaton, 1834), 532.

[28]*Marbury v. Madison,* 5 U.S. 137 (1803).

[29]*Dred Scott v. Sandford,* 60 U.S. 393 (1857).

[30]Charles Evans Hughes, *Addresses of Charles Evans Hughes* (New York: G. P. Putnam's Sons, 1916), 185–186.

[31]*Barron v. Baltimore,* 32 U.S. 243 (1833).

[32]Ibid.

[33]On the debate over whether the Fourteenth Amendment was intended to apply to the sates, see Horace E. Flack, *The Adoption of the Fourteenth Amendment* (Baltimore: John Hopkins Press, 1908; Charles Fairman, *Reconstruction and Reunion, 1864–88* (New York: Macmillan, 1971); and Raoul Berger, *Government by Judiciary* (Cambridge, Mass.: Harvard University Press, 1977).

[34]*Gitlow v. New York,* 268 U.S. 652 (1924).

[35]For an excellent history of the nationalization of the Bill of Rights, see Richard C. Cortner, *The Supreme Court and the Second Bill of Rights: The Fourteenth Amendment and the Nationalization of Civil Liberties* (Madison: University of Wisconsin Press, 1981).

[36]*Griswold v. Connecticut,* 381 U.S. 479 (1965).

[37]Felix Frankfurter, "The Zeitgeist and the Judiciary," in *Law and Politics,* ed. A. MacLeish and E. Prichard (New York: Capricorn, 1939), 6.

[38]Edward White, "The Supreme Court of the United States," *American Bar Association Journal* 7 (1921), 341.

[39]For background and reference to much of this discussion, see Ralph Blumenthal, "The Supreme Court: The Plaintiff," *New York Times,* March 3, 2005.

[40]"Ten Commandments before High Court," http://www.cnn.com; May 17, 2005.

3

Federalism in Theory and in Practice

Introduction

THE FRAMERS OF THE CONSTITUTION were concerned about the protection of individual rights and liberties. They knew that in a democracy, a system in which those with the greatest number tend to prevail, the rights of the minority could be threatened. That is why they created a federal system of government in which power was divided between the national government and the states in addition to the separation of powers among the three branches of the national government. As James Madison put it,

> In the compound republic [a term Madison used to describe federalism] of America, the power surrendered by the people is first divided between two distinct governments, and then the portion allotted to each subdivided among distinct and separate departments. Hence a double security arises to the rights of the people. The different governments will control each other, at the same time that each will be controlled by itself.[1]

More than 200 years later, in 2001, Supreme Court Justice Clarence Thomas echoed Madison's belief in the protection afforded individual rights and liberties by a federal form of government:

> But what has escaped notice of late . . . is that the framers established another structural safeguard for individual liberty, and I am speaking here of federalism. The framers did not believe that separating powers alone would be sufficient to guard against tyrannical government. They saw for example, that the three branches of the national government could collude in an unconstitutional exercise of power. In order to protect against this possibility the framers created a federal, not purely national, system of government. . . . In other words, federalism provides a check on the national government when the separation of legislative from executive from judicial powers alone cannot do the job or does not do it. Madison does not say that federalism necessarily exists to protect the sates as institutions, although that's a subsidiary effect. Rather, federalism, like the separation of powers, exists to protect the rights of the people.[2]

Considerable consensus exists among the American public, and the country's political leaders, over the theoretical value of federalism. Recent surveys indicate that more than 75 percent of the American public agrees with the statement, "A federal form of government, in which power is divided between a national government and state and local governments, is preferable to any other kind of government."[3] And President George W. Bush, in a speech delivered to the nation's governors at the outset of his administration, proclaimed, ". . . let me make this pledge to you all: I'm going to make respect for federalism a priority in this administration. Respect for federalism begins with an understanding of its philosophy. The framers of the Constitution did not believe in an all-knowing, all-powerful Federal Government. They believed that our freedom is best preserved when power is dispersed."[4]

In practice, however, federalism is far more controversial, even for President Bush. Although he had pledged to make federalism "a priority" in his administration, in many areas he has actually increased the power and size of the national government through his policies of education reform, with national incentives for local schools; Medicare restructuring, with national drug coverage for the elderly; airline security, with a new federal bureaucracy, the Transportation Security Agency; and anti-terrorism legislation, which enhanced the national government's surveillance powers. Further, President Bush also voiced his support for a constitutional amendment that would outlaw same-sex marriages in all the states. Commenting on actions such as these, Senator Lamar Alexander (R-TN) stated, "The principle of federalism has gotten lost in the weeds."[5]

The administration's actions have not gone unnoticed or unopposed. More than thirty states have voiced serious objections to President Bush's "No Child Left Behind" education reform law. The state of Utah has withdrawn entirely from the Bush school plan.

So although widespread consensus exists on the principle of federalism, considerable controversy can develop when those principles are implemented. A good example of the controversy is illustrated by the reaction to the Violence Against Women Act. After finding that some states were treating offenses against women less seriously than those against men, Congress enacted this legislation in 1994. It permits victims of rape, domestic violence, and other crimes "motivated by gender" to sue their attackers in federal court.

The first case brought under the Violence Against Women Act was initiated by Christy Brzonkala, a then student at Virginia Polytechnic Institute.

© AP/Wide World Photos

Should the federal government or the states decide if physicians may prescribe medication to end the life of terminally ill patients? Ruth Gallaid from Eugene, Or., who supports physician assisted suicide, protests in front of the Supreme Court Wednesday, Oct. 5, 2005, the day on which the Court heard the case of *Gonzales v. Oregon*. In its ruling issued three months later, the Court held that Attorney General Ashcroft exceeded his authority when he threatened doctors with criminal prosecution if they, acting under the Oregon statue, provided lethal drugs to a patient who wished to die.

Brzonkala accused two varsity football players at that school of raping her in her dormitory room. As provided in the act, she brought suit against them in federal court. The defendants, however, challenged the constitutionality of the act on the ground that Congress did not have authority in such areas. This case, known as *United States v. Morrison*,[6] reached the Supreme Court, which decided that, indeed, those provisions of the act were unconstitutional. The Court's majority opinion stated, "Gender-motivated crimes of violence are not, in any sense of the phrase, economic activity" and therefore do not fall within the scope of congressional authority.

Despite possible state bias against women in cases such as these, the Court ruled that such matters are not of legitimate federal concern but should remain with the states: "The Constitution requires a distinction between what is truly national and what is truly local, and there is no better example of the police power, which the founders undeniably left reposed in the States and denied the central government, than the suppression of violent crime and the vindication of its victims."[7] Commenting on the Court's judgment, Senator Joseph R. Biden (D-DE), sponsor of the law, stated simply, "this decision is really all about power."[8]

Senator Biden is correct: Federalism is all about power. It also is about the controversy that the struggle for exercising that power generates. Throughout the nation's history, Americans have and continue to debate, the respective roles of the national government, the states, and local governments. In nonfederal countries such as Great Britain, political debate ordinarily is limited to whether the government should become involved in some activity. In the United States, however, the debate is about not just whether government should be involved but also which level of government should be responsible for a particular activity.

Questions to Ponder

- Which level of government—national, state, or local—do you think should be responsible for protecting women against acts of domestic violence?
- Which level should be responsible for firearm regulation?
- Which level should be responsible for setting education standards, deciding whether same-sex couples can marry, deciding when extraordinary life-saving measures should be abandoned, establishing abortion laws, setting environmental rules and regulations, regulating businesses and professions, and establishing welfare policies?
- Which level should set minimum wage rates for public- and private-sector employees, determine the appropriate age for alcohol consumption, set speed limits on roads and highways, and determine the legality of marijuana use for medical purposes?

The answers to these questions were not spelled out by the framers of the Constitution; they were left for future generations to decide. Those decisions ensure that although federalism in theory is almost universally applauded, in practice it can be very controversial.

3.1 In Theory . . .
Federalism

Students sometimes view federalism as simply a concept forced on the drafters of the Constitution as a compromise between those factions wanting to create a strong central government and those wanting to protect the status of individual states. The adoption of federalism—a system recognizing the sovereign independence of both national government and state governments—was necessary simply to placate the independent states that feared distant, centralized authority.

But the framers of the U.S. Constitution viewed federalism as a key feature for the protection of individual rights and liberties. James Madison called federalism one of the Constitution's "auxiliary precautions" that, along with the separation of powers principle, would prevent tyranny in government (see *The Federalist,* No. 51). For the framers, federalism helped provide the "balance of power" that would permit each level of government to control the excesses of the other and thus protect individual rights from the encroachment of either. In Madison's words, "the [national] legislature will not only be restrained by its

continued

3.1 **In Theory . . .** *continued*

dependence on the people . . . but it will be moreover watched and controlled by the several [state] legislatures" (*The Federalist,* No. 52).

And, as Alexander Hamilton put it, "the general government will at all times stand ready to check the usurpations of the state governments, and these will have the same disposition toward the general government" (*The Federalist,* No. 28). Further, Hamilton said, "The state legislatures . . . will be ready enough, if anything improper appears, to sound the alarm to the people and not only to be the voice, but, if necessary, the ARM of their discontent" (*The Federalist,* No. 26).

These principles have served as fundamental pillars of American government and democracy from the drafting of the Constitution to the present. In an important case decided in 1991, the U.S. Supreme Court declared that "perhaps the principal benefit of the federalism system is a check on abuses of government power. . . . In the tension between federal and state power lies the promise of liberty" (*Gregory v. Ashcroft,* 501 U.S. 452).

Justice Clarence Thomas made similar points in a speech he delivered at James Madison University on March 15, 2001, on the occasion of Madison's 250th birthday. He stated that "the Framers did not believe that separating powers alone would be sufficient to guard against tyrannical government.

In order to protect against [tyranny] the Framers created a federal . . . system of government." And Supreme Court Justice Sandra Day O'Connor in her recently published book (*The Majesty of the Law,* 2003) declares federalism to be a constitutional principle "nearly as dear to the American people" as the Bill of Rights.

Federalism, then, is a fundamental principle to the American theory of government and governing. For the framers, as well as for contemporary members of the U.S. Supreme Court, federalism is viewed as a key restraint on the concentration and abuse of governmental power, and consequently as a key protector of individual rights and liberties.

Federalism as a Political Issue

In creating federalism, the founders "introduced an entirely new concept" to political discourse, according to historian Forrest McDonald.[9] And in so doing, they provided no clear designation of the precise relationships among the various levels of government. What has resulted is a continuous struggle between state and national governments over such issues as the regulation of business and labor, civil rights, and environmental protection, to name but a few of the areas in which the levels of government have collided.

Ostensibly the fight is over policy, but frequently it takes the form of a struggle over authority—which government has the right to make the policy. People who believe that state and local governments are likely to support their views on an issue—be it same-sex marriages, welfare, gun control, abortion, or prayer in public schools—will argue that the Constitution "clearly" reserves authority for such decisions to the states and communities. The federal system will suffer, they say, if such decisions are "nationalized." People who believe that the national government is likely to be supportive of their views will make the opposite argument. The Constitution, they say, "obviously" delegates responsibility in these areas to the national government.

In this chapter, we examine conflict and consensus on the theory and practice of federalism. We trace the evolution of the American federal experience, focusing on the ways in which the national government and the states and localities attempt to regulate and influence one another's behavior. We also discuss the effect of federalism on democratic government. Our case study at the end of the chapter, the regulation of handguns in the public schools, illustrates the continuing conflict and confusion over national versus state rights.

The Changing Nature of American Federalism

The concept of federalism has been evolving since 1787. It is, as some people say, "unfinished business."[10] Here we present a summary of that evolution and the conflict and consensus that have characterized it.

National Supremacy Versus State Rights, 1787–1865

During the period from the ratification of the Constitution to the end of the Civil War, debate over the proper role of governments in the American system persisted. Those who supported **nation-centered federalism**—the Federalists—believed that the Constitution emanated from and was applicable to the American people as a whole, that it was not simply a pact among the states. From the Federalist perspective, the national government had a legitimate interest in protecting and promoting the health, safety, and welfare of the people; its interests and obligations did not end with its dealings with state governments. As Chief Justice John Marshall stated in 1819 in the case of *McCulloch v. Maryland*, the national government "is the government of all; its powers are delegated by all; it represents all, and acts for all."[11]

> **nation-centered federalism** A view of federalism held in the pre–Civil War era that advocated an active and expanded role for the national government.

Marshall and other Federalists saw the Constitution as a document of and for national unity. They believed that the national government could draw on a rich array of delegated and implied powers to promote the general welfare of the country. As Secretary of the Treasury Alexander Hamilton put it, the test for determining whether an act of Congress is constitutional is the end, or goal, that it addresses:

> If the end be clearly comprehended within any of the specified powers, and if the measure have an obvious relation to that end, and is not forbidden by any particular provision of the Constitution, it may safely be deemed to come within the compass of the national authority.[12]

In contrast, those who supported **state-centered federalism**—the Anti-Federalists—believed that the Constitution was a compact among the states and that the states themselves were the legitimate center of power and authority in the federal system. This position was eloquently advanced in 1798 in the Virginia and Kentucky Resolutions, which were drawn up by James Madison and Thomas Jefferson in opposition to the Alien and Sedition Acts of 1798 and were passed by the legislatures of both Virginia and Kentucky.[13] The resolutions implied that the national government did not have all government power, that its powers were limited by the language of the Constitution, that some rights were reserved for the states, and that states could protect their rights.[14]

> **state-centered federalism** A view of federalism held in the pre–Civil War era that opposed increasing national power at the expense of the states.

doctrine of nullification
Doctrine of the claim, associated most closely with South Carolina Senator John C. Calhoun, that states could declare acts of Congress null and void within their borders.

This position was taken to its extreme in the 1820s and 1830s by many advocates of states' rights, and especially by Senator John C. Calhoun of South Carolina, whose **doctrine of nullification** argued that sovereignty—ultimate government power—could not be divided among levels of government but instead resided with the states. The Constitution, Calhoun believed, was an agreement among sovereign states that established a central government to perform certain tasks for them. Viewing the central government as an agent of the states, he argued that whenever a state found an act of Congress to be in violation of the Constitution, that state could declare the congressional act null and void within its own borders. This position was clearly at odds with the views of those advocating a nation-centered form of government.

By the 1840s, slavery had become the dominant issue, dividing advocates of the nation-centered and state-centered notions of federalism. As always, both groups pointed to the Constitution for support. Opponents of slavery cited the due process clause of the Fifth Amendment, which states that "No person . . . shall be . . . deprived of life, liberty, or property, without due process of law." They further argued that because Congress had full sovereignty over the territories by virtue of its treaty and war powers, Congress could limit or abolish slavery in the territories as it wished.

Relying on positions similar to those advanced by Calhoun, proponents of slavery argued that because the national government was merely an agent of the states, it could not administer the territories against the interest of any state. Therefore, they said, slaveholders had a constitutional right to bring slaves into any territory without legal hindrance. They also relied on the Fifth Amendment, arguing that because slaves were property, legislation abolishing slavery would be a destruction of property without compensation and therefore a violation of the amendment's due process protections. This argument was accepted by Chief Justice Roger Taney in the *Dred Scott* case.[15]

Scott, a slave, had been taken by his owner from Missouri, where slavery was legal, to Illinois, where it was illegal, and later to the Minnesota Territory, where it was prohibited under the Missouri Compromise. When his owner died, Scott sued for his freedom, claiming that the years he had spent in Illinois and the free territory had ended his bondage. The case made its way through the state courts in Missouri, moved into federal court, and in 1857 was decided by the Supreme Court.

The Court ruled against Scott, stating that he could not sue because as a Negro and as a slave he was not a citizen of the United States. As for the issue of slavery in the territories, Chief Justice Taney's opinion stated that the federal government had no general sovereignty over the territories. Congress had only the powers associated with the right to acquire territories and prepare them for statehood; it could not exercise internal police powers. This meant that Congress could not prevent slavery in the territories and that the Missouri Compromise, which had excluded slavery from the northern territories, was unconstitutional.

The *Dred Scott* decision greatly intensified the crisis that led to the Civil War. It is often said that even though the decision did not "cause" the war, it was the straw that broke the nation's back.

Redefining State and National Roles, 1865–1933

The Civil War permanently altered federal–state relations. The doctrine of nullification was discredited by the outcome of the strife, and the Union was preserved. Since that time, few Americans have seriously proposed that a state can declare an act of Congress null and void or can secede from the Union.

Between 1865 and 1933, a new relationship known as **dual federalism** emerged; it recognized separate and distinct spheres of authority for national government and state governments. The staunchest advocates of dual federalism viewed the distribution of power among the levels of government as fixed and unchangeable. The states were judged to be on an equal plane with the national government, and the Tenth Amendment was cited as constitutional evidence for an area of authority reserved for the states.[16]

dual federalism
A view of federalism held between the time of the Civil War and the mid-1930s that attempted to recognize and maintain separate spheres of authority for the national government and state governments.

This philosophy can be seen in the Supreme Court's ruling in the case of *Texas v. White* (1869), which tested whether Texas was responsible for bonds issued by its Confederate government during the Civil War. Chief Justice Salmon P. Chase stated that

> Under the Constitution, though the powers of the States were much restricted, still all the powers not delegated to the United States, nor prohibited to the States, are reserved to the States, respectively, or to the people. . . . Not only . . . can there be no loss of separate and independent autonomy to the States, through their union under the Constitution, but it may be not unreasonably said that the preservation of the States, and the maintenance of their governments, are as much within the design and care of the Constitution as the preservation of the Union and the maintenance of the National Government. The Constitution, in all its provisions, looks to an indestructible Union, composed of indestructible States.[17]

During this period the United States was industrializing rapidly, and the public began looking to government at all levels for greater social and economic regulation. However, because state attempts to curb business excesses and monopolies have largely proven ineffective, it fell to Congress to regulate economic practices and the social effects of big railroads and other industrial giants. Much of the debate over proper federal–state relations centered on the interpretation of the interstate commerce clause of the Constitution (Article I, Section 8) and on the proper role of Congress in regulating the nation's commerce.

Attempting to distinguish between *interstate* commerce, which Congress could regulate, and *intrastate* commerce, which was under the authority of the states, the Supreme Court invalidated several regulatory actions by Congress on the ground that they usurped state authority. In 1895, for example, the Court significantly weakened the effects of the Sherman Anti-Trust Act of 1890 (a federal act that attempted to prevent monopolies) by declaring that monopolistic manufacturing activities were not within the scope of national regulatory influence because manufacturing is not commerce.[18] During the 1890s, the Court also severely curtailed the powers of the Interstate Commerce Commission, which had been created in 1887 to regulate commerce, particularly the railroads.

The case of *Hammer v. Dagenhart* (1918) presents most forcefully the doctrine of dual federalism. In that case, the Supreme Court invalidated the federal Child Labor Act of 1916—which barred any commodities produced by manufacturers employing children from interstate commerce—on the ground that the act invaded an area reserved for state activity. In the words of Justice William R. Day,

> In interpreting the Constitution it must never be forgotten that the nation is made up of states to which are entrusted the powers of local government. And to them and to the people the powers not expressly delegated to the national government are reserved. . . . The power of the states to regulate their purely internal affairs by such laws as seem wise to the local authority is inherent and has never been surrendered to the general government.[19]

Justice Day's use of the term "expressly" in the *Dagenhart* decision altered the meaning of the Tenth Amendment, because almost 130 years earlier the framers had deliberately rejected use of the term there.

The Court's affirmation of dual federalism lasted until the Great Depression of the 1930s. After President Franklin Roosevelt took office in 1933, he proposed several actions to speed the nation's economic recovery. One of these, the National Industrial Recovery Act of 1933 (NIRA), created a massive public works program and attempted to establish uniform codes and regulations for much of the nation's business and industry. Reflecting the philosophy of dual federalism, the Court struck down the NIRA in 1935 in the case of *Schechter Poultry Corporation v. United States,* noting that "the authority of the federal government may not be pushed to such an extreme as to destroy the distinction . . . between 'commerce among the several states' and the internal commerce of a state."[20] But nullification of the NIRA proved to be the last significant Court decision supporting the concept of dual federalism.

Expansion of the Federal Government, 1933–1968

cooperative federalism
A view of federalism held between the mid-1930s and the 1960s that stressed a partnership and sharing of government functions between the states and the national government.

The Great Depression ended an era and ushered in **cooperative federalism,** which stressed a partnership and a sharing of functions, responsibilities, and programs between the states and the national government. Since the late 1930s, the courts have generally extended the national government's control and regulation of business and commerce through their interpretation of the Constitution. In the case of *United States v. Darby Lumber Company* (1941),[21] for example, the Supreme Court upheld the Fair Labor Standards Act of 1938, which, among other provisions, prohibited the shipment in interstate commerce of goods produced by child labor and thus effectively overturned the *Dagenhart* decision. And as we mentioned at the beginning of this chapter, subsequent actions by Congress and the courts have greatly enlarged the role of the national government in such areas as education, housing, transportation, civil rights, environmental protection, and social services.

grants-in-aid
Programs through which the national government shares its fiscal resources with state and local governments.

The period from 1933 to 1968 was marked by the increased use of **grants-in-aid,** that is, programs through which the national government shares its fiscal resources with state and local governments (grants-in-aid are described in detail later in the chapter). By 1930, fifteen grant programs were allocating about $120 million to the states annually. Between 1930 and 1960, the number of grants-in-aid programs increased dramatically. During the period sometimes called the "First New Deal"—about 1933 to 1935—new grant programs were enacted for the distribution of surplus farm products to the needy and for free school lunches, emergency highway expenditures, emergency relief work, general relief, administration of unemployment insurance, and assistance in meeting local government costs. During the "Second New Deal"—about 1935 to 1939—additional grant programs were created for child welfare, mothers' and children's health, services for children with disabilities, old-age assistance, aid to dependent children, aid to the blind, general health services, fire control, wildlife conservation, public housing, emergency road and bridge construction, and control of venereal disease and tuberculosis.

By 1960, there were some 132 grant programs, allocating a total of almost $7 billion annually. Most grants made available during this period went to state governments; a few went directly to cities. Because most grants were for specific purposes or programs defined by Congress, the regulatory role of the national government (in the form of rules that had to be followed and conditions that had to be met for grants to be awarded) increased significantly. So did national reliance on the grants-in-aid system for achieving a range of objectives, especially in social welfare, housing, and transportation.[22]

The Elementary and Secondary Education Act, originally passed in 1965, has allocated over $200 billion in federal aid to the nation's elementary and secondary schools. Reauthorized in 2002, the act incorporated President Bush's "No Child Left Behind" legislation, more closely tying federal assistance to school performance.

During the 1960s the number of federal grants available to state and local governments exploded. Under President Lyndon B. Johnson's Great Society social program, grants were used to expand the range of federal activity; in 1965 and 1966 alone, Congress enacted 130 new grant programs. By 1968, almost $19 billion was allocated through the grant programs, many of which provided money directly to cities, bypassing state governments.

From Grants-in-Aid to Mandates and Regulations, 1968–1994

coercive federalism
Term some apply to the period after the 1960s when the national government began forcing state and local government to conform with nationally set goals and objectives.

new federalism
The view of federalism associated with Presidents Nixon and Reagan, which stressed greater flexibility in the use of grants-in-aid by the recipients and, in the Reagan years, reductions in the total amount of grants.

The next several decades are described by many as a period of **coercive federalism,** one in which the national government assumed many powers that had previously been exercised by the states and forced the states to implement certain nationally set priorities. When he took office in 1968, President Richard M. Nixon proposed an approach that he called **new federalism.** He deemphasized the use of grants for specific purposes and focused instead on large grants to local governments in general policy areas. In theory, such grants, known as *block grants,* gave the recipient governments greater discretion in the expenditure of funds, and they removed from the national government a degree of control over how the funds were spent. Throughout the 1970s, the amount of money allocated through grants-in-aid programs continued to grow. By 1980, the national government was allocating $91.5 billion to states and localities annually.

In 1980, President Reagan announced a program also known as new federalism, but his approach differed from Nixon's. Reagan called for a significant slowdown in the rate of increase in the funding of grant programs, and in both 1982 and 1987 the amount of money made available declined. In addition, the number of programs declined significantly, as did the proportion of state and local budgets funded by grants. In 1980, grants-in-aid accounted for 25.8 percent of total state and local spending, but by the end of the decade the amount had dropped to about 17 percent. This trend turned around somewhat in the early 1990s, and more than sixty new grant programs were enacted from 1993 to 1995. In 1995, grants represented about 22 percent of state and local spending and almost 15 percent of the federal budget. But most of these increases occurred in grants targeted for individuals (such as Medicaid), not in grants going to local governments for general purposes.

The Reagan administration deemphasized grants-in-aid as a tool for national policymaking. But a higher proportion of grants went to state governments than to local governments, and states had greater authority over the funds. This policy continued during the George H. W. Bush administration, contributing to what some observers believed to be a revitalization of state governments. However, it also left local governments with considerably less revenue to deal with the myriad problems facing America's cities. President Bill Clinton proposed a few modest assistance programs for distressed cities and neighborhoods, but his focus on deficit reduction precluded any major new spending on grants-in-aid.

Throughout this period, whether grants were expanding or shrinking, the federal government—through various mechanisms discussed later in the chapter—greatly increased its monitoring and regulation of state and local activities. From 1970 to 1990, for example, it issued more than 200 "preemptive statutes" that displaced or replaced state and local laws. This was twice as many such statutes as had been passed in the entire history of the United States until then.

Throughout this period, too, the Supreme Court adopted an increasingly nationalistic perspective on issues of federalism. In an important 1976 case, *National League of Cities v. Usery,* the Court held that some areas of state activity—in this instance, the setting of minimum wages for municipal employees—are exempt from encroachment by the national government. The Tenth Amendment, the Court ruled, provides absolute protection for at least some areas of state (and municipal) government functions: "There are attributes of sovereignty attaching to every state government which may not be impaired by Congress . . . because the Constitution prohibits [Congress] from exercising [its] authority in that manner."[23]

Soon, however, the Court began issuing decisions that severely eroded the principle of state sovereignty established in the case.[24] In *Garcia v. San Antonio Metropolitan Transit Authority* (1985), the Court ruled that local governments must adhere to minimum-wage standards set by Congress (at a cost to local governments of about $1.75 billion annually).[25] In this 5–4 decision, the Court ruled that, except in rare situations, the Constitution does not limit the national government's power to interfere in state affairs. The notion of state functions beyond the control of Congress, the Court said, is "both impracticable and doctrinally barren."[26]

To some, these and related court decisions seemed to have virtually eliminated any vestige of protected state or local sovereignty. As Justice Sandra Day O'Connor lamented in her dissenting opinion in the *Garcia* case, "The States as States retain no status apart from that which Congress chooses to let them retain." Together, the cases seemed to imply that officials of the national government would be the sole judges of the limits of national power and that almost no arena of state activity was beyond the regulatory authority of the national government.

Devolution Federalism, 1994–?

Many observers see the period beginning from the mid-1990s and extending to the present as one of **devolution federalism.**[27] Devolution federalism implies an era marked by a return to state and local governments of many responsibilities that in recent years have been assumed by the federal government, an action that in effect reverses decades of centralization of power in the American federal system.

In 1994, Republicans ran on a platform they called Contract with America, much of which dealt with federal–state relations. Among other provisions, the contract promised a reduction in unfunded mandates—federal requirements

devolution federalism
A possible contemporary trend, beginning with the 1994 Republican congressional victories, in which many federal government responsibilities may be returned to state and local governments.

imposed on state and local governments without any federal funding to cover the costs of implementation. The contract also promised reductions in grants-in-aid and greater emphasis on block grants.

After winning majorities in the House and Senate, Republicans were quick to introduce many of their ideas into proposed legislation. Among the first significant pieces of legislation passed by the new Congress—in March 1995—was one limiting congressional use of unfunded mandates; it requires Congress to study the costs of a mandate before imposing it and to find ways to pay those costs—or to vote specifically to waive the funding requirement in that case. A few months later, Congress repealed the national 55-mile-an-hour speed limit it had established twenty-one years earlier, saying that states should be permitted to decide their own speed limits. As Senator Don Nickles (R-Oklahoma) explained, "I just happen to think that the State of Oklahoma and the State of Virginia are just as concerned about safety as the Federal Government."

By far the strongest indication of the shift to devolution federalism, however, was congressional action in 1996 that converted the Aid to Families with Dependent Children (AFDC) program, a central component of the nation's welfare policy, to block grants—an action that virtually ceded control of national welfare policy to the states. Although similar proposals to convert the Medicaid program, along with various employment and job-training programs, to block grants were not enacted, the abolition of AFDC alone represented a significant change of direction in federal responsibilities.

But the center of action for the new emphasis on devolution has been the U.S. Supreme Court. Beginning in the early 1990s, the Court (led in most cases by five justices known as the "Federalism Five"—Justices Kennedy, O'Connor, Rehnquist, Scalia, and Thomas) issued several decisions that were "friendly" to state governments at the expense of the national government. Relying mainly on the current Court's interpretation of the interstate commerce clause of the Constitution, as well as the Tenth and Eleventh Amendments, the Court significantly curtailed the authority of the national government and reasserted constitutional protection of state governments from certain congressional actions. Although in these decisions the Court did not explicitly overturn the *Garcia* decision discussed previously, it did significantly limit federal authority and restore state powers in many important areas.

In the 2000 case of *United States v. Morrison* (noted earlier), the Court ruled that gender-motivated crimes of violence do not fall within the scope of federal authority. In 1995, the Court had struck down the 1990 Gun-Free School Zones Act, a federal law banning possession of guns in or near schools.[28] Control of guns in and around public schools, the Court reasoned, was a legitimate area for state but not federal regulation. A year later, the Court ruled that the Eleventh Amendment protects states from being sued in federal courts by groups who believe that they are victims of wrongdoing.[29]

In 1997 the Court ruled that a 1993 act of Congress requiring state and local officials to perform background checks on prospective gun purchasers was an unconstitutional extension of federal powers into the authority of states.[30] And in 1999 it extended state immunity against private suits to include state courts, as well as federal courts—a decision that meant that state employees could no longer sue to enforce the Fair Labor Standards Act of 1938 on state governments.[31] In a case decided in 2000,[32] the Court ruled that state employees could no longer sue to force states to adhere to the federal Age Discrimination in Employment Act of 1967. And in 2001 the Court ruled that private parties cannot sue states for violations of the federal Americans with Disabilities Act.[33]

In the 2002 case of *Federal Maritime Commission v. South Carolina Ports Authority,*[34] the Court significantly expanded Eleventh Amendment protections granting immunity to states from private lawsuits to include immunity from actions by private parties against executive branch agencies. Two cases decided in 2003 signaled the Court's willingness to extend state authority. One of these was a ruling from a federal appeals court in Arkansas that the Court let stand allowing that state to force a convicted murderer to take drugs to make him sane enough for execution. The other was a South Carolina Supreme Court case upholding the murder conviction of a woman who had used crack cocaine before delivering her stillborn baby.

Although many of these pro-state cases may seem to have invalidated little-known laws and obscure federal statutes, the cumulative effect has been stunning—amounting to what some have called a "counterrevolution" in federal–state relations.[35] For the first time in decades, the Court seems more than willing to consider issues from the perspective of federalism, to draw sharp distinctions between national and state spheres of authority, and in the process, to extend state immunity from the reach of federal law. As Justice Stephen Breyer stated in his dissent to the 2002 *Federal Maritime Commission* case, these cases are reversing the "modern understanding of federal supremacy."[36]

Most recently, however, there seems to be evidence that the Court is retreating, at least a bit, from its pro-state position. In a case decided in 2004, the Court upheld by a 5–4 decision the right, under the Americans with Disability Act passed by Congress in 1990, of disabled people to sue state governments that did not make their courts fully handicapped accessible (*Tennessee v. Lane*).[37] In a decision reached in 2005, the Court invalidated state laws that permitted in-state, but not out-of-state, wine shipments, and in another 2005 decision it upheld the power of Congress to prohibit the use of marijuana for medical purposes, even in those states that permit it (*Gonzales v. Raich*).[38] And, in a case decided in 2006 (*Central Virginia Community College v. Katz*), the Court ruled that states are not immune from private law suits brought under federal bankruptcy laws. As these decisions make clear, the struggle between national and state representatives continues, with proponents of greater state and local responsibility arguing that governments closest to the people make better decisions for their citizens and opponents suggesting that these governments may not be able to carry out these responsibilities adequately and fairly.

© AP/Wide World Photos

Beverly Fox, who suffers from severe arthritis and an eye condition similar to glaucoma, puffs on a pipe filled with marijuana, Thursday, Oct. 23, 1997, in the offices of the Green Cross Patient Co-op. Fox, who smokes marijuana several times a day, says using marijuana greatly eases her pain and helps to clear her vision. In 2005, the Supreme Court ruled that the Federal government can bar use of marijuana, even for medical purposes.

Do these recent developments represent fundamental shifts in American federal–state relations? Some believe that they have. Richard Nathan, for example, has stated "It is finally beginning to dawn on people that this is a big deal. This could produce a series of changes in domestic policy bigger than the Great Society."[39] Others are more cautious in their appraisals. John Kincaid finds that although there has been some "nudging toward restoring some state powers . . . no wholesale devolution" has yet taken place.[40] Indeed, in some of its most recent decisions, the Court seems to have retreated from its pro-state philosophy, and, as mentioned at the outset of this chapter, many of the policies and activities of the Bush administration have resulted in a greater centralization of power in Washington. Regardless, these developments show that the principle of federalism, created more than 200 years ago by the framers of the Constitution, remains a central feature of American politics today. Federalism, we noted earlier, is "unfinished business." It continues to adapt in response to changing situations and changing public attitudes.

Review Questions

1. In the early days of the Republic, those who held what might be called a "state-centered" view of federalism were called

   A. Anti-federalists
   B. Federalists
   C. Nationalists
   D. Loyalists

2. The period between about 1865 and 1933 that recognized separate and distinct spheres of authority for the national government and the state governments is known as the period of

   A. New federalism
   B. Dual federalism
   C. Cooperative federalism
   D. Creative federalism

3. The period between about 1933 and 1968 that stressed a partnership and sharing of functions between the national government and the state governments is known as the period of

   A. New federalism
   B. Dual federalism
   C. Cooperative federalism
   D. Creative federalism

4. One prominent feature of the period known as cooperative federalism, between about 1933 and 1968, was the increasing use of

   A. Revenue sharing
   B. State Tax exemptions
   C. Grants-in-aid
   D. Federal Regulations

Answers:

   1. A
   2. B
   3. C
   4. C

Conflict and Consensus in Review

Americans share a general consensus on the value of our Federal system of government. When asked, most Americans will say that a federal system of government, like ours, is preferable to any other arrangement. But since the beginning of our Republic, the actual

continued

practice of federalism has been marked by debate, disagreement, and conflict between the national government and the states.

The conflict has taken the form of disputes over public policy. The greater resources and more representative character of the Congress (as compared to many state legislatures) have prompted the federal government to act when states were hesitant to do so. The Supreme Court has refereed this struggle, determining when the federal government has crossed the line by improperly imposing national policy on the states. The Court's composition, the politics of the times, and the policy environment has influenced its judgment on this question.

Although conflict generates the judicial issue, consensus emerges over time and, sometimes reluctantly, as a consequence of the Court's decision. That consensus, however, gives way to conflict as new policy issues emerge, new solutions are debated, and new legal challenges are initiated. Federalism has clearly been an invitation for struggle between the states and national government, but the principle upon which that struggle is predicated, the desirability of a federal system of government, is one in which most Americans concur.

Federal–State–Local Relations: Power and Politics

The federal system of the United States poses particular challenges for the national government, as it attempts to influence and regulate local governments, and for local governments, as they attempt to affect activities at the national level. The national government, in its attempts to regulate states and localities, may issue direct orders and may preempt state and local activities. Also, through grants-in-aid and the conditions attached to these grants, the national government may encourage certain state and local activities and discourage others.

National Regulation of States and Localities

Direct Orders Occasionally the national government issues mandates or **direct orders** that local governments must comply with or else face civil or criminal penalties. For example, the Americans with Disabilities Act of 1990 requires local governments to see to it that all fixed-rate public transportation systems are made accessible to the disabled, that all new buses and transit facilities are equipped with wheelchair lifts, and that transit services are provided to people who cannot use public transit facilities. In 1991, the Environmental Protection Agency issued a ruling requiring all municipal landfills to meet certain conditions designed to prevent contamination of soil and underground water supplies—at a cost to local governments of about $330 million per year—thereby establishing the first comprehensive federal standards for city dumps.

The Help America Vote Act, passed by Congress in 2002, mandated the upgrading of voting equipment and training of poll workers, and the REAL ID Act,

direct orders
Legal measures adopted by the national government, and enforced by civil or criminal penalties, that require certain actions by state and local governments.

passed in 2005, required states to ensure that by 2008 drivers' licenses comply with nationally set standards (at an estimated cost to state and local governments in excess of $100 million). Although there have been attempts to curtail the imposition of such requirements—especially those unfunded or underfunded—it is estimated that today the gap between the funds provided by Congress to state and local governments to carry out such mandates and their actual cost exceeds $30 billion annually.[41]

Preemption Early in the nation's history, Congress assumed the authority to **preempt,** or remove from state activity, policy areas with broad national implications. When Congress decides to exercise this authority, the authority of state and local governments is weakened. The Copyright Act of 1790 and the Bankruptcy Act of 1898, for example, stipulated that all regulatory activity in these fields would be exercised exclusively by the national government. In 1995, Congress preempted all state and local requirements pertaining to the sale and distribution of cigarettes and smokeless tobacco that were different from federal requirements. In 2000, Congress passed the American Homeownership and Economic Opportunity Act that preempted states' authority to set standards for installing manufactured housing. In 2005 Congress passed the Protection of Lawful Commerce in Arms Act that preempts state laws by prohibiting civil liability actions in state courts against firearm manufactures, dealers, or importers when their products are unlawfully used, and in 2006 a bill was introduced in Congress which, if eventually passed, would preempt state and local eminent domain authority by prohibiting states and localities from taking privately-owned land for the purpose of economic development.

Preemption, of course, is controversial and is frequently opposed by state and local governments. One of the criticisms voiced against the "Patient's Bill of Rights" debated by Congress several years ago was the preemption that federal legislation would impose on state insurance and health laws. Another equally contentious issue was raised by Attorney General John Ashcroft in November of 2001 when he threatened prosecute any doctors who provided lethal medicines to patients wishing to end their life. Ashcroft's threat would have effectively nullified Oregon's Death with Dignity Act, which was approved by voters in a state-wide referendum. The Supreme Court in a narrow ruling in 2006 stated that Aschroft did not have the authority under a federal law, the Controlled Substances Act, to prosecute state doctors.[42]

A process known as **partial preemption** occurs when the national government establishes minimum standards in certain areas and authorizes state and local governments to exercise primary responsibility for the function, as long as they maintain standards at least as high as those set by the national government. States may impose stricter standards, but if a state or locality fails to enforce the base-level standard set by Congress, the national government assumes responsibility for doing so. When Congress passed the Water Quality Act of 1965, it gave states one year in which to set acceptable standards of quality for interstate waters within their boundaries. After that year had passed, the Secretary of Health, Education, and Welfare (and, more recently, the head of the Environmental Protection Agency) was authorized to enforce federal standards in any state that failed to do so. Similarly, the Clean Air Act of 1970 set air quality

preempt
The removal of an area of authority from state and local governments by the national government.

partial preemption
The national government's establishment of minimum standards in a policy area and its requiring state and local governments to meet those standards or lose their authority in that area.

standards throughout the nation and required the states to develop effective plans for their implementation. In 1990, amendments to this act established strict regulations that cities must meet in reducing urban smog and required state agencies to prepare new studies of pollution in cities.

Since the ratification of the Constitution, more than 500 preemption statutes have been enacted by Congress. However, only a few were passed before 1900, and more than half have been adopted in the past three decades. This concentration reflects the growing complexity of contemporary policy issues and the need for uniform national standards in many areas. But the increased use of preemptive legislation mirrors political considerations as well. In the 1930s, liberals championed the use of preemptive tactics as a means of overcoming the reluctance of many states to pass progressive economic and labor legislation. In the 1960s, liberals again relied on preemptive legislation as a key weapon in implementing policies in the areas of civil rights, fair housing, age discrimination, voting rights, and environmental issues.

In the 1980s and early 1990s, on the other hand, business and industry groups (especially in banking, communications, and transportation) repeatedly sought federal preemption as protection from more aggressive state regulations. For example, the Bus Regulatory Reform Act, signed by President Reagan in 1982, nullified the authority of states to engage in economic regulation of the busing industry. Today virtually all authority to engage in economic regulation of airline, bus, and trucking activities has been removed from the states. Another example is the 1990 Nutritional Labeling and Education Act, signed into law by President George H. W. Bush, which preempted state nutritional-labeling requirements. And in 2006 legislation supported by the food industry was introduced in Congress that if ultimately adopted would preempt all state food safety regulations that are more restrictive than federal statutes.

Grants-in-Aid

The use of grants-in-aid is an even more common, and in many instances a more effective, way for the national government to achieve its objectives at state and local levels. The Sixteenth Amendment to the Constitution, ratified in 1913, gave Congress the power to impose an income tax, and the greatly increased revenues obtained by this means enabled the national government to share extensive resources with the states. This sharing took the form of grants-in-aid.

Today over $400 billion is allocated annually through more than 900 grant-in-aid programs. These grants enable state and local governments to carry out many activities that would not be possible without federal aid. They also have enabled the national government to motivate state and local governments to pursue objectives that otherwise might have been politically difficult or impossible. Grants-in-aid have been used to fund projects in mass transportation, urban renewal, housing, drug rehabilitation, crime reduction, health care, low-income home energy assistance, pollution control, nuclear-waste disposal, solid-waste disposal, highway beautification, and aid to homeless youth, as well as in many other areas.

Conditions of Aid Federal money comes with "strings." The many conditions that recipients must satisfy to receive federal grants can influence state and local policies. These conditions are of two types: crosscutting requirements and crossover sanctions.

Crosscutting requirements, which are attached to almost all federal grants, pertain to nondiscrimination, environmental protection, planning and coordination, labor standards, and public access to government information and decision making. As an example, the 1964 Civil Rights Act guarantees nondiscrimination in all federally assisted programs. Today there are approximately sixty crosscutting requirements.

Crossover sanctions impose national sanctions or penalties in one area to influence state or local policy in another area. The Intermodal Surface Transportation Act of 1991, for example, contained more than a dozen crossover sanctions, including one requiring states to adopt mandatory motorcycle helmet and seatbelt laws by 1994. (The motorcycle helmet provisions of this act were repealed in 1995.) States that failed to adopt these laws had to spend up to 3 percent of the federal funds they received for highway projects on highway safety activities. The same strategy had been used in 1984, when Congress passed a law that withheld a portion of federal highway funds from any state that did not set its minimum drinking age at twenty-one or higher. In 1996, the Health and Human Services Administration issued a ruling threatening states with the loss of federal grants to fight drug and alcohol abuse unless they reduced the easy access of teenagers to cigarettes and other tobacco products. Also in 1996, when Congress renewed the Ryan White Act—a measure that funneled millions of dollars to state and local governments to help with the care of people with AIDS—it included a provision to cut off funds to states that do not establish mandatory procedures to test newborns for the virus that causes the disease. And in 2001, Congress included a provision in the transportation spending bill of that year stipulating that

crosscutting requirements
Conditions imposed on almost all grants-in-aid to further various social and economic objectives, such as nondiscrimination or environmental protection.

crossover sanctions
Conditions imposed on grants-in-aid in one program area that are designed to influence state and local government policy in another area.

Figure 3.1 Federal Aid to State and Local Governments in 2004

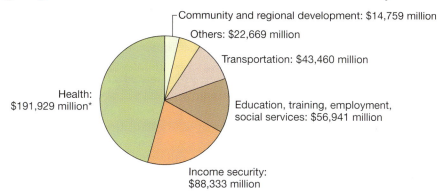

Community and regional development: $14,759 million
Others: $22,669 million
Transportation: $43,460 million
Health: $191,929 million*
Education, training, employment, social services: $56,941 million
Income security: $88,333 million

*$191,929 million represents $191,929,000,000

© AP/Wide World Photos

A new round of federal highway funding provides millions of dollars for the Warren Bridge over the Palmer River in Rhode Island. The federal government has allocated more than $77 million for bridge projects in Rhode Island, where one quarter of bridges are structurally deficient.

states failing to comply with a national standard for drunken driving (set at 0.08-percent blood alcohol content) would lose 2 percent of their federal highway grants starting in 2004, a figure that rises to 8 percent by 2007.

Although conservatives often criticize federal regulations as undesirable and unnecessary intrusions on the states and local areas, they, too, have used such instruments to achieve broader policy objectives. Ronald Reagan, who came to office promising to eliminate or reduce grant-related regulations, actually increased the number of federal regulations in several policy areas. At the urging of the trucking industry, for example, his administration supported a transportation bill that denied federal highway funds to states that did not approve the use of larger trucks carrying more weight than many states permitted at the time. The administration did so for political reasons—to maintain the support of the trucking industry and the labor unions that represented teamsters (drivers). The Bush administration, in 2005, threatened to withhold federal highway money from New Jersey unless the state's governor, James McGreevey, reversed an executive order dealing with the process by which that state awarded state contracts.

categorical grants
Grants-in-aid that can be used only for narrowly defined purposes, such as education for homeless children or prevention of drug abuse.

Types of Grants   Historically, there have been three types of grants: categorical grants, block grants, and general revenue sharing. **Categorical grants** are made for specific purposes defined by Congress, such as library construction, child welfare, adoption assistance, and bridge and road construction. Such grants can be used only for the purposes stated in the legislation that creates and funds the program, and state and local decision makers thus have little discretion over how the grant money is spent. As of 2003, there were approximately 900 categorical grants, the largest number in history. Among the more recently approved are the Drug Abuse Prevention and Education Relating to Youth Gangs program (approximately $12 million per year), the Emergency Community Services for the Homeless program (about $19 million per year), and the AIDS Education program (about $14 million per year).

Block grants allow appropriated funds to be used in broad policy areas such as job training, health, and public housing. Congress establishes the areas in which the funds are to be used, and state and local officials determine how the money is spent. Today there are sixteen block grants in the areas of education, health and human services, housing, criminal justice, job training, and transportation. Mainly because of the consolidation of smaller categorical grants, more block grants were approved during the Reagan administration than during any previous administration. President George H. W. Bush continued the trend with his proposal to create a $20 billion block grant by consolidating several existing grant programs, and in his 1996 budget proposal President Clinton called for combining 271 categorical grant programs into a few block grants. However, the only additional block grant approved in 1996 was the one that replaced the national government's welfare program, AFDC.

General revenue sharing, created by the State and Local Fiscal Assistance Act of 1972, distributed approximately $6 billion annually to state and local governments until 1980 and about $4 billion annually to local governments thereafter, until the program was terminated in 1986. These monies were allocated with almost no "strings" attached to nearly 39,000 local governments: The recipient governments could use general revenue sharing money for any purpose, as long as they did not spend it in a discriminatory manner.

General revenue sharing was the centerpiece of the domestic program proposed by President Nixon, who saw in it opportunities for managerial and political reform. From a management perspective, general revenue sharing countered the complex and largely unregulated growth of federal grants. Politically, by giving state and local governments maximum flexibility in spending the funds, the program shifted power from Congress, the national bureaucracy, and Washington-centered interest groups, all of which Nixon viewed as loyal principally to the Democrats and Democratic constituents. The successful passage of the program also demonstrated the growing political influence of a new interest group: the intergovernmental lobby, which consists of organizations representing state and local governments.

General revenue sharing expired in 1986 as a result of President Reagan's budget reduction efforts and congressional and presidential concern about large federal deficits, and has not been reinstituted.

Politics of Grants-in-Aid In general, block grants are popular among conservatives and advocates of states' rights. Presidents Nixon and Reagan supported these grants partly because they knew that most local electorates and local

block grants
Grants-in-aid that state and local governments can spend as they wish within specified broad policy areas, such as housing, transportation, or job training.

general revenue sharing
A federal program existing between 1972 and 1986 in which grants-in-aid were distributed to state and local governments with few strings attached.

officials would not want to use them for liberal social programs, especially those designed to sharply redistribute resources from upper- to lower-income populations. Block grants also tend to be popular among state and local officials because they give them greater discretion in spending the funds.

Categorical grants are more appealing to liberals, particularly those who believe that the national government should be actively involved in addressing highly pressing social and urban problems. Congress, too, generally prefers categorical grants, because they allow greater congressional influence in determining and monitoring how the money is spent.

Categorical grants frequently are supported by private-interest groups, which put pressure on Congress to approve programs to address their particular needs. Thus, each grant tends to build a constituency of people whose programs or projects are funded largely by it. These people naturally become protective of "their" grant and feel threatened when it is considered for termination or conversion to another type. Consider the 1995 testimony of the Reverend Fred Kammer, president of Catholic Charities USA, presented to Congress during its consideration of the proposal to convert many categorical welfare grants to one, or just a few, large block grants administered by the states. Kammer stated that

> We [Catholic Charities USA] administer model WIC [Special Supplemental Nutrition Program for Women, Infants, and Children] programs, we operate the Commodity Supplemental Food Programs, the Child and Adult Care Food Programs, and the Summer Food Programs, and Catholic schools use the school breakfast and lunch programs to help students from poor families. Catholic Charities USA opposes block-granting Federal nutrition programs because of the impact on the nation's poorest families. . . . Serious questions exist about the will or ability of the states to protect our poorest families from the worst ravages of hunger and poverty. Despite recent political promises of some governors, state AFDC [Aid to Families with Dependent Children] reforms are as yet untested and unproved. States have allowed welfare benefits to decline steadily for over 20 years . . . and many states have been very punitive toward poor families. The proposed . . . block grant would deny food to millions of low-income people, a profoundly wrong social, political, and moral outcome.[43]

Figure 3.1 shows the distribution of federal aid to state and local governments by major program areas.

Distribution Criteria   Grants may be categorized as formula grants or as project grants, depending on the criteria used for distribution of the money. **Formula grants** follow a formula applied proportionally to all eligible recipients. For example, a grant program to aid education might allocate money to all school districts, with the amount for each district determined by the number of pupils in the district whose families' incomes are below a certain level. By simply calculating the number of pupils who fall into this category, all school districts across the country will immediately know how much they are entitled to receive.

The political controversies surrounding formula grants concern the elements to be included in the formula and the weighting of those elements. For example, a bitter fight broke out in 1988 when Congress considered changing

formula grants
Grants-in-aid distributed on the basis of a formula applied to all eligible recipients.

the formula for distributing money through the Alcohol, Drug Abuse, and Mental Health (ADAMH) block grant. The original formula included a factor that benefited states receiving funds under older categorical grants that had been eliminated when the ADAMH block grant was approved. Critics argued that this element of the formula gave too much of the ADAMH money to northern states and too little to southern and western states. As an aide to Representative Henry Waxman of California said, "You won't find anyone with a dispassionate interest who would not say the existing formula is an outrage." On the other hand, the deputy director for government and community relations at the New York State Division of Substance Abuse Services commented about the proposed change, "I don't see anything equitable in a proposal which would entail closing down drug treatment programs in high-risk areas like New York."[44]

Project grants are ones for which potential recipients must apply directly to the agency responsible for administering the grant. That agency reviews the proposals and determines which ones are to be funded and at what level. Because there is not enough money to fund every potential project, competition for the funds may be keen.

project grants
grants-in-aid for which potential recipients must apply to a federal agency; such grants are usually awarded on a competitive basis.

Federal agencies and departments maintain greater control and authority over project grants than over formula grants. Project grants, which proliferated in the 1960s, have been used for policy areas that might not receive sufficient attention from state and local decision makers in the absence of national funding—areas such as education for disabled youth, programs for the aging, AIDS research, drug rehabilitation, and bilingual education. Like formula grants, however, project grants are often a focus of much political controversy. Those whose applications are not approved may blame federal bureaucrats who make poor decisions or are out of touch with local problems. They argue that project grants place too much control at the national level, ignore the specialized needs of local areas, and give an advantage to jurisdictions large and wealthy enough to hire staffs with the skills required for drafting complex federal grant proposals.

The Regional Controversy over Grant Distribution As the controversy over the ADAMH formula suggests, conflicts sometimes arise over the regional distribution of grants-in-aid funds. Some states and regions receive considerably higher per-person allocations than do others. Figure 3.2 shows the per-person distribution of federal grants-in-aid to all states with the top and bottom five states highlighted.

State and local officials in the Frostbelt (the Midwest and Northeast) often express the opinion that their social and economic problems, such as decaying cities and aging industrial infrastructures, justify higher proportions of federal grant assistance. On the other side, officials in the Sunbelt (the South and Southwest) argue that rapid population growth in their sections of the country brings with it unique problems that call for increased federal aid. The dispute has led to clashes among coalitions of legislators, mayors, and governors over distribution formulas, a rivalry that has been described as a "regional war."[45]

In 1995, for example, when Congress was debating welfare reform, representatives from the Frostbelt states generally wanted each state's share of the proposed welfare block grant to be based on what it had previously received from the federal government in categorical grants for welfare programs. Representatives from the Sunbelt states, however, argued that funding should favor those regions with high population growth rates. Criticizing the Frostbelt proposal, Senator Bob Graham (D-Florida) complained, "We start under the banner of 'we're going to end welfare as we've known it,' and yet distribute the money based on a formula which is predicated on welfare as we knew it."[46]

Regional disputes broke out again over the allocation of federal homeland security aid following the terrorist attacks of September 11, 2001. After those attacks, Congress set aside close to $10 billion in terrorism preparedness grants for state and local governments. The funds, however, were disbursed throughout the country primarily on the basis of population and not concentrated in areas most vulnerable to future attacks. Public officials from the northeastern states, and especially from New York, have been especially prominent in expressing their displeasure with the proportion targeted to their area. New York Mayor Michael Bloomberg, for example, called the distribution system "irrational, tragically misguided, and creating grave hazards not just for New Yorkers but for all Americans."[47] Sarcastically explaining why New York City's share of funding to be received through the Urban Areas Security Initiative—the program designed specifically to deliver security funds to at-risk cities—is only 7 percent of all aid allocated through that program and why Louisville—a city not particularly threatened by terrorist attacks—was slated to receive $9 million from this program in 2005, an aid to Mayor Bloomberg explained that "The chairman of the

© AP/Wide World Photos

Bullard volunteer firefighters Justin Doniny, right, and Dustin Rounsavall load a 5,000-watt generator onto their fire truck in Whitehouse, Tx., as Stacy Posey stands nearby, Tuesday, May 18, 2004. The generator, along with such items as thermal imaging cameras and global positioning systems, are part of a Homeland Security allocation grant that distributed the equipment to Smith County, Tx. fire departments.

Figure 3.2 **Federal Aid to State and Local Governments per Capita 2004**

State	Dollars	Rank
United States	1,366	(X)
Alabama	1,329	21
Alaska	3,713	1
Arizona	1,361	24
Arkansas	1,498	16
California	1,317	22
Colorado	982	48
Connecticut	1,431	23
Delaware	1,341	25
District of Columbia	6,485	(X)
Florida	1,045	44
Georgia	1,080	43
Hawaii	1,429	29
Idaho	1,364	30
Illinois	1,176	40
Indiana	1,117	45
Iowa	1,222	36
Kansas	1,072	46
Kentucky	1,511	14
Louisiana	1,555	15
Maine	2,005	7
Maryland	1,196	37
Massachusetts	1,659	13
Michigan	1,207	38
Minnesota	1,241	39
Mississippi	1,825	11
Missouri	1,341	26
Montana	2,032	12
Nebraska	1,329	31
Nevada	897	49
New Hampshire	1,160	41
New Jersey	1,247	34
New Mexico	2,232	4
New York	2,213	3
North Carolina	1,329	32
North Dakota	2,074	6
Ohio	1,265	35
Oklahoma	1,401	18
Oregon	1,382	20
Pennsylvania	1,453	19
Rhode Island	1,833	10
South Carolina	1,319	33
South Dakota	1,800	9
Tennessee	1,547	17
Texas	1,142	42
Utah	1,105	47
Vermont	2,051	5
Virginia	884	50
Washington	1,266	28
West Virginia	1,864	8
Wisconsin	1,250	27
Wyoming	3,125	2

X	Not applicable
red	top 5 in rank
blue	bottom 5 in rank

Source: U.S. Census Bureau. Federal Aid to States for Fiscal Year 2003.

[House] Appropriations Committee is from Kentucky. He wants to take some [of the money] home, too."[48]

Regional variances in attitudes toward the treatment received from the federal government are not limited only to public officials. Surveys have shown that considerable variance exists among the general public as well. Paralleling attitudes of officials, citizens from the Northeast region (including the states of New York, New Jersey, and Pennsylvania) are considerably more likely than citizens from most other regions to say that their states are not treated with the respect they deserve in the United States federal system of government.[49]

Research centers have sprung up in Washington, D.C., whose sole purpose is to identify and promote public policies that would benefit particular regions. These so-called think tanks often engage in small skirmishes among themselves. In the late 1980s, for example, the Sunbelt Institute (representing the eleven states of the old Confederacy and five border states) issued reports asserting that southern states, on average, send to the national government more than $1.50 in taxes for every dollar returned in federal aid, whereas some northern states receive far more in federal aid than they contribute to the federal treasury. The Northeast-Midwest Institute (representing eighteen northeastern and midwestern states) immediately issued its own report criticizing the Sunbelt Institute's figures. Congressional representatives from each region were drawn into the debate. To the Sunbelt Institute's charges, New York Senator Daniel Patrick Moynihan curtly replied that "everybody is entitled to their own opinions, but not their own facts."[50]

Competition for federal funds has been growing as the proportion of dollars distributed by the federal government through grants-in-aid programs has been declining. So regional clashes over federal aid are likely to continue and increase in intensity. Even though the pie has gotten smaller, the hunger for federal funds has not abated.

State and Local Influences on National Policymaking

Officials of state and local governments, and local constituencies in general, use certain tools of their own in an attempt to influence national policymaking, including the allocation and distribution of grants. All national legislators are elected from states or local districts and are responsible to voters at the local level. Thus, members of Congress are sure to give some attention to the concerns of their constituents.

State and local governments can also go to court to challenge the actions of the national government and therefore may halt or delay national initiatives, at least temporarily. In protest of President George W. Bush's education reform law, the state of Connecticut, in 2005, filed suit against the Department of Education; and in 2006 five states—California, Texas, Kentucky, New Jersey, and Missouri—joined in a suit of the federal government over provisions of the newly-enacted Medicare drug benefit program. Sometimes just the threat of court action will influence an agency or department to modify its policies. In 1995, for example, such a threat by several states persuaded the Environmental Protection Agency to relax significantly its proposed timetable and other requirements for states to set up testing programs for automobile exhaust systems.

States may consider refusing to accept federal grants entirely to avoid being bound by the strings that may be attached to them. An example of this occurred in 1997, when Congress made available to states $250 million for sex education if states would agree to teach, among other things, that sex outside of marriage "is likely to have harmful psychological and physical effects." The requirements were so strict that some states considered not applying for their share. As one Maine official stated, "The limits on what you can say are so restrictive that we decided we could not use the money for classroom programs or anywhere else where there was face-to-face contact." And a Connecticut official stated "we ought not to pursue [funds through this program] if handcuffs come with the bill."[51]

In summary, state and local governments may depend on their locally elected officials to press their concerns and represent their interests in Congress; they may challenge federal action through the courts; and sometimes they may simply decline federal grants and the rules and regulations their acceptance brings. Two additional tools that local officials may use to influence national policies are grantsmanship and the intergovernmental lobby.[52]

Grantsmanship

The efforts of local officials to maximize the amount of federal grants they receive and to have grant rules interpreted so that they achieve the best funding distribution for their areas are termed **grantsmanship.** Cities and states most capable of exploiting the various options and opportunities provided by the grant program are able to garner far more than their "fair" share of federal grants. Consider the comments of John Chafee, a former governor of Rhode Island:

grantsmanship
Efforts by state and local governments to maximize the federal aid they receive.

> Let us take the case of a 1-year-old boy on aid to dependent children who has a hearing problem that can be corrected. There is the temptation—and I must say this is a very real one—to refer such a patient, not to the program that is best organized to meet his particular need, but to the program in which the State obtains the best financial advantage. The Federal government will pay 50 percent of the cost when the care is provided by the Crippled Children's Division; it will pay 56 percent under Title XIX since he is on aid to dependent children; and, if he is cared for by vocational rehabilitation, the Federal government will soon pay 75 percent of the bill. Each of these programs has some variation in standards for eligibility, but nonetheless the differences in Federal reimbursement seem extremely puzzling.[53]

Grantsmanship is frequently criticized by those who believe that federal grants should go to local areas because of demonstrated problems or needs, not because of officials' skills in obtaining grants. Moreover, officials at the national level seek to prevent what they consider the "manipulation" of grant programs. In 1991 the George H. W. Bush administration issued rules preventing states from using money collected from donations or from special taxes paid by hospitals as matching money to qualify for federal Medicaid payments. That ruling cost state governments between $3 billion and $5 billion per year.

The Intergovernmental Lobby

intergovernmental lobby
The group of state and local government organizations, such as the National League of Cities and the National Governors' Association, that lobby the national government for legislation and decisions favorable to state and local governments.

One of the most effective strategies used by state and local governments in recent years has been to organize the **intergovernmental lobby.** Following the explosion of grants-in-aid in the 1960s, representatives of state and local governments began organizing themselves into lobby groups and organizations to press for more federal aid for states and communities, to see that grants are designed to meet state and local needs, and to keep abreast of new rules and regulations affecting grants. Unlike other Washington lobbies, the intergovernmental lobby is funded almost exclusively with public money—state and local funds and even federal grants.

The most important organizations in the intergovernmental lobby are listed in Table 3.1. But these organizations are just a few of the dozens of groups that represent state and local interests. Other members of the growing intergovernmental lobby include the American Association of State Highway and Transportation Officials, the Association of State and Interstate Water Pollution Control Officers, the National Association of Attorneys General, the American Association of School Administrators, the National Association of State Budget Officers, the National Association of State Mental Health Program Directors, the Council of State Community Development Agencies, the National Association of State Units on Aging, and the National Association of State Alcohol- and Drug-Abuse Directors.

In addition, many states and cities, believing that these national organizations cannot adequately represent their particular interests, have opened their own offices in Washington. By the mid-1990s, about 30 states, 100 cities, and 12 counties maintained offices there. California had the largest presence in Washington of all states: separate offices represented the state, twenty-three cities, and seven counties. Sometimes all of this lobbying activity can lead to awkward situations and even conflicting efforts. The state of New York, for example, has separate lobbyists serving the interests of the governor, the state assembly, and the state senate. In the debate over President Reagan's block grant proposals, lobbyists for the Democratic-controlled New York state assembly opposed the block grants, and lobbyists for the Republican-controlled state senate supported them.

The 1960s and 1970s were in many ways a golden age for the intergovernmental lobby. Federal aid to states and cities rose steadily during that time, reaching $91.5 billion by 1980—just over 25 percent of total state and local fiscal outlays. The passage of the general revenue sharing program in 1972 was perhaps the crowning achievement of these organizations. By contrast, the Reagan–Bush years, 1981–1992, were a time of declining political influence for the intergovernmental lobby. It was unable to prevent the elimination of the general revenue sharing program and the urban development action grants, and it could not overcome a slowdown in federal funding for housing, transportation, and many social programs.

With the elections of two former governors to the presidency (Bill Clinton in 1992 and George W. Bush in 2000), the intergovernmental lobby hoped for

Table 3.1. **The Intergovernmental Lobby**

Organization	Approximate Number of Employees	Approximate Budget	Some Recent Issues
National Conference of State Legislatures 40,000 (approx.) Legislators and staff of 50 U.S. states, commonwealths, and territories	210	$26,000,000	Terrorism Health Care Education Electric Utilities
National League of Cities 20,000 (approx)	100	$16,000,000	Homeland security Youth and education Public safety
United States Conference of Mayors Cities with over 30,000 (approx. 1000)	50	$9,000,000	Homelessness Economic security Affordable housing
National Association of Counties	80	$20,000,000	Homeland security Education reform Unfunded mandates
National Governors' Association 55 state and territorial governors	100	$16,000,000	Medicaid Electric utilities Safe drinking water
National Association of Towns and Townships Local governments in small and rural areas mostly with populations of 25,000 or less	6	$1,000,000	Water Homeland security Environment

Source: Authors' interviews with officials of each organization.

more productive relationships with the federal government. With the Republican Congress elected in 1994, the intergovernmental lobby did succeed in passing the Unfunded Mandates Reform Act in 1995, making it more difficult for Congress to impose costly mandates and certain conditions of grants-in-aid on state and local governments. And in 1996 the intergovernmental lobby, particularly the National Governors' Association, was instrumental in effecting welfare reform. In 2001, the National Governors' Association, along with other local and private organizations, was able to modify and lessen the severity of sanctions against states that were not abiding by the drunk driving standards included in the transportation bill enacted that year.

3.2 **Politics in the 21st Century**

Some Features of Other Federal Countries

The U.S. Constitution was the first to establish a federal system of government—one in which authority is divided between the national government and the state governments and in which the sovereignty of each is guaranteed.

So the framers had no models to choose from; they created the first. Today some two dozen other nations have selected the federal system of governing, but there is considerable variation in the arrangements that those federal systems have adopted.

Consider the following features found in some federal countries. If you were drafting the U.S. Constitution today—to serve for the twenty-first century—which of these, if any, do you believe would be worth considering for the U.S. federal system?

1. The federal constitution of *Brazil* provides formal recognition of municipalities (along with states and the national government); provides for three senators to be selected from each state, serving eight-year terms; and provides for a minimum of six representatives from each state.

2. The federal constitution of *Ethiopia* provides for states' right of secession.

3. The federal constitution of *Malaysia* gives the national government the right to expel member states.

4. The federal constitution of *Belgium* provides recognition for some ethnic and language groups, as well as for provinces.

5. The federal constitution of *Canada* establishes a parliamentary form of government with a prime minister who appoints most of the members of the national senate.

6. The federal constitution of *Austria* allocates to states seats in the upper house of its national legislature in proportion to state population, and members are selected by vote of state parliaments.

7. In *Australia,* the federal constitution provides for twelve senators from each state and two from each territory.

8. In *Mexico,* approximately one-quarter of senators are elected from the country at large, not from any particular state.

9. In *Germany,* half the members of that country's highest court are elected by the lower house of the German legislature; the other half are elected by the upper house.

10. Finally, if a "constitutional revision convention" were held today, do you think the United States would opt for a federal system at all?

An interesting new addition to the intergovernmental lobby groups appeared in 2004 when the governors of the four largest states—California, New York, Texas, and Florida—joined together to form a lobby organization they call the "Big Four." Concerned with what they believe to be the disproportionately large share of federal grants going to the smaller states, the Big Four hope that through their organization they will be able to successfully influence Congress to direct greater shares of federal aid to their states.

Federalism in Action: Setting National Standards for Alcohol Consumption

Recent attempts by Congress to establish minimum national standards for alcohol consumption illustrate many of the issues discussed in this chapter. For most of the nation's history, individual states have assumed the authority to set rules and regulations concerning the sale and use of beer, wine, and liquor—including the minimum age required for purchase and consumption and drunk driving standards based on blood alcohol content.[54] Before 1984, twenty-eight states had established minimum ages below twenty-one for the purchase of some or all categories of alcohol. The national government had provided grants to states for the purpose of developing programs to reduce drunk driving but had not formulated policy in this area.

In the early 1980s, however, as drunk driving began to arouse public concern and grassroots organizations such as Mothers Against Drunk Driving (MADD) were formed, national officials became more interested in the problem. In 1982, President Reagan appointed a commission to examine the drunk driving issue. In its report, released in 1983, the commission recommended that each state establish twenty-one as the minimum age for possession of alcohol and that federal grants for road construction projects be denied to states that did not comply with the age recommendation. Although the second recommendation proved controversial, it eventually became the means by which the national government exerted authority in an area that had previously been reserved to the states.

Congressional opposition centered on the issue of states' rights. New Hampshire Senator Gordon Humphrey asked, "Who are we, the national legislature, who have done a perfectly abysmal job of managing our own business, to tell the state legislatures . . . how to conduct their business?"[55] In a similar vein, Montana Senator Max Baucus said, "The real issue is whether the Federal Government should intrude into an area that has traditionally and appropriately been left to the States and force them into accepting its solution to the problem of drunk driving."[56]

However, the majority of the members of Congress did not share this view, and in 1984 the National Minimum Drinking-Age Act was enacted into law. Reflecting on the act's possible usurpation of state authority, President Reagan commented that "the problem [of drunk driving] is bigger than the individual States. It's a grave national problem, and it touches all our lives. With the problem so clear-cut and the proven solution at hand, we have no misgivings about this judicious use of federal power."[57]

The National Minimum Drinking-Age Act specified that larger proportions of highway funds would be denied to states the longer they delayed in establishing the required minimum age. The effectiveness of this provision is seen in that by 1993 all states had raised to twenty-one the minimum age for buying liquor.

When considering the 2001 transportation spending bill, Congress turned its attention to setting a standard for drunk driving based on blood alcohol content. This aspect of the legislation pitted traffic safety groups against alcohol and restaurant lobbyists and various state and local organizations in a fierce battle. In the end, Congress did approve a national standard for drunk driving of 0.08-percent blood alcohol content. States that fail to comply with this standard are threatened with loss of federal highway funds.

As explained earlier in the chapter, federal regulatory activities of this type are called crossover sanctions: The federal government threatens to withhold funds in one program area (in this case, highway funds) to achieve policy objectives in another area (in this case, the minimum age required for alcohol purchase and consumption and minimum national standards for identifying drunk driving). The growth of federal grant programs in recent decades and the increased reliance of state and local governments on these grants have made crossover sanctions a potent policy tool. The national government has used this tool successfully to achieve uniform state policies in areas such as highway beautification and energy conservation, as well as in establishing national standards for alcohol consumption.

Review Questions

1. When Congress authorizes states to exercise primary responsibility for a particular function, as long as the states maintain standards at least as high as those set by the national government, this is a form of national regulation known as

   A. Direct order
   B. Preemption
   C. Partial preemption
   D. Grants-in-aid

2. Those federal grants made for specific and narrowly defined purposes—such as library construction and bridge and road repair—are known as

   A. Categorical grants
   B. Block grants
   C. Revenue sharing grants
   D. Imposed grants

3. Those federal grants that may be used in broad policy areas—such as job training or housing—are known as

   A. Categorical grants
   B. Block grants
   C. Revenue sharing grants
   D. Imposed grants

4. In attempting to influence the national government, local governments may

   A. Rely on their locally elected officials
   B. Challenge federal action in the courts
   C. Refuse federal aid
   D. All of the above

continued

Answers:

1. C
2. A
3. B
4. D

Conflict and Consensus in Review

This chapter has shown that the American federal democracy frequently appears to be best described as a tug-of-war. On the one hand, there are those who argue that on any given issue the national government ought to have the final say; on the other, there are those who say that state and local governments should be the ones to decide a particular issue. When and under what circumstances is each level of government appropriate to decide the particular issues involved?

Conflict among the levels of government is not inevitable. When there is a policy problem with which most of the public agrees, such as the need to reduce drunk driving, racial discrimination, and polluted air and water, Congress can impose national standards with little or no opposition, especially if it sweetens the pot with federal funds. Unfortunately, there is usually much more consensus on the problem than there is on the solution. The result is the politics of federalism in which various governments strive to achieve the strategic advantage in the making and implementation of public policy.

Politics in Action

National Versus State Rights: Who's in Charge?

On March 10, 1992, Alfonso Lopez Jr., a senior at Edison High School in San Antonio, Texas, was caught carrying a .38-caliber handgun, along with five bullets, to school. Although Lopez was initially arrested under Texas law, those charges were dropped by the state when federal law enforcement agents charged him with violating the Gun-Free School Zones Act. The act, which banned the possession or discharge of guns in or near schools, was passed as part of the federal Crime Control Act of 1990.

Although Lopez was carrying the gun to school to sell it, there was no mention of commercial activity in the charges against him. He was charged on a single count that he had violated the federal law prohibiting the possession of a gun in or near a school. Lopez and his attorneys requested that the charge be dismissed on the ground that it was unconstitutional for the federal government to regulate activity related to local schools. The court denied this request, however, and Lopez was convicted in U.S. district court and sentenced to six months in prison and two years of probation.

Lopez appealed the lower court's decision, claiming that in passing a law regulating schools Congress had

continued

Politics in Action *continued*

overstepped its boundaries. The regulation of public education, Lopez and his attorneys argued, should be a state matter, not an issue appropriate for federal action; the control of guns in and around public schools, and the establishment of a gun-free school zone, was a legitimate area only for state regulation. The federal government argued that its constitutional authority to regulate interstate commerce gave it jurisdiction over such issues: gun violence represents a drain on national commerce because guns affect learning and learning affects the nation's economic strength. They also argued that the costs associated with violent crime were significant, and because that increased insurance prices, the costs were incurred by the whole country. In addition, they made the case that violent crime would make individuals less likely to travel to areas within the country that they perceived as unsafe.

As it turns out, in its 1995 decision the Supreme Court ruled that Lopez and his attorneys were correct: this is not a matter for federal regulation. For many, this was a stunning decision. This case marked the first time in more than sixty years that the Court had limited the reach of national authority under the interstate commerce clause of the Constitution. Many interpreted the *Lopez* case as a reversal of the trend toward increased federal control over state and local issues.

In their decision, the majority of the justices argued that there were three broad categories of activity that Congress could regulate under its commerce power: the use of channels of interstate commerce; the instrumentalities of interstate commerce and the people or things in interstate commerce; and things having a substantial effect on interstate commerce, even if the threat came from intrastate activities. The majority opinion rejected the notion that the carrying of a gun in a school zone was an issue of interstate commerce, stating that it was "in no sense an economic activity that might, through repetition elsewhere, substantially affect any sort of interstate commerce." This was particularly true, according to the Court, given that Lopez was a student at a local school who had not had any recent activity in interstate commerce. Writing for the majority, Chief Justice Rehnquist stated: "If we were

to accept the [federal] Government's arguments, we are hard pressed to posit any activity by an individual that Congress is without power to regulate." Ultimately, the Court ruled in favor of maintaining "a distinction between what is truly national and what is truly local."

In a dissenting opinion, Justice John Paul Stevens stated, "The Welfare of our future . . . is vitally dependent on the character of the education of our children. [Therefore] Congress has ample power to prohibit the possession of firearms in or near schools." In a concurring opinion, Justice Stephen Breyer stated that "in determining whether a local activity will likely have a significant effect upon interstate commerce, a court must consider, not the effect of an individual act (a single instance of gun possession), but rather the cumulative effect of all similar instances (i.e., the effect of all guns possessed in or near schools)." Breyer further stated that the majority decision in favor of Lopez would create three legal problems: It ran "contrary to modern Supreme Court cases that have upheld congressional actions despite connections to interstate or foreign commerce;" it would be difficult to reconcile this decision with earlier cases "because it made a critical distinction between commercial and noncommercial transaction[s];" and finally, it threatened to "create legal uncertainty in an area of law that, until this case, seemed reasonably well settled."

Despite the Court's message that Congress did not have constitutional authority over crime based on the interstate commerce clause, in 1996 Congress reinstated gun-free school zones when it passed the appropriations act for fiscal year 1997, a 2,000-page federal defense spending bill. The bill declares it unlawful "for any individual knowingly to possess a firearm that has moved in or that otherwise affects interstate or foreign commerce at a place that the individual knows, or has reasonable cause to believe, is a school zone." With the reinstatement of gun-free school zones, Congress reasserted its authority to regulate crime at the state level, an action that will likely result in another tug-of-war over state versus federal powers and perhaps another test case of the issue in the federal courts.

What Do You Think?

1. What do you think? Do you think issues such as the regulation of guns in and around public schools should be a matter for federal legislation, or are these matters most appropriately left to state and local governments? Why is this so?
2. What areas of the Constitution can you point to that sustain your position?
3. How do you think the Court would have ruled on this case if it had being decided in the 1980s, instead of in 1995? How about if it were decided today?
4. Do you believe this is a decision that will remain unchallenged for many years, or is it one that is likely to soon be overturned? What factors might relate to whether this decision remains unchallenged?
5. Do you believe this was the correct decision? Why or why not?

| Summary |

Although a general consensus exists among Americans, and America's leaders, about the value of the federal form of government, the nation's history has been rife with conflicts over the application of federal principles to particular situations. During the period following ratification of the Constitution, those who favored more power and responsibility for the national government were opposed by those who sought to protect and enhance the rights of individual states. Those with a nation-centered view believed that the Constitution was applicable to the American people as a whole. Those with a state-centered view believed that the Constitution was a compact among the states, which were the legitimate center of power and authority. Advocates of states' rights argued that if the national government overstepped its legitimate boundaries, its acts should be null and void; this position is known as the doctrine of nullification.

The conflict over national supremacy versus states' rights intensified with opposition to slavery, finally culminating in the Civil War. After the war, the nullification theory was discredited and a new relationship known as dual federalism emerged. It recognized separate and distinct spheres of authority for the national government and state governments. During this period, much of the debate over federal–state relations centered on the proper role of Congress in regulating the nation's commerce. The Supreme Court invalidated several regulatory actions by Congress on the ground that they usurped state authority.

The Great Depression of the 1930s ushered in a period of cooperative federalism, which stressed a partnership and a sharing of functions, responsibilities, and programs between the states and the national government. This era was marked by increased use of grants-in-aid, programs through which the national government shared its fiscal resources with state and local governments. By 1960, there were about 132 grant programs, with most grants for specific purposes defined by Congress. The number of grants increased dramatically during the 1960s, especially as part of President Johnson's Great Society social program.

After 1968, however, President Nixon's new federalism deemphasized the use of grants for specific purposes and focused instead on large grants in general policy areas. These gave the recipient governments greater discretion in the expenditure of funds and decreased the national government's control. During the Reagan administration, there was a slowdown in the rate of increase in the funding of grant programs, but under President George H. W. Bush spending began to rise faster again.

For much of the past half-century, Supreme Court rulings have been interpreted by many as eliminating—or at least significantly reducing—state and local sovereignty. But in recent years some Court decisions seem to have restored a measure of state and local independence. Moreover, the Republicans who won control of Congress in the 1994 elections mounted a strong effort to return to the state and local governments many responsibilities that had been assumed by the federal government in recent decades, such as welfare, job training, and Medicaid. These shifts suggested a trend toward a new era in intergovernmental relations, one that some have called devolution federalism.

In its attempts to regulate states and localities, the national government may issue direct orders, preempt state and local activities, or use grants-in-aid to encourage certain activities and discourage others. Occasionally the national government issues direct orders, such as antidiscrimination and environmental regulations, that local governments must comply with or else face civil or criminal penalties. Preemption removes a certain policy area, such as regulation of copyrights or cable television rates, from state authority. Partial preemption occurs when the national government establishes policies and delegates the responsibility for implementing them to state and local governments, provided that they meet certain conditions or standards.

A more common approach to regulation is the use of grants-in-aid. Grants have been used to fund projects and efforts in areas ranging from mass transportation to nutrition programs for the elderly.

National influence over state and local policies is accomplished through the conditions and requirements that recipients must satisfy to receive the aid. Crosscutting requirements apply across the board and deal with issues such as environmental protection and labor standards. Crossover sanctions impose national sanctions in one area to influence state or local policy in another.

Historically, there have been three types of grants. Categorical grants are made for specific purposes defined by Congress and give the recipient states and localities little discretion in terms of how the money is to be spent. Block grants allow appropriated funds to be used in broad policy areas, with state and local officials determining how the money is actually spent. General revenue sharing, which existed from 1972 to 1986, was a system in which federal funds were allocated to state and local governments to be used for virtually any purpose, provided that the money was not spent in a discriminatory manner.

Grants may also be categorized by their criteria for distribution. Formula grants are distributed according to a formula applied proportionally to all eligible recipients. Project grants are those for which potential recipients must apply directly to the agency responsible for administering the grant; the agency determines which proposals are to be funded and at what level.

Some states and regions receive considerably higher per-person allocations of grant funds than do others. As a result, controversies and conflicts sometimes arise over the regional distribution of grant funds. In particular, officials in Frostbelt and Sunbelt states often clash over the formulas for distribution of federal funds.

State and local governments naturally attempt to influence the adoption and distribution of federal grants. Grantsmanship refers to efforts by local officials to maximize federal grants received and influence the interpretation of grant rules in ways that are favorable to their locality. State and local governments have also organized an intergovernmental lobby to press for more federal aid, see that grants are designed to meet their needs, and keep abreast of new rules and regulations.

Key Terms

nation-centered federalism
state-centered federalism
doctrine of nullification
dual federalism
cooperative federalism
grants-in-aid
coercive federalism

new federalism
devolution federalism
direct orders
preempt
partial preemption
crosscutting requirements
crossover sanctions

categorical grants
block grants
general revenue sharing
formula grants
project grants
grantsmanship
intergovernmental lobby

Discussion Questions

1. Why did James Madison and other framers of the Constitution view the concept of "federalism" as important? In your view, does it continue to be important today?

2. Discuss the evolution of American federalism from 1787 until today. What political, social, and economic factors seem to be associated with varying interpretations of our federal system?

3. Is there evidence that we may today be witnessing a significant change in the relationship among national, state, and local governments? What do you think the nature of U.S. federalism will look like in twenty-five years and in fifty years?

4. Is there any way that the U.S. Supreme Court can recognize state authority and still issue national guidelines in key policy areas such as representation (one person, one vote) or religion (no prayer in public schools)?

5. Discuss some of the ways the national government attempts to influence state and local governments. Discuss some of the ways state and local governments attempt to influence the national government. Which of these are most effective? Why?

Topics for Debate

Debate each side of the following propositions:

1. The concept of "federalism" was adopted simply as a way of achieving compromise at the Constitutional Convention.

2. The Congress overstepped its authority when it made federal highway funds contingent upon a state establishing the age of 21 for the public consumption of alcoholic beverages.

3. In protecting the rights of the minority, the Supreme Court has usurped the rightful authority of the states and local governments.

4. Federal assistance to state and local governments should be allocated proportionally according to the population so that all recipients receive their "fair share."

5. The use of marijuana for medical purposes (or gay marriages or deciding when lifesaving measures should be abandoned) is a clear example of an issue that should be left for state and local governments to decide.

Where on the Web?

The Federalism Project, **www.federalismproject.org/**

The Constitution Society, **www.constitution.org/**

Federalism & Intergovernmental Relations, **www.apsafederalism.org/**

Forum of Federations, **www.forumfed.org**

Go to **www.thomsonedu.com/thomsonnow** to learn about a powerful online study tool. You will get a personalized study plan based on your responses to a diagnostic Pre-Test. Once you have mastered the materials with the help of interactive learning tools, activities, timelines, video case studies, simulations, and an integrated E-Book, you can take a Post-Test to confirm you are ready to move to the next chapter.

Selected Readings

Conlan, Timothy. *From New Federalism to Devolution.* Washington, D.C.: Brookings Institution, 1998.

——————. *New Federalism: Intergovernmental Reform from Nixon to Reagan.* Washington, D.C.: Brookings Institution, 1988.

Griffiths, Ann L., ed. *Handbook of Federal Countries, 2005.* Montreal: McGill-Queens' University Press, 2005.

Keleman, R. Daniel. *The Rules of Federalism.* Cambridge, Mass.: Harvard University Press, 2004.

Kincaid, John, and G. Alan Tarr. *Constitutional Origins, Structure, and Change in Federal Countries.* Montreal: McGill-Queen's University Press, 2005.

Riker, William H. *The Development of American Federalism.* Boston: Kluwer Academic Publishers, 1987.

Schleicher, David, and Brendon Swedlow, eds. *Federalism and Political Culture.* New Brunswick: Transaction Publishers, 1998.

Tarr, G. Alan, Robert F. Williams, and Josef Marko. *Federalism, Subnational Constitutions, and Minority Rights.* Westport, Ct: Praeger, 2004.

Walker, David B. *The Rebirth of Federalism.* Chatham, N.J.: Chatham House Publishers, 1995.

Wills, Gary. *Explaining America: The Federalist.* New York: Penguin Books, 1981.

Wootton, David, ed. *The Essential Federalist and Anti-Federalist Papers.* Cambridge, Mass.: Hackett Publishing Co., 2003.

Notes

[1] James Madison, *The Federalist,* No. 51. In Clinton Rossiter, ed., The Federalist Papers (New York: The New American Library, 1961), 320–325.

[2] From a speech delivered by Justice Clarence Thomas at James Madison University, March 15, 2001.

[3] Richard L. Cole, John Kincaid, and Alejandro Rodriguez, "Public Opinion on Federalism and the 'Federal Political Culture' in Canada, Mexico, and the United States: Results of the 2004 Survey," *Publius: The Journal of Federalism* (Summer 2005).

[4] President George W. Bush, "Remarks at the National Governors' Association Conference," *Weekly Compilation of Presidential Documents,* February 26, 2001. From the 2001 Presidential Documents Online via GPO Access.

[5] Quoted in Franklin Foer, "The Joy of Federalism," *New York Times,* March 6, 2005.

[6] *United States v. Morrison,* 529 U.S. 598 (2000).

[7] Cited in "Excerpts from the Supreme Court's Decision on the Violence Against Women Act," *New York Times,* May 16, 2000.

[8] Senator Biden's remarks are cited in Linda Greenhouse, "Women Lose Right to Sue Attackers in Federal Court," *New York Times,* May 16, 2000.

9 Forrest McDonald, *Novus Ordo Seclorum: The Intellectual Origins of the Constitution* (Lawrence: University of Kansas Press, 1985), 262. Charles McCoy, however, argues that the theory of federalism precedes the American Constitution by many years. See McCoy, "Federalism: The Lost Tradition?" *Publius: The Journal of Federalism*, 31:2 (Spring 2001), 1–14.

10 Many excellent historical chronicles of American federalism exist. One of the best of these is David B. Walker, *The Rebirth of Federalism* (Chatham, N.J.: Chatham House Publishers, 1995), upon which much of the following discussion is based.

11 *McCulloch v. Maryland,* 17 U.S. 316 (1819).

12 Quoted in Alfred H. Kelly and Winfred A. Harbison, *The American Constitution* (New York: W. W. Norton & Co., 1955), 180.

13 The laws known as the Alien and Sedition Acts were four separate acts. The Naturalization Act raised from five to fourteen years the length of time an alien had to wait to acquire citizenship. The Alien Act empowered the president to order out of the country all aliens judged dangerous to the peace and safety of the nation. The Alien Enemies Act empowered the president in case of war to remove or detain as enemy aliens all male subjects of a hostile power. The Sedition Act provided for fines against or imprisonment of any person found to be conspiring against the U.S. government.

14 It should be noted that the Virginia and Kentucky Resolutions were written to address specific political issues of the time and that neither Madison nor Jefferson governed as president in a way that was congruent with the resolutions. Further, neither accepted Calhoun's extended nullification theories. For further discussion, see Andrew C. McLaughlin, *A Constitutional History of the United States* (New York: Appleton-Century, 1935).

15 *Dred Scott v. Sandford,* 60 U.S. 393 (1857).

16 See Edward S. Corwin, *The Twilight of the Supreme Court* (New Haven, Conn.: Yale University Press, 1934), ch. 1.

17 *Texas v. White,* 74 U.S. 700 (1869).

18 *United States v. E. C. Knight Company,* 156 U.S. 1 (1895).

19 *Hammer v. Dagenhart,* 247 U.S. 251 (1918).

20 *Schechter Poultry Corporation v. United States,* 295 U.S. 495 (1935).

21 *United States v. Darby Lumber Company,* 312 U.S. 100 (1941).

22 For elaboration, see Walker, *The Rebirth of Federalism,* 76–91.

23 *National League of Cities v. Usery,* 426 U.S. 833 (1976).

24 See *Hodel v. Virginia Surface Mining & Reclamation, Inc.,* 452 U.S. 264 (1981), and *EEOC v. Wyoming,* 460 U.S. 226 (1983).

25 *Intergovernmental Perspective* 11, No. 2/3 (Spring–Summer 1985): 23. In response to this "Garcia update," it should be noted that in 1986 Congress amended the Fair Labor Standards Act to allow states and localities to use compensatory time in lieu of overtime pay for their workers. See John J. Harrigan, *Politics and Policy in States and Communities* (New York: HarperCollins, 1991), 58.

26 *Garcia v. San Antonio Metropolitan Transit Authority,* 469 U.S. 528 (1985).

27 For further discussion of the devolution issue, see Richard P. Nathan, "The Devolution Revolution: An Overview," *Rockefeller Institute Bulletin* (Albany, N.Y.: Nelson A. Rockefeller Institute of Government, 1996), 5–13; Timothy Conlan, *From New Federalism to Devolution* (Washington, D.C.: The Brookings Institution, 1998); and Richard L. Cole, Rodney V. Hissong, and Enid Arvidson, "Devolution: Where's The Revolution?" *Publius: The Journal of Federalism* 29:4 (Fall 1999), 99–112.

28 *United States v. Lopez,* 514 U.S. 549 (1995).

29 *Seminole Tribe v. Florida,* 517 U.S. 44 (1996).

30 *Printz v. United States,* 521 U.S. 898 (1997).

31 *Alden v. Maine,* 527 U.S. 706 (1999).

32 *Kimel v. Florida Board of Regents,* 528 U.S. 62 (2000).

33 *Board of Trustees of the University of Alabama v. Garrett,* 531 U.S. 356 (2001).

34 *Federal Maritime Commission v. South Carolina Ports Authority,* 535 U.S. 743 (2002).

35 Linda Greenhouse, "Battle on Federalism," *New York Times,* May 17, 2000.

36 As cited in Linda Greenhouse, "The Nation: 5–4, Now and Forever; Dissent Over States' Rights Is Now War," *New York Times,* June 9, 2002.

37 *Tennessee v. Lane,* 541 U.S. 509 (2004). Even here, however, the Court specifically stated that the decision applied only to courthouses and court services and made it clear that the ruling did not necessarily apply to other state-run facilities, such as swimming pools or hockey rinks.

38 *Gonzales v. Raich,* 545 U.S. ___ (2005).

39 Quoted in Rochelle L. Stanfield, "Holding the Bag?" *National Journal* (September 9, 1995): 2206.

[40]John Kincaid, "The Devolution Tortoise and the Centralization Hare," *New England Economic Review* (May/June 1998), 38.

[41]National Conference of State Legislatures, "Mandate Monitor," January 18, 2005, www.ncsl.org. In response to the growing burden placed on state and local governments, Congress, in 1995, passed the Unfunded Mandates Reform Act, which was designed to ensure that Congress is informed about the costs to state and local governments of such imposed mandates.

[42]As quoted in Robert Pear, "States Dismayed by Federal Bills on Patient Rights," *New York Times,* August 13, 2001.

[43]Statement of Reverend Fred Kammer, president of Catholic Charities USA, at a hearing titled *Reforming the Present Welfare System* before the Subcommittee on Department Operations, Nutrition, and Foreign Agriculture of the Committee on Agriculture, U.S. House of Representatives, 104th Cong., 2nd sess., February 14, 1995, 555–556.

[44]For background on this controversy, see Ann Markusen and Jerry Fastrup, "The Regional War for Federal Aid," *The Public Interest* 53 (Fall 1978): 87–99.

[45]For an interesting look at these regional debates, see Dick Kirschten, "Formula Friction," *National Journal* (February 2, 1991): 272–273.

[46]*Jeffrey L. Katz, "Sunbelt Senators Revolt Over Welfare Formula," Congressional Quarterly Weekly Report* (June 24, 1995): 1,842.

[47]Quoted in Christopher Logan, "Politics and Promises," April 3, 2005, www.governing.com.

[48]See Ryan Lizza, "Bush to New York: Here's Your $20 Billion—Now Drop Dead," *New York Magazine,* June 14, 2004, www.nymag.com/.

[49]John Kincaid and Richard L. Cole, "Public Opinion on Issues of U.S. Federalism in 2005: End of the Post-2001 Pro-Federal Surge?" *Publius: The Journal of Federalism* (Spring 2005).

[50]Quoted in Dick Kirschten, "Formula Friction," *National Journal* (February 2, 1991): 272–273.

[51]Cited in Tamar Lewin, "States Slow to Take U.S. Aid To Teach Sexual Abstinence," *New York Times,* May 8, 1997. It is interesting to note that all states did eventually accept funds through this program, although many found ways to get around the bill's most controversial provisions.

[52]An interesting study of states attempting to influence the congressional process is provided by John Dinan, "State Government Influence in the National Policy Process: Lessons from the 104th Congress," *Publius: The Journal of Federalism,* 27:2 (Spring 1997), 129–142.

[53]Quoted in John Rehfuss, *The Job of the Public Manager* (Chicago: Dorsey Press, 1989), 154.

[54]For an excellent discussion of this issue, see Sarah F. Liebschutz, "The National Minimum Drinking-Age Law," *Publius: The Journal of Federalism* 15 (Summer 1985): 39–51.

[55]Quoted in *Congressional Quarterly Weekly Reports,* June 30, 1984, 1,557.

[56]Ibid.

[57]President Ronald Reagan, "Remarks on Signing H.R. 4614 into Law," July 17, 1984.

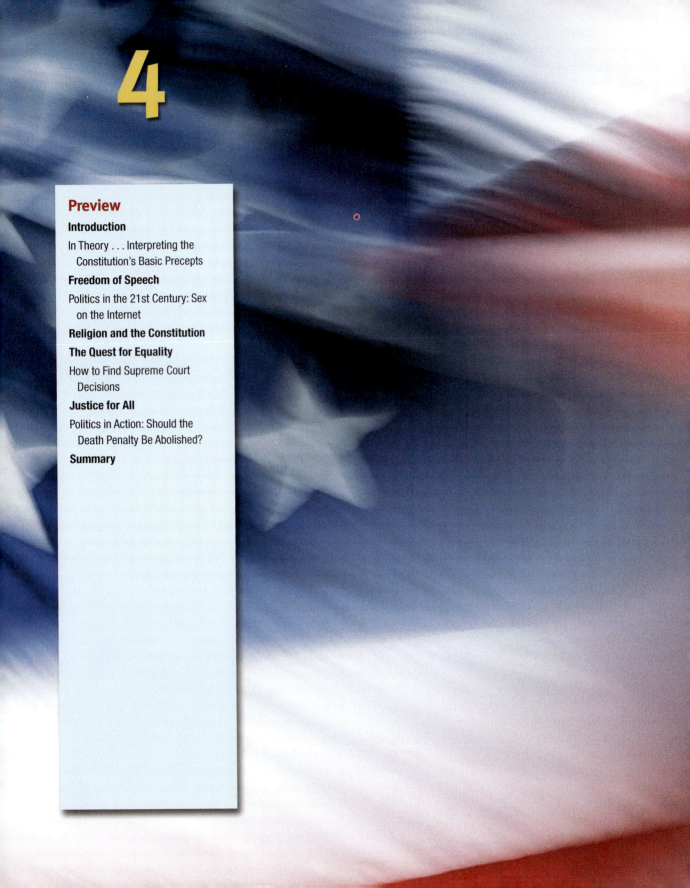

4

Issues of Freedom, Equity, and Justice

Introduction

OUTSIDE THE 1984 REPUBLICAN National Convention in Dallas, Gregory "Joey" Johnson and other members of the Revolutionary Communist Youth Brigade held a rally to protest of the Reagan administration's policies toward Latin America and its support of the contras in Nicaragua. After a march through the streets, Johnson set fire to an American flag while the crowd chanted, "America, the red, white, and blue, we spit on you." Police officers moved in and arrested Johnson.

During Johnson's trial his attorney argued that like the Vietnam War protesters of the 1960s and 1970s, Johnson had burned the flag as a means of political expression, a form of expression protected by the First Amendment guarantee of freedom of speech. Nevertheless, Johnson was convicted of violating a Texas law forbidding abuse and destruction of the American flag. He appealed to the Texas Court of Criminal Appeals, which reversed his conviction on First Amendment grounds. The ruling was then appealed to the Supreme Court by the state's attorney general in *Texas v. Johnson* (1989).

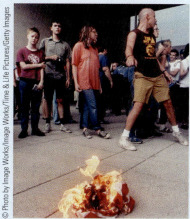

© Photo by Image Works/Image Works/Time & Life Pictures/Getty Images

TEXAS, UNITED STATES—1984: Demonstrators surrounding burning American flag expressing their First Amendment rights to freedom of speech.

The Supreme Court has often been involved in controversies over the flag. In 1943, for example, the Court struck down a law requiring children in public schools to salute the flag at the beginning of each school day. In that case the Court upheld the claim of a Jehovah's Witness that the law denied his First Amendment rights by forcing his children to worship a graven image in violation of their religious beliefs. Subsequently the Court overturned the convictions of a protester who had

burned the flag of an individual who had worn a small flag on the seat of his pants, and of a student who had hung a flag upside down with a peace symbol attached to it from the window of his dormitory room.

Despite the more conservative composition of the Court in the late 1980s, it again upheld the First Amendment protection of political expression. Not only did the Court strike down the Texas law, but it also voided laws in forty-seven other states that made it a crime to desecrate the American flag. In the opinion announcing the majority's decision in *Texas v. Johnson*, Justice William J. Brennan wrote, "If there is a bedrock principle underlying the First Amendment, it is that the Government may not prohibit the expression of an idea simply because society finds the idea itself offensive or disagreeable."[1]

President George H. W. Bush immediately denounced the Court's ruling. "Flag burning is wrong—dead wrong," exclaimed Bush, echoing a theme from his 1988 presidential campaign.[2] In the aftermath of the Court's ruling, numerous congressional leaders in both parties joined the president in calling for a constitutional amendment to reverse the Court's judgment. Instead, Congress passed the Federal Flag Protection Act of 1989, which authorized the prosecution of individuals who desecrate the American flag. That law was immediately challenged, and it was overturned by the Court in *United States v. Eichman* (1990).[3] Following the ruling, another attempt to overturn the Court's ruling through a constitutional amendment failed. Despite the overwhelming opposition, even outrage, of the American people, the Court's decision still stands. Had Congress enacted the same law more than a decade later, after the terrorist attacks of September 11, 2001, do you think the Court would have rendered the same judgment? Do you think it would have even taken the case on appeal?

The case of *Texas v. Johnson* illustrates the difficult role the Supreme Court plays in safeguarding the rights of minorities and those who express unpopular views. It illustrates the controversy that the Court can generate when it makes an unpopular decision, one that the majority of people find objectionable. Nonetheless, the flag decision has stood the test of time and continues to prevent legislators from making desecration of it a crime, testifying to the consensus shared by the people and their elected representatives that the Supreme Court is and should be the final interpreter of the Constitution— that its judgment, no matter how unpopular, must be observed until it is reversed by the Court itself or by amending the Constitution. Finally, it demonstrates that the Court cannot avoid political issues as it makes judicial judgments.

Questions to Ponder

- How has (and should) the Supreme Court interpret the meaning of the Constitution?
- What has been (and should be) the criteria by which the Court makes its judgments: the meaning of words in the Constitution at the time they were written, the intentions of the framers as revealed in the debates at the Constitutional Convention and during the ratification period, or evolving precedent and changing times?
- Should the Supreme Court consider contemporary public opinion when it interprets the meaning of the Constitution at a particular time?
- To what extent do (and should) the prohibitions on Congress apply to states?
- How can the Supreme Court protect the majority's rights to determine public policy by their legislative representatives and the minority's rights to equal protection under the law?

4.1 **In Theory . . .**

Interpreting the Constitution's Basic Precepts

The Constitution guarantees basic liberties and rights. But these rights are not absolute. As in other areas of public policy in which the interests of the majority and a minority clash, the Supreme Court must establish rules for determining the boundaries between permissible and impermissible behavior. Historically, it has done so by ensuring that freedoms are enjoyed equally by everyone, not just those in the majority. However, the Court must also consider the right of a community to determine public policy through its elected and appointed public officials. In other words, the Court must balance the right of self-government with the protections granted to individuals and groups by the Constitution.

The Court's role as constitutional interpreter is not easy. Its decisions are bound to upset one or more of the contending parties. Even though the Supreme Court ruling ends the conflict among the parties involved in the case and settles the issue, at least in the short run, it may result in new or related issues being brought into the judicial arena as individuals or groups probe the parameters of the Court's judgment. Conflict continues although there is a consensus that the Court's decision is final, unless and until the Court changes it or it is modified by constitutional amendment.

Freedom of Speech

One of the basic tenets of a democratic society is free speech, the right of people to express their views no matter how unpopular those views may be. The logic behind this principle is that truth and wisdom will prevail over falsehood and ignorance in a free and open marketplace of ideas. The framers of the First Amendment accepted this principle and the logic on which it is based when they prescribed that Congress shall make no law abridging freedom of speech. Yet the history of American politics and government provides numerous examples of people and their elected representatives trying to constrain words, expressions, and even nonviolent demonstrations within the public arena.

In 1798, seven years after the adoption of the Bill of Rights, Congress passed the Alien and Sedition Acts, making it a crime to "utter false, scandalous and malicious" statements about the government. It did so to silence criticism from those who opposed the policies of the Washington administration and its Federalist-controlled Congress. But when prosecutions were brought under the act, conflict ensued. The public reacted violently to the restrictions on speech. After his election in 1800, President Thomas Jefferson pardoned those who had been convicted under the act. The legislation expired in 1801.

There have been many other examples of controversial government policies that limited First Amendment liberties for individuals and groups. Before the Civil War, abolitionist literature was confiscated and burned by authorities in both the North and the South. Later, many states passed laws forbidding obscene and indecent publications, a category interpreted to include such now-classic works as

James Joyce's *Ulysses,* Henry Miller's *Tropic of Cancer,* and Theodore Dreiser's *An American Tragedy.* In the late nineteenth century, fears of the spread of "subversive" ideas and doctrines such as anarchism, socialism, and communism led to a rash of prosecutions during and after World War I and World War II.

Apparently the meaning of the First Amendment's guarantee of free speech was not self-evident. The Supreme Court has had to interpret it and apply it to changing social conditions and beliefs. In doing so, the Court has developed several tests or standards that define the scope of protected speech.

Protected Speech

The Court's best-known test was formulated by Justice Oliver Wendell Holmes in *Schenck v. United States* (1919).[4] In that case, the Court upheld the conviction of Charles T. Schenck under the Espionage Act of 1917 for urging resistance to the draft and distributing antidraft leaflets during World War I. Schenck's antidraft advocacy at a time of war constituted, in the Court's view, "a clear and present danger" to the country. In Justice Holmes's familiar words:

> The character of every act depends upon the circumstances in which it was done. . . . The most stringent protection of free speech would not protect a man in falsely shouting fire in a theater and causing a panic. . . . The question in every case is whether the words used are used in such circumstances and are of such a nature as to create a clear and present danger that they will bring about the substantive evils that Congress has a right to prevent. It is a question of proximity and degree.[5]

clear and present danger doctrine
A doctrine used by the Supreme Court to determined the bounds of speech protected by the First Amendment; it asserts that unless the speech presents "a clear and present danger" it is protected by the Constitution.

Despite the Court's ruling against *Schenck,* the **clear and present danger doctrine** was seen as a broad judicial guideline that would protect individuals against prosecution for unpopular ideas. Yet the Court rejected Holmes's test only six years later.

Amid the hysteria over subversive speech following World War I, the Supreme Court upheld the conviction of Benjamin Gitlow under New York's criminal anarchy statute.[6] As noted in Chapter 2, the Gitlow case was the first in which the Supreme Court applied the Bill of Rights to the states. The New York law made it a crime to preach or advocate the overthrow of the government by force. Because Gitlow had written a book calling for a Russian-type revolution in New York, he was prosecuted and found guilty under the statute. In upholding his conviction, the Court majority argued that as long as the law against it was reasonable and that the speech could "bring about the substantive evil which the legislative body might prevent," that speech could be punished. They described as subversive speech that tends to corrupt public morals, incite crime, and disturb the public peace. Justice Holmes filed a vigorous dissenting opinion.

preferred freedom
A Supreme Court doctrine that asserts free speech has a higher priority than other constitutional protections; therefore, any law that restricts speech will be viewed more closely and critically than laws that restrict the exercise of other freedoms and rights.

As the public mood changed, so did the position of the Court. In the 1940s it expanded the protection of free speech, acknowledging it to be a **preferred freedom.** By placing a higher priority on the exercise of this liberty, the Court not only placed it in a separate category but also looked more critically at any law that restricted it.

But in the aftermath of World War II and the perceived threat of international communism, the Court again cut back on the protection of free speech when it upheld the Alien Registration Act of 1940 (the Smith Act), the first federal legislation restraining political speech since the ill-fated Alien and Sedition Acts. The ruling came in the case of *Dennis v. United States* (1951), in which the Court upheld the convictions of eleven leaders of the American Communist Party for advocating overthrow of the government, even though they had not done anything illegal other than teach and advocate their communist beliefs. Using a test first proposed by an appeals court judge, Learned Hand, the Supreme Court articulated a new speech test known as the **gravity of evil doctrine:** whether the gravity of evil, "discounted by its improbability, justifies such invasion of free speech as is necessary to avoid the danger."[7]

The Court gradually expanded First Amendment freedoms in a series of rulings beginning in the late 1950s. By 1969, the Supreme Court had come to the position that only the advocacy of immediate, violent, and illegal action may be subject to criminal prosecution. *Brandenburg v. Ohio* was the case in which the Supreme Court stated this position.

Charles Brandenburg, a leader of Ohio's Ku Klux Klan, had been arrested, tried, and convicted under the state's criminal syndicalism statute, which made it a crime to advocate violence or terrorism as a means of political reform and to assemble with a group that taught or advocated such beliefs. Standing before a burning cross, Brandenburg had addressed a small group of hooded men, some of whom carried firearms, declaring (among other things) that if the president, Congress, and the Supreme Court continued "to suppress the white, Caucasian race, it's possible that there might have to be revenge taken."[8] The Supreme Court unanimously reversed Brandenburg's conviction and struck down the Ohio law as unconstitutional. Today, the protections accorded by freedom of speech remain quite broad.

Speech that has **social redeeming value,** because it addresses matters of public concern, is now fully protected. The government may neither prevent individuals from engaging in speech or publications that touch on political, scientific, literary, or artistic matters nor punish them for doing so. Even speech that might threaten national security is protected. At the height of the Vietnam War in 1971, for example, the Court rejected the Nixon administration's attempt to prevent the *New York Times* and the *Washington Post* from publishing excerpts from *The Pentagon Papers,* a forty-seven–volume documentary history of America's involvement in the war that had been classified as top secret. In this watershed ruling, the Court maintained that the government "carries a heavy burden" of justifying its attempts at censorship.[9]

Determining what speech has social redeeming value, however, is often controversial. The desire of communities to silence speech that is not **politically correct,** that does not accord with the dominant view of acceptable language or expression, conflicts with the rights of individuals to express themselves in any manner they choose. In the late 1980s and the 1990s, for example, more than thirty states, as well as numerous localities, colleges, and universities, enacted "hate-crime" and "hate-speech" laws. St. Paul, Minnesota, made it a crime to place on public or private

gravity of evil doctrine
A doctrine to determine the bounds of protected speech; the doctrine asserts that speech is protected so long as the gravity of evil discounted by its improbability of occurrence is not at such a level as to threaten people individually or collectively and thereby justify constraints placed on that speech.

social redeeming value
That which is deemed to have merit and benefit for society.

politically correct
That which accords with the dominant view at the time; it pertains to words and actions.

property a burning cross, a swastika, or any other symbol likely to arouse "anger, alarm, or resentment in others on the basis of race, color, creed, religion, or gender." But the constitutionality of that ordinance was challenged by Robert A. Vicktora, who with several other white youths burned a cross after midnight on the lawn of the only African American family in his neighborhood. In *R. A. V. v. City of St. Paul, Minnesota* (1992), the Supreme Court ruled that the ordinance violated the First Amendment because it punished certain kinds of speech on the basis of its content. Writing for the Court, Justice Antonin Scalia observed that "the First Amendment does not permit St. Paul to impose special prohibitions on those speakers who express views on disfavored subjects."[10] Nonetheless, hate crimes, which can be differentiated from other criminal acts because they are directed against people primarily because of their race, ethnicity, religion, or sexual orientation, can be given more severe penalties.[11]

Unprotected Speech

As the Court's decisions indicate, the protection of freedom of speech is not absolute. In *Chaplinsky v. New Hampshire* (1942), which upheld the conviction of Walter Chaplinsky for calling a police officer "a goddamned racketeer," Justice Frank Murphy explained the Court's rationale for defining some categories of speech as unprotected and outside the scope of the First Amendment:

> There are certain well-defined and narrowly limited classes of speech, the prevention and punishment of which has never been thought to raise any Constitutional problem. These include obscenity, libel and slander, commercial speech, and symbolic expression and conduct. Yet defining standards for each category has proven extraordinarily vexing. In this section we look briefly at each of these categories.

obscenity

Words or visual depictions that appeal to prurient interests, describe or show sexual behavior in an offensive way, and lack social value; obscene materials are not protected by the First Amendment to the Constitution.

Obscenity   For centuries, **obscenity** has been subject to government censorship, but defining what is obscene in the light of evolving social mores and community beliefs has been a persistent problem. Before *Roth v. United States* (1957), federal courts permitted state and local governments to ban books on the basis of isolated passages that might "deprave and corrupt those whose minds are open to such immoral influences." This broad standard allowed communities to remove major literary works from their public libraries and, if applied aggressively, could eliminate virtually all literature "except that only fit for children," according to Justice Felix Frankfurter.

In the *Roth* decision, the Court held that obscenity is "not within the area of constitutionally protected speech," but it also rejected the broad standard that had been previously adopted for determining what is obscene. In explaining the Court's ruling, Justice William Brennan articulated a new obscenity test: "whether to the average person, applying contemporary community standards, the dominant theme of the material taken as a whole appeals to prurient interests."[12]

Basically, the *Roth* test meant that only hard-core pornography was outside the scope of First Amendment protection. But the justices remained unable to agree what is obscene. That problem led Justice Potter Stewart to confess that although he could not define it, "I know it when I see it."

4.2 Politics in the 21st Century
Sex on the Internet

The Internet as the newest communications channel has posed some vexing public policy issues. Few of them have invoked more passion and public concern than the depiction of sexual activities on sites accessible to minors. In 1996, Congress reacted to these public pressures by banning the dissemination of "indecent" and "patently offensive" material to minors on the Internet, with penalties of prison terms and large fines for violators.

Civil libertarians, medical educators, and companies offering online and computer services immediately objected to the new legislation, arguing that it would allow the government to act as a censor. Public officials would be in a position to determine what was or was not allowed. Would a medical journal that depicted parts of the human anatomy or discussed the transmission of AIDS through sexual relations be subject to prosecution under the law? What about a nature journal that discussed and depicted procreation among a species of animals? Would paintings or photographs, prominently displayed at public art galleries, that showed nudity or depicted people engaged in sexual activities be subject to prosecution if they were displayed on the Internet? Would print images or images permitted in movies also be banned? And what about material originating from sources outside the United States? How would the U.S. government enforce its laws against foreigners subject to different legal standards and perhaps different social mores?

Despite the difficult questions raised by the imposition of government standards, proponents of the legislation argued that Congress has a right, indeed an obligation, to protect children. It also has a duty to be responsive to the wishes of the American people and to make policy that reflects community standards and accords with the will of most of the people. That is what democratic government is all about.

In trying to resolve this contentious issue, the Supreme Court has tried to balance two social rights: that of individuals to exercise free speech and that of a community to govern itself in accordance with the wishes of the people as reflected by the decisions of their elected representatives. The Court has invalidated overly vague laws and those that affect communication among adults. It has ruled that Congress cannot make virtual imagery depicting sexual relations a crime, but it has also approved the use of various devices, such as V chips and pornography filters, to edit or remove material deemed harmful to children by their parents, guardians, or librarians and may be required of libraries if they accept federal government funds.

What do you think? Has the Court found an acceptable middle ground, or has it gone too far or not far enough in protecting children and preserving freedom of speech? What about violence on the Internet? Should depictions of violence be subject to the same rules as pornography?

The *Roth* ruling ignited considerable controversy because it appeared to open the floodgates for purveyors of pornographic materials. Presidential commissions studied the problem, and state and local law enforcement agencies sought tougher standards. In the 1970s, under pressure to overturn *Roth*, a more conservative Court redefined the basis for determining obscenity. In *Miller v. California* (1973), the Court stipulated three tests for judging allegedly obscene material: (1) whether the average person, applying local community standards, would find that a work, taken as a whole, appeals to a prurient interest; (2) whether the work depicts in a patently offensive way sexual conduct specifically defined as "obscene" in law; and (3) whether the work, taken as a whole, lacks "serious literary, artistic, political, or scientific value."[13]

Although many law enforcement agencies thought that the *Miller* decision gave them broader power to prosecute purveyors of obscenity, the Court subsequently reaffirmed that only hard-core pornography lay outside the First Amendment's protection. The use or public display of "four-letter words" may not be banned. However, students in public schools may be disciplined for the use of indecent, as well as obscene, language. Moreover, states may forbid the sale of pornographic materials to minors (those under the age of eighteen), completely ban pornography depicting minors, and prohibit sexually explicit live entertainment and films in bars. In addition, municipalities may use exclusionary zoning to regulate the location of adult bookstores and theaters.[14]

The Federal Communications Commission (FCC), which regulates the broadcast media, also has the power to prohibit the use of indecent and obscene language on the airwaves. The FCC has used this power to ban certain words and images from the public airwaves on the grounds that children and unsuspecting listeners otherwise could not be completely protected from "patently offensive, indecent material."[15] But the ban does not apply to subscription cable or satellite channels.

The Supreme Court has also taken a dim view of government attempts to regulate communication on the Internet. In the case of *Reno v. American Civil Liberties Union* (1997), the Court struck down federal legislation that made it a crime to put indecent and obscene materials that minors could access on the Internet.[16] Subsequently the Court negated another provision of the act, which criminalized the creation, distribution, and possession of "virtual" child pornography computer imagery. But in 2003 the Court upheld the right of Congress to require public libraries that receive federal funds to install pornography filters on certain computers with access to the Internet and to require minors to use only those computers.[17]

libel
A false statement about a person or defamation of a person's character by print or visual portrayal; for a "public" person, libel must be accompanied by evidence of actual malice to recover damages.

slander
A false statement or defamation of character by speech.

Libel and Slander   In legal terms, **libel** is a false statement about a person or defamation of his or her character in print or in a visual portrayal on television. **Slander** is such a statement or defamation by speech. Both damage an individual's reputation by holding the person up to contempt, ridicule, and scorn, and both may be subject to civil lawsuits. In *New York Times Co. v. Sullivan* (1964) the Supreme Court expressly noted that criminal libel is inconsistent with the values of the First Amendment.[18]

The Court's ruling in this landmark case established criteria by which public figures had to prove libel to recover damages. Those in the public spotlight must show "actual malice." They not only have to demonstrate the falsity of the statements but also must prove that the statements were made with knowledge of their falsity or with reckless disregard for their truth. The reason that the Court imposed such a high standard for public figures is that it did not want to discourage the press from performing its critical watchdog role in a democratic society. But by doing so, the Court also reduces the penalty for careless and inaccurate reporting, for presenting rumors and half truths as if they were facts, for rushing to judgment before a sufficient amount of information is available, and for relying on leaks from people who may have an ax to grind.

This high standard makes it exceedingly difficult for public figures to win libel awards. The conflict here is between the public's need and right to know and the individual's right to privacy or, if that individual is in the public arena, to fair, accurate, and unbiased reporting. Private individuals, those who neither hold public office nor have been thrust into the limelight, may recover damages on a lesser standard. They simply must show that the statements were false and that the publisher was negligent in its reporting.

Commercial Speech Advertising or **commercial speech** was for many years deemed to be outside the scope of First Amendment, ostensibly because it did not bear on political matters. Moreover, governments have important interests in regulating truth in advertising. Nevertheless, the Court has extended First Amendment protection to some commercial speech. It has overturned state and local laws forbidding advertising of alcohol, routine legal services, the cost of prescription drugs, the availability of abortion services, and other kinds of professional services. In addition, it has ruled that corporations' advertisements, newsletters, and mailings are protected under the First Amendment.[19] But claims in the ads must still be accurate. The government may require warning labels on products that could adversely affect the health and safety of people such as tobacco, liquor, and medicines.

commercial speech
Advertising that is truthful and not deceptive may fall under the protections of the First Amendment; however, the government may require labels on products that could adversely affect the health and safety of those who use them.

Symbolic Expression and Conduct

Besides extending First Amendment protection to virtually all forms of speech, the Supreme Court has ruled that certain other kinds of expression are protected by the First Amendment because they involve the communication of ideas. These include symbolic speech, and speech-plus-conduct.

Conduct that involves the communication of political ideas, often as a protest, is known as **symbolic speech.** The Court has held, for example, that wearing a black armband in school and turning the American flag into a peace symbol to protest a war are protected forms of expression under the First Amendment. Failure to pay taxes because of opposition to a government policy, however, is not protected by the First Amendment.

Speech-plus-conduct also involves the communication of ideas, but the ideas are conveyed through marching, picketing, and holding sit-ins on sidewalks and streets and in other public areas. Protection for these kinds of expression is rooted not only in the First Amendment's guarantee of free speech but also in its provision for freedom of association and "the right of the people peaceably to assemble, and to petition the government for a redress of grievances."

In public places such as streets and parks, individuals have the right to engage in political activities, subject only to reasonable time, place, and manner restrictions. Thus, cities may limit the hours that parks may be used or the times that sound trucks may travel on city streets and other public areas where protests may or may not occur, such as directly in front of the White House.

symbolic speech
Expressions of beliefs, such as wearing armbands to protest a war or turning an American flag into a peace symbol, are a form of protected speech.

speech-plus-conduct
The communication of ideas by marching, picketing, and demonstrations is protected provided that the conduct is not disruptive of public or private property. In the interests of public safety and order, the government may require permits or restrict the places in which such activity may occur.

People going from door to door to proselytize for their beliefs, however, may not be restricted.[20]

Freedom of Association   The constitutional protection of **freedom of association** is broader than that of freedom to organize rallies and peaceful protests. It also includes the right to join political parties and religious, economic, and other kinds of organizations. As a result, the disclosure of an organization's membership list cannot be compelled by election officials or legislative investigating committees. Nor may individuals be dismissed from employment because of their political associations or be required to disclose their associations to gain admission to the bar.[21]

However, the Court has ruled that freedom of association may be limited in certain ways when there are overriding social issues. For example civil servants who work for the federal government are prohibited from engaging in electoral campaigns for national office or assuming leadership positions in political parties.[22] These limits, established by the Hatch Act of 1940, have been upheld as necessary to protect the political neutrality of the civil service system. Similarly, federal workers may join unions, but they are not allowed to strike.

Private groups may also prescribe rules for their associates. The Girl Scouts do not have to admit boys. Intercollegiate sport teams do not have to be integrated by gender, but schools must provide equal opportunities for men and women to participate in sports and equal facilities for them to do so.

One of the most controversial cases of discrimination based on sexual orientation involved the Boy Scouts. All scouts take an oath in which they promise to do their best "To do my duty to God and my country and to obey the Scout Law; To help other people at all times; To keep myself physically strong, mentally alert, and morally straight." Acting on the belief that being an avowed homosexual was not being morally straight, the Boy Scouts expelled an assistant scoutmaster who had been a former Eagle Scout before he publicly declared his homosexuality. A deeply divided Court sided with the Scouts and upheld the expulsion of the assistant scout master on the grounds that private organizations can define a code of conduct for their members.[23] Nonetheless, it is unlikely that the Court's decision in this case will be the final word on state laws that prohibit discrimination on the basis of sexual orientation.

In summary, by protecting the rights of individuals and minorities to express their political views, no matter how unpopular, through marches, pickets, other kinds of demonstrations, and even cross burnings, and by allowing people to associate with whomever they choose as long as the group has not violated the law, the Court has challenged the views of the majority and invited more political controversy. Yet in defending the right to express unpopular views, it has also acknowledged that freedom of public discussion and debate is essential to democratic self-governance and a free society, a belief that most Americans shared in theory but not necessarily in practice.

The distinction between free speech and speech that crosses the line because it is obscene, false and malicious, or leads to illegal behavior is often very difficult to discern and repeatedly involves the judiciary in deciding where to draw that line and on the basis of what criteria.

Religion and the Constitution

Establishment of Religion

To most Americans, freedom of religion occupies a hallowed place in their country's hierarchy of political values. It ranks with that of speech as a fundamental tenet to which most citizens subscribe. But the early settlers in the new world did not display much tolerance for religions other than their own. Many of them came to the colonies to escape persecution and state churches in England and on the European continent. They established their own churches in America and made their religion a criterion for holding public office, thereby excluding Catholics, Jews, and atheists, as well as Protestants belonging to non-established sects. Some people were even persecuted for their refusal to convert to the dominant faith.

By the time the Constitution was ratified in 1789, religious freedom and tolerance had become more widely accepted. Four of the original thirteen colonies never had established churches, and three others abandoned theirs during the American Revolution. After the Revolution, all states gradually accepted religious diversity and extended their support to all Christian faiths.

The Constitution states that "no religious test shall ever be required as a qualification to any office or public trust under the United States" (Article VI). The Bill of Rights provided an even broader and more explicit protection for the exercise of religious beliefs. In prohibiting government from enacting any law establishing a religion or prohibiting the free exercise of religion, the Constitution guarantees that individuals can worship without fear of government imposing a set of religious beliefs on them. The **establishment clause** expressly forbids the creation of a national religion; it separates church and state. The **free exercise clause** guarantees that individuals may worship as they please.

As we noted in Chapter 2, these two provisions, however, raise more vexing questions than they settle. Does the Amendment forbid the establishment of a national church or all religious activity such as prayers in schools or in government institutions, such as Congress or the military? Does it preclude the mere mention of God such as the expression "In God We Trust," which appears on U.S. currency? Does any state aid to religious schools or do only certain forms of aid constitute an establishment of religion? Religious beliefs are protected, but how far may states go in prohibiting certain religious practices? And what should be done when the provisions for separation of church and state and those for free exercise of religion conflict?

Separation of Church and State

According to James Madison and Thomas Jefferson, the establishment clause embodies "a high wall of separation" between church and state. In the 1960s, this high wall was taken to mean that no religious activity, such as beginning the school day with a prayer, a practice that had become customary in many parts of the country, could be permitted.

establishment clause
The separation of church and state; government may not establish religion, including prayer or other religious activities in public schools; it may, however, provide funds to religious organizations for nonreligious purposes, such as free lunches for needy students or busses to take them to and from school.

free exercise clause
Individuals have the right to worship as they please; the government, however, may prevent people from engaging in religious practices that are harmful to society.

The first school prayer case, *Engle v. Vitale* (1962), involved a recommendation of the New York State Board of Regents that a brief nonsectarian prayer be uttered by schoolchildren at the beginning of the day: "Almighty God, we acknowledge our dependence upon Thee, and we beg Thy blessings upon us, our parents, our teachers, and our country." The prayer was voluntary. Children whose parents objected to their saying it could be excused from the room. Nevertheless, parents who objected to their children's participation in government-sponsored religious activity challenged the constitutionality of the prayer. The Supreme Court agreed. In writing the majority opinion, Justice Black stated:

> There can be no doubt that New York's state prayer program officially establishes the religious beliefs embodied in the Regents' prayer. . . Neither the fact that the prayer may be denominationally neutral nor the fact that its observance on the part of the students is voluntary can serve to free it from the limitations of the Establishment Clause.[24]

But what about a prayer that was not composed by the state, such as the Lord's Prayer? One year later the Court once again said "no" to that prayer in the case of *Abington School District v. Schempp.*[25]

These Court rulings were widely criticized at the time. Numerous constitutional amendments to overturn them were introduced in Congress. Although those attempts failed, state and local governments found ways to evade the decisions. By 1983 almost half of the states had enacted laws permitting voluntary moments of silence or prayer in public schools. But again some parents challenged the constitutional validity of these practices. In 1985, the Court overturned an Alabama law that required a "moment of silent meditation or prayer" on the ground that it did not have a clear secular purpose. Subsequently, the Court decided that prayers during a high school graduation ceremony and during sporting events also run afoul of the First Amendment's establishment clause. Private schools, however, are not prohibited from conducting religious services as part of their educational program.

Accommodating Church and State

accommodationist or preferentialist approach
The government may aid or extend benefits to religious groups for their nonreligious activities that benefit the community. President George W. Bush's faith-based initiative is based on such an approach.

In recent years the Court has moved away from its strict interpretation of "a high wall of separation" between church and state and has adopted instead an **accommodationist** or **preferentialist approach.** This position holds that government may aid or extend benefits to religion as long as it does not prefer one religion over another. In advancing this view, the Court has evolved a three-part test to determine the constitutionality of laws that indirectly aid religion. To be valid, such laws must have a secular legislative purpose, their primary effect must neither advance nor inhibit religion, and they must avoid excessive government entanglement with religion.

The accommodationist approach requires the Court to draw some fine lines in determining the scope of the establishment clause as the recent decisions on the Ten Commandments illustrate (see Chapter 2, pp. 60–61). Laws sponsoring

school prayer and the posting of the Ten Commandments in classrooms have been overturned, as have laws banning the teaching of evolution or requiring instruction in "creation science."[26] In a recent case, a district court went so far as to proscribe warnings placed on texts that evolution was only a theory.

On the other hand, the Court has permitted the study of the Bible and religion as part of secular education in public schools.[27] And as we noted in Chapter 2, the Court did not rule on the question, do the words *under God* in the Pledge of Allegiance represent state-sponsored religion?

The Supreme Court has approved the busing of children to private and parochial schools, the lending of books and other services from public schools to private religious schools, a tax exemption for religious schools, and tax deductions for parents who send their children to parochial schools.[28] Aid to education that indirectly helps a religious institution may be constitutional, but direct support for religious institutions or state-sponsored religious activity is not.

Another controversial issue concerns the issuing of vouchers by a municipality to help defray the costs of attending private or parochial schools. In 2002, the Supreme Court upheld such a program designed by the city of Cleveland, Ohio, to allow parents to use vouchers at private, as well as parochial, schools. Chief Justice William Rehnquist, who wrote the majority opinion, claimed that the plan was neutral between the religious and the secular choices, but the dissenting justices believed that the use of government vouchers at religious schools violated the separation of church and state.[29]

The Exercise of Religion

The free exercise clause embodies the principle of government neutrality with respect to different religious beliefs. Although the government cannot take sides, preferring one religion over another, it may regulate and even ban actions or practices that grow out of religious beliefs. In other words, beliefs are protected but certain religious practices may not be.

In making this distinction, the Supreme Court has followed a **secular regulation rule** that requires all laws to have a reasonable secular purpose and to not discriminate on the basis of religion. People may not, however, claim exemption from reasonable government regulations on religious grounds

secular regulation rule
A Supreme Court rule that requires all laws to have a reasonable secular purpose and not discriminate on the basis of religion.

because such an exemption would be favoring one religion over another. In *Reynolds v. United States* (1879), for instance, laws forbidding polygamy were upheld over the objections of Mormons, even though at the time the practice was part of Mormon religious beliefs.[30] Subsequently, the Court ruled that states may require schoolchildren to have smallpox vaccinations, denying claims of exemption by Christian Scientists.

The Court has also upheld laws restricting the sale of pamphlets and books in public buildings, dismissing objections by the Hare Krishna that such sales are part of their religious rituals. It has ruled that the Amish may be required to pay Social Security taxes even though doing so is contrary to their faith. And it has upheld "blue laws" requiring businesses to close on Sundays, despite claims that Sunday closing could cause economic hardship to members of religious groups that observe their Sabbath on other days of the week. In all these cases the Court has ruled that the state can regulate religious activity when protecting the health and well-being of all citizens.

The Supreme Court has not always sided with the state, however. It has also ruled that parents have the right to send their children to religious schools instead of to public schools as long as those schools are certified by the state. Nor may children be forced to attend school beyond the eighth grade if such a requirement would contradict their religious beliefs and cultural practices.[31] Similarly, students cannot be required to salute the American flag if doing so violates their religious convictions (as it does those of Jehovah's Witnesses).[32]

In these and other cases, the Court has avoided trying to define religion. The First Amendment guarantees the right of each person to define his or her own religious beliefs. In the words of Justice Robert H. Jackson, "If there is any fixed star in our constitutional constellation it is that no official, high or petty, can prescribe what shall be orthodox in politics, nationalism, or religion, or other matters of opinion, or force citizens to confess by word or act their faith therein."[33]

Review Questions

1. Freedom of speech is protected by the Constitution because

   A. In a democracy people should be able to say whatever they want whenever they want to do so
   B. In a democracy there should be a free marketplace of ideas
   C. In a democracy, words can't hurt; only actions can
   D. In the American colonies, the rights of Englishmen were denied to the settlers

2. Freedom of the press implies

   A. That newspapers can publish information that is classified without fear of government retribution
   B. That reporters never have to reveal their sources

continued

C. That the press may criticize public officials without fear of criminal penalty

D. That television broadcast news must be free to viewers

3. The establishment clause in the Constitution prohibits

   A. Public schools from requiring all students to pray silently at the beginning of the school day

   B. Public schools from denying students from praying silently at the beginning of the school day

   C. Public schools from teaching evolution

   D. Public schools from giving religious groups a room in which to conduct after-school activities

4. Freedom of religion means

   A. Organized churches can do whatever they please

   B. All religious activity is protected by law

   C. The government must give everyone their own Sabbath off

   D. The government cannot jail people suspected of terrorist activities because of their religious beliefs

Answers:

1. B
2. C
3. A
4. D

Conflict and Consensus in Review

Thus far, we have discussed the conflict over the meaning and application of the First Amendment and how the Supreme Court has attempted to resolve it. But how do the American people feel about the First Amendment today? A survey conducted by the First Amendment Center in 2005 indicates that most people support it. When asked to agree or disagree to the following statement: "The First Amendment goes too far in the rights its guarantees," 56 percent strongly disagreed and 16 percent mildly disagreed. Pluralities indicated that the press had just about the right amount of freedom, that Americans have just about the right amount of religious freedom, and that high school students have just about the right amount of freedom to express themselves. However, pluralities also said that public school students have too little religious freedom and that the American people have too little access to information about the federal government's war on terrorism.[34]

The Quest for Equality

The concept of equality and equal freedoms for all citizens is not mentioned in the Constitution or the Bill of Rights. Nevertheless, it is the bedrock of a democratic political system. The Declaration of Independence was emphatic about equality of political freedoms: "We hold these truths to be self-evident: That all men are created equal." But not until 1868, with the ratification of the Fourteenth Amendment, did the Constitution expressly provide that no person shall be deprived of "the **equal protection of the laws.**" Achieving that equality in practice has proven extraordinarily difficult. There remains no greater struggle in American politics than the struggle to guarantee all citizens their basic rights and liberties. That struggle reflects the success of social movements in changing the discriminatory attitudes and practices of the past.

equal protection of the laws
The principle that all people are equal under law and must be protected equally by the law.

The Extension of Voting Rights

The narrow victory of General Ulysses S. Grant in the 1868 presidential election convinced the Republican Party that to maintain its control of Congress it needed the votes of former slaves living in the South. This political need generated support for the Fifteenth Amendment (ratified in 1870), which forbade the abridgment of any citizen's right to vote "on account of race, color, or previous condition of servitude."

Although the amendment did not mention discrimination on the basis of gender, some women hoped that they might win the right to vote, or at least the right to vote in federal elections, by claiming that this right was implicitly guaranteed by the Fourteenth Amendment's prohibition against the states abridging the "privileges and immunities" of any of their citizens. But when Susan B. Anthony was prosecuted for voting in a federal election in 1872, her Fourteenth Amendment defense was rejected by a federal court. Three years later the Supreme Court held that "the Constitution of the United States does not confer the right of suffrage upon anyone."[35]

Pressure for giving women the right to vote mounted during World War I as large numbers of women entered the workforce and contributed to the war effort. In 1918 President Woodrow Wilson endorsed women's suffrage, and during the next year Congress enacted the Nineteenth Amendment granting women the right to vote. It was ratified in 1920.

Although African Americans were guaranteed the right to vote by the Fourteenth and Fifteenth Amendments and many were elected to office in the South during Reconstruction, white-dominated state governments and party organizations soon erected barriers such as poll taxes and literacy tests that effectively reduced their opportunities to vote. **Poll taxes** required a payment to vote and thereby discouraged the poor from voting. Likewise, **literacy tests** were used in the South to deny or discourage African Americans from voting by requiring them to answer questions—often obscure ones—about the Constitution, law, and politics. By the turn of the century, most African Americans in the South were effectively disenfranchised.

poll taxes
Fees formerly charged to individuals to pay the cost of conducting elections in states. Such taxes are now banned by the Fourteenth and Twenty-Fourth Amendments to the Constitution.

literacy tests
Tests formerly conducted by states, theoretically to determine whether a person had sufficient knowledge to make an informed voting decision but actually used to discriminate against poor, uneducated white and African American citizens. Today such tests are essentially banned by the Voting Rights Act of 1965 and its amendments.

In 1937 the Supreme Court ruled that poll taxes did not violate the Fourteenth and Fifteenth Amendments, a decision that sparked a campaign by citizen groups to convince the states and Congress to abolish them. The campaign had considerable success; by 1960, only five southern states retained poll taxes. The Twenty-Fourth Amendment, ratified in 1964, finally banned such taxes in federal elections, and two years later, the Court decided that the Fourteenth Amendment's equal protection clause forbade them in state elections as well.

The civil rights movement of the 1950s and 1960s initiated a drive to eliminate all barriers to voting for African Americans. But voter registration drives in the South still met widespread and often violent resistance. It was not until the passage of the Voting Rights Act of 1965 that suffrage for African Americans was effectively guaranteed by federal legislation.

The Voting Rights Act bans the use of literacy tests and other requirements that voters prove "good moral character" or present certificates verifying their qualifications in districts in which less than 50 percent of the citizens of voting age were registered to vote. Moreover, it authorizes the justice department to appoint federal examiners to register voters where the attorney general deems it necessary for the enforcement of the Fifteenth Amendment.

Because it limits the powers of the states to determine the qualifications for voting, the Voting Rights Act has remained controversial. However, the Supreme Court affirmed its constitutionality in 1966, and the act has been extended several times since then. In the 2000 election, for the first time the proportion of African Americans who voted was similar to that of the white majority.

Redistricting and Equal Representation

Besides striking down poll taxes and other barriers to voting, the Supreme Court has become involved in the issue of **redistricting,** the redrawing of legislative district boundaries. Traditionally, the courts avoided such matters on the ground that they involve "political questions," which must be resolved by legislative bodies. However, in a landmark decision, *Baker v. Carr,* 1962, the Court ruled that such controversies contain issues of fairness and justice that open them to judicial review.[36]

Once the Court conceded that the matter was "justiciable" (that it could be adjudicated in a court of law, the justices had to define the standard by which districting plans could be evaluated in accordance with the constitutional prescriptions of the Fourteenth Amendment. In two cases in the 1960s, the Court articulated this standard—one person, one vote—and applied it to every electoral district within the country except for ones specifically exempted by the Constitution: the U.S. Senate and the Electoral College.[37]

One of the most contentious issues involving the judiciary has been legislation drafted to ensure minority representation. Citing a provision of the 1982 Voting Rights Act and several Supreme Court decisions, the Justice Department, beginning in the administration of George H. W. Bush and continuing through those of Bill Clinton and George W. Bush, pressed state legislatures to create

redistricting
The process of redrafting legislative district boundaries within states. All legislative districts within a state must be approximately equal in population. They cannot vary by more than 0.005 percent.

more districts in which minority groups within the state were in the majority to increase the proportion of minority legislators. Although, the number of minority candidates elected to the House of Representatives more than doubled, the public policy consequences were not nearly as favorable to minority groups and their liberal supporters. Because African Americans and Hispanics tend to vote Democratic, their heavy concentration in certain districts made other, "whiter" districts more likely to elect Republicans and thus provided congressional Republicans with an overall advantage. White Democrats in some southern states challenged the constitutionality of such "racial gerrymandering," and in a series of rulings in the 1990s a bare majority of the Court agreed that racial gerrymandering violates the Fourteenth Amendment's equal protection clause.[38]

The issue came to a head in Georgia following the 2000 census, when a Democratic legislature drafted a redistricting plan that reduced the concentration of minority voters in congressional districts to improve the chances of Democratic candidates in others. The plan was immediately challenged by Republicans who called it "a retrogression," a retreat into the discriminatory past. But the Supreme Court disagreed. A majority upheld the new Georgia plan. In doing so, the Court gave the states greater flexibility in determining the equity of its representational system for minority voters.[39]

Ending Racial Discrimination

Despite the Fourteenth and Fifteenth Amendments (as well as the Thirteenth, which prohibited slavery), new barriers to racial equality emerged in the late nineteenth century in the form of so-called **Jim Crow laws.** These laws separated the races in public transportation and accommodations and discriminated against African Americans in other ways. Segregation persisted in housing, education, and employment. In 1883 the Court struck down as unconstitutional the Civil Rights Act of 1875, which had forbidden discrimination in public accommodations such as hotels, theaters, and railroad carriages. According to the Court, Congress had exceeded its power under the Fourteenth Amendment by prohibiting individuals from discriminating; the amendment, in the Court's view, forbade only state discrimination.

Subsequently, in the case of *Plessy v. Ferguson* (1896), the Supreme Court affirmed the **separate but equal doctrine** by upholding Louisiana's law requiring separate but equal facilities for the races in railroad cars.[40] Although it struck down laws specifically denying or limiting the right of nonwhites to acquire property, it upheld until 1948 the enforcement of **restrictive covenants,** that is, contracts in which property owners agree not to sell or lease their property to members of certain racial or religious groups.

The Brown Decision

Beginning in the 1930s, however, organizations such as the National Association for the Advancement of Colored People (NAACP) began filing lawsuits to force the end of racial segregation in housing, education, and employment. Like the

Jim Crow laws
Laws enacted in many southern states after the Civil War to separate the races in public transportation, hotels, restaurants, and other places of public accommodation.

separate but equal doctrine
The Supreme Court doctrine that upheld Louisiana's law requiring separate but equal facilities for the races in railroad cars and other forms of public transportation. In actuality, however, most facilities were not equal.

restrictive covenants
Contracts in which the sellers of private property agree not to sell that property to members of certain religious, racial, or ethnic groups. Restrictive covenants have been deemed unconstitutional and, therefore, invalid since 1948.

Segregated seating on Atlanta buses in 1956.

other branches of government, the Court was slow to respond to these demands. Not until 1954 did it step firmly into the racial discrimination controversy with its landmark school desegregation decision in *Brown v. Board of Education of Topeka* (1954).[41] In that case the Court rejected the separate but equal doctrine, holding instead that racially segregated public schools violated the equal protection clause of the Fourteenth Amendment.

Even in *Brown*, the Court was reluctant to press too hard too quickly to rectify the situation. It feared a negative public reaction and even the outright refusal of some school districts to abide by its decision. It was another year before the Court handed down its remedial decree that school boards must proceed with "all deliberate speed to desegregate public schools at the earliest practical date."[42] The decree of "all deliberate speed" was a compromise between requiring precise deadlines for school desegregation and simply allowing states and localities to comply with *Brown's* mandate at their own discretion.

The *Brown* decision and its enforcement decree did meet with massive resistance in the form of widespread evasion, occasional violence, and even the yearlong shutdown of an entire school system. The vagueness of the phrase "with all deliberate speed" actually served to justify noncompliance; progress toward achieving integrated schools was deliberately slow and uneven. In addition,

President Dwight Eisenhower refused to use the power of the executive branch to ensure compliance until he was forced to send the National Guard to quell resistance to the desegregation of Central High School in Little Rock, Arkansas, in 1957. Eisenhower sent the troops not because he favored the Court's ruling but because it was the law of the land and he as president had to enforce that law. In the decade after the *Brown* decision, less than 2 percent of all African American students in the South attended desegregated schools.

The Civil Rights Act of 1964

The major advance in ending racial segregation, not only in education but also in housing and employment, came with the passage of the Civil Rights Act of 1964. Title VI of this act forbids schools from discriminating "on the ground of race, color, or national origin in any program or activity receiving federal assistance." Besides authorizing the withholding of federal funds from schools that discriminate, the Department of Justice was authorized to enforce the act and the mandate of *Brown*. Title II of the act forbids discrimination in public accommodations—inns, hotels, restaurants, theaters, and the like—and Title VII makes it illegal for employers in any business or industry with fifteen or more employees to discriminate on the basis of race, color, national origin, religion, or sex. Subsequent amendments extended all parts of the act to forbid discrimination based on gender and age, as well as discrimination against people with disabilities and against Vietnam veterans.

By the late 1960s the Supreme Court also made it clear that it would no longer accept delays in complying with its *Brown* mandate. In proclaiming that continued operation of racially segregated schools under the standard of "all deliberate speed" was no longer permissible, the Court instructed school districts to end their dual school systems based on race immediately and operate only unitary school districts.[43]

School Integration

de facto segregation
Segregation that exists as a consequence of living patterns, not because of law or official government policies.

de jure segregation
Segregation on the basis of law or official government policies. The Supreme Court has declared that the Fourteenth Amendment to the Constitution forbids this type of segregation.

During the 1970s, 1980s, and early 1990s, the issue of bringing an end to segregated schools was replaced by the issue of how to achieve integrated schools. This was a particularly troublesome question in the North and West, where schools were segregated as a result of housing patterns (**de facto segregation**), not because of laws and official policies (**de jure segregation**). One device for overcoming de facto segregation was to bus children to schools outside of their neighborhood, schools that they would not have ordinarily attended. Although busing can be a means of achieving integrated schools, it violates the tradition of neighborhood schools, creates lengthy travel for some students, and sometimes increases racial tensions within schools.

The Supreme Court has upheld the power of federal judges to order busing *within* school districts but not *between* them as a remedy for segregated schools.[44] The racial composition of many urban school districts, which may be

Box 4.3 How to Find Supreme Court Decisions

Cases pending before the Supreme Court are analyzed in *Preview of United States Supreme Court Cases,* published regularly during each Court term by the Public Education Division of the American Bar Association. Each discussion summarizes the issues, facts, background, significance, arguments (for and against), and amicus briefs (for and against) for each case. *Preview* is an excellent source of clearly written descriptions of the cases awaiting decision; it can be found in law and research libraries.

When a Supreme Court decision is referred to, or cited, in a formal text, a specific format is followed. Court citations always begin with the names of the parties to the case, starting with the appellant (the person or party bringing the case), followed by *v.* (meaning "versus," or "against"), followed by the name of the appellee (the person or party responding)—all usually underscored or italicized. Next is the volume number of the *United States Reports* in which the decision appears, followed by the page number on which the decision begins. Next, if a specific quotation from the decision is being cited, the word *at* and the page number of the quote appear. In parentheses following the page number is the year in which the decision was made. For example, the case *McCulloch v. Maryland,* 17 U.S. 316 at 317 (1819), is found in volume 17 of the *United States Reports* starting on page 316, with the particular quote cited appearing on page 317; the decision was made in 1819.

Information about Supreme Court decisions can also be found in commercial publications such as *Supreme Court Reporter, United States Law Week,* and *United States Supreme Court Reports, Lawyer's Edition.* In addition, computerized legal databases such as LexisNexis contain Supreme Court decisions.

Sources like these are found in all law libraries and in many research libraries.

Supreme Court decisions have been available on the Internet since 1991. The opinions can be accessed from several university servers, such as Cornell University's Legal Information Institute website (supct.law.cornell.edu/supct/index.html). They may also be located at FindLaw's Supreme Court Opinions page (www.findlaw.com/casecode/supreme.html).

The oral arguments in many landmark Supreme Court cases may also be heard by downloading, at no cost, a RealPlayer media player (www.real.com) and going to the Oyez site at www.oyez.org/oyez/frontpage. Oyez also has brief biographies of the justices and some of their speeches, as well as excellent coverage of cases on the docket for the current term and the previous one.

The home pages of other federal and state courts may be located at the United States Courts Home Page at www.uscourts.gov.

overwhelmingly minority, has not enabled proponents of integrated public schools to achieve their goal even with busing. However, opposition to busing may have contributed to the movement of families from the cities to suburban neighborhoods.

Disproportionate resources among school districts within a state aggravate the problem. With property taxes the principal source of revenue for school funding, poorer districts—those in which property is not highly assessed—have to depend on the state or federal government for additional support. Providing such support for schools that improved their educational standards was one of the primary objectives of the reforms that President George W. Bush proposed and Congress enacted in 2001 in the so-called No Child Left Behind Act. But the legislation, thus far, has had mixed results.

Nonracial Discrimination

All legislation and government policy, by its very nature, discriminates in some way because it confers burdens or benefits on some groups and not on others. For example, most states require individuals to be at least sixteen years old and pass a driving test before they can operate a motor vehicle and to be twenty-one years old before they can purchase alcoholic beverages in public bars and restaurants. Others deny licenses to aliens who have entered the country illegally even though they are required to pay state and federal taxes. From the standpoint of civil rights, the question is whether laws and regulations are reasonable and do not unfairly discriminate against particular groups, such as younger people in the driving and liquor examples.

Minimal Versus Strict Scrutiny

minimum scrutiny test
The lowest standard that the Supreme Court uses to determine the constitutionality of state laws. According to this standard, laws must have a rational purpose to be valid.

When considering challenges to law and policy under the Fourteenth Amendment's equal protection clause, therefore, the Supreme Court must decide whether the discrimination is *invidious,* in which case it is unconstitutional because it unfairly discriminates against an individual or group, or whether it is *reasonable,* in which case it may be constitutional because there is a logical basis for making the distinction. During the mid-1950s and the 1960s, the Court evolved a two-tier approach to applying the equal protection clause. When reviewing challenges to legislation that deals solely with economic matters, it uses a **minimal scrutiny test,** meaning that it simply looks at whether the legislation in question has a rational basis. Using this test, the Court has not struck down any federal or state economic legislation under the equal protection clause since 1937.

strict scrutiny test
A higher standard for determining the constitutionality of federal or state laws; the state must demonstrate a "compelling interest" in laws that limit or deny people rights or that discriminate on the basis of race, national origin, or religion.

When legislation is based on a "suspect classification" or denies individuals their "fundamental rights," the Court uses a **strict scrutiny test** for determining its constitutionality. The strict scrutiny test puts the burden of proof on the state, which must demonstrate a "compelling interest" to justify the law or policy in question. Suspect classifications include distinction made on the basis of race, ethnicity, and alien status. Because those characteristics are immutable—individuals cannot choose or change their race or ethnicity—laws that impose burdens or deny benefits on the basis of such characteristics invariably fail to pass the Court's strict scrutiny test.

The Exacting Scrutiny Test

strict rationality or exacting scrutiny test
A middle standard for determining the constitutionality of laws that involve nonracial discrimination such as gender, age, or wealth; the laws must further some legitimate government interest in a reasonable way to be constitutional.

In the past two decades the Court has confronted an increasingly broad range of claims of nonracial discrimination, including claims of discrimination based on gender, age, and wealth. In response to these new challenges, the Court has created a third, intermediate test—the **strict rationality test,** also known as the **exacting scrutiny test.**

Under the strict rationality test, legislation must in a reasonable way further some legitimate government policy. Such a standard is necessarily more subjective or flexible than the strict scrutiny standard. For example, gender-based discrimination has been upheld by the Court in cases challenging an all-male military draft, the enforcement of statutory rape laws against males but not females, the sale of 3.2-percent beer to males (but not females) under age twenty-one, the assignment of female guards to prisons in which women are incarcerated, and the denial of health benefits to women who miss work because of pregnancy leave.[45] On the other hand, the Court has struck down laws discriminating against women in cases involving denial of benefits for dependents of female (but not male) military personnel and denial of seniority status to women who take pregnancy leave from work.[46] Moreover, in 1986 the Court unanimously agreed that female employees could sue employers for sexual harassment under the Civil Rights Act.[47]

Age discrimination in employment is another area in which the Court has encountered claims of invidious discrimination. Responding to pressure brought by groups of senior citizens and to demographic changes in the U.S. population, Congress prohibited age discrimination under the Age Discrimination in Employment Act of 1967, which was amended in 1975 and 1978. The Supreme Court has upheld several claims under this legislation. However, it has found no constitutional objection to a state law requiring police officers to retire at the age of fifty. Nor did the Court find any constitutional violation on the basis of age when, in *Gregory v. Ashcroft* (1991), it upheld a Missouri law requiring state judges to retire at seventy.[48]

In other areas of nonracial discrimination—in which, for example, benefits for illegitimate children or the treatment of the mentally disabled or homosexuals are at issue—the Court applies either its rational basis or its exacting scrutiny test, taking each case on its own merits. Basically, the Court tries to balance the interests of government against the claims of individuals to equal protection of the laws, and the results are sometimes unpredictable. For example, in *Romer v. Evans* (1996) the Court invalidated an amendment to Colorado's constitution that forbade localities from enacting laws that prohibited discrimination against gays and lesbians.[49] Applying the rational basis test, the Court held that the amendment merely expressed "animus" (hatred) toward homosexuals and thus, having no rational basis, violated the Fourteenth Amendment's equal protection clause.[50]

Affirmative Action

Affirmative action in education and employment has been especially controversial. Designed to help women and minorities advance in areas in which they have historically been discriminated against, **affirmative action,** which originated with Lyndon Johnson's Democratic administration in 1964–1965, gives special consideration to women and minorities. Consequently, these programs have been attacked for practicing **reverse discrimination**—that is, for penalizing whites and males in violation of their rights under the Fourteenth Amendment's equal protection clause. Critics argue that what affirmative action does is move beyond the principle of **equality of opportunity** in education and employment in an effort to ensure **equality of result.**

affirmative action
A program instituted to correct past discriminatory practices aimed people identified as part of certain racial, ethnic, and gender-based groups. It provides hiring and promotion opportunities for members of these groups.

reverse discrimination
Refers to discrimination of the majority that occurs when minorities or other groups are given additional advantages or opportunities.

equality of opportunity
The principle that all people should have an equal chance to pursue their goals and interests and to achieve them in the political, economic, and social system.

equality of result
Relates to the consequences of economic, social, or political activities—the results should be equal. The principle has limited applicability in a free-enterprise, capitalistic system.

During the presidencies of Richard Nixon, Gerald Ford, and Jimmy Carter, affirmative action programs were promoted and defended by their respective administrations. Under Ronald Reagan, George H. W. Bush, and George W. Bush on the other hand, the Department of Justice challenged the constitutionality of such programs. The Clinton administration supported them, but the president did order a review of federally sponsored policies to narrow their scope and end those that had achieved their goals. Regardless of which party has controlled the executive branch, however, affirmative action programs adopted at the state and local levels have been bitterly contested in the courts.

Defenders of affirmative action argue that because women and minorities had been denied equal opportunities in education and employment for many years, they frequently do not have the education, training, or seniority necessary for some jobs and promotions, and judging them by the criteria used to judge white males will perpetuate the disadvantage of these disadvantaged groups. Critics, however, claim that affirmative action programs go too far in the pursuit of greater equality; they discriminate against the majority.

When confronted with challenges to affirmative action programs, the Supreme Court initially was sharply divided. One of the most important cases was *Regents of the University of California v. Bakke* (1978).[51] Alan Bakke, a white man who had been denied admission to the medical school at the University of California at Davis, contended that his application had been rejected because the school set aside 16 out of 100 admissions for African Americans, Chicanos, Asians, and Native Americans—groups that had previously been underrepresented in the student body. He claimed that this policy violated his rights under the Civil Rights Act and the Fourteenth Amendment, because some of the minority students admitted under the school's affirmative action program had grade-point averages and test scores lower than his.

The Court partly agreed with Bakke. The majority opinion stated that quota systems (programs that set aside a specified number of openings for minorities) like the one at the University of California are unconstitutional. At the same time, however, the Court upheld the principle of affirmative action programs that consider race as one among many factors in student admissions.

This ruling was reaffirmed twenty-five years later, when another deeply divided Court upheld the admission policy of the University of Michigan law school. In its decision, the Court majority, acknowledging the prerogative of a university to consider the diversity of the student body as part of the overall educational experience, stated that race and ethnicity could be considered in the making of admission decisions as long as it was done on an individual, not a collective, basis. Minority candidates could not be put on a separate track because that would deny members of other groups equal protection of the laws. However, the race or ethnicity of an applicant could be counted as a plus in the overall evaluation of a person's application for admission in the university's attempt to achieve a racially diverse student body.[52]

In a related case, the Court invalidated Michigan's undergraduate program, which was based on a point system that automatically awarded certain students

20 points simply because they were minorities. In rejecting such a plan as discriminatory, the Supreme Court reiterated its opposition to quotas or separate tracks for different races and ethnic groups.[53]

Affirmative action programs in employment have proven even more divisive for the Court. In 1979, it ruled that employers and labor unions may agree to adopt private affirmative action programs despite the objections of white members of the union. In three out of four rulings during the 1980s, the Court upheld the constitutionality of affirmative action programs, basing its decisions on its exacting scrutiny test. But by 1989, changes in its composition that resulted in a conservative majority reversed the Court's orientation toward most affirmative action programs in the private sector.

In *City of Richmond v. J. A. Croson* (1989) the Supreme Court struck down a program in Richmond, Virginia, that required nonminority building contractors to subcontract 30 percent of all city-awarded projects to minority-owned businesses.[54] In announcing the Court's ruling, Justice Sandra Day O'Connor noted that Richmond's affirmative action program was not narrowly targeted to the city's African Americans, because minority-owned businesses from all over the country were eligible to bid on projects. The ruling held that state and local governments may no longer adopt affirmative action programs unless they are designed specifically as remedies for past discrimination. On a parallel track, the Supreme Court also restricted the application of the Americans with Disabilities Act by narrowing the definition of disabilities to those that are central to daily life, not to the workplace alone.[55]

But the debate is far from over. In 1990, a bare majority of the justices upheld affirmative action programs adopted by the federal government and approved by Congress. One year later Congress enacted a civil rights act that barred discrimination in all phases of employment, not just in hiring practices, and extended protection against discrimination based on race, religion, gender, and national origin to employees of U.S. companies who are stationed abroad. In addition, Congress reversed other rulings that had made it more difficult for African Americans and women to prove discrimination in employment and made it easier for whites to challenge court-ordered affirmative action programs.[56]

Conflict and Consensus in Review

The American people strongly support the concept of equality, but they disagree over the extent to which that equality has been achieved. Whites are more likely than African Americans to perceive race relations as satisfactory; they are also more likely to believe that minorities do have opportunities to succeed in academia and the workplace.[57] Whites did not believe that the government's slow response to the victims of Hurrricane Katrina was due to racial prejudice; African Americans did.[58] On the issue of homosexuality, a plurality of people support the right of consenting adults to engage in homosexual relations; a large majority thinks that homosexuals should have equal job opportunities; but a majority still does not believe in homosexual marriage.[59]

| Justice for All |

Criminal justice is another area of constitutional interpretation. It, too, is rooted in the principles of the English common-law tradition and embodied in the Bill of Rights. It, too, has been made applicable to the states through the Fourteenth Amendment, which prohibits government from depriving any person of due process of law. But what is due process?

Due Process of Law

It is helpful to think of due process as being divided into two basic kinds: procedural and substantive.

procedural due process
Concerned with the processes by which law is implemented and enforced; the enforcement must be fair and equitable for everyone.

Procedural due process is concerned with how the law is carried out—whether by police, judges, legislatures, or administrative agencies. Although procedural due process often pertains to the specific rights and procedural guarantees mentioned in the Bill of Rights, the Supreme Court has sought to enforce a more general standard of fairness in criminal procedures and law enforcement. In *Rochin v. California* (1952), for example, the Court reversed the conviction of Antonio Richard Rochin for selling and possessing narcotics. Police with no arrest or search warrant had broken into Rochin's home and found him in bed, where he immediately swallowed two morphine capsules that were on a table next to the bed. The police attempted to make him cough up the evidence, repeatedly kicking him and trying to make him gag. Finally they took him to a hospital and ordered a doctor to pump his stomach. At Rochin's trial the prosecution introduced the regurgitated morphine as evidence. In an opinion for the Court overturning Rochin's conviction, Justice Felix Frankfurter observed that the conduct of the police "shocks the conscience. . . Due process of law [means that] convictions cannot be brought about by methods that offend 'a sense of justice.'"[60]

During the 1960s and 1970s, the Court greatly expanded the requirements of procedural due process by applying them to administrative agencies and other government institutions. For example, it held that individuals must be given some kind of hearing or opportunity to challenge the termination of welfare benefits, the suspension of students from school, and the disconnecting of electric, gas, and water services by public utilities. In the 1980s and 1990s, however, the Court became more conservative and more resistant to expanding procedural due process. During this period the Court let stand certain criminal convictions even though the accused's rights were not fully honored because some "harmless error" was made by the prosecution at the trial.[61]

substantive due process
Subjects laws to a standard of reasonableness; it has been used to limit what government may do in certain areas, such as privacy.

Substantive due process is concerned with the subject matter of a law, regulation, or executive order; it places limitations on what government may do. The Court looks at the substance of the law itself, why it was enacted, and whether it is "unreasonable," "irrational," or "arbitrary." Because the Court may overturn laws made by elected officials and thereby change public policy, substantive due process is highly controversial.

In the late nineteenth and early twentieth centuries, the Court was dominated by conservatives opposed to most social-welfare legislation. During this period it often used substantive due process to strike down government regulation of economic activities, including laws that governed prices, wages, hours of work, and job conditions. It did so on the basis of a "liberty of contract," which, although not specifically mentioned in the Constitution, the Court found to be implicit in the concept of due process. Between 1897 and 1937, more than 200 state and federal laws were overturned as unreasonable and infringing on the liberty of contract.

This use of substantive due process to promote the interests of business became a major political issue—particularly when the Court invalidated much of the early New Deal economic legislation of the 1930s, which was intended to alleviate the effects of the Great Depression. In 1937, President Franklin Roosevelt retaliated. He proposed that the number of justices be increased from nine to fifteen so that he would be able to appoint new justices and thereby secure a majority willing to uphold his New Deal program. Although his opponents denounced him for trying to "pack" the Court, the Supreme Court appeared to change its interpretation at that point by handing down a series of decisions that humorists called "the switch in time that saved nine." Since 1937, no economic regulation has been struck down on grounds of substantive due process.

More recently, however, the Court has employed substantive due process to overturn laws infringing on noneconomic civil liberties. Notably, in the 1965 case of *Griswold v. Connecticut*,[62] the Court invoked the **right to privacy** under the Fourteenth Amendment's due process clause to overturn a law prohibiting the use of contraceptives. In its highly controversial 1973 ruling in *Roe v. Wade*, it went even further by striking down most laws forbidding abortion. It did so on the basis of the right of privacy and a balancing of the interests of women against the interests of the state. Now, more than three decades later, the Court has ruled that laws that require parental or spousal consent, provide for a short waiting period, or limit the use of taxpayer funds for abortion services or even information on abortion are constitutional even though prohibiting abortion is not.

For the past thirty years, the Court has been reluctant to rely on substantive due process to protect or extend benefits to individuals. It refused to extend marital protections of privacy to homosexual couples[63]; it refused, in the case of *Bowers v. Hardwick,* to overturn a Georgia law that criminalized sodomy.[64] However, in 2003 the Court reversed its position and voided a Texas sodomy law directed against same-sex partners. In doing so, Justice Anthony Kennedy specifically rejected the decision of the Court in *Bowers* as "not correct when it was decided, and it is not correct today."[65] By indicating that states have no right to criminalize private sexual activities between two consenting adults, the Court essentially invalidated all sodomy laws, including those that applied to opposite-sex couples. Angered by Kennedy's decision, conservative groups criticized him and began a campaign to get more socially conservative justices appointed to the federal bench.

In summary, whereas liberals attacked the pre-1937 Court for imposing its own values (in economics) under the doctrine of liberty of contract, conservatives criticized the post-1937 Court for doing precisely the same thing (in moral standards) through its application of the right of privacy. The use of

right to privacy
A right that may be inferred from the protections enunciated in the First, Third, Fourth, and Fifth Amendments and applied to the states through the Fourteenth.

substantive due process will always be hotly contested because it pits the Court against the forces of the legislative majority. Indeed, whenever the Court sides with the individual or with a minority against the state, its decisions are likely to be controversial.

Unreasonable Searches and Seizures

unreasonable searches and seizures
Searches and seizures by enforcement officials that are arbitrary, unreasonable, or too general; these are usually prevented by requiring the enforcement officials to obtain a search warrant from a judge.

Like many other rights, the freedom from **unreasonable searches and seizures** is rooted in the history of English common law and the American colonial experience. During the colonial period, royalist judges issued writs of assistance or general warrants, which allowed British authorities to search and ransack homes. The purpose of the Fourth Amendment was to prevent such an intrusion—to forbid police from conducting "arbitrary," "unreasonable," and "general" searches and seizures.

The key to this protection is the requirement that a magistrate issue a warrant before a search or an arrest can be made. To obtain a warrant, the police must swear under oath that they have "probable cause" for its issuance, and the warrant must describe the specific places that will be searched and the people or things to be seized. The police are barred from conducting more wide-ranging searches. Exceptions to the warrant requirement may be allowed when the arrest is made in a public place, when the police are in "hot pursuit" of a suspect, or when someone's life is in danger.[66]

In response to the growth of government and the rise of the administrative state, in which government agencies regulate many kinds of activities, the Court has ruled that in some circumstances administrative officials (such as housing inspectors and agents of the Occupational Safety and Health Administration) must obtain a warrant before searching a home or business without the owner's consent. However, in 1985 the Court upheld a school principal's warrantless search of a student's purse and locker, and two years later it upheld the warrantless search of an employee's office by her supervisor. The Court has also upheld drug testing of federal employees, alcohol testing of employees involved in serious accidents, and random drug testing of student athletes and those involved in extracurricular activities. In 1997, however, in *Chandler v. Miller,* the Court struck down as unreasonable a Georgia law requiring all candidates for public office to submit to drug tests to be placed on the ballot.[67]

Other threats to personal privacy posed by new technologies and changing law enforcement techniques have been addressed by the Court. The drafters of the Fourth Amendment could not have foreseen the use of wiretaps, electronic eavesdropping devices, and secret television cameras. When initially confronted by the issue of whether wiretapping constituted an unreasonable search and seizure, a bare majority of the Court in 1928 said "no."[68] But almost forty years later, in *Katz v. United States* (1967), the Court reversed itself when it held that police must obtain a search warrant before conducting wiretaps—even wiretaps placed in public telephone booths—because the Fourteenth Amendment safeguards individuals' "reasonable" and "legitimate expectations of privacy."[69] Following the Court's decision, Congress established federal guidelines for the use of electronic surveillance by

Police officer and dog search for bomb after the school received a threatening telephone call.

law enforcement officials and forbade any unauthorized person from tapping telephones and using other kinds of electronic listening devices in the Crime Control and Safe Streets Act of 1968. These guidelines were revised and expanded in the USA Patriot Act of 2001, enacted after the terrorist attacks on the World Trade Center and the Pentagon. The manner in which the Justice Department implemented this law, however, was criticized by Arab American groups and subsequently challenged in the courts by the American Civil Liberties Union (ACLU).

Government Interrogations

Individuals enjoy several rights under the Fifth and Sixth Amendments, which bar the government from coercing confessions and forcing the disclosure of incriminating evidence. One of the best known of these rights is the right against **self-incrimination** guaranteed by the Fifth Amendment to the Constitution. The phrase "taking the fifth" refers to people who invoke this constitutionally protected right when they refuse to answer questions before a congressional committee, administrative hearing, or grand jury. But people may invoke that protection only when their disclosures would prove incriminating, not merely embarrassing.

self-incrimination
The principle of being innocent until proven guilty includes the right not to testify against yourself or provide incriminating evidence.

Grants of Immunity

grant of immunity
Protection given to people who have information that the government desires; in exchange for providing such information, the government agrees that none of it can be subsequently used in a criminal trial against the person who provided that information.

The privilege against self-incrimination may be waived by an individual who is offered a **grant of immunity** by a prosecutor, grand jury, or congressional investigatory committee; such a grant must be approved by a judge. Grants of immunity are offered when the government is more interested in obtaining information about some criminal activity, such as drug trafficking or corporate corruption, than in prosecuting a particular individual. In exchange for immunity from subsequent prosecution on the basis of evidence presented at the hearing, the witness may no longer claim the protection of the Fifth Amendment or refuse to testify.

Plea Bargaining

plea bargaining
The practice of allowing a person charged with a crime to plea guilty to a lesser offense; it is used when law enforcement officials need information or do not want to go through the process of a long and expensive trial.

The Supreme Court has also sanctioned the practice of **plea bargaining,** in which an accused person pleads guilty to a lesser offense than the one with which he or she was originally charged. In exchange for the lighter sentence, defendants who plea-bargain must surrender their constitutional right against self-incrimination, as well as their rights to a speedy and public jury trial and to confront witnesses against them.

Plea bargaining is advantageous for the government, as well as for the accused, because it eliminates the time and cost of going to trial and provides the government with information that it might not otherwise be able to obtain. The desire to "get the goods" on members of Congress who may have accepted trips, meals, and sports tickets from lobbyist Jack Abramoff in exchange for performing legislative favors for him was a principal motive behind the government's offer of a plea bargain to Abramoff and his associates, which they accepted.

Limits on Police

The most controversial extension of the protection against self-incrimination is the Supreme Court's use of it to limit police interrogations of criminal suspects. For years the Court reversed convictions based on coerced confessions and police brutality. But this practice meant that the Court had to examine all circumstances in each case to determine whether the accused's rights had been violated. Doing this provided little guidance for the police and added to the Court's workload.

To rectify this problem and safeguard the rights of the accused, in the 1960s the Court handed down several landmark rulings that had wide-ranging consequences for the criminal-justice system. In *Escobedo v. Illinois* (1964), it held that whenever a person becomes the primary suspect in a criminal investigation, he or she has the right to request the assistance of counsel.[70] A year earlier, in *Gideon v. Wainwright* (1963), it had ruled that any individual who is accused of a criminal offense but is too poor to hire a lawyer has the right to a court-appointed attorney.[71] Both cases acknowledged that without the assistance of counsel, individuals may not fully understand their rights and may be intimidated by police and by the judicial process.

Subsequently, in *Miranda v. Arizona* (1966), Chief Justice Earl Warren sought to establish objective standards for determining whether confessions had been coerced.[72] Ernesto Miranda, a twenty-three-year-old indigent with a ninth-grade education, had been arrested and charged with kidnapping and raping an eighteen-year-old girl on the outskirts of Phoenix, Arizona. At the police station the rape victim identified Miranda in a police lineup; two officers then took him into a separate room for interrogation. At first denying his guilt, Miranda eventually confessed and wrote and signed a brief statement admitting and describing the crime. After his trial and conviction Miranda's attorneys appealed, contending that the use of a confession obtained during police interrogations, in the absence of an attorney, violated Miranda's Fifth Amendment right against self-incrimination. The Court agreed, holding that confessions cannot be introduced at trial unless the police have initially informed the suspect of his or her constitutional rights. This procedural safeguard, known as the **Miranda warnings,** have gained widespread notoriety on the numerous law enforcement shows on television.

The Miranda Warnings

1. You have the right to remain silent and refuse to answer questions. Do you understand?
2. Anything you do say may be used against you in a court of law. Do you understand?
3. You have the right to consult an attorney before speaking to the police and to have an attorney present during any questioning now or in the future. Do you understand?
4. If you do not have an attorney available, you have the right to remain silent until you have had an opportunity to consult with one. Do you understand?
5. If you cannot afford an attorney, you have the right to have one appointed for you. Do you understand?
6. Now that I have advised you of your rights, are you willing to answer questions without an attorney present?

Like the Court's rulings on the exclusionary rule, the *Miranda* decision has been widely criticized for "handcuffing" the police and making law enforcement more difficult. The Court has become more sensitive to these concerns, and although it has upheld its *Miranda* decision, it has also recognized certain exceptions, such as police no longer have to use the precise language of the Miranda warnings when informing suspects of their rights under the Fifth Amendment.

Right to Counsel

Escobedo, Gideon, Miranda, and other rulings are crucial to ensuring individuals' Sixth Amendment right to counsel and to achieving equality before the law for rich and poor citizens alike. Subsequent decisions have held that the right to counsel applies to virtually every stage of the criminal-justice

Miranda warnings
The warnings that police are usually required to give those whom they arrest on suspicion of having performed a crime; the warnings contain a list of the rights people have, including to remain silent and to have an attorney present during police interrogations.

process—from initial police interrogations and preliminary hearings, through trials and sentencing, to the first appeals of convictions and sentences. Only when individuals do not face the possibility of imprisonment has the Court held that they have no right to a court-appointed attorney. Thus, immigrants who entered the United States illegally are not entitled to state-provided counsel during deportation hearings, although they may have private attorneys present. In the aftermath of the September 11 terrorist attacks, the Justice Department has initiated proceedings to deport thousands of illegal aliens.[73]

The Court's rulings protecting the rights of the accused have made law enforcement efforts more costly and more difficult. Sometimes guilty individuals are allowed to go free as a result of mistakes made by arresting officers or prosecution attorneys. Nevertheless, the Court's rulings are designed to preserve the presumption of innocence and to put the burden of proof on the government.

Other Protections

When a criminal case goes to trial, several other safeguards come into play to ensure that the accused receives a fair trial. In addition to being guaranteed the assistance of counsel, accused individuals are guaranteed the right to be informed of the nature and cause of the accusation against them. They have the right to confront witnesses. One of the principal objections to the trials of terrorists in the United States was the government's refusal to identify sources that provided the evidence presented against the accused.

It is the responsibility of the prosecutor, the attorney representing the government and the public, to bring the charges. Usually this is done through an indictment by a **grand jury.**[74] Not all states require grand jury **indictments,** however. About half permit the prosecution to present a **bill of information,** a document specifying the charges and evidence against an accused, to a judge at a preliminary hearing. The attorney for the accused may then seek to exclude particular evidence from being used at the defendant's trial.

In criminal cases, defendants have the right to be tried by a **petit jury,** traditionally consisting of twelve people selected from members of the community by the judge and the prosecuting and defense attorneys. The jury determines the guilt or innocence of the accused. The judge imposes the sentence on those found guilty. However, the Supreme Court has recently held that judges may not impose a death penalty; only a jury may do so.[75]

Criminal suspects may also not be subject to **double jeopardy,** retrying a person for the same offense in the same court, whether state or federal, after being acquitted of the crime. However, they may be tried in both state and federal courts for different offenses.

The Sixth Amendment requires the federal government to give a person accused of a crime a speedy and public trial before an impartial jury, and the Seventh Amendment guarantees the right to a jury trial in civil cases involving controversies concerning amounts that exceed $20. Although the Sixth Amendment does not explain what constitutes a speedy trial, Congress has tried

grand jury
A group of twelve to twenty-three people who decide whether the evidence presented is sufficient for an indictment.

indictment
A formal statement of charges brought against a criminal defendant by a prosecuting attorney.

bill of information
A document that specifies the charges and evidence against a criminal defendant; in some cases, such a document may be obtained by state prosecutors from a judge rather than a jury.

petit jury
A jury usually consisting of twelve people selected from members of the community to sit in judgment during a trial.

double jeopardy
The legal principle that a person cannot be tried for the same offense twice.

to do so by enacting the Speedy Trial Act of 1974. According to this legislation, a person who is arrested must be charged with a specific crime within thirty days, arraigned ten days later, and tried by a jury within two months of arraignment.

However, those requirements are not always met because of the large number of criminal cases, procedural delays requested by defendants, and the frequency of plea bargaining. In the aftermath of the terrorist attacks of September 11, 2001, there have been frequent accusations that people have been held for long periods, sometimes in solitary confinement, without charges being brought against them, much less presented to a grand jury.

Although trials have historically been conducted in public, widespread newspaper and television coverage of sensational trials may create a conflict between the defendant's right to a fair trial and a reporter's claims to freedom of the press. Judges may employ several safeguards and remedies to protect the rights of the accused against the effects of prejudicial publicity. If pretrial publicity can reasonably be expected to threaten the chances of obtaining an impartial jury, the defendant may ask for a **change of venue**—that is, for the trial to be moved to another locality where there has been less publicity. The Virginia trials of the two men charged with ten sniper killings in the Washington, D.C., metropolitan area in 2002 were shifted to other parts of the state because of the fear that the extensive media coverage given to these crimes on local and national television and newspapers had prejudiced local residents against the defendants.[76]

Juries must be not only impartial but also representative of a fair cross section of the community. This does not mean, however, that defendants are entitled to a jury that includes members of their own race, gender, religion, or national origin or one that is representative of the proportions of such groups in the community. Rather, the defendant's rights and those of potential jurors are considered to be denied only if members of a particular group are denied the opportunity to be selected for jury service.

Traditionally, juries need a unanimous verdict to determine guilt "beyond a reasonable doubt." The standard of proof beyond a reasonable doubt applies for all criminal cases tried in federal courts and in state criminal cases.[77]

After trial and conviction, the accused is sentenced. In federal and most state courts the laws provide for a range of terms of imprisonment for particular offenses, and judges and juries have some discretion in sentencing within that range. The federal government and some states, however, have systems of **determinate sentencing,** in which a mandatory length of imprisonment is specified for each offense.

The only limitation on sentencing and punishment provided in the Constitution is the Eighth Amendment, which forbids the levying of "excessive fines" and the inflicting of "cruel and unusual punishment." According to the Supreme Court, the ban on cruel and unusual punishment limits sentencing in two ways. First, it prohibits barbaric forms of punishment, such as torture and unnecessary infliction of pain. Second, it forbids punishment that is grossly disproportionate to the crime.

These broad standards do not always provide clear guidelines in particular cases. In 1910, for instance, the Court struck down a law allowing twelve years of

change of venue
The practice of moving a trial from the area in which the crime was committed to another area in order to increase the chances for obtaining a fair trial and unbiased jury.

determinate sentencing
The practice of specifying a mandatory length of imprisonment for an offense; it does not allow the sentencing judge discretion.

hard labor for anyone convicted of falsifying a government document, but in 1980 it upheld the life sentence imposed on a man for three thefts that totaled $289.[78] And in 2003 a sharply divided Court upheld California's "Three Strikes and You're Out" law, which imposes severe penalties on people who have been found guilty of three felonies. The Court ruled that these harsher penalties do not violate the Constitution's ban on cruel and usual punishment even though the defendants, who had prior convictions, in the cases the Court considered received sentences of twenty-five years without parole for stealing three golf clubs and fifty years without parole for two shoplifting convictions involving merchandise valued at $150.[79]

The Supreme Court's 2005–2006 Term: Major Decisions

Abortion: *Ayotte v. Planned Parenthood of Northern New England*
Declared New Hampshire's abortion law, which required parental notification and a waiting period for teenagers who wanted an abortion, unconstitutional because it did not permit exceptions for medical emergencies.

Authority of the Federal Government: *Gonzales v. Oregon*
Held that Attorney General John Ashcroft exceeded his authority when he threatened to prosecute doctors who assisted in helping patients end their lives in accordance with Oregon's Death with Dignity Act.

Capital Punishment: *Hill v. McDonough*
Ruled that prisoners facing execution can challenge the state's choice of drugs used in lethal injections as well as the way in which they are administered. In another case, *House v. Bell,* the Supreme Court stated that new evidence, including DNA tests, can be introduced in order to gain a new hearing for a person who has unsuccessfully appealed his or her conviction.

Freedom of Speech: *Rumsfeld v. Forum for Academic and Institutional Rights*
Decided that universities that prevent military recruiters at their law schools deny the military freedom of speech. This decision upheld a federal law that precludes federal funds for universities if they do not provide military recruiters with the same access they provide other employers.

Presidential Power: *Hamdan v. Rumsfeld*
In a major refutation of the power that President Bush has claimed and exercised after 9/11, the Court ruled that the establishment of military tribunals for foreigners suspected of terrorist activities against the United States violated the Geneva Convention and was not authorized by congressional statute.

Redistricting: *League of United Latin American Citizens v. Perry*
The Court upheld Texas's right to redraft its legislative districts prior to the 2004 election but held that its restructuring of a district in the southwestern part of the state with a majority of Hispanic voters denied this group its rights guaranteed by the Voting Rights Act.

Review Questions

1. In their admission policies, public colleges and universities may do all of the following except

   A. Discriminate on the basis of intelligence
   B. Give preference to the children of alumni
   C. Use diversity as a criterion in deciding who to admit
   D. Discriminate on the basis of age

2. Due process of law means

   A. Laws apply to every citizen equally
   B. All people accused of crimes are assumed to be guilty until proven innocent
   C. The process by which laws are applied should be fair and just for everyone
   D. The substance of the law should be fair and just for everyone

3. The right to privacy is

   A. Explicitly protected by the First Amendment to the Constitution
   B. Implicitly protected by the First Amendment to the Constitution
   C. Not protected by the First Amendment to the Constitution
   D. Protected by the Constitution itself

4. When individuals take the fifth, they invoke their right

   A. To drink a pint of Scotch
   B. To a fair trial
   C. Not to testify against themselves
   D. To enter a plea bargain

   Answers:

   1. D
   2. C
   3. B
   4. C

Conflict and Consensus in Review

Americans strongly believe in the concept of justice for all, but only one in four in 2005 expressed a great deal or quite a lot of confidence in the criminal justice system and 41 percent in the Supreme Court.[80] A plurality of Americans (41 percent) believes that the Patriot Act is about right in how it balances people's civil rights with the need to investigate suspected

continued

terrorism while 30 percent think that the legislation goes too far.[81] But when asked, "Which comes closer to your view: The government should take all steps necessary to prevent additional acts of terrorism in the U.S. even if it means your basic civil liberties would be violated, (or) the government should take steps to prevent additional acts of terrorism but not if those steps would violate your basic civil liberties?", the results were as follows:

	Take steps, even if civil liberties violated (%)	Take steps but not violate civil liberties (%)	No opinion (%)
2005 Dec 16–18	31	65	4
2003 Nov 10–12*	31	64	5
2003 Aug 25–26*	29	67	4
2003 Apr 22–23	33	64	3
2002 Sep 2–4*	33	62	5
2002 Jun 21–23	40	56	4
2002 Jan 25–27	47	49	4

*Asked of a half sample
Source: "Poll Topics and Trends: Civil Liberties," Gallup Poll (accessed September 16, 2005).

Similarly Americans are divided over the president's authorization of telephone monitoring of calls without first obtaining a court-issued warrant to do so. A slight majority opposed the president's actions. Public opinion was strongly affected by partisanship with eight out of ten Republicans approving and eight out of ten Democrats opposing the president's unilateral decision.[82]

In short, the consensus on the need to respect civil liberties gives way to conflict over the application of this principle. As with other basic rights, it is much easier to agree on principle than it is to agree on practice. The court continually has to decide where to draw the line between the need of government to protect national and personal security and the desire of people to exercise their constitutional rights.

In the past few decades a major controversy has centered on the imposition of the death penalty. Should it be abolished as it is in many European countries and in 12 states plus the District of Columbia or should it continue as a deterrent to murder and as a penalty for it? The case study in Politics in Action examines this question in the light of recent Supreme Court decisions.

Politics in Action

Should the Death Penalty Be Abolished?

The execution of Kenneth Boyd brought newspaper head-lines around the country. Boyd, a former Vietnam veteran who had been found guilty of murdering his estranged wife and her father, was the one thousandth person executed in the United States since the states rewrote their death penalty statures after the Supreme Court decision in *Furman v. Georgia* that the death penalty was not cruel and unusual punishment, but that states had to establish pre-cise standards for imposing it. The Furman decision had invalidated most state death penalty laws at that time because they lacked those standards. Over the next decade, a majority of states redrafted laws that imposed the penalty. Today, 38 states have death penalty laws. The state of Texas has executed the most people; California has the most on "death row."

Americans, by and large, support the imposition of the death penalty. As Gallup Poll data indicate, about two out of three people favor the penalty for a person convicted of murder. (See Figure 4.1.)

Despite the relatively high level of public support, the death penalty has been under increasing criticism in recent years as a result of several highly publicized inquiries in which people on death row were found innocent of the crimes for which they had been convicted, some on the basis of new DNA evidence. A principal argument used by those opposed to the death penalty is that as long as there is a pos-sibility that innocent people are being put to death, the death penalty should not be used. And studies have found high numbers of judicial errors in America's capital-punishment system.[83] But these studies have not appeared to change public opinion. Perhaps because DNA evidence is now being used by prosecutors to establish a case, most people believe that the execution of innocent people is rare.[84]

In addition to the argument that innocent people may be put to death, another related charge is that the death penalty has been applied in a discriminatory manner. African American men are more likely than whites to receive death sentences when convicted of capital offenses. From 1976–2005, 34 percent of those put to death have been African Americans compared to 58 percent white. Yet, African American men constitute less than 10 percent of the total population.[85] If the law, the judicial system, and the penalties imposed discriminate against a particular group, then certainly that group is not receiving equal justice under the law as the Constitution prescribes.

A third problem with the application of the death penalty concerns the mental capacity of people who are found guilty of murder. Should people who are mentally retarded be put to death? Should juveniles receive the same sentence as adults convicted of murder? And what about the administration of the death penalty? Are certain methods of ending life—the guillotine, a firing squad, the electric chair, a lethal injection—more odious than others? Do any or all of them rise to the level of cruel and unusual punishment that the Eighth Amendment prohibits?

The Supreme Court has been concerned with these issues since its 1972 decision that upheld the constitution-ality of the death penalty, but required states to rewrite their death penalty laws to ensure that there were precise standards by which the penalty would be used. Although the Court has not reversed its decision that the death penalty was constitutional, it has narrowed the type of cases in which it may be imposed. The death penalty can only be given for the crime of murder, not rape or torture. It cannot be mandatory for certain crimes such as the killing of a law enforcement officer. Judges and juries must have discretion in rendering the sentence. They must be able to consider all extenuating circumstances. Nor can the sentence be imposed by a judge alone. It must result from a jury verdict.

In 2002, the Court went further. In the case of *Virginia v. Atkins,* a majority held that mental retardation was grounds for voiding a death sentence. Atkins had been convicted of murder; the prosecutor urged the death penalty based on

continued

Politics in Action *continued*

© Bettmann/CORBIS

This is a composite photograph, posed and reconstructed by artist John Wolters, which has for its background the death chamber in the State Prison, Trenton, New Jersey. The person to be executed is Bruno Richard Hauptmann, the man convicted of kidnapping and murdering the infant son of Charles Lindbergh, the first person to fly solo across the Atlantic Ocean. Despite compelling evidence, Hauptmann maintained his innocence until his death by execution.

the defendant's history of violent crime. Previously, he had been convicted of maiming, grand larceny, breaking and entering, abduction, five counts of robbery, and eight counts of use of a firearm in the commission of a felony.[86] Atkins's attorneys did not deny his past crimes nor that he killed a person; they argued, however, that he was mentally impaired. They called an expert witness, who testified to Atkins's IQ of 59, a measurement that places him in the bottom one percent of IQ levels. Although the prosecution also presented an expert witness who disagreed with the defense's contention that Atkins was mentally retarded, the

Court had sufficient doubt to void his death sentence.[87] The majority worried that "mentally retarded defendants may be less able to give meaningful assistance to their counsel and are typically poor witnesses, and their demeanor may create an unwarranted impression of lack of remorse for their crimes."[88] They were also more likely to be manipulated by police and prosecutors, act on the basis of impulse, and not appreciate the consequences of their actions.

Justice Scalia, author of the dissenting opinion, strongly disagreed with the majority's reasoning.

continued

Politics in Action *continued*

Figure 4.1 Death Penalty

Question: Are you in favor of the death penalty for a person convicted of murder?

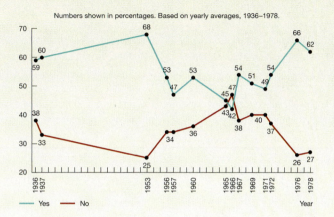

Numbers shown in percentages. Based on yearly averages, 1936–1978.

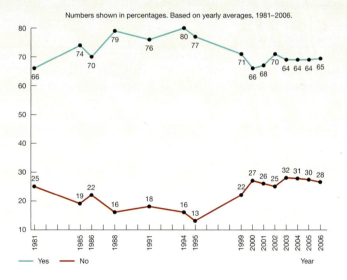

Numbers shown in percentages. Based on yearly averages, 1981–2006.

Source: Gallup Poll, "Poll Topics and Trends: Death Penalty." http://www.gallup.com/contents/default.aspx?ci=1606 (accessed February 1, 2006). Used by permission.

continued

Politics in Action *continued*

"What scientific analysis can possible show that a mildly retarded individual who commits an exquisite torture—killing is 'no more culpable' than the 'average' murdered in a holdup-gone-wrong or a domestic dispute? . . . Surely culpability, and deservedness of the most severe retribution, depends not merely (if at all) upon the mental capacity of the criminal (above the level where he is able to distinguish right from wrong) but also upon the depravity of the crime. . . . Once the Court admits (as it does) that mental retardation does not render the offender morally blameless . . . there is not basis for saying that the death penalty is appropriate retribution, no matter how heinous the crime."[89]

More recently, the Court has also held that juvenile offenders should not be executed. In 2006, the Court stayed the execution of two Florida men convicted of murder while it was deciding whether the lethal injection used by state authorities to terminate life causes great pain and suffering, thereby violating the cruel and unusual clause of the Constitution, but subsequently denied appeals from death row inmates of both states who had questioned the constitutionality of the manner of their execution.

What Do You Think?

1. Should a person's mental ability and/or chronological age be considered in rendering a verdict or imposing the death penalty? Should the victim or the accused's race or ethnicity be considered in determining the sentencing? Regardless of how you answer this question, what can and should be done about the fact that poor people and some racial minorities disproportionately receive the death penalty?

2. Is the death penalty, in and of itself, cruel and unusual punishment, and thus, should it be banned?

3. Which institution should be responsible for interpreting public standards of morality and for deciding what penalties should be imposed on those who commit criminal acts: the legislature, the executive, or the judiciary?

4. On balance, do you favor or oppose the imposition of the death penalty?

Summary

We began this chapter by noting that the Supreme Court has become the institution that applies the Constitution and determines its meaning. On this, most Americans are agreed. They also believe in the basic rights and liberties that the Constitution guarantees. Where they are more likely to disagree is over the constitutionality of particular words or deeds. It is job of the Supreme Court to determine the boundaries between legal and illegal actions.

The Court cannot determine these boundaries once and for all times. Its decisions must resonate with evolving social mores, economic conditions, and political beliefs. As America has changed, so too has constitutional interpretation. In other words, the Constitution has meaning, but that meaning is not set in stone. Here is how the Court has responded to the political controversies in which individual freedom, social equality, and justice for all collide.

The First Amendment provides broad protection against government infringement of basic freedoms, but those freedoms cannot be regarded as absolute. Speech that touches on political matters or has redeeming social value is protected, but obscenity and "fighting words" are not. Written communications in the press are protected, but libelous statements and innuendos are not. Religious beliefs and practices are protected, but activities, conducted in the name of religion, that are harmful to society are not. Nonverbal expression is protected, but expression that violates the rules and mores of an institution, such as a school, may not be. The right to associate with like-minded individuals is protected, but all actions of the groups that result from that association are not.

Government may not impose religious activities, such as prayer in public schools, but it also may not discriminate against religious groups by denying them access to facilities that other groups may use. Moreover, it may indirectly aid such groups through programs designed to promote the health and welfare of society and improve economic conditions within communities.

Government must make laws that apply equally to everyone. Similarly, all adult citizens must have the opportunity to express their beliefs and to vote in elections. However, states do have flexibility in conducting elections and designing legislative districts, as long as they conform to the one person, one vote dictum and do not undercut the goals of redistricting plans aimed at increasing minority representation.

Government may ban invidious discrimination on the basis of race, ethnicity, gender, and sexual orientation to give everyone equal protection of the laws, but it may not end legal discriminatory practices—that is, those in which there is a legitimate basis for making a distinction, such as having the academic qualifications for admission into a college or university. Thus far, having a heterosexual orientation has been viewed as a reasonable criterion for military service.

Reversing decades of discrimination against women and minorities has proven difficult. The Supreme Court has been supportive of equality of opportunity but not equality of result. It has approved the principle of affirmative action but not practices or programs that establish quotas or in other ways directly discriminate against individuals in the majority.

The Court has also found it difficult to achieve justice for all and simultaneously allow communities to govern themselves. The rights of individuals are frequently pitted against those of the community when questions of due process and equal opportunity are raised. The Court's judgment shifts with changing social practices and political beliefs, as evidenced by its recent death penalty decisions.

Key Terms

clear and present danger
  doctrine
preferred freedom
gravity of evil doctrine
social redeeming value
politically correct
obscenity
libel
slander
commercial speech
symbolic speech
speech-plus-conduct

freedom of association
establishment clause
free exercise clause
accommodationist or preferentialist approach
secular regulation rule
equal protection of the laws
poll taxes
literacy tests
redistricting
Jim Crow laws
separate but equal doctrine

restrictive covenants
de facto segregation
de jure segregation
minimum scrutiny test
strict scrutiny test
strict rationality or exacting
  scrutiny test
affirmative action
reverse discrimination
equality of opportunity
equality of result
procedural due process

substantive due process
right to privacy
unreasonable searches and
    seizures
self-incrimination

grant of immunity
plea bargaining
Miranda warnings
grand jury
indictment

bill of information
petit jury
double jeopardy
change of venue
determinate sentencing

Key Constitutional Law Cases

Speech

Schenck v. United States (1919)
Dennis v. United States (1951)
Brandenburg v. Ohio (1969)
Chaplinsky v. New Hampshire (1942)

Roth v. United States (1957)
Miller v. California (1973)
Reno v. American Civil Liberties Union (1997)
New York Times Co. v. Sullivan (1964)

Religion

Engle v. Vitale (1962)
Abington School District v. Schempp (1963)

Reynolds v. United States (1879)

Equality Under Law

Baker v. Carr (1962)
Plessy v. Ferguson (1896)
Brown v. Board of Education of Topeka (1954)
Gregory v. Ashcroft (1991)

Romer v. Evans (1996)
Regents of the University of California v. Bakke
(1978)
City of Richmond v. J. A. Croson (1989)

Due Process of the Law

Rochin v. California (1962)
Griswold v. Connecticut (1965)
Roe v. Wade (1973)
Bowers v. Hardwick (1986)
Chandler v. Miller (1997)

Katz v. United States (1967)
Escobedo v. Illinois (1964)
Gideon v. Wainwright (1963)
Miranda v. Arizona (1966)
Furman v. Georgia (1972)

Discussion Questions

1. Under what circumstances can and should speech be limited by the government?
2. Does freedom of speech protect politically incorrect language from government interference? Should it? Does it protect it from a university or college's code of conduct? Should it?
3. Does the establishment clause prevent public schools from teaching creationism? Why or why not?
4. Should freedom of religion protect the practice of religion, or are there some practices that can and should be restricted?

5. Can government promote political equality for all without discriminating against the majority?
6. Is discrimination ever valid? Should it be?
7. Do all procedural due process protections of the Constitution go too far in preventing government officials from punishing criminal behavior?
8. Should the assumption of innocence until proven guilty apply to those suspected of terrorist activity against the United States?

Topics for Debate

1. A free and open society should permit all forms of speech, including obscenity.
2. Observing Christmas as a national holiday violates the establishment clause of the U.S. Constitution.
3. Prohibiting prayer in public schools discriminates against religion and therefore violates the constitutional guarantee of freedom of religion.

4. Equality under law should not be achieved by discriminating against those in the majority.
5. Discrimination on the basis of gender, race, ethnicity, and sexual orientation is immoral.
6. The procedural due process protections of the Constitution should apply only to American citizens.
7. Government officials who permit torture of American prisoners should be punished.

Where on the Web?

Death Penalty Information Center **www. deathpenaltyinfo.org**

Campaign to End the Death Penalty **www. nodeathpenalty.org**

Pro-deathpenalty.com **www.prodeathpenalty.com**

Go to **www.thomsonedu.com/thomsonnow** to learn about a powerful online study tool. You will get a personalized study plan based on your responses to a diagnostic Pre-Test. Once you have mastered the materials with the help of interactive learning tools, activities, timelines, video case studies, simulations, and an integrated E-Book, you can take a Post-Test to confirm you are ready to move to the next chapter.

Selected Readings

Abramson, Jeffrey. *We, the Jury: The Jury System and the Ideal of Democracy.* New York: Basic Books, 1994.

Black, Charles L. Jr. *Capital Punishment: The Inevitability of Caprice and Mistake.* New York: W. W. Norton & Co., 1974 (rev. ed., 1982).

Bowen, William G., and Derek Bok. *The Shape of the River: Long-Term Consequences of Considering Race in College and University Admissions.* Princeton, N.J.: Princeton University Press, 1998.

Cole, David. *No Equal Justice: Race and Class in the American Criminal Justice System.* New York: New Press, 1999.

Etzoni, Amitai, and Jason H. Mason. *Rights v. Public Safety after 9/11: America in an Age of Terrorism.* Lanham, Md.: Rowman & Littlefield, 2003.

Friendly, Fred W. *Minnesota Rag: The Dramatic Story of the Landmark Supreme Court Case That Gave New Meaning to Freedom of the Press,* reissued ed. Minneapolis: University of Minnesota Press, 2003.

Ivers, Gregg, and Kevin T. McGuire, eds. *Creating Constitutional Change.* Charlottesville: University of Virginia Press, 2004.

Klinker, Philip A., and Rogers M. Smith. *The Unsteady March: The Rise and Decline of Racial Equality in America.* Chicago: University of Chicago Press, 2000.

Lewis, Anthony. *Gideon's Trumpet,* reissue ed. New York: Vintage Books, 1989.

Perry, Michael J. *We the People: The Fourteenth Amendment and the Supreme Court.* New York: Oxford University Press, 1999.

Rosen, Ruth. *The World Split Open: How the Modern Women's Movement Changed America.* New York: Viking Press, 2000.

Scheck, Barry, Peter Neufeld, and Jim Dwyer. *Actual Innocence: Five Days to Execution, and Other Dispatches from the Wrongly Convicted.* New York: Doubleday, 2000.

White, Welsh S. *The Death Penalty in the Nineties.* Ann Arbor: University of Michigan Press, 1991.

Notes

[1] *Texas v. Johnson,* 491 U.S. 397 (1989).

[2] Quoted in David M. O'Brien, *Storm Center: The Supreme Court in American Politics* (New York: W. W. Norton & Co., 1996), 124.

[3] *United States v. Eichman,* 496 U.S. 310 (1990).

[4] *Schenck v. United States,* 249 U.S. 47 (1919).

[5] Ibid.

[6] *Gitlow v. New York,* 268 U.S. 652 (1925).

[7] *Dennis v. United States,* 341 U.S. 494 (1951). The decision was not unanimous. Two vigorous dissents were filed by Justices William Douglas and Hugo Black. Douglas pointed out that the convictions were for mere advocacy of theories, not for illegal actions. Justice Black championed an "absolutist interpretation" of the First Amendment:

> I read "no law abridging" to mean no law abridging. The First Amendment, which is the supreme law of the land, has thus fixed its own value on freedom of speech and press by putting these freedoms wholly "beyond the reach" of federal power to abridge. . . . Consequently, I do not believe that any federal agencies, including Congress and this Court, have power or authority to subordinate speech and press to what they think are "more important interests."

Black's judicial colleagues did not accept his absolutist interpretation.

[8] *Brandenburg v. Ohio,* 395 U.S. 444 (1969).

[9] *New York Times Co. v. United States,* 403 U.S. 670 (1971).

[10] *R. A. V. v. City of St. Paul, Minnesota,* 505 U.S. 377 (1992).

[11] In *Wisconsin v. Mitchell,* 508 U.S. 476 (1993), the Court upheld laws that give defendants longer prison terms if they commit crimes determined to have been motivated by racial, religious, or gender bias. In that case, an African American who said "go get that white boy" and then assaulted the individual received a four-year instead of a two-year prison sentence under Wisconsin's prison-enhancement statute for so-called hate crimes.

[12] *Roth v. United States,* 354 U.S. 476 (1957).

[13] *Miller v. California,* 413 U.S. 15 (1973).

[14]The relevant cases that established these rulings are as follows: *Cohen v. California,* 403 U.S. 15 (1971); *Bethel School District No. 403 v. Fraser,* 478 U.S. 675 (1986); *New York v. Ferber,* 458 U.S. 747 (1982); *California v. LaRue,* 409 U.S. 109 (1972); *Barnes v. Glen Theatre,* 501 U.S. 560 (1991); and *Renton v. Playtime Theatres,* 475 U.S. 41 (1986).

[15]*Federal Communications Commission v. Pacifica Foundation,* 438 U.S. 726 (1978).

[16]*Reno v. American Civil Liberties Union,* 521 U.S. 844 (1997). In *Ashcroft v. Free Speech Coalition,* 535 U.S. 234 (2002), it negated another section of the act that criminalized the creation, distribution, and possession of "virtual" child pornography, computer imagery that portrays children engaging in sexual acts.

[17]*United States v. American Library Association,* 539 U.S. 194 (2003). The law permits but does not require librarians to unblock sites at the request of an adult.

[18]*New York Times Co. v. Sullivan,* 376 U.S. 254 (1964).

[19]*Pacific Gas and Electric v. Public Utilities Commission of California,* 475 U.S. 1 (1986).

[20]*Watchtower Bible and Tract Society v. Village of Stratton,* 536 U.S. 150 (2002).

[21]*Brown v. Socialist Worker '74 Campaign Committee,* 459 U.S. 87 (1982); *Gibson v. Florida Legislative Investigating Committee,* 371 U.S. 539 (1963); *Elfbrandt v. Russell,* 384 U.S. 11 (1966).

[22]*United States v. Harris,* 347 U.S. 612 (1954).

[23]*Boy Scouts of America, et al. v Dale,* 530 U.S. 640 (2000).

[24]Justice Hugo Black, *Engle v. Vitale,* 370 U.S. 421 (1962).

[25]*Engle v. Vitale,* 370 U.S. 421 (1962); *Abington School District v. Schempp,* 374 U.S. 421 (1963).

[26]In 2003, the Supreme Court refused to review a court of appeals' decision that forbid the chief judge of the Alabama Supreme Court from placing a large sculptured plaque containing the Ten Commandments inside the courthouse.

[27]*Lee v. Weisman,* 505 U.S. 577 (1992).

[28]In 1948, the Court had overturned a law that permitted children to attend religious classes in the public school during the regular school days. However, a few years later it upheld a "released time" program that gave students the option of attending classes in religious instruction held *off* school grounds. In 1997, a bare majority of the Court held that public school teachers may be sent into parochial schools to provide remedial education to disadvantaged children. *Agostini v. Felton,* 521 U.S. 203 (1997). This decision overturned *Aguillar v. Felton,* 473 U.S. 402 (1985).

[29]*Zelman v. Simmons-Harris,* 536 U.S. 639 (2002). In general, the Court tries to distinguish between legitimate state aid to students, even those in sectarian schools, and illegitimate state sponsorship of religion. It approved a state's giving higher-education grants to blind students even though one recipient chose to study at a Christian college in the case of *Witters v. Washington Department of Service for the Blind,* 474 U.S. 481 (1986). The Court also has held that a university could not deny funds used for extracurricular student activities to a Christian student group that published a newspaper in the case of *Rosenberger v. the Rector and Visitors of the University of Virginia,* 515 U.S. 819 (1995).

[30]*Reynolds v. United States,* 98 U.S. 145 (1879).

[31]*Wisconsin v. Yoder,* 406 U.S. 208 (1972).

[32]Recently the Court has signaled that it may no longer exempt religious minorities from generally applicable laws. In a case involving the claims of two Native Americans that they were denied state unemployment compensation after they had been dismissed for using peyote (an intoxicating drug produced from mescal cacti) during religious ceremonies of the Native American Church, the Court rejected their claims. This decision was so controversial, however, that a range of religious groups persuaded Congress to override it with the Religious Freedom Restoration Act of 1993. But the Supreme Court struck down that act on the grounds that Congress, under the Fourteenth Amendment, may enact legislation enforcing constitutional rights that the Court has recognized but may not expand or enlarge those rights beyond what the Court has held. See *Employment Division, Department of Human Resources of Oregon v. Smith,* 494 U.S. 872 (1990), and *City of Bourne v. Flores, Archbishop of San Antonio,* 521 U.S. 507 (1997).

[33]*West Virginia State Board of Education v. Barnette,* 319 U.S. 624 (1943).

[34]"State of the First Amendment 2005," First Amendment Center. www.firstamendementcenter.org (accessed September 16, 2005).

[35]*Minor v. Happersett,* 88 U.S. 162 (1875).

[36]*Baker v. Carr,* 369 U.S. 186 (1962).

[37]The Court's rulings meant in effect that that district lines for congressional, state, and local elections must be redrawn every ten years, after the national census, to ensure that they remain equal in population. This requirement has mired the judiciary in partisan political controversies.

[38]*Shaw v. Reno,* 509 U.S. 630 (1993); *Miller v. Johnson,* 512 U.S. 622 (1995); *Bush v. Vera,* 517 U.S. 952 (1996).

[39]*Georgia v. Ashcroft,* 539 U.S. 461 (2003).

[40]*Plessy v. Ferguson,* 163 U.S. 537 (1896).

[41]*Brown v. Board of Education of Topeka,* 347 U.S. 483 (1954).

[42]*Brown v. Board of Education of Topeka,* 349 U.S. 294 (1955).

[43]*Alexander v. Holmes County Board of Education,* 396 U.S. 19 (1969).

[44]In *Milliken v. Bradley,* 418 U.S. 717 (1974), for instance, the Court held that lower federal courts could not order the busing of schoolchildren to and from Detroit's overwhelmingly black inner-city school district and fifty-one predominantly white suburban school districts.

[45]*Rostker v. Goldberg,* 453 U.S. 57 (1981); *Michael M. v. Superior Court,* 450 U.S. 464 (1981); *Craig v. Boren,* 429 U.S. 190 (1976); *Dothard v. Rawlinson,* 433 U.S. 321 (1977); *Geduldig v. Aiello,* 417 U.S. 484 (1974).

[46]*Frontiero v. Richardson,* 411 U.S. 677 (1973); *Nashville Gas Co. v. Satty,* 434 U.S. 136 (1977).

[47]*Meritor Savings Bank, FBD v. Vinson,* 477 U.S. 57 (1986). In 1991 the Court overturned a fetal protection policy of Johnson Controls, a Milwaukee, Wis.-based manufacturer of automobile batteries. Under Johnson Controls's policy, fertile female employees were barred from certain jobs that exposed them to high levels of lead, which can pose severe health risks to developing fetuses. The Court struck down that discriminatory policy as a violation of the rights of women under the Civil Rights Act of 1964 and the Pregnancy Discrimination Act of 1978. *International Union, Automobile Workers, Aerospace, Agricultural Implement Workers of America, UAW v. Johnson Controls Co.,* 499 U.S. 187 (1991).

[48]*Gregory v. Ashcroft,* 501 U.S. 452 (1991).

[49]*Romer v. Evans,* 517 U.S. 620 (1996).

[50]Another statute, which may be subject to constitutional challenge, is Vermont's civil union, or as it is popularly known, same-sex marriage statute.

[51]*Regents of the University of California v. Bakke,* 438 U.S. 265 (1978).

[52]*Grutter v. Bollinger,* 539 U.S. 306 (2003). The Court majority added a caveat to its approval of a diversity-based admission policy, however. It stressed that the policy should be considered temporary, not permanent, and should be used only as long as necessary to rectify past discrimination. The Court expressed the hope that such a program would not be necessary after another twenty-five years. Although the Court's minority did not directly challenge the principle of affirmative action, two of the justices dissenting in this case, Antonin Scalia and Clarence Thomas, indicated that they believed that race and ethnicity are not appropriate criteria to consider in admission's decisions.

[53]*Gratz v. Bollinger,* 539 U.S. 244 (2003).

[54]*City of Richmond v. J. A. Croson,* 488 U.S. 469 (1989).

[55]*Toyota Motor Manufacturing Inc. v. Williams,* 534 U.S. 184 (2002).

[56]It overturned the following cases: *Price Waterhouse v. Hopkins,* 490 U.S. 228 (1989); *West Virginia University Hospitals v. Casey,* 499 U.S. 83 (1991); *Lorance v. AT&T,* 490 U.S. 900 (1989); and *Martin v. Wilks,* 490 U.S. 755 (1989).

[57]"Poll Topics and Trends: Homosexual Relations," Gallup Poll, September 14, 2005.

[58]"Blacks Blast Bush for Katrina Response," Gallup Poll, September 14, 2005.

[59]"Poll Topics and Trends: Homosexual Rights," Gallup Poll (accessed September 16, 2005).

[60]*Rochin V. California,* 341 U.S. 165 (1952).

[61]*Gray v. Mississippi,* 481 U.S. 648 (1987); *Rose v. Clark,* 478 U.S. 570 (1986).

[62]*Griswold v. Connecticut,* 391 U.S. 145 (1965).

[63]*Romer v. Evans* 517 U.S. 620 (1996).

[64]*Bowers v. Hardwick,* 478 U.S. 1986 (1986).

[65]Justice Anthony Kennedy in *Lawrence v. Texas,* 539 U.S. 558 (2003).

[66]Even when the police arrest or "seize" a person in a public place, they must still have probable cause to believe, or a reasonable suspicion, that the person had committed or was about to commit a crime. But if they arrest that person, they may search him or her, as well as whatever area and items are in "plain view."

> The provisions of the Fourth Amendment apply not only to people's houses but also to their apartments, their offices, and (under some circumstances) their cars and other personal effects, such as clothing and luggage. In general, the Court has held that the amendment "protects people, not places" and applies in cases in which the Court deems someone to have a "reasonable expectation of privacy."

[67]*Chandler v. Miller,* 520 U.S. 305 (1997). The Court has also ruled that individuals do not have reasonable expectations of privacy and Fourth Amendment protection against warrantless searches of papers or records held by third parties such as banks, accountants, and lawyers; of garbage in trash cans; or of the interior and contents of cars. Nor does the Fourth

Amendment protect individuals against police helicopters flying over their property in search of marijuana plants.

[68]*Olmstead v. United States,* 277 U.S. 438 (1928).

[69]*Katz v. United States,* 389 U.S. 347 (1967).

[70]*Escobedo v. Illinois,* 378 U.S. 478 (1964).

[71]*Gideon v. Wainwright,* 372 U.S. 335 (1963).

[72]*Miranda v. Arizona,* 384 U.S. 436 (1966).

[73]Individuals accused of crimes not only have a right to counsel but also have a right to a competent defense and may ask for a new trial if they can demonstrate that the defense they received was inadequate. Convicted defendants who cannot afford to hire lawyers must be given transcripts of their trials so that they can prepare an appeal. (*Griffin v. Illinois,* 360 U.S. 252 [1959]). If sanity is an issue in the defense, the state must provide access to a psychiatrist. (*Ake v. Oklahoma,* 470 U.S. 68 [1985]). Prison officials must also provide an adequate law library to enable those who are incarcerated to file "meaningful appeals." (*Bounds v. Smith,* 430 U.S. 817 [1977]). And indigents may not be held beyond the maximum term or imprisoned solely because they cannot pay a fine. (*Tate v. Smith,* 401 U.S. 395 [1971]).

[74]A grand jury is composed of twelve or more citizens who first hear the government's charges against a suspect on the basis of a preliminary presentation of the evidence and then many approve an **indictment,** a written statement of the charges or offenses for which the accused will stand trial.

[75]*Ring v. Arizona,* 536 U.S. 584 (2002).

[76]When the jury is being selected, the defendant's attorney may question potential jurors about the publicity and their views of the defendant; on the basis of that questioning, the attorney may ask the judge to disqualify those jurors. In addition, during the trial the jurors may be sequestered and forbidden to read or watch news coverage of the trial. Finally, a judge may declare a mistrial if any of the safeguards are violated, and a defendant always retains the right to appeal a conviction on the ground that prejudicial publicity prevented a fair trial.

[77]Some states have adopted smaller juries and permit non-unanimous verdicts to reduce the costs of conducting jury trials.

[78]*Rummell v. Estelle,* 445 U.S. 263 (1980).

[79]*Ewing v. California,* 538 U.S. 11 (2003); *Lockyer v. Andrade,* 538 U.S. 63 (2003).

[80]"Poll Topics and Trends: Confidence in Institutions," Gallup Poll (accessed September 16, 2005).

[81]"Poll Topics and Trends: Civil Liberties," Gallup Poll (accessed September 16, 2005).

[82]Joseph Carroll, "Slim Majority of Americans Say Bush Wiretapping Was Wrong," Gallup Poll, January 2006, www.gallup.com/contents/default.aspx?ci=21058.

[83]Found at justice.policy.net/jpreport/executivesummary.html.

[84]According to a Gallup poll fielded in May 2005, one-third of respondents believe that there have been no wrongful deaths, and two-thirds believe that only 1 to 5 percent of those executed have been innocent in the last five years. Jeffrey M. Jones, "Americans' Views of Death Penalty More Positive This Year," Gallup Poll, May 19, 2005, poll.gallup.com/content/default.aspx?CI=16393.

[85]Death Penalty Information Center, January 23, 2006, www.deathpenaltyinfo.org (accessed January 23, 2006).

[86]Two key witnesses were called to show Atkins's violent tendency. A man who worked in pizza delivery testified how he had been abducted by Atkins, taken to a secluded swamp, and told to run because on the count of five Atkins would shoot at him. Atkins drove off in the man's car and did not fire, but the similarity to the Nesbitt shooting made the court think that Atkins was not remorseful and had not learned from previous punishment. A woman who lived near Atkins testified that he had approached her while mowing her lawn, hit her over the head with a handgun, and then shot her in the stomach at close range, leaving her hospitalized for twenty days. "Commonwealth's Brief in Opposition," filed February 1, 2001, in *Atkins v. Virginia,* 536 U.S. 304 (2002).

[87]"Brief for Petitioner," filed September 29, 2001, in *Atkins v. Virginia,* 536 U.S. 304 (2002).

[88]Majority opinion, Stevens, *Atkins v. Virginia.*

[89]Dissenting opinion by Justice Scalia, filed June 20, 2002, in *Atkins v. Virginia,* 536 U.S. 304 (2002). Found at supct.law.cornell.edu/supct/html/00-8452.ZD1.html.

5

Political Socialization, Public Opinion, and Participation

Introduction

THIS IS A STORY ABOUT PUBLIC OPINION and democratic government, about interpreting that opinion and acting on it to make public policy. It is also a story about consensus and conflict on a major policy issue, Social Security, and about ambiguities and shifts in opinion on that issue. It is also about public officials accurately discerning that opinion as they make policy judgments.

The story begins with the pending retirement of the baby boomers and the problems that retirement poses for the Social Security system. In the relatively near future, around 2014, the system will be paying out more money than it is taking in; in the more distant future, about thirty-five years from now, the system will have exhausted its reserves and be unable to pay its beneficiaries the full amount they would be entitled to under existing law. A consensus exists that something needs to be done to keep the system solvent, but policymakers and outside experts disagree over the best way to do so.

During his campaign for the presidency in 2000, George W. Bush suggested that Americans be able to put some of their Social Security payroll tax into private accounts that could be invested in stocks and bonds. Bush argued that the expected revenue from such an investment would exceed the amount that people would receive from Social Security. Investors would be better off and so would the country, Bush argued. Americans would save more, the Social Security system would pay out less, and the dependence of senior citizens on government would be reduced. The president saw it as a win-win situation.

With younger people fearful that the Social Security trust fund would be depleted by the time they retired, personal accounts seemed appealing. Twice as many people liked the idea according to Gallup polls taken toward the beginning of the Bush's first term as president.[1] Although the level of support for such accounts declined somewhat over the next several years, more people continued to favor the idea than opposed it.[2]

Following his victory in the 2004 presidential election, George W. Bush made partial privatization of Social Security a key item in his second-term agenda, surprising Republican and Democratic members of Congress who referred to Social Security as "the third rail of politics." Touch it and you're dead. When Ronald Reagan proposed making Social Security voluntary in 1981, the Republican Senate responded with a 96–0 vote against his proposal.

For Bush, however, fresh from his election victory and desirous of creating a domestic policy legacy of greater individual responsibility, an ownership society for all, the idea seemed like its time had come. With the words, "To keep the promise of Social Security alive for our children and grandchildren, we need to fix Social Security now once and for all . . . [and] "make it a better deal for our younger workers by allowing them to put part of their payroll taxes in personal retirement accounts," Bush made Social Security reform his number one legislative priority in 2005.[3]

The initial public reaction was favorable, especially among people under thirty. But even older Americans supported the president's plan (see Tables 5.1a and 5.1b).

Although the poll numbers looked good, public opinion is not always what it seems to be and first reactions are usually based on little information.

Table 5.1a The Public, the President's Plan, and Perceptions of Social Security

"Do you favor or oppose giving individuals the choice to invest a portion of their Social Security contributions in stocks or mutual funds?"

	Favor (%)	Oppose (%)	Unsure (%)
ALL	60	28	12
Under 30 Years	76	16	9
30–45	65	24	10
46–55	54	33	13
Over 55	56	31	14

Table 5.1b Public Fears of Social Security Insolvency

"How concerned are you that the Social Security system will not have enough money to pay you your full benefits when you retire: very concerned, somewhat concerned, not very concerned, or not at all concerned?"

	Concerned (%)	Not Concerned (%)	Retired/Already Receive (%)	Unsure (%)
ALL	54	23	20	2
Under 30 Years	84	9	2	4
30–45	77	2	—	1
46–55	74	20	4	2
Over 55	28	28	42	2

Source: *FOX News*/Opinion Dynamics Poll conducted March 29–30, 2005 of 900 registered voters nationwide. Margin of error ±3 (for all registered voters).

The public knew little about the president's plan and even less about its consequences for Social Security solvency in general and the payment people could expect to receive in particular. Polls taken in December 2004 indicated that three out of four people had heard little or nothing about the president's proposal; three months later, a majority still said that they were relatively unfamiliar with the issue.[4]

The educational campaign by opponents of the president's initiative began almost immediately. In December 2004 the giant American Association of Retired Persons (AARP), representing some 35 million senior citizens, announced its opposition to private accounts and launched a $5 million advertising campaign to alert the public to its dangers. Congressional Democrats, in disarray following their loss of seats in the

2004 election, found the issue to be one on which they could unite and fight back. Interest groups across the political spectrum began to take sides. Business and investment communities supported the president's plan, and labor unions and groups sympathetic to the plight of poorer Americans opposed it. The fight had begun.

As more people became aware of the trade-offs that would have to be

Table 5.2 Individual Accounts versus Reduced Benefits

"As you may know, one idea to address concerns with the Social Security system would allow people who retire in future decades to invest some of their Social Security taxes in the stock market and bonds but would reduce the guaranteed benefits they receive when they retire. Do you think this is a good idea or a bad idea?"

	Good Idea (%)	Bad Idea (%)	No Opinion (%)
2005 APR 1–2	33	61	6
2005 MAR 18–20	33	59	8
2005 FEB 7–10	36	60	4
2005 FEB 4–6	40	55	5
2005 JAN 7–9	40	55	5

Source: "Polls and Trends: Social Security," Gallup Poll, http://www.gallup.com (accessed July 1, 2005). Used by permission.

made if personal accounts were created, support for the president's plan declined. Gallup polls taken during the spring and summer of 2005 found an increasingly skeptical public (see Table 5.2).

To rally his backers, President Bush engaged in a sixty-day, sixty-city tour in which he addressed the issue and his plan for dealing with it. The White House campaign helped the president firm up his base, but it did not change public sentiment. Rarely do speeches alone affect short-term public opinion.[5] Over the long haul, events, conditions, and public debate can shift the mood and may even affect political attitudes. But the president's campaign did not do so.

By July 2005, the Republicans were looking for an exit strategy on the Social Security issue, and the president changed his focus, leaving the task of working out a deal to Republican legislators. In his 2006 State of the Union

© AP/Wide World Photos

President Bush pushes his Social Security reform message to an audience gathered at the Kentucky Center for the Performing Arts in Louisville, Ky., Thursday, March 10, 2005. The carefully selected audience was responsive to his proposal but the country was not.

Address when the president said, "Congress did not act last year on my proposal to save Social Security . . .," Democrats cheered.

The Social Security controversy points to the difficulty of changing public opinion, much less deep-seated beliefs about "entitlement" programs.

It also points to the role that opinion can play in setting guidelines within which government officials operate.

Public opinion matters. It is important for those in government to assess that opinion. But assessment can be difficult. Surveys can be misleading; questions may not address the heart of the matter or may generate unreliable responses; people may not tell pollsters what they really believe or how deeply they feel about an issue. Yet government officials rightfully believe that they have a duty to evaluate opinion and act in accordance with it; they also have political incentives to do so. That duty and those incentives explain why public opinion is so critical in a democratic society and why we have devoted the first chapter on political behavior in this section to the formation, interpretation, and effect of public opinion on the politics of American democracy.

We begin by discussing the process by which people acquire their political values and beliefs, a process called political socialization. We then turn to the content of the beliefs themselves. Here we describe the two dominant political ideologies that comprise the American belief system, liberalism and conservatism, as well as issues that arise from them: What is the proper role of government; do citizens have the capacity to affect that government; and how much support do the people really have for democratic processes and institutions and for public policies that emanate from them? From beliefs we move to more transitory knowledge about public affairs and opinions on current issues and the relationship among knowledge, opinion, and governmental policymaking. In the final part of the chapter we turn from opinions to actions. We note various forms of participation, attributes of those who do and do not participate, and theories about how public participation affects the vitality of our democratic system. Our case study at the end of the chapter examines the shifts in public opinion over U.S. policy toward Iraq and how those shifts have pressured the Bush administration to adjust its policy goals.

Questions to Ponder

- What role should public opinion play in a democratic society?
- How do people gain information, acquire beliefs, and form opinions about the key issues of the day?
- How can these beliefs and opinions be expressed or otherwise discerned? Is the intensity with which they are held a relevant and measurable factor?
- To what extent should government officials take public opinion into account in policymaking?
- On what issues do Americans agree or disagree, and on what issues do they hold ambiguous opinions?

5.1 In Theory . . .
The Role of Public Opinion

Public opinion is obviously important in a government based on the consent of the governed. But when and how that consent is given, by whom, and whether those in positions of authority should follow or lead public opinion is not nearly as clear. In an ideal democracy, public opinion sets the agenda for government, frames the issue debate, and affects the formulation and execution of public policy. But opinion may be uninformed; it may be contradictory. What then? Moreover, opinions are held with different degrees of intensity. Some people may have no opinion, and others may feel strongly about an issue. Some are able to convey their opinions directly to public officials, but others cannot or choose not to do so. To whom should those in power turn for guidance? Finally, what about the obligation of those in the know and those in positions of authority? Should they be the principal opinion leaders?

The broad parameters of public opinion establish the framework within which political disagreements occur. Politicians and public officials react to that opinion, but they also try to shape it. It is a two-way process. If there is a consensus, those in power will usually act in accordance with it. If there is not, they have more discretion when deciding what to do, but they do so within the general parameters of the debate. But as we argued in Chapter 1, a representative democracy orients government policymakers toward their principal constituencies, be they a geographic area, clientele groups, a political party, or some combination of these. Thus, in any event, the interests and beliefs of some group tend to guide policy decisions and, after those decisions are made, hold those who made them accountable. This is why the role of public opinion is such an important topic in the study of American democracy.

The Development of Political Orientations and Attitudes

Genetic Predispositions

Children often look and think like their parents. Why? The answer has to do with the genes they inherit from their biological mother and father. Those genes help explain physical appearances; they also may contribute to psychological dispositions, intelligence, and even political attitudes—at least, that is what recent research on identical and fraternal twins suggests.[6]

Genetic inheritance may not dictate these beliefs and the behaviors that follow from them. After all, children are not carbon copies of their biological parents. Moreover, genetics and the environment in which we live interact to affect our thinking, our being, and our reactions to situations and events. Just how they do so is still a mystery, but the evidence is clear that hereditary factors matter as people develop and move through the life cycle.

Most political science research has been directed toward the effect of environment, not genetics, largely because environmental variables have easier to identify and measure than genetic traits. The field of study that examines the effect of living patterns and associations on the development of political attitudes is known as political socialization, and it is to that subject that we now turn.

The Socialization Process

political socialization
The process by which people acquire the values, beliefs, and opinions that affect their involvement in the political system.

citizenship
The responsibilities that people have by virtue of their birth or naturalization in a particular country.

Political socialization is the process by which people acquire the values, beliefs, and opinions that motivate their involvement and condition their activities in the political system. That process is designed to teach and reinforce patriotism and good **citizenship,** the responsibilities that inhabitants of a country have by virtue of their birth or naturalization. When the process is successful, it invigorates and perpetuates the society and its governing institutions as each new generation comes of age. When it does not, the society can become unstable because a portion of it may be alienated, angry, and even rebellious. People who live in communities in which there is much poverty, and those who find themselves stuck at the bottom of the socioeconomic ladder with little hope of advancement and political power, naturally will be less supportive of the government and the political system and less willing to assume the duties and obligations of citizenship than their more advantaged peers.

Political socialization starts early in life, when the family is the dominating influence on a child's development. Later, school, church, and other collective experiences contribute to the socialization process.

No one is sure exactly how early the process begins, but by the second grade many children already possess some knowledge and ideas about the country in which they live. Most of them are aware of the existence of a government and are able to identify two important authority figures: the president of the United States and the local police officer. They may also be familiar with political symbols such as the flag, the national anthem, and George Washington.

In the preadolescent period, the majority of American children develop positive feelings about their nation's government and its leaders. Most see the police officer as a helper and protector and the president as a good and wise person interested primarily in the welfare of the nation. Many children in this age group compare the president to their father and place this leader near the top of their list of favorite people. Children become patriotic before they have acquired enough information to understand the loyalty they feel.[7]

The positive character of most children's early perceptions of the American political system is important because it facilitates the bonding between people and government that is essential to recognizing the right of government to make laws and the obligation of people to obey them. If people do not believe that their government is legitimate, they are unlikely to participate faithfully in its processes or support its decisions. Fortunately, in the United States most people believe in the legitimacy of their government and the system for choosing electoral officials, although they may not agree with what the government does or may not be happy with the outcome of an election. Nonetheless, there is a consensus within the American populace that

Future president Bill Clinton, a teenage boy, shakes the hand of
President John F. Kennedy (1917–1963) as other American Legion
Boys Nation delegates look on during a trip to the White House in
Washington DC. From an early age, Clinton wanted to be president.

people should abide by the government's decisions (or accept the penalties for
not doing so) even as they try to change those decisions. Americans also
believe that change should be accomplished in a lawful manner.

As children move into adolescence, their perceptions of the political world
become more sophisticated. They begin to recognize that there is more to government than presidents and police officers; they become aware of Congress,
courts, cabinet members, and the distinctions among various levels of government. Also emerging at this point is a sense of the conflict that pervades politics.
As children begin to recognize that individuals may take sides in disagreements
among candidates, political parties, and interest groups on controversial issues,
they are confronted by the need to choose a side, to position themselves within
the political universe. This is a critical stage in the process of political socialization because it shapes the lifelong attitudes and provides the basis for social and
economic diversity from which political conflict ensues.

Party Affiliation One of the most important of these attitudinal choices is identifying with a political party. This identification begins as early as elementary school for many children and structures their orientation toward politics throughout their lifetime. In the early grades, many children have a notion of the existence of Republicans and Democrats and can identify themselves with one party or the other. Several studies carried out in the 1960s found that more than half of the fifth-graders questioned had a party preference. By the twelfth grade, according to another study, almost two-thirds of a national sample had a preference. Today, however, there are larger numbers of children who are identifying themselves as independents or adopting no partisan preference.[8]

As you might expect, most of these early partisan attachments are based on little substantive knowledge. Children who identify themselves as a Republican, Democrat, or independent usually cannot express an ideological or issue-based explanation for their choice. In some cases they can cite a prominent political personality: They have identified with the Republicans, for instance, because they admire President George W. Bush or with the Democrats because they dislike something they have heard about him or his policies. Few, however, are able to go beyond a superficial knowledge of individual political figures in explaining their partisan preference. Not until high school do most people acquire an understanding of the substantive differences between political parties.[9]

Political Cynicism With the increase in knowledge about politics and partisanship that occurs in the adolescent years comes a modification of the positive attitudes held in earlier years. Teenagers' political views become more realistic, and teens begin to perceive political figures in less heroic terms as they begin to understand the complexities and controversies of politics. It is also during the teenage years that most people begin to perceive government as placing constraints on personal behavior through such means as local curfews, minimum ages for driving and drinking, compulsory drug tests for athletes, and even school attendance requirements.

Cynicism in political attitudes tends to develop in early adulthood and to increase, in varying degrees, throughout adult life. This delayed development is not surprising, because children and early adolescents are not encouraged to become involved. With young adulthood comes broader exposure to the daily realities of politics, government, and public policy, as well as the first significant opportunities to participate in political activities. Although some adults remain unaffected, for many this new experience results in diminished faith in the effectiveness of political institutions and decreased trust in political leaders and their motives.

Major Political Events The acquisition of political attitudes and attachments is further shaped by major political events that occur during a person's lifetime. Each generation of Americans is exposed to a different set of stimuli because each lives through a different period of history.

Major events, especially those that occur during the formative years, may have lifelong effects on the generation that experiences them. For example, the generation of southern whites who came of age during and immediately after the Civil War mostly learned to view Republicans as the villains of that war and as "carpetbaggers" who rode roughshod over the South during the Reconstruction. Their allegiance to the Democratic Party was tightly forged as a result of this experience. Similarly, the generation of Americans who reached adulthood during the Great Depression of the 1930s tended to blame the Depression on President Herbert Hoover and the Republicans; they therefore attached their loyalties to the Democrats. In both cases, party allegiances remained in place long after the events that created them. The New Deal generation, for instance, remained a core component of the Democratic Party for decades after Franklin Roosevelt's first election to the presidency in 1932.

People who came of age politically between the mid-1960s and the 1990s were affected by tensions within society produced by the civil rights, antiwar, and women's rights movements, combined with the lingering effects of the Vietnam War, the Watergate break-in, and the Iran-contra affair. An increasing critical news media that focused on scandals in government and the scandalous behavior of politicians reinforced discontent with government, its personnel, and its policies. This discontent was manifest in the apathy of the electorate as voting turnout declined for a period of about thirty years beginning in the 1960s.

This period coincided with the coming of age of the baby boomers, the generation of Americans born during and in the aftermath of World War II. This generation was to have a profound effect on the social fabric of American society (as indicated in Box 5.2).

Box 5.2 **The Social Impact of the Baby Boomers**

The year 1947 saw the beginning of a demographic development that has deeply influenced American life and politics well into the twenty-first century. Although it was not much noticed at the time, Americans began to have babies by the millions. In 1940, 2.6 million babies were born in the United States; by 1947, that number had grown to 3.8 million, and it stayed above 3.6 million until the mid-1960s.

This "baby boom" produced the largest population cohort in American history. The effect on public life was dramatic. As the baby boomers reached school age in the early 1950s, an unprecedented wave of school construction began, with major effects on government budgets and tax rates. By 1965, the pressure on local school budgets had grown so great that the federal government began to provide aid to education for the first time. By 1979, a new cabinet-level Department of Education had been created to supervise the myriad programs that had grown up in the wake of that initial decision.

As family size grew during the 1950s and 1960s, the demand for more and larger houses grew as well, accelerating the move to the suburbs and the decline of the tradition of the multigenerational extended family living under one roof. Not only were there a lot of baby boomers, but they had access to more disposable income than any previous generation. Those with products to sell took notice. As the baby boomers reached puberty and early adulthood, they quickly became the favorite target of mass marketers; as they passed through adolescence, crime rates increased; after they graduated from high school, they

continued

Box 5.2 *continued*

enrolled in college in record numbers; as they reached working age, they required more new and skilled jobs; as their incomes grew to the highest levels in history, they created a vast new market for consumer electronics, luxury cars, pricey restaurants, and other amenities of the good life; and as they have aged, they are beginning to blaze yet another trail into the golden years.

By 2035, almost one-fourth of the U.S. population will be over the age of sixty-five—more than double the current figure—increasing the demand for more recreational activities, more retirement communities that provide independent and assisted living, and more health benefits, including subsidized or lower-cost prescription drugs.

The baby boomers have also become a potent political force. Their proportion of the electorate, their relatively high rates of voting, and the time, money, and interests they have to engage in political activities have increased their political clout. Elected officials and policymakers have had to take notice. They are another example that in a democracy large numbers of people, common interests, and the capacity to organize and become involved matter.

Source: Paul C. Light, *Baby Boomers* (New York: W. W. Norton and Co., 1988), 144–145.

For some, the antigovernment attitude made the ideology of economic and social conservatism more appealing. Individual initiative, private ownership, and the "Protestant work ethic" were lauded; public service, except for the military, was not. Government was seen as inefficient and ineffective, hopelessly mired in red tape, and promoting "giveaway" programs that kept an underclass overly dependent on federal and state aid. More traditional family values, religious experiences, and local government autonomy replaced the relativism, secularism, and big-brother approach of government that had characterized American politics since the New Deal. The economic prosperity of the 1980s and the mid-1990s reinforced for many the wisdom of these conservative policies, with the Republican Party the principal beneficiary.[10] These conservative trends continued through the 1990s with Democrat Bill Clinton declaring the era of big government over, reducing the size of the federal work force by 400,000, reversing the perennial budget deficits that plagued the federal government for so long.

It is unclear whether the dotcom boom (and bust) in the 1990s, the terrorist attacks of 2001, the wars and occupations in Afghanistan and Iraq, and the immigration from south of the border will affect the political views of the current generation, the one acquiring political consciousness now as it moves into the political arena. It is probably too early to tell for certain, but the feelings of complacency and invulnerability that resulted from the end of the Cold War and the status of the United States as the only remaining superpower seem to have given way to fears of further terrorist attacks, a growing debate over national security strategy, and deepening cleavages within society between Republicans and Democrats, men and women, sectarians and secularists, the old and the young, and the haves and have-nots.

Agents of Political Socialization

How do young people acquire information and develop attitudes about politics? Two theories have been proposed.[11] According to one of them, individuals are taught most of what they come to know and feel about politics by **agents of political socialization**—that is, people and institutions with an active interest in influencing their beliefs. The other theory suggests that individuals have considerable autonomy in acquiring the political information they find useful and the political attitudes they find comfortable.

The two theories are not necessarily at odds with each other. In American society, as in every other society, certain agents attempt to socialize young people to accept and adapt to the prevailing political culture. But American society also gives young people ample opportunities to shape their own political socialization through independent acquisition and evaluation of political information, although some contend that the government, especially in times of crises, exercises too much control over the information available to citizens.

agents of political socialization
Factors that affect political socialization: family, school, peers, mass media, religion, party, and social groups.

The Family The family is the most potent agent of political socialization in the early years. Until children begin school, they spend most of their waking hours with one or more members of their family. Even during children's school years, the family normally remains an important reference point.

Although parents are in an unusually good position to influence their children's political attitudes, they do not always make their influence felt. Studies have indicated that the potential for family influence is likely to be realized only when three conditions are met: (1) a close relationship among family members, (2) significant agreement among adults in the family on political values and attitudes, and (3) frequent communication of those values and attitudes to the child. Thus, if both parents are active partisans who discuss politics regularly, their children are more likely to be interested in politics and to think of themselves as partisans. Political scientists have found that there is a strong statistical correlation between the party identification of children and that of their parents, especially if the parents' identification is strongly felt.[12] The role of the family as a socializing agent may be weakening, however, as more women enter the away-from-home workforce and the proportion of single-parent households grows.

Schools Schools are also an important socializing agent. Not only do they occupy many waking hours of children but as instruments of instruction they orient young students toward becoming patriotic citizens. However, studies have shown that civics courses per se have little effect on knowledge or attitudes.[13] Nor is there significant evidence that teachers are likely to have much independent impact on their students' political attitudes.[14]

Nevertheless, a lot of ritualistic patriotic activity takes place in schools: saluting the flag, saying the Pledge of Allegiance, singing patriotic songs, and so on. After the terrorist attacks in 2001, President Bush asked American children to help poor children who were suffering from the war in Afghanistan. Many did. Such activities may reinforce children's support for the political system, but they do not appear to have a lasting effect on adult attitudes or political behavior.

Rather than having much independent impact on political socialization, schools tend to complement other, more important socializing forces in a child's life. Because public education in the United States is locally controlled, teachers and curricula usually reflect, within certain broad limits, the prevailing values of the community in which a school is located. For many decades after the Civil War, for example, southern schoolteachers often referred to that conflict as the War of Northern Aggression. Today, in school districts close to military bases or defense manufacturing plants, patriotism is usually given greater emphasis in the curriculum than it receives in districts where military influence is absent. It would be unusual indeed to find local public schools fostering values that were at odds with popular beliefs in their communities, and this congruence of values helps explain why schools reinforce rather than challenge community attitudes.

By equipping people to comprehend and participate in the political world, however, schools have traditionally influenced political socialization in a more indirect way. The more formal education people have, the more interested and better informed they are likely to be about politics and the more likely they are to take part in political activities.[15] Thus, people who are well educated may be better equipped to direct their own political socialization than those who are not.

Peers Peer groups share some of the advantages of families and schools in influencing the political socialization of individuals. In some ways their capacity to instill and reinforce values and beliefs are even greater. Interaction with a peer group usually persists into adulthood as exposure to family and school declines. Most people are members of peer groups throughout their lives and tend to be receptive to communications received from them. In fact, people are often more attentive and accommodating to members of groups than they are to others in their schools or families.

The Mass Media Anyone who has grown up in the contemporary United States would expect the communications media, especially television, to have a significant effect on the way citizens perceive their political environment. After all, Americans spend a great deal of time watching television, listening to radio, reading newspapers and magazines, and increasingly, using the Internet as a source for news and entertainment.

Yet there is little evidence that documents the role of the mass media as agents of political socialization. One explanation for this finding is that most people use the media primarily for entertainment; viewing or reading material with specific political content consumes only a small portion of the time they spend watching television or reading a daily newspaper. Indeed, a significant number of Americans have little more than a peripheral interest in politics. Furthermore, most people who watch political programs or read political articles tend to gravitate toward those that support their existing views and partisan preferences. Thus, conservatives are more apt to watch Fox news and Democrats more likely to listen to *All Things Considered* on public radio.[16] Psychologists refer to this phenomenon as **selective perception.**

selective perception
The tendency of people to see what they are looking for; information that accords with existing beliefs.

Even if the mass media do not seem to shape partisan or ideological preferences to any significant extent, they may affect political socialization in another, perhaps more profound way. Some recent studies have suggested that the cumulative effect of watching television may be to increase disaffection and cynicism. The lengthening of election campaigns, combined with extensive television coverage, often leads to boredom rather than to heightened interest, and the news media's intensive scrutiny of political scandals and the private lives of public officials, along with their tendency to emphasize the negative, inevitably make American leaders seem less heroic than they often appeared in the days before television.[17] During 1998, for example, no single story received more coverage than the investigation of the sexual relationship between President Bill Clinton and White House intern Monica Lewinsky. Similarly, the reconstruction of Iraq received far more attention and far more negative comments than any other issue area in the period after President George W. Bush had announced that the military phase of the war had ended.[18] Running for reelection, the president received twice as much negative as positive coverage.[19] The accumulation of negative news stories reduces support for the political system and esteem for its leaders.

Secondary Groups Americans start joining organizations in early childhood and continue to do so throughout their lives. Sociologists refer to groups that people join voluntarily as **secondary groups,** in contrast to **primary groups,** such as the family or cliques at school, in which there is close person-to-person interaction. Typical of the secondary groups to which Americans belong are professional associations, social or service clubs, labor unions, and political action organizations and political interest groups.

Membership in a group may have some effect on an individual's political socialization if three important conditions are met: (1) the individual identifies closely with the group's values or objectives; (2) those values or objectives are directly related to some aspect of politics; and (3) the group engages in promotional activities designed to inspire specific political attitudes or actions on the part of its members. In recent years, for instance, the Roman Catholic Church and some fundamentalist Protestant sects have made aggressive efforts to persuade federal and state governments to prohibit the practice of abortion and funding for groups that promote it. The efforts of these church groups have had an effect on both the attitudes and the political activities of some of their members. We discuss the effect that these secondary groups have on people, government, and policymaking in the next chapter.

As noted earlier, political socialization is a dynamic process, one that continues throughout the life cycle. Although important aspects of belief systems and political attitudes begin to take shape before adulthood, these are not etched in stone. But they also do not change easily; for political attitudes formed in the preadult years to change, a person who holds these beliefs must be exposed to potent stimuli in adulthood. And because those stimuli appear only infrequently—partly because people tend to associate with others who are like them—attitudes formed early in life usually remain at the core of an individual's belief system throughout life.

secondary groups
Organizations and associations to which people belong that often help shape and reinforce their views.

primary groups
Family or a group of people with whom a person lives and associates regularly; such groups shape personalities and help provide an orientation toward life.

Review Questions

1. Which of the following factors contributes the least to political socialization?

   A. Ancestry
   B. Family
   C. School
   D. Peer associations

2. Which of the following events is likely to have the most influence on the beliefs of your generation?

   A. End of the Cold War
   B. Controversy over the 2000 presidential election
   C. Terrorist attacks of September 11, 2000
   D. Hurricane Katrina

3. Liberals and conservatives disagree on all of the following *except*

   A. The balance between national security and personal liberty
   B. The basic nature of people
   C. The priorities attached to liberty and equality
   D. The need for some type of government

4. Which of the following best characterizes American public opinion on most issues?

   A. Apathy
   B. Activism
   C. Agreement
   D. Accommodation

Answers:

   1. A
   2. C
   3. D
   4. A

Conflict and Consensus in Review

Biology and sociology interact to reproduce and reinforce values and beliefs, including views of citizenship and government. To the extent that people undergo a shared political experience based on a common history, culture, and language, that experience is apt to contribute toward an agreement on the norms, values, and attitudes that underlie American democracy. To the extent that this experience differs by virtue of where people live; what they believe; and how they go about their daily lives; the values, interests, and orientations are apt to differ as well. It is from these differences that political conflict ensues.

Political Belief Systems

What is a **political belief system,** and how does it affect perceptions and opinions on contemporary issues? Simply put, a belief system is a set of interrelated attitudes that shape judgments about political issues and reactions to them. Another word for such a system is **ideology.** It provides a lens, a mindset, through which we organize our thoughts, formulate our opinions, and evaluate events occurring around us.

political belief system or ideology
A set of beliefs that relate to one another and shape judgments about political issues.

Liberalism and Conservatism

In the United States the two dominant political ideologies are **liberalism** and **conservatism.** Perhaps no two words in the English language have been used more often, and with less consistency, than these. As political ideologies, they have represented different beliefs to different people at different times.

Contemporary liberalism stems from the writings of the British philosopher John Locke, whose arguments about the purposes and ends of government in his *Second Treatise of Civil Government* influenced Thomas Jefferson when he drafted the Declaration of Independence. Locke contended that government is a necessary evil, created to protect the basic values of life, liberty, and property.[20]

Contemporary liberals and conservatives both subscribe to these basic values, but they emphasize different aspects of them. Liberals stress individual political freedoms, such as the right to express beliefs in speech or print, no matter how unpopular those beliefs might be. Liberals tend to be leery of governmental attempts to restrain speech and the political activities that result from it. Conservatives, on the other hand, are more tolerant of such restraints, particularly if their purpose is to maintain social order and community values.

When it comes to the exercise of economic freedoms, the positions of liberals and conservatives are reversed. Conservatives favor maximum freedom for individuals to acquire, own, and use personal property as they see fit; they tend to criticize governmental efforts to restrict such activity. Conservatives believe that the free-enterprise system invigorates and benefits the entire society, whereas liberals are more skeptical that everyone benefits, often pointing to the economic and social inequalities that this type of economic system frequently produces and sustains.

For liberals, inequalities interfere with the pursuit of happiness for those who are disadvantaged and have fewer opportunities to improve their condition. They see government as a potential equalizer if people are unable to improve their own condition. They ask, what other way is there to help those who cannot help themselves and defend those who cannot defend themselves? Thus, liberals have supported government intervention to protect civil rights and promote equal opportunity for minorities and others who have not been accorded the same benefits and opportunities as other members of society.

Conservatives, in contrast, see economic and social inequality as a natural consequence of the human condition and the price society must pay for the benefits of an economic system in which individual initiative and competition spur scientific and technological progress. Conservatives thus oppose government restrictions

liberalism
An ideology that places the greatest value on political freedom and social and economic equality; liberals tend to favor the use of government to redistribute resources from the wealthy to the poor and to provide a minimum standard of living for everyone.

conservatism
An ideology that places the greatest value on economic freedom and social order; conservatives favor the use of government to maintain law and order, protect national security, and preserve and protect property.

that might impede private enterprise. They are especially wary of government attempts to redistribute wealth by increasing the taxes paid by those with the highest incomes. They are also wary of government programs that undercut the economic incentives for people to better themselves through their own efforts. Because they are more accepting of social conditions, conservatives tend to be more resistant to large-scale change than liberals. They desire stability, believing that it is necessary if people are to enjoy and protect the fruits of their labor. Underlying this desire, however, is a more pessimistic view of human nature than liberals tend to have. Conservatives are more sympathetic to the thinking of Thomas Hobbes, another British political philosopher, who theorized that life without government would be "solitary, poor, nasty, brutish, and short." Hobbes saw the primary role of government as preserving life and protecting the exercise of those liberties that would not jeopardize social order. Conservatives thus value law and order; they believe that the principal function of government is to preserve it and to protect society from those who threaten it, either from within or from outside.

Since World War II, conservatives have generally supported a foreign policy based on military strength and aid, primarily in the form of arms, to governments politically allied with the United States. In contrast, liberals, although not denying the need for a strong defense, have tended to favor diplomatic policies that promote accommodation among nations. The Democrats have emphasized working with and supporting international organizations; they have tended to place less emphasis on the use of force as an instrument of diplomacy and more on providing social and economic aid to nations with the greatest needs, especially those in less industrialized regions of the world.

Do people actually think along these ideological lines? Do they use liberalism and conservatism as a basis for formulating opinions and making decisions? The evidence suggests that they do. It also suggests that the more information and education people have, the more likely they are to maintain views on policy issues that are consistent with their basic ideological orientation.

Ideology provides cues for making political judgments, such as taking a stand on an issue or voting. In recent years, there has been a strong association between people's ideological self-identification and their political allegiances and voting behavior. Liberals tend to identify with the Democratic Party and vote for Democratic candidates and conservatives with the Republican Party and Republican candidates.[21] Ideology, in short, influences the composition and policy positions of the two major parties more clearly today than it did in the past.

If ideology is more important, then how do Americans classify themselves today? Table 5.3 shows the patterns of ideological self-identification. Although conservatives have maintained an advantage over liberals throughout this period, that advantage increased markedly in the last two decades of the twentieth century and the beginning of the twenty-first century.

Who are the liberals and conservatives in the American electorate? The data in Table 5.3 suggest that men are more conservative than women, whites are more conservative than nonwhites, and older Americans are more conservative than younger Americans.

Table 5.3 Ideological Self-Identification

	Conservative (%)	Moderate (%)	Liberal (%)	N =
TOTAL	41	39	19	4,036
Men	44	39	16	1,928
Women	39	39	21	2,108
Whites	43	38	18	3,175
Blacks	30	47	22	440
High School Diploma or Less	42	41	16	1,573
Some College Education	45	37	18	1,316
College Graduate	39	39	21	557
Postgraduate Education	31	41	28	577
Republicans	70	26	4	1,307
Independents	29	47	22	1,521
Democrats	25	43	31	1,193
18–29 Years	32	40	27	762
30–49 Years	42	39	19	1,625
50–64 Years	42	40	18	901
65 Years and Older	47	40	11	719

Source: "Most American Identify as Either Conservative or Moderate," Gallup Poll, November 11, 2003, http://www.gallup.com. Used by permission. The data in the table are based on a combined sample of 4,036 interviews conducted in October and early November 2003.

In recent years American politics has become more ideological. Candidates for office, officials in office, and parties and their partisan supporters have become more clearly differentiated along ideological lines. This differentiation has affected the American electorate, which has become more polarized.

The ideologicalization of American politics has made compromise more difficult. There is more distance to move to reach an accord, and perhaps less incentive to do so. It is harder for those in government to find a middle ground.

Conflict and Consensus in Review

Liberals and conservatives have helped shape American beliefs about the role of government and its importance. From the 1930s through most of the 1960s, the liberal persuasion was dominant and views of government more positive. Since the 1980s, the conservative view that government should be smaller and less intrusive in the domestic and economic spheres has been in the ascendancy. Evaluations of social and economic conditions and the ability of government to

continued

affect them have reduced trust in government and personal efficacy. People have become more cynical, the press more critical, and politicians and partisans more polarized. These changes have heightened conflict within the political arena. To some extent, they have also widened the perceived gap between government and the governed.

Beliefs About Democratic Government

Political attitudes have an effect in four areas that are critical to the operation of a democracy: the proper role of government, trust in public officials, political efficacy, and public support for democratic processes, and tolerance of others.

The Proper Role of Government   What do the American people see as the proper role of government? In the economic realm, support for government intervention to promote employment, control inflation, and foster growth has remained fairly consistent since the Great Depression. However, there has been considerable disagreement over how much the government should be involved in the economy and how much it should regulate economic activity. This disagreement is often couched in partisan and ideological terms, with Democrats, liberals, and women supporting a larger governmental role in this area than Republicans, conservatives, and men.

Trust in Government and the People Who Run It   As the economy improved, first in the early 1980s and again in the mid-1990s, confidence and trust in government increased, only to decline again when allegations of personal wrongdoing and abuses of power made headlines. After the terrorist attacks of September 11, 2001, and the government's response, trust and confidence in government increased, a consequence of the Bush administration's strong response, bipartisan support of that response by Congress, and a unified, optimistic, patriotic spirit that the country's strength and determination would prevail. But as the economy weakened, the stock market fell, large corporations went bankrupt, and their improper accounting practices became known, trust declined yet again, not only in government but also in big business, big labor unions, and big media conglomerates. The political scandals involving members of Congress and officials of the Bush administration, which became public toward the end of 2005, further eroded public trust. Figure 5.1 and Table 5.4 illustrate this decline.

Does the decline in confidence and trust in government matter? It certainly does. If citizens lack confidence in government and cannot trust public officials to mean what they say and do what they promise, they are less likely to participate in the political process. Without confidence, government cannot operate successfully; without trust, the motives of public officials will always be suspect and their actions will be subject to misunderstanding and misinterpretation.

Figure 5.1 **Trust in Government**

How much of the time do you think you can trust government in Washington to do what is right—just about always, most of the time, or only some of the time?

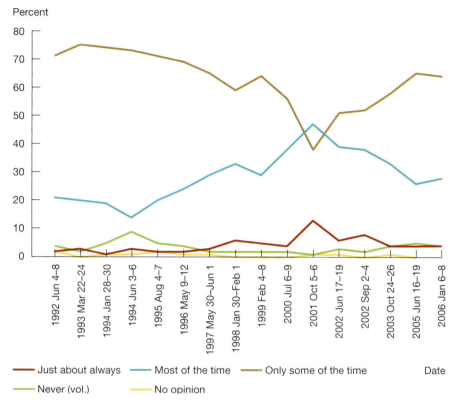

Source: "Poll Topic and Trends: Trust in Government," Gallup Poll, http://www.gallup.com/content/default. aspi?ci=5392 (accessed March 12, 2006). Used by permission.

Levels of trust are not uniform throughout the population. Young people had traditionally exhibited more trust in government than their elders did. However, political trust among young people declined during the late 1960s and early 1970s. By the mid-1970s, young people were again as trusting as people in other age groups, and they have remained so since then despite their wariness about whether government will be as important an influence on their lives as it has been on the lives of their parents. Political trust also varies among racial groups. African Americans show less political trust than the rest of the population.

Trust has partisan implications as well. Before the terrorist attacks, Democrats were more trusting of government than Republicans. After September 11, 2001, however, the relationship between partisanship and trust shifted, with Republicans and conservatives indicating more trust in government than

Table 5.4 Confidence in Institutions

"Now I am going to read you a list of institutions in American society. Please tell me how much confidence you, yourself, have in each one—a great deal, quite a lot, some, or very little?" (The percentages listed below combine the responses "a great deal" and "quite a lot.")

	A. (%)	B. (%)	C. (%)	D. (%)	E. (%)	F. (%)	G. (%)	H. (%)	I. (%)	J. (%)	K. (%)	L. (%)	M. (%)	N. (%)	O. (%)
2005	53	74	41	49	37	28	22	28	24	44	63	42	26	22	17
2000	56	64	47	46	37	37	24	36	25	42	54	40	24	29	16
1995	57	64	44	43	40	30	21	33	26	45	58	41	20	21	—
1990	56	68	47	36	45	39	24	—	27	—	—	—	—	25	—
1985	66	61	56	51	48	35	39	—	28	—	—	—	—	31	—
1981	64	50	46	46	42	35	29	—	28	—	—	—	—	20	—
1975	68	58	49	—	—	—	40	—	38	—	—	—	—	34	—

Key: A. The church or organized religion; B. The military; C. The Supreme Court; D. Banks; E. Public schools; F. Newspapers; G. Congress; H. Television news; I. Organized labor; J. The presidency; K. The police; L. The medical system; M. The criminal justice system; N. Big business; O. Health maintenance organizations (HMOs).
Source: "Poll Topics and Trends: Confidence in Institutions: Military Again Tops 'Confidence' in Institutions List," Gallup Poll, June 1, 2005, http://www.gallup.com (accessed June 2, 2005). Used by permission.

Democrats, largely because they approved of the actions of the Bush administration and because those actions were in the national security sphere.

As noted earlier, the lack of trust in government has serious implications for a democratic society. It increases public cynicism, decreases confidence in government, and discourages participation in the political process. It reduces the discretion public officials have in fashioning policy solutions and shortens the length of time people are willing to wait for those solutions to have their promised effect. It also contributes to feelings of alienation, a sense that people cannot affect what government does or how it influences their lives. Table 5.5 provides a measure of this alienation.

Political Efficacy and Public Support for Democratic Processes If people believe that they cannot make a difference, they are said to have a low sense of **political efficacy.** As a group, both African Americans and Hispanics have a lower sense of efficacy than whites do. Their lower levels of education explain some of the difference, because studies conducted since the 1950s have consistently found that education is correlated with higher levels of political efficacy. Yet an increase in educational levels in the general public has not resulted in a corresponding increase in political efficacy, nor has it led to an increase in the portion of the population that votes.

Trust and efficacy are related. People who trust the government tend to feel that they can affect its decisions, whereas those who lack trust often feel helpless and become alienated and angry.[22]

political efficacy
The perception that individuals can make a difference, that they can affect what government does and when it does it.

Table 5.5 Feelings of Efficacy

	Agree (%)	Disagree (%)
"People like me don't have any say about what the government does."		
2003	47	51
2002	46	51
1999	47	52
1997	46	53
1994	54	46
1992	50	49
"Generally speaking, elected officials in Washington lose touch with the people pretty quickly."		
2004	66	26
2003	75	22
2002	74	22
1999	77	21
1997	76	23
1994	83	16
1992	84	15

Source: "2004 Political Landscape: Evenly Divided and Increasingly Polarized," Pew Research Center for the People and the Press, November 5, 2003; and "Beyond Red vs. Blue: Republicans Divided about Role of Government—Democrats by Social and Personal Values," Pew Research Center for the People and the Press, May 10, 2005.

Although many Americans have been critical of their government, they strongly oppose taking violent actions against it, as can be seen in the public's reaction to the Oklahoma City bombing in 1995 or to paramilitary groups. Public support for the principles of majority rule and minority rights remains high, and there is a consensus in the basic values that underlie the American political system.[23]

Political Tolerance Surveys conducted during the last two decades have also found greater **political tolerance,** especially among the young. (See Table 5.6.) There are also differences in tolerance between the elites, people in leadership positions, and the general population.[24] The key finding of this research is that the elites tend to be more supportive of the political rights of others than the general population. Does the fact that the general public is less tolerant than the governing elites and less supportive of the norms and practices of democracy threaten the democratic character of the system? According to a group of scholars known as democratic elitists, the answer is "no." As long as those in power make decisions and take actions in accordance with democratic principles, they

political tolerance
A general acceptance of people with different lifestyles, beliefs, and opinions on public policy issues.

Table 5.6 Changing Attitudes about Race and Sexual Orientation

Year of Survey	Born: Pre-1913	WWII (1913–27)	Silent (28–45)	Boomer (46–64)	Gen X (65–76)	Gen Y (77–)
"I think it's all right for blacks and whites to date each other." (Agree, %)						
1987–1988	26	31	41	59	64	—
2002–2003	—	49	60	77	85	91
"We've gone too far in pushing equal rights in this country." (Agree, %)						
1987–1988	49	52	47	38	34	—
2002–2003	—	50	58	48	42	34
"School boards ought to have the right to fire teachers who are known homosexuals." (Disagree, %)						
1987–1988	22	27	38	51	47	—
2002–2003	—	37	46	62	70	71

Source: "2004 Political Landscape: Evenly Divided and Increasingly Polarized," Pew Research Center for the People and the Press, November 5, 2003.

argue, the character of the system is not threatened (although public support of basic democratic values is still essential).[25]

authoritarian personality
A personality type that requires structured environment with clear rules of behavior; a person prone to doctrinaire views.

In addition to education, another factor that affects tolerance is personality. The need for a more structured and ordered existence makes some people less able to accept behavior that violates the norms of society than others, who can function in a looser, less structured environment. The term **authoritarian personality** is often used to describe people who are prone to doctrinaire views and willing to follow those who preach them.[26] In general, when behavior becomes more threatening—when it adversely affects someone's job, property, or lifestyle—it is more difficult for people to be tolerant.

Review Questions

1. Both Republicans and Democrats agree that government should

   A. Provide for a strong defense
   B. Stimulate the economy
   C. Enforce community values
   D. Give Welfare to those who need it

continued

2. Since the 1960s have the levels of trust in government been

   A. Increasing
   B. Decreasing
   C. Remaining the same
   D. Fluctuating wildly

3. Which of the following groups has the highest level of tolerance on social issues?

   A. Old college graduates
   B. Young college graduates
   C. Women
   D. Men

4. In which government organization do people express the most confidence today?

   A. President
   B. Supreme Court
   C. Congress
   D. Military

Answers:

   1. A
   2. B
   3. B
   4. D

Conflict and Consensus in Review

Americans agree about the need for government to protect their personal and national security; there is less agreement about the government's involvement in these and other political, economic, and social spheres. That disagreement has become more polarized along partisan lines. Trust in government has declined as people perceive an increasing gap between the promises and performance of public officials. Although Americans continue to support the democratic processes, they are still pessimistic about their ability to affect these processes. The country has gone through a period of major social and economic change since the 1960s with young people better able and more willing to accept these changes.

Public Opinion and Democratic Governance

Belief systems are important because they provide a framework for perceiving and interpreting the world around us. They influence but do not dictate public opinion. In a democracy, public opinion is important for several reasons. It helps establish the **salience** of issues and, to some extent, identifies acceptable and unacceptable policy alternatives. A high level of public interest and concern indicates

salience
Importance, relevance; salience usually refers to the importance of public policy issues at a given point in time.

that an issue is important and, usually, that something must be done about it. If there is a dominant mood or opinion, public officials tend to follow it. Scholars who have studied opinion change and policy outcomes have found a correlation between the two[27]; they have also found that opinion change precedes rather than follows policy change, a pattern that would be expected in a democracy.[28]

For most issues, however, there is not a single dominant opinion but a variety of opinions. These opinions are developed, publicized, and communicated by the opinion leaders, people who have the skills, contacts, and motivation to try to convert them into public policy decisions. Specific courses of action are more likely to be influenced by the interchange between opinion makers and government officials than by the general public. However, the values, beliefs, and opinions of the people are still important because they establish the boundaries within which policy debate occurs and policy decisions are made.

Do officials respond to the public's opinions, or do they shape them? The answer is that they try to do both. At the national level, government officials regularly use polls to discern prevalent public opinions and political attitudes. Since the 1960s, presidents have regularly consulted with pollsters, who gauge the public's reactions to their policies and actions, to learn about the public's mood. But using polls to assess public opinion or focus groups to discover the words or phrases that resonate the most with different groups is different from using them to make public policy decisions. According to Dick Morris, chief political strategist for Bill Clinton's 1996 presidential reelection campaign, "Clinton . . . consults polls as if they were giant wind socks that tell him which way the wind is blowing. And then he asks the pollster to help him determine which current he should try to harness to move him closer to his destination. He sails with that air current until he has gone too far to the left. . . . He polls again, reverses his tack, and this time aims a little to the right. . . . He ends up . . . in the middle."[29]

George W. Bush has also been sensitive to shifts in public opinion; his political aides have kept him informed of national polling data and factored that information into the advice they have given him on public policy decisions[30] (see Box 5.3).

5.3 Politics in the 21st Century
Polling and Policymaking

Public opinion polling is a fact of life for politicians and policymakers. They conduct polls to get elected, and they keep abreast of poll results to remain popular with their constituents. But

should they? Should polls serve as a guide to public policy decisions and actions? To find out, the Kaiser Family Foundation and the journal *Public Perspective* conducted a poll in 2001.

This poll on polling revealed the American public to be somewhat ambivalent on the question, how closely public officials should follow polls. Nevertheless, more people expect their representatives to reflect their views (54 percent) than want them to use their best judgment (42 percent). Similarly, more people express a great deal or a fair amount of confidence "in the public when it comes to making

continued

5.3 **Politics in the 21st Century** *continued*

judgments about what general direction elected and government officials should take on various issues facing the nation" (54 percent) than express little confidence or none (45 percent).

Do government officials reflect what the majority wants? Again the public is divided, but a majority believes that "officials in Washington" do not (52 percent). Why not? Some of the reasons given are as follows: "They don't understand what the public wants" (51 percent); "They do not believe the public is informed enough on the issues" (60 percent); "Officials choose to follow what special interests want instead" (65 percent); "Officials are doing what they believe is ultimately in the best interest of the public" (47 percent).

How can government officials become informed about public desires and opinions? The public does not place much faith in polls. Only 25 percent think that "conducting a public opinion poll is the best way for officials to learn what the majority of people in our country think about important issues." Although the general public is skeptical of the accuracy and validity of polls as a reflection of public opinion, policy leaders and media representatives place more confidence in them (46 percent and 52 percent, respectively).

If not by polling, then how can public officials find out what the people want and need? Town meetings are viewed as more effective by 43 percent of the American people, and 15 percent think that personal contact initiated by individuals is the best way for government officials to become informed. Policy leaders and media representatives have less faith in town meetings and much less in people who call them.

The public's faith in the majority's judgment, with its skepticism about polling, puts government officials in a quandary. Should they follow public opinion, even if it goes against their own best judgment? If so, how can they be sure what that opinion actually is and how informed it may be? Moreover, national polls may not reflect constituency views, and local polls, conducted by the news media or interest groups, may not be as reliable or valid as larger-scale countrywide surveys. Besides, opinions change and vary in intensity, two components of the public perspective that may or may not be captured in a poll. Is it possible to have a government "of the people, by the people, and for the people" at the same time?

Source: "Polling and Democracy," *Public Perspective* (July/August 2001): 16–24.

Because government officials have been extremely sensitive to public opinion, they have been accused of both pandering to it and of manipulating it to their advantage. Such accusations, however, do not take account of the fine line between leading and following. A good leader moves out in front, but not too far. Although Americans may fault their political leaders for failing to heed public opinion or to lead it, government officials still must make their decisions without knowing exactly how the public will react.

Moreover, effective policy may demand that decision makers do what they think is right and what will benefit the country the most in the long run, regardless of the public mood and the short-run consequences of a decision. But there is a danger here, too. American history is filled with examples of policies such as prohibition, the Vietnam War, Clinton's health-care reforms, and Bush's Social Security proposals, which failed or had to be curtailed because of lack of public support.

Finally, what is the effect of public opinion on the politics of American democracy? Opinion differences lead to political conflict. But overall consensus on the merits of the system, the rules of the game, and the need to express beliefs and pursue interests within the letter and spirit of the law have contributed to a more vibrant society that encourages political debate and activities but simultaneously prevents these vital inputs into a democratic political system from getting out of hand.

The public's values and beliefs constitute the intellectual foundation on which the political system rests; public opinions frame the policy debate and influence the decisions of government officials. Those decisions in turn are continuously subjected to the public in the form of polls, elections, and political activities initiated by individuals and groups.

Because public opinion is a critical component of democratic politics, it is important to measure and interpret it accurately as the opening to this chapter suggests. For much of American history, this interpretation was the result of observations and educated guesses by journalists, politicians, and other students of government. During the 1930s, public opinion pollsters, such as George Gallup, began to conduct survey for commercial use. Using scientific methods to determine his sample and analyze data, Gallup correctly predicted the results of the 1934 congressional elections and the 1936 presidential election, whereas organizations that conducted larger but less scientific surveys did not.[31] Gallup's success demonstrated the importance of using scientific methods and the value of polling in revealing the characteristics of American public opinion.

© AP/Wide World Photos

Dr. George Gallup, director of the American Institute for Public Opinion, and the institute's chief statistician, Edward G. Benson (standing), are working together, using slide rules, at an office in Princeton, NJ, on August 7, 1941.

Determining Public Opinion

Polls indicate the direction, the stability, and to some extent the intensity of public opinion. **Direction of public opinion** refers to the proportion of the population that holds a particular view. Evaluations of direction over time indicate the fluidity or the **stability of public opinion.** Over the last three decades, for example, national surveys have asked the American people whether they support or oppose abortion. Their responses have been remarkably consistent (stable), as indicated in Figure 5.2. There has been a little more fluidity in the public's support for homosexual rights, as seen in Figure 5.3.

Intensity of public opinion refers to the depth of feelings. Because opinions are easy to express, even without much information, intensity is a good indicator of whether people will act on the basis of their opinions. It is measured by asking people how strongly they feel about a particular issue such as keeping the words "under God" in the Pledge of Allegiance. Naturally, the more intensely people feel about an issue, the more likely they are to do something about it. Consider the advocates of gun ownership, for example. Although polls indicate that most Americans favor stricter gun control laws, Congress has found that it is difficult to enact such restrictions because of lobbying and public advocacy by the National Rifle Association (NRA).[32]

direction of public opinion
The largest proportion of the population that holds a particular view.

stability of public opinion
The constancy of opinion; how much it changes over time.

intensity of public opinion
The depth of feelings on an issue; the greater the intensity, the more likely a person will become politically involved.

Figure 5.2 Public Opinion on Abortion

Do you think abortions should be legal under any circumstances, legal only under certain circumstances, or illegal in all circumstances?

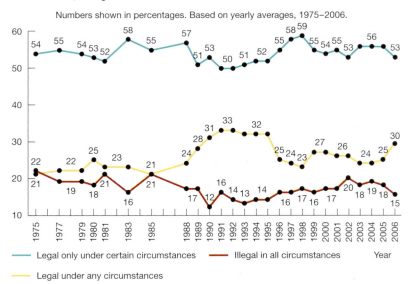

Numbers shown in percentages. Based on yearly averages, 1975–2006.

— Legal only under certain circumstances   — Illegal in all circumstances   Year

— Legal under any circumstances

Source: "Topics and Trends: Abortion," Gallup Poll, http://www.gallup.com content/default.aspx?ci=1576 (accessed March 12, 2006). Used by permission.

Figure 5.3 Public Opinion on Homosexual Rights

Do you think homosexual relations between consenting adults should or should not be legal?

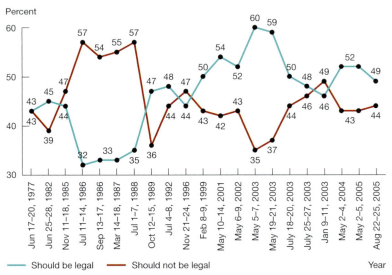

Source: "Topics and Trends: Homosexual Rights," Gallup Poll, http://www.gallup.com/content/
default.aspx?ci=1651 (accessed March 12, 2006).

Surveys of public opinion not only reveal which groups of people are most likely to support certain policies, be concerned about different issues, and vote for particular candidates but also can indicate which issues do not generate much public interest or awareness and therefore may not have to be addressed by government officials. Polls cannot predict what opinions people will hold in the future. Rather, they present a snapshot of society at a particular point in time. By asking the same questions, however, they can plot trends in opinion over time. For a snapshot, or a series of them, to be accurate, however, the people who participate must be representative of the whole population. The only way to achieve this is randomly selecting respondents from the population.

In a **random sample,** every element in the population must have an equal chance of being included in the sample, and the choice of any one element must not preclude the choice of any other. Because sampling is based on a mathematical theory of probability, the odds of being right can also be calculated. These odds become better as the size of the sample increases. The more the sample approximates the size of the population, the more likely it is to be accurate and the more confidence can be placed in the findings. However, enlarging the sample adds to its costs. And those costs can be considerable: A straightforward national poll of about 1,000 people, sampled randomly by telephone number and interviewed for about fifteen minutes, could cost $50,000 or more. The longer the interview and the more complex the analysis, the higher the cost will be. At some point a law of diminishing returns sets in: The gain in accuracy is small, but the increase in cost is considerable.

random sample
A sample in which every element in the populations has an equal chance of being included. Variations are used to survey national public opinion. The probability of accuracy can be calculated on the basis of the number of people included.

In assessing the results of a random sample, two factors must be considered: sampling error and level of confidence. Both result from the process of random selection itself and the odds of being wrong. **Sampling error** refers to the degree to which the sample could deviate from the population. Thus, if a poll with a sampling error of ±3 reported that 50 percent of those surveyed thought the president was doing a good job, pollsters could generalize that anywhere from 47 to 53 percent of the entire population held that opinion.

Even within the range of sampling error, however, there is always a chance that the results of the sample (the findings of the survey) might not be accurate for the population as a whole; the smaller that chance, the greater the degree of confidence that can be placed in the results. Most national surveys are based on a **level of confidence** of 95 percent, meaning that nineteen times out of twenty the results of the sample are probably within the range of its sampling error. But occasionally the results will not be. To illustrate, in almost every election cycle there is at least one major poll that differs from the others. That difference immediately attracts attention because the results are surprising and newsworthy. Moreover, the candidate who moves up in the standings is likely to point to the poll as evidence of a campaign that is gaining momentum. Although the news media inevitably suggest that opinion has shifted, another explanation would be chance error—that one chance in twenty that the poll was wrong.

The Hazards of Polling

In addition to the possibility of a sampling error, polls may present an inaccurate picture because of the way their questions are worded, the way surveys are constructed, or the way responses are interpreted. Bias can be introduced by question wording, by using emotional or controversial words, or by phrases that imply the "right" answer, phrases such as "don't you believe?" or "isn't it true?" Even slight changes in wording can produce large differences in responses; this is why most pollsters carefully pretest the wording of their questions or items to detect any implicit bias in the wording or the order in which they are asked.

Here is an example of how question wording makes a difference. In September 2003, Gallup conducted a survey in which half of the respondents were asked one question:

> Do you think the federal government has become so large and powerful that it poses an immediate threat to the rights and freedoms of ordinary citizens, or don't you think so?

Thirty-nine percent replied yes.
The other half were asked the following question:

> Do you think the federal government poses an immediate threat to the rights and freedoms of ordinary citizens or not?

Thirty percent said yes.
Gallup concluded that difference in responses was because of the words "large and powerful" included in the first question but not the second.[33]

The choice of closed- or open-ended questions also may affect the kinds of responses obtained. **Closed-ended questions** force a person to choose among a

sampling error
The difference between the results of the sample and the whole population, usually represented by ± the number. The difference tends to decrease as the size of the sample increases.

level of confidence
The amount of certainty placed in the findings of a survey (within the range of sampling error).

closed-ended questions
Questions or responses selected from a list of items.

open-ended questions
Questions that have no predetermined answers; respondents can say whatever comes into their minds.

list of responses, whereas **open-ended questions** have no predetermined answer. Although responses to closed-ended questions can be categorized and analyzed more easily than responses to open-ended ones, they may also lead people to express opinions on issues about which they have little or no information or do not feel strongly, or they may force responses into categories that do not accurately reflect the respondent's opinion.

The order in which questions are asked also can shape the responses people give. Information included in the early questions may be used to answer later questions. Similarly, answers to the initial questions may affect answers to later questions, particularly if people try to be consistent in their answers. Even the interview itself can affect the response. People tend to give more socially acceptable or desirable responses to personal interviewers than they do on relatively impersonal questionnaires. In other words, people try to give the "right" answers, which may or may not reflect their true opinions, beliefs, or behaviors. For example, when asked whether they voted in the last election, more people will say they did than actually do vote; similarly, more will say that they voted for the winner than really do so. Pollsters are aware of the tendency of people to try to provide the "right" answers, and they attempt to compensate for this tendency by wording the question in such a way that no one answer appears more appropriate than any other one. Finally, error can also be introduced by the way survey results are interpreted.

Public Knowledge

The political opinions of most people rest on an extremely limited information base. Why are some people more informed, interested, and involved in political life than others? Why do some have more consistent political beliefs, look to the government for solutions to problems, or show greater tolerance of minority rights? The answer has a lot to do with their education, their ideology, and their understanding of democracy.

Survey after survey conducted during the past thirty years has shown that the general public is poorly informed about government officials and political issues. Not only do Americans know little about specific issues, but most people would be hard-pressed to name their representatives in Congress and their state legislature, much less recall those representatives' performance in office unless they have been involved in a scandal or abused their position. For example, recent national polls conducted for the Pew Research Center for the People and the Press found that only 61 percent of respondents correctly identified the current vice president and 43 percent the current secretary of state.[34]

People have more knowledge about entertainers and celebrities than they do about leading public officials. Moreover, many retain myths about government that they find hard to reject. A large majority of people continue to believe that the government spends more on foreign aid than on Medicare when, in reality, 11 percent of the budget is spent on Medicare and less than 0.005 percent on foreign aid.[35]

Higher levels of education and income are associated with greater political information. Thus, it seems that as Americans received more education they would have become more knowledgeable about politics and government. But alas, there is little evidence that suggests people are more knowledgeable today than they were in the past.[36]

Age is also strongly associated with a person's level of information on political issues. As people grow older and develop higher stakes in their community and profession, they become more aware of the effects of political decisions on their lives and well-being. As the number of government policies affecting senior citizens increases, older people have an incentive and the time to remain informed and involved.

Generational differences may also be a factor. The Pew Research Center for the People and the Press analyzed polling data during the last decade and found that Americans under thirty represented "a generation that knew less, cared less, and read newspapers less than previous generations of young people." It found that only one out of five people between the ages of eighteen and twenty-nine pays close attention to the news.[37] Nor have the terrorist attacks and their consequences changed this pattern. According to a more recent Pew publication, the younger people are, the less likely they will watch the news on a regular basis.[38]

What implications does the low level of information have for the politics of American democracy? For one thing, it gives government leaders more discretion in making policy decisions. With less direction from the public, they have more flexibility in crafting policy solutions. This is particularly evident in foreign affairs and in complex economic and technological issues, such as telecommunications policy, nuclear energy, and biomedical research. In contrast, when the public is better informed on issues that deal with unemployment, inflation, or crime, issues that affect them directly in the course of everyday life, public officials have much less leeway, their policy decisions will be scrutinized more closely, and the first sign of unsatisfactory results will prompt criticism.

Another consequence of limited public knowledge is that it contributes to unrealistic expectations of government and, therefore, greater disappointment in its performance. The more uninformed people are about what government does for them, the more negative they are likely to be toward it. Moreover, limited knowledge encourages public officials to seek policies that have an immediate impact. Thus, members of Congress feel the need to demonstrate to their constituents what they have done for them lately; executive branch officials constantly educate the public on the services they provide. The public tends to be impatient, demanding results here and now. These demands are readily converted into political pressure on government officials for quick fixes rather than longer-term solutions.

Similarly, low levels of public information increase the power of interest groups and their leaders. When many people are uninformed and uninterested, opinion leaders, particularly those who represent large and powerful groups, have more clout and use it, if only to justify their leadership position (and, in most cases, their large salaries). The bottom line is that a poorly informed public is easier to manipulate than a well-informed public. Perceptions of manipulation, even if they do not accord with empirical reality, undermine support for the political system and those who work in it.

Americans regularly express the view that elected officials should pay more attention to public opinion, yet as we have noted the public is leery of public opinion polls. Americans believe that government would improve if officials did what the people want, but opinions are frequently divided and often uninformed. As a consequence, public officials seem to spend as much time trying to lead the public as they do trying to follow it.

Public Opinion and Political Participation

In assessing public opinion, pollsters divide the population into three broad groups based on the relative level of information they people possess: the general public, the attentive public, and the opinion makers. The **general public** is the largest group (approximately three-fourths of the population), the least informed, and the most apathetic most of the time.[39] Because that group is subject to the greatest swings in mood and shifts in opinion, it is also the most easily manipulated of the three groups, at least for the short periods when its attention can be directed toward certain issues and proposals for dealing with them.

The second group is the **attentive public** (perhaps as much as one-fifth of the population). Better informed and more interested than the general or mass public, the attentive public comprises people who have a general awareness of issues, candidates and officials, and politically relevant events. They tend to have well-developed and consistent opinions on many issues, follow them in the news media, and discuss them with others. However, members of this group generally refrain from most political activities other than voting.

As its name suggests, the third group, the **opinion makers** (less than 5 percent of the population), consists of those who inform and shape the views of others. Their interest level, knowledge, and political activities set them apart. Included in this smallest group are party leaders, elected and appointed government officials, business executives, labor leaders, some members of the media, educational and religious leaders, and other interest group representatives. The opinion makers tend to hold the most consistent political beliefs.

The opinion makers, the attentive public, and the general public differ not only in their level of information but in their political attitudes as well. In particular, political scientist Herbert McClosky found significant differences between elite and mass attitudes toward the principles and practices of democracy. Although most people value freedom of speech in the abstract, they differ about how that freedom should be applied. The **political elite** (most of the opinion makers and some of the attentive public) express more support for individual civil liberties than does the general public.[40]

Whereas the attentive public and the general public determine the direction and intensity of opinion on a particular issue, the opinion makers define the alternatives—that is, the specific policies that are considered—and lead the public debate. That debate conditions the coverage that issues receive from the news media, which in turn can capture the attention of the general public.

general public
The general or mass public tends to be less informed and more apathetic than political elites.

attentive public
People who have a general knowledge; they tend to be more interested and involved than the general public.

opinion makers
A small group of people in and out of government that inform and shape the views of others.

political elite
A relatively small group interested, informed, and involved in politics; people who tend to exercise the greatest influence on government and its decisions.

The stronger someone's opinion, the more likely that person will participate in the political process. Political participation encompasses a variety of activities, from campaigning, to contacting public officials, to engaging in cooperative and even uncooperative activities such as protest demonstrations, sit-ins, rent strikes, riots, and other forms of nonviolent behavior. Only 1 or 2 percent of the population engage in such activities. An even smaller percentage may cross the line and participate in activities that violate community norms and even the law itself. These activities range from heckling a speaker, to protesting the meetings of a group, to blockading clinics that perform abortions, to bombing, kidnapping, and assassination.

Voting is the most prevalent form of campaign activity, followed by persuading others to give their support, distributing literature, attending rallies, making contributions, and doing other work for specific candidates and their parties. Contacting a public official is the most frequent form of citizen participation in the governing process. In most cases of contacting, however, interest group leaders organize and orchestrate a public response.

A sizable number of Americans do not participate in political activities. They do not vote regularly, contribute to political campaigns, or engage in direct contact with public officials. They are not members of any group involved in political action, and they do not participate in unconventional forms of political activity. They are politically inactive.

Among these inactive citizens are several types of people: those who are elderly and infirm, mentally incompetent, or incarcerated in prisons or other

© AP/Wide World Photos

Nation of Islam leader Louis Farrakhan addresses the Million Man March, Monday Oct. 16, 1995 on Capitol Hill. Farrakhan proclaimed divine guidance in bringing to Washington the largest assemblage of black Americans since the 1963 March on Washington.

confining institutions; those who live lives of poverty and desperation and lack the skills, confidence, or energy necessary to take part in political life; and those who believe that politics is inherently corrupt, unfair, or inequitable, so why bother? Still others are inactive because they are basically satisfied with their own lives and with the state of national affairs and see no reason to invest time or effort in political activities directed toward change. Whatever their reasons, approximately one-fifth of American adults are politically inactive. During the 2004 election cycle, only seven percent indicated that they attended a political meeting or rally, three percent said that they worked for a party or candidate, 21 percent claimed that they wore a button or put a bumper sticker on their car, and 13 percent said that they gave money to help a campaign.[41]

Who does become involved? One of the most consistent findings of studies of American political participation is that involvement is closely linked with an individual's **socioeconomic status (SES)**, or social and economic standing relative to other citizens. The higher one's SES, the greater the likelihood that one will participate actively in politics. Most citizens who are active participants are well educated and well off; among the totally inactive or those whose only activity is voting are a disproportionate number of people with low levels of education and income.

What accounts for the strong correlation between SES and participation? An important study of a sample of more than 15,000 Americans led political scientists Henry Brady, Sidney Verba, and Kay Lehman Schlozman to propose what they call a "resource model of political participation." They argue that three resources are essential for political activity—time, money, and civic skills—and that these critical resources are distributed unequally among groups defined by SES. Those who are higher on the SES ladder have more money; because they are well educated, they are also likely to have acquired more knowledge about the workings of the political system (that is, civic skills). Free time, on the other hand, is related not to SES but to other variables such as having a job, a spouse, or children at home. Nevertheless, people in the higher SES groupings are more likely to apply whatever time they do have to political activities because they see a greater benefit in doing so. Their higher levels of political interest motivate them to participate.[42]

The relationship among interest, participation, and SES is not surprising. Because of their greater knowledge of politics, higher-SES individuals are more likely to follow political issues on television and in the press, they are more likely to have a substantial financial interest in many public policy decisions, and they also have higher levels of political efficacy; in other words, they think they can make a difference.

Although no other demographic characteristic matches the effect of SES on participation, several others appear to influence participation. Age is one of them. Participation levels increase with age until the individual is affected by health and old age. Race, gender, and religion may also be factors in participation. African Americans, for example, are less likely than whites to be politically active, partly because they are overrepresented in the lower SES groups. Women are less likely to be active than men, although the gap between the sexes has been narrowing in recent years and has reversed itself entirely in voting participation.

socioeconomic status (SES)
The social and economic standing of people relative to others in the society.

Women now vote at higher rates than men. And people who participate significantly in religious activities are more likely to be politically active than people who don't attend religious services regularly.

How do the variations in participation affect the democratic character of the political system? Some argue that the critical issue in a democracy is not who actually participates but whether most people have the opportunity to do so. As long as this opportunity is available, they say, individuals are free to choose whether they will participate or not. And if policy decisions are made primarily by those who participate actively, that is all right as long as all citizens can participate when they choose. Those who question this view, however, point out that there is an important difference between the legal right to participate in politics and the actual possession of the skills and incentives necessary to do so. Nonparticipation is rarely just the exercise of free choice.

If participants and nonparticipants were scattered randomly throughout the population, the actual level of participation might not make much difference in terms of public policy. But as we have suggested, participation patterns are not random. Those who are older, with more education and higher incomes, participate at a higher level than do those who lack these characteristics. Moreover, their political views are often quite different from those of non or irregular participants.[43] To the extent that policy decisions are a response to what officials hear from the public, that response is skewed toward the views of those most likely to make themselves heard. Thus, the haves tend to speak with a louder, steadier, and more influential voice than the have-nots, and by doing so, they can maintain their advantage.

Review Questions

1. Which of the following contribute the most to a person's political participation?

   A. Level of knowledge
   B. Intensity of feeling
   C. Parental involvement
   D. Political beliefs

2. The most common type of political participation is

   A. Voting
   B. Writing a member of Congress
   C. Joining a demonstration
   D. Contributing money to a political campaign

3. People who tend to be most involved in politics are distinguished by all of the following *except*

   A. Education
   B. Religion

continued

    C. Sexual orientation

    D. Socioeconomic status

4. Which of the following groups comprise today's political elite in the United States?

    A. High school Merit Scholars

    B. Professional Athletes

    C. Interest Group Leaders

    D. Political Scientists

Answers:

    1. B

    2. A

    3. C

    4. C

Conflict and Consensus in Review

Political elites tend to give more support to the system and the need to participate in it than does the general public. The elites are in the forefront of the policy battles, bringing in their supporters to demonstrate the popularity of their views. Hence, conflict is led by elites, may involve the attentive public, and captures the interest and concern of the general population only for a few of the most salient issues. Where consensus exits, there is less need for the elites to lead and to mobilize support. Congress and the president tend to reflect the public mood when that mood has gelled into a policy consensus. The problem that policy makers face, however, is that there is usually much more consensus in the problem than how that problem can be solved.

Politics in Action

Public Opinion and Operation Iraqi Freedom

"I don't really care what polls and focus groups say. What I care about is doing what I think is right." This statement, often heard from candidate George W. Bush during his 2000 presidential campaign, was designed to differentiate his style of leadership from that of Bill Clinton, whose administration regularly conducted and used public opinion polls to set its agenda, fashion its priorities, embolden its rhetoric, and evaluate public perceptions of its performance.

Despite Bush's campaign assertion, his top political aides have kept abreast of public opinion by following the national polls and private surveys conducted by the Republican National Committee.[44] The Bush White House has even tried to anticipate potential shifts in public opinion by engaging in a continuous public relations campaign, replete with prepackaged information kits, television clips, and high officials designated for interviews with national

continued

Politics in Action *continued*

and local news media. The administration's defense of its war on terrorism is a case in point. Fearing that public support of the administration's efforts, particularly the military actions in Afghanistan and Iraq, would dissipate over time, top administration officials from the president down warned the American people from the outset that the war on terrorism would not be easy or short. The administration was right, but its warning was insufficient to stem the decline in public support for military actions and occupations abroad.

At the beginning of the war in Iraq, the American people approved of the president's handling of the situation. Gallup polls conducted at the time of the "preemptive attack" by the United States and its allies indicated that between two-thirds and three-fourths of the public believed that the use of force to remove Saddam Hussein's regime from power was merited. Seventy percent of the population supported the president's decision for a military response, despite strong international opposition to it. This high level of domestic support for the president's policy continued throughout the war. On May 1, 2003, when the president declared the military operation over, 86 percent of those surveyed said that things were going moderately or very well, and the president's approval rating stood at 69 percent. By the end of July, Americans were still optimistic that weapons of mass destruction would be found (52 percent), Saddam Hussein would be captured (68 percent), a stable democratic government could be established (58 percent), and the war had solved more problems than it had created for the United States (53 percent). Overall, 63 percent still thought that the situation in Iraq was worth going to war; 56 percent believed that things were going well; and the president's popularity hovered near 60 percent. It remained at that level through August 2003.[45]

Public opinion began to shift that September as the news media reported more Iraqi resistance to the U.S. occupation, more American soldiers being killed or wounded, more reservists being called to active duty for longer periods, and more money needed to fund the operation. The administration requested an additional $87 billion for reconstruction in Iraq and for the costs of keeping more than 100,000 U.S. troops there. With international opposition to the American-controlled occupation persisting and no weapons of mass destruction found, the wisdom of the policy, the credibility of the president, and the veracity of the intelligence on which he had based his decision to go to war were all called into question.[46]

The criticism of the Bush administration was amplified by the campaign for the Democratic presidential nomination, which accelerated in the winter as the 2004 caucuses and primaries neared. Howard Dean, a persistent opponent of the war in Iraq, emerged as the front-runner largely on the basis of his antiwar views, which were shared by many Democrats. By the end of November, support for the war had decreased to 56 percent and disapproval of the peacekeeping operation had reached 66 percent.[47]

The president clearly had been pushed off the pedestal he had occupied since the administration's response to the terrorist attacks of September 11, 2001. Bush's approval rating, which had been higher than that of any other president for a longer period, had fallen to 50 percent, the lowest of his presidency; at the end of November 2003, 47 percent disapproved of the job he was doing.[48]

With the 2004 presidential election fast approaching, Republican fund-raising well under way, and the 108th Congress debating several critical domestic issues at the end of its first session, the administration felt compelled to act. First, the president put his special assistant for national security, Condoleezza Rice, in charge of overseeing the Iraqi operation; the Pentagon's role was diminished. Also put on the fast track were plans to train more Iraqi police, army, and paramilitary to assume responsibility for the country's internal security. For the first time since the official end of the war, the president visited wounded service personnel and commiserated with families who had lost loved ones; he also made a surprise trip to Iraq to have Thanksgiving dinner with the troops.

Bush also began to pay more attention to domestic issues. The administration worked behind the scenes with Republican congressional leaders to reach an agreement on a Medicare reform bill, complete with a prescription drug

continued

Politics in Action *continued*

benefit; it launched a major public relations campaign to build pressure on Congress, and, at the request of House leaders, personally lobbied a few conservative Republicans who had voiced their opposition to the bill to change their votes—which they did. In addition, the president approved a bill to prohibit partial-birth abortions and a measure to reduce the risks of wildfires by clearing brush and trees, and he rescinded tariffs on imported steel to prevent economic retaliation by the European Union.

The administration had responded to public opinion as much as it could before the 2004 presidential election, in which the Bush campaign emphasized the war on terrorism, tying the military action and occupation in Iraq to that issue. After the election, Bush changed his focus to his domestic agenda.

Continued American casualties, highlighted by the news media; adverse reactions to those casualties and the situation in Iraq; and the high costs of the war could no longer threaten his tenure. Nevertheless, it reduced his political capital and the success with which he was able to achieve his new domestic goals. The public's increasingly critical evaluation of administration policy and progress in Iraq lowered approval of the president's job performance; reduced his political influence, particularly with his own party; constrained his domestic agenda; and threatened Republican control of Congress as the 2006 midterm election approached. The people had spoken.

What Do You Think?

1. Should public officials watch the polls and react to them? Should President George W. Bush have adjusted his administration's policy in Iraq as public opinion became more negative?
2. What role should public opinion play in a democratic society? Should government officials lead or follow? Does your answer vary for members of Congress, for their party leaders, and for the president?

3. Is public support a critical component of a democratic policymaking process? Should it be? If so, must policy change when opinions change?
4. Do elections increase public influence on government? Do they facilitate compromise and improve accountability, or do they water down policy and result in more parochial political decisions?

| Summary |

The public should be the driving force in a democracy. The people's values, beliefs, and opinions guide government officials in their decisions and actions. Moreover, the public's judgment of how those in office perform their roles, whether the policies they make and implement satisfy the needs and interests of the country, and how much faith and trust they place in government are important criteria for assessing the strength and vitality of a democratic system. Thus, the development of political beliefs, their conversion into public opinion on salient issues, and the activities that stem from them are topics of considerable importance to democratic governance.

Political socialization is the process by which individuals acquire the information, beliefs, attitudes, and values that help them comprehend the workings of a political system and orient themselves within it. Socialization begins early in life, initially with positive information about the nation's leaders and what they do and later with more complex information about what government should do and what policies it should pursue. Major political events can affect these value judgments.

Agents of political socialization include family, school, and religious groups. Later, peer interaction becomes more influential. Secondary groups such as professional associations, labor unions, and other interest groups affect political socialization when three conditions are met: (1) a person identifies closely with the group's values; (2) those values are directly related to some aspect of politics; and (3) the group engages in promotional activities designed to inspire specific political attitudes or actions on the part of its members.

Most Americans adopt a belief system, a set of simplified ideas that help them understand and cope with the world around them. A political belief system that shapes responses to policy issues and positions is frequently referred to as an ideology. The two dominant political ideologies in the United States are liberalism and conservatism. Liberals tend to support government intervention in social and economic programs—especially to protect civil rights and promote equal opportunity—and to oppose governmental actions that might deprive individuals of basic political freedoms. Conservatives tend to oppose government involvement, especially in the economic sphere, contending that a free market produces the prosperity that solves many of the country's social ills. But they are more supportive of governmental actions designed to curb behavior that conflicts with the norms of society. Conservatives lean heavily toward the Republican Party and liberals toward the Democratic Party.

Ideology influences beliefs about government. Although most Americans agree that government should promote employment, control inflation, and foster growth, they disagree over how extensive that involvement should be. Indeed, attitudes toward the proper role of government vary widely, as do levels of trust and efficacy. In general, however, the American people support the concept of democracy and the principles of majority rule and minority rights, and they oppose behavior that violates the law and disobeys the government. They are also concerned about security and the need to protect the nation against terrorism.

People vary in the knowledge they possess about politics and government. The general public is the least informed, most apathetic, and most easily manipulated; the attentive public is more informed and interested but takes little political action beyond voting. Opinion makers are the most informed and involved. They shape policies and influence public debate.

Higher income and more education are correlated with higher levels of political information. As people age, they become more aware of how political decisions affect them. A poorly informed public gives government leaders more flexibility in making policy decisions that have a direct and immediate effect, but it also discourages longer-term solutions, as the Social Security debate indicates.

Public opinion does affect politics and policy-making, and it should do so in a political system in which government rests on the consent of the governed. It does not dictate policy, but it does establish the salience of issues, the contours of debate, and the limits that define acceptable policy choices. A high level of public interest indicates that an issue is important and requires action. But in most cases opinions are divided on the most appropriate solution. The persistence of these different opinions, based partly on differing beliefs, generates continuous conflict, which elections and policy judgments help resolve—at least in the short run. The consensus rests on the systems for resolving differences, not on the election outcomes or the policy judgments themselves.

| Key Terms |

political socialization
citizenship
agents of political socialization
selective perception
secondary groups
primary groups
political belief system (ideology)
liberalism
conservatism

political efficacy
political tolerance
authoritarian personality
salience
direction of public opinion
stability of public opinion
intensity of public opinion
random sample
sampling error

level of confidence
closed-ended questions
open-ended questions
general public
attentive public
opinion makers
political elite
socioeconomic status (SES)

| Discussion Questions |

1. Discuss the ways in which growing up conditions the development of political orientations and attitudes. Illustrate your answer with examples from your personal experience.
2. What have been the principal factors that have contributed to the conservative shift in political attitudes in the United States since the beginning of the 1960s? Are these factors likely to persist and affect political attitudes in the foreseeable future?
3. How do the opinions and beliefs of young Americans in your generation differ from those of people in your parents' and grandparents' generations? Are these differences a cause for concern?

4. What is the relationship between public opinion and public policymaking in a democratic society, and what should that relationship be?
5. What effect does the low level of public knowledge about the issues of the day have on politics and government? Does this relatively low level of information undercut the democratic fabric of American society?
6. What are the principal values, attitudes, and opinions on which most Americans agree?
7. What are the issues that produce the greatest range of disagreements?

| Topics for Debate |

Debate each side of the following propositions:

1. Pollsters have too much influence on American politics today.
2. Ideological purity is dangerous for a democratic society.
3. Public opinion should guide government decision making in a democracy.

4. It is undemocratic for government officials to act on the basis of the intense feelings and political activities of a minority of the population.
5. Government officials such as the president should be required to consult with public opinion polls on at least a weekly basis.

| Where on the Web? |

Current Public Opinion Pollsters

Gallup Organisation **www.gallup.com**

Joint Center for Political and Economic Studies
www.jointctr.org

New York Times/CBS News Poll
www.nytimes.com/ref/national/polls_index.html?r=1

Pew Research Center on the People and the Press
www.people-press.org

Polling Report **www.pollingreport.com**

Public Opinion Data Libraries and Data Archives

Cornell Institute for Social and Economic
Research **www.ciser.cornell.edu/ASPs/datasource.asp**

Electronic Data Service (Columbia University)
www.columbia.edu/acis/eds

Inter-University Consortium for Political and
Social Research (University of Michigan)
www.icpsr.umich.edu/

Go to **www.thomsonedu.com/thomsonnow** to learn about a powerful online study tool. You will get a personalized study plan based on your responses to a diagnostic Pre-Test. Once you have mastered the materials with the help of interactive learning tools, activities, timelines, video case studies, simulations, and an integrated E-Book, you can take a Post-Test to confirm you are ready to move to the next chapter.

| Selected Readings |

Alvarez, R. Michael, and John Brehm. *Easy Answers, Hard Choices: Values, Information, and American Public Opinion.* Princeton, N.J.: Princeton University Press, 2002.

Asher, Herbert. *Polling and the Public.* 6th ed. Washington D.C.: Congressional Quarterly, 2004.

Delli Carpini, Michael X., and Scott Keeter. *What Americans Know and Why It Matters.* New Haven, Conn.: Yale University Press, 1996.

Dionne, E. J. *Why Americans Hate Politics.* New York: Simon and Schuster, 1991.

Dunn, Charles W., and J. David Woodard. *The Conservative Tradition in America.* Lanham, Md.: Rowman & Littlefield, 1996.

Greenstein, Fred I. *Children and Politics.* New Haven, Conn.: Yale University Press, 1965.

Herbst, Susan. *Numbered Voices: How Opinion Polling Has Shaped American Politics.* Chicago: University of Chicago Press, 1995.

Jacobs, Lawrence, and Robert Y. Shapiro. *Politicians Don't Pander.* Chicago: University of Chicago Press, 2000.

MacManus, Susan A. *Young v. Old: Generational Combat in the Twenty-First Century.* Boulder, Colo.: Westview Press, 1996.

McClosky, Herbert, and Alida Brill. *Dimensions of Tolerance: What Americans Believe about Civil Liberties.* New York: Russell Sage, 1986.

McClosky Herbert, and John Zaller. *The American Ethos: Public Attitudes toward Capitalism and Democracy.* Cambridge, Mass.: Harvard University Press, 1984.

Nye, Joseph S. Jr., Philip D. Zelikow, and David C. King, eds. *Why Americans Don't Trust Government.* Cambridge, Mass.: Harvard University Press, 1997.

Rosenstone, Steven J., and John Mark Hansen. *Mobilization, Participation, and Democracy in America.* New York: Macmillan Publishers, 1993.

Stimson, James A. *Public Opinion in America: Moods, Cycles, and Swings,* 2nd ed. Boulder, Colo.: Westview Press, 1998.

Verba, Sidney, Kay Lehman Schlozman, and Henry Brady. *Voice and Equality: Civic Voluntarism in American Politics.* Cambridge, Mass.: Harvard University Press, 1995.

Warren, Kenneth F. *In Defense of Public Opinion Polling.* Boulder, Colo.: Westview Press, 2001.

Wills, Gary. *A Necessary Evil: A History of American Distrust of Government.* New York: Simon and Schuster, 1999.

Zaller, John. *The Origins and Nature of Mass Opinion.* New York: Cambridge University Press, 1992.

Notes

[1] *CNN/USA Today/*Gallup Poll conducted October 24–26, 2003.

[2] "A proposal has been made that would allow people to put a portion of their Social Security payroll taxes into personal retirement accounts that would be invested in private stocks and bonds. Do you favor or oppose this proposal?"

	Favor (%)	Oppose (%)	Unsure (%)
10/03	62	34	04
11/02	57	40	03
9/02	52	43	05
6/02	57	39	04
4/02	63	33	04
1/02	63	33	04
11/01	64	31	05
8/01	62	34	04
3/01	63	30	07
6/00	65	30	05

Source: *CNN/USA Today/*Gallup Poll conducted October 24–26, 2003 of 1,006 adults nationwide. Margin of error ±3.

[3] George W. Bush, "Strengthening Social Security for Future Generations," http://www.whitehouse.gov (accessed July 5, 2005).

[4] "Beyond Red vs. Blue: Republicans Divided about Role of Government—Democrats by Social and Personal Values," Pew Research Center for the People and the Press, May 10, 2005, question 7, http://people press.org/reports/print.php3? PageID=953 (accessed May 11, 2005).

[5] George C. Edwards III, *On Deaf Ears* (New Haven, Conn.: Yale University Press, 2004).

[6] John R. Alford, Carolyn L. Funk, and John R. Hibbing, "Are Political Orientations Genetically Transmitted?" *American Political Science Review* 99 (May 2005): 153–167.

[7] Fred I. Greenstein, *Children and Politics* (New Haven, Conn.: Yale University Press, 1965).

[8] See M. Kent Jennings and Richard G. Niemi, "Patterns of Political Learning," in *Political Opinion and Behavior,* eds. Edward C. Dreyer and Walter A. Rosenbaum (North Scituate, Mass.: Duxbury Press, 1976), 80–97; and Martin P. Wattenberg, *The Decline of American Political Parties* (Cambridge, Mass.: Harvard University Press, 1984).

[9] Jennings and Niemi, "Patterns of Political Learning."

[10] Michael X. Delli Carpini, *Stability and Change in American Politics* (New York: New York University Press, 1986).

[11] For a discussion of different explanations of the socialization process, see David O. Sears, "Whither Political Socialization Research? The Question of Persistence," in *Political Socialization, Citizenship Education, and Democracy,* ed. Orti Ichilov (New York: Teachers College Press, 1989), 69–97.

[12] R. W. Connell, "Political Socialization in the American Family: The Evidence Re-Examined," *Public Opinion Quarterly* 36 (1972): 330.

[13] M. Kent Jennings, Kenneth P. Langton, and Richard G. Niemi, "Effects of the High School Civics Curriculum," in *The Political Character of Adolescence,* eds. M. Kent Jennings and Richard G. Niemi (Princeton, N.J.: Princeton University Press, 1974), 181–206.

[14] M. Kent Jennings, Lee H. Ehman, and Richard G. Niemi, "Social Studies Teachers and Their Pupils," in *The Political Character of Adolescence,* 207–228.

[15] Frank P. Scioli and Thomas J. Cook, "Political Socialization Research in the United States: A Review," in *Political Attitudes and Public Opinion,* eds. Dan D. Nimmo and Charles M. Bonjean (New York: McKay Press, 1972), 154–174.

[16] Thomas E. Patterson, *Doing Well and Doing Good: How Soft News and Critical Journalism Are Shrinking the News Audience*

and Weakening Democracy—And What News Outlets Can Do about It (Cambridge: Mass.: The Joan Shorenstein Center, Harvard University, 2000).

[17]See, for example, Douglas Kellner, *Television and the Crisis of Democracy* (Boulder, Colo.: Westview Press, 1990); and Thomas Patterson, *The Vanishing Voter* (New York: Alfred A. Knopf, 2002), 63–98.

[18]"TV News Turned Sour on Bush after Iraq War Ended," Center for Media and Public Affairs, press release, December 17, 2003, http://www.cmpa.com/pressReleases/TVNews TurnedSour.htm (accessed June 1, 2004).

[19]"George Bush's Postwar Blues," *Media Monitor* (November/December 2003): 3–5.

[20]John Locke, *Second Treatise of Civil Government* (New York: Liberal Arts Press, 1952).

[21]In 1988, approximately 80 percent of people who identified themselves as conservative supported the Republican nominee for president, and a similar percentage of self-identified liberals supported the Democratic candidate. Although the candidacy of independent H. Ross Perot in 1992 and 1996 reduced these percentages, 68 percent of the liberals still voted for the Democratic candidate in 1992, 78 percent in 1996, 80 percent in 2000, and 86 percent in 2004. Conservatives were equally supportive of the Republican presidential candidate, who received 65 percent of the conservative vote in 1992, 71 percent in 1996, 81 percent in 2000, and 83 percent in 2004.

[22]See Martin B. Abravnel and Ronald J. Busch, "Political Competence, Political Trust, and the Action Orientation of University Students," *Journal of Politics* 37 (February 1975): 57–82; and Joel Aberbach and Jack L. Walker, "Political Trust and Racial Ideology," *American Political Science Review* 64 (December 1970): 1,199–1,219.

[23]Henry F. Brady, Sidney Verba, and Kay Lehman Schlozman, "Beyond SES: A Resource Model of Political Participation," *American Political Science Review* 89 (1995): 271–294.

[24]See Herbert McClosky, "Consensus and Ideology in American Politics," *American Political Science Review* 58 (June 1964); Herbert McClosky and Alida Brill, *Dimensions of Tolerance* (New York: Russell Sage, 1983); Clyde Z. Nunn, Harry J. Crockett Jr., and J. Allen Williams Jr., *Tolerance for Nonconformity* (San Francisco: Jossey-Bass, 1978); and James L. Gibson and Richard D. Bingham, *Civil Liberties and the Nazis: The Skokie Free-Speech Controversy* (New York: Praeger Publishers, 1985).

[25]This position is well stated in Stephen Earl Bennett, "'Know Nothings' Revisited: The Meaning of Political Ignorance Today," *Social Science Quarterly* 69 (June 1988): 476–490.

[26]Their behavior pattern of dominance and submission is thought by some to compensate for deeply held feelings of insecurity.

[27]See Benjamin I. Page and Robert Y. Shapiro, "Effects of Public Opinion on Policy," *American Political Science Review* 77 (March 1983): 175–190; and Gerald C. Wright Jr., Robert S. Erikson, and John P. McIver, "Public Opinion and Policy Liberalism in the American States," *American Journal of Political Science* 31 (November 1987): 980–1,001.

[28]Robert S. Erikson, Norman Luttbeg, and Kent L. Tedin, *American Public Opinion: Its Origins, Content, and Impact,* 5th ed. (New York: Random House Publishers, 1997), 332.

[29]Dick Morris, *Behind the Oval Office* (New York: Random House Publishers, 1997), 84.

[30]Katie Dunn Tenpas, "Words and Deeds: President George W. Bush and Polling," *Brookings Review* (Summer 2003), http://www.brookings.edu/press/review/summer2003/tenpas.htm (accessed December 4, 2003).

[31]*The Literary Digest,* a popular monthly magazine, mailed thousands of ballots to people on lists of automobile owners and in telephone directories in an effort to predict the outcome of presidential elections starting in 1924. Its surveys correctly predicted the winner until 1936, when the *Digest* forecast a huge victory for Alf Landon. Roosevelt won by a landslide. What went wrong? The *Digest* mailed 10 million ballots and received 2 million back. The problem was that automobile owners and telephone listings did not reflect the electorate in 1936 during the Great Depression. The sample was unrepresentative. The *Digest* subsequently went out of business, but Gallup and other pollsters continued to poll, refined their techniques, and mostly have been able to determine American public opinion at a certain point in time.

[32]"Topics and Trends: Guns," Gallup Poll, April 2005 (accessed June 1, 2005).

[33]David W. Moore, "Government an Immediate Threat? Question Wording Makes a Difference," Gallup Poll, September 16, 2003, http://www.gallup.com.

[34]Pew Research Center for the People and the Press: "Public's News Habits Little Changed by September 11," http://people-press.org/reports/display.php3?ReportID=156, and "Beyond Red vs. Blue: Republicans Divided about Role of Government—Democrats by Social and Personal Values," May 10, 2005, question 8 from poll conducted December 2004, Part I.

[35]Pew Research Center for the People and the Press, *Deconstructing Distrust: How Americans View Government,* 1998, 86.

[36]The relationship between income and information can be attributed partly to the demands of a professional or business life, which require people to be aware of what is going on in the political arena. The relationship may also be because of people's efforts to protect their income or profession from those who might threaten it. In addition, education and income tend to be associated with each other. Better-educated people generally make more money, and those who make more money tend to be better educated.

[37]Pew Research Center for the People and the Press, *Younger Americans and Women Less Informed,* 1996, 7.

[38]Pew Research Center for the People and the Press, *Trends 2005: Media, More Voice, Less Credibility,* 2005.

[39]James N. Rosenau, ed., *Public Opinion and Foreign Policy* (New York: Random House Publishers, 1961), 34–35.

[40]See Herbert McClosky, "Consensus and Ideology," 363; and Herbert McClosky and Alida Brill, *Dimensions of Tolerance,* 239.

[41]The American National Election Study Guide to Public Opinion and Electoral Behavior, 2004. http://www.umich.edu/~nes/nesguide/toptable/tab6b_2,3,4, and5.

[42]Brady, Verba, and Schlozman, "Beyond SES: A Resource Model of Political Participation."

[43]Sidney Verba, Kay Lehman Schlozman, and Henry E. Brady, *Voice and Equality: Civic Voluntarism in American Politics* (Cambridge, Mass.: Harvard University Press, 1955), 186–268.

[44]Katie Dunn Tenpas, "Words and Deeds."

[45]"Topics and Trends: Iraq," Gallup Poll, http://www.gallup.com (accessed November 12, 2003).

[46]A poll conducted in November 2003 by the Center on Policy Attitudes and the Center for International and Security Studies at the University of Maryland found most Americans doubtful that the Bush administration had acted on the basis of correct assumptions about the threat posed by the government of Saddam Hussein to the security of the United States and the international community, particularly countries in the Middle East. A Gallup poll ("Trends and Trends: Iraq") revealed that, in October 2003, 50 percent of the population disapproved of the way the United States has handled the situation in Iraq since the major fighting ended.

[47]"Majority Believes U.S. Acted on Incorrect Assumptions in Rush to War," Center on Policy Attitudes and the Center for International and Security Studies at the University of Maryland, press release, November 13, 2003, http://www.pipa.org/OnlineReports/Iraq/IraqReeval_Nov03/IraqReeval%20Nov03%20pr.pd (accessed November 13, 2003).

[48]"Trends and Trends: Iraq," Gallup Poll.

6

Political Interest Groups

Introduction

Over the last half-century, Congress has reacted to gun violence by enacting laws that curb the right to purchase firearms. The Gun Control Act of 1968, written in the wake of the assassinations of Robert F. Kennedy and Martin Luther King Jr., makes it illegal for convicted felons, noncitizens, mentally ill individuals, and people under the age of eighteen to buy or possess firearms. Retailers cannot sell firearms without registering the sale with an agency of the federal government. Furthermore, the law prohibits the sale of some types of nonsporting guns, including automatic machine guns, to the public.

Despite the intent of the 1968 legislation—to reduce the rate of violent crime in which firearms are used—crimes involving guns have increased. Although states passed additional measures to control the ownership and use of guns, the federal government did not do so until the attempted assassination of President Ronald Reagan and the serious injury sustained by his press secretary, Jim Brady, refocused attention and generated pressure for greater limits to be put on gun purchases. Brady's wife, Sarah, organized a group that

Children checking out guns at the Annual National Rifle Association Meeting in Orlando, Fla. April 27, 2003.

"works to reform the gun industry and educate the public about gun violence through litigation and grassroots mobilization."[1] In 1993, after a lengthy public relations and lobbying campaign, her efforts were finally successful. Congress enacted the so-called Brady Bill, which banned the commercial sale of all types of handguns to people under the age of twenty-one and required retail sellers to obtain background checks for all gun purchasers.

However, opponents of the new law, notably the National Rifle Association (NRA), quickly realized that there was a way around the restrictions. Although the legislation applies to gun sellers who are federally licensed, it does not prevent private gun owners from selling their collections to whomever they wish. Because many people buy and sell weapons at gun shows, the NRA alerted those interested in buying and selling firearms that private sales were not subject to background checks.

Believing that the Brady Bill and other federal regulatory efforts violate the Second Amendment (see Appendix B), the NRA has mounted a continuing lobbying campaign to deter Congress from enacting any law that infringes on the people's rights to keep and bear arms. It issues legislative and political alerts to its 4 million members, sponsors speakers and conferences, publishes a monthly newsletter, and maintains an up-to-the-minute website that responds to criticism by gun control advocates and their sympathizers. The organization has also become heavily involved in election activities and keeps in close touch with its "friends" in Congress, primarily but not exclusively Republicans. According to one liberal Democratic member of Congress, Barney Frank (D-Massachusetts), "The NRA does the best job of any group in lobbying members. They don't have marches, they don't have demonstrations, they don't shoot their guns in the air. It's just good, straight democracy."[2]

In the face of the NRA's success in deterring Congress from passing additional gun control legislation, the Brady campaign and other gun control groups have tried to keep the issue alive. They have sponsored a Million Mom March, are involved in election campaigns, and lobby their "friends" on Capitol Hill to close the loophole in gun purchases, expand the national registry in which people prohibited from purchasing firearms are listed, and extend the ban on assault weapons that expired in 2004. They have also supported legislation that would make gun manufacturers liable for lawsuits by victims of gun violence and their families. But they have not been successful. In fact, the NRA helped convince Congress in 2005 to enact legislation that specifically exempts gun manufacturers from civil liability in lawsuits stemming from the use of their weapons.

The political struggle between the proponents and the opponents of gun control pits groups of people with strong feelings against one another, but it does so within the framework of the democratic system. This group struggle illustrates democracy at work, but it has also made the politics of democracy more contentious. The struggle has encouraged participation in the political process, an indication of the vitality of the democratic character of the political system, but it has also given advantage to groups with more members, greater resources, and more effective leadership, thereby giving credence to the perception, held by many, that America's is a government of, by, and for the special interests.

Is it? Does the group struggle invigorate the democratic process for the benefit of the entire society, or does it direct those benefits toward the rich and powerful? Does it provide opportunities for all or advantages for a few? This chapter will try to answer these questions. It will do so by addressing the political dimensions of the group struggle: the composition of groups, the functions they serve, the methods they use, the ways in which they affect the electoral and governing processes, and the policies that result from their activities. It will also address the inevitability of the clash between the pursuit of self-interest and the desire to promote the public good. To begin, however, we ask you to think about the following questions.

Questions to Ponder

- Does the pursuit of self-interest by groups reflect and reinforce the principle of liberty? Does it also undercut political equality? Does the overall effect that groups have on and in policy processes benefit or hurt the society?
- Was James Madison right when he warned in *The Federalist,* No. 10, about the evils of factions and the need to prevent any one of them from controlling the government?
- Do interest groups, such as the NRA and Handgun Control, Inc., facilitate or impede the operation of the political system and the functioning of government?
- Should the activities of interest groups in elections and government be regulated? Can they be regulated without violating the First Amendment to the Constitution?

6.1 In Theory . . .
Interest Groups

The ebb and flow of interest group activity is another aspect of the politics of American democracy at work. This activity occurs within a political system that encourages people to organize to pursue their objectives, protects them when they do so, and rewards those who are able to do so most effectively.

Political interest groups add to the politics of American democracy by increasing public awareness, providing an outlet for public expression, and encouraging participation in the political process. In this way they energize the political system, extend democracy, and channel self-interested behavior into legitimate and productive political activity. The civic activities in which groups engage contribute to the country's social cohesion.

But group activity can also weaken democracy if the competition among groups is uneven—that is, if certain groups become dominant because of their size, status, access to policymakers, or skill at influencing them.

Domination by political interest groups is precisely what James Madison warned of in *The Federalist*, No. 10. He argued that people naturally join together to pursue common interests. They form *factions* (Madison's term for political interest groups), which have the potential to influence government decisions on public policy. The danger, according to Madison, was that a faction would be able to dominate decision making because of its size, resources, or leadership. To prevent such domination from occurring, the framers of the Constitution divided power between the national government and the states, as well as within the national government itself.

Madison praised this division of powers as infinitely better than a direct democracy, in which a majority faction could more easily gain control of government and thereby shape public policy to further its own interests rather than those of the whole society. As long as the government remained a republic, based directly or indirectly on the consent of the governed, Madison believed that it would serve the interests of all people, not just the few or even the many.

Americans value their right to join groups. They point to freedom of association as an important constitutionally protected right. Political interest groups add a dimension to representation, but they can also detract from representation, depending on how well they reflect the interests and needs of the general public. Similarly, they can make governing easier or more difficult, depending on how well their interests and needs are transformed into policies.

The group struggle is a continuous one; it extends from the electoral arena to the governing arena and to the public policy that government formulates, implements, and adjudicates. The effect that this policy has on society in turn fuels and refuels the group struggle.

The openness of the American political system to outside interests is consistent with democracy; the advantages certain groups have and the benefits they receive may not be, however. Therein lies the dilemma of interest group politics for a democracy.

Individuals, Groups, and Society

People join and participate in groups throughout their lives. The family is the first and most basic social unit. As people grow older, they associate with others because of where they live, what they believe, and what they like to do. Neighborhood, religious, and recreational groups form the basis of these early associations.

By providing a sense of community and security, groups contribute to a person's social identity and self-enhancement. They help people reinforce their values, clarify their goals, and identify their achievements. Belonging to a group can be a source of economic benefit. Labor unions, business groups, and professional associations regularly seek to promote the financial interests of their members. Examples include the American Federation of Labor and Congress of Industrial Organizations (AFL-CIO), the U.S. Chamber of Commerce, and the National Education Association. But groups also promote noneconomic interests, such as the environment (Sierra Club), religious or ethical values (Christian Coalition), ideological beliefs (American Civil Liberties Union), or the welfare of particular groups of people (National Gay Rights Organization).

To achieve their objectives, groups have to become involved in the political and governing processes. Those that do so are referred to as **political interest groups.** They have three primary characteristics: (1) shared interests and goals, (2) an organizational structure, and (3) a desire to influence public policy.

If a group does not become involved in the political process to influence public policy, it is not a political interest group. A local bridge club, for example, is not a political interest group, whereas the American Farm Bureau Federation, the Teamsters Union, and the Family Research Council are. Institutions such as universities and corporations also become involved in political activities and are often referred to as organized interests. They, too, band together in pursuit of their common objectives.

Political interest groups differ from political parties in several ways. First, they tend to have a narrower membership base than parties, especially the major parties—the Democrats and the Republicans. In addition, political interest groups are more focused on policy issues than are political parties, which are concerned primarily with elections and, if their candidates are successful, with the organization and operation of government. Whereas parties take positions on a range of issues, most political interest groups direct their political involvement to matters directly related to their interests. The NRA is concerned with the possession of firearms but not with farm subsidies, taxes, or abortion. The Republican Party, however, has taken strong positions on all four issues.

In many ways, political interest groups supplement the role of political parties in the political process by representing and promoting interests on a range of public policy issues. Political interest groups broaden and strengthen the ties between representatives and their constituents. However, they also heighten and extend political struggles. Many diverse, overlapping, and conflicting groups compete for access and influence within government, within the parties, within the electorate, and increasingly, within the electoral arena.

Interest group formation is not a uniquely American phenomenon; in most democratic societies, interest groups supplement political parties in making

political interest groups
Organized groups of people with shared interests and goals who seek to influence public policy.

demands on government. However, the nature of the groups varies. The United States has a pluralistic system in which a variety of groups such as business, labor, and professional associations and ethnic, racial, and religious organizations flourish and compete with political parties for influence. In Germany and some of the countries of northern Europe, interest groups are comparatively larger and more centralized than they are in the United States and often work with political parties to affect government decision making.[3]

Regardless of how groups are organized, they struggle with one another to gain and exercise influence over politics and policy. Some people believe that this competition is beneficial to a democratic society, that interest groups perform a useful, necessary, and natural function. Others are not so sure, fearing that groups promote their own interests at the public's expense. The automobile industry's objections to strict auto emissions standards, the NRA's campaign to protect and promote gun ownership, and the Tobacco Institute's attempt to limit its liability for smoking-related illnesses are three illustrations of interest group positions and activities that some would regard as harmful to society even though those policies may benefit the groups that promote them.

The Origins and Evolution of Political Interest Groups

What are the factors that contribute to group formation and involvement in the political process, and how have these factors changed over the years?

Theories of Group Formation

One of the first political scientists to address these questions was David Truman.[4] Writing in the 1950s, Truman postulated that major disturbances within the political environment produce conditions that encourage group activity.[5] He reasoned that people whose interests are adversely affected by these conditions will band together to improve their lot. In the process, he suggested, their group activities may be directed at the government for help in addressing the problem that sparked their initial involvement.

Truman went on to argue that the creation of political interest groups spurs others to organize to promote their interests. The process of competitive mobilization that is initiated in this way generates additional group formation and activity, until at some point a balance among groups is achieved and the activity stabilizes. The equilibrium lasts until a new group responding to new concerns reactivates the group formation-activity cycle.[6]

Truman's theory assumes the existence of an active and informed citizenry that has the will and the capacity to organize to pursue its interests and redress its grievances. A problem not addressed by this theory, however, is that all people do not have the same will and capability to organize themselves; some have greater incentive to do so than others. The differences in people's incentives led economist Mancur Olson to suggest that the principal reason for joining a group

selective benefits
Economic, social, or political benefits that result from group membership.

is the **selective benefits** that people receive from being members.[7] These may be economic, social, or political benefits that would usually be unavailable to those who did not join the group. Take the American Association of Retired Persons (AARP), for example. In addition to working for the collective good of Americans over the age of fifty, the AARP offers its members benefits such as insurance, mutual funds, credit cards, travel services, and a mail-order pharmaceutical service, plus a newsletter and magazine.

A problem with Olson's theory of selective benefits, however, is that it does not appear to be equally applicable for all types of groups. As might be expected, people who join economic groups tend to be motivated more by direct economic benefits than those who join issue-oriented or ideological groups. Indeed, the incentive for joining a pro-life or pro-choice group is different from the incentive for joining a labor union or being part of a business association.

Another political scientist, Robert Salisbury, used the analogy of the marketplace to explain why some groups prosper and others do not. A group that has a valuable product and is able to promote it, he suggested, will probably be successful in creating and maintaining its organization. Salisbury saw the group's leaders as entrepreneurs who hold the key to this success.[8]

Not only do groups try to influence what the government does, but the government itself stimulates group formation, mobilization, and actions as a consequence of the new legislation and regulations it issues.[9] More than half the groups representing senior citizens were organized after the passage of Medicare legislation and the Older Americans Act in 1965.[10] Similarly, groups promoting civil rights, women's issues, and social diversity were activated by judicial decisions, executive orders, and legislative enactments in those areas. In short, there is a relationship among group formation, government actions, and public policy outcomes.

The Proliferation of Group Activities

The history of group formation also testifies to the effect of communications technologies on mobilization efforts. Take the publicity given to the dissident political movements of the 1960s and 1970s by television news. TV coverage of mass demonstrations provided an impetus for like-minded people to become involved. It also encouraged those upset with the demonstrations or the goals of these groups to dig in their heels and oppose those efforts. The reporting of the civil rights struggles, the protests against the Vietnam War, and the movement for greater equality for women sparked activism by a lot of people, pro and con, people who had previously been content to sit on the sidelines.

Faster and cheaper means of mass communication, first by telephone trunk lines, fax machines, and computerized mailings and later by e-mail and home pages on the Internet, have made it possible for organizations to reach out and broaden their membership, raise more money, promote their issues, and mobilize grassroots support. Moreover, the potential membership base of many public interest, citizen, and consumer advocacy groups has grown greatly over the last fifty years because of the increasing proportion of the population with some college education, who are more likely to see the value of joining and supporting these types of organizations.

© AP/Wide World Photos

Gov. Haley Barbour, second from left, confers with, from right, Camile Young, a Mississippi lobbyist for Northrop Grumman, Jim Schoppenhorst of United Defense, LP, Parsons Corporation, Jeff Bruno of Northrop Grumman, and James Clarke of the Staubach Co., at the Capitol in Jackson, Miss., Friday, Feb. 11, 2005.

A final factor contributing to the expansion of group activity has been changes in the nature and operation of the political system—notably the changes in the political parties' nomination processes, laws regulating campaign contributions and expenditures, and the opening of government to greater public scrutiny. These changes have made candidates for office more eager for interest group support and public officials more sensitive to organized interests and pressures. The proliferation of groups has transformed the politics of American democracy, making it more pluralistic and competitive and forcing government to be more responsive to outside pressures. Washington D.C. has become a city of lobbyists, political consultants, and public relations specialists, employing an estimated 100,000 people, more than 26,000 of whom have registered as lobbyists, a figure that has more than doubled over the last decade.[11] There are so many lobbyists today that they have formed their own association, the American League of Lobbyists, to lobby on behalf of lobbyists.

And a lot of money is spent on lobbying in Washington. A recent report in the *National Journal* listed the twenty-five top Washington, D.C. lobbying firms as earning almost $350 million in 2004, employing almost 800 lobbyists, and representing practically every major U.S. corporation and trade association plus state and local governments.[12]

Politicalmoneyline.com estimates total lobbying expenditures for that year at $2.1 billion. The health care industry alone spent $325.6 million.[13] Moreover, lobbyists were active contributors and fund-raisers for the 2004 federal elections. Lobbying, in short, has become a big business.

Sources of Group Influence

A group's influence varies with its size, composition, and unity, as well as with the popularity of the issue the group is pursuing. Naturally, interests or objectives that lay outside the mainstream of public norms, values, or beliefs—the legalization of narcotics, prohibition of research on animals, or abolition of military forces—are not apt to attract as many supporters as those that appeal to a significant portion of the population. Resources, both human and material, also contribute to a group's ability to exert political clout.

Groups with a large membership base such as AARP, with more than 35 million members, or the American Automobile Association (AAA), with about 44 million members, exert muscle by virtue of their large size. Similarly, labor unions such as the AFL-CIO, business federations such as the U.S. Chamber of Commerce, and groups such as the National Organization for Women also have large membership bases and can be powerful if their members are unified and aroused over the issue. The AARP's opposition to President George W. Bush's proposal to permit workers to put part of their Social Security payroll takes into personal investment accounts is a case in point. When the association launched a $5 million advertising campaign against President George W. Bush's Social Security reforms, members of Congress took notice. Even Republicans became dubious of the merits of the president's proposal when they returned home and heard their constituents voicing the AARP's concerns.

In addition to size, the emotional intensity that the issue generates among members of the group is also important. In fact, to some extent, depth of feeling can compensate for lack of numbers.

Take the NRA's campaign against gun control. As noted in the opening case study, its members feel so strongly about their right to have firearms that they have been able to persuade Congress not to control the sale of guns with the exception of sales to minors and background checks on purchasers despite the fact that a majority of Americans have consistently favored stricter gun control laws.[14]

Emotional intensity raises the salience of issues such as abortion, school prayer, and marriage between same-sex partners. But intensity may also make the problem more difficult to resolve. President Bill Clinton found this out the hard way in 1993, when he raised the question of whether homosexuals who acknowledge their sexual orientation should be permitted to serve in the military. The president proceeded to irritate all principal groups involved by raising but not satisfactorily resolving the issue of gays in the military. President George W. Bush's decision to prohibit government funding for stem cell research also divided rather than unified his partisan supporters.

The geographic distribution of a group's members and their social and professional status can also affect a group's influence. Having sufficient financial resources is critical as well. The more financial resources a group has, the more likely its communications facilities and grassroots lobbying efforts will be state of the art.[15] The AARP, with annual revenues in excess of $520 million, has a website that is constantly updated, a monthly magazine, and legislative alerts that are regularly e-mailed to its members. The U.S. Chamber of Commerce, which regularly collects $90 million just from its largest corporate members, has an operating budget of $150 million. For the first six months of 2004, it spent $30 million on lobbying activities, contributed $4 million to affiliated groups that supported the reelection of President Bush and other Republican candidates, sent 215 political operatives to thirty-one states to mobilize the business community, mailed 3.7 million letters to targeted voters, made 5.6 million telephone calls, and sent 30 million e-mails—all to get out the business-oriented vote.[16]

Another example of wealth contributing to group influence is the pharmaceutical industry. According to *Public Citizen,* one of Ralph Nader's public interest groups, the industry hired 675 lobbyists from 138 firms and spent more than $600 million contributing to candidates, running issue ads, and lobbying public officials in 2002 alone.[17]

Many large political interest groups have both an elected leadership to establish policy and an administrative staff to run the organization. Often, however, the administrative staff, with its professional expertise and day-to-day involvement, assumes de facto policy leadership. For organizations with staffs in Washington, an important source of influence is contacting the right people at the right time in the right place. Washington is full of former members of Congress and former executive branch officials, including senior White House aides, who leave government to represent organized interests in the private sector, a practice referred to as **revolving-door politics.** According to a recent study by Congress Watch, a public interest group, 43 percent of the members of Congress who left that institution between 1988 and 2004 have taken positions as lobbyists. This includes half of the former Republican members and one-third of Democratic members.[18] Members of Congress are not alone in their desire to gain advantage from their government experience. Former top-level Department of Defense officials, both military and civilian, leave government for jobs in the private sector that deal primarily with the department's needs.

revolving-door politics
The practice of moving from the public to private sector and vice versa; individuals tend to work in the areas of their expertise, using their contacts to affect government decision making.

Review Questions

1. Interest group activities and their consequences are most often inconsistent with which of the following basic tenets of a democracy?

   A. Liberty
   B. Equality
   C. Social welfare
   D. Minority rights

continued

2. In *The Federalist,* No. 10, Madison defends the Constitution on the grounds that it would

   A. Prohibit factions from influencing government
   B. Prevent a faction from easily and continually dominating the government
   C. Encourage citizens to form political interest groups and thereby strength the democratic foundation of society
   D. Place factions under the protection of the First Amendment

3. Which of the following has *not* contributed to the expansion of political interest groups in the United States since the 1970s?

   A. Partisan reforms in the nomination process
   B. Campaign finance laws
   C. New communications technology
   D. The end of the Cold War

4. Sources of interest group power include all of the following except

   A. Size of the group
   B. Wealth of the group and willingness to spend it on electoral campaigns
   C. Geographic location of the group
   D. Diversity of the group

Answers:

   1. B
   2. B
   3. D
   4. D

Conflict and Consensus in Review

The group struggle has been part of American politics since the country became independent and its government established. The struggle preceded the development of the party system and has functioned along side of it. Part of the struggle occurs within the parties themselves.

In the contemporary period, however, groups have proliferated and professionalized, and their struggles have increased along social, economic, and political lines. To a large extent, the increase in group activity has been a product of social trends and technological advances. The group struggle emphasizes conflict more than consensus. It does so because the news media considers disagreement more newsworthy than agreement, and because a consensus on the rules of the games facilitates as well as constrains the struggle among groups and the public policy outcome. In that struggle, groups tend to be more effective in articulating and pushing their own interests than they are in identifying and organizing more broad-based social interests, another reason why conflict, not consensus, is seen as the dominant force.

Electoral Activity

How do interest groups influence electoral politics? They do so in three ways: They direct resources in the form of financial, structural, and operational support to candidates and parties; they run parallel candidate and issue campaigns; and they provide a linkage to their members that encourages political activity and reinforces voting decisions.

Political interest groups have become extremely active in political campaigns. Before the 1970s, they channeled most of their electioneering through Democratic and Republican parties at a time when these organizations exercised more control over nominations and election campaigns than they do now. Today, however, election laws encourage interest groups to raise and spend money on their own.

Groups engage in the electoral process not only to elect candidates sympathetic to their interests but also to make sure that they have access them and others in positions of power. Fortune 500 companies, which "invested" heavily in Republican candidates in 2004, were rewarded by the early legislative priorities of the 109th Congress: a bill to make it more difficult for people to declare bankruptcy to avoid paying credit card and other debts and a bill that moves class-action lawsuits from state to federal courts, where the verdicts and financial penalties have been more favorable to businesses. Had the Democrats won, labor unions, trials lawyers, and liberal groups would undoubtedly have seen legislation that supported their policy concerns: an increase in minimum wage, no limits on class-action lawsuits, and greater protections for personal liberties in the war on terrorism.

Federal election law does not allow business organizations and labor unions to make direct contributions to candidates for national office, but it does permit them to form **political action committees (PACs)** composed of their employees, stockholders, or members to raise and spend money to promote issues of importance to them and influence the outcome of elections. PACs can contribute up to $5,000 to individual candidates (except for the major parties' presidential and vice presidential nominees), but they can spend an unlimited amount of money independently in support of or in opposition to particular candidates, as well as engage in educational efforts to inform, mobilize, and register voters. In addition to contributing to federal candidates, PACs can contribute to state and local candidates and to congressional and national party committees, but their principal efforts are aimed at educating and turning out voters.

As expected, there are partisan patterns to PAC giving. Labor PACs contribute overwhelmingly to Democrats, business PACs give more to Republicans, and the contributions of nonconnected groups are more evenly divided. Table 6.1 indicates the twenty PACs that contributed the most money during the 2003–2004 election cycle.

In general, PACs play a more important role in congressional politics than they do in presidential politics. Within Congress, PAC money is more critical for members of the House of Representatives than it is for members of the Senate (even though senators receive more PAC money, it is a smaller percentage of their total funds). At the presidential level, PAC contributions account for a small percentage of the total contributions candidates receive in their quest for

political action committees (PACs)
Groups of employees, stockholders, and others associated on the basis of common beliefs or interests groups involved in election activity; they raise money for and promote specific candidates and issue positions.

Table 6.1 Partisan Dimensions of the Twenty Largest PAC Contributions, 2003–2004

PAC Name	Total Amount	Democrat (%)	Republican (%)
National Assn. of Realtors	$3,787,083	47	52
Laborers Union	$2,684,250	86	14
National Auto Dealers Assn.	$2,603,300	27	73
International Brotherhood of Electrical Workers	$2,369,500	96	4
National Beer Wholesalers Assn.	$2,314,000	24	76
National Assn. of Home Builders	$2,201,500	33	67
Assn. of Trial Lawyers of America	$2,181,499	93	6
United Parcel Service	$2,142,679	28	72
American Medical Assn.	$2,092,425	21	79
United Auto Workers	$2,075,700	98	1
Carpenters & Joiners Union	$2,074,560	74	26
Credit Union National Assn.	$2,065,678	42	58
Service Employees International Union	$1,985,000	85	15
American Bankers Assn.	$1,978,013	36	64
SBC Communications	$1,955,116	35	65
Machinists/Aerospace Workers Union	$1,942,250	99	1
Teamsters Union	$1,917,413	88	11
American Hospital Assn.	$1,769,326	44	56
American Federation of Teachers	$1,717,372	97	3
Wal-Mart Stores	$1,677,000	22	78

Note: Totals include subsidiaries and affiliated PACs, if any. For ease of identification, the names used in this section are those of the organization connected with the PAC, rather than the official PAC name.
Source: Center for Responsive Politics, "Top 20 PAC Contributors to Federal Candidates, 2003–2004," http://www.opensecrets.org/pacs/topacs.asp. Reprinted by permission.

their party's nomination, only about 1 percent. The total PAC contributions in the 2003–2004 election cycle are indicated in Table 6.2. In addition to the $310 million that PACs gave in contributions to candidates for Congress and the presidency, they spent an additional $57.3 million independently for ($48.6 million) and against ($8.7 million) candidates.[19]

One of the most controversial developments in recent years has been the explosion of **issue advocacy groups**, many of them nonprofit, which have spent millions of dollars on advertising and grassroots activities to promote *their* issues and candidates who support them. The sheer volume of these ads and organizational efforts can dominate a political campaign, literally controlling its issue agenda. Under federal law, issue ads cannot endorse or promote a particular candidate directly; they cannot even mention that candidate's name in their

issue advocacy groups
Groups that advocate their own policy positions and support candidates with similar stands on their issues.

Table 6.2 PAC Contributions During the 2003–2004 Election Cycle

Type	No. of PACs	Total (in millions)	President	Senate	House	Republican	Democratic
Corporate	1,402	$115.6	1.6	32.2	81.8	78.6	37.1
Labor	206	52.1	0.2	8.4	43.5	6.6	45.4
Nonconnected	819	52.5	0.7	15.8	35.9	33.9	18.5
Trade/Membership/ Health	722	83.2	0.4	18.0	64.9	52.9	30.3
Cooperative Corporations	34	2.9	0.001	0.5	2.4	1.4	1.4
Without Stock	75	4.2	0.006	1.2	2.9	2.6	1.6
TOTAL	3258	$310.5	3.0	76.1	231.4	176.0	134.3

Source: Federal Election Commission, "PAC Financial Activity, 2003–2004," April 13, 2005.

advertisements 30 days or less before a primary and 60 days or less before the general election. The 2003–2004 election campaign saw an explosion of particular campaign entities known as 527s and 501c groups. These numbers represent the section of the Internal Revenue Code that permits non-profit groups to engage in political activities. In previous election cycles, 527s and 501c groups had not been subject to the federal contribution limits imposed on people who wish to contribute money to the group. As a consequence, these groups can raise large amounts of money from a relatively few wealthy donors. In the 2003–2004 election cycle, financier, George Soros, and insurance executive, Peter Lewis, gave Democratic groups $46.5 million between them to help their party and candidate's campaigns at the presidential level. Republican groups were also active, although they raised and spent less than the Democrats in the 2004 election.[20] (See Chapter 8 for a discussion of this type of campaign spending.)

The increasing involvement of groups in the electoral process has generated considerable criticism, centering on the advantages that economic groups with access to money have in elections and how this access carries over to governing and public policy. Many people believe that public officials make decisions that favor special interests rather than the public interest.[21] A recent survey conducted by the Pew Research Center asked whether the government is run for the benefit of all people. About half of the respondents said "no."[22]

Groups direct their contributions and expenditures not only toward the reelection of incumbents but also toward the reelection of party leaders and the chairs of committees and subcommittees. Interest groups believe that these individuals have the most power to help or hurt them. The more money a candidate receives from a particular group, association, or industry, the more difficult it will be for elected officials to make independent decisions about issues of concern to their benefactors— or so it is alleged by critics of group involvement in the election process.

If all segments of society were equally represented by this group-oriented election activity, the consequences might even out, but they are not equally represented. Corporate and trade association PACs raise and spend more money than do their chief adversaries, organized labor and consumer group PACs.

Although charges of undue influence may be justified, it is difficult to know for certain why legislators make particular decisions. Nevertheless, there is some evidence of a relationship between money and influence. Political scientists Richard L. Hall and Frank W. Wayman studied the participation of members of the House of Representatives on three committees in three issue areas (milk price support, job training, and natural gas deregulation). They found that the more a group had given to committee members, the more time and effort those members devoted to the issues in which that group had an interest. Hall and Wayman concluded that, although election contributions may not buy votes, they do "buy the marginal time, energy, and legislative resources that committee participation requires."[23]

Another controversial aspect of group activity during the electoral process is the effect on political parties. Many political scientists believe that the involvement of PACs and issue advocacy groups hurts parties by siphoning off funds that would otherwise go to them. However, the parties have continued to raise increasing amounts of money, and they benefit from the supplementary spending of groups that have similar interests and support their party's candidates. Besides, the money contributed and spent by interest groups helps finance elections, reducing the burden on taxpayers and the general public; groups provide information that educates voters and encourage people to vote. Moreover, by supporting candidates who are sympathetic to their points of view and are in a position to help them achieve their policy objectives, PACs and interest groups link the public with its representatives—another important objective of democracy.

Review Questions

1. The principal problem with the involvement of interest groups and others in the electoral political process is the public perception that

   A. Groups exercise special influence
   B. Groups provide too much erroneous information
   C. Groups undercut the foundation for political parties
   D. Groups make American society look more divided than it really is

2. Political action committees and other groups influence the electoral process for all but which one of the following reasons?

   A. To help candidates who are sympathetic to their interests get elected
   B. To advocate their own special interests to the electorate
   C. To help set the agenda for the new government
   D. To change public attitudes on politics and government

continued

3. Groups involved in the electoral process at the least can usually expect to gain congressional

   A. Votes
   B. Access
   C. Influence
   D. Social standing

4. Which of the following is the most effective way to exert influence in a political campaign?

   A. Give a lot of money to both parties
   B. Mount an issue advocacy advertising campaign in which certain candidates are named
   C. Formally endorse a candidate
   D. Urge members of group to get-out-to-vote.

Answers:

   1. A
   2. D
   3. B
   4. B

Conflict and Consensus in Review

Nonparty groups have become increasingly active in the electoral arena, an arena that political parties had dominated for most of the nineteenth and twentieth centuries. Reforms in the major parties' nomination processes, new campaign finance legislation, and access to the rapidly changing means of communication have spurred this group activity. The result has been more competition over campaign agendas, candidate appeals, and even organizational structures. Candidates and parties no longer exercise total control over the election and its outcome.

Campaigns reveal the amount of conflict within the body politic. Election results are about conflict resolution. Just about the only consensus in the campaign is that too much money is being raised and spent, that the nonparty groups are exercising too much influence over partisan candidates and issues and are not being held sufficiently accountable for their actions, and that the public perceives that those group expenditures buy influence and favors from the candidates and party they supported.

| Lobbying |

Once an election is over, what can a group do to ensure that its point of view is forcefully presented when issues of concern arise on Capitol Hill or in a state legislature? It can **lobby,** that is, provide information to public officials in an attempt to affect their policy decisions. The term *lobbying* is said to have originated during the Grant administration. President Ulysses S. Grant used to go to the Willard Hotel, located near the White House, after dinner for brandy and

lobby
The practice of influencing public officials in their formulation and execution of public policy.

a cigar. Supplicants, aware of the president's habit, would wait for him in the lobby. The hotel staff referred to these special pleaders as "lobbyists" and the term stuck. Today lobbyists frequent the halls of Congress, executive branch agencies, and whenever possible, the White House in their efforts to make their case to government officials.

Most lobbyists contend that their principal function is to provide public officials with information to use when making policy judgments. Because lobbyists typically deal with the same officials repeatedly, they must take care to ensure that the information they provide is reliable, relevant, and above all, truthful. Their ability to persuade is directly related to their own credibility; if they mislead, either purposely or accidentally, their information and arguments will always be viewed skeptically by those they are trying to influence.

Underlying all lobbying is an implicit promise and threat, however. Help us and we will help you; ignore us and we may ignore you—or, worse yet, mobilize our political supporters against you and your policy positions. This promise and threat are taken seriously by officials, particularly those most vulnerable in the electoral arena.

Types of Lobbying

Lobbying can take many forms: a memo or statement indicating a group's position, a trip by influential constituents to Washington to plead an organization's case, a grassroots campaign in which millions of people participate and millions of dollars are spent.

Lobbyists attempt to influence the policymaking process directly by testifying at public hearings and providing detailed policy statements, briefings, and supporting material to public officials in positions of power. Sometimes they even draft proposed bills or regulations for use by a committee considering legislation or an agency attempting to implement a law. Even when lobbyists do not testify or prepare memoranda detailing their group's position on the issue, they make a point of attending hearings when proposals in which they are interested are being considered and usually follow up on the session by contacting individual members of Congress and their staffs.[24]

Groups also engage in indirect lobbying. They write speeches for their proponents to deliver, and they mount public relations campaigns, using computer technology to target large groups and generate letters and telephone calls from them to public officials.

Direct mail has been a major reason for the financial success of ideological and issue groups since the 1970s, when Richard Viguerie, a conservative direct mailer, put together more than 300 mailing lists with the names of more than 25 million contributors to various conservative causes. Not only were these people likely donors for fund-raising drives, but they also constituted a large number of potential activists for the causes themselves. Computerized telephoning has also been used to achieve these goals; when used for political purposes, such phoning is not subject to "do not call" restrictions. E-mail alerts are also used to activate a group's base of supporters

© AP/Wide World Photos

Cindy Sheehan of Vacaville, Calif., a mother who had lost her son in Iraq, holds two flowers in her hands as she stands in front of the group of tents on the side of a road that leads to President Bush's ranch, Wednesday, Aug. 10, 2005, in Crawford, Texas. Sheehan, 48, wished to speak with the president but he refused to do so. His refusal extended and brought more antiwar protestors to Crawford, Texas to demand an end to U.S. military involvement in Iraq.

and direct their response to the officials responsible for making the policy decision of which the group is interested.

Grassroots campaigns can generate a public response that seems to be spontaneous. Such campaigns are often called **astroturfing,** because they are designed to evoke or magnify a response from the public, one that is larger and more focused than a spontaneous response would probably be. A case in point was the campaign of the American Tort Reform Association to reform liability laws on the state and federal levels. The object of this campaign was to make it more difficult and less profitable for individuals to sue builders, manufacturers, or service providers. To create the impression that there was broad public support for this effort, the Tort Reform Association publicized the community groups, such as little leagues and school boards, that supported their coalition, but not the large manufacturers, insurance companies, and retail chains that actually paid for it and would be its principal beneficiaries. Congress enacted product liability legislation in 1996, but President Clinton vetoed it. Proponents of the legislation, including the American Tort Reform Association, immediately charged that the president was beholden to special interests, in this case trial lawyers who had contributed heavily to his campaign and opposed the limits on monetary awards.[25]

astroturfing
A public relations campaign designed to give the impression of broad grassroots support for a particular issue or candidate.

6.2 Politics in the 21st Century
Internet Advocacy

It started in 1998 when Wes Boyd and his wife, Joan Blades, became impatient with the extended attacks on President Bill Clinton that culminated in his impeachment by the House of Representatives. They wanted Congress to censure the president for his behavior and move on to more important, pressing national issues. To demonstrate support for their goal, they mobilized their friends with an e-mail campaign that alerted them to the couple's new website, Moveon.org. Within days, more than 500,000 people had indicated their personal, and in some cases financial, support for the campaign. More than $13 million dollars was raised in 1999 alone.[26] The movement did not stop the Clinton impeachment, but it did demonstrate the power of Internet advocacy.

Moveon.org has continued to advocate liberal political causes. It has conducted a peace campaign, urging restraint in the use of force following the terrorist attacks. The organization has also mounted a grassroots effort to censor President George W. Bush for misleading Americans about the threat Iraq posed to the United States before the U.S. military action against the regime of Saddam Hussein. It opposed government efforts to ease the restrictions on the ownership regional television, radio, and newspapers.

Economic advocacy groups have also used the Internet to generate public support. Take the case of Citizens for Better Medicare, a group that listed a variety of health care providers and users as its members, but whose activities were funded almost entirely by the pharmaceutical industry. To reach a broad audience, the group, through its website, offered individuals $10 if they would have their grandparents contact the group to receive helpful information about their health benefits. The site provided information, links to other groups of similar persuasions, and various ways in which letters, e-mails, and telephone calls could be initiated to members of Congress from the site. One of the major goals of the group was to promote President Bush's proposal to restructure Medicare and add a privately-insured drug benefit to it. After adverse publicity in which the drug industry's role in the group became public, the Citizens merged their organization into the United Seniors of America (http://www.USAnext.org), a conservative counterweight to the AARP.

For grassroots organizing and advocacy, the Internet has become a cheap, quick, and relatively easy way to reach and engage millions of potential supporters.

Radio is another medium that has been used extensively to generate a public reaction. Conservative talk show hosts and Christian fundamentalist ministers regularly employ this medium to rally support for or against government policies.[27]

Targets of Lobbying

Most Americans tend to equate lobbying with efforts to influence the legislative process. However, any experienced lobbyist knows that legislation is only one activity of the government, and not always the most important one for a particular group on a particular issue. At the national level, the president plays an active role in the legislative process and the executive agencies have a great deal of discretion in the administration of laws. Moreover, the courts have the power to interpret and, in some cases, invalidate laws passed by Congress. At the state level, similar patterns of interaction and spheres of influence are evident. What determines the best place for a group to lobby, and what kinds of activities are most successful in different branches or levels of government?

Legislatures   Sometimes getting legislation passed or defeated is vital to a group's interests. This was the case in 2005, when business groups, such as those in the high-tech industry, banned together to support a bill to establish a Central American Free Trade Agreement, and in 2002, when agriculture groups supported legislation to provide cash subsidies to farmers and thereby reverse Congress's attempt to end these subsidies and move to a free-market system. Congressional action was also required when domestic manufacturers sought protection against foreign competition, when exporters wish to sell advanced technology to other countries, and when public interest groups want to open government deliberations and documents to the public view (through so-called sunshine laws). When the credit card industry sought to make it harder for people to shield their personal assets from bankruptcy proceedings, they, too, turned to the legislative process, as did the pharmaceutical industry during the debate over the costs of prescription drugs.[28]

Legislators are relatively easy to lobby. They are open and accessible; as elected representatives, they have to be sensitive to outside pressures, particularly when those pressures emanate from their districts. Lobbyists can also provide resources that legislators need and want: information about how a particular bill will affect their constituents, political support for the legislation, and financial backing, advertising campaigns, and even grassroots activities in the next election cycle. These benefits open doors for lobbyists in the halls of Congress and state legislatures.

© Time Life Pictures/Getty Images

Capitol Hill hallway crowded with lobbyists during legislating of tax reform.

How successful lobbyists are in getting what they want from legislators is another matter. The main challenge facing those who hope to influence legislative bodies is the relatively large size of most legislatures and the number of people, both members and their staffs, who must be contacted and persuaded. It takes time and costs money.

A second problem, particularly at the national level, stems from the degree of activity, the number of lobbyists, and the diverse perspectives they present. Lobbyists are rarely alone in presenting their position or unified in the advice they give. And they usually encounter opposition from other lobbyists.

The proliferation of lobbying has resulted in coalition building among diverse political interest groups. The formation of alliances in support of and in opposition to the Bush administration's Social Security proposals is a case in point. Groups supportive of the plans—the Business Roundtable, the National Association of Manufacturers, the U.S. Chamber of Commerce, and the Financial Services Forum—formed the Coalition for the Modernization and Protection of Social Security. Their efforts were augmented by several smaller groups: Alliance for Worker Retirement Security, Progress for America, and Woman for a Social Security Choice. On the other side were Americans United to Protect Social Security, a coalition of over 200 interest groups and labor unions.

A third limitation on the ability of lobbyists to get their way is that legislators frequently behave as if they do not owe lobbyists anything. They may use the professional and personal services provided by lobbyists (such as legislative research, political support, financial contributions, electoral endorsements, and grassroots activity) without promising anything in return. They may also accept invitations to participate in and relax at conventions held in plush resorts, with the organization sponsoring the event picking up the tab. Their spouses must pay, however.

Legislators can even pressure firms to change their lobbyists. After the Republicans took control of Congress in the mid-1990s, House Republican leaders adopted a "K Street strategy" to encourage groups to replace their Democratic lobbyists with Republicans.[29] Upon taking office, the administration of George W. Bush pursued a similar strategy for groups and associations that wished to gain access to the executive branch.

The Executive Branch   Chief executives, the president and the state governors, and their administrative agencies have also become a focus of lobbying activities. As in the legislature, lobbying in the executive branch is viewed as legitimate and usually is not discouraged. Indeed, lobbyists and executive branch officials tend to have mutual needs and interests. Whereas interest groups desire access, visibility, and support for their objectives, chief executives and their administrations require political allies to work on their behalf and get the word out and, if necessary, build public support.

Lobbying the lobbyists is not a recent phenomenon. In 1978, the White House set up an office of public liaison to initiate and coordinate group support for the administration's key priorities. This office has also become involved in political activities. The Clinton administration was notorious for using the trappings of the White House to benefit the president's reelection prospects, as well as the Democratic party's campaign coffers. Large donors were invited to dinner parties and coffee hours and given special briefings by cabinet officials. Delegations of American executives were also asked to join the secretary of commerce on trade missions abroad.

The administration of George W. Bush has been more circumspect in its use of government facilities, wanting to avoid allegations of impropriety that plagued the Clinton White House. Nevertheless, Vice President Dick Cheney held a large reception for Republican donors at his home on the grounds of the Naval Observatory, provoking outrage from the Democrats, negative publicity from the news media, and allegations that the Bush administration seemed impervious to the lessons of the past.

In addition to trying to influence policymaking in the executive branch, interest groups try to shape the content and application of rules governing the implementation of public policy. Indeed, executive agencies are required to publish proposed regulations, hold public hearings on them, and solicit reactions from affected and interested groups *before* issuing a regulation. Group representatives are invited to testify at these hearings, provide written comments on proposed rules, and make direct contact with individuals they know in the departments and agencies. Moreover, many lobbyists specializing in executive branch activities have served in the very departments and agencies they seek to influence. They know how the game is played, who the principal players are, and which arguments and information are likely to be most persuasive to decision makers.

Groups may also try to influence the selection of political appointments. For example, public interest groups representing consumers were instrumental in defeating George W. Bush's nomination of Sheila Galt as chairperson of the Consumer Product Safety Commission by publicizing what they contended were her anticonsumer positions and votes when she was a member of the commission.

Nonetheless, legislative lobbying tends to exceed the lobbying that occurs within the executive branch. Public interest groups, especially, focus their efforts on policymaking rather than policy implementation.[30]

The Judiciary Judicial nominations have also been a focus of interest group activity. Although the judicial selection process is often portrayed as nonpolitical, partisan considerations are almost always involved in the nomination and confirmation processes. The vast majority of federal judicial nominees are of the same party as the president. Although most nominations of judges for the lower courts are confirmed by the Senate without much challenge, nominations for appellate courts and the Supreme Court nominees undergo more rigorous scrutiny and sometimes are the subject of extensive public campaigns, initiated by various interest groups, for or against their appointment. During his first term, President George W. Bush was unable to convince the Senate to confirm several of his appellate court nominees even when the Republicans were in the majority. He had more success in his second term, even though his Supreme Court nominees, John Roberts and Samuel Alito Jr., faced a barrage of questions from skeptical senators, primarily Democrats who were reflecting the concerns of their interest group supporters. It is not unusual for groups to lobby the Senate by testifying before the Judiciary

Committee, providing written statements, placing "op-ed" pieces in major newspapers, appearing on news or talk shows, and generating a letter writing, e-mail, and/or telephone campaigns.

Another way for outside groups to influence the judiciary is through the initiation of test cases to challenge the constitutionality of some law or its application. For those who wish to prevent a hostile majority from depriving them of what they consider their basic rights, the courts are a last resort. The National Association for the Advancement of Colored People (NAACP) has effectively used the courts to change public policy; advocates of women's rights have initiated test cases against alleged discrimination; and business groups have regularly gone to court to invalidate government attempts to regulate their operations. In the early part of the twentieth century, business groups successfully challenged state and national laws that limited the hours employees could work and established the minimum wage they could be paid. Today they continue to contest restrictions on how they do business, including regulations on health, safety, and environmental concerns and even personnel practices such as hiring, firing, and promoting.

amicus curiae brief
A "friend of the court" legal argument, submitted in written form by a group or individual who has an interest in the outcome of a case but is not formally a party to the proceedings.

In addition to instituting legal challenges, an interest group may file an **amicus curiae brief,** or "friend of the court" brief. This is a legal argument that a group presents in an effort to influence the decision on a pending case. More than 100 different groups filed briefs with the Supreme Court in 2000 arguing for and against the University of Michigan's affirmative action plan for admission to its undergraduate and law schools.

Efforts to influence the justices through legal arguments have been supplemented by more visible demonstrations of public support. One pro-choice group organized a campaign to send 1 million postcards to the Supreme Court. Both sides on the abortion issue have engaged in extensive and expensive media campaigns, including full-page advertisements in newspapers that the justices were likely to read, such as the *Washington Post* and the *New York Times,* as well as organizing marches on Washington and demonstrations outside the Supreme Court building, frequently on the anniversary of landmark decisions.

Public rallies, private correspondence, and media advertising serve interest groups' needs for visibility and public education (and, indirectly, help them with their own fund-raising efforts), but whether these activities greatly affect Supreme Court decisions is questionable. However, the Court is not oblivious to the outside world. In their 1989 and 1990 opinions stating that burning the American flag is a form of protest protected by the First Amendment to the Constitution, the justices went to great lengths to explain their decisions in anticipation of an adverse public reaction.

Changes in Lobbying and Lobbyists

As American society grows more pluralistic, more groups are seeking to influence government. Lobbying activities have increased many fold, not only in Washington, D.C., but in most state capitals as well. Foreign interests have also found new ways to be represented to influence policymaking and its implementation in the United States.

Before the 1980s, most non-American companies used the commercial sections of their countries' embassies to promote their interests. Although embassies still provide their nationals with diplomatic and consular services, foreign governments and privately-owned businesses and multinational corporations have increasingly turned to American firms to represent them in Washington and the states in matters that affect their industries, workers, or trade interests. And they turn to people with Washington experience, and especially with contacts, to do so: former White House aides, congressional leaders, senior executives, and legislative staff who have moved into the private sector.

The expenditures for this type of lobbying are considerable. Foreign governments and corporations spent more than $150 million for political representation in the United States for the first six months of 2003, according to a study published in the *National Journal*.[31] One large American lobbying firm, Patton Boggs, earned more than $10 million in 2004 for representing the interests of just three relatively small countries, Qatar, Angola, and Saudi Arabia.[32]

Legal changes have affected lobbying as well. "Sunshine laws" mandating that congressional committee meetings and executive agency deliberations be open to the public have forced lobbyists and decision makers to operate in the public spotlight much of the time. New ethics and finance laws have imposed more stringent requirements on public officials who interact with lobbyists, and the news media regularly report lobbying activities, particularly those that may involve improprieties, illicit influence, or economic gain at the public's expense.

There are many other examples of abuses. To cite just one, several years ago a scheme was uncovered in which a grassroots lobbying firm hired to generate opposition to a telecommunications bill that Congress was considering generated letters and telegrams to members from constituents. However, in some cases the constituents had no knowledge of communications that they allegedly sent. One member of Congress received a letter from himself, or at least from a constituent with the same name as his but a bogus address. Another representative received a letter from a dead constituent; the next day he received another letter from the same (apparently persistent) deceased person.[33]

In another highly publicized case in 2004, a senior Defense Department employee in charge of purchasing for the Air Force negotiated a deal to lease refueling jets from the Boeing Corporation for $30 billion. After the contract was completed, the official resigned her government position to accept a well-paid job at Boeing, an obvious conflict of interest. Pressure from members of Congress on the Armed Services committees forced the Air Force to cancel the contract. The official who negotiated it went to jail.

The most serious lobbying infraction of recent years has concerned lobbyist Jack Abramoff and his associates who funneled thousands of dollars to congressional campaigns; provided all-expense trips for members of Congress to resorts around the country and abroad; and free dinners, skybox tickets at sporting events, and jobs for congressional spouses and former staffers, all allegedly in exchange for legislative favors.[34] These favors included the introduction of legislation, amendments, and earmarks to existing authorization and appropriation bills; speeches on the floor of Congress and insertions into the congressional record;

Jack Abramoff, foreground, leaves Federal Court in Washington Tuesday, Jan. 3, 2006 after a plea bargain in which he plead guilty to charges of conspiracy, tax evasion, and mail fraud. Abramoff promised to cooperate with prosecutors investigating illegal influence peddling on Capitol Hill and in the Executive Branch.

and the exercise of informal influence within congressional committees. Congress reacted to the scandal by proposing more restrict lobbying legislation while the Justice Department investigated possible criminal prosecutions against those members of Congress caught in the web of Abramoff's wheeling and dealing.

Regulation of Lobbying

Some activities are obviously illegal—kickbacks and bribes, for example. Other actions may be legal but unethical—using the perquisites of the office (such as invitations to the White House, trips on *Air Force One,* offers to play golf with the president) to raise campaign funds. The biggest problem with lobbying, however, is not the illegal or unethical activities but the perception that certain groups exercise disproportionate influence because of their superior resources. Whether true or not, this perception is damaging to democracy because it leads to a loss of trust and confidence in government, greater anger among some people and apathy among others, and growing cynicism that can undercut the legitimacy of the system and the policies it formulates. What can be done?

The act of lobbying is protected by the Constitution, but lobbyists can still be required to register and file a financial report. However, Congress's first attempt to do so was a failure. The law, enacted in 1946, was immediately subject to legal challenge. Although the Supreme Court upheld the law, it interpreted its registration requirements narrowly. As a result, few people actually registered as lobbyists.

In 1995, Congress tightened the registration and reporting requirements and broadened the definition of lobbying beyond simply contact with government officials. The new law also included the preparation of information to influence those officials as a component of lobbying and, therefore, reportable. Today, people who spend at least 20 percent of their time lobbying members of Congress, their staffs, and executive branch officials are required to register and report the identity of their clients, the issues on which they were involved, and the amount of money they were paid for their services.

The lobbying law also precludes members of Congress and presidential appointees from accepting gifts or even free meals from lobbyists. (Receptions with "finger food," however, are legal). But as the old saying goes, where there is a will, there is a way, and lobbyists have designed legal ways to circumvent this rule. They have created and funded nonprofit, educational groups whose only function is to sponsor and pay for travel. From 2000 to the middle of 2005, members of Congress, their families, and their staffs took more than 5,900 privately funded trips at a cost of $17.6 million. These have included trips to the Napa Valley in California to learn about the wine industry, to Germany and other countries in western Europe to learn about DaimlerChrysler and the European automobile industry, and to Scotland to learn about—you guess. The lobbyists who paid for these trips went as well. Although members of Congress are permitted to attend educational seminars and trips hosted by nonprofit, educational groups—such as the Aspen Institute, Brookings Institution, and Harvard University—these institutions do not permit their own lobbyists to attend.[35]

Lobbyists not only find ways to interact with government officials but also, as we have noted, hire them once they leave office. Legislation that sets ethical standards for members of Congress and the executive branch does little to discourage revolving-door politics, although it does prevent executive branch officials from working on an issue in the private sector that they have worked on in government. Nor can they contact their former associates in the office in which they worked for one year. Initially, President Clinton extended this ban on personal contacts to five years, but after complaints by his own staff, he retreated to the one-year rule.

Are such restrictions necessary? Some people argue that they are because the careers of many public officials begin and end in the private sector. Thus, it is necessary to reduce the temptation for private gain at public expense. Others, however, fear that the requirements for financial disclosure and the limits placed on private employment after government service, when combined with relatively low salaries in government compared with those in the private sector, may keep some of the best-qualified people out of government. The loss of privacy and the constraints on behavior that come from intense media scrutiny also make public service at the top echelons of government less attractive for many people.

| Consequences of the Group Struggle |

What are the consequences of the American system of interest group representation? Does it have an effect on national policy? Does it diminish government's ability to pursue nationwide policies and long-term interests and instead favor those with narrower, more immediate, and direct appeal? Does it allow certain groups to dominate the policymaking process?

When resources are limited, it is almost inevitable that some people will benefit more than others. In 1960, E. E. Schattschneider suggested that the beneficiaries of the struggle among political interest groups are the people in higher socioeconomic brackets, those with the most money, the best organizations, and the greatest influence.[36] More than four decades later, there are many more organized interests, but the system still favors the haves in the sense that it is resistant to large-scale policy change. Moreover, corporations, educational institutions, and local governments still outnumber public interest and consumer groups and have a larger and more pronounced presence in Washington. They have more resources to hire high-powered lawyers, lobbyists, and public relations firms, which they believe give them greater ability to influence policymakers' decisions.

The effectiveness of political interest groups in actually affecting policy outcomes partly depends on how much competition there is among groups within a particular policy sphere. In general, if there is little competition, an interest group seeking change will be more likely to get what it wants than if there is much competition among groups with comparable resources. A good example of a noncompetitive situation is **pork-barrel legislation,** such as farm subsidies, grants for medical research, public works projects, or corporation tax credits, in which the benefits are concentrated but the costs are widely dispersed. (See Chapter 14, pages 536–537, for a description for distributive policy.) In such a situation, those who stand to gain a lot from creation of the programs or lose a lot from their elimination have much more incentive to organize and try to influence policy than do those who will pay or save a relatively small amount as a result of the change.

pork-barrel legislation
Legislation that contains public works and other projects that provide specific benefits for congressional constituencies.

But if there is competition among groups, such as between environmental and industry groups over automobile emissions or water purification standards or among motorists, truckers, and insurance companies over highway speed limits, there may be a standoff until the competitors can make a deal (as in the case of the 2003 Medicare bill) or until one side wins (as in the case of removing the national speed limit of fifty-five miles per hour on interstate highways). In general, the American system puts the burden on those who wish to change a policy, not on those who wish to maintain it. Change is possible, but it usually occurs in small increments.

In short, organized interests try to influence what government does, but their influence may be offset or deflected by other interests, the public mood, or skilled political leadership. Thus, political interest groups do not usually dictate policy, but they certainly influence it, especially in a government system designed to respond to public pressures.

Review Questions

1. In recent years the amount of lobbying in Washington has

    A. Increased
    B. Decrease
    C. Remained about the same
    D. There is no record kept of Washington lobbying

2. Which of the following legislative lobbying activities is illegal today?

    A. Lobbyists making political donations to a member's reelection campaign and then asking to see the member
    B. Lobbyists inviting members to join them on an all-expense paid visit to the Augusta National Golf Course during the PGA tournament to discuss items of common interest
    C. Lobbyists donating $1 million to a member's favorite charity and then asking that member to consider a client's position on pending legislation
    D. Lobbyists offering to get their sympathizers to vote for a member's pet bill if that member will vote "right" on legislation that the lobbyist favors

3. What are the restrictions placed on revolving-door lobbyists in the executive branch?

    A. They have to be partisans of the party and have contributed to an official's election or reelection
    B. They cannot ever lobby officials in their former office
    C. They cannot ever lobby on an issue on which they worked in government
    D. They cannot lobby an official of the government with whom they are having an illicit affair

4. Which one of the following would not be considered an effective form of judicial lobbying?

    A. Providing public support for or against a judicial nominee on the basis of that nominee's past statement and judicial decisions
    B. Filing an amicus curiae brief
    C. Generating a letter-writing campaign to the Supreme Court
    D. Planting an article on a issue currently before the Court in a law journal that the justices and their clerks read

Answers:

1. A
2. B
3. C
4. C

Conflict and Consensus in Review

Interest group politics is all about conflict over costs and benefits, values and beliefs, and philosophies and ideologies. The conflict occurs within the political arena as groups attempt to influence government decisions on public policy. There is a consensus that such activities are natural and necessary in a democratic political system and that they are protected by the First

continued

Amendment of the Constitution so long as they do not violate federal or state laws. But Americans also believe that special interests exercise disproportionate influence, particularly over legislatures, and thereby gain their goals at the expense of society at large. This perception of unfairness increases criticism of government, reduces the trust people place in it, and may ultimately undermine the legitimacy of that government in the eyes of those who see themselves disadvantaged time and time again.

Politics in Action

The Struggle Between the Forces of Energy and the Environment

Americans desire plentiful sources of cheap energy, but they also care about the environment. Since the 1970s, these concerns and the interests that support them have continually clashed, and today they are doing so again. On one side is the energy industry: the companies that extract, refine, and sell fossil-based fuel such as oil, gas, and coal; the companies that build and maintain hydroelectric and nuclear power plants and sell the energy that those plants produce; the unions that represent their blue-collar employees; and their consumers—the electric industry, mass transportation, home heating companies, and the general public, particularly automobile drivers. On the other side are environmental interests represented by such groups as the Sierra Club, the National Wildlife Federation, the Environmental Defense Fund, Greenpeace, and Earth First. Their allies include environmental officials from state and local governments and concerned members of the scientific community and the general public.

In their battles over legislation to establish environmental standards and regulations to implement them, each side has developed a strategy for achieving its policy objectives. Each has worked with its own allies on Capitol Hill and in the executive branch. Each has tried to mobilize public support. And each has been involved in electoral politics.

For years the energy industry was blessed with abundant resources and minimum regulations. However, as the country became more concerned with the effect of energy development and usage on the environment, government became more involved. The first comprehensive environmental legislation was enacted during the administration of Richard Nixon, and the Environmental Protection Agency (EPA) was created at that time. The EPA was responsible for issuing regulations, monitoring activities, and prosecuting violators. But concern about energy usage and its effect on the environment continued.

With the election of Republican Ronald Reagan, however, the clout of environmental interests began to decrease. The Reagan administration, more sympathetic to the concerns of the business community, desired fewer government regulations and weaker enforcement of them. As a consequence, the EPA was forced to relax its aggressive enforcement of environmental regulations. For its part, Congress resisted new and more far-reaching environmental legislation.

The battle between energy producers and environment forces has continued into the 1990s and the Twenty-First Century. In 1990, the administration of President George H. W. Bush and the Democratic Congress reached an accommodation for tighter controls on utilities that burned soft coal and for tougher auto emission standards. Environmentalists did not think the legislation went far enough; the energy industry, particularly automobile manufacturers and businesses that burned soft coal, thought it went too far.

With the 1992 election looming, President George H. W. Bush refused to issue stringent rules for implementing the legislation; his successor, Bill Clinton, tried to do so, but the Republican-controlled Congress had different ideas.

continued

Politics in Action *continued*

Not only did they oppose the higher standards for air and water that the Clinton administration proposed, but they set out to cut the EPA's enforcement budget and reduce its rule-making authority. The president threatened to veto any legislation that weakened the EPA and curtailed its enforcement powers. Congress and the presidency remained at loggerheads. In the final days of his administration, Clinton used his executive powers to issue new and more stringent standards for air and water.

Once he became president, George W. Bush put a temporary hold on the new Clinton rules and subsequently modified those that went into effect. He also supported a national energy strategy designed by Vice President Dick Cheney, but during his first term, Congress was unable to agree on the details of such a strategy and none was legislated. In 2005, Congress enacted energy bill that provided tax incentives to encourage the exploration of new fossil-fuel energy resources and renewable sources of energy. To obtain sufficient support for the proposal, the legislation provides for greater use of ethanol, a product of corn.

But the growing dependence of the U.S. on foreign oil—President Bush called it an addiction in his 2006 State of the Union Address—the sharp rise in energy prices, and the volatility of conditions in the countries that supply much of the world's oil, led the Bush administration to support the development of alternative sources of energy, such as the reprocessing of nuclear fuel and the construction of new nuclear energy plants despite their vulnerability to a terrorist attack. Environmental groups, which had opposed the expansion nuclear energy after the accident at the plant at Three Mile Island in Pennsylvania and the explosion of the Chernobyl nuclear facility in Russia, took a new and more sympathetic look at this source of energy in addition to advocating better conservation and more renewable sources.

The battle between generating sufficient energy and protecting the environment has been a persistent one since the 1970s. It has been fought not only among strong domestic groups but in the international arena as well. The Clinton administration negotiated an international agreement on the environment, known as the Kyoto treaty, but the Bush administration has refused to support it. Nevertheless, more than 100 state and local governments have enacted laws based on the protocol established in the treaty. American companies selling or manufacturing goods for European countries that abide by the new and tougher emission standards have had to comply despite the increased costs of doing so. Is that fair?

What Do You Think?

1. Is the struggle among political interest groups harmful to democratic government?
2. Does the struggle between energy and environmental interests demonstrate that special interests have an advantage? If so, how; if not, why not?
3. How does the international market affect the energy–environmental debate in the United States?
4. Can the world have cheap and abundant energy without damaging its environment in the short or long run? If so, how? (If you think you know the answer to this question, write it out and send it to the president and your congressional representatives. They should be interested in what you have to suggest.)

Summary

We began this chapter by asking whether groups are helpful or harmful to a democracy, whether their activities can be controlled, and whether the advantages that certain groups have because of their size, wealth, or leadership undercut the principal of political equality upon which American democracy is based. Hopefully, we have provided you with enough information to begin to answer these questions.

Interest group politics is the inevitable consequence of a political system based on popular consent, which permits individuals to organize into groups and petition their government for specific policy outcomes. Although political interest groups have existed throughout the nation's history, they have undergone their greatest development since the 1970s. Their rapid expansion has been spurred by the growth of government programs, regulatory activity, and political movements; changes in the political system; and advances in communications technology.

Groups play an active role in elections. They solicit contributions from their members and make donations to candidates. They also engage directly in campaign activities, supporting or opposing particular candidates and advocating specific issues. The amount of money spent by these groups has led some observers to conclude that public officials are bound to be influenced by their electoral activities. Proponents of group involvement in the electoral process, however, respond that groups help finance elections, increase public knowledge of the issues, and encourage voting. Besides, such activity is legal and protected by the Constitution.

Groups are also active in government. They lobby officials in the legislative and executive branches and try to influence the judiciary. They demonstrate the concern of their members, and launch public relations campaigns to broaden their popular support.

In recent years there have been several changes in the nature of lobbying. The amount of lobbying activity in Washington, D.C., and in state capitals has increased dramatically. Before 1920, only one major company, US Steel, maintained a permanent office in the nation's seat of government.

Fifty years later that number had grown to 175; today it exceeds 600. Lobbying expenditures have also mushroomed.

Foreign companies and governments now hire American firms to represent them. The lobbying business has also become more specialized, with law firms being joined by public relations, issues management, and accounting firms. Sunshine laws force lobbyists to conduct more of their work in public view, and new ethics and finance laws and regulations have imposed stringent requirements on public officials who interact with lobbyists or become lobbyists after leaving office. Nonetheless, illegal and unethical activities persist, receive considerable media attention, and contribute to the public perception that America's government is of, by, and for the special interests.

The extent to which political interest groups actually affect policy outcomes is largely determined by the degree of competition among groups in a particular policy area, such as energy and the environment, and by the distribution of benefits and costs among them and the general public. If there is little competition, groups active in the political process are in a better position to get what they want, particularly if costs are distributed widely among the population. If there is competition between groups and the groups represent equally powerful constituencies, the results are not as predictable. The principal democratic issue, however, is not the existence of groups or their involvement in the political arena; rather, it is that they do not equally represent all segments of society. Those with the greatest resources are advantaged.

Nonetheless, political interest groups can strengthen the democratic process by educating people about their civic responsibilities, increasing public awareness, providing an outlet for public expression, and encouraging participation in the political process. However, when certain groups come to dominate decision making, they shape policy in their interests. Herein lies danger if the same interests tend to win most of the time and others tend to lose. Such a result undermines a basic tenet of democracy—political equality.

Key Terms

political interest groups   (PACs)   amicus curiae brief
selective benefits   issue advocacy   pork-barrel legislation
revolving-door politics   lobby
political action committees   astroturfing

Discussion Questions

1. Why has election activity and lobbying for special interests increased so much in the last thirty-five years? How has that increased activity affected the way in which election campaigns are conducted and government makes decisions today?
2. How have lobbying activities affected the type of legislation Congress has enacted in recent years? Do lobbyists influence the behavior of members of Congress? Do they affect the public policy that Congress does or does not enact?
3. What are the most effective ways to lobby the executive branch? What about the courts?
4. Does the activity of special interest groups undermine or contribute to the politics of democratic government in the Untied States?
5. Can the activities of special interest groups be restricted under the U.S. Constitution? Should they be? If so, which activities? If not, why not?

Topics for Debate

Debate each side of the following propositions:

1. Successful lobbying results in the inequitable distribution of costs and benefits and is therefore inconsistent with a democratic process.
2. All lobbyists should be forced to take lie-detector tests to make sure that they are not influencing government officials illegally.
3. Revolving-door politics undercuts the public interest and should be prohibited.
4. In a democratic society, everyone is potentially a special interest lobbyist.
5. Organizations that contribute to candidates, design and air issue ads, and communicate with government officials provide critical services for a democratic electoral process and should be allowed to continue their election activities without restrictions on their contributions or expenditures.

Where on the Web?

American Association of Retired Persons (AARP) **www.aarp.org**

American Federation of Labor and the Congress of Industrial Workers (AFLCIO) **www.aflcio.org**

American League of Lobbyists **www.alldc.org**

Center for Responsive Politics **www.openscrets.org**

Common Cause **www.commoncause.org**

Federal Election Commission **www.fec.gov**

Green Peace **www.greenpeaceusa.org**

Public Citizen **www.citizen.org**

Go to **www.thomsonedu.com/thomsonnow** to learn about a powerful online study tool. You will get a personalized study plan based on your responses to a diagnostic Pre-Test. Once you have mastered the materials with the help of interactive learning tools, activities, timelines, video case studies, simulations, and an integrated E-Book, you can take a Post-Test to confirm you are ready to move to the next chapter.

| Selected Readings |

Baumgartner, Frank R. and Beth L. Leech. *Basic Interests: The Importance of Groups in Politics and in Political Science.* Princeton, NJ: Princeton University Press, 1998.

Berry, Jeffrey M. *The Interest Group Society,* 4th ed. New York: Longman, 2001.

_____. *The New Liberalism: The Rising Power of Citizen Groups.* Washington, D.C.: Brookings Institution, 1999.

The Capital Source, Washington, D.C.: The National Journal (semiannual).

Cigler, Allen, and Burdett A. Loomis, eds. *Interest Group Politics,* 6th ed. Washington, D.C.: Congressional Quarterly, 2002.

Heinz, John P., Edward O. Launmann, Robert L. Nelson, and Robert H. Salisbury. *The Hollow Core: Private Interests in National Policy Making.* Cambridge, Mass.: Harvard University Press, 1997.

Herrnson, Paul, Ronald G. Shaiko, and Clyde Wilcox. *The Interest Group Connection,* 2nd ed. Washington, D.C.: Congressional Quarterly, 2005.

Vogel, David. *Kindred Strangers: The Uneasy Relationship between Politics and Business in America.* Princeton, N.J.: Princeton University Press, 1996.

Walker, Jack L. Jr. *Mobilizing Interest Groups in America: Patrons, Professions, and Social Movements.* Ann Arbor: University of Michigan Press, 1991.

Wright, John R. *Interest Groups and Congress: Lobbying Contributions, and Influence.* New York: Allyn & Bacon, 1996.

| Notes |

[1]Found at http://www.bradycampaign.org/about/mission.asp (accessed December 19, 2003).

[2]Barney Frank as quoted in "Elements of Successful Activism," NRA-ILA, http://www.nraila.org/ActionCenter/GrassRoots-Activism.aspx (accessed December 19, 2003).

[3]For an extended discussion of interest groups and political systems, see Gabriel A. Almond and G. Bingham Powell Jr., *Comparative Politics Today* (New York: HarperCollins Publishers, 1992), 61–73.

[4]Truman's theory was built on the writings of another student of social and political movements, Arthur F. Bentley, who was the first to study group behavior systematically. He wrote about his findings in *The Process of Government* (1908).

[5]David B. Truman, *The Governmental Process* (New York: Alfred A. Knopf, 1960).

[6]Ibid., 97.

[7]Mancur Olson Jr., *The Logic of Collective Action* (New York: Schocken Books, 1968).

[8]Robert H. Salisbury, "An Exchange Theory of Interest Groups," *Midwest Journal of Political Science* 13 (February 1969): 1–32. The resources available to groups are not equal. In another influential study of interest groups, Jack Walker argued that group formation and activity, particularly in contemporary times, are closely tied to the nature of a group's financial base. Start-up funds need to be sufficient to begin the group and support its operations. At least initially, Walker noted, these funds must be obtained from outside the membership base, although over time the membership may be able to sustain itself financially. Jack L. Walker, "The Origins and Maintenance of Interest Groups in America," *American Political Science Review* 77 (June 1983): 390–406.

[9]Mark P. Petracca, "The Rediscovery of Interest Group Politics," in *The Politics of Interests,* ed. Mark P. Petracca (Boulder, Colo.: Westview Press, 1992), 14.

[10]Walker, "The Origins," 403.

[11]Politicalmoneyline.com, July 13, 2005 (accessed February 8, 2006).

[12] Bara Vaida and Lisa Caruso, "Billable Hours," *National Journal*, March 26, 2005, 912–918.

[13] Politicalmoneyline.com, July 13, 2005 (accessed February 8, 2006).

[14] Gallup Poll: "Trends and Topics: Guns." http://www.gallup.com/content/default.aspx?ci+1645 (accessed February 8, 2006).

[15] Jeffrey H. Birnbaum, "A Quiet Revolution in Business Lobbying," *Washington Post*, February 5, 2005, A1, 11.

[16] "Influence, Inc.: Lobbyist Spending in Washington," 2000 ed., Center for Responsive Politics, http://www.opensecrets.org/pubs/lobby00/summary.asp (accessed June 26, 2005).

[17] "Drug Industry Employs 675 Washington Lobbyists, Many with Revolving-Door Connections, New Report Finds," *Public Citizen*, press release, June 23, 2003, http://www.citizen.org/pressroom/release.cfm?ID=1469 (accessed August 12, 2005).

[18] Jeffrey H. Birnbaum, "Hill a Steppingstone to K Street for Some," *Washington Post*, July 27, 2005, A19. These contributions apparently paid off in 2005 when the Justice Department substantially reduced the amount of money that it would request from a judgment against the industry in a landmark civil racketeering case.

[19] "PAC Activity Increases for 2004 Elections," Federal Election Commission, press release, April 13, 2005, http://www.fec.gov/press/press2005/20050412pac/PACFinal2004.html.

[20] Ibid.

[21] "Expecting More Say: A Study of American Public Attitudes on the Role of the Public in Government Decisions," Center on Policy Attitudes, February 9, 1999, 9.

[22] Pew Research Center for the People and the Press: "2004 Political Landscape: Evenly Divided and Increasingly Polarized," November 5, 2003, http://www.people-press.org (accessed December 18, 2003).

[23] Richard L. Hall and Frank W. Wayman, "Buying Time: Moneyed Interests and the Mobilization of Bias in Congressional Committees," *American Political Science Review* 84 (September 1990): 814.

[24] A new business has even been created to help lobbyists perform this task. Because congressional committee rooms have a limited seating capacity and are filled on a first-come, first-served basis, a service now exists to save places in line for busy, high-paid lobbyists. Students are paid by the hour to wait until the committee room opens. Sometimes the lineup for an extremely popular hearing will begin the previous day and involve camping outside the House and Senate office buildings throughout the night until the doors open the next morning.

[25] Trial lawyers have maintained their Democratic sympathies. In the 2003–2004 election cycle, they contributed $86.4 million, 80 percent of which went to Democratic candidates. The American Tort Reform Association and other business groups, however, have continued efforts on behalf of Republican candidates.

[26] Robert J. Klotz, *The Politics of Internet Communication* (Lanham, Md.: Rowman & Littlefield, 2004), 87.

[27] In 1993, the Christian Coalition stimulated 50,000 telephone calls to the White House, ten times their normal volume, to object to President Clinton's plan to permit homosexuals to serve openly in the military. During this campaign, Congress received more than 500,000 letters in a single day.

[28] According to the Center for Responsive Politics, "MBNA, the nation's largest credit card firm, spent $860,000 in the last six months of 1998, $640,000 in the first six months of 1999, and $800,000 in the last six months of 1999. By and large, MBNA's lobbying followed the fortunes of legislation to deregulate the financial services industry and to change bankruptcy laws" (http://www.opensecrets.org/pubs/lobby00/summary.asp [accessed July 23, 2005]).

[29] According to the *Washington Post*, House Majority Whip Tom DeLay suggested to one corporate CEO that if his company wanted to see DeLay, it needed to hire a Republican. David Maraniss and Michael Weisskopf, "Speaker and his Directors Make the Cash Flow Right," *Washington Post*, November 27, 1995, A8.

[30] Scott R. Furlong, "Exploring Interest Group Participation in Executive Policymaking," in *The Interest Group Connection*, eds. Paul S. Herrnson, Ronald G. Shaiko, and Clyde Wilcox, 2nd ed. (Washington, D.C.: Congressional Quarterly, 2004), 291–295.

[31] Robert Gettlin and Bara Vaida, "FARA Tab $157 Million in Early 03," *National Journal* (February 28, 2004): 648.

[32] Vaida and Caruso, "Billable Hours," 918.

[33] See David Segal, "The Tale of the Bogus Telegrams," *Washington Post*, September 28, 1995, A1, A8; and Juliet Eilperin, "Police Track Down Telecom Telegrams," *Roll Call*, August 7, 1995.

[34] Abramoff plead guilty to defrauding Native American tribes, tax evasion, conspiracy to bribe legislators, and inducing congressional staff and executive officials to intercede on issues in which he had an interest.

[35] Jim Drinkard, "Lobbyists Showing Congress the World," *USA Today*, June 22, 2005, A1, A2.

[36] E. E. Schattschneider, *The Semi-Sovereign People: A Realist's View of Democracy* (Hillsdale, Ill.: Dryden Press, 1960), 34–35.

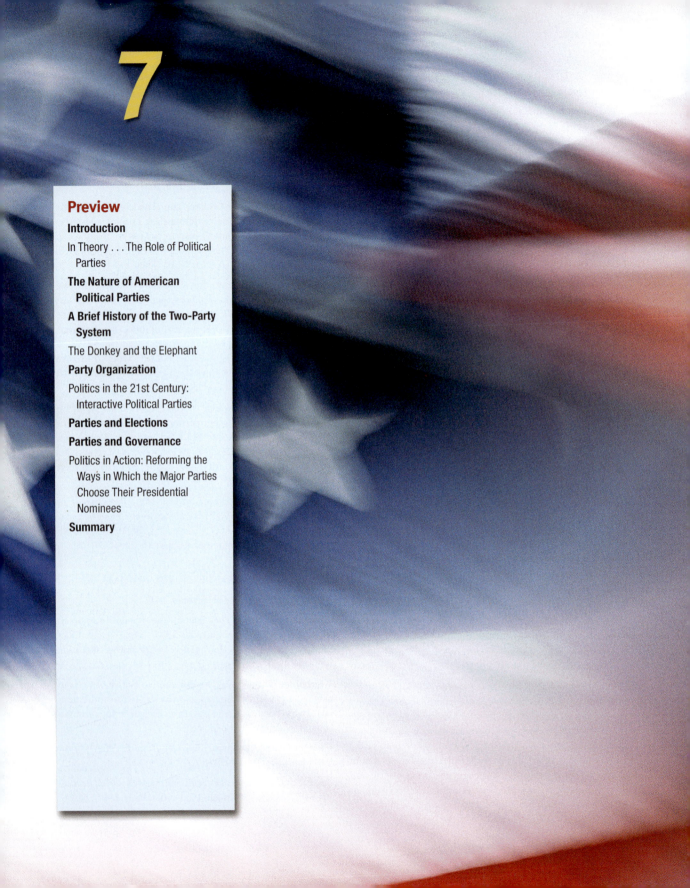

7

Political Parties

Introduction

THEIR BATTLE BEGAN DURING the Reagan years, and it is still being waged today. An army of believers, mostly evangelical Christians, wish to shape social policy on the basis of their faith-oriented values. An umbrella group known as the Christian Coalition had been trying, with increasing degrees of success, to gain effective control over state and national Republican Party organizations to recruit its own candidates, highlight its own issues, and promote its own policy agenda. Opposing them, initially, were much of the Republican establishment, the party's moderate wing, and conservatives more concerned with economic and national security matters than moral issues and social policy.

Ronald Reagan was the first Republican president to win the votes of evangelical Christians. Although his programs were oriented toward revitalizing the economy and strengthening the military, he articulated the social values and beliefs of his religious constituency, which overwhelmingly supported him for reelection.

People who considered themselves religious fundamentalists also voted solidly for George H. W. Bush in 1988, but they became increasingly dissatisfied with his administration as it progressed. Although the president stressed family and community values that were important to these religious believers, he did not pursue them as diligently as his predecessor had. In 1992, this dissatisfaction manifested itself in the electoral support that Pat Buchanan, a Roman Catholic, received from "born-again" Christians in his challenge to Bush for the Republican nomination, in the debate over the Republican platform at the party's convention, and in the substantial decline in the religious right's vote for Bush in the 1992 election.

By 1993, Christian fundamentalists who were active in two-party politics had a new political opponent, Bill Clinton, a president who was hostile to much of their policy agenda and whose secular and pragmatic views, not to mention his personal behavior, were antithetical to many of their beliefs, values, and norms of behavior. Fueled by talk radio, church sermons, and a well-organized, well-organized and funded public relations campaign, groups such as the 1.7-million–member Christian Coalition grew increasingly influential in state and national Republican politics. The group mobilized millions of its adherents in get-out-the-vote campaigns. The Christian Coalition's political activities were a critical factor in the Republicans' winning control of Congress in the 1994 election.[1]

The coalition has continued to back Republican candidates. Its support for President George W. Bush, who himself advocated the positions of the Christian right on such issues as abortion, school prayer, and homosexuality has remained strong, but it also has caused divisions within the Republican Party on other issues, such as stem cell research, prayer and the teaching of evolution in public schools, and judicial nominations.

The strains within the Republican Party between the Christian right and the Republican establishment are characteristic of internal divisions that have plagued the major parties in the United States since they were organized. Over the last three decades, the Democrats have also had their share of internal strife. So-called hawks and doves fought over America's involvement in the Vietnam War and have continued to differ over the use of the military in foreign policy. African American and Hispanic minorities have disagreed with the party's white rank and file over the government's role in ensuring civil rights and providing social welfare. The national Democratic Party's adoption of policies that appealed to these minority groups eventually led to the defection of southern whites from the party and the declining electoral support from white voters. More recently, labor and commercial interests within the Democratic Party have split over the desirability of free trade, liberals and moderates over eligibility and work requirements for welfare, and environmentalists and commuters over highway construction.

These internal divisions are not surprising in a large and diverse country such as the United States, but a country that has a dominant two-party system. How could those parties have survived for so long if they had not appealed to a range of interests? However, their internal diversity, which is an explanation for their longevity and a source of strength, is also a source of weakness when it produces differing priorities, competing goals, and candidates whose beliefs vary across a range of policy issues. Although internal divisions within the parties continue to exist on some issues, conflict between the major parties has taken on an ideological coloration with the Democrats more liberal and the Republicans more conservative.

So, as with other aspects of the American political system, conflict and consensus characterize American political parties today. We explore this conflict and consensus in this chapter by examining the relationship between parties and democratic politics. The chapter begins by noting the roles parties play in the political system. After describing the nature of parties and their functions, the chapter traces the evolution of American political parties from just after the founding of the Republic to contemporary times. In doing so, it examines the shifting components of each major party's electoral coalitions, its principal interests, and the tensions that diverse views have created within and between the parties. We then turn to the structure of the major parties and their primary arenas of political activity: elections and government.

Questions to Ponder

- Can two major parties effectively represent the interests and opinions of a country as large and diverse as the United States?
- Can they do so if they become more ideologically distinct from each other?
- Can moderates be effectively represented if both Republican and Democratic parties are increasingly responsive to their most active, ideological supporters?
- Why have third parties played such a minor role in American politics? Are they likely to fill the schism between Republican and Democrats today?
- Are political parties necessary for representative government? Do they contribute to or detract from the politics of American democracy?

Political parties are essential to democracy. They connect people with government by orienting and organizing the electorate; by nominating candidates and linking them on the basis of shared values, beliefs, and issue stands; by providing direction and structure for government; and by holding those in government accountable for their actions. These linkages are essential for a democratic political system that operates within a diverse society such as the United States.

Parties provide a mechanism for aggregating diverse interests, articulating them in their platforms and in candidate appeals during campaigns, and helping transform these positions into public policy. They achieve that transformation by providing a collective vision and organization that helps orient their elected and appointed officials to govern: to establish an agenda, to structure the government, and to mobilize internal and external coalitions. Moreover, parties also provide a basis for assessing collective responsibility for the decisions and actions of government.

Not only do the partisan allegiances of public officials provide a criterion by which the public and the electorate can evaluate the performance of those in office, but they also provide a kind of running tally on how well the party represents the public.[2] This accumulated judgment helps voters make informed judgments in the next election.

The Nature of American Political Parties

The roles that **political parties** play in the electorate, elections, and government are used to define their composition and function today. Within the electorate, the parties shape attitudes toward policy and government; during the election, they debate issues and provide a basis of agreement for their candidates; and within the government, they provide organization and give coherence and stability to public policy outcomes. Thus, we define parties as public organizations designed to mobilize people—their partisans and others within the electorate—to support the candidates who run on their label, subscribe to their principal policies, and if successful, pursue these policies once in office.

A political party consists of three interacting groups: professionals, candidates and elected officials, and rank-and-file supporters. The professionals are the smallest of these groups. They are paid workers. The party is their employer: the organization to which loyalty is owed, for which work is performed, and from which compensation is received. That work includes raising money, mobilizing sympathizers, developing positions, projecting images, making appeals, and continuing political traditions. In performing these functions, party professionals compile and maintain lists of supporters, provide a liaison to elected party leaders at all levels of government, coordinate events and on-going party activities, and handle the administrative chores of running a large but decentralized organization.

political parties
Public organizations whose goals are to nominate and elect candidates for office, organize government, and affect public policy.

For members of the second group—the party's candidates for public office and elected officials—the party is a source of funds and services. Simply running as a Republican or a Democrat activates the support of a sizable portion of the electorate, something that running as an independent does not automatically do. Most candidates need that support to win office, and a party needs to have people who are loyal to it, who run on its label and agree with its policies.

Whereas professionals and candidates both carry the party's banner, the rank-and-file **partisans** are more difficult to identify. In the United States people with allegiance to a party rarely carry membership cards or attend political meetings. They may not even vote. In most cases, all they have to do is think of themselves as Republican or Democratic partisans or state that they are if they want to participate in a party's primary election.

The Major Parties

The two major American parties share characteristics that distinguish them from the major parties in other democratic political systems. They are more diversified in composition, are more decentralized in structure, and in the past, were more pragmatic in their approach to policymaking than their counterparts in many European countries. The composition and orientation of American politics have permitted the two-party system to survive, even prosper.

Why has such a diverse country, such as the United States, had only two principal parties for most of its existence? Part of the answer has to do with the federal system of government. The major parties reflect its decentralized structure. Candidates are recruited at the state or local level and are responsive primarily to their own state or local constituencies. At the national level, the major parties consist of representatives of state parties; at the state level, they consist of local party representatives. This state–local orientation affects the policy positions that parties take and the decisions that their elected officials make.

A second reason for the existence of a two-party system in the United States is the structure of the election system. Most public officials in the United States are chosen in a **single-member district.** The victorious candidate in such a system reflects the choice of the plurality of voters. There is no prize for coming in second. Candidates of smaller parties have little chance of winning in this type of electoral system. In contrast, in many European countries, legislators are elected in **multimember districts** in which a number of people are elected in proportion to the vote that they or their parties receive.[3] The Democrats use a proportional electoral system to select their convention delegates in presidential primaries.

A third reason has to do with the tradition of two major parties and their adaptability to changing times. Because the principal parties consist of broad-based coalitions, they have tended to adopt positions that are acceptable to as much of the electorate as possible. A consensus among most of the electorate on basic political values, goals of government, and objectives of public policy has until recently kept the parties in the mainstream of public attitudes and opinions.

Today, however, the major parties are more ideological than they were in the past, a consequence of changes in their nomination processes that began to

---

partisans
People who identify their political allegiances with a political party.

single-member district
A legislative district in which one candidate is elected to represent the people who live within that district; it benefits the candidate of the dominant party in that district.

multimember district
A legislative district in which several people are elected, usually on the basis of the total proportion of the vote they or their party receive; more amenable to minority and third-party representation than a single-member district.

occur in the 1970s. The ideological orientation of contemporary parties has realigned the most ideological voters. Liberals now overwhelmingly identify with the Democrats and conservatives with the Republicans.

But the ideological restructuring of the major parties has also alienated some moderates who cannot identify with the extreme rhetoric or policy stands of either party. Some observers believe that this alienation has contributed to the rise in cynicism and apathy in the body politic.[4] If people find themselves disagreeing with the rhetoric and positions of the political parties, they have greater difficulty identifying with either party, are less likely to participate in campaigns, and are even less likely to vote. Yet voting turnout increased in the 2004 presidential election, an indication of activism not apathy.

The closeness of the vote, greater efforts to bring out the vote, and stronger partisan allegiances are three factors that may have contributed to the increased turnout. Strength of partisanship also contributes to the evaluations of the candidates, parties, and public officials who may be running for reelection. Since 1988 there has been a high correlation between the partisan identity and voting behavior, so much so that many politicians and political scientists claim today that not only are the major parties evenly divided but they are increasingly, deeply divided.

The polarization of the American electorate, to which public officials both contribute and reflect, is seen as a product of greater regional homogeneity (e.g., the persistence of voting patterns in the blue and red states at the presidential level); more electoral districts, particularly in the House of Representatives, dominated by a single party; nomination politics that advantage and reflect the voting decisions of party activists; and the current political debate that reinforces ideological cleavages more than it builds a general consensus.[5]

Other students of American politics, however, perceive elected officials to be more deeply divided than the country. According to Professor Morris P. Fiorina and his associates, the American electorate is ambivalent on most issues and closely divided on the electoral choices it is offered, but it is not deeply divided on the most salient issues of the day. The major parties, their most ardent supporters, and the public officials they elect, however, are highly polarized.[6]

Minor Parties

Minor parties have been a part of the American political landscape since 1831, when a small party known as the Anti-Masons held a national convention to nominate candidates and propose a set of governing principles. Although minor parties have come and gone quickly, some of the shortest lived have exerted the greatest influence by convincing one or both of the major parties to address their concerns.

In general, minor parties in American history have had three types of orientations: ideological, issue, and candidate. The latter are of more recent origin. (See Table 7.1 for a list of some of the most significant minor parties.)

Of the three types, **ideological parties,** such as the Socialist Party, the Communist Party, and the Libertarian Party, have had the greatest staying power but the least political impact. Because their beliefs lie outside the dominant views of mainstream America, their followings have been loyal but not large.

ideological parties
Political parties whose members subscribe to a common belief system, such as socialism or communism.

Table 7.1 Types of Minor Parties

Party	Life Span	Platform
IDEOLOGICAL PARTIES		
Socialist Party	1901–	Replacement of much private enterprise with a worker-run state
Communist Party	1924–	Overthrow of capitalism and establishment of a socialist state
Libertarian Party	1971–	Opposition to most government regulation and, particularly, to state-sponsored social programs
ISSUE PARTIES		
Free Soil Party	1848–1852	Position to the extension of slavery to new territories
Know-Nothing Party	1854–1856	Opposition to immigration
Greenback Party	1876–1884	Inflationary paper money to raise the prices of farm products
Populist Party	1892–1908	Inflationary monetary policy through the free coinage of silver; government ownership of railroads; direct election of senators; graduated income tax
Green Party	1984–	Promotion of environmental issues, community involvement, and nonviolent positions on international issues
CANDIDATE-ORIENTED PARTIES		
Progressive Party: Theodore Roosevelt	1912	Antitrust laws; direct primary; unemployment insurance
American Independent Party: George Wallace	1968–1972	Opposition to civil rights legislation; hawkish stance on the Vietnam War
National Unity Party: John Anderson	1980	Independent, nonideological, moderate leadership
United We Stand America: H. Ross Perot	1992–1995	Deficit reduction; streamlining of government; citizen activism
Reform Party: H. Ross Perot	1995–	Deficit reduction; government reform; citizen participation

issue parties

Political parties whose members subscribe to a similar position on an issue that is important to them.

Issue parties have had more political success. Created out of dissatisfaction with one or both of the major parties when they ignored important issues or took unpopular stands on them, these parties have sought to convince the major parties to change their positions. They have done so largely by attracting support for their own candidates, thereby reducing the size of the electoral coalitions of the major parties. Although issue parties have not usually managed to get their candidates elected, they have drawn attention to their interests and diverted

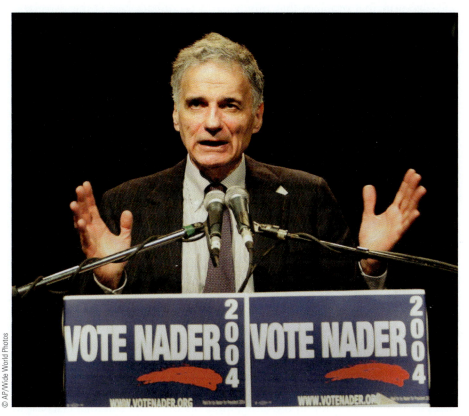

© AP/Wide World Photos

Ralph Nader speaks with supporters who attended a signature-gathering event to get Nader and his Green Party on the ballot in Oregon for the 2004 election. The effort failed, however, because Nader did not secure enough signatures of registered voters in the state.

votes from the major parties and their candidates. A good example of this was seen in Florida in 2000, when the Green Party's presidential nominee, Ralph Nader, received almost 100,000 votes. Exit polls suggested that had Nader not been on the Florida ballot, Al Gore would have won the popular vote in that state and, with that, an Electoral College victory.[7]

The **Green Party,** which is issue oriented, has been active in the United States since the mid-1980s. The party supports environmental concerns, labor movements, urban revitalization, and issues of social justice. It is also opposed to expansion of nuclear energy.

Most contemporary third parties have been **candidate-oriented parties.** And they have had short lives. When the candidate for whom the party was established is defeated, the organization loses its *raison d'étre* and usually fades from the scene, as did George Wallace's American Independent Party, John Anderson's National Unity Party, and perhaps H. Ross Perot's **Reform Party.**

Green Party
A party oriented toward a cleaner and safer environment; organizes on the local and national levels but has only received a small proportion of the national vote even though consumer advocate, Ralph Nader ran for president on its label in 2000 and 2004.

candidate-oriented parties
Parties organized to support a particular candidate and that candidate's major policy positions. The American Independent Party (George Wallace) and the Reform Party (H. Ross Perot) are examples.

Reform Party
A party organized and funded by Texas billionaire H. Ross Perot. The Reform Party has run candidates for the presidency since 1992.

The principal problem that minor party candidates face is the two-party bias of the American electoral system. Third-party and independent candidates encounter legal obstacles to getting on the ballot and raising sufficient funds to run a viable campaign. Most states require new parties to obtain the signatures of a specified percentage of registered voters to appear on the ballot many months in advance of the election, an expensive and labor-intensive effort, especially for small parties with limited resources.

Third parties are also disadvantaged at the presidential level by the mechanics of the Electoral College, which benefits candidates who can win a statewide popular vote. To make matters worse for third-party presidential candidates, even if they win enough electoral votes to prevent either major party candidate from receiving the required majority, they are greatly disadvantaged in the next step in the process when the House of Representatives determines the winner, because almost all elected representatives are aligned with one of the major parties.

Third parties also have a financial disadvantage. Their presidential candidates do not automatically receive government funding unless they received at least five percent of the vote in the previous election, but they are still subject to the legal limits on individual and group contributions during the campaign. The only way to skirt these limits is for candidates to use their own money, not the federal government's, as H. Ross Perot did in 1992 as the presidential nominee of the Reform Party, when he spent about $63.3 million, most of it his own. In 1996, he accepted federal funds, as did Reform Party candidate Pat Buchanan in 2000. Because Buchanan, did not receive 5 percent of the vote in that election, the Reform Party was not eligible for federal funding in 2004. Nor is it eligible in 2008.

Lack of adequate news media coverage is another reason minor party candidates have difficulty. Without the recognition, organization, and financial base of the major parties, third-party and independent candidates need more press coverage but they usually receive less. The horse-race orientation of election coverage by the major news networks, combined with the perception that third parties and independents can't win, reduces the amount of coverage minor party candidates receive, shapes the story line about them and reinforces the traditional parties' appeal: "Do not waste a vote on a third-party or independent candidate."

Finally, when third-party and independent candidates find a new issue on which there is substantial public support, the major parties usually rush to embrace it without necessarily embracing the messenger who delivered it. For these reasons, third parties have been unable to sustain a foothold among the American electorate for an extended period.

A Brief History of the Two-Party System

American political parties have changed significantly over the years. That evolution has been influenced not only by the federal character of the political system in the United States but also by major events such as the Civil War, the recession of the early to mid-1890s, the Great Depression of the 1930s, and for many in the South, the civil rights movement of the 1960s. How the parties reacted to these conditions, how they dealt with the economic and social consequences that followed, and to which groups they appealed for support have all affected the composition of the parties and their success or failure in winning elections and governing the country. The history of American political parties has been a history of adapting to changing economic and social conditions by appealing to broad-based electoral constituencies. In this section we examine that history in some detail.

The Development of National Parties, 1789–1824

Parties are not mentioned in the Constitution and did not exist before to its ratification and the presidency of George Washington. They came into being largely to support or oppose the first administration's policies: the assumption by national government of the Revolutionary War debt, the taxation of imported goods to protect domestic industry, and the establishment of a national bank to regulate currency. In general, Washington's supporters included commercial interests—merchants, manufacturers, bankers, creditors, and speculators—whereas farmers, laborers, debtors, and other less advantaged members of society opposed him. Those who believed their interests to be adversely affected by Washington's policies turned to Thomas Jefferson, who had resigned from his cabinet position because of his disagreement with the administration's policies.

The political groupings that emerged during this period also differed in their foreign policy orientations. Those who backed the administration, the so-called **Federalists,** tended to be more pro-British; they supported the treaty that Ambassador John Jay had negotiated to end the official state of hostilities between Britain and its former colonies. Jefferson's supporters, known as **Democratic-Republicans** or simply **Republicans,** opposed it.[8] Although the Jay Treaty was ratified by the Senate, it gave rise to a partisan debate and vote, the first such partisan vote in Congress.

Partisanship was also evident in the elections of 1796 and 1800. So unified were the Democratic-Republicans in the presidential election of 1800 that all their electors voted for Jefferson and Aaron Burr, the party's candidates. The result was a tie that forced the House of Representatives, still controlled by the Federalists, to choose between the two candidates with the most votes, Jefferson and Burr.[9]

By 1800, the Federalist and Republican Parties were competing within most states and at the national level.[10] Neither of them, however, had much popular backing; their most active supporters were primarily elected officials and others who desired to hold public office. Of the two, it was the Democratic-Republicans who expressed more confidence in the common people. Blessed with a succession of prestigious presidential candidates—the so-called Virginia dynasty of Jefferson, James Madison, and James Monroe—they were able to expand their base, becoming the majority party by 1800 and the only national party by 1820. The last Federalist candidate for president ran in 1816 and received only a handful of electoral votes.

The early party system contributed to the nation's evolving political tradition in several important respects. By channeling the debate about how the

Federalists
The party that supported the economic and foreign polities of the George Washington and John Adams administrations.

Democratic-Republicans (Republicans)
The party, led by Thomas Jefferson, that was agrarian based and became the first opposition party in the United States.

nation should develop, what role the government should play, and which national policies should be pursued, it provided a framework for resolving differences of opinion about public issues. In addition, it created an institutional mechanism for recruiting public officials and influencing their policy judgments. Finally, it forced candidates to listen to public opinion and forced public officials to pay attention to their constituents' interests.

The Regionalization of Parties, 1828–1852

By the mid-1820s, the Republicans had become victims of their own success. Without a rival party, they split into feuding factions, with five candidates campaigning for the presidency in 1824. Two dominant groups survived the factional feuds. One, the National Republicans, supported John Quincy Adams; the other, the Democratic-Republicans, backed Andrew Jackson. Although Jackson won a plurality of votes in the Electoral College, he was defeated in the House of Representatives. Four years later, having organized a broad-based political coalition and engaged in grassroots campaigning, Jackson was elected.

The 1828 election was the first in which the electors in a majority of the states were chosen in direct popular elections. Besides accelerating the movement toward popular election of the president, Jackson's victory spurred a shift of power from the national government to the states. The congressional party caucus, which had been used to nominate presidential and vice presidential candidates between 1800 and 1824, was replaced by national nominating conventions dominated by state party leaders. Increasingly, members of Congress owed their nomination and election to their state party and its leadership.

Jackson's new electoral coalition also changed the landscape of American politics. His principal backing came from economically disadvantaged groups: small farmers and newly enfranchised voters in the West and South, along with Catholics and new immigrants in the East. Known simply as the **Democrats,** Jackson's following soon dominated the Democratic-Republican Party, which dropped "Republican" from its name.

A new party, the **Whigs,** emerged in opposition to Jackson. A diverse group composed of prosperous farmers in the South and West, commercial interests in the East, and antislavery advocates in the Northeast and Appalachia, the Whigs held themselves together in national campaigns by running military heroes as candidates.[11] By 1840, the Democrats and Whigs were competitive throughout the country. Their vigorous competition increased voter turnout to a high of approximately 80 percent of eligible voters (almost exclusively white men) in the 1840 presidential election, nearly double the highest rate attained earlier.[12]

Three minor parties emerged during this period. The Anti-Masons, which favored issue-oriented protectionist economic policies and government-sponsored internal improvements; the Liberty Party, which opposed the existence of slavery; and the Free Soil Party, which opposed the extension of slavery into the western territories and the influx of new immigrants into the country. Although none of these parties generated much popular support or staying power, they revealed growing discontent within the two major parties. This discontent would

Democrats
The faction of the Democratic-Republican Party, led by Andrew Jackson, that represented various economically disadvantaged groups and sought policies that would benefit these groups.

Whigs
A disparate group that opposed Jackson. The Whigs were composed of more prosperous farmers in the South and West, commercials interests in the East, and antislavery advocates.

lead to the breakup of the two-party system in the period before the Civil War. The new **Republican Party** was organized in 1854. Its constituents included disillusioned Whigs, who feared and opposed new immigrants; Anti-Masons; Free Soilers; and others opposed to slavery (abolitionists) or its expansion (white laborers, small farmers, and some entrepreneurs). In 1856, the Republicans ran their first presidential candidate, John C. Frémont, who did surprisingly well. Although he was not elected, he received 40 percent of the vote.

The Civil War and Its Aftermath, 1856–1892

By 1860, the Democrats had split over slavery, with northern and southern factions each running their own presidential candidate. The Whigs, controlled by antislavery forces, lost their support in the South and suffered so many defections in the North over their anti-immigration stand that they were no longer a viable political force. With the opposition divided, the Republican candidate, Abraham Lincoln, won the 1860 election with only 39.8 percent of the popular vote, the smallest winning percentage in U.S. history.

Out of the turmoil created by the Civil War, the Reconstruction, and the rapid expansion of industrialization, new partisan coalitions emerged. The Republicans evolved from their beginnings as a party of small business, labor, and farmers into a party increasingly dominated by big business. Banking and commercial interests also influenced the northern wing of the Democratic Party, but its southern wing remained controlled by the white supremacists who sought to reimpose the pre–Civil War social and economic structure in the South. African Americans were effectively disenfranchised in the South after the withdrawal of federal troops in 1876.

Minor parties, such as the agricultural Greenback Party and the urban Socialist Labor Party, organized to appeal to farmers and workers whose grievances had not been adequately addressed by the major parties. In addition, new parties opposing the consumption of alcohol (the Prohibition Party) and favoring more participation by the people in government (the Populist Party) were created. (The Prohibition Party, which still exists, is the oldest third party in the United States.)

The Republican Era, 1896–1928

A recession in 1893, during the Democratic administration of Grover Cleveland, led to a shifting of political forces that culminated in the Republicans becoming the majority party. They gained adherents in the Northeast, and the Democrats picked up support in the grain-producing states of the prairies and the silver-mining states of the Rockies. Farmers and townsfolk, who were adversely affected by the pro-business, *laissez-faire* policies of the government, supported Democrat William Jennings Bryan, an advocate of unlimited coinage of silver. Although Bryan lost that and subsequent elections (1900 and 1908), his movement helped transform the Democrats from a party sympathetic to the more conservative interests of the business community to a party that was more supportive of the needs of small farmers, immigrants, and industrial workers.[13]

Republican Party
Founded in 1854, the Republicans opposed the expansion of slavery and, in some cases, the institution of slavery itself. It was pro-labor and anti-immigration. Abraham Lincoln was the nation's first Republican president, elected in 1860.

William Jennings Bryan, Democratic candidate for president in 1896, made 159 speeches in three months, 24 of them in 24 hours. He won the Democratic Party nomination with powerful oratory in which he criticized the big business-orientation of the party and urged delegates to adopt a free silver policy with the words, "You shall not crucify mankind upon a cross of gold!"

Partisan conflict also took on regional coloration during this period, with the Democrats gaining support in the Midwest and maintaining it in the South and the Republicans enlarging their voter base in the Northeast and Middle Atlantic states. Ethnic and religious divisions also began to emerge. The newer wave of immigrants (largely Catholics and primarily from southern and eastern Europe) turned to the Democratic Party, whereas those who had immigrated earlier (largely Protestants from northern Europe) stayed Republican.

Smaller parties that appealed to the plight of industrial workers in the cities, such as the Socialists and Communists, also gained a foothold during this period. Progressives, who advocated social justice and industrial democracy, supported Theodore Roosevelt's attempt to win the Republican presidential nomination from incumbent William Howard Taft in 1912 and his subsequent independent candidacy in the general election. Although Roosevelt received the largest share of votes (27.4 percent) of any third-party candidate in American history, he split the Republican vote, thereby enabling Democrat Woodrow Wilson to win the presidency.

Despite Wilson's victory and his reelection four years later, the Republicans or **Grand Old Party (GOP),** as they came to be called, maintained their northern European, Protestant-dominated national politics until the 1930s.[14] During the period from 1896 to 1928, the Democrats controlled Congress for only six years and the White House for only eight. In the 1920s, however, the flow of new immigrants, combined with unpopular Republican policies (particularly Prohibition), led urban-based ethnic groups to enlarge the Democrats' electoral

Grand Old Party (GOP)
Another name, coined during the last decades of the nineteenth century, for the Republican Party.

Box 7.2 The Donkey and the Elephant

Today, it is the late-night entertainers and news reporters on Comedy Central that create and disseminate the caricatures and stereotypes that satirize contemporary politics and politicians. Before the television entertainers, it was the political cartoonists who performed this task. Thomas Nast was one of the most famous of those cartoonists. It was his cartoons in the *New York Herald* and *Harper's Weekly* that led to the association of the donkey with the Democratic Party and the elephant with the Republican Party.

In 1874, Nast depicted a donkey wearing a lion's skin, labeled "Caesarism," frightening away animals in New York City's Central Park. One of the animals was an elephant that Nast labeled "the Republican vote." The cartoon, titled "Third Term Panic," suggested that Democrats would invoke the fear of Caesarism to frighten away Republican voters if President Ulysses S. Grant were to run for a third term, which was being rumored at the time.

Thereafter, the donkey and the elephant became associated with the Democratic and Republican Parties. The Republicans even went so far as to adopt the elephant, which they saw as a strong and intelligent animal, as their official symbol. The Democrats, of course, had another view of the elephant. In the words of Adlai Stevenson, Democratic presidential candidate in 1952 and 1956: "The elephant has a thick skin, a head full of ivory, and as everyone who has seen a circus parade knows, proceeds best by grasping the tail of its predecessor."

In contrast, the Democrats saw the donkey as a symbol of the party's humility, courage, and stubbornness, recalling Andrew Jackson's 1828 presidential campaign in which the old warrior was pictured on a donkey to demonstrate that he would not cave in to the desires of the eastern moneyed interests by supporting a second Bank of the United States. Republicans, of course, have used other terms to characterize the donkey, such as *stupid* and *obstinate* or, more simply and directly, *jackass.*

Party symbols: The first appearance of the Republican Elephant, with a fox in the bottom right corner representing the Democratic party, was in a political cartoon by Thomas Nast that appeared in November 1874.

base. By 1928, the Democrats won a majority of the vote in the large cities for the first time since the Civil War.

The Roosevelt Realignment, 1932–1968

In the 1932 election, which occurred during the most severe economic depression in the nation's history, the Republicans lost control of both the presidency and the Congress. The Democrats expanded their electoral coalition, gaining support from white southerners, Catholics, and organized labor. By 1936, when Roosevelt was reelected to the second of his four terms, African Americans had abandoned the party of Lincoln for the party of Roosevelt. Jewish voters, attracted by the president's anti-Nazi foreign policy, also shifted their allegiance to the Democrats. And although the Republicans retained their hold on northern Protestants, the Democrats made inroads among this group as well, particularly among those at the lower end of the socioeconomic scale. The electorate thus was divided along economic class lines, with less prosperous voters more likely to be Democratic and more prosperous ones Republican. The principal exception to this pattern was in the South, where regardless of their socioeconomic status, most white voters remained loyal to the Democratic Party.

The economic division between the parties became evident in the policy perspectives they adopted. The Democrats looked to government, particularly the national government, to help rectify the nation's most severe economic and social problems, whereas the Republicans were more leery of government efforts to regulate private industry and expand social services.

It is difficult to say precisely when the Roosevelt realignment that gave the Democrats a secure hold on the allegiance of a majority of voters was completed. But after World War II, the party's electoral coalition was strained by divisive new issues such as civil rights, American military involvement in Korea and then Vietnam, and deterioration of the nation's cities and their associated problems of crime and drugs. By taking liberal policy positions on issues of race and social welfare, the national Democratic Party alienated southern whites and many of its blue-collar, white ethnic supporters. The party's stand on women's rights, its pro-choice stand on abortion, its opposition to discrimination based on sexual orientation, and its position in favor of the separation of church and state irritated Christian fundamentalists, who had voted Democratic through the mid-1970s. Finally, the economic gains of labor, the growth of a larger and more inclusive middle class that included blue-collar workers, and the decrease in the proportion of low-income voters in the electorate depleted the party's dependable base of support. The Democrats lost their dominance at the presidential level in 1968, and their status as the majority party eroded even further after that.

The Composition of the Major Parties Today

The Democratic coalition built during Franklin Roosevelt's presidency has undergone major changes since then. One of the most significant and enduring of these changes has been the defection of white southerners, who had supported the party since the Civil War. The seeds of this defection were sown in 1948, when the Democratic National Convention adopted a strong civil rights plank in its party platform; some southern delegates walked out of the convention and later supported J. Strom Thurmond's independent candidacy that year. In the 1960s, the exodus of white southerners from the party accelerated with the advocacy of school desegregation, civil rights legislation, and other social programs designed to help poor, socially-disadvantaged people who tended to be disproportionately racial and ethnic minorities. Even when southerners Jimmy Carter and Bill Clinton headed their respective Democratic presidential tickets, a majority of southern white voters continued to support Republican presidential candidates.

But the Democratic vote declined in other areas as well. Some attribute this erosion of support to the cultural and social issues that alienated working-class whites.[15] Others saw it as a sign of prosperity, the movement of many lower-income people up the socioeconomic ladder and their adoption of middle-class values and lifestyles. The Republican Party's appeal of individual initiative, private ownership, and financial success resonated with these new middle class voters. According to this class-based theory of partisan change, the increasing gap between haves and have-nots has worked to the Republicans' advantage not only because American society has prospered but also because those in the lower income brackets do not turn out to vote as often as those who make more money.[16] Similarly, the growth and political activism of Christian fundamentalists has helped the Republicans and shaped that party's value-oriented appeal. These shifts in partisan attitudes have a regional coloration with both the South and Southwest increasingly Republican and the Northeast and Pacific Coast, increasingly Democratic. The Midwest has remained more evenly divided and has become the principal battleground for recent presidential elections.

The increasing importance of social issues, continuing class divisions, and the expanded role of party activists in the nomination and election processes have clarified and made distinctive the ideological appeals of the major political parties, unifying the parties internally but enhancing their differences externally. Elected public officials have reflected these increasingly ideological divisions. Political pragmatism has suffered at the hands of ideology. Strident rhetoric characterizes contemporary political discourse. Compromising public policy positions has become more difficult.

Today, the Democratic Party's electoral coalition consists first of organized labor, although that group's proportion of the population has declined significantly since the New Deal coalition was formed in the 1930s. Catholic support has also declined, especially among the Catholic groups that immigrated to the United States in the first half of the twentieth century, Irish and Italians. The newly arriving Hispanic population, however, has shown a greater tendency to vote Democratic, primarily for economic reasons. African Americans have remained a loyal and stable part of the Democrats electoral coalition, as have Jewish voters.

Since 1980, clear gender differences have emerged within the American polity, with women more likely to identify with the Democrats and men with the Republicans. In presidential voting, this "gender gap" increased with each election until 2004; the gender gap has tended to be larger among whites than among nonwhites (because of the latter's overwhelming Democratic support regardless of gender), larger among better-educated and wealthier voters than among less advantaged groups, and larger among unmarried people than among married ones.

In short, the Democrats have become a diverse party in which ethnic and racial minorities constitute core constituencies; women—especially younger single women—are part of this coalition as well. Although the party still receives overwhelming support from those with the lowest incomes and those who live in central cities, the relatively small size of these groups within the total electorate and their lower turnout at the polls have made them less important components of the Democratic voting block than they were in the past. Some other traditionally Democratic-oriented groups, such as union members and Catholics, also provide less support than in the past. Clearly, the Democrats' New Deal coalition has eroded, as has its position as the dominant party.

As for the Republicans, they have gained adherents, probably as much from new voters as from changes in the political allegiances of older ones. As an electoral coalition, Republicans have become more Caucasian, male, and suburban. The GOP has maintained the traditional loyalties of white Protestants, and the party has gained support from Protestant fundamentalists and conservative Catholics. The core constituency of the contemporary Republican Party thus consists of members of racial and religious majorities, particularly regular churchgoers, and higher socioeconomic groups.

As the United States enters the twenty-first century, the major parties are at or near parity (see Table 7.2).

Table 7.2 The Partisan Identification of the American Electorate, 1980–2004

YEAR	1980	1984	1988	1992	1996	2000	2004
PARTY IDENTIFICATION							
Strong Dem.	18	17	18	17	18	19	17
Weak Dem.	24	20	18	18	20	15	16
Independent-Leaning Dem.	12	11	12	14	14	15	17
Independent	13	11	11	12	08	12	10
Independent-Leaning Rep.	10	13	14	13	12	13	12
Weak Rep.	14	15	14	15	16	12	12
Strong Rep.	09	13	14	11	13	12	16

Source: The American National Election Studies, "The ANES Guide to Public Opinion and Electoral Behavior."
http://www.umich.edu/~nes/nesguide/toptable/tab2a_1.htm.

There has also been an increase in the percentage of the population that identifies itself as **independent.** Much of that increase came in the 1970s and early 1980s when dissatisfaction with the parties was high. The growth of independents also coincided with the increasing candidate-orientation of elections, which itself was a product of the changes the major parties initiated in their nomination processes, new campaign finance laws, and the use of television as the principal campaign medium by which candidates communicated with voters.

Although about one-quarter of the population identifies itself as independent today, fewer people actually vote independently. Most lean in a partisan direction and vote more or less consistently for one party's candidates. The bottom line is that partisanship is alive and well in American politics.

independent
A voter who does not formally think of him or herself as a party partisan; the numbers of people who claim to be independent grew in the 1970s and early 1980s.

Review Questions

1. The two major parties in the United States have always been

   A. Ideological
   B. Decentralized
   C. Homogeneous
   D. Structurally dissimilar

2. The major parties differ most from minor parties in the United States on the basis of their

   A. Election orientation
   B. Emphasis on the issues
   C. Diverse composition
   D. Ideological content

3. Which of the following regions of the country provides the Republicans with the most support today?

   A. North
   B. South
   C. East
   D. West

4. Which group is not part of the Democrats' electoral coalition?

   A. Hispanics
   B. African Americans
   C. Labor unions
   D. White men

5. Which of the following groups has provided the Republicans with the highest percentage of support in recent years?

   A. Mainline Protestants
   B. Protestant fundamentalists

continued

    C. Catholics
    D. Jews

Answers:

    1. B
    2. C
    3. B
    4. D
    5. B

Conflict and Consensus in Review

The merits of the major parties are that they permit diversity yet build a candidate and policy consensus. They contribute to American democracy by reinforcing the tie between the people and their elected representatives and between their candidate choices and their government's policy decisions. The major parties help find common partisan ground; they unify their partisans into a cohesive electoral coalition, their issue positions into an agenda for governing, and their winning candidates into an organization for making policy decisions. Yet they differ from each other increasingly on ideological grounds.

Party Organization

In the decentralized organization of the major political parties, there are separate structures at the national, state, and local levels. Although each exercises autonomy over its nominations and, to a lesser extent, its campaigns, the influence of the national party has grown in recent years. Its growth is a product of three factors: fund-raising and the distribution of monies to national candidates and to state parties and candidates, information technology used to extend the word and reach of the national organizations, and well-trained political professionals who help state and local party affiliates.

The National Level

Until the 1970s, the national parties were relatively weak. When parties first emerged, there was no effective party organization at the national level. Informal congressional caucuses decided on the party's national candidates and instructed electors from their states for whom to vote. Only after national conventions replaced the congressional caucuses in the 1830s did the parties establish national committees to make arrangements for the conventions and coordinate national campaigns more effectively.

The Democratic National Committee (DNC) was organized in 1848, the Republican National Committee (RNC) in 1856. Initially, each was composed of an equal number of representatives from each state party. The Republicans have maintained this principle of equal representation, but the Democrats have not.[17]

The Democrats provide representation to the states on the basis of their population and their past support for their party's nominees, a rule that has given larger states such as California, New York, Texas, and Florida more influence on the national committee and its decisions. Before World War I, neither party had a headquarters, a staff, or a full-time paid chairperson.[18] Today, both have all three.

After they were created, both national committees operated like confederations of state parties rather than independent entities. Changes began to occur in the late 1960s, a consequence of Democratic Party rule changes, Republican Party fund-raising prowess, and the use of new communications technologies to activate and reinforce partisan attitudes.

Reforms in the presidential and congressional nominating process, which the Democrats initiated and many of which the Republicans adopted, have nationalized the presidential nominating process. Democratic rules, to which state party affiliates must adhere, determine the period during which primaries and caucuses may occur, the procedures for allocating the vote, and the demographic balance of the convention delegates chosen in the states. Although the Republicans do not mandate most of these reforms on their state parties, they do provide services to their state parties and many of their candidates who run for office.

The Republicans have led the way in national fund-raising in the 1970s and 1980s. They created a large list of donors by using direct mail, telephone solicitation, and major fund-raising events to fill their campaign war chest. The Democrats, saddled with a divided party and a sizable debt from their 1968 presidential campaign, were unable to match the GOP's initiative. Until the Bill Clinton presidency, the Democrats lagged behind their Republican counterparts in the financial support they could provide their candidates for office. The Clinton presidency proved to be a boon to the Democrats financially, but their manner of using their position in power and government facilities to solicit contributions raised ethical questions.[19]

The Republicans also took advantage of their control of Congress in the 1990s and the White House after 2000 to raise large amounts of money, but they were more careful than the Democrats to avoid the appearance of improprieties. In the 2003–2004 election cycle, both parties raised and spent more money than ever before even though they could no longer accept very large individual contributions. In addition to providing financial support, both parties have established state-of-the-art technical facilities to help their candidates and officeholders communicate to the voters. These include in-house media, such as television studios, party-generated programming, and satellite linkups; an easy-to-use, updated website; and computerized voter registration and get-out-the-vote lists. In 2004, the Bush campaign, in association with the RNC, mounted an effective voter mobilization effort in the key battleground states, increasing turnout by about 6 percent from the 2000 presidential election. Both parties have also established effective campaign committees in the House and Senate to help recruit and fund their congressional candidates.[20]

As a result of these activities, the number of professionals working for the national parties have increased enormously, particular during elections. These professionals provide valuable support and services for the state parties and their candidates at all levels.

The chief spokesperson for the national party is the chairperson of the national committee, who also acts as a liaison to elected officials and state party leaders. The chairperson oversees the party's administrative operations, although sometimes day-to-day responsibilities are performed by another person if the general chairperson holds another position, such as that of an elected official.

7.3 Politics in the 21st Century
Interactive Political Parties

Reaching out to their online supporters, both major political parties have created interactive websites. Naturally, both want donations—the more the better—because large contributions for get-out-the-vote and other party activities are no longer permitted. But the parties want more than simply dollars. They want to expand their base; they want to involve their rank and file, register them, energize them, and make them feel a part of the team, and get them to contribute money, volunteer for the campaign, and make sure that they vote on election day. Both sites have a blog for like-minded partisan commentary.

Party websites provide one-stop shopping. Those who want to find out about the party and its history, its candidates and their positions, or its opponents and their weaknesses need only to read the banner headlines that stream across the site, the press releases and research reports that are merely a touch away, or the speeches, advertisements, and platform that can be easily accessed. The web page lists upcoming events and provides a running commentary on the campaign. There is a photo gallery, even a store to purchase party paraphernalia. Need to know the names of the party's national officers and how to reach them, find out who the chairperson and contact people are for the conventions, or contact state or local party leaders? That information is available on the website as well.

Both national parties try to engage partisans, sympathizers, and others with attractive and easy to use websites.

continued

7.3 Politics in the 21st Century *continued*

There are links to the various groups affiliated to the parties: College Democrats and Republicans; African American, Hispanic and other ethnic groups; veterans, seniors, women, and even gay and lesbian groups. It is easy to subscribe to these list serves or formally join the groups. More interested in issues? You can also link up to issue-oriented groups, join marches and protests, or show your support. The Republicans list talk radio stations you can call and newspapers to which you can write.

The parties' facilitate voter registration and voting. By indicating the state in which you reside and then providing some basic information, you can obtain a personalized registration form, sign it, and just put it in the mail to the address indicated. If you need other information about when and where to vote, you can also access it from the parties' websites. (See the Where on the Web section at the end of the chapter for a listing of party web addresses.)

The State Level

Some developments that have changed the national party organizations have also affected their state counterparts. The organizational structure of many of them has been strengthened, and their operations have become standard. Most state parties now have a permanent staff. Their fund-raising capabilities have been substantially improved; their operating budgets have increased; and their ability to train and assist candidates in the general election has been enhanced.[21]

The strengthening of state party organizations has not been easy. For one thing, the growth of primary elections, which make it easier for candidates to appear on the ballot and encourage them to mount their own campaigns and make their own appeals to voters, has made it more difficult for state party leaders to exercise control over the nomination process. Similarly, the influence of television as a vehicle for communicating to the electorate has weakened the capacity of parties at all levels to control the messages their candidates present to voters. Moreover, the growth of the civil service system in state and national governments has reduced the powers of party leaders and elected officials to find government jobs for their loyal workers and supporters.

State party structures are decentralized. In most states, there is a party committee composed of representatives from different geographic subdivisions, usually counties. State party committees vary in size, composition, and function. Some elect their members in primary elections, others in local caucuses, and still others at state conventions. Because most state party committees meet infrequently, the chairperson has considerable discretion in the conduct of party affairs. In only a few states, however, is the position of party chairperson a full-time paid job. Turnover remains high: a state party chairperson averages less than three years in office.[22]

Electing candidates to state and national office remains the primary goal of state parties, although they have become involved in a variety of other activities, ranging from taking official positions on salient issues, to holding meetings and conventions, to conducting fund-raising and membership drives. State parties recruit potential nominees and help with their campaigns. Like the national parties, in recent years state parties have improved their capacity to raise money, compile lists of voters, and provide organizational support to candidates. All of these developments have strengthened the state parties and increased their electoral effectiveness. They have not, however, eliminated the need for candidates to obtain funds on their own, build their own grassroots organizations, or hire their own campaign consultants.[23]

The Local Level

wards or precincts
The smallest unit within the state in which elections occur.

Local parties also have their own organizations built around geographic subdivisions, usually counties or cities. The county or city organization is made up of representatives from still smaller units, called **wards or precincts.** Usually the key figure in directing the party's efforts is the chairperson of the county committee or the mayor of the town or city, assisted by precinct captains and ward leaders.

party machines
Tightly organized local parties that exercise control over nominations, job distribution, and other social benefits in certain counties or cities.

It was primarily at the local level, particularly in cities, that political organizations referred to as **party machines** (because of the effectiveness of their operation and their top-down hierarchical structure) and their leaders, referred to as **party bosses** (because of their near-total control over party affairs), flourished during the second half of the nineteenth century and the first half of the twentieth. For their supporters, many of whom were newly arrived immigrants, these organizations provided help in securing jobs, obtaining housing, learning English, and more generally, becoming integrated into the life of American cities. In exchange for this help, the machine received their votes.

party bosses
The elected political leaders of party organizations that hold considerable influence over their partisans within the locality in which their organization dominates.

The machines weakened and eventually lost their hold over city politics as a result of several factors. Not only did immigrants gradually become assimilated into American society but urban governments expanded their social and economic services, reducing the need for those provided by parties. Also, a civil service system based on merit gradually replaced a political appointment system based on partisanship. Other political reforms, such as the direct primary election, reduced the power of party leaders to control nominations. Today only a few strong party machines still exist, and none operates in the dictatorial manner of the old-style bosses.

Local party organizations tend to be loosely structured. Most of their leaders and workers are volunteers; there may be no paid staff. Most of their activities, as with those of the state parties, are organized around election campaigns: arranging fund-raising events, contributing money to candidates, and publicizing themselves and their candidates through media advertising, press releases, telephone campaigns, and the distribution of campaign literature. The local organization also maintains lists of registered voters and organizes get-out-the-vote campaigns.

In recent years, the power of ethnic and racial minorities in local parties has grown substantially. Beginning in the 1970s and continuing into the twenty-first century, African Americans, Hispanics, and Asian Americans have won control of local party organizations in areas where they are dominant population

Republican Party headquarters, Manchester, N.H., 1992.

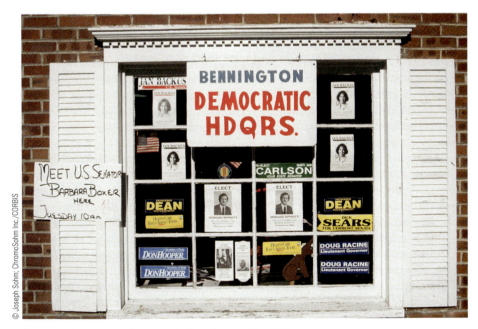

Democratic Party headquarters in Bennington, Vt., 1992.

groups. This control has enabled them to nominate and elect candidates sensitive to their needs, many of whom are themselves minorities. The gains of these groups, especially in many of the nation's largest cities, mirror those of European immigrants a half-century earlier. Women, too, have achieved increased electoral success at local and higher levels of government.

In sum, on all three levels, the party provides a mechanism for organizing its professional and partisans into electoral and governing coalitions, thereby serving as a cohesive force in a diverse polity.

Parties and Elections

As noted earlier, parties are election oriented. Their principal function is to win elections. However, the parties exercise less influence over the conduct of elections today than they did in the past.

For the first 100 years of partisan politics in America, the methods used by parties to get out the vote were often sneaky, if not downright dishonest. Parties printed and distributed ballots listing only their own candidates, and they paid people to take time off work to vote. Because voting was open and public, enormous pressure was exerted on people to vote for the party's ticket. Allegations of fraud against the parties for registering ineligible voters, "stuffing" ballot boxes with illegal votes, and miscounting the results were frequent.

Toward the end of the nineteenth century, fraudulent activity was reduced by the passage of state laws governing the conduct of elections. Uniform procedures for voting were established; standard ballots, designed by state officials, were introduced, as was the requirement for secret voting. Today voting machines and machine-scan ballots have replaced paper ballots, further reducing but not eliminating ballot tabulation problems, as the results of the Florida vote in the 2000 presidential election attest. In 2002, Congress and several states enacted laws to computerize voter registration, update voting machines, and standardize procedures for resolving registration disputes and other voter challenges.

Primary Elections

Party organizations have been affected by other changes in the electoral process, especially the evolution of the nomination process. When the congressional caucus system for nominating presidential and vice presidential candidates began to break down in the 1820s, it was replaced by state and national party conventions, which were usually controlled by party leaders. Local precincts chose delegates to county conventions, which in turn chose delegates to state conventions, which in their turn chose nominees for state office and delegates to the national nominating conventions.

This system, however, was neither as representative nor as receptive to popular control as it appeared to be. Party leaders could use their clout to affect the choice of delegates and influence their behavior at the conventions. Not only did the nomination process minimize the effectiveness of the party's rank and file, but in areas of one-party dominance it effectively denied a voice to supporters of the minority party. The nomination was, in effect, the election.

The capacity of the system to be manipulated by party leaders, combined with the selection of unpopular, unimaginative, and in some cases unethical candidates, led to demand for reform. At the beginning of the twentieth century, the Progressive movement responded to these demands by urging a direct primary election in which party partisans, not simply party leaders, would choose the nominees. In 1904, Florida became the first state to hold such an election. Others followed suit. By 1916, twenty states had some type of primary; by the mid-1950s, most of them did. Today every state does so, although at the presidential level some states still use a multistage caucus system to choose delegates to the party's national nominating convention. In a caucus system, local precinct meetings select representatives to a state convention, which in turn selects delegates to a national convention.

Primaries are more democratic than multistage delegate selection processes because they allow more people to participate. However, even in primaries, those who participate may not be an accurate reflection of the general electorate or even of the party, as we noted in our previous discussion of the shifting composition of the major parties. The better-educated, higher-income, more professional supporters of the party tend to be overrepresented, as do the most ideological partisans. In short, primaries have increased rank-and-file participation, but they have also increased the influence of party activists, many of whom have stronger and more consistent belief systems than do other partisans. Party leaders no longer control who is nominated or what appeals those nominees make in the general election.

Modern Campaigns

Campaigns are important. They affect election outcomes and public policy. Without a strong campaign, it is difficult for a challenger to gain sufficient recognition to defeat an incumbent, an officeholder running for reelection. Without a strong campaign, it is difficult for candidates of parties who do not command the loyalties of a majority or plurality of the electorate to overcome this disadvantage. Without a strong campaign, it is even difficult for a candidate to win an open seat or a nonpartisan election.

And what occurs on the campaign trail influences governance. The promises candidates make often become the agenda they pursue once in office. Moreover, their followers become the core of the coalitions on which they depend to build support for their policy initiatives.

The demands of modern campaigning, and particularly the increased use of radio and television, have reduced the traditional role of parties as the principal link between candidates and voters. Because candidates need to raise much of their own campaign money and be aware of public opinion, they have increasingly turned to a new group of professionals who have rivaled and in many instances replaced party pros as campaign strategists and technical advisers. They have also turned to nonparty groups to supplement their campaign efforts.

And the campaign never ends. Once in office, elected officials immediately position themselves for reelection by taking politically popular stands, cultivating their interest group ties, soliciting contributions, and making themselves visible to their constituents. The persistent campaign elevates the importance of maintaining good press and public relations for those who hold public office, but it also keeps government officials in close touch with the people they serve, an essential component of a vibrant democracy.

Parties structure the electoral process. In doing so, they channel conflict within the electorate over candidates and issues into political activity that ultimately results in these conflicts being resolved in a democratic manner. That resolution provides a foundation for governing.

Parties and Governance

Despite its emphasis on elections, the party's ultimate objective is to shape the machinery of government in order to influence the formulation of public policy in accordance with the interests and needs of its supporters. These interests and needs are articulated by the party in its platform (which can be accessed on its website), by its candidates during the campaign, and by its leaders and elected officials during non-election periods.

Determining the Party's Positions

party platform
A statement of the issue positions of the national party ratified by delegates at the party's national nominating convention.

A **party platform** is a formal statement of beliefs, opinions, and policy stands tied together by a set of underlying principles based on the party's ideological orientation. It is drafted by a platform committee composed of delegates to the party's national convention and then approved (occasionally with modifications) by the convention. The prospective nominee usually is able to exercise the greatest influence over the results of this drafting process because that nominee usually controls the selection of a majority of the members of the platform committee. Besides, platform drafters are not eager to create a rift between their party's positions and those of its nominee.

Over the years, the platforms of the two major parties have differed significantly despite the allegation frequently voiced in the late 1960s and the 1970s that there is not "a dime's worth of difference" between them.[24] Between 1944 and 1976, for example, more than two-thirds of the pledges made in each party's platform were not made in the others.[25]

The sharpest distinctions between Democrats and Republicans have been evident in relation to the economy, welfare, and social and cultural issues. The Democrats favor greater government involvement on economic issues, and the Republicans support government-imposed community standards on social issues such as abortion, prayer in school, and homosexuality. On the other hand, the Democrats have consistently favored government-imposed requirements for registering firearms, and in some cases their prohibition, whereas the Republicans have not. Foreign affairs have not produced as many clear-cut or consistent differences between the two parties except during and immediately after wars, such as those in Vietnam and Iraq. Disagreement on the extent to which the United States should support international organizations, such as the United Nations, the World Bank, and the International Monetary Fund, and agreements such as the nonproliferation treaty, the Kyoto accords on global warming, and the treaty banning the production and use of chemical and biological weapons has also differentiated the parties. Democratic presidents have been more willing to engage in multilateral diplomacy than have their Republican counterparts. President George W. Bush's decisions not to sign the Kyoto treaty on the environment, not to make American citizens subject to the International Court of Criminal Justice, not to continue the Anti-Ballistic Missile Treaty, and not to wait for a United Nations resolution to invade Iraq illustrate a more unilateral approach to foreign policy than was practiced in the Clinton and Carter administrations.

Differences between party platforms are important because elected officials attempt to redeem the promises they and their parties make. There have been several studies of party platforms and campaign promises made during presidential election campaigns in the twentieth century. These studies have found that presidents have acted on most of their campaign promises and those of their party platforms. They have achieved about one-third of them fully and another one-third partially. A smaller percentage, anywhere between 16 and 27 percent, has not been redeemed either because Congress objected or because the times had changed and the promises no longer were feasible and/or desirable.[26] Well-known examples of promises not kept include Ronald Reagan's to balance the budget, George H. W. Bush's not to raise taxes, and Bill Clinton's to stimulate the economy. George W. Bush's promise to restructure Social Security by adding personal accounts has also met with considerable opposition, as the opening of this chapter suggests.

Sometimes campaign promises create unrealistic expectations that politicians are unable to fulfill. Take Newt Gingrich's promise to consider the major items in the Republicans' 1994 Contract with America. As Speaker of the House and with a Republican majority, he was successful in convincing that chamber to vote for nine of the ten proposals that comprised the Contract. However, the Republican Senate did not follow suit, and of course, President Clinton was opposed to many of these GOP initiatives.

Converting Positions into Public Policy

The successful conversion of a partisan agenda into legislative enactments and executive actions is an important measure of **responsible party government**— that is, holding the party that controls the government accountable for its platform and the promises made by its candidates for national office.[27]

Officials who abandon their party's positions risk losing the benefits they receive from their party's leaders—such as legislative committee assignments

responsible party government
A model for governing in which the major parties take dissimilar policy positions during the campaign. The party that wins the election is expected to pursue its campaign agenda when governing. Such a model enhances public accountability of the party in power.

and financial support. However, this threat may not be a serious risk to popular incumbents who can easily win reelection on their own.[28]

A party organization has limited leverage over public officials, regardless of their partisan affiliation. The heterogeneous nature of the major parties and their decentralized structures result in policy positions that are not equally attractive and salient to all candidates and officeholders. Their platforms also can become dated. Even though legislators of both parties maintain committees and caucuses to reach agreement on their party's priorities and legislative policy positions, they still may have difficulty obtaining unified support. Normally, items high on the president's legislative agenda are a focus of congressional attention and provide the president's party with a set of priorities to pursue.

Partisan Influence on the Legislature

Parties shape the structure and operation of Congress, as they do for most state legislatures. The vote on legislative leadership occurs along party lines: the Speaker of the House and the Senate majority leader are chosen on straight party votes. When Senator James Jeffords renounced his Republican Party affiliation in 2001, he stated that he would vote with the Democrats to reorganize the Senate, which had been evenly divided between the two parties before his defection. As a result, the Democrats gained a member on each of the standing committees and its leadership determined which bills reached the Senate's floor and when they did so.

When members deviate from their party's policy positions, however, there is little party leaders can do to keep them in line. Unlike their counterparts in the United Kingdom, for example, where members of Parliament who do not support their party may be denied the opportunity to run for reelection, party leaders in the United States cannot control or in some cases even effectively influence the nomination, campaign, and election of those who run on its label but do not support its issue stands. Although sanctions can be imposed by not giving renegade members campaign funds collected by party committees and others, this practice is rarely used, especially if it might result in the election of a candidate of the opposite party. More likely, the leadership will use its influence within the party to reward loyal members with choice committee assignments and pass over those who do not adhere to the party line as often, especially on key votes.

In the end, the ability of the leadership to affect legislative decision making rests primarily on its powers of persuasion, particularly in the U.S. Senate, a body whose rules permit individual senators to delay or even prevent voting on policy and personnel issues. In situations in which constituency, executive, or other strong pressures push against the party position, however, persuasion may be difficult. Party leaders will not ask their fellow partisans to commit political suicide by voting against the wishes of most of their constituents.

Although the effect of partisanship on substantive policy matters varies with the issue, it tends to be greater than any other factor in affecting the outcome of voting in Congress at the final stage of deliberation.[29] Partisan voting patterns have become even more prevalent in recent years as the ideological divide between Republicans and Democrats has widened. According to data assembled by the *Congressional Quarterly* for the last twenty-five years, partisan majorities have opposed each other on a majority of the votes in Congress.[30]

Congress is more polarized today—a consequence of more unified congressional parties. Political scientists explain this unification phenomenon, particularly in the House of Representatives, on the basis of the increasingly distinctive electoral districts they represent. In the words of Jeffrey M. Stonecash, Mark D. Brewer, and Mack D. Mariani, "Democratic candidates win in districts that are low income, have a relatively high percentage of nonwhites, and are urban. Republicans now dominate elections in districts are relatively affluent, largely white, and rural or suburban."[31]

The homogeneity within districts—the result of migration, immigration, and legislative drafting—has produced greater ideological differences among congressional districts oriented toward the Democrats and those leaning toward the Republicans.[32] Partisan divisions are less extreme in the Senate, a consequence of greater diversity within the state as a whole than in the House legislative districts within those states and more flexible rules that permit individual senators to influence the process and product of legislation more than their counterparts in the House of Representatives. Nonetheless, there is still more partisan unity in the Senate than there was two or three decades ago. These changes have affected Congress's internal dynamics. They have made compromise more difficult, especially when government is divided (with one party controlling the White House and the other controlling one or both houses of the Congress). They have also produced more heated rhetoric and less civility. When government is unified, however, partisanship has the opposite effect. It facilitates the legislative process in accordance with the wishes of the party in power with the president, the principal beneficiary.

Partisan Influence on the Executive and the Judiciary

Traditionally, chief executives perform several functions that may be subject to party influences. They set the agenda for public debate, choosing which initiatives they wish to emphasize. They nominate certain people to high-level executive positions and, in the federal government, to judicial positions. They even exercise some discretion over the performance of government services through their management initiatives, policy priorities, and political appointments. In each of these activities, they are affected by partisan considerations, but they also influence those considerations.

Even if a president, governor, or mayor does not hold a formal position within a party, he or she is considered the party's leader at the national, state, or local level and, as such, can make policy decisions and exercise personnel choices. Sometimes, however, the chief executives, especially presidents neglect their party because of the time and energy required for partisan activities, and occasionally they make judgments to which a sizable portion of their partisan or electoral constituency may object. George H. W. Bush did so when he supported a tax increase in 1990, as did Bill Clinton when he pursued free-trade agreements and fast-track legislation;

George W. Bush angered his conservative supporters when he signed into law legislation dealing with campaign finance reform, farm subsidies, tariffs on imported steel, and Medicare reform with an added prescription drug benefit.

Internal party divisions can reduce a president's political capital as they did for George W. Bush following his reelection. Some House Republicans objected to Bush's support of a bill to establish a national intelligence director with budget authority to oversee the intelligence community. With the president's attention diverted elsewhere, these Republicans blocked the intelligence bill, much to the embarrassment of the newly reelected president who had boasted of his political capital after his electoral victory. Similarly, a unified congressional Republican party forced President Bush to back off his threat to veto a bill that prohibited the United States from using torture to gain information from suspected terrorists.

Nonetheless, legislators of the president's party are more likely to support a chief executive of their own political persuasion because they share similar goals and objectives. Their political fates are also usually bound together. Republican unity on the tax cuts proposed by President George W. Bush is a good illustration of how ideological, partisan, and presidential influences combine to produce a unified party effort.

In trying to extend their political clout, presidents can bestow rewards such as patronage appointments, campaign resources, and media exposure. On the other hand, an unpopular president or governor can hurt the party and affect the success of legislators running on the same ticket in the next election. In 1994, for example, many conservative and some moderate Democrats "jumped ship," distancing themselves from President Clinton and the liberal policies associated with his administration. In 1998, however, most remained loyal to the president after he was accused of sexual improprieties and during his subsequent impeachment. The difference was that the public was critical of Clinton's performance in office in 1994 but supportive of it in 1998.

Partisanship is an important consideration in the appointment of federal judges and some state judges, and partisan divisions are evident even in states where judges are selected on the basis of merit alone.[33] However, the influence of party on judicial decision making is more difficult to determine. Although studies have found that Republican and Democratic judges differ on certain types of issues, these studies have not been able to determine whether the differences are a result of partisanship or differing values, ideology, and judicial philosophy.[34]

Moreover, judges are required to make their decisions on the basis of law, not politics, although personal and partisan factors may intrude on these decisions. The sentence given to a person convicted of a heinous crime could affect a state judge's reelection; the determination of whether a redistricting plan accords with federal guidelines could affect a party's chances in the next election. Nevertheless, partisan considerations affect the judiciary, but not in the same way they do the legislative or executive branches.

The political party is thus an instrument for governance, although it is rarely able to exercise total control over the operation of government. What it does is link institutions on the basis of common ideas and overlapping interests and promote cooperation through a system of rewards and occasional sanctions.

Parties help produce an agenda and contribute to consensus building within institutions and among the general public. In theory, this linkage between politics and government also contributes to holding a party responsible for the decisions and actions of its elected officials, although weak party discipline and separate institutions that may be controlled by different parties make that responsibility harder to achieve in practice. Nevertheless, the performance of a party in office affects the election prospects of others who run on the same party label. The crucial relationship between party and government puts a premium on building and maintaining partisan unity.

Only by converting public choices into coherent partisan positions can parties minimize internal struggles and thereby maximize their chances of winning. Party unity also facilitates governance. It promotes accountability by making it easier for the public to allocate responsibility for the government's decisions and actions. That is why political parties are an important component of a democratic system, and partisan politics are essential to its operation.

Review Questions

1. Which of the following campaign activities is not performed by the major political parties today?

   A. Convincing partisans to register to vote
   B. Turning out voters
   C. Overseeing the vote
   D. Tabulating the vote

2. Party voting in Congress has_____ in recent years.

   A. Increased
   B. Decreased
   C. Remained stable
   D. Fluctuated wildly

3. Presidents can influence elections in all but one of the following ways:

   A. Raising money
   B. Taking a position on an issue
   C. Making speeches
   D. Nominating an Executive Branch official

4. Partisan affiliation affects the federal judiciary primarily through which of the following processes?

   A. Nominations
   B. Litigation
   C. Appeals
   D. Impeachment

continued

Answers:

1. D
2. A
3. D
4. A

Conflict and Consensus in Review

The party provides the cohesion for governing. It provides an agenda on which most of its winning candidates will agree, a caucus in which legislative leadership can be determined and internal policy issues resolved, and ultimately a record upon which it can be judged by the American people. In these ways it contributes to democratic government.

Politics in Action
Reforming the Nomination Process: The Democrats Try It Again

The major parties have a dilemma: how to pick their strongest nominees for office but do so in a more democratic fashion. Before the 1970s, party leaders exercised tight control over the selection of their presidential nominees. More often than not, they used this control to choose the candidate who was most acceptable to the party's rank and file and had the best chance of winning. In 1968, Democratic Party leaders selected Vice President Hubert Humphrey to be the party's presidential nominee, even though Humphrey had not entered the Democratic primaries. His selection in the face of the party's division over the Vietnam War and a primary process in which Democrats Robert F. Kennedy and Eugene McCarthy received the most votes prompted a revolt by delegates who felt that their voice and that of the people they represented had not been heard.

A party commission led by Senator George McGovern proposed a series of changes in the procedures for choosing convention delegates aimed at increasing participation by the party's rank and file. Convention delegates were also required to be more demographically representative of the party's electorate. Since then, the Democrats have been tinkering with their rules but not with their goals, as have the Republicans.

Now, almost four decades later, the nomination process has still not achieved most of its desired ends. It has increased participation a little but still has not energized most of the party's electoral coalition. It has reduced the influence of party leaders, but it has also increased that of activists and the groups that represent them. It has enlarged the pool of potential nominees, but still gives an advantage to those with greater name recognition, financial resources, and organizational skills. Moreover, it has extended the election calendar, increased the costs of running, and attracted a more negative news media, but has not always resulted in the selection of the strongest party candidate.

Why? What is the problem with presidential nominations today? For one thing, the process starts too early, more than two years before the election. It is also heavily front-loaded and as a consequence usually ends too early, leaving a period of several months between the unofficial determination of the winner and the political convention in which the candidate officially receives the nomination. Moreover, most

continued

Politics in Action *continued*

of the public is not tuned into the nomination process at its most decisive stage in the early rounds.

The first states to hold contests, Iowa and New Hampshire, are not representative of the party's electorate, yet these states receive most of the candidates' attention and resources and exercise the most influence over the outcome.

The winner of either of these two contests may not be the most popular within the party or the candidate best able to win the general election. It is this problem, the unrepresentative character of Iowa and New Hampshire, that Democratic Party officials tried to remedy by changing the nomination calendar for 2008.

Following the 2004 election, the party established a Commission on Presidential Nomination Timing and Scheduling to recommend ways to make the nomination process more geographically balanced, more participatory for Democratic voters, and more likely to reflect the views of the party's broad-based electoral coalition. The commission met in party forums around the country; heard appeals by state party officials, partisans, and experts on the electoral process; and decided to recommend changes that would expand the first phase of the nomination contest and, if possible, back-load the calendar. In August 2006, the party's national committee accepted these recommendations for the 2008 nomination process. The party added contests at the beginning of the nomination process, before the official period in which states could hold their caucus or primary. They also provided incentives for other states to hold their caucuses and primaries later in the spring, including a bonus system that would increase the number of state delegates at the national nominating convention for states that held their contests later in the nomination process.[35] Both of these scheduling rule changes were accompanied by sanctions to be imposed on states that violated them and candidates who campaigned in those states.

In what was proposed as a compromise between Iowa and New Hampshire on one hand, and other states wanting to go first on the other, the commission invited two states—Nevada, which has a large Hispanic community, and South Carolina, with a sizable African American vote—to hold their contests early. Nevada's caucus would follow Iowa's, and South Carolina's primary would be held a week after New Hampshire's. The next week would open the official nominating calendar, which would last until the second Tuesday in June. The committee anticipated the following schedule:

Democratic Nomination Schedule for 2008
January 14, 2008: Iowa Caucus
January 19, 2008: Nevada Caucus
January 22, 2008: New Hampshire Primary
January 29, 2008: South Carolina Primary

Naturally, party officials in Iowa and New Hampshire were not happy to share the limelight with other states and threatened to move their contests even earlier. Kathleen Sullivan, chair of New Hampshire's Democratic Party, complained:

> By compressing Iowa, Nevada, New Hampshire, and South Carolina into 15 days, our candidates will not face the test of speaking to average voters about the issues that will matter in November 2008. Our nominee will be chosen by the end of January, a nominee who will be chosen by fewer than 500,000 voters. That is not democracy, that is not diversity.[36]

The changes are modest and are not expected to decrease front-loading very much. The early period still promises to be the most important for candidates seeking the nomination and for the press covering the campaign, but probably not for the average partisan who has not yet tuned in to a presidential election still many months away. Nor are the changes expected to shorten the two-year nomination cycle, the high costs of running, or the candidates' dependence on the mass media for reaching voters. In fact, the changes may have the opposite effect.

Party activists and organized interest groups will probably continue to exercise disproportionate influence. Appealing to these activists, who tend to be the most ideological, and to groups with specific agendas will still be necessary for candidates seeking their party's nomination. The moderate middles in both major parties will continue to

continued

Politics in Action *continued*

suffer as a result of the rhetoric necessary to win over the more extreme groups. Moreover, voters in the general elec-

tion may still see the party's presidential nominees as being too ideological and out of step with their own opinions.

What Do You Think?

1. Are there still inequities in the presidential selection process that undercut a democratic election system? Will the changes that the Democrats instituted for 2008 affect these inequities in any meaningful way?
2. How can a party conduct a process that stimulates turnout and energizes its rank and file but does not exacerbate party divisions, which would put it at a competitive disadvantage for the general election?
3. Does candidates' ability to "nominate" themselves to run produce a set of nominees that are ideologically,

psychologically, or politically distinct from candidates whom party leaders might have chosen if they had been given the opportunity to do so?

4. If a political party asked you for suggestions on how to reform its presidential nomination process, what change would be at the top of your list? Note the arguments for and against such a change. Do you think this change will ever happen?

Summary

We began this chapter by pointing to conflict and consensus within and between the major parties. Both naturally agree on the merits of the two party system. Over the years both have supported legislative measures that have strengthened it on the federal and state levels.

Partisans also tend to concur in their party's basic philosophy, many of its policy positions, and most of the candidates who run on its label in the general election. The heterogeneous composition of the parties does permit issue and candidate differences which may be resolved by the nomination process or at least submerged in the general election by overarching loyalties and a common interest in defeating their partisan opponents.

Parties are an essential component of a democratic political system. They provide a critical link between the electorate and its government. They structure elections, nominate candidates, provide a set of policy goals, and if successful, present an organization for governing and an orientation toward certain policy objectives and outcomes. They also enhance the collective responsibility of government, particularly when the same party controls the executive and legislative branches.

In the electorate, parties shape the public's political attitudes. These attitudes, in turn, act as a lens though which political events can be interpreted, candidates evaluated, and voting decisions made. Parties not only affect how people think about politics but also provide an association through which various demographic, issue-oriented, and economic groups can find a home. Just as important, they offer a channel through which groups may pursue their diverse interests. That pursuit generates conflict within and between the parties.

In elections, parties provide a framework for nominating candidates and a set of beliefs, policy positions, and priorities to which those candidates may subscribe. They also are a source for much of the personnel and financial support needed to mount a successful campaign.

Parties help organize government. They provide the means by which members of Congress choose their legislative leaders and committee chairperson or ranking members and hire loyal and competent staffs. Their caucuses meet to establish priorities and positions, as well as to achieve and maintain as much collective unity as possible. In the executive branch, they affect personnel selection and the president's policy agenda. The judiciary is less subject to partisan influence, except in the selection phase of the process.

Parties have become the cohesive mechanism that links governmental institutions and provides a kind of collective mindset for governing. To the extent that a single party controls an institution of government, it can be held accountable for its performance in that institution. That accountability also extends to individual public officials who identify themselves as and behave as partisans. During recent years, these personal factors have been more visible and have received greater attention from the news media.

In short, partisanship remains an important mechanism for informing the electorate, for structuring elections, and for deciding how to vote. It also provides a framework in which diverse interests can be resolved and public policy decisions made. The political perspective to which partisanship contributes can help overcome the constitutional separation of powers when government is unified, but it also can reinforce that separation when government is divided. The partisanship of elected officials also becomes a criterion for evaluating their individual and collective accountability in office.

Key Terms

political parties	Reform Party	independent
partisans	Federalists	wards or precincts
single-member district	Democratic-Republicans	party machines
multimember district	(Republicans)	party bosses
ideological parties	Democrats	party platform
issue parties	Whigs	responsible party government
Green Party	Republican Party	
candidate-oriented parties	Grand Old Party	

Discussion Questions

1. On what issues today do the Republicans and the Democrats agree more than they disagree?
2. How have the two major parties in the United States survived for so long as viable political entities?
3. Why have third-party and independent candidates had so much difficulty winning elections in the twentieth and twenty-first centuries?
4. How have reforms in the major parties' nomination processes affected the distribution of

power within the parties? Do these reforms contribute to conflict or consensus within the parties? Do they render the parties better or less able to govern?

5. Are parties really essential for democratic government? Explain.

6. Has the increasing ideological nature of the major parties contributed to or detracted from responsible party government?

7. What are the ways in which parties affect the structure and operation of the legislative and executive branches of government?

8. What effect, if any, do political parties have on the federal judiciary?

Topics for Debate

Debate each side of the following propositions:

1. The two-party system is essential for American democracy.

2. Voting in a party's primary election should be restricted to those who register as partisans of that party.

3. National party conventions are irrelevant and should be abolished.

4. Political appointments in the executive and judicial should be made solely on the basis of merit, not partisanship.

5. A new third party should be created that speaks for the average American.

6. A unified government is better than a divided government.

Where on the Web?

Democratic Party Organizations

Democratic National Committee **www.democrats.org**

Democratic Congressional Campaign Committee **www.dccc.org**

Democratic Senatorial Campaign Committee **www.dscc.org**

Go to **www.thomsonedu.com/thomsonnow** to learn about a powerful online study tool. You will get a personalized study plan based on your responses to a diagnostic Pre-Test. Once you have mastered the materials with the help of interactive learning tools, activities, timelines, video case studies, simulations, and an integrated E-Book, you can take a Post-Test to confirm you are ready to move to the next chapter.

Republican Party Organizations

Republican National Committee **www.rnc.org**

National Republican Congressional Campaign Committee **www.nrcc.org**

National Republican Senatorial Committee **www.nrsc.org**

Other Party Organizations

Reform Party **www.reformparty.org**

Green Party **www.greenparty.org**

| Selected Readings |

Abramson, Paul R., John H. Aldrich, Phil Paolino, and David W. Rohde. "Third-Party and Independent Candidates: Wallace, Anderson, and Perot." *Political Science Quarterly* 110 (Fall 1995): 349–367.

Aldrich, John H. *Why Parties? The Origin and Transformation of Political Parties in America.* Chicago: University of Chicago Press, 1995.

Beck, Paul Allen, and Marjorie Randon Hershey. *Party Politics in America,* 9th ed. New York: Longman, 2001.

Black, Earl, and Merle Black. *The Rise of Southern Republicanism.* Cambridge, Mass.: Harvard University Press, 2002.

Cotter, Cornelius P., James L. Gibson, John F. Bibby, and Robert Huckshorn. *Party Organizations in American Politics.* Pittsburgh: University of Pittsburgh Press, 1989.

Fiorina, Morris P., with Samuel J. Abrams and Jeremy C. Pope. *Culture Wars: The Myth of a Polarized America.* New York: Pearson/Longman, 2005.

Herrnson, Paul S., and John C. Green. *Multiparty Politics in America,* 2nd ed. Lanham, Md.: Rowman & Littlefield, 2002.

Jacobson, Gary C. "Party Polarization in National Politics: The Electoral Connection" in *Polarized Politics: Congress and the President in a Partisan Era.* Edited by Jon R. Bond and Richard Fleisher. Washington, D.C.: Congressional Quarterly, 2000, 9–30.

Key, V. O. Jr. *Southern Politics.* Knoxville: University of Tennessee Press, 1984.

Mayhew, David R. *Electoral Realignments: A Critique of an American Genre.* New Haven, Conn.: Yale University Press, 2002.

O'Connor, Edwin. *The Last Hurrah.* Boston: Little, Brown & Co., 1985.

Rosenstone, Steven J., Roy L. Behr, and Edward H. Lazarus. *Third Parties in America,* 2nd ed. Princeton, N.J.: Princeton University Press, 1996.

Shafer, Bryon E., and William J. M. Claggett. *The Two Majorities: The Issue Context of Modern American Politics.* Baltimore: Johns Hopkins University Press, 1995.

Smith, Steven S., and Gerald Gamm. "The Dynamics of Party Government in Congress" in *Congress Reconsidered.* Edited by Lawrence C. Dodd and Bruce I. Oppenheimer. Washington, D.C.: Congressional Quarterly, 2001, 245–268.

Stonecash, Jeffrey M., Mark D. Brewer, and Mack D. Mariani. *Diverging Parties: Social Change, Realignment, and Party Polarization.* Boulder, Colo.: Westview Press, 2003.

Warren, Robert Penn. *All the King's Men.* New York: Bantam Books, 1990.

Wattenberg, Martin P. *The Decline of American Political Parties, 1952–1996.* Cambridge, Mass.: Harvard University Press, 1998.

White, John K., and Daniel M. Shea. *New Party Politics: From Jefferson and Hamilton to the Information Age.* Boston: Bedford/St. Martin's, 2000.

Williams, T. Harry. *Huey Long.* New York: Vintage Books, 1981.

| Notes |

[1] John C. Green, James L. Guth, Lyman A. Kellstedt, and Corwin E. Smith, as quoted in "Religious Voters in 1994," *American Enterprise* (November/December 1995): 20.

[2] Morris Fiorina, *Retrospective Voting in American National Elections* (New Haven, Conn.: Yale University Press, 1981), 84.

[3] Third-party and independent candidates would do better in a multimember district, in which the winners are determined by the proportion of the votes they or their party receives. In elections decided by proportional voting, there is an incentive for candidates to affirm their party's positions and downplay their own beliefs. A multimember district system also encourages more parties to run candidates, because to win they need not finish first but only make a strong showing. Some states and cities conduct elections in multimember districts, as do countries such as France, Germany, and Spain.

[4]David C. King, "The Polarization of American Political Parties and Mistrust of Government," working paper, Politics Research Group, Kennedy School of Government, Harvard University. Available at http://www.ksg.harvard.edu/prg/king/polar.htm (accessed July 1998).

[5]Paul R. Abramson, John H. Aldrich, and David W. Rohde, *Change and Continuity in the 2004 Elections* (Washington D.C.: Congressional Quarterly, 2006), 182–206; Gary C. Jacobson, *The Politics of Congressional Elections*, 6th ed. (New York: Pearson/Longman, 2004), 230–253.

[6]Morris P. Fiorina with Samuel J. Abrams and Jeremy C. Pope, *Culture War? The Myth of a Polarized America* (New York: Pearson/Longman, 2005).

[7]According to the large exit poll conducted for the news media on the day of the election, 70 percent of Ralph Nader's supporters said that they would have participated had Nader not been on the ticket. Of this group, two out of three preferred Al Gore to George W. Bush.

[8]Jefferson's Republicans were not the forerunners of the modern Republican Party, which was organized in 1854 and nominated its first presidential candidate in 1856. Democrats, however, claim Jefferson as their first president and trace their party's origins to the Democratic-Republican Party at the end of the eighteenth century.

[9]This is the only time a tie occurred. Upon taking office, Jefferson and his supporters proposed a constitutional amendment that required electors to cast separate ballots for president and vice president. The Twelfth Amendment was ratified in 1804.

[10]For a more extended discussion of the creation of the American party system, see William Nisbet Chambers, *Political Parties in a New Nation: The American Experience, 1776–1809* (New York: Oxford University Press, 1963). Another helpful interpretation of the beginning of parties in the United States can be found in Wilfred E. Binkley, *American Political Parties: Their National History* (New York: Alfred A. Knopf, 1959).

[11]The politics of these new parties reflected their bases of support. Jackson's Democrats advocated an agrarian society in which the national government had a limited role and greater economic opportunities were available for the average person. In contrast, the Whigs, like their Federalist predecessors, envisioned a more industrial society in which a strong central government promoted policies designed to stimulate economic development.

[12]For an extended discussion of voter turnout during this and subsequent periods, see Walter Dean Burnham, "The Turnout Problem," in *Elections American Style*, ed. A. James Reichley (Washington, D.C.: Brookings Institution, 1987), 112–133.

[13]Binkley, *American Political Parties*, 315–319.

[14]"Origin of GOP," Republican National Committee, http://www.gop.com/About/Default.aspx (accessed July 23, 2004).

[15]See Robert Huckfeldt and Carol W. Kohfield, *Race and the Decline of Class in American Politics* (Urbana: University of Illinois Press, 1989), 84; and Benjamin Ginsberg, "The 1994 National Elections: A Debacle for the Democrats," in *Do Elections Matter?* (New York: M. E. Sharpe, 1996), 9.

[16]See Jeffrey M. Stonecash, *Class and Party in American Politics* (Boulder, Colo.: Westview Press, 2000); and Jeffrey M. Stonecash, Mark D. Brewer, and Mack D. Mariani, *Diverging Parties: Social Change, Realignment, and Party Polarization* (Boulder, Colo.: Westview Press, 2003).

[17]The DNC consists of state party chairpeople and other elected and appointed party leaders.

[18]For a history of the RNC and the DNC, see Ralph M. Goldman, *The National Party Chairmen and Committees* (Armonk, N.Y.: M. E. Sharpe, 1990).

[19]Coffee hours and sleepovers in the White House, trade missions and trips on *Air Force One,* and briefings by cabinet members and White House staff were all employed to fill the party's coffers.

[20]For an excellent discussion of the strengthening of national party organizations in their campaign activities, see Paul S. Herrnson, *Party Campaigning in the 1980s* (Cambridge, Mass.: Harvard University Press, 1988).

[21]James L. Gibson, Cornelius Cotter, John F. Bibby, and Robert J. Huckshorn, "Assessing Party Organizational Strength," *American Journal of Political Science* 17 (May 1983): 193–222.

[22]John F. Bibby, *Politics, Parties, and Elections in America*, 2nd ed. (Chicago: Nelson-Hall, 1992), 104.

[23]For a good study of trends in state parties, see Robert J. Huckshorn and John F. Bibby, "State Parties in an Era of Political Change," in *The Future of American Political Parties*, ed. Joel L. Fleishman (Englewood Cliffs, N.J.: Prentice-Hall, 1982), 70–100.

[24]This phrase was used by Governor George Wallace in his 1968 campaign for president as an independent candidate.

[25]Gerald M. Pomper with Susan S. Lederman, *Elections in America* (White Plains, N.Y.: Longman, 1980), 161.

[26]Ibid., 42–43. See also Jeff Fishel, *Presidents and Promises: From Campaign Pledge to Presidential Performance* (Washington, D.C.: Congressional Quarterly, 1985), 37–38; Michael G. Krukones, *Promise and Performance: Presidential Campaigns as Policy Predictors* (Lanham, Md.: University Press

of America, 1984), 124; and William G. Mayer, "Why Presidents Break Promises," in *Readings in Presidential Politics*, ed. George C. Edwards (Thomson/Wadsworth, 2006), 5–11.

[27]For a discussion of the concept of responsible party government, see the Committee on Political Parties of the American Political Science Association, *Toward a More Responsible Two-Party System* (New York: Holt, Rinehart and Winston, 1950); and Austin Ranney, *The Doctrine of Responsible Party Government* (Urbana: University of Illinois Press, 1962).

[28]Take the case of Phil Gramm. In 1981, when he was a Democratic representative from Texas, Gramm supported the Reagan administration's proposals to reduce domestic spending. Moreover, he allegedly conveyed to the Republicans the content of confidential Democratic discussions on these budget proposals. The Democratic leadership punished him by denying him a seat on the budget committee in the next Congress. Gramm responded by switching parties and winning reelection as a Republican, an example that was not lost on subsequent party leaders. In 1995, when Senator Mark Hatfield of Oregon broke ranks to oppose a major Republican proposal (a constitutional amendment to require a balanced federal budget), a meeting composed of all Republicans in the Senate that considered his actions decided not to censure him.

[29]See David W. Rohde, "The Reports of My Death Are Greatly Exaggerated: Parties and Party Voting in the House of Representatives," in *Changing Perspectives on Congress*, ed. Glenn R. Parker (Knoxville: University of Tennessee Press, 1990); and Malcolm E. Jewell and David M. Olson, *Political Parties and Elections in American States* (Chicago: Dorsey Press, 1988), 246–249.

[30]Harold W. Stanley and Richard G. Niemi, *Vital Statistics on American Politics 2005–2006* (Washington, D.C.: Congressional Quarterly, 2006), 217.

[31]Stonecash, Brewer, and Mariani, *Diverging Parties*, 28.

[32]James G. Gimpell, *Separate Destinations: Migration, Immigration and the Politics of Places* (Ann Arbor: University of Michigan Press, 1999), 13–14, 326.

[33]Paul Allen Beck and Frank J. Sorauf, *Party Politics in America*, 7th ed. (New York: HarperCollins Publishers, 1992), 423.

[34]This subject is discussed for federal judges in Robert A. Carp and Ronald Stidham, *The Federal Courts* (Washington, D.C.: Congressional Quarterly, 1985), 142–148; also see Craig Ducat and Robert L. Dudley, "Federal District Judges and Presidential Power During the Postwar Era," *Journal of Politics* 51 (February 1989): 98–118. An examination of the influence of party on state judges can be found in Stuart Nagel, "Political Party Affiliation and Judges' Decisions," *American Political Science Review* 55 (December 1961): 843–850; and David W. Adamany, "The Party Variable in Judges' Voting: Conceptual Notes and a Case Study," *American Political Science Review* 63 (March 1969): 57–83.

[35]During this period, the public usually loses interest and money is in short supply, yet the prospective nominee must still stay in the news to reunify the party, recast his or her image, and articulate the themes for the general election campaign. It is difficult to do so using only free media.

[35]States that held their caucus or primary during the period of March 4–17 would receive a bonus of 15 percent additional delegates; March 18–April 7, 20 percent more; April 8–April 28, 30 percent more; and April 29–June 10, 40 percent more.

[36]Kathleen Sullivan, quoted in "Democrats Shake Up Primary Schedule," CBS News, August 19, 2006.

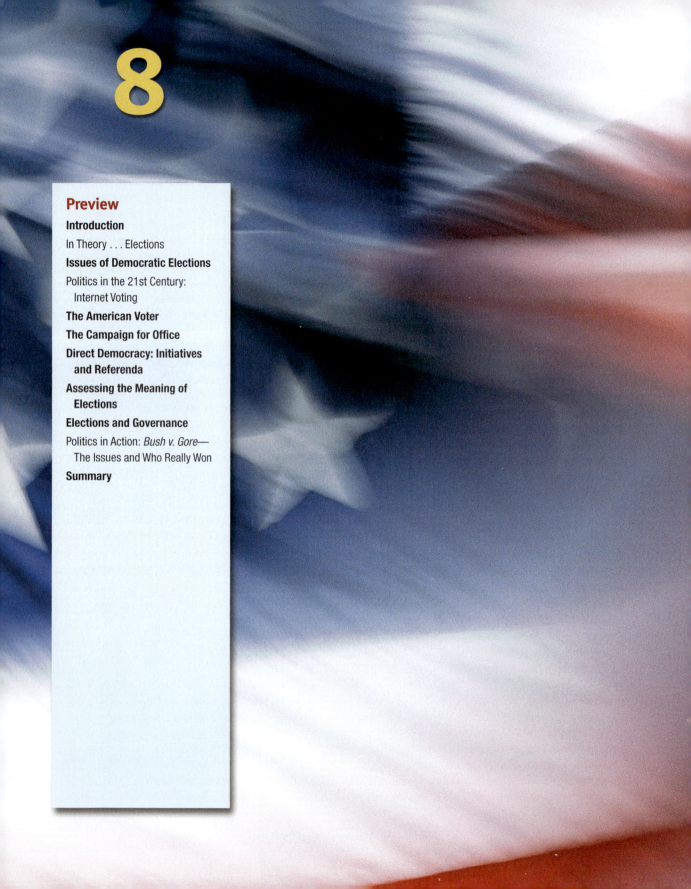

8

Campaigns and Elections

Introduction

THEY WERE AT THE TOP OF THEIR GAME—powerful legislators, articulate party spokesmen, and nationally recognized leaders. Republican Tom DeLay was the Majority Leader in the House; Joe Lieberman was a prominent senator and Democratic Party vice-presidential nominee in 2000. Who would have thought that several years later the voters would have rejected them at the polls?

DeLay's rise to power and fall from grace was rapid. Elected to Congress in 1984, he first became Majority Whip and later Majority Leader. DeLay's political action committees contributed millions to Republican candidates. Known as "the hammer" for his persistence, drive, and clout, he orchestrated GOP victories on such key issues as Medicare reform, fast-track authority for the president, and school vouchers for the District of Columbia. He criticized excessive government regulations, weakening the authority and budgets of the Environmental Protection Agency (EPA) and Occupational Safety and Health Administration

(OSHA) in the Department of Labor. When he became Majority Leader in 2002, he shook up the lobbying community by demanding that groups hire Republican lobbyists if they wanted access to his office.

Who would have thought that such a powerful member of Congress, a leader who knew how to stretch the rules to gain political advantage, would have been brought down by these same rules and the laws that regulate the behavior of government officials? But that is exactly what happened. DeLay crossed the line. He went too far to help his party and to benefit himself. The House Ethics Committee admonished him for his heavy-handed threats to hire Republican lobbyists, for the access he gave to large contributors, for the government resources he used to try to influence the Texas legislature's decision to redraw the lines of its congressional districts, and for promising to endorse a Representative's son if that Representative voted in favor of a particular piece of legislation. In addition, his close relationship with Jack Abramoff—a lobbyist who subsequently pleaded guilty to charges of conspiracy, tax evasion, and mail fraud—and

the free trips he accepted from him, the money DeLay's wife received from Abramoff for consulting, and the ways DeLay used his position to help Abramoff's clients all raised questions about DeLay's ethics, judgment, and behavior.

But it was his indictment by a Texas grand jury for violating the state's campaign finance law and the possibility of a long and costly trial that ultimately did him in. Republicans forced him to give up his position as Majority Leader and eventually to resign from Congress. He did so, but not before being renominated by his constituents. Unable to remove his name from the ballot, DeLay was defeated in 2006 by former Democratic representative Nick Lampson, who had earlier lost his congressional seat as a consequence of DeLay's Texas redistricting plan.

Joe Lieberman's problem with the voters of Connecticut was quite different. A moderate senator and a person who emphasized moral and ethical behavior—he was the first Democrat to criticize President Clinton for his actions in the Monica Lewinsky affair—Lieberman was an unabashed supporter of President Bush's decision

©Reuters/CORBIS

Democratic vice presidential candidate Senator Joseph Lieberman (D-CT) raises his fist while addressing delegates during the third day of the Democratic National Convention at the Staples Center in Los Angeles, August 16, 2000. Senator Lieberman is the first Jewish-American to run on a major party's presidential ticket in the United States.

to go to war in Iraq, the president's policy of keeping American troops in that country despite the cost in money and personnel, his expanded use of executive powers in the war on terrorism, his faith-based initiative, and his restructuring of homeland security and national intelligence. Lieberman's agreement with the Republican president on all of these issues put him on a collision course with Connecticut's Democratic electorate. Lieberman lost a close primary election to the wealthy but inexperienced Ned Lamont. Prior to his defeat, however, the senator indicated that he would run as an independent candidate if he did not win the nomina-

tion, thereby infuriating party officials and the Democratic electorate that voted for his opponent. Moreover, he depended largely on contributions from Republicans to fund his independent candidacy and their votes to reelect him.

Here, too, the voters had the last word. They reelected Lieberman, preferring his independent, moderate views to the more ideological stands of his Democratic and Republican opponents.

The cases of DeLay and Lieberman illustrate the challenges and dangers elected officials face in office. They also show why electoral choice, be it by peers in the House, partisans in Connecticut, or the general electorate in Texas, is central to a democratic political process. Elections are important because they tie elected officials to their electoral base. They are a mechanism for making leadership choices. They are also a constraint on the exercise of power. Because most elected officials desire to remain or move up in elective office, want the adulation and respect of their constituents, and believe in representative government, they are motivated to make decisions and take actions that accord with the values, beliefs, and opinions of—and are directed toward the needs and interests of—those they represent. Remove the election cycle and this motivation declines.

Elections also provide an opportunity for learning. They are predicated

on people having sufficient information to make an enlightened judgment. By forcing candidates to express their opinions on salient policy issues, elections shape and anticipate their decisions and actions in office. The collective judgment of the electorate thereby helps determine an agenda for governing. Elections also reveal much about the character and qualifications of those who run for elective office.

Finally, elections provide a periodic mechanism for resolving conflict in a way that is agreeable to the vast majority of Americans. There is a consensus that elections are an acceptable way to give the people a voice in determining the composition and, indirectly, the disposition of government.

This chapter begins by discussing the critical relationship between elections and democracy. Next it turns to the electorate—who votes and why. The third part of the chapter examines the environment in which elections occur and the various stages of the electoral process, from organizing a campaign to raising money and mobilizing voters to employing certain strategies and tactics. The final part of the chapter turns to the outcome of the election, its meaning and its implications for government and public policy. The case study at the end examines the 2000 Florida electoral controversy and its resolution by the Supreme Court.

Questions to Ponder

- Why are elections so critical to a democratic political process?
- How do they resolve conflict and for whom?
- Do most elections meet the standard for fairness? Does everyone have an equal chance to run, win, or affect the outcome of the vote?
- Does the electoral process facilitate a discussion of the issues and of the candidates' qualifications for office? What role does the press play? Do the news media provide "fair and balanced" coverage that is sufficient for voters to make an informed choice on election day?
- How do elections affect governing? Do election results provide an agenda and a mandate for the new administration?

8.1 In Theory . . .

Elections

Elections are a mechanism for making important political choices. They frame policy debate, select candidates for public office, determine who wins, and influence the decisions and actions of elected officials in office. They also are the principal means by which the electorate can hold those in government accountable for their actions. In short, elections are necessary for a democracy because they establish and reaffirm the principle and practice of popular control.

If elections are to link the people to their representatives, they must meet the democratic criteria of liberty (voters must be able to exercise a free, informed, and meaningful choice) and equality (all citizens must have the opportunity to vote and all votes must be counted equally). They must also be sufficiently comprehensive so that voters can make an informed judgment on election day. Finally, the results of the vote should be reflected accurately and fairly in the composition of the elected government and the policy that its officials pursue.

To the extent that elections meet these criteria, the politics of American democracy is working well; to the extent that they do not, the public can become apathetic or angry, cynical or distrustful, and support or oppose what government does and how it does it. The stakes are high because elections are such a critical component of democratic governance. If they are suspect, then the fabric of that government is suspect as well.

Issues of Democratic Elections

Elections are a major component of democracy. They allow citizens to choose the people who will make and oversee the implementation of public policy, policy that settles political disputes among different groups within society. Elections also provide a coalition for governing, at least initially. How long that coalition lasts varies with the success that the government has in satisfying the interests and demands of this coalition.

Suffrage: Who Should Be Able to Vote?

In 1787, the framers of the Constitution struggled with the electoral component. They struggled because they were leery of a government in which one group could gain control through the electoral process. Moreover, they had to contend with two related but controversial issues: who should vote and how should representation be based. An unpopular decision on either issue could have threatened the ratification of the new Constitution.

In theory, the convention delegates favored a government of, by, and for the people. In practice, they feared that the self-interested behavior of the masses could lead to what is often referred to as a **tyranny of the majority.**

tyranny of the majority
A term used to suggest that a majority of people can be as tyrannical as a few or one. Fear of the tyranny of the majority is one reason James Madison and others preferred a republican form of government to a direct democracy.

One way to prevent such a tyranny was to restrict suffrage—that is, to limit the right to vote. Such restrictions, however, would not have been consistent with the political rights defined in the Declaration of Independence or the preamble to the Constitution. Moreover, they would have jeopardized the ratification of the Constitution. So the framers took another tack by designing a system to represent three constituencies: (**1**) the nation (president and vice president), (**2**) the states (Senate), and (**3**) the people (House of Representatives). To avoid the potentially divisive issue of who would be eligible to vote, they made the states responsible for resolving that question, retaining for Congress the power to legislate on these matters if it so desired.

Initially, most states required citizens to have a stake in their community—that is, own property—as a condition of voting. Because most property was owned by white men, this requirement effectively disenfranchised women and racial minorities. Some states imposed an additional requirement: belief in a Christian God.

In the early nineteenth century, pressure developed to expand the franchise to enable more people to vote. By the middle of the 1830s, property ownership and religious beliefs had been dropped as qualifications for voting in most states. However, gender and racial barriers remained, and it took the enactment of constitutional amendments to remove them. The Fifteenth Amendment, ratified in 1870, abolishes race, creed, and national origin as qualifications for voting, at least in theory. In practice, formal and informal restrictions effectively prevented large-scale voting by African Americans in the South for another 100 years. The Nineteenth Amendment, ratified in 1920, prevents states from denying women the right to vote. At that time, only a few states permitted woman's suffrage. Moreover, the Twenty-Sixth Amendment, ratified in 1971, requires states to

Suffragettes march for the right to vote.

extend the right to vote to citizens eighteen years of age or older. Each of these amendments was passed as a result of successful struggles in the public arena—political struggles—by those who favored the expansion of suffrage and those who opposed it.

The restrictions on suffrage had benefited those in power, generally the more well-to-do members of society. As suffrage gradually expanded, however, government became more representative and more responsive to more people within society. Moreover, political parties became more competitive at all levels of government, and within the parties there were more opportunities for the rank and file to be heard and to influence the selection of nominees for public office.

How Should Elections Be Structured and Conducted?

In the early days of the republic, states had extensive authority to determine the conduct of federal elections. Subsequently, constitutional amendments and congressional statutes limited that discretion, such as the right to set qualifications for voting and, more recently, procedures for voter registration. Nevertheless, state laws that control ballot access, electoral challenges, and even the time, place, and manner of voting continue to have an important effect on the electoral process. Take touch screen voting, for example. California recently decertified the use of many of its touch screen voting units on the grounds that their accuracy and security could not be ensured (see Box 8.2).

8.2 Politics in the 21st Century

Internet Voting

For most Americans, especially those who remember the 2000 Florida voting controversy, with its confusing butterfly ballots, hanging and dimpled chads, and registration foul-ups, electronic voting is an appealing concept. Why couldn't computer technology be used to systematize registration procedures nationally and make the act of voting easier and the counting of the votes more reliable?

For the elderly, the infirm, and the disabled, touch screen voting could reduce inadvertent voting errors. It could help those who do not have a command of the English language and who might be unable to complete a paper ballot. The votes could be tabulated automatically, thereby providing instant and accurate results at the end of the election.

In theory, every voter benefits from electronic voting. In practice, however, the technology might not be sufficiently developed to ensure the integrity of the voting process. What would happen if the screen froze or the computer crashed? And how would voters and election officials know that votes were properly cast and counted unless there was a paper trail?

Although electronic voting is still in its infancy, election officials are beginning to experiment with it, and Congress is helping them to do so. The 2002 Help America Vote Act authorized $3.9 billion in assistance to states and localities to upgrade their election equipment and created an Election Assistance Commission to administer the funds.

The commission met in May 2004 but has a long way to go before standards are established and the new equipment has passed tests for accuracy and security. Experiments thus far with touch screen voting have been disappointing. In Maryland, some new touch screen voting machines did not work. In California, the electronic voting units made by one company were actually decertified because of security concerns; others were used only if they produced a paper ballot that allowed voters to confirm their touch screen vote and election officials to confirm the results of the machine tabulation with the paper ballots that the machine produced.

An even more futuristic possibility is voting on the Internet. Proponents contend that voting on a home computer would improve turnout, allow voters to take their time and presumably make a more reflective judgment, and allow many Americans who are out of the country to vote. Opponents, however, think it is a dangerous idea that would subject election to Internet terrorism and undermine public confidence in the results. Moreover, with computer ownership and access still skewed in the direction of the better-educated, higher-income portion of the population, online voting might initially benefit the economically advantaged at the expense of the less affluent and less well-educated. Democratic candidate Al Sharpton, a candidate for the 2004 Democratic nomination, apparently thought it would do so when he objected to the plan of Michigan Democrats to allow online voting in lieu of attendance at one of the party's regular caucuses.

On the other hand, with so many U.S. citizens living, working, and traveling abroad, voting on the Internet could enfranchise thousands of people. It would certainly be easier and less time-consuming for most people than obtaining an absentee ballot, having it postmarked and in some cases even notarized, and then mailing it back to the proper address at the proper time. The Defense Department found the idea so appealing that it launched an online voting initiative in 2002, the Secure Electronic Registration and Voting Experiment (SERVE). Ten expert political and computer scientists were asked to determine the feasibility for armed services personnel.

In the end, however, Defense Department experts were divided. Some criticized the proposal, calling the system's current technology unstable, unsafe, and insecure. Others, however, saw potential in the idea, although they admitted there were problems with the Internet as it exists today. But the critics won. They leaked their objections to the proposal to the *New York Times,* which ran a front-page story on the dangers of Internet voting: its vulnerability to hackers, its susceptibility to viruses that could alter voters or change outcomes, and even its potential for terrorists who might want to disrupt the vote. These concerns and the public outcry they produced led the Pentagon to abandon the plan, at least for the foreseeable future.

But hope remains that technology can be developed to conduct a secure and reliable election online. Britain and Switzerland are looking into Internet-facilitated voting, as are U.S. election reformers and companies that hope to profit from this new technology.

Electoral choice is affected by the rules for appearing on the ballot. States can make it tough or easy to run for office. They can impose residence requirements on candidates, make them pay a filing fee, and require them to obtain the signatures of a certain number or percentage of registered voters before their names can be placed on the ballot. The more rigorous these requirements, the fewer the candidates and the greater the party's control over its nominees are likely to be. H. Ross Perot's Reform Party in 1992 and 1996 and the Green Party in 2000 had to spend considerable time and money collecting signatures simply to get the names of their candidates to appear on the ballot.

The authority of the states to conduct general elections extends to primaries. Primaries are elections in which party partisans decide on the candidates who will run on their party's label in the general election. The type of primary, the date for holding it, the requirements for entering it, and the rules for determining the winner are all established by state laws. In some cases, these laws have elicited considerable controversy, particularly when they conflict with national party rules. In other cases, they have worked to the advantage of candidates who have the backing of state party leaders and their organizations and can obtain the required number of signatures to appear on the ballot.

In two landmark decisions, *Cousins v. Wigoda* (1975) and *Democratic Party of the U.S. v. La Follette* (1981), the Supreme Court held that the parties may determine their own rules for delegate selection and refuse to seat delegates at their national conventions who are not chosen in accordance with those rules.[2] Despite these rulings, however, popular participation in the nomination process has weakened the ability of party leaders and organizations to select candidates for office. As a result, the party activists exercise more influence over candidate selection, and those who are elected tend to be more responsive to these activists' beliefs and demands. The democratic character of the political system has been enhanced, but divisions between the parties have widened.

Should Citizens Be Able to Spend as Much as They Desire in Political Campaigns?

The criteria of making sure that all citizens have an equal voice and vote in the electoral process have generated a decades-long debate over campaign finance, and specifically over whether the American tradition of unrestricted private funding of political campaigns undercuts the basic principles of political equality in which all adult citizens should have an equal opportunity to affect the outcome: one person, one vote Before the mid-1970s, campaigns were financed entirely by individual contributions with both parties depending on a small number of wealthy donors.[3] As campaign expenditures increased, primarily as a result of rising costs of modern communications technology (such as polling, computerized mailings and targeting of campaign appeals, and extensive radio and television advertising), questions began to be raised about the connection between giving and governing. Do the wealthy exercise a disproportionate influence? What do they receive for their money? Can elected officials be responsive to large donors and to the general public at the same time? Do the high costs of running discourage qualified individuals from seeking office? These questions, which have persisted over the years, have prompted Congress to regulate campaign contributions and expenditures to reduce the inequalities in the campaign finance system.

Congress enacted laws in the 1970s to limit campaign spending and provide government support for presidential nomination and election campaigns. The Federal Election Campaign Act (FECA) required public disclosure of all contributions and expenditures above a certain amount and created the Federal Election Commission to monitor activities and oversee compliance. Parts of the legislation were highly controversial. Did the prescribed limits on contributions restrain freedom of speech? In *Buckley v. Valeo* (1976) the Supreme Court said "no." Arguing that personal expenditures can be a form of expression but that campaign finance can be regulated, the Court upheld the right of Congress to restrict the amount of money that individuals and groups could contribute to candidates in any federal election, but it also allowed these same individuals and groups to spend unlimited amounts independently of the candidates.[4]

The Court's decision did not end the controversy,[5] although initially it reduced the partisan inequalities that existed and also the amount of money available to presidential campaigns at a time when turnout was decreasing. With limited federal funds available to them, the presidential campaigns spent most of it on television advertising, not on grassroots mobilization. Some members of Congress attributed the decline in turnout to the lack of money spent on get-out-the-vote activities in 1976. As a result, Congress amended the law to allow unlimited contributions and expenditures on party-building efforts such as voter turnout campaigns. This amendment became known as the **soft money** loophole.

soft money

Campaign contributions not subject to federal limits of $2,000 per candidate per election and $5,000 per nonparty group. Political parties can no longer accept soft money contributions.

The goal was laudable—to increase voter information and participation in the electoral process—but the results were disastrous. The new amendment essentially encouraged political parties to solicit large donations from the rich and powerful, using their perquisites of office to do so. Invitations to the White House, trips on *Air Force One* and trade missions, special briefings by cabinet officials and members of Congress, ambassadorships, and other political appointments were among the inducements made available to big donors. The successful solicitation of soft money by the major parties effectively undermined the contribution limits that the law had imposed on federal candidates.[6] The system had broken down. Table 8.1 indicates the amount of soft money that parties raised and spent in recent election cycles.

It was not until 2002 that sufficient support could be built in Congress to try to fix it. The Bipartisan Campaign Reform Act (BCRA), also known by the names of two of its most prominent Senate sponsors, John McCain and Russ Feingold, barred the national parties from soliciting soft money after the 2002 midterm elections. It also placed constraints on nonparty groups, which were prohibited from mentioning candidates by name in their issue ads 30 days or less before a primary and 60 days or less before the general election. Table 8.2 lists the current contribution limits.

Table 8.1 Party Fund-Raising and Expenditures in Recent Federal Elections, 1999–2004

	1999–2000			2001–2002			2003–2004
	Hard	**Soft**	**Total**	**Hard**	**Soft**	**Total**	**Hard**
DEMOCRATS							
Revenue	$275.2	$245.2	$520.4	$217.2	$246.1	$463.3	$683.8
	(53%)	(47%)		(47%)	(53%)		
Expenses	$265.8	$244.8	$510.7	$208.7	$250.6	$459.3	$655.6
	(52%)	(48%)		(45%)	(55%)		
REPUBLICANS							
Revenue	$465.8	$249.9	$715.7	$441.6	$250.0	$691.6	$784.8
	(65%)	(35%)		(64%)	(36%)		
Expenses	$427.0	$252.8	$679.8	$427	$258.9	$685.9	$752.6
	(63%)	(37%)		(62%)	(38%)		

Source: "Party Committees Raise More Than $1 Billion in 2001–2002," Federal Election Commission, http://www.fec.gov/press/press2003/20030320party/20030103party.html (accessed March 14, 2006). "Party Financial Activity Summarized for the 2004 Election Cycle," Federal Election Commission, http://www.fec.gov/press/press2005/20050302party/Party2004final.html (accessed March 14, 2006)

Table 8.2 Federal Contribution Limits

	To Any Candidate (per Election*)	To National Party Committee (per Calendar Year),	To Any Other PAC, State or Local Party, or Other Committee (per Calendar Year)	Aggregate Total
Individual May Give[†]	$2,000	$25,000	$5,000	$25,000 per year; $95,000 per electien cycle[§]
Multicandidate Committees[‡] May Give	$5,000	$15,000	$5,000	No limit
Other Political Committees May Give	$1,000	$20,000	$5,000	No limit

*Primary and general elections count as separate elections.
[†]Individual contribution limits are to be indexed to inflation.
[‡]Committees with fifty or more contributors that have been registered for at least six months.
[§]To federal candidates per election cycle—$37,500. To national party committees per election cycle—$20,000–$57,000. To all other committees per election cycle—$37,500.
Source: Federal Election Commission, *The FEC and the Federal Campaign Finance Law* (Washington, D.C.: Government Printing Office, 1978), 4, as amended by the Campaign Finance Reform Act of 2002.

The legislation was immediately challenged by a variety of groups, including the Republican Party, which argued that it abridged the party's constitutional rights, but a sharply divided Supreme Court disagreed. In *McConnell v. FEC* (2003), the Court upheld the major parts of the legislation.[7]

Meanwhile the parties and their allies began to explore other ways to circumvent the law legally in order to supplement their campaign spending. They created nonparty, nonprofit groups, known as 527s, the numbered provision in the Internal Revenue code that permitted such groups to form and engage in political activities. These groups organized to raise large sums of money and used it to mount effective advertising and grassroots campaigns to supplement the parties' effort.[8] Although public interest groups and a Republican-oriented advocacy group challenged the legality of these fund-raising operations, the Federal Election Commission decided not to intervene during the 2003–2004 election cycle, rejecting a proposal to subject nonparty groups to the soft money prohibition. As a result, both parties turned to advocacy groups to supplement their campaigns. These groups raised almost $597 million and spent $610 million in the 2004 election, highlighting once again the issue of the influence that large donors and the organizations they represent have on the election, on the parties, and on the people they elect. The public perceives that they have a lot of influence, and so do the mass media. Such perceptions, whether accurate or not, have contributed to increased public cynicism and distrust of politicians, especially those in elective office.

Review Questions

1. Elections are considered democratic when which of the following criteria is met?

   A. When everyone votes
   B. When everyone has the opportunity to vote
   C. When all adult citizens have the opportunity to vote
   D When there is no controversy over the election outcome

2. Suffrage has expanded in the United States as a result of all of the following except

   A. Constitutional amendment
   B. Federal law
   C. Political tradition
   D. State action

3. Which of the following factors contributes the most to how people vote?

   A. Partisan allegiances
   B. Issue positions
   C. Candidate images
   D. Prospective judgments

continued

4. Recently, federal laws have been enacted to regulate all of the following except

    A. Campaign contributions
    B. Campaign expenditures
    C. Issue advocacy advertising
    D. Independent expenditures

Answers:

    1. C
    2. C
    3. A
    4. D

Conflict and Consensus in Review

In short, Americans agree that there are issues that affect the democratic character of elections. Who can vote, when and how elections are held, and how much money is spent are three such issues that have produced conflict over the years. A consensus for extending suffrage to all adult, law-abiding citizens, for making voting easier and more accessible, and for limiting the size of contributions and expenditures is building, but problems of how to achieve these objectives without constricting the liberties that the US Constitution protects continue to generate controversy.

The American Voter

Who can vote and who does vote are two different questions. The expansion of suffrage has made the American political system more democratic—at least in theory. In practice, however, there has always been a gap between eligible voters and actual voters, a gap that has traditionally been widest for newly eligible voters.

U.S. election laws are part of the problem. For years, voting turnout in the United States has trailed that of many other democratic countries, in part because most states require registration *before* voting[9] whereas other countries permit its citizens to register when they vote or do not require registration, using other official records to determine eligibility.

The enactment of the "motor voter" bill in 1993 was aimed at making it easier for people to register to vote. Since the law went into effect in 1995, the proportion of the voting-age population (VAP) registered to vote has increased slightly, from 66 percent of the VAP to about 80 percent.[10] Nevertheless, the percentage of the voting-age population turning out to vote has declined since 1960. Table 8.3 indicates turnout percentages in recent federal elections. Notice how much lower turnout has been in nonpresidential election years. For a country that prides itself on its democratic values and promotes democracy abroad, the turnout figures are a cause of concern and embarrassment.

Table 8.3 Turnout in National Elections

Year	Turnout (%)
1980	59.2
1982	48.5
1984	59.9
1986	46.0
1988	57.4
1990	45.0
1992	61.3
1994	44.6
1996	54.2
1998	41.9
2000	54.7
2002	34.2
2004	60.7

Source: *Statistical Abstract of the United States: 2004.* United States Census Bureau, 256; updated by authors.

Who Votes and Why?

Why do some people always vote, others vote only occasionally, and still others never cast a ballot in a national, state, or local election? One reason for the varieties of voting behavior is that the decision is up to the individual. There are no penalties for not voting, as there are in some other countries, such as Australia, Belgium, and Chile. Citizens in those countries who fail to vote are fined, whereas in the United States not voting is considerable a viable and, for many, an acceptable option.

Another reason is that there are a substantial number of adult citizens who have lost their right to vote or who are not citizens and thus ineligible to vote.[11] In most states, prisoners cannot vote; in many states, those convicted of a felony or dishonorably discharged from the military also lose their right to vote. These prohibitions have disproportionately affected African American males, disenfranchising about 1.4 million out of approximately 10.4 million in the population.[12]

A more fundamental reason, however, is apathy. Many people lack interest in the campaign, concern about the outcome, feelings of civic responsibility, or a belief that their vote will make a difference.[13] These people tend to have weak, if any, partisan affiliations. Generally, people who identify strongly with a political party are more motivated to vote, more likely to be contacted during the campaign, and consequently, more likely to vote.

Why do so many people not care about voting? Some political scientists argue that the public's increasingly negative feelings about the performance of those in government have led to greater apathy, more cynicism, and lower efficacy (see Chapter 5). A study of voting behavior by three political scientists,

Paul R. Abramson, John H. Aldrich, and David W. Rohde, found that 80 percent of the decline in turnout can be attributed to the combined effects of weaker partisan affiliation and feelings of decreasing political effectiveness, "with the decline in feelings of political efficacy being about three times as important as the decline of party identification."[14]

Demographic characteristics also contribute to or detract from political involvement. The more educated a person is, the more likely it is that he or she will vote.[15] Education enhances an individual's ability to understand the issues, follow the campaign, and recognize the differences between the candidates' positions. More education also usually leads to higher income, which in turn may increase a person's perceived stake in the outcome of elections.[16] However, given the effects of education and income on voting, it is surprising that the electoral turnout has generally decreased since 1960 even though education and income levels have increased. To understand why this has occurred, it is necessary to look at other factors, such as the increasing number of immigrants who have come to America in recent years. These people, many of whom may be newly arrived, may not speak English, may come from impoverished backgrounds with little formal education, and may not have the skills or motivation to vote. In fact, they may not want to call attention to themselves by registering with a government agency to vote.

Another factor has to do with age. Studies have shown that the youngest group of eligible voters, those under thirty, register to vote less regularly than people in the middle age groups.[17] People over seventy-five also are a little less likely to vote, for reasons having to do with health. Trends that have resulted in larger proportions of younger and older voters may have contributed to the decline in turnout.

Turnout has partisan implications as well. Republican partisans, who tend to be better educated and have higher incomes than Democrats, vote more regularly than Democrats. The higher Republican turnout has helped the GOP counter the numerical advantage in the electorate enjoyed by the Democrats from the 1930s through the 1970s. This boost in turnout was apparent in 2004 when a concerted drive by the Republican Party increased turnout in battleground states by 4.4 percent compared to 3.6 percent for the Democrats.[18]

Who votes matters for another reason. The winning candidates are more likely to reflect the interests of those who elected them when they make public policy decisions than the interests of those who stood on the sidelines. Thus, if there is a class bias in voting, if voters tend to be more educated and have higher incomes than do nonvoters, then public policy is likely to reinforce rather than reallocate the economic advantages that those with higher incomes and greater education enjoy and would like to perpetuate.

This reasoning explains why the question of who actually votes is as important to a democracy as the question of who is eligible to vote. Turnout indicates the extent to which the ideal of equal participation and influence is being achieved; indirectly, it reveals the levels of satisfaction and dissatisfaction within the populace; and finally, it forecasts how representative the government is likely to be, which segments of the society are likely to benefit the most from its decisions and actions, and how much support or opposition the government's public policy decisions may receive from this population.

Is it desirable to try to encourage as large a turnout as possible for the sake of the democracy? Opinion on this question is divided. Some contend that it not— that simply having more uninformed, uninterested, and uninvolved people voting is not desirable. It dilutes the influence of those who care, those who believe that elections are important, that citizens should become informed and involved to make an intelligent voting decision, and that the right not to participate is just as fundamental a freedom as the right to do so. Others, however, point to the hypocrisy of government policy promoting democratic institutions abroad when Americans do not practice democracy to the fullest extent at home. They also note the discrepancy that exists between the electorate and the population as a whole and argue that this discrepancy contributes to the perception and even the reality of a government of, by, and for the few. If this discrepancy were eliminated or reduced, confidence and trust in government should improve and the legitimacy of its decisions and actions would be heightened.

Why Do People Vote in Certain Identifiable Ways?

Although who votes obviously influences the outcome of the election, so do the political attitudes and social groupings of the electorate. Voters do not come to an election with completely open minds; they come with preexisting beliefs and attitudes. Of these, the most important is their **partisan identification**.[19] As noted in the previous chapter, about two thirds of the electorate still identify with a political party, a commitment that has been relatively stable and has both direct and indirect influences on voting (see Table 7.2).

partisan identification
The allegiances that people have toward political parties; these allegiances affect campaign participation and voting behavior.

Partisanship   Party identification is important because it provides a framework for analysis; it offers cues for evaluating the candidates and their stands. In general, the less that is known about the candidates, particularly those running for state or local office, the greater the influence of partisanship is apt to be on voting behavior. When more information about the candidates is available, as is usually the case in presidential elections, partisanship competes more with personality and the issues. Nevertheless, even when voting for president, partisanship has been clearly evident in recent elections.

Group Pressures   In addition to having individual political attitudes, most people see themselves as members of groups. To the extent that groups believe their interests are best served by particular parties, candidates, or issues, they will tell their members how to vote in a given election.

Group associations generate social interaction, which has consequences for the political process. These pressures work to activate and reinforce partisan inclinations. Occasionally, they may undermine them by creating cross-pressures that give mixed signals to voters.[20] In other words, partisan and group loyalties tend to make voting decisions easier for most people. Parties and candidates go to great lengths to coordinate their messages and target them to specific electoral constituencies. Their goal is to move people in the direction in which their political sympathies and personal associations lie.

Candidates and Issues Other influences on voting include the candidates themselves and the issues of the day. Voters' perceptions of candidates have become more important in recent years, largely because of the greater use of television in campaigns. Moreover, the news media emphasize personality and leadership issues at the expense of substantive policy debates. The specific issues that affect voting behavior vary with the election, the constituency, and the candidates. Whether issues—be they jobs, crime, education, environment, health and the elderly, or national and homeland security—are salient depends on four factors:

1. How much attention they receive from the media
2. How directly they affect voters
3. How much the candidates differ on them
4. Voters' awareness of candidates' differences

The more direct the perceived effect of the issue, the more likely it is to have a discernible effect on the voter. For Arab Americans in 2004, the Bush administration's strong support of Israel, combined with its vigorous enforcement of the USA Patriot Act, turned this community against the president; on the other hand, George W. Bush's outspoken support of the Christian right's position on social issues maximized the votes the president received in his reelection bid from this population group.

In every election there are multiple influences on voting. Because these influences, either singly or together, can affect the outcome of the election, candidates and parties try to shape them by designing a campaign strategy that puts their best case to the voters, one that emphasizes their strengths and their opponent's weaknesses. A single campaign may be too short a period to change political attitudes or alter group associations, but it is long enough to affect perceptions and influence voting.

Models of Decision Making

How do people weigh various factors in arriving at their voting decisions, and what questions do they try to answer? Political scientists have proposed two models of voting: retrospective and prospective. **Retrospective voting** is based on an assessment of the past performance of the parties and their elected officials in light of the promises they made, any political events that have occurred, and the conditions that currently exist.[21] In this model, voters base their judgment on their accumulated political experience, asking themselves, "Am I better off now than I was when the other party and its leaders were in power?" The retrospective model also produces a cumulative evaluation of political parties, one that can change over time as the electorate reexamines and reevaluates the party's issue stands and those of the candidates who run on its label.

In contrast, prospective voters look to the future. They ask, "Will I be better off with a certain candidate and party in office, given their issue positions and my personal beliefs?" **Prospective voting** anticipates the actions of candidates once they assume office. Voters compare their values, beliefs, and opinions with those of the

retrospective voting
A judgment made primarily on the basis of the past performance of the parties and their elected officials.

prospective voting
A judgment made primarily on the basis of the promises candidates make about the priorities and policies they will pursue if elected. People tend to vote for the candidate whose views and positions are closest to their own.

candidates and parties; then they base their judgment on their sense of which party and which candidates are more likely to benefit them the most after the election.

The retrospective and prospective models are theoretical formulations of the thought processes that people go through when they decide how to vote. In practice, voters undoubtedly do both—they look both backward and forward to arrive at their electoral judgments. They evaluate the candidates and their parties and how well they have done largely on the basis of how good or bad present conditions seem to be. If the economy is strong, society appears harmonious, the nation feels secure, and the government seems to be functioning normally, people assume that their leaders must be doing a good job and tend to reelect them.[22] If conditions are not favorable, they tend to blame those in power, especially the president. This judgment—how conditions are and who is responsible for them—is part of the voting decision, but not the only part. Voters must also anticipate which of the candidates and parties, given their records of past performance, are likely to do better in the future. Thus, both retrospective and prospective analyses help people arrive at the rationales they use for their voting decisions.

The Campaign for Office

Every candidate's objective is to convince voters that she or he is well qualified and will do the best job. The campaign is the vehicle for achieving this objective. Candidates often must conduct two campaigns: one to gain their party's nomination and another to compete in the general election. Because they are conducted at different times under different rules, appeal to different constituencies, and often emphasize different issues, these campaigns are quite distinctive.

The Presidential Nomination Process

Of the two, the presidential nomination campaign has changed the most in the last century. Formerly an internal matter decided by party leaders, the quest for nomination today occurs within the public arena, usually in primary races among self-declared aspirants for office. Candidates are selected on the basis of their appeal to partisans in the primary elections. If successful, they must run again in the general election, refocusing their campaign and usually broadening and moderating their message for the entire electorate. In doing so, they may have to soften their ideological rhetoric, reposition themselves toward the center of the political spectrum, and stress issues and personal traits that will attract the votes of independents, supporters of the other party, and partisans of their own party who did not vote for them in the primaries.

The quest for office is also conditioned by the rules and processes that govern the election, the environment in which that election occurs, and the electorate to which the candidates must appeal. Of these, the economic and social environment is the most variable factor, changing from one election to the next. The rules are more predictable, but they too have changed, particularly those that pertain to the presidential nomination process. The electorate is stable but not static.

Party Reforms and Their Effect In theory, national nominating conventions still designate the major parties' nominees for president and vice president and formulate the platforms on which they will run. In practice, party activists have the greatest influence on those judgments. The movement toward increased popular control of the nomination process began during the 1970s, when the Democratic Party revised its rules for delegate selection to its nominating convention to encourage greater public participation and more equitable representation of rank-and-file voters.

These changes made primary elections the preferred mode of selection. Today more than three fourths of the delegates pledged to particular candidates at both the Democratic and the Republican national conventions come from states that hold some form of **primary,** an election preceding the general election in which partisans select their party's nominee. Most of the remaining delegates come from states that use party **caucuses,** which are meetings conducted first at the precinct level and later at county and state levels in which partisans begin the process of selecting representatives who will choose their state's convention delegates.[23] In addition to these delegates pledged to support particular candidates, the Democrats choose several unpledged delegates from among the party's elected and appointed leaders; in 2004 these **superdelegates,** as they are called, constituted about 18 percent of the total number of delegates who attended the Democratic convention.

Another major objective of the Democratic rule changes was to more accurately reflect popular preferences in the selection of delegates. That is why the Democrats adopted the principle of **proportional voting,** in which delegates are awarded to each candidate in a primary or caucus in proportion to the number of popular votes that candidate receives. To be eligible for delegates, however, a candidate must receive a minimum percentage of the total vote, or *threshold,* usually 15 percent.[24] Beginning in the 1980s the Democrats have also required that the state delegations be evenly divided between men and women.

The Republicans have not imposed similar national rules on their state parties except for a prohibition against discrimination on the basis of race, ethnicity, or gender. Nevertheless, state Republican parties operate under rules that have increased rank-and-file participation and broadened representation at their conventions. The chief difference is that the Republicans permit states to have winner-take-all voting within states and the Democrats do not.

The changes in the way the parties select their delegates initially resulted in greater public involvement in the nomination process. In 1968, before the reforms, only 12 million people participated. Four years later, that number rose to 22 million. By 1988, with two contested nominations, it was over 35 million. With competitive contests in both parties in 2000, about 36 million people participated. In 2004, however, with only the Democratic Party embroiled in a nomination contest—George W. Bush was unopposed for the Republican nomination—16.4 million voted and an additional 650,000 participated in their state's caucus selection process.[25]

The lack of participation by the party's rank and file gives the activists in each party more influence than they might otherwise have over the selection of

primary
An election in which partisans choose candidates to run for specific offices on their party's label in the general election.

caucuses
Meetings at the local level in which partisans conduct party business, including voting for candidates for president (or delegates pledged to them).

superdelegates
Elected and appointed party officials who automatically serve as delegates at their party's nominating convention.

proportional voting
A voting rule for the Democratic Party's presidential nomination in which candidates receive delegate support in proportion to the popular vote they receive in a primary; in several democratic European countries, a proportional voting system is used to select legislative delegates or representatives.

their party's nominee. Activists tend to be more ideological than rank-and-file partisans and much more ideological than the general electorate. Naturally, they choose candidates and delegates pledged to these candidates who reflect their views and their ideological orientations. Studies of recent conventioneers have found Republican delegates to be more conservative and Democratic delegates more liberal than the average voter in their party, much less the country.[26] The stronger ideological position of the delegates helps explain why party platforms take unequivocal stands on controversial issues such as abortion, taxes, capital punishment, the balanced budget, and gun control. On a demographic level, however, convention delegates are more diverse than was the case in the pre-reform period.

The changes in the rules have affected party leaders as well, reducing their ability to choose delegates and influence them at the convention. They have also encouraged more candidates to seek the nomination and more party and non-party groups to become involved, as recent presidential nominations attest. Candidates must also raise their own money, build their own organizations, hire their own consultants, and campaign actively for many months, even years, to win the nomination. A two-year quest has become standard for most serious presidential candidates.

Candidate Strategy and Tactics   Campaigns usually start long before the first caucuses and primaries are held because most candidates need to do well early if they are to have any chance of winning. There are three basic reasons for starting so early: money, media, and momentum. It takes time, a lot of time, to raise the necessary funds to make a viable challenge. Millions of dollars are necessary to build an organization, pay its expenses, move around the country, and project an appeal. Financial pressures have forced candidates to devote much of their time to fundraising, especially because individual donors cannot contribute more than $2,000 per candidate per election and groups cannot contribute more than $5,000.

Successful fund-raising long before the first contests is particularly significant for those who do not begin the quest for their party's nomination with a national reputation, such as Michael Dukakis in 1988, Bill Clinton in 1992, and Howard Dean in 2004. The ability to raise relatively large amounts of money early gives a candidate an edge in gaining media coverage, which in turn helps in achieving recognition, obtaining endorsements from party leaders, and projecting a message. Conversely, an inability to obtain sufficient funds is viewed by political leaders, major contributors, and the news media as a sign that the candidacy lacks the popular support necessary to win the nomination. Smart money flows to the candidate perceived to have the best chance to win, whereas belief money goes to the candidate with similar views as the donor.

front-loading
The concentration of presidential primaries and caucuses at the beginning of the nomination process, normally in January, February, and early to mid-March of the election year.

The increasing use of the mass media, particularly television, by aspirants for their party's nomination has also upped the financial ante. Television is not cheap, especially during prime time. Most candidates spend the bulk of their money on it. They feel that they have no choice but to do so, because people increasingly obtain more information about the campaign from the electronic media than from any other source. The **front loading** of caucuses and primaries also adds to the need for early money.

In addition to the costs of media, the expenses of building a campaign organization and conducting public opinion polls have increased the financial burden on contemporary candidates in recent elections. Candidates who gain the endorsement of state party leaders and the support of their political organizations have an advantage. Endorsements from political and entertainment celebrities are much less important, as Al Gore and Bill Bradley's endorsements of Howard Dean in 2004 attest.

With intentions clear, money in hand, and an organization in place, a candidate must next ascertain public sentiment. Polling provides an accurate reflection of general public opinion. Focus groups are used to explore perceptions of the issues, the intensity with which beliefs are held, and the effect of specific words and phrases on groups of voters.

The early primaries tend to be the most important, particularly for candidates who lack national reputations. Doing well in these initial contests gives candidates credibility, helps in fund-raising, and increases the amount of news media coverage that a campaign receives; doing poorly, however, can have the opposite effect, effectively ending a quest for the nomination before it has had time to get off the ground. Howard Dean's ability to raise large amounts of money on the Internet gave his early campaign greater notoriety than he might have expected to gain as a little-known governor of a small state, Vermont. However, it also made him the focus of more scrutiny by the news media and more critical attacks by his opponents. Dean did not fare well under this microscope of public attention.

Those who are better known have greater flexibility and are in a better position to take advantage of their reputation and political influence to build a strong organizational and financial base. They can also lose without being knocked out of the race. In 1988, for example, George H. W. Bush built what his campaign manager referred to as a "firewall" in South Carolina by raising more money, collecting more endorsements, creating larger state organizations, and running more television advertisements than his principal opponent, Bob Dole. His son, George W. Bush, adopted the same strategy twelve years later, relying on the Republican state party organization in South Carolina and grassroots support from the Christian Coalition to blunt the momentum that McCain had gained from his surprising win in New Hampshire in 2000. John Kerry also used his personal wealth and status as a decorated war hero to remain a viable candidate, even as rival Dean was receiving most of the attention and contributions as the Iowa caucus neared.

The Spring Interregnum After the nomination has been effectively decided, there is usually an interim period of several months during which the winning candidate tries to repair the damage caused by the contest: reaching out to partisans who supported other candidates, refashioning a presidential image that may have been marred by political opponents, and remolding a policy appeal from the emotion-laden rhetoric and sharp ideological positions that may have been taken with party activists in mind.

Reconciliation within the party is important. The winning candidate is expected to reach out to his political opponents and to the partisans who backed them. In return, the prospective nominee desires the endorsement of his opponents and their promise to help the party and its standard bearers in the general election.

Image reconstruction may also be necessary during this period. Battered and bruised from the nomination battle, the would-be candidate needs to polish an image that has undoubtedly been tarnished by the personal negativity that characterizes modern media-oriented campaigns. Bill Clinton, beset by allegations of sexual infidelity, draft dodging, and "pot smoking" and criticized by liberal Democrats for being too conservative became the boy from Hope, Arkansas in 1992, a new Democrat. George W. Bush billed himself as a reformist governor and a compassionate conservative; John Kerry presented himself as a centrist with strong national security credentials. All three nominees emphasized their mainstream policy positions and issues associated with the other party. Meanwhile the press and the opposition party point to the inconsistencies, discrepancies, and contradictions in the candidates' new imagery. During this period, there is also endless speculation in the news media on the vice presidential selection, speculation fueled partly by the element of surprise and by the secrecy with which the prospective nominees usually decide on their running mates. All of this hype and political maneuvering rivet public attention as the candidates gear up for their national nominating conventions.

National Nominating Conventions: Pure Theatre The functions of conventions have changed. It used to be that convention delegates came together to make important decisions. They decided on disputed delegates, adopted rules for their deliberations, approved the planks of their platform, and with much pomp and circumstance, chose their standard bearers. Today these decisions are almost all preordained by the results of the primaries and caucuses. What is

A Democratic delegate displays his wares.

left for the convention is the show: choreographed speeches, tailored film clips, orchestrated demonstrations of enthusiasm for the party's heroes—all of which are designed with the television audience in mind. Naturally, the size of the audience that watches the conventions and the number of hours watched has shrunk as conventions have become less newsworthy and more theatrical and as viewers have more news and entertainment options at the time the convention is aired.

The absence of the unexpected has led the broadcast networks to show the highlights of the conventions during prime time. C-Span and the all-news cable networks provide more complete coverage for those who desire it, which are usually the party faithful. Despite the small television audience, the conventions are still items in the news. Their effect on the general population is amplified by the coverage they receive. People learn about the parties and candidates and their issue stands from this coverage.[27]

Political scientists have suggested three major effects of conventions on voters: (1) They heighten interest, thereby potentially increasing turnout; (2) they arouse latent attitudes, thereby raising awareness of the partisan issues; and (3) they color perceptions, thereby affecting the electorate's judgments about the candidates, the parties, and their positions.

The Presidential Election

Whereas the nomination process has undergone many changes in recent decades, the general election process has been more stable. That stability has been a product of the **Electoral College** system, which directs candidate strategies and determines the real winner.

The Legal Environment: The Electoral College When the framers of the Constitution fashioned the system for choosing the president and vice president, they rejected the idea of a direct popular vote, preferring instead an indirect method in which a group of **electors** would choose the president. Their plan was to have states choose electors in any manner they desired. The electors, who would be equal in number to the total number of senators and representatives from a state, would then exercise their own judgment in selecting the president and vice president. It was anticipated that they would select the most qualified candidates, not necessarily the most popular ones.

Today electors are chosen directly by the voters and are expected to cast their votes for the candidates of their party. In all but two states, Maine and Nebraska, the candidate who wins the most popular votes receives *all* the state's electoral votes. In Maine and Nebraska, one elector is chosen in each state congressional district and two are selected at large, making a divided electoral vote possible. The winner-take-all method of voting in the other forty-eight states is known as the **general ticket system.** A majority of the votes in the Electoral College, 270 out of 538, is needed to win. A candidate can win a majority in the Electoral College and thus be elected president without winning a majority or even a plurality of the total popular vote. This situation has occurred three times: in 1876, 1888, and 2000.

Electoral College
The electoral body that chooses the president and vice president; it consists of electors from the states, equal in number to their congressional delegation.

electors
Individuals nominated by their party and elected by the voters in states to cast the official votes for president and vice president. They may not hold an office in the federal government.

general ticket system
A method of voting that elects the entire slate (of electors) by virtue of the popular vote (for president).

If no candidate wins a majority in the College, the House of Representatives selects the president, with each state's delegation casting one vote. If no vice presidential candidate receives a majority, the Constitution assigns the responsibility for choosing a vice president to the Senate. The Senate has chosen a vice president in this manner only once, in 1837.[28] The structure and operation of the Electoral College give the largest states a disproportionate degree of influence because they have the most electoral votes and cast those votes as a bloc. The large state advantage also benefits groups that reside in those states and vote cohesively, such as Jews in New York, Hispanics in Texas and California, and African Americans living in urban areas of the large industrial states. Voting in the Electoral College also gives advantage to the smallest states, which receive a minimum of three electoral votes regardless of their size, one for each senator and one for each representative.

Presidential candidates take the Electoral College into account when planning their strategy for the general election. Their primary objective, to win a majority of the College not necessarily a plurality of the popular vote, forces them to concentrate their resources in the larger and most competitive states. Those states in which one party tends to be dominant receive less attention from the presidential candidates and the groups that support them. In 2000 and again in 2004, only about one-third of the states fit into the competitive category at the beginning of each campaign and only about five to seven were still there in the closing days. A disproportionate amount of time, money, advertising, and grass-roots organizing are devoted to these battleground states.

The Political Environment: Advantages of Incumbency   Another strategic factor has to do with incumbency. In every presidential election between 1956 and 2004, an incumbent president or vice president has received a major party nomination. When incumbents run, they are usually advantaged by their status, experience, and accomplishments. Of the fifteen presidents who sought reelection in the twentieth century, ten have won. Franklin Roosevelt was reelected three times. Incumbency can be a two-edged sword, however. It can strengthen or weaken a president's claim to leadership depending on the nature of the time. It helps in good times and when national security issues are salient; it hurts during periods of economic recession or social turmoil as Gerald Ford, Jimmy Carter, and George H. W. Bush can attest. Incumbency also helps resolve character issues. It conveys knowledge and experience, which challengers have to demonstrate but incumbents usually do not.

Nonpresidential Nominations and Elections

Some changes that have affected presidential selection have affected the election campaigns for other offices. The strategy and tactics for nomination campaigns are similar for national, state, and local offices. The principal differences in these contests involve the cost of the campaigns, the use of media, and the ability to employ sophisticated campaign techniques, including public opinion polling. Most money tends to be spent in races for state governor and U.S. senator. These statewide nomination contests are also likely to depend more on visual media, primarily television geared to local markets. All candidates rely on radio and print journalism to generate coverage in the local news. Similarly, public opinion surveys, a staple for presidential, senatorial, and gubernatorial candidates, may be too expensive for most other candidates, who must depend more on their own impressions, instincts, and skills and on smaller surveys that their campaign commissions or those done by a local newspaper, television news outlet, or university's social science research center.

The level of competition in congressional, state, and local elections varies. There is more competition for open seats than for seats held by an incumbent seeking reelection, more competition in areas where the party organization is not supporting a particular candidate than in areas where it is, and more competition when the parties are evenly matched than when one party dominates a particular area.

The amount of competition affects turnout. Contested primaries attract more voters than uncontested ones. Even so, only a minority of the electorate regularly participates in these nonpresidential nomination contests, particularly when they are not held on the same day as the presidential nomination. The smaller the turnout, the greater the effect a strong party organization can have, because it can identify and mobilize support.

Nonpresidential Elections All elections except the presidential election are conducted by the states according to state laws. These laws establish the districts in which elections are held and the rules and procedures by which they are conducted and the winners determined. Of these factors, the process known as redistricting, the redrafting of the boundaries for legislative districts, can be especially controversial (see Chapter 4).

The Legal Environment: Reapportionment and Redistricting The Constitution requires that seats in the House of Representatives be redistributed among the states every ten years on the basis of the national census. The stakes are high in this redistribution, known as **reapportionment,** because it may affect not only the number of congressional representatives a state has but also the amount of federal aid it receives.[29]

If the number of congressional seats allocated to a state changes, after each census the state legislature may have to redraw the boundaries of the state's congressional and other legislative districts to reflect shifts in its population. The party in control of the legislature uses its power to draw the district boundaries in such a way as to maximize its political advantage, having its partisans constitute a stable but not overwhelming majority in as many districts as possible. The practice of drawing legislative districts for political gain is referred to as **gerrymandering.** This term, coined in 1812 or 1813, described the shape of a particular legislative district in Massachusetts that looked a little like a salamander (see Figure 8.1) during the governorship of Elbridge Gerry—hence, "Gerry-mander."

Gerrymandering is a powerful political tool. In states in which one party is clearly dominant and refuses to change the legislative district borders, the only way for the party out of power to effect a change is to gain control of the legislature. But because of the way the district lines are drawn, it cannot gain control of

reapportionment
The reallocation of state seats in the House of Representatives on the basis of population shifts, as indicated in the latest census.

gerrymandering
The drawing of legislative district boundaries to achieve partisan advantage. Named for Elbridge Gerry, a governor of Massachusetts after the Constitution was ratified.

Figure 8.1 **The First Gerrymandered Congressional District and North Carolina's Twelfth Congressional District, Which Was Invalidated by the Supreme Court in 1996**

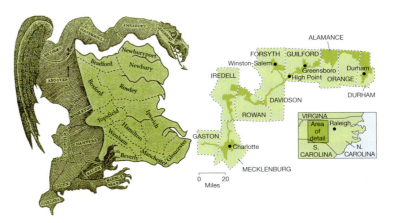

Source: Data for Massachusetts from Library of Congress; for North Carolina from *New York Times*, July, 29, 1993, A12.

the legislature without a large influx of new voters who favor its candidates and positions or a major shift of sentiment against the party in power. Therefore, changes in the partisan composition of an electorate are slow to be reflected in the composition of its legislative representatives.[30]

For most of American history, states enjoyed complete discretion in drawing their legislative district boundaries. Beginning in the 1960s, however, a series of judicial decisions set limits on that discretion. One limitation concerns the size of the population within a district. In the case of *Wesberry v. Sanders* (1964), the Supreme Court held that all congressional districts within a state must be approximately equal in population so that no individual voter will be overrepresented or underrepresented. To do otherwise, the Court said, would be inconsistent with the principle of "one person, one vote."[31] Today the populations of congressional districts within a state usually cannot vary by more than 1.5 percent. However, from one state to another, the populations of districts can vary considerably. Montana, for example, had one at-large congressional district with a population of 926,865 in 2004; Wyoming had one with 506,529 people. The population of the average congressional district is about 690,000.

From the 1930s through the 1980s, the principal beneficiaries of gerrymandering were the Democrats, who used it to preserve their dominance of both state legislatures and the House of Representatives. After the 1990 census, the Republicans benefited from redistricting. They were helped by the creation of congressional districts, largely in the South, in which a majority of voters were members of racial or ethnic minorities. How would the creation of majority–minority districts help the Republicans? It concentrated minority voters in a few districts, which helped the Republicans win the other districts by decreasing the number of Democratic voters within them. These changes resulted in more minority representatives in Congress but also in more conservative Republicans being elected.

The newly drawn legislative districts were challenged in court. Opponents contended that the redistricting amounted to "racial gerrymandering." The Supreme Court agreed. In a series of redistricting decisions, the Court held that no plan in which race is the dominant factor can meet the standards and conditions of the equal protection clause of the Fourteenth Amendment.[32] However, the Court's decision did not prevent states from redrafting districts to favor the party in power, such as the Republican-controlled Texas legislature did in 2003.

The Political Environment: Advantages of Incumbency Partisan gains from redistricting have been reinforced by incumbency. Barring a high level of public dissatisfaction, the electorate is more likely to vote for candidates it knows than for those it does not, and challengers are usually not nearly as well known as incumbents.

Incumbents can use the perquisites of their office to help themselves get reelected. The availability of staff, travel funds, and free mailings gives them a head start and discourages qualified people from running against them.[33] In addition, incumbents have a fund-raising advantage. Potential contributors see incumbents as better able to help them because of their established position in government. The ability of incumbents to raise money, which they do from the moment they take office, combined with the high costs of running (particularly for statewide office), also discourage would-be challengers.

Those who oppose incumbents are often placed in a catch-22 situation: They cannot obtain sufficient funds, coverage, or voluntary support because their chances are not viewed as promising, and they cannot improve their chances without the necessary funds, coverage, and voluntary support. One by-product of this predicament is an increase in the number of challenges to incumbents by wealthy individuals with little political experience but sufficient resources to launch an effective campaign; another is the tendency of the party out of power to run its strongest candidates in districts where an incumbent is not running again. A third, and perhaps most important consequence, is the high rate of reelection of incumbents.

During the last several decades, approximately 95 percent of incumbents in the House of Representatives were reelected and 86 percent of incumbents in the Senate (see Table 8.4).

In addition to its effect on individual candidates, the incumbency advantage works to perpetuate the ruling group within all levels and branches of government, whether that group is defined in partisan, demographic, or ideological terms. This advantage is one of the reasons that women, who constitute a majority of the population and vote at the same or higher rates than men, have not achieved elective office in anywhere near the proportions that men have. Table 8.5 indicates the percentages of women in elective national, state, and local offices.

Table 8.4 Congressional Incumbency and Reelection, 1980–2004

Year	Incumbents Running in General Election		Incumbents Defeated in General Election		Percentage Successful	
	House	**Senate**	**House**	**Senate**	**House**	**Senate**
1980	398	29	31	9	90.7	55.2
1982	393	30	29	2	90.1	93.3
1984	411	29	16	3	95.4	89.7
1986	394	28	6	7	98.0	75.0
1988	409	27	6	4	98.3	85.2
1990	406	32	15	1	96.0	96.9
1992	368	28	24	4	88.3	82.1
1994	387	26	34	2	91.0	92.3
1996	384	21	21	1	94.2	90.5
1998	401	29	6	3	98.0	90.0
2000	400	29	6	6	97.8	90.1
2002	398	24	8	3	96.0	85.7
2004	402	27	7	1	98.3	96.1

Source: *Statistical Abstract of the United States: 2004.* United States Census Bureau, 250; updated by authors.

Table 8.5 Women in Elective Office, 1975–2005

Level of Office	1975	1977	1979	1981	1983	1985	1987	1989	1991	1993	1995	1997	1999	2001	2003	2005
U.S. Congress	4%	4%	3%	4%	4%	5%	5%	5%	6%	10%	10%	11%	12%	14%	13.6%	15%
Statewide (Executive)	10	10	11	11	11	14	14	14	18	22	26	26	28	27	25.6	25.7
State Legislatures	8	9	10	12	13	15	16	17	18	21	21	22	23	22	22.3	22.5

Source: Center for the American Woman and Politics, Eagleton Institute of Politics, Rutgers University, http://www.cawp.rutgers.edu/Facts/Officeholders/elective.pdf (accessed July 16, 2005).

Strategy and Tactics Candidates for Congress and those for state and local office conduct their own campaigns, using similar types of campaign organizations, strategies, and tactics. The components of a campaign organization are dictated by the functions that have to be performed: raising and spending money, traveling and giving speeches, monitoring opinion and creating an image, formulating and targeting a message, obtaining free media coverage and running paid advertisements, and launching efforts to get out the vote.

In developing and implementing a strategy, candidates must design and project a basic appeal. The appeal indicates why people should vote for them. Partisanship plays a major role in the appeal, especially for the candidate of the dominant party in the area where the election occurs. In articulating partisan themes, candidates normally stress issues that conjure up positive associations within their party and community and have the most direct effect on constituents, such as jobs, taxes, and crime and other social issues. Negative images of the opposition party are also part of most campaign messages. Democratic candidates refer to the Republicans as the party of the rich, big business, and special interests, a party that has been insensitive to the plight of the less fortunate. Republicans, in turn, describe the Democrats as the party of big government, big spending, and high taxes.

Traditionally, foreign affairs have not played as large a role as domestic affairs in most campaigns, even at the congressional level. However, in recent elections the effect of foreign policy on the economy, homeland security, and leadership itself has been sufficient to force candidates for national office to address international

Ribbons, buttons, and bumper stickers have provided color, creativity, and character in American elections.

matters, such as American military intervention, peacekeeping operations, economic aid, open markets and free trade, and even human rights. In 1980, the presence of U.S. diplomats held hostage in Iran was a major issue. In 2004, U.S. military presence in Iraq fueled considerable campaign debate. The movement of American jobs to other countries in which the costs of labor were much lower than in the United States has also captured public attention in election years.

Personal appeals are important. Incumbents point to their experience, record, and performance in office; challengers describe their potential for office, criticize their opponents' record, and claim that they can and will do better.

The speeches, advertising, and occasional rallies and parades may seem and sound more like theatre than political discourse, but campaigns remain important to a democratic system. They raise issues, present alternative viewpoints, and provide opportunities for both candidates and voters to be heard, and set an agenda for those who win. Elections offer the electorate a choice among the people who will make public policy decisions and, indirectly, the policies that they will pursue, at least initially. They also provide a referendum on past performance, a mechanism for holding those in government accountable, and an incentive for public officials to remain responsive to their constituents.

© Kenneth James/Corbis

Schwarzenegger wins election for California Governor. California Governor-Elect Arnold Schwarzenegger and wife Maria Shriver at the victory celebration held at the Los Angeles Ballroom in the Century Plaza Hotel, staged in true Hollywood style for the viewing audience.

Review Questions

1. The nomination process has become more democratic in all of the following ways except one:

   A. It has provided more opportunities for rank-and-file partisans to participate
   B. It has allowed party activists to exercise more influence over the selection of the nominee
   C. It has resulted in the selection of delegates who are more representative of the party's demographic profile
   D. It has allowed more candidates to run for the nomination

2. Which of the following groups has been disadvantaged by the changes in the presidential and congressional nomination processes?

   A. Moderates
   B. Ideologues
   C. Activists
   D. Politicians with access to money

3. On which principle underlying democratic elections do most American agree?

   A. Proportional representation in multimember districts
   B. Plurality or majority rule in single-member districts
   C. Winner-take-all systems in state primaries
   D. State voting in the House of Representatives

4. Incumbents are advantaged in elections for all of the following reasons except one:

   A. They tend to be able to raise more money
   B. They have greater name recognition
   C. They are better and more compelling as candidates
   D. They probably have performed constituency services

Answers:

   1. B
   2. A
   3. B
   4. C

Conflict and Consensus in Review

Campaign professions and political scientists agree that political attitudes affect turnout and voting behavior. They differ in exactly how the attitudes interact with the environment in which the election occurs and with the campaign itself to influence the outcome of the election. The consensus seems to be that the partisan composition of the electorate, economic and social conditions, and campaign organizations and strategies all play some role, but knowing the precise combination during any particular election cycle seems to be beyond the scope of current knowledge.

Direct Democracy: Initiatives and Referenda

citizen ballot initiatives
Policy questions or constitutional amendments initiated by citizens, put on the ballot through a petition process, and voted on by the general electorate.

legislative referenda
Policy questions or constitutional amendments put on the ballot by state legislatures for the approval or disapproval of the voters.

Most elections in the United States are among candidates vying for office; some, however, involve policy choices. **Citizen ballot initiatives** in which individuals or groups put policy questions before the voters are permitted in twenty-four states; **legislative referenda,** policy issues that the legislature places before the electorate, are allowed in fifty states. Both are forms of direct democracy in which the electorate determines public policy.

Oregon was the first state to permit citizen initiatives. It did so in 1904. Since then, the initiative process has spread, primarily in the western states. Six states—Arizona, California, Colorado, North Dakota, Oregon, and Washington—have traditionally placed the most initiatives on their statewide ballots. In 2004, thirty-four states did; in 2006, thirty-seven did.

In recent years the number of ballot proposals has declined. In 2004 there were 162; in 2006, there were 205. Some of these initiatives were wtarted by citizen petition and most of the rest by state legislatures. People in twenty states voted in 2004 and 2006, usually by large majorities, to support amendments to their state consititutions that defined marriage as being between a man and a woman. Arizona was the first state to reject such an amendment. Other states decided whether to legalize various aspects of gambling, prohibit abortion, decriminalize various uses of marijuana, increase taxes on tobacco, restrict the right of eminent domain, approve the issuance of bonds, or raise the minimum wage in addition to voting on a host of education issues.[35]

Ballot initiatives are a form of direct democracy, but they are a costly form. To get the proposition on the ballot, a certain percentage of the state's eligible

© AP/Wide World Photos

Supporters of gay marriage march down Market St. in San Francisco, Monday, March 14, 2005.

voters must sign a petition within a specified period. The higher the percentage of signatures and the shorter the time frame, the more difficult and expensive it is to get on the ballot, and that is just the first step. A public relations campaign for or against the initiative must also be waged during the election period. Lawsuits challenging the constitutionality of the initiative are often filed after the vote.

Ballot initiatives are not only costly but also remove issues from the purview of state legislatures, which may be in a better position than the average voter to render an expert judgment. Moreover, these initiatives give special interest groups with a strong financial base disproportionate influence. They may also increase the time required for voting. In short, ballot initiatives are at best a mixed blessing for a democratic electoral process.

Assessing the Meaning of Elections

When the campaigns are over and the voters have made their decisions, political pundits, media analysts, party officials, and the winning and losing candidates evaluate the election. This analysis is important for several reasons. It helps the winners define and claim an electoral mandate, whether or not they actually have one. It helps the losers know why they lost and, equally important, what they might do to win the next time. For other observers, it helps clarify the meaning of the election, an important concern for a government based on popular consent that wants to maintain political support for its policies.

To understand who voted for whom and why, researchers conduct surveys in which voters are asked to identify the principal reasons for their choices and how they feel about the candidates and issues. The two most frequently cited surveys of this sort are the large exit polls conducted for the major news networks, newspapers, and wire services on Election Day (see Table 8.6) and a smaller but comprehensive pre- and post-election survey conducted by the American National Election Studies. Interpretations of data from these surveys are undertaken to discern the dominant issues, images, and partisan allegiances that seem to have shaped the retrospective and prospective judgments of the electorate.

Contemporary Presidential Elections

In 1976 it was the Watergate scandal, President Gerald Ford's pardon of former President Richard Nixon, and a shaky economy that contributed to challenger Jimmy Carter's victory. That Carter was a southern Democrat, a moderate, and a Washington outsider at a time insiders were viewed with suspicion helped him defeat the incumbent Republican president.

When Carter sought reelection four years later, however, being a Democrat, a southerner, a moderate, and an incumbent was not enough. His poor performance ratings overcame the advantage that partisanship and incumbency usually bring to the president of the dominant party, which the Democrats had been since 1932. The first time Carter ran for president, he had been judged on the basis of his *potential* for office; the second time, he was judged on his *performance* in office, and that judgment was harsh.

Ronald Reagan was the beneficiary of the electorate's decision that Carter did not deserve another four years as president. By 1980, it was Reagan, not Carter, who voters believed had the greater potential for leadership. That potential was the primary reason he won: not his ideology, policy positions, or his personal appeal.

Four years later, it was a different story. Then, Reagan's personal appeal, policy successes, and strong leadership contributed to his victory. Voters rewarded him for what they considered a job well done. Although they had voted *against* Carter in the previous election, they voted *for* Reagan in 1984.

This trend of retrospective voting continued in 1988. George H. W. Bush won because the electorate evaluated the Reagan administration positively, associated Bush with that administration, and concluded that he, not his Democratic opponent Michael Dukakis, would be better able and more likely to maintain the good times and the policies and leadership that produced them.

Analysis of the 1992 election also suggests that it was primarily a retrospective vote, but one that worked to the president's disadvantage. An unhappy electorate turned Bush out of office because it was disgruntled with his domestic policy leadership, particularly his economic policies or lack thereof. Although people had serious reservations about Bill Clinton's character and national governing experience, they still saw him as more likely to stimulate the economy, reduce the deficit, and reform the national's welfare and health-care systems.

The 1996 election was a referendum on the Clinton presidency, and Clinton won. The economy was stronger, crime had decreased, and the nation remained at peace—all conditions that favored the incumbent. Despite misgivings about the president's character, voters saw Clinton as more caring, more in touch with the times, and more visionary than his Republican opponent, Robert Dole.

The 2000 election could also have been a referendum on the Clinton-Gore administration had Al Gore chosen to run on its record, but he did not. Gore's decision to sever his ties with the Clinton administration reduced the positive effect on his campaign that peace, prosperity, and the president's high approval ratings normally bring to the incumbent vice president. An evenly divided electorate split along partisan lines, with Gore winning a small popular-vote victory and Bush eking out a narrow Electoral College majority.[35]

With a few minor exceptions, the same divisions were seen in the electorate in 2004, but the issues had changed. Bush's leadership became the focal point for most voters. Republicans saw that leadership in a positive light, particularly the administration's response to the terrorist attacks of 2001; Christian Coalition voters liked the president's moral standards and positions on social issues; and conservatives praised the tax cuts and military build up. Democrats had a different and much more negative perspective. Separating the war in Iraq from the need to maintain a high level of homeland security, Democrats raised questions about the president's credibility, his judgment, and his go-it-alone foreign policy. They challenged the administration's insensitivity to civil and personal rights; the equity of its economic policies, particularly the tax cuts; and the president's position on such divisive issues as stem cell research, gay marriage, and abortion.

These issues produced clear and expected voting patterns among partisans and ideologues, with Republicans and conservatives overwhelmingly supporting the president and Democrats and liberals opposing him. There were also gender, racial, and ethnic differences, although they were not as pronounced as in 2000. The sectarian–secular divide was, however. These voting patterns can be seen in Table 8.6.

Bush won in 2004 because he was the incumbent during a period in which national security issues continued to be important. He won because he was able to demonstrate those personal characteristics associated with strong leadership: strength, conviction, consistency, and vision. Finally, he won because he stayed on message, his party turned out a large Republican vote, and his Democratic challenger did not connect to his base as well as Bush connected to his.

The presidential elections of 2000 and 2004 indicate the stability of voting behavior. They reveal a strong correlation among partisanship, ideology, and voting. The familiar red state–blue state divisions persist with only three states, New Hampshire, Iowa, and New Mexico, moving from one color to the other in the two elections. See Figure 8.2.

The 2006 Midterm Election

The 2006 midterm election, however, reversed some of these trends, particularly the voting patterns in a number of red states. In this election the Democrats picked up enough seats to control both houses of the 110th Congress and also claimed a majority of the state governors. They gained 29 seats in the House, defeating 22 Republican incumbents, and 6 seats in the Senate, defeating 6 incumbent senators.

The election results were interpreted by the news media and political pundits as a rebuke to the Bush administration and its policy in Iraq as well as to the Republican-controlled 109th Congress, its leadership, its strong ideological stands, and the unethical behavior and allegedly illegal actions of some Republican members. As a consequence of the election, Nancy Pelosi (D-Cal.), the new Speaker of the House, became the first woman to occupy this position. Harry Reid, Democratic minority leader in the 109th Congress, took over as the majority leader.

The president responded to the Democratic victory by asking for the resignation of Secretary of Defense Donald Rumsfeld, nominating Robert Gates to replace him, and saying that he would work with the new Democratic leadership.

Table 8.6 Portrait of the American Electorate, 1996–2004

Percentage of 2004		1996			2000			2004		
		Clinton	**Dole**	**Perot**	**Bush**	**Gore**	**Nader**	**Bush**	**Kerry**	**Nader**
	Total Vote	49%	41%	8%	48%	48%	3%	50%	49%	1%
46	Men	43	44	10	53	42	3	54	45	1
54	Women	54	38	7	43	54	2	47	52	1
77	Whites	43	46	9	54	42	3	57	42	1
11	Blacks	84	12	4	9	90	1	11	89	0
9	Hispanics	72	21	6	35	62	2	42	55	2
2	Asians	43	48	8	41	55	3	41	59	—
63	Married	44	46	9	53	44	2	56	43	1
37	Unmarried	57	31	9	38	57	4	40	59	1
17	18–29 Years	53	34	10	46	48	5	44	54	1
28	30–44 Years	48	41	9	49	48	2	51	47	1
30	45–59 Years	48	41	9	49	48	2	50	49	1
25	60+ Years	48	44	7	47	51	2	53	46	0
4	Not H.S. Grad	59	28	11	38	59	1	49	50	0
22	H.S. Grad	51	35	13	49	48	1	51	48	1
31	Some College	48	40	10	51	45	3	53	46	0
26	College Grad	44	46	8	51	45	3	51	47	1
17	Postgraduate	52	40	5	44	52	3	43	55	1
53	White Protestant[†]	36	53	10	56	42	2	58	41	0
27	Catholic	53	37	9	47	50	2	51	48	1
3	Jewish	78	16	3	19	79	1	24	76	—
22	White Born-Again Christian[‡]	26	65	8	80	18	1	77	22	1
24	Union Household	59	30	9	37	59	3	39	60	1
8	Family Income Under $15,000	59	28	11	37	57	4	36	63	1
15	$15,000–$29,999	53	36	9	41	54	3	41	58	0
22	$30,000–$49,999	48	40	10	48	49	2	48	51	0
23	$50,000–$74,999	44	48	7	51	46	2	55	44	1
14	$75,000—$99,999	41	51	7	52	45	2	53	46	0
11	$100,000+	38	54	6	54	43	2	56	43	1
	Family's Financial Situation Is									
31	Better Today	61	35	3	36	61	2	79	20	0
39	Same Today	46	45	8	60	35	3	48	50	1
28	Worse Today	27	57	13	63	33	4	19	80	1

continued

Table 8.6 *continued*

Percentage of 2004		1996			2000			2004		
		Clinton	Dole	Perot	Bush	Gore	Nader	Bush	Kerry	Nader
22	Northeast	55	34	9	39	56	3	43	56	1
25	Midwest	48	41	10	49	48	2	51	48	1
31	South	46	46	7	55	43	1	58	41	0
21	West	48	40	8	46	48	4	45	53	2
37	Republicans	13	80	6	91	8	1	93	7	0
26	Independents	43	35	17	47	45	6	47	50	2
37	Democrats	84	10	5	11	86	2	10	89	0
21	Liberals	78	11	7	13	80	6	13	86	1
45	Moderates	57	33	9	44	52	2	44	55	0
33	Conservatives	20	71	8	81	17	1	83	16	1
60	Employed§	48	40	9	48	49	2	52	46	1
40	Unemployed§	49	42	8	48	47	3	49	50	1
11	First-Time Voters	54	34	11	43	52	4	45	54	1
52	Approve of Clinton's/Bush's Performance				20	77	2	90	9	1
46	Disapprove of Clinton's/Bush's Performance				88	9	2	5	93	1
	Most Important Issue for Voting									
5	Taxes							56	44	0
4	Education							25	75	—
15	Iraq							25	74	0
19	Terrorism							84	14	0
20	Economy/Jobs							18	80	1
22	Moral Values							79	18	2
8	Health Care							22	78	—

*N = 13,660.

[†]Includes all Protestants in 2000 and 2004.

[‡]Includes all people who identified themselves as part of the religious right in 2000 and 2004.

§The 1996 question: Are you employed full time? In 2000 and 2004: Do you work full-time for pay? "Yes" answers were categorized as "employed," "no" answers as "unemployed."

Source: General Exit Poll in 1996 and 2000 conducted by VNS for the National Election Pool, a consortium of the major news networks; General Exit Poll in 2004 conducted by Edison Media Research and Mitofsky International for the National Election Pool.

Figure 8.2 The Politics of the Electoral College Today: A Red and Blue Country

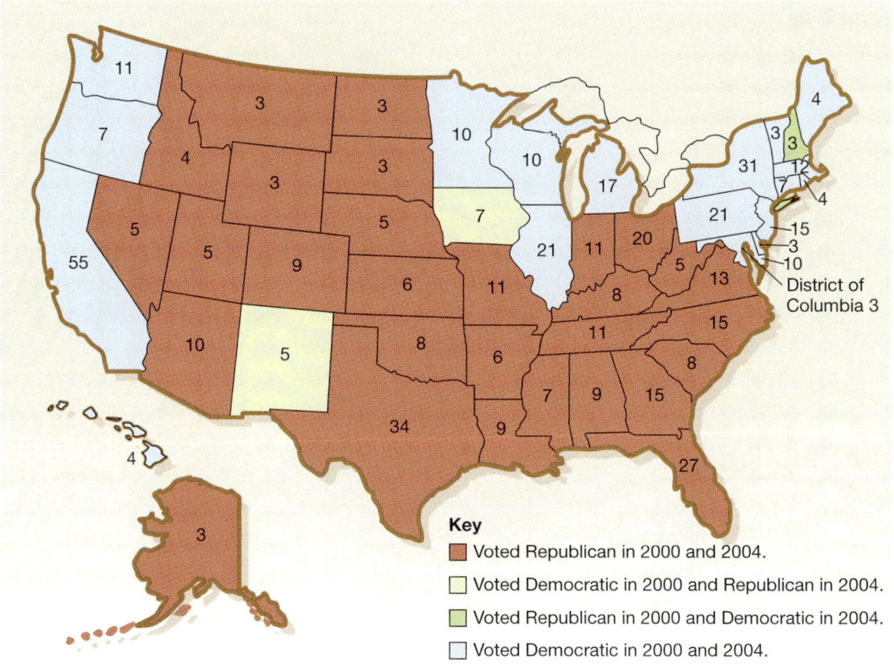

Key

■ Voted Republican in 2000 and 2004.
□ Voted Democratic in 2000 and Republican in 2004.
■ Voted Republican in 2000 and Democratic in 2004.
□ Voted Democratic in 2000 and 2004.

Congressional Elections

Most midterm elections do not lend themselves as easily to a single interpretation as do presidential elections, although the interpretation of a presidential election may carry over to that of Congress, especially if the president's party does well, as the Republicans did in 2004, or poorly, as the Democrats did in the midterm election of 1994. Successful presidential candidates who help members of their party get elected to Congress are said to have **coattails** to which other candidates cling. Franklin Roosevelt in 1932, Dwight Eisenhower in 1952, and Ronald Reagan in 1980 fit into this category. Since Reagan's election in 1980, however, presidents have tended to run behind their party's congressional nominees, not ahead of them. The absence of presidential coattails weakens presidents in their initial dealings with Congress because fewer members believe that they owe their win to the help they received from a popular president.

During midterm elections, national trends are less evident, despite the news media's attempts to read them into almost every election. For most voters most of the time, the dominant concerns are local—the candidates, their personalities, and constituency-related issues. The congressional elections of 1946 and 1994 were exceptions, however. In 1946, the voters reacted against sixteen years of Democratic control; a Democratic president, Harry Truman, who lacked the

coattails

The political influence that a leading candidate (usually for the presidency) exerts to help others on that candidate's ticket get elected.

stature of his much-revered predecessor, Franklin Roosevelt; and various scandals that had marred the Truman presidency. In 1994, they did the same thing: They protested Democratic leadership, policies, and behavior in office, reacting against a Democratic president who had not lived up to expectations, a Democratic Congress that seemed unable or unwilling to follow his lead, a Democratic Party that was internally divided over a multitude of issues, and a Democratic philosophy of government that seemed out of tune with the antigovernment, anti-Washington mood of many Americans.

The midterm elections of 2002 were also different. Normally the president's party loses seats in midterm elections. The opposition party is able to attract stronger candidates and often better funding when the president is not running. And usually some of the electorate are dissatisfied because the new administration has not met their policy and leadership expectations. President George W. Bush's high approval rating after his response to the terrorist attacks of September 11, 2001; his successful fund-raising and campaigning for Republican candidates in the 2002 congressional election; and the Democrats' inability to articulate a convincing plan that could improve the economy helped the GOP win back control of the Senate in addition to maintaining their majority in the House. For the first time since 1954, the Republicans controlled the presidency and both houses of Congress.

Elections and Governance

In theory, elections are critical not only for whom they elect to office but also for what these elected officials will say and do while in office. Contrary to popular belief, campaign promises and party platforms matter. Election officials try to redeem their campaign promises and have had reasonable success in doing so.

On the other hand, elections are rarely mandates, even though public officials may claim that they are. The GOP sweep in 1994 could hardly be considered a mandate for the Republicans' Contract with America, a set of ten policy positions that all Republican candidates for the House endorsed. Only about 25 percent of the voters ever heard of the Contract, much less knew its ten principal propositions. Nor did Republican senators declare their support for the Contract.

A mixed electoral judgment is not unusual. Differing national, state, and local constituencies tend to produce outcomes that mirror the political system's decentralization and diversity rather than generating a dominant public mood. Moreover, people may vote for the same candidate for different reasons, and they may vote for different candidates for the same reason. They also vote for many different officials. As a consequence, the results of the election may be ambiguous, even contradictory. One party may win the White House, and another may gain or maintain control of one or both houses of Congress. More ideological candidates on both the left and the right may be elected, thereby making consensus more difficult to achieve. The policy positions of newly elected members of Congress may also differ.

On the other hand, presidential or congressional elections in which the candidates of one party do well usually produce an agenda for the new administration and Congress; they also provide the basis for building and maintaining a governing coalition. And regardless of the results, elections generate a debate on the salient issues that carries over to the new government. As time passes, however, that debate becomes less relevant as new issues emerge that the government must address. Unless these issues are resolved satisfactorily, they will probably become campaign issues during the next election cycle.

Review Questions

1. Ballot initiatives are a form of what type of democracy?

   A. Representative
   B. Direct
   C. Indirect
   D. Constitutional

2. Which of the following provides the most useful data for explaining the meaning of an election?

   A. The actual election results
   B. The tabulation of the actual vote
   C. The statements made by the winning and losing candidates
   D. The large exit poll conducted on election day

3. Which of the following election results would produce the most potentially difficult problem for a new installed government?

   A. An election that results in divided control of the government
   B. An election that produces a unified government
   C. A close election in which the dominant party loses seats
   D. An election with low turnout and allegations of voter fraud

4. Elections affect government in all of the following ways except one:

   A. They hold government officials accountable for their decision and actions
   B. They provide the basis for an initial governing coalition
   C. They select the most qualified people for the government
   D. They provide the agenda for the government

Answers:

   1. B
   2. D
   3. A
   4. C

continued

Conflict and Consensus in Review

Most people concede that elections are critical because they choose the people, identify the issues, and provide a blueprint for governing. The disagreement stems from the mixed messages that voters send, the difficulties of interpreting the meaning of the election, and the contradictory results that they may produce: incompatible winners, unprioritized issues, conflicting policy agendas, and divided control of government. Whatever conflict is not settled by the election continues into the government as do the pressures to resolve that conflict.

Politics in Action

Bush v. Gore—The Issues and Who Really Won

The 2000 presidential election was one of the most remarkable in American history. Throughout the evening following the vote and into the early hours of the next morning, Americans did not know who their next president would be. First Al Gore was in the lead, then George W. Bush, then no one. It took five weeks, much political rhetoric, and lots of legal maneuvering, before a 5–4 Supreme Court decision resolved the issue in Bush's favor.

What was the controversy about, and who really won? The answers to these questions are quite complex. They depend on which Floridians exercised their franchise and which ones were erroneously or illegally prevented from doing so; they depend on the clarity of the Florida ballot and the accuracy with which punch-card and paper ballots were tabulated. And they depend on the judgment of hundreds of people—from county boards of elections to state election officials, to the Florida legislature that designed the election law, to various state courts that interpreted it, and finally to Supreme Court members' judgment about the constitutionality of the decisions of the Florida courts.

The morning after the election, Americans woke up to a political nightmare and legal dispute of the first order. It was unclear who had won. Here's what happened.

Early in the evening of election day, it looked as if Gore would be the eventual victor. At 8 p.m. EST, when polls were still open in the western part of Florida, the networks predicted a Democratic victory in that state on the basis of the Voter News Survey (VNS) exit poll. But shortly before 10 p.m. EST, with the Bush campaign publicly disputing that Florida would

go for Gore, the VNS noted a discrepancy between its forecast and the actual vote in the key precincts surveyed. After being alerted to the problem, the networks quickly withdrew their prediction that Gore had carried Florida.[36]

The state stayed in the undecided column until 2 a.m., when Bush's lead in the actual votes counted reached about 50,000. At that point, a Fox News network official, who also happened to be Bush's cousin, announced that the Republican candidate had won Florida. The other networks quickly followed suit. Upon hearing the news, Gore proceeded to his Tennessee campaign headquarters, telephoned Bush, and conceded the election. He was about to speak to his supporters when a Florida Democratic operative reached a Gore aide to say that the contest was far from over. Several of the vote-counting machines had malfunctioned. When they were fixed, 56,000 votes were quickly added to Gore's total. Gore called Bush again, this time to retract his concession. At 3:50 a.m., the networks also withdrew their prediction that Bush would win Florida. The vote in that state was simply too close to call.

The next day, a frantic post-election campaign began in the Florida counties in which each side argued that its ballots had been undercounted. Each side sought recourse in the courts and in the arena of public opinion.

The Gore team rushed to convince four counties to recount the vote. In Palm Beach County, normally a Democratic stronghold, a confusing ballot had generated a large number of voided votes, as well as a sizable number for Reform Party candidate Pat Buchanan despite the

continued

Politics in Action *continued*

county's sizable elderly Jewish population. Most election analysts viewed the Buchanan vote as evidence of the confusion with the "butterfly ballot" in which the punch holes, or "chads" as they were called, were not lined up evenly with the candidates' names. Moreover, some of the punch cards were not punched through completely. The chads were left hanging or indented, which impeded the machine count.

But how much of the chad had to be punched for a vote to register? That was the issue Florida's Republican secretary of state, Katherine Harris, who was charged with certifying the vote, had to answer. Harris ruled that only square chads with at least two corners dislodged should be counted. Using this criterion, the Palm Beach election board canvassed 1 percent of the county's ballots and found that Gore had netted nineteen more votes than had been recorded by the machines. On the basis of this finding, the board decided to do a full recount of the county's ballots.

Harris reminded election officials that she had only seven days to certify the vote. She asserted that the only exceptions to this seven-day rule were votes from a machine that had malfunctioned or an act of God, such as a hurricane that prevented election workers from doing their job. Hence, a hand count would have to be completed within this time frame, according to Harris.

The secretary of state's decision prompted an outcry by Democrats and a contrary judgment by the state's attorney general, the highest-ranking Democrat holding elective office in the state. The controversy—how much time the county had to recount and submit a revised vote tabulation—was ultimately decided by the Florida Supreme Court, which permitted late filings until November 26, almost three weeks after the election. Gore also asked for recounts in three other counties with high concentrations of Democrats: Broward, Dade (Miami), and Vollusia.[37]

On the extended certification date that the Florida Supreme Court had established, Bush was officially recorded as the winner of Florida's twenty-five electoral votes. If Gore was to continue to contest the election, he had to do so in court. The Gore camp filed suit in two heavily

Republican counties that had misprinted their absentee ballots, leaving off a key voter identification code. The suit asked that all absentee ballots in those counties be disqualified, but the courts ruled otherwise.

Gore gained a temporary victory, however, when a divided Florida Supreme Court reversed a lower-court decision and ordered a hand recount of all ballots statewide. The state court did not provide guidance on the standards to be used by election officials in determining the actual vote. The individual county canvassing boards had to decide on their own standard. Bush appealed the decision of the Florida Supreme Court to the U.S. Supreme Court, arguing that use of different standards by different counties for deciding votes was unconstitutional because it diminished the votes of other Floridians, who followed the rules and voted according to the proper procedure in violation of the equal protection clause of the Fourteenth Amendment. Bush's brief, submitted on behalf of his campaign, also contended that modifying voting standards and deadlines after the election amounted to changing the rules of the game after it had been played, a violation of state and federal law.

Gore's legal team countered that every vote had to be counted; otherwise, the true intent of the Florida electorate would not be known. They also argued that there was sufficient time to complete such a count before the Electoral College met.

A divided Supreme Court sided with Bush. Seven of the nine justices contended that the equal protection clause was violated when counties employed different standards in determining votes; five of the seven justices also believed that there was not enough time to establish and implement a state-wide standard by date that the Florida legislature had set for notifying the federal government of the state's electoral vote. Two of the justices disagreed however, however, noting that federal law gave the state more time to report its vote if it chose to use that time. The two other dissenters did not see a violation of the equal protection clause. Rather, they saw an activist Supreme Court eroding the power of the states to choose their electors.

continued

Politics in Action *continued*

Bush was declared the winner, but did he really win? Two groups of newspapers, one headed by *USA Today* and the other by the *New York Times,* tried to answer this question by recounting the entire Florida vote. But, like the election itself, the newspapers' recounts did not provide clarity. The *USA Today* group found that under three of the four standards that counties used, Bush would have been elected had all undervotes been examined. Gore would have been elected by three votes if the clean-punch standard had been used. The irony is that Gore's camp had advocated using the loosest standards to count votes. If those standards had been adopted, Bush would have won by the largest margin, 1,665 votes.[38] The *New York Times* group found that Gore probably would have lost even with a hand recount in all sixty-seven counties, which had been ordered by the Florida Supreme Court.[39]

What Do You Think?

1. What were the significant constitutional issues in the Florida recount?
2. Could or should these issues have been resolved at the state level? If so, by which branch of state government—legislature, executive, or judicial?
3. Did the U.S. Supreme Court make the right decision in taking the case and in deciding it?
4. How do you think election controversies, such as the one in Florida, can be prevented in the future?
5. Does the Florida vote controversy suggest that we should abolish the Electoral College? Why or why not?

| Summary |

We began this chapter by noting the extent to which elections resolve conflict and contribute to the legitimacy of government. We also noted that the resolution of conflict is only temporary, because some issues remain unresolved and new ones are created, partly by the policy decisions a government makes and implements. These new issues precipitate a debate that often extends into the next election cycle.

Those conflicts, however, are set within a framework upon which there is considerable consensus. Elections are a critical component of democracy. Elections frame policy debates, select legislative and top executive officials, and influence the decisions these officials make, as well as the initial agenda they pursue. In this way, electoral politics shape the "who," "when," and "what" of American government. It would be difficult to conceive of how representative democracy could function and public policy be formulated without regular elections, competing candidates, and partisan divisions.

Yet in the early years of the nation, suffrage was extremely limited. It has taken three amendments to the Constitution to remove racial and gender barriers to voting and extend suffrage to citizens eighteen years of age and older. States still establish the rules and procedures for elections and set the requirements for voting, subject to federal regulation. The more rigorous those requirements are, the lower voter turnout is likely to be. State laws also govern primary elections. If these laws conflict with party rules, however, the Supreme Court has held that parties may determine and enforce their own rules for the selection of delegates to their national nominating conventions.

In recent years, an emerging consensus on the desirability of universal suffrage, easy access to voting, and accurate and rapid tabulation of the vote has been developing. A contentious democratic issue, however, is the use of private resources in election campaigns. Do the wealthy exercise disproportionate influence on the electoral process through their ability to spend unlimited amounts or contribute unregulated amounts to nonparty groups? A second democratic issue is participation. Although the expansion of suffrage increased the number of eligible voters, it has not increased the percentage of the voting-age population that actually votes. In fact, turnout declined as the electorate was expanding. A third issue is representation. If legislative elections are decided by a plurality vote, then how can a minority be represented effectively?

Candidates and parties design their campaigns to influence the judgments of voters. There are usually two campaigns: one is to gain a party's nomination; if that is successful, the other is to win the general election. Of the two, the quest for the nomination changed the most during the last three decades, particularly at the presidential level.

The campaigns start earlier because it takes time to raise the amount of money needed for a serious campaign—money to build an organization, pay for television, conduct public opinion polls, and develop voter appeals. Moreover, the presidential selection process has become heavily front-loaded,

and candidates have no choice but to enter the early primaries and caucuses to gain recognition and win delegates. Once they have effectively won the nomination, they begin to conduct their presidential campaign—well before the national nominating conventions are held. Although the convention officially crowns the candidates, determines the platform, and approves the party's rules, most of these decisions are preordained by the primaries and caucuses. Presidential candidates take the Electoral College into account when devising their campaigns.

Some changes that have affected the presidential selection process have also affected nonpresidential selection as well. Primaries have become the route to nomination at most levels of government. These primaries have led to more competition within the parties and have left them more factionalized. To win the nomination, candidates must build their own organization, raise their own money, design their own strategy, and launch a campaign that appeals to those partisans who are most likely to participate.

The rules and procedures governing the general election have also changed, but not as much as the nomination process. Two of the most important of these changes are the increasing emphasis placed on the electronic media, including the Internet, and the increasing amounts of money needed to pay for the campaign. Media and money, combined with recognition, contribute to the incumbent's advantage, particularly in good times. The playing field is not level. Being in office is usually advantageous for staying in office.

Elections are important because they provide an agenda of priorities and a potential coalition of supporters. It is up to those in power to convert that agenda into a series of proposals and mobilize the coalition to support them. They usually claim an election "mandate" to do so, although they may not have such a mandate.

Key Terms

tyranny of the majority
soft money
partisan identification
retrospective voting
prospective voting
primary

caucuses
superdelegates
proportional voting
front-loading
Electoral College
electors

general ticket system
reapportionment
gerrymandering
citizen ballot initiatives
legislative referenda
coattails

Discussion Questions

1. What are the principal criteria for a democratic election process? How democratic are U.S. elections are today?
2. What are the major factors that affect voter turnout? Who votes and what difference does it make?
3. Which factors today seem to have the greatest influence on how people vote? How do campaign officials take these factors into account when designing their campaign strategies and candidate's appeals?
4. Do campaigns matter? Explain why or why not.
5. Why is it so hard for a winning presidential candidate to claim a mandate? Did George W. Bush have a mandate in 2000? Did he have one in 2004? Explain.

Topics for Debate

Debate each side of the following propositions:

1. Universal suffrage is neither necessary nor desirable for a democratic society.
2. The way to convince more people to vote is to penalize those who don't do so.
3. Campaign advertising that is not truthful should be banned from the public airwaves.
4. The advantages that incumbent candidates have are unfair and undemocratic. Congress should level the paying field.
5. All federal elections should be publicly funded, with no additional monies spent on them.
6. Exit polls should be part of the election itself so that the meaning of the election is clearer to those who are elected.

Where on the Web?

American National Election Studies **www.election studies.org**

Center for Responsive Politics **www.crp.org**

Democracy in Action **www.gwu.edu/~action/**

Election Assistance Commission **www.eac.gov**

Electoral College **www.archives.gov/ federal-register/electoral-college**

Federal Election Commission **www.fec.gov**

League of Women Voters **www.lwv.org**

Politics1 **www.politics1.com**

Go to **www.thomsonedu.com/thomsonnow** to learn about a powerful online study tool. You will get a personalized study plan based on your responses to a diagnostic Pre-Test. Once you have mastered the materials with the help of interactive learning tools, activities, timelines, video case studies, simulations, and an integrated E-Book, you can take a Post-Test to confirm you are ready to move to the next chapter.

Selected Readings

Abramson, Paul R., John H. Aldrich, and David W. Rohde. *Change and Continuity in the 2004 Elections*. Washington, D.C.: Congressional Quarterly, 2006, and volumes for previous elections.

Abramson, Paul R., John H. Aldrich, and David W. Rohde, "The 2004 Presidential Election: The Emergence of a Permanent Majority?" *Political Science Quarterly*, 120 (Spring 2005), 33–57.

Beck, Paul Allen, Russell J. Dalton, Steven Greene, and Robert Huckfeldt, "The Social Calculus of Voting: Interpersonal, Media, and Organizational Influences on Presidential Choices," *American Political Science Review*, 96 (March 2002), 57–73.

Campbell, Angus, Philip E. Converse, Warren E. Miller, and Donald E. Stokes. *The American Voter*. Chicago: University of Chicago Press, 1960.

Campbell, James E. "Why Bush Won the Presidential Election of 2004: Incumbency, Ideology, Terrorism, and Turnout," *Political Science Quarterly*, 120 (Summer 2005), 219–241

Jacobson, Gary C. "Polarized Politics and the 2004 Congressional and Presidential Elections," *Political Science Quarterly*, 120 (Summer 2005), 199–218.

Keith, Bruce E., et al. *The Myth of the Independent Voter*. Berkeley: University of California Press, 1992.

McDonald, Michael P. and Samuel L. Popkin, "The Myth of the Vanishing Voter," *The American Political Science Review*, 95 (December 2001), 963–974.

Morris, Dick. *Behind the Oval Office*. New York: Random House Publishers, 1997.

Rosenstone, Steven J., and John M. Hansen. *Mobilization, Participation, and Democracy in America*. New York: Macmillan Publishers, 1993.

Wattenberg, Martin P. *Where Have All the Voters Gone?* Cambridge, Mass.: Harvard University Press, 2002.

Wayne, Stephen J. *The Road to the White House, 2008*. Belmont, Calif.: Wadsworth, (forthcoming).

White, Theodore. *The Making of the President, 1960*. New York: Atheneum, 1989.

Wolfinger, Raymond E., and Steven J. Rosenstone. *Who Votes?* New Haven, Conn.: Yale University Press, 1980.

Woodward, Bob. *The Choice*. New York: Simon and Schuster, 1996.

Notes

[1]David W. Moore, "One Year after Election, Controversy over Winner Appears Less Serious," Gallup Poll, November 6, 2001.

[2]*Cousins v. Wigoda*, 419 U.S. 477 (1975); *Democratic Party of the U.S/ v. Wisconsin ex. rel. LaFollette*, 450 U.S. 107 (1981).

[3]For an extended discussion of the early history of campaign finance, see Herbert E. Alexander, *Financing Politics: Money, Elections, and Political Reform* (Washington, D.C.: Congressional Quarterly, 1984), 1–54.

[4]*Buckley v. Valeo*, 424 U.S. 1 (1976).

[5]Republicans have opposed limits on spending for practical and philosophical reasons. Not only do they believe that limits on individual contributions deny their party its traditional financial advantage, but they feel that the government had no business telling the people what they could do with their money, much less using taxpayers' money to subsidize elections. Democrats, in contrast, contend that equalizing the amount of money available to candidates would produce a more democratic result, one in which money would not determine the outcome. They see nothing wrong with the government helping to defray the costs of election.

[6]The national parties circumvented not only contribution limits on federal candidates with soft money but also spending limits on the parties and their presidential nominees. Ostensibly, they gave the soft money they solicited to their state party affiliates to help them in party-building and

get-out-the-vote activities. In practice, the money was given to those states in which close contests for the presidency were anticipated, with instructions on how and when to spend the money.

[7]*McConnell v. FEC*, 540 U.S.93 (2003).

[8]These included both Republican-oriented groups such as Progress for America and the Leadership Forum and groups sympathetic to the Democrats such as American Coming Together and the Media Fund. Wealthy financier George Soros and insurance executive Peter Lewis contributed millions to these and other pro-Democratic groups.

[9]North Dakota does not require registration; Wisconsin permits it on election day at the time people vote.

[10]However, only about 70 percent of the registrants are classified as active, people who have voted in the precincts in which they are registered or have responded to a verification notice indicating that they still reside there. "The Impact of the National Voter Registration Act of 1993 on the Administration of Elections for Federal Office, 2001–2002: A Report to the 108th Congress," Federal Election Commission (2003): 4, http://www.fec.gov (accessed January 15, 2004). See also, "A Slight Rise in Registration," *Washington Post*, October 29, 2004, A4.

[11]Voter turnout in the United States is calculated on the basis of the voting-age population, some members of whom are not eligible to vote. Immigrants who are not citizens cannot vote. Two political scientists, Michael P. McDonald and Samuel L. Popkin, calculated that turnout would increase by 4 to 6 percent if just the eligible voting-age population were considered. Michael P. McDonald and Samuel L. Popkin, "The Myth of the Vanishing Voter," *American Political Science Review* 95 (December 2001): 966–967.

[12]Michael A. Fletcher, "Voting Rights for Felons Win Support," *Washington Post*, February 22, 1999, A1, 6.

[13]Angus Campbell, Philip E. Converse, Warren E. Miller, and Donald E. Stokes, *The American Voter* (New York: Wiley, 1960), 101–107.

[14]Paul R. Abramson, John H. Aldrich, and David W. Rohde, *Change and Continuity in the 2004 Elections* (Washington, D.C.: Congressional Quarterly, 2006), 99.

[15]Raymond E. Wolfinger and Steven J. Rosenstone, *Who Votes?* (New Haven, Conn.: Yale University Press, 1980), 13–26.

[16]Ibid., 18–20, 35–36.

[17]Among the young, greater mobility, weaker partisanship, and a less developed sense of community contribute to lower rates of participation, as does not having voted in the past. See also Eric Plutzer, "Becoming a Habitual Voter: Inertia,

Resources, and Growth in Young Adulthood," *American Political Science Review* 96 (March 2002): 41–56.

[18]Curtis Gans, "President Bush, Mobilization Drives Propel Turnout to Post-1968 High; Kerry, Democratic Weakness Shown," Committee for the Study of American Elections, November 4, 2005.

[19]This theory was first postulated in a classic study by Campbell et al., *The American Voter*.

[20]The theory of cross-pressures was first advanced by Paul Lazarsfeld, Bernard Berelson, and Hazel Gaudet in *The People's Choice* (New York: Columbia University Press, 1944). See also Bernard Berelson, Paul Lazarsfeld, and William McPhee, *Voting* (Chicago: University of Chicago Press, 1954).

[21]Morris Fiorina, *Retrospective Voting in American National Elections* (New Haven, Conn.: Yale University Press, 1981), 65–83.

[22]See Edward Tufte, *Political Control of the Economy* (Princeton, N.J.; Princeton University Press, 1978); and M. Stephen Weatherford, "Economic Conditions and Election Outcomes: Class Differences in the Political Response to Recession," *American Journal of Political Science* 22 (1978): 917–938.

[23]These caucuses usually come in stages: the first is held at the precinct level, the second at the county level, and the third at the state level. In the third stage representatives elected by the previous level's caucus meet to choose the delegates to represent the state at the party's national convention. The vote in the initial caucus round is usually reflective of the vote in the final round unless candidates have dropped out of the race during the period in which these multistage caucuses take place.

[24]Initially the Democratic Party also established rules implying that minorities and women had to be represented on the state delegations in proportion to their numbers within the state. Protests over the establishment of what some people considered quotas led the Democrats to substitute language that prescribed affirmative action guidelines for designated minority groups to achieve a delegate composition that reflected the party's electoral constituency.

[25]Rhodes Cook, "2004: The Voting Begins," http://www.rhodescook.com/primary.analysis.html (accessed June 30, 2004).

[26]John S. Jackson, Barbara Brown, and David Bositis, "Herbert McClosky and Friends Revisited: 1980 Democratic and Republican Party Elites Compared to the Mass Public," *American Politics Quarterly* 10 (1982): 158–180; and Martin Plissner and Warren J. Mitofsky, "The Making of the Delegates, 1968–1988," *Public Opinion* 3 (September–October 1988): 46.

[27]"Despite Limited Convention Television Coverage, Public Learned about Campaign from Democrats," National Annenberg Election Survey, August 29, 2004.

[28]Because of a personal scandal, Richard Johnson, Martin Van Buren's running mate, fell one vote short of a majority in the Electoral College. The Senate elected him anyway.

[29]The state of Utah went to court to protest the 2000 census count, which awarded an extra congressional seat to North Carolina rather than Utah. With a large Mormon population for whom overseas religious activity is a part of their religious beliefs and heritage, Utah disputed the Census Bureau's refusal to count citizens living abroad as part of the domestic population, eligible for congressional representation. Utah also objected to the Census Bureau's technique of estimating data on households that it was unable to contact during the period in which the census was taken. The Supreme Court rejected Utah's arguments. D'Vera Cohn, "Court Denies Utah House Bid," *Washington Post,* June 21, 2002, A8.

[30]The significant political ramifications of the census help explain why the count has been subject to challenge. After the 1990 census, several cities, states, and citizen groups alleged that several million people, primarily in the inner cities, had been missed. However, they were unable to convince the Census Bureau to adjust its population count or the courts to force the agency to do so.

[31]*Wesberry v. Sanders,* 377 U.S. 533 (1964).

[32]*Shaw v. Reno,* 509 U.S. 630 (1993).

[33]In many local governments in the United States, officials are chosen in nonpartisan elections in which issue positions and candidate images are the central elements of the campaign. Party labels are not used.

[34]"Ballotwatch: 2004 Election Summary," Initiative and Referendum Institute, University of Southern California, December 29, 2004. http://www.iandrinstitute.org (accessed July 18, 2005). "Ballotwatch: Election Results, 2006," November 7, 2006.

[35]Paul R. Abramson, John H. Aldrich, and David W. Rohde, *Change and Continuity in the 2000 Elections* (Washington, D.C.: Congressional Quarterly, 2002), 148, 166.

[36]Howard Kurtz and Edward Walsh, "Battleground State," *Washington Post,* November 8, 2000, A31.

[37]There were ballot problems in addition to the tabulation of the punch card. Florida law permits absentee ballots to be tallied as long as they are postmarked on or before election day. However, some ballots, which were collected and bundled by the military, were not postmarked because they were sent through an internal military mailing system. The Democrats challenged these ballots, and the Republicans launched a counteroffensive by raising the patriotism issue. When Democratic vice presidential candidate Joseph Lieberman appeared on the Sunday talk shows, he undercut the Democrats' position by stating that he would give the benefit of the doubt to ballots coming from military personnel. Democrats quietly dropped the issue, and Bush picked up 200 additional votes from a recounting of absentee ballots.

[38]Dennis Cauchon, "Newspaper's Recount Shows Bush Prevailed in Fla. Vote," *USA Today,* April 4, 2001, 1A.

[39]John M. Broder and Ford Fessenden, "Study of Disputed Florida Ballots Finds Justices Did Not Cast the Final Vote," *New York Times,* November 12, 2001, A1.

9

Media and Politics

Introduction

THE NEWS MEDIA PRESENTED a highly positive portrayal of the military phase of the war in Iraq. From the beginning of hostilities on March 19, 2003, to the fall of Tikrit on April 14, 2003, coverage of the war on the major broadcast networks' evening news shows and on the Fox news channel was considerably more favorable (62 percent) than unfavorable (38 percent), according to a study conducted by the Center for Media and Public Affairs.[1] Assessments of the president's policy were also more positive (56 percent) than negative (34).[2] Moreover, the public gave the news media high marks for its efforts. Three out of four Americans rated coverage of the war as good or excellent.[3]

With much pomp and ceremony, President Bush announced the end of the hostilities on May 1, 2003, abroad the aircraft carrier *USS Abraham Lincoln* in a speech viewed by millions of Americans. The Gallup poll that followed the president's announcement indicated that 69 percent of respondents approved of Bush's performance in office and 72 percent believed that sending troops to Iraq was appropriate, not a mistake.[4]

With the Iraqi resistance to the U.S. occupation rising, the coalition forces unable to find weapons of mass destruction, the economic costs of the operation skyrocketing, and the human toll rising, news coverage of the United States' presence in Iraq became more critical. Seventy-seven percent of evaluations of the U.S. reconstruction and peacekeeping efforts were negative in the six months from May 1, 2003, the date of the president's announcement, to October 31. Positive media assessments of the president during this period also fell to 32 percent.[5] Public opinion changed as well. In a Gallup poll taken in the middle of November 2003, only 42 percent of respondents said that they approved of how the United States was handling the situation in Iraq. The president's job approval rating dropped to 50 percent and his disapproval rose to 47 percent, the highest since he took office.[6]

The White House responded by coordinating a blame-the-media campaign, limiting journalists' access to senior civilian and military authorities in Iraq, keeping camera crews out of hospitals and preventing them from filming the return of the bodies of American soldiers who had lost their lives, and excluding noncombat deaths and injuries from the casualty lists distributed to the press. The president referred to the "filtering" of the news from Iraq[7] and attributed public impatience with the occupation in the United States and abroad to "the news cycle," a contention with which Republicans agreed but Democrats and Independents did not.[8]

In response to the negative news coverage, the administration also launched a public relations campaign. The president met with Iraqi leaders at the White House, used a Veterans Day appearance to emphasize U.S. resolve, and met with military families who had lost loved ones in Iraq. He even shared Thanksgiving dinner with the troops in a surprise visit to Baghdad. In addition, the president began to devote more attention to domestic issues he had neglected during the military build up that followed the terrorist attacks and continued to neglect during the war in Iraq.

What is the relationship today among events, news coverage of them, and public evaluations of presidential leadership? This chapter explores that question. It begins by reviewing the critical role of a free and informative press in a democratic society. In this discussion, we examine the tension between the goals of a private news media—to inform, to entertain, and to profit—and those of a responsive partisan government—to explain, to justify, and to promote its policy and the beneficial effect that will result from it.

The relationship between the press and the government is symbiotic; it is a love–hate relationship. The news media need information from public officials about what they are thinking and doing, yet the media are leery of the information they receive. Elected and appointed officials know that the press is their principal vehicle for communicating with the people, but they, too, are fearful that their story will be distorted. The general public is caught in the middle, needful of information to evaluate their government but also desirous of the types of information they find most interesting, information that may not be conducive to a fair and balanced assessment of how the government is doing.

Public interests condition media coverage just as these interests affect government decision makers and the public policy they formulate. This chapter also looks at the news media's effect on public perceptions and the effect of those perceptions on politics and government.

Although there is a consensus in America about the need for a free press, there is also conflict over how well the press performs its role. Much of that conflict stems from a partisan reaction to the news that is reported, how it is reported, and what conclusions can be drawn from it about the decisions and actions of government officials.

Republicans tend to be more critical of news coverage than are Democrats. Independents are the least critical.[9] They are also the least knowledgeable, which suggests that they pay less attention to the news and do not have as well defined a mindset from which to view it. Republicans and Democrats, on the other hand, interpret the news through a partisan lens—hence their stronger reaction to it. We explore these competing perspectives: how they shape public reaction to the news and how they affect the presentation of that news to the American people.

We begin our discussion by asking why a free press is so important to democracy: what critical functions the news media perform, how they have performed those functions, and how that performance has changed over time—a consequence of a capitalist system, technological advances, and changing norms of political and social discourse and behavior. In our discussion, we pay particular attention to television and the Internet and their impact on the younger generation's knowledge of politics and government. The news media's coverage of electoral politics and governing institutions is explored in some detail in a final section. The case study at the end of the chapter deals with the increasing attention that has been directed at "character" issues by the press. Is such attention merited? Is it relevant? Is it desirable?

Questions to Ponder

- Why is a free press so important to a democracy?
- Should government place limits on the press in the interests of national security, social morality, or economic competition?
- Do the news media provide the people with the coverage they want and need to make informed judgments?
- How well does the press perform its role as watchdog of government?
- Should government officials be able to use taxpayer funds for public relations campaigns that promote their policy proposals?
- Is the media's emphasis on private behavior relevant to public performance in office?

9.1 In Theory . . .
The Role of the Press

A free and diversified press is essential to a democratic society. It provides the channels through which information flows from the people to their government and from the government back to the people. The press serves as a watchdog, enabling the public to evaluate the performance of government officials on a continuing basis; it also acts as an incentive for officials to keep the public interest in mind when making policy decisions. The exposure of the White House connection to the Watergate burglary during the Nixon administration, the reporting of atrocities committed by the U.S. military during the Vietnam War, the nightly television news programs about American diplomats held hostage in

Iran, the revelation of arms sales to Iran, and more recently, the pictures of Iraqi prisoners being humiliated and maltreated by their American captors all helped focus public attention on major problems, forced government officials to react to them, and set off a series of decisions and events that ultimately affected government, public policy, and the political environment.

The news media affect the politics of American government in a variety of ways: They direct attention to salient issues; create a time frame in which those issues should be addressed; influence the content, tone, and scope of public debate; and convey and evaluate the decisions and actions of those in power.

But their coverage of events also affects the realities that they purport to describe and assess. That is why they are often referred to as the fourth branch of government.

Reporting on politics and government requires access; it may also require protection of news sources. The press's watchdog role was what the drafters of the First Amendment had in mind when they prohibited laws that abridged freedom of speech. But how great should the scope of that freedom be if it adversely affects the nation's security, wrongly accuses innocent people, or presents a distorted picture of reality? These are difficult questions, ones that Congress debated during its consideration of the USA Patriot Act in 2001 and the extension of many of its provisions in 2005 and 2006. These issues must be continually addressed in a democracy with a free, largely private, and competitive news media.

The Role of the News Media

Most Americans agree that the news media need to operate freely, although they disagree over how extensive that freedom should be. A recent survey taken by the Freedom Forum found that 47 percent of the respondents indicated that the press has had just about the right amount of freedom, 39 percent said that it had too much, and 10 percent asserted that it did not have enough.[10]

The theory behind the need for a free press is straightforward. In a government based on the consent of the governed, the people need to know what public officials say and do, what decisions they make and the reasons that they make them, and how well those decisions and actions address the salient issues and rectify the problems of the day. The press provide a critical link by which information is conveyed from and to the government, information that directs public officials and provides a basis for evaluating their performance.

Democracy and a Free Press

Government officials also have a duty to inform the public, but they wish to do so in a way that justifies their decisions and actions. When the news media investigate or question what they have been told by public officials, tension can be generated. This tension reduces the openness with which those in government operate. It also motivates them to try to shape the news coverage they receive, to put their "spin" on events. Such a motivation encourages members of the press to suspect that they are not hearing the whole truth, that government officials are not being candid, or that they may be hiding something. This suspicion motivates them to dig more deeply, to assume that they are being given the administration's line, and to play "gotcha" journalism with those in positions of power. The tension between news reporters and government officials can impede the search for truth, it can result in false accusations, and it makes the press–government relationship an adversarial one much of the time.

There is another problem. The public's right to know and the press's obligation to report the news can clash with the government's ability to function efficiently, to protect the confidentiality of internal communications, to facilitate decision making, and to prevent the premature release of information that might give an unfair advantage to certain individuals or groups within society or might even damage national security.

Congress addressed these issues in 1966, when it enacted the Freedom of Information Act. Designed to facilitate access to government documents, this law places on the government the burden of showing why a document should not be released to the public.[11] However, the news media have not used the act as much as anticipated because of the long time it takes to process information requests, the court battles that ensue when government officials say information should not be released, and because it is easier, quicker, and cheaper to obtain the information from "leaks" than from formal requests.

Sometimes, however, Congress acts on behalf of the public to obtain information about executive branch activities. Armed with the power of subpoena, Congress can force executive officials to provide such information. If they fail to do so, they can be held in contempt of Congress.

Occasionally the two institutions come to loggerheads over an issue that the judiciary may have to resolve. During the first year of George W. Bush's presidency, Vice President Dick Cheney declined to reveal the names of people from the private sector with whom he consulted in formulating the administration's energy policy. After rolling brownouts in California and the failure of the Enron Corporation, a congressional subcommittee looking into the matter requested that the Government Accountability Office (GAO), its investigative arm, obtain this information. Cheney refused to provide it. He said that the president could consult with whomever he pleased and did not have to reveal the identity of his advisers.

The GAO subsequently went to court to force the administration's hand, but after the terrorist attacks of September 11, 2001, the GAO dropped its lawsuit. A public interest group reinstituted the legal challenge. The case eventually reached the Supreme Court; but the Court sent it back on a technicality to the U.S. Court of Appeals in Washington, D.C., which had originally considered the issue.

Subsequently, the appeals court ruled unanimously that the vice president did not have to make the information available.[12]

The public's right to know has other limits. Classified information may be withheld for extended periods. Government officials do not have to reveal information that they believe would threaten the nation's security. For example, it is against the law to identify covert intelligence and law enforcement agents. Doing so can result in criminal prosecution.

Take the case of Valerie Plame, a covert agent for the Central Intelligence Agency (CIA), whose name was leaked to several reporters—apparently in retribution for her husband's criticism of President George W. Bush's contention that Saddam Hussein was trying to obtain uranium to build nuclear weapons.[13] The reporter who was first leaked the information of Plame's association, Robert Novack, refused to identify his source, as did several other reporters who heard about the story from government officials who requested anonymity. The reporters contended that the First Amendment protected their confidential relationships with informants.

A special investigator, charged with determining whether a crime had been committed, subpoenaed White House aides and reporters to appear before the grand jury investigating the matter. Two reporters initially refused to do so, although one later recanted after his editors at *Time* magazine made his notes of a conversation with a top presidential aide, Karl Rove, available to the grand jury. The reporter later said that Rove released him from his promise of confidentiality. The other journalist, Judith Miller of the *New York Times,* went to jail rather than appear before the grand jury.[14] Miller's position and that of her newspaper was that the reporter–informant relationship is similar to that between a lawyer and a client, a doctor and a patient, or the clergy and a confessor. Without such a relationship, they argued, a reporter's ability to obtain information about the government would be severely hampered and the very notion of freedom of the press would be undercut.

Not everyone agrees with the contention that reporters should have immunity from prosecution for failing to reveal their sources. Although the general public strongly supports the principle of a free press, that same public is leery of unnamed sources and the accuracy of information they provide.[15]

Nevertheless, leaks have become commonplace. Sometimes they are made purposefully by government officials to gauge public reaction to a proposed policy initiative; sometimes they are the consequence of a public official unhappy with a government policy decision or the procedure by which that decision was made; and sometimes leaks are initiated by a person who believes that fraudulent activity is occurring or improper influence is being exerted. A person who reveals such information is often referred to as a **whistleblower.** Congress has enacted legislation to protect whistleblowers from discipline or dismissal by their superiors.

Members of the press contend that unless they have complete freedom to report the news, unless they are shielded from prosecution when refusing to divulge their sources, and unless a stringent test is used to decide cases of libel and slander, they cannot perform their role as the watchdog of the American

whistleblower
A person who alerts the public, usually through the news media, to improper or unethical decisions or actions occurring within an organization, often the national government.

© AP/Wide World Photos

New York Times reporter Judith Miller leaves U.S. District Court in Washington with her attorney Robert Bennett, right, in this October 12, 2005, file photo. The vice president's chief of staff, I. Lewis "Scooter" Libby Jr., was indicted October 28, 2005, on charges of obstruction of justice, perjury, and making false statements in the CIA leak investigation.

people. In response, the government has argued that a free press is not impaired by legitimate restrictions essential to the functioning of government, restrictions to protect national security and to ensure that the president receives candid opinions and sage advice.

As noted in Chapter 4, the Supreme Court has not held that First Amendment freedoms are absolute. Rather it has contended that the needs of the press to obtain information, to organize and analyze it, and to print, air, or otherwise transmit it must be balanced by individual rights of privacy, truthfulness, and fairness. It is up to the judiciary to determine the boundaries between freedom of the press and individual and societal rights. It is interesting to note that in determining these boundaries, the Court has not judged all media by the same standard. The limits placed on print journalism and cable and satellite television are less extensive than those placed on the broadcast media, which use the public airwaves and thus are available to everyone with a television rather than simply to subscribers.[16]

Capitalism and a Fair Press

A free press with a watchdog role cannot be controlled by a government. It must operate independently of the government or outside it entirely; otherwise, it will be viewed as an instrument of the government without the credibility and objectivity it needs to perform reporting and evaluative functions.

In the United States the press began and has continued to be primarily a profit-making enterprise. Although there is a Corporation for Public Broadcasting that receives some government funding and noncommercial public radio and television networks that obtain private contributions, most of American media is private, and this means that it is motivated largely by the need to make a profit.

Not only are the news media in the United States private, but they also are big business. Almost 1,500 papers are published daily.[17] Most of them are part of newspaper chains such as Gannett, Scripts-Howard, Hearst, and Times Mirror; the twelve biggest chains account for more than 400 daily newspapers, with a total circulation of more than 35 million. The chains also maintain their own news bureaus, which distribute reports, features, and news analyses to member papers. The papers' editors determine what material provided by the bureau is published.

The largest of the chains, Gannett, publishes more than 95 newspapers, with a total daily circulation of more than 6 million; it also owns more than 300 nondaily papers and operates 22 television stations and 19 radio stations.[18] It is this combination of media outlets that causes particular concern.[19] Some fear that concentrated ownership will reduce the number of sources of information and impose the perspective of a few large corporations on the shape and content of the news.[20] For this reason, many members of Congress, both Republican and Democrat, opposed the decision by the Federal Communications Commission (FCC) in 2003 to allow the major media giants to own a greater share of the radio and television stations in a given market. Although the president sided with the FCC, the White House did agree to a compromise that set the percentage of media outlets that could be owned by the same company to a maximum of 39 percent of the regional market, ending the dispute but not satisfying either business or consumer advocacy groups.

The profit motive drives the news media to capture and maintain as large an audience as possible. That is how they make money. To attract and hold such an audience, they must provide a product that people want: they must please their readers, listeners, or viewers or face the risk of losing them. Their dilemma is how to meet market demands by satisfying their audience and simultaneously fulfill their role in a democracy, particularly if the majority of people do not desire much information about, or critical evaluations of, politics and government.

The news media have attempted to resolve this dilemma mostly by making the news entertaining. They emphasize action rather than ideas, politics rather than policy, people rather than institutions and processes. They focus on conflict, drama, and the human dimension because these topics spark the most interest. Moreover, to save time and money and to report the news quickly, even instantaneously, they may become overly dependent on a few sources and fail to devote enough resources to verifying the information they receive, much less providing alternative perspectives. The pressure to beat the opposition can undercut the democratic process and make the news media imperfect instruments for performing their important educational and informational roles.

Review Questions

1. Most Americans agree that a free press is

   A. Essential to a democratic society at all times
   B. Essential to a democracy except in times of war
   C. Desirable but not always critical for a democracy
   D. Dangerous and should be constrained

2. Americans disagree most over

   A. The role of the news media
   B. The accuracy of the news media
   C. The spin of the news media
   D. The privatization of the news media

3. Newspapers continue to be the prime sources of news for which population group?

   A. The youngest age cohort in the electorate
   B. White women
   C. Older members of society
   D. Ethnic and racial minorities

4. The evolution of the news media in the United States today has resulted in

   A. Continuing competition among news providers
   B. An increase in government control
   C. A decreasing number of news outlets
   D. The expansion of print journalism

Answers:

   1. A
   2. C
   3. C
   4. A

Conflict and Consensus in Review

Contemporary audiences have evidenced less confidence in the veracity of news reports and the correspondents and anchors who reported them than they did in the immediate past. Although Americans believe in a free press and support its watchdog role, they have become increasingly critical of how that role is being performed—a subject that we will address later in this chapter. First, however, we turn to a history of the press—how the news media has changed and how those changes have affected the news and the audience to which it is directed.

A Brief History of the News Media in America

The tension between the democratic goal of informing the public and the economic value of maintaining as large an audience as possible is apparent in the history of the news media in the United States—a history marked by professional change, economic competition, and technological advances.

Print Media: Newspapers

Even before American independence, newspapers were published and circulated in the colonies. The first known paper, *Publick Occurrences, Both Foreign and Domestick,* was published in 1690 but lasted for only one issue. Colonial officials viewed its content as so offensive that they forbade future publication. Throughout the colonial period, other papers also had to contend with British authorities who wished to suppress criticism of their government.

Such criticism erupted during the Revolutionary War. Most newspapers supported the revolution and became an important source of information and propaganda. After the war, the debate over the new government was carried on in the press. The most famous and eloquent defense of the Constitution, *The Federalist Papers,* appeared as a series of essays written under an alias by James Madison, Alexander Hamilton, and John Jay; those opposed to the Constitution published their own criticism in Anti-Federalist newspapers.

Newspapers at this time were not aimed at the masses; they were written for the educated upper class, and their content consisted primarily of business and political news and opinions. Congress enlarged the potential market for these newspapers by its enactment of the Post Office Act of 1792, which created a national postal system and subsidized newspaper distribution by charging low mailing rates. The general availability of newspapers, an increase in literacy, and the movement toward greater public involvement in the political process led to a boost in readership beginning in the 1830s. Technological advances, which made mass production of newspapers possible, contributed to the "penny press," newspapers sold for a penny. These papers were oriented toward the less prosperous members of society and offered interesting, lively, even scandalous content— local news, human interest stories, and accounts of crime and violence.

The penny press revolutionized American journalism. Newspapers began to rely on advertising supplemented with larger over-the-counter sales as their primary sources of income. To attract advertisers, they had to have many readers. To attract readers, their content had to be different and eye-catching. As a result, there were changes in what was reported and how it was reported.[21]

With more newspapers targeted at a general readership, a higher premium was put on gathering news quickly and reporting it in an engaging, easy-to-read manner. The invention of the telegraph helped make it possible for reporters in Washington to communicate information about government to the entire country. Sensationalism and aggressive crusading began to dominate the news, giving rise to **yellow journalism,** a term that originated in a battle between two newspaper chains for the rights to a popular comic strip titled "The Yellow Kid."

yellow journalism
News stories that emphasize the sensational or feature aggressive reporting and undercover investigations by the press.

Table 9.1 Daily Newspapers with the Largest Circulation (2005)

Newspaper	Circulation
USA Today	2,281,830
Wall Street Journal	2,070,498
The New York Times	1,136,433
Los Angeles Times	907,997
The Washington Post	751,871
New York Daily News	735,536
New York Post	678,086
Chicago Tribune	573,744
Houston Chronicle	527,744
San Francisco Chronicle	468,739

Source: "State of the Industry," *Washington Post,* May 3, 2005, E3.

In the early 1900s, the number of daily newspapers, which had exceeded 2,000, started to decline. The economics of publishing, which made it essential to achieve lower unit costs and higher advertising revenues by increasing circulation, caused many newspapers to fold or merge with their competitors. Less competition and more consolidation resulted in the growth of newspaper chains. By 2005, only three daily newspapers had circulations of more than 1 million, and the number of daily newspapers has been decreasing. (Table 9.1 lists the dailies with the largest circulation.)

The proportion of the population receiving most of its news from newspapers remains large; however, it is only about half as large as the proportion who watches television regularly to obtain news and about the same as people who listen to radio to get their news.[22] There is also a generational divide between newspaper readers and television viewers. Younger people are much less wedded to the print press than those who grew up before the age of television. According to a recent survey conducted by the Pew Research Center for the People and the Press, although younger Americans are still more likely to acquire their news from newspapers than the Internet, the gap between these two sources of information is closing rapidly[23] (see Table 9.2).

Electronic Media

Radio The first radio station began operating in 1920, and radio remained the principal electronic medium from the 1920s to the 1950s. Dominated by the major national networks, CBS and NBC, it broadcast entertainment and news programs to a national audience. At first, radio stations did not provide regular news coverage, but they excelled at covering special events as they were happening. The 1924

Table 9.2 Principal Sources of News For Americans

"How have you been getting most of your news about national and international issues? From television, from newspapers, from radio, from magazines, or from the Internet?" [Directions to interviewers: Accept two answers: If only one response is given, probe for one additional response.]

	June 2005	Sept. 2001 (after 9/11)	Sept. 2001 (before 9/11)	Sept. 1995	Jan. 1991
TELEVISION	74	90	74	82	82
NEWSPAPERS	44	11	45	63	40
RADIO	22	14	18	20	15
INTERNET	24	5	13	—	—
MAGAZINES	5	*	6	10	4
OTHER	2	1	1	1	1

*Don't know.
Source: "Public More Critical of Press, but Goodwill Persists," Pew Research Center for the People and the Press, June 26, 2005, http://people-press.org/reports/display.php3?ReportID=248 (accessed June 27, 2005).

presidential election was the first to be reported on radio; the conventions, major speeches, and election returns were broadcast to a national audience. During the 1928 election, both major presidential candidates, Herbert Hoover and Alfred E. Smith, spent campaign funds on radio advertising.

Radio soon became the most important medium for reporting fast-breaking news stories. Whereas the speed with which newspapers could bring current events to readers was limited by the time required for printing and delivery, a radio station could have a story on the air in a matter of minutes.

In addition to being faster, radio had the advantage of being better able to convey the excitement and color of an event. Politicians soon became aware of the power of radio to transmit ideas. Franklin Roosevelt was the first president to use radio to appeal directly to the people and mobilize support for his political agenda. Roosevelt's "fireside chats" fostered a personal relationship with the public that became a model for his successors in the White House.

Although radio lost its national audience to television in the 1950s, it did not fade away. Instead, stations began broadcasting specialized programming aimed at smaller, local, more homogeneous audiences. Today there are more radio stations operating than there were in radio's supposed "glory days" in the 1940s. One factor that has kept radio alive and well has been the increasing amount of time Americans spend in their cars; unlike reading, watching television, or even talking on a cell phone, listening to the radio is not difficult or dangerous to do while driving.

Because it is relatively cheap and accessible and can be targeted to different types of people, radio remains a major communications medium for candidates seeking public office and officials and organizations attempting to affect public policy. President Ronald Reagan used radio effectively to deliver policy statements on Saturdays, a practice that has been continued on this generally slow news day by his successors. The 1990s saw the expansion of "talk radio," in which listeners were encouraged to telephone the host with questions and comments. Many of the people who host such shows have strong ideological convictions that they share with like-minded listeners. Conservatives commentators and audiences tend to outnumber liberal commentators and listeners who listen to talk radio. Listeners tend to be middle aged and male, although the size of the talk-radio audience is declining.[24]

Broadcast Television After World War II, television quickly transformed the American public into a large viewing audience. In 1950, only 9 percent of households in the United States had televisions; within the next decade that percentage grew to 87. Today it is more than 98 percent, with most households averaging more than two TV sets.[25] Television, which had been a curiosity item that only the rich could afford, had become a necessity for most Americans. Today the average person watches about 4.6 hours of television per day.[26]

When television started to dominate the American media, three networks—ABC, CBS, and NBC—began to dominate television. During this formative period, most commercial stations in the United States were affiliated with one of these three networks, which provided the bulk of their entertainment programming and national news.

Television featured daily newscasts almost from the outset, but its political effect was initially felt more strongly through its coverage of special events such as the Senate hearings on organized crime in 1950–1951. The chairperson of the committee that conducted the inquiry, Senator Estes Kefauver (D-Tennessee), became a national hero and subsequently a presidential candidate through the visibility and notoriety he gained as a result of the television coverage of the hearings. Kefauver's rise to prominence demonstrated the potential of television as a vehicle for increasing name recognition and enhancing personal image. It soon became a major medium through which campaigns were directed and elections were observed.

In presidential elections, the effect of television was felt as early as 1952. The most important news event of that campaign was a speech by General Dwight Eisenhower's running mate, Richard Nixon. Accused of obtaining secret campaign funds in exchange for political favors, Nixon defended himself in a national television address. He denied accepting contributions for personal use, accused the Democratic administration of President Harry Truman of being soft on communism, criticized his Democratic opponents in the presidential campaign, and vowed that he would never force his children to give up their dog, Checkers, who had been given to the Nixons by political supporters. The emotion of the speech, and particularly the reference to Checkers, generated a favorable public reaction, ended discussion of illicit campaign funds, and kept Nixon on the Republican ticket.

Paid television advertising by the political parties also first appeared during the 1952 election. The marketing of candidates on television revolutionized the electoral process, particularly the strategy and tactics of campaigning. It enabled candidates to craft their own images and challenge those of their opponents.

Over the next two decades, television's power to shape personal images was demonstrated repeatedly. In 1954, it contributed greatly to the downfall of Senator Joseph McCarthy (R-Wisconsin), who had made a name for himself by charging that communists had infiltrated the government, particularly the State Department, and the military. During eight weeks of televised hearings by McCarthy's committee into possible communist influence in the Army, the public was able to view and evaluate the senator's unsubstantiated charges and brow-beating of witnesses and others who denied his allegations.

Another example of the power of television came during the four debates held in 1960 between the two major presidential candidates, Senator John F. Kennedy and Vice President Richard Nixon, especially the first debate. In that confrontation, the vice president appeared pallid; the color of his suit blended into the background; he seemed to need a shave; and he shifted nervously in his seat with his eyes darting back and forth. He did not look nearly as good as he sounded. In contrast, Kennedy appeared fresh; his clothes made him stand out; and his facial expressions and gestures came across well on television. Those who heard the debate on radio judged Nixon the winner; those who saw it on television were more impressed by Kennedy. The television exposure that both candidates received during the debates contributed to Kennedy's narrow victory.

Television coverage of the civil rights movement, particularly the 1963 protest staged in Birmingham, Alabama, by Dr. Martin Luther King Jr., and the reaction to it by the police (with attack dogs, water cannons, and cattle prods), created unforgettable images for viewers. For much of the public, television provided the evidence that justified the struggle for civil rights. Coverage of the Vietnam War, the first "living-room war," provided another vivid illustration of the power of television. Nightly pictures of the pain and suffering of the war's victims, including

© MPI/Getty Images

The first television debate occurred in 1960 when Republican Richard M. Nixon debated Democratic candidate, John F. Kennedy.

American military casualties, and persistent, critical evaluations of the progress of the war by correspondents in the field had a powerful cumulative effect on the public's conscience and helped turn national sentiment against the war.

The decade of the 1960s also saw the increasing importance of television network news and the growth of a large Washington press corps. In 1948, NBC and CBS began airing 15-minute evening newscasts; by 1963, they had extended their coverage to a half-hour. Since then, Americans have cited television as their principal and most believable source of news, although viewership of evening network news has declined markedly since the availability of twenty-four-hour cable news and expanded local news shows. Today only about one in three Americans report that they watch the nightly news shows on the broadcast networks on a regular basis compared to almost 60 percent who watch local news.[27]

The ascendancy of television news has affected the print media as well. Because electronic media can report events at or close to the time when they happen, newspapers and magazines had to supplement their coverage and commentary to provide an additional dimension and thereby maintain a product that people would want to buy. Moreover, they had to "find" news by investigating activities that on the surface might not have appeared newsworthy.

The *Washington Post's* reporting of the Watergate scandals during 1972 and 1973 is a good example of the power and profitability of investigative journalism. The *Post* reported that White House aides had broken into the Democratic National Committee's headquarters at the Watergate complex and that President Nixon had participated in a cover-up of the attempted burglary.

W. Mark Felt, the anonymous source whom *Washington Post's* Bob Woodward called "deep throat," is pictured here on CBS' "Face The Nation" in 1976. Felt provided Woodward with important clues during the Watergate investigation.

Attacked by high-level officials, including the president and the vice president, the *Post* stuck to its story, producing one revelation after another and eventually prompting a congressional investigation, the hiring of a special prosecutor, and the resignation of President Nixon. *Post* reporters Bob Woodward and Carl Bernstein, who broke the Watergate story, helped usher in a new era of investigative reporting.[28]

The Vietnam War and Watergate were turning points in the relationship between the press and the government. The press accused the government of withholding and falsifying information, and the administrations of Lyndon Johnson and Richard Nixon accused the media of being unfair and biased in their coverage of events. The so-called credibility gap between the news media and the government has continued, as have accusations of cover-ups and bias by the press and of sensationalism in the news by those in politics and government.

Today the news media no longer give public officials the benefit of the doubt: they assume that when officials speak on the record, they are providing their own perspective, the most favorable one for them. Members of the press view their job as uncovering the truth, not simply reporting the "spin" that government "PR" presents. In doing so, the news media tend to be aggressive in their questioning and critical in their reporting, usually more negative than positive. Predictably, government officials see this media coverage as hostile.

Cable and Satellite A major change in the electronic media has been the growth and accessibility of cable and satellite television. Although cable began to operate in the early 1950s, largely to improve television reception in areas when it was difficult to receive a clear picture, it took several decades for the entire country to become wired for cable and for companies to offer a wide selection of programming on the new medium. Similarly, satellite-directed television required the positioning of satellites in space and the availability of relatively cheap "dishes" for reception of the signal. By the 1990s, both were readily available and affordable. More than two-thirds of households in the United States subscribe to one of these services.[29]

The proliferation of stations on cable and satellite has had the opposite effect from that of broadcasting. Instead of appealing to the broadest possible audience, stations included in cable and satellite packages offer specialized programming designed for targeted audiences. For those interested in politics and government, the all-news and public affairs stations provide "24/7 coverage."

The Cable News Network (CNN) was the first to do so. Its worldwide news bureaus, correspondents, and satellite hookups challenged the major broadcast networks' near monopoly on national and international news coverage. Several other regional and national cable networks have followed CNN into the twenty-four–hour news business, and one, Fox News, has even surpassed it in viewership. The character of the audiences also varies from one news service to another. Conservatives and Republicans are more likely to watch Fox, and liberals and Democrats are more likely to depend on the broadcast networks, CNN, and public radio and television.[30] The partisan character of the cable news audience cannot help but affect the type of stories that are reported and the spin placed on these stories by correspondents, anchors, and their editors.

For public affairs, the Cable Satellite Public Affairs Network (C-SPAN) began covering official proceedings of the House of Representatives in 1979 and those of the Senate in 1986. This congressional coverage has been extended to include committee sessions and leadership press conferences. Press conferences by the president and other executive cabinet officials, major speeches and events, even academic conferences are now regularly broadcast on one of the three C-SPAN channels. Although C-SPAN is generally available, it has a small audience, only about 5 percent of all viewers. On the other hand, 16 percent indicate that they regularly listen to National Public Radio or watch *The News Hour with Jim Lehrer* on public television.[31]

Not only has the diversity of programs increased, but so has the capacity of viewers to shift quickly from one channel to another by using remote controls. These devices have had a profound effect on news coverage and the news audience. There are many inadvertent viewers who turn to news in the process of "surfing" their channels. These viewers tend to watch for shorter periods. To hold them longer, the news networks have speeded up the action, shortened the statements by candidates and public officials that they air (producing sound bites), and emphasized argumentation and conflict in these individuals' on-the-air remarks. Programs are purposefully designed to be as controversial as possible. Nonetheless, people are spending less time watching the news than they did a decade ago. Moreover, they are watching local news more, national news less, and international news least of all with the exception of terrorism and the War in Iraq.[32]

The Internet   The Internet was created in 1969 by experts in the Department of Defense who feared that the military communications system could be sabotaged or disrupted by a nuclear attack. To reduce the system's vulnerability to hostile forces, they decentralized it, creating a network of communications among computers. This network broke information into pieces and sent those pieces to designated points in the system where they were reassembled to produce a message. If for any reason one route was blocked, the packet of information would seek an alternative route.

At first, the system connected just the Pentagon's computers. By the 1980s, it extended to researchers and scholars at universities and to officials in other government agencies. By the 1990s, it had expanded into the private sector. By the beginning of the twenty-first century, it had become a mass medium. Today more than 75 percent Americans report that they have access to a computer in their home, workplace, or school; 60 percent say that they go online on a regular basis.[33] Although the Internet is still a secondary source of news for most Americans, its use as a primary source is growing.[34] One out of four people say that they regularly go online to get the news.[35] Young people especially are inclined to use the Web to get information, communicate with their friends, and engage in political interchanges on Blogs.

The most recent development has been the growth of broadband that permits high-speed Internet access. Here too younger people with such access are more likely to cite the Internet as their principal source of news about politics than people older than 35.[36]

E-Government In 1993, the Clinton administration became the first to establish a White House website. Congress established its own site shortly thereafter. In 1995, a database system, named Thomas, after Thomas Jefferson, was established by the Library of Congress. It contains the full text of all bills that have been introduced into Congress since 1973, reports of congressional committees, transcripts of their hearings, and testimony of public officials, as well as the congressional schedule, a listing of day-to-day activities, and even historical and research-oriented materials pertaining to Congress. In addition, all members of Congress have their own sites at which they provide their constituents with a lot of "how to" information, such as how to obtain an internship in their office or how to gain an appointment to a military academy, and answers to questions about Medicare and its new drug coverage and Social Security.

The information provided by the White House and Congress is supplemented by information made available by executive agencies. The Federal Election Commission, for example, now places the quarterly reports it receives from candidates for federal office, in addition to its summaries of overall campaign contributions and expenditures, on its website; thus, these are available to journalists, academics, and even to opposition candidates. Census material is available from the Census Bureau, located in the Commerce Department; immigration data can be obtained from the Immigration and Naturalization Service in the Department of Homeland Security; treaties and alliances viewed at the State Department website—the list is almost endless.

The George W. Bush administration has initiated an Internet initiative to encourage electronic communications within government and to those the government serves.[37] And Americans have done so in large numbers. The Pew Internet project reports that 97 million people have accessed government websites, 38 million have corresponded with government officials in an effort to influence their policy decisions, and 29 million have done research or applied for government benefits using the Web.[38]

Although the judicial branch has lagged behind the other two branches, the Administrative Office of U.S. Courts has developed a website (http://www.uscourts.gov/) and the Federal Judicial Center has established a website (http://www.fjc.gov/).

As the information explosion changes the ways in which people obtain political and other information, the types and amount of information they receive, the ways in which they contact their government, and the time frame in which public officials respond, politics and government are bound to be affected. Each of the major news organizations and many Internet companies have established news websites. Table 9.3 lists the number of users who regularly access these sites; Table 9.4 presents a profile of Internet users.

New political issues have also been created (see Box 9.2). The next two sections examine some of that effect by describing contemporary news media coverage of elections and government and exploring how that coverage affects the events reported. In the final case study, the news media's increasing emphasis on character issues is discussed.

Table 9.3 News Sites and Audiences on the Internet

Company	Audience (in hundreds)
Yahoo News	24,917
MSNBC	23,760
CNN	21,353
AOL News	17,393
Gannett	11,351
New York Times	11,157
Internet Broadcasting	10,836
Knight Ridder Digital	9,878
Tribune Newspapers	9,047
USA Today	8,611
Washington Post	8,475
ABCNews	7,687
Google News	7,177
Hearst Newspapers	6,938
World Now	6,236
Fox News	6,013
CBS News	5,863

Source: Nielsen/NetRatings.

Table 9.4 Who Uses the Internet?

Gender	
Men	61%
Women	66%

Age	
18–29	78%
30–49	74%
50–64	60%
65+	25%

Race/Ethnicity	
White, nonHispanic	67%
Black, nonHispanic	43%
Hispanic	59%

continued

Table 9.4 *continued*

Community Type	
Urban	62%
Suburban	68%
Rural	56%
Household Income	
Less than $30,000/yr.	44%
$30,000–$50,000	69%
$50,000–$75,000	81%
More than $75,000	89%
Educational Attainment	
Less than High School	32%
High School	52%
Some College	75%
College+	88%

Source: Pew Internet and American Life Project, May-June 2004 Tracking Survey, "Trends 2005," Pew Research Center for the People and the Press, p. 63.

9.2 Politics in the 21st Century

The Internet

The Internet is rapidly becoming a channel for campaign communications because so many people go online to follow elections and communicate with their friends and fellow partisans. In its study of Internet usage, the Pew Research Center found that more than half the adult population uses the Internet on a regular basis compared to about 80 percent for teenagers. The Pew study estimates that 84 million American used the Internet in 2004 to obtain political news and get information about the campaign. With so many people going online, candidates and parties cannot afford to ignore an increasingly large group of voters.[39]

The communications revolution has been rapidly expanding. During the 1990s, having an Internet site was newsworthy. Politicians and public officials who had a web address were deemed to be on the cutting edge of the communications revolution. Today, not having a site is almost as newsworthy. Candidates for federal office and public officials in office now regularly use their campaign website to provide information, solicit input, raise money, and build an organization of supporters.

Much was made of John McCain's success in the 2000 Republican nomination in raising more than $7 million from his website, much of it after his surprising victory in the New Hampshire primary against George W. Bush.

continued

9.2 **Politics in the 21st Century** *continued*

McCain's efforts, however, paled by comparison to those of Howard Dean. Launching his site in March 2003, Dean obtained most of his money and gained most of his supporters through an interactive Internet campaign. Dean's site featured a Blog, short for web log, in which people were encouraged to chat with campaign staff, express their concerns, make suggestions, and even vote whether Dean should or should not accept federal matching grants. By the beginning of 2004, more than 500,000 people had signed up on the Dean site as volunteers, contributors, or simply activists in their own communities, a figure that Dean pointed to as evidence of his large and growing base of support. General Wesley Clark also used his website as a principal vehicle for establishing a financial and volunteer foundation upon which to build his campaign for the Democratic nomination.

George W. Bush had a website as well, but one that did not emphasize the interactive component. Bush's site did, however, provided supporters with information and alerted them to other resources that they could use in advancing the president's candidacy.

Interactive websites are not limited to the candidates. Both major political parties created sites for their political conventions and for links to their national committees' official sites. Activist groups such as Moveon.org, Rock the Vote, Leadership in Action, and others too numerous to name also operate inactive sites to energize and mobilize their sympathizers.

Politics and the News Media

Objectivity in reporting the news is a goal but one that is difficult to achieve. Most news media coverage of politics and government is not neutral. It is colored by the vantage point, information, and journalistic priorities of the person reporting the story. What do the news media choose to emphasize, and toward whom are their stories directed? How do candidates for political office react, and how do they try to shape the news to their advantage? Finally, what effect does all this have on voters?

The News Slant

The key to news media coverage of political events (as well as other kinds of events) is their newsworthiness. This complex concept includes timeliness, importance, conflict, drama, and surprise. To be considered **newsworthy,** an event must have the potential to capture the attention of the public: readers, listeners, and viewers. From the news media's perspective, their job is to emphasize events with this potential.

newsworthy
Items that are most likely to capture and hold public attention; items that are new, unexpected, surprising, or conflict oriented or that generate human interest.

What is reported as news is also influenced by factors such as access and convenience. With limited resources, the news media have to decide what to cover and how much time to devote to it. Along with newsworthiness, the cost of coverage and the amount of time and effort it will take figure in that decision.

How does the slant of the news color the coverage of an event? Consider an electoral campaign. Above all else, in the view of the media, election news must be exciting. Thus, campaigns are reported as if they were sporting contests, with correspondents stressing the competitive aspect: which of the candidates is winning and losing, who is doing better than expected, and who is doing worse. The game of politics is not only emphasized but usually is stressed at the expense of substantive policy issues—particularly at the beginning of the electoral process, when "horse race" stories tend to dominate the coverage. Once a front-runner emerges, builds a lead, and thus makes the race less interesting, the focus shifts to questions about the candidates' character and to conflicts among candidates, their advisers and staff, and even the news media covering the campaign.

In close presidential contests, such as those of 1992 and 2000, horse race stories dominate campaign coverage; in elections in which one candidate has a large lead, they do not. Coverage in 2004 was more balanced, with horse race and policy issues receiving about the same amount of attention (see Table 9.5). The likely victory of the leading candidate, often an incumbent, makes the race less newsworthy than the candidates' campaign strategies and their personal characteristics and behavior. Issue positions are covered in both types of elections, but they are not usually examined in great depth. Newspapers, particularly large national and regional ones such as the *New York Times,* the *Washington Post,* the *Los Angeles Times,* and the *Wall Street Journal,* provide more extensive policy analysis.

The focus on the private lives and personalities of the candidates and their staffs has become a fixture of news media coverage of politics and government. This focus began during the 1980 presidential primaries, when the news media turned their attention to Senator Edward Kennedy's troubled marriage and his 1969 car accident in Chappaquiddick, Massachusetts, in which a young woman drowned. Similarly, in 1988 news reports about Senator Gary Hart's female guest at his townhouse in Washington raised questions about his marital fidelity, his credibility, and his judgment. In the 1992 Democratic primaries, Bill Clinton also faced a barrage of questions about his personal life, questions that continued throughout his presidency.

Unlike Kennedy and Hart, however, Clinton survived the ordeal to become president, and despite the persistence of such allegations throughout his presidency, particularly in the period during and after his reelection, he maintained high performance ratings even though the public's evaluation of his personal character became more negative. Similarly, George W. Bush's high school and college records, his alcoholic escapades (one of which included an arrest for drunk driving), and rumors of his drug use were reported during his 2000 presidential campaign but did not seem to be a major factor in the election. Senator John Kerry's record as a Vietnam veteran, and after leaving active duty service as a war protester, received considerable coverage during the 2004 election. This coverage, reinforced by ads sponsored by his opponent's supporters, however, seemed to have only a minor effect on the outcome of the election.

One reason that personality issues have received considerable media attention is public interest. Allegations of scandalous behavior command attention because people find such information interesting, even entertaining. How relevant such information is to performance in office is another question, one that we explore in the case study at the end of the chapter.

Another explanation for the focus on the personal dimension has to do with the medium of television. News stories tend to be short; they provide sufficient time to present a titillating item for public consumption but not enough for an in-depth policy analysis.

In addition to the requirement that an item must be newsworthy, it is usually fit into the framework of a larger story. According to political scientist Thomas E. Patterson, a dominant **story line** emerges and much of the campaign is explained in terms of it. In 1992, it was George H. W. Bush's weakness as a president running for reelection. Patterson writes:

story line
The framework within which the news is fit to help explain it within a larger context.

> Bush's bad press was mainly a function of journalistic values. The news form itself affected both the content and the slant of most of his coverage. Bush's story was that of a reelection campaign in deep trouble—much like the story of a baseball team that was favored to win the pennant but stumbled early and never regained its stride.[40]

Patterson's point is that the press fits the news of the campaign into the accepted story line rather than creating a new story line from the changing events of the campaign. It is the mindset in which reporters and correspondents view the campaign. That mindset affects the electorate's perception of what is happening.

news spin
The value judgment and meaning that people in the news, including reporters and commentators, give to a speech, decision, action, or event.

Not only is the news fit into a story line, but increasingly the news presented is bad. In an analysis of the evening news on the three major television networks during recent presidential campaigns, S. Robert Lichter and his associates found that the **news spin** has been negative for Republican candidates and mixed for Democrats (see Table 9.5).

Table 9.5 General Election News: 1988–2004*

	2004	2000	1996	1992	1988
AMOUNT OF COVERAGE					
Number of Minutes	1,007	805	788	1,400	1,116
Number of Stories	504	462	483	728	589
Average Number of Stories per Day	9	7.3	7.7	11.5	10.5
Average Sound Bite (seconds)	7.8	7.8	8.2	8.4	9.8
FOCUS (PERCENTAGE)					
Horse Race	48	71	48	58	58
Policy Issues	49	40	37	32	39
TONE OF COVERAGE (SPIN) (PERCENTAGE OF GOOD PRESS)					
Democratic Nominee	59	40	50	52	31
Republican Nominee	37	37	33	29	38

*Based on an evaluation by nonpartisan sources of election stories on the ABC, CBS, and NBC evening newscasts.
Source: "Campaign 2004 Final," Media Monitor (November/December 2004): 5.

Does the negativism represent an ideological or political bias? Most people think that it does. They believe that the presentation of news is often inaccurate, and many perceive a partisan bias. Conservative Republicans, in particular, believe that the press has a liberal Democratic bias, but liberal Democrats see it the other way around. A study of people in the news media found that journalists' political views tend to be more liberal than those of the average population.[41] However, most media owners and editors are conservative and Republican.

Partisan perceptions of media bias have decreased confidence people have in the accuracy and objectivity of news reporting. Today one in three people question the credibility of the media compared to one in seven in 1985.[42] Accordingly, trust and confidence in the press has declined more than it has in most other American institutions.

Content analyses of the news, however, do not reveal a consistent ideological bias. But they do suggest a journalistic bias. That bias is evident in the definition of what is news. A new face winning or an old face losing is news; an old face winning or a new one losing is not. Similarly, the first time a politician states a position, it may be newsworthy; the second time, it is not. Because candidates or

© AP/Wide World Photos

Democratic presidential hopeful, former Vermont Gov. Howard Dean's famous "I have a scream speech." Here Dean attempts to cheer up his supporters after a disappointing third place finish in Iowa.

public officials cannot provide positions or new ideas every time they address a group—in fact, candidates normally give the same speech many times—the correspondents who cover these events look for other things to report. Verbal slips, inconsistent statements, and other mistakes receive more attention than a speech that was well delivered or warmly received but which had been given previously by the candidate. Similarly, how the public reacts to what candidates say and do has become almost as newsworthy as the statement, event, or action itself.

Another aspect of contemporary news coverage that adversely affects a candidate's ability to appeal to voters is the mediating role that correspondents play. News programs devote less time to the candidate's own words and more to the interpretations of correspondents and the reaction of others. In 1968, the average length of a quotation from a candidate on the evening television news was 42.3 seconds. In 2000 and 2004, the average length of a **sound bite** was less than 8 seconds (see Table 9.5).

sound bite
A small part of a speech, interview, or conversation used to highlight an aspect of the communication.

The candidates today account for only a small percentage of the airtime devoted to campaign stories; the reporters and others they interviewed account for most of the airtime. Media spokespeople defend this allocation of time by citing the watchdog role they are expected to play. But another reason is that television professionals are more interested in holding their audience (and giving themselves visibility) than in allowing the candidates to present their case in their own words. Under the circumstances, it is not surprising that politicians attempt to manipulate the coverage of their campaigns.

Manipulation of the News

Staging   People in the news, especially politicians, try to affect the coverage they receive. They do so by scheduling and staging events, releasing information and granting access to reporters, preparing speeches and responses, or being unavailable to reporters if the news is potentially embarrassing or damaging politically.

Some politicians behave as if they were celebrities. They regularly appear on popular entertainment and talk shows such as *Oprah, Saturday Night Live,* and even MTV, shows on which their hosts tend to be more cordial and less adversarial than news commentators and reporters. Moreover, the audience is different; many of the people who watch these programs are less oriented toward partisan politics, have less information about the candidates, and thus may be more amenable to influence.

When to release information and how to do so are also critical components of a successful public relations strategy. It should come as no surprise that politicians and elected officials want to maximize their good news and minimize their bad news. One device often used to prolong a favorable story is the "artful leak." Giving a story to a single reporter first can extend its coverage for two days as other news outlets are forced to report the story after it initially "broke." With bad news, however, the tendency is to suppress or down play it entirely.

To accommodate television's need for good visual images, newsmakers often pose in dramatic settings to create the image they wish to convey. Reagan's appearance on the shores of Normandy on the fortieth anniversary of the Allied invasion of Europe during World War II, George H. W. Bush's Thanksgiving dinner with the troops on the Arabian desert during the 1990 buildup of U.S. forces for the Persian Gulf War, and his son's Thanksgiving dinner with U.S. armed forces in Iraq in 2003 are illustrations of how contemporary presidents have used their position to their own advantage. George W. Bush's announcement of the end of the military phase of the Iraq War on the deck of the *USS Abraham Lincoln* is another, but one that he may have come to regret as resistance to the occupation mounted.

Political Advertising Paid advertising is also used to convey political messages. Associated primarily with election campaigns, it has been increasingly used to generate public support on a range of political issues. The banking, pharmaceutical, telecommunications, and health industries among others have launched "PR" campaigns to promote or prevent legislative action. One of the most effective advertising campaigns in recent years was launched in 1994 by the Health Insurance Industry of America. The ads featured an average American couple, Harry and Louise, who voiced their fears that the Clinton health plan would not allow them to choose their own doctors, would cost them more money, and would involve them in more government paperwork and red tape. The ads contributed to growing public mistrust of the Clinton proposal and to its demise in Congress.

The objectives of advertising are to gain recognition, create images, and most importantly, evoke a favorable response from those who read, watched, or listened to it. Advertising can have either a positive or a negative spin. With the increasing emphasis placed on personal factors in elections, political ads have become more negative. Researchers have estimated that at least half the advertising in the last four presidential campaigns fall into this negative category, and most people expect it to continue largely because media consultants are convinced that such advertising works.[43] It informs the electorate and energizes a candidate's base.[44]

Some ads, particularly during elections, have evoked strong emotions. "The Daisy Girl," aired during Lyndon Johnson's 1964 presidential campaign, featured a young girl plucking the petals of a daisy as a stern-sounding voice counted down from ten. When the announcer reached zero a nuclear explosion appeared on the screen while President Johnson's voice was then heard saying, "These are the stakes—to make a world in which all of God's children can live, or go into the dark. We must either love each other, or we must die."

The implication of the Daisy girl ad was clear: Republican Barry Goldwater was more likely to start a nuclear war than was Democrat Lyndon Johnson. Naturally, Goldwater and his supporters were furious and protested vigorously, so much so that the ad became a news item. Even though it was aired only once, parts of it were played repeatedly as news from the campaign. The Democrats had made their point, and the media had reinforced it.

Another highly controversial commercial was aired in 1988, this time by a group that supported George H. W. Bush. It featured a mug shot of Willie Horton, an African American prisoner who had raped a white woman while on a weekend furlough from a Massachusetts jail. Aimed at those who were fearful of crime, of African Americans, and of liberals and their "do-good" social policies, the ad placed Bush's opponent, Michael Dukakis, who had supported the furlough plan when he was Massachusetts' governor, squarely in the liberal, do-gooder camp. The Bush campaign also produced ads of its own to reinforce the crime issue to its advantage. Cumulatively, the advertising left the impression that Dukakis released hardened criminals, who then committed additional heinous crimes against other innocent victims. Dukakis's failure to respond quickly and forcefully to the inference that he was soft on crime allowed that impression to stick.[45]

During the 2004 presidential campaign, a Republican-oriented group, Swift Boat Veterans for Peace, designed a series of commercials that questioned Democratic candidate John Kerry's record as a Vietnam War hero. These ads effectively neutralized the leadership image Kerry was attempting to project from his active service duty in Vietnam.

The Effect of the Media on Electoral Politics

With all of the effort and energy put into news coverage, public relations, and political advertising, one would expect that the news media to have a significant effect on the outcome of elections. Yet that effect is difficult to measure.

The media's coverage tends to affect voters' awareness and impressions of candidates more than it influences their political attitudes or cause them to change their opinions. The media do, however, elevate the importance of certain issues by calling attention to them. In this way, they shape criteria that people use to evaluate candidates, their positions, and their parties and by that process decide for whom to vote.

Moreover, news coverage and political advertising are important sources of information, particularly for those who are less attentive, informed, and partisan. The press's influence tends to be greater at the beginning of a campaign, when people have less knowledge about the candidates and their stands, than at the end when they have more. The disproportionate coverage given to certain candidates in the early caucuses and primaries can be crucial. Howard Dean's early rise in the polls during the 2004 Democratic nomination process was boosted partly by the attention he received from reporters for his successful fundraising activities on the Internet and for the endorsements of his candidacy by prominent party leaders. Similarly, favorable or unfavorable coverage at the nominating conventions can solidify partisan support or weaken it.

By emphasizing certain issues and personal characteristics, the press sets the campaign agenda and helps shape public debate. By evaluating the candidates and their campaigns, reporting public sentiment, and forecasting the likely outcome, the news media became participant observers in the campaign.

The news media also affect political parties by becoming the principal vehicle through which campaigns are communicated to the electorate. Voters no longer need to turn to the parties for information about candidates. Conversely, candidates gain independence from party organizations by mounting direct media-based appeals.

President Bush gestures toward his Democratic challenger, John Kerry, during their first debate. The bulge in the back of Bush's suit jacket suggested to some that the president was being fed answers through what appeared to be a receiver in the form of a small box. The White House denied the charges and made sure that the President's suit fit better during their second debate.

Finally, the news media shape the environment for governing. Candidates who emphasize their leadership capabilities, and media that focus on these qualities, create expectations that may be difficult to achieve or ignore. "Telegenic" candidates (those who look good on television) are expected to be telegenic leaders, to use the style of campaigning that got them into office to stay in office. Moreover, they are expected to fulfill the promises they make during the campaign. Those promises become a scorecard by which their early efforts are judged.

Review Questions

1. The predominant bias of the news media is

    A. Its pro-business orientation
    B. Its political partisanship
    C. Its ideological perspective
    D. Its journalistic orientation

continued

2. Contemporary election coverage in the United States has increasingly emphasized which of the following:

   A. Policy
   B. Public Relations
   C. Personality
   D. Party

3. The primary analogy that the press uses for its coverage of elections is

   A. Sex
   B. Scandal
   C. Sports
   D. Statistics

4. People obtain most of their news about elections from which of the following sources?

   A. Television
   B. Radio
   C. Newspapers
   D. The Internet

Answers:

   1. D
   2. C
   3. C
   4. A

Conflict and Consensus in Review

The consensus is that campaign coverage is essential to an informed electorate. The conflict is over the substance and spin of that coverage. That conflict is increasingly affected by the partisan division within the electorate. Partisanship affects perceptions of objectivity; these perceptions have contributed to increasing criticism of news media bias, which in turn has led to a decrease in the confidence in which the public views the accuracy of the news that is reported. The news media, especially cable news networks, have responded to this crisis of confidence by catering more to their specialized audiences, shaping the news in a way that appeals to their audience and thereby becoming part of the politics they purport to describe.

Government and the News Media

Certain journalistic conventions condition the reporting and presentation of national news. The focus on government activities centers on people and politics rather than on institutions and policy, partly because most issues and operations of government are so complex that they are difficult to explain in a news story.

Little background or contextual information is provided, particularly by the electronic media. Instead, the human dimensions of the story tend to be emphasized. The media's preoccupation with the sensational is illustrated by the attention given government officials when they engage in activities that seem to violate public norms.[46]

News coverage often stresses the style and strategy employed by government officials to pass or defeat a particular piece of legislation, rather than the effect the policy might have on the country. This is a variation of the "horse race" journalism that commonly appears in election coverage. Policy issues are presented as two-sided arguments. Congressional votes are portrayed as either wins or losses for the president, the congressional leadership, or one of the political parties; conflicts within agencies or committees are seen as pluses or minuses for one individual or group against another. The news media regularly describe the debate and division over how to balance the budget as a tug of war between the administration and Congress, between a president of one party and a Congress in which one or both branches are controlled by the other, and among and between Democrats and Republicans, liberals and conservatives, budget doves and hawks.

In their coverage of government, the news media tend to emphasize failures rather than successes, what does not work rather than what does. Take President George W. Bush, for example. Not only did he receive more critical press than his opponent in the 2004 presidential election, but he also faced a barrage of negative commentary as he began his second term. During the so-called "honeymoon period," the first 100 days of his new term, two out of three stories on the major networks' evening news shows contained more negative than positive commentary, including 78 percent of the judgments made about the president's Social Security proposals and 71 percent of the comments about the war in Iraq.[47] Analyses of the coverage Bush's predecessors received suggest that they have been treated as harshly by the news media.

Why all the negative spin? Much of it has to do with the news media's perception of their role as watchdog of government. Presenting the other side helps the news media fulfill this role; it also contributes to political debate, a critical component of a democratic political system. A second reason for the negative tone has to do with the gap between promise and performance, between expectations that candidates create and the actual consequences of the decisions and actions of elected officials. Part of the problem may also have to do with White House attempts to shape the coverage it receives. By restricting the access of the media, controlling the information that is made available, and spinning the story to present the most favorable interpretation, the White House encourages reporters to be on their guard and to question the accuracy and adequacy of the news they receive. Bad news is almost always reported; good news may not be.

Coverage of the President

Of the three branches of government, the national news media focus the most on the presidency. When a White House scandal erupts, such as President

Clinton's sexual liaison with a White House intern, coverage can approach a **feeding frenzy.**

Even without a scandal, the president and the executive branch still receive much more coverage than any other branch of government. They do so because the president is seen as the principal initiator and the prime mover of the political system, the head of the government and the head of state, and a chieftain with multiple roles, all deserving public attention. Moreover, the presidency provides a "handle" for evaluating the many facets of government. The president personifies the government, at least in the eyes of the news media and often in the eyes of the American people.

The amount of coverage devoted to the rest of the executive branch varies. Certain departments (State, Defense, Justice, and Treasury) usually receive more attention than the others because of the critical issues with which they must deal regularly, the policies they implement, or the personalities and behaviors of those who run them. The bureaucracy that actually implements policies is given even less attention, except for instances of fraud, waste, and abuse or when government has to deal with such problems as a potential pandemic, such as the Avian flu, terrorist activities, or a natural disaster.

The White House is a prime information source. With limited time and resources to discover presidential news, reporters tend to depend on the White House for pictures and stories. The press is even more reliant on the information the White House makes available when the president is traveling. The White House also orchestrates interviews given by key administration officials. It has even gotten into the business of prepackaging news by designing a video that includes a news story presented by a person who resembles an on-the-scene reporter. These look-a-like news clips are distributed to local stations around the country to be included in their news reports.

Coverage of Congress

Congress is less newsworthy than the president most of the time. The twenty-four-hour news networks occasionally offer live coverage of events such as major speeches, committee hearings, and floor debates. In recent years, these have included Senate hearings on the confirmation of controversial executive and judicial nominees and congressional hearings on campaign finance, national intelligence, prisoner abuses, the federal response to Hurricane Katrina, and secret wiretaps order by the president. Other congressional events that have received live coverage include the Clinton impeachment proceedings, investigations of the Iran-contra affair during the Reagan administration, and hearings on Watergate and related scandals during the Nixon administration.[48]

With 535 members, most eager for public attention, Congress tends to be hospitable to media coverage. The focus of congressional coverage tends to be on the final stages of the lawmaking process and often on the final vote that will determine a bill's fate. The early steps in the process by which a bill becomes a law—the introduction of a bill, subcommittee and committee hearings—are largely ignored, except for controversies over presidential initiatives and investigations by key committees. Moreover, the major media give little emphasis to the substance of policy and its consequences for society. When substantive policy is discussed, it is often simplified and described as a divisive partisan struggle. Newspapers and news magazines provide more in-depth coverage of policy issues than do the electronic media, but the most in-depth coverage comes from the specialty press—journals that focus primarily on Congress, such as *Congressional Quarterly, Roll Call,* and *The Hill,* and the newsletters of interest groups.

Instead of policy, the news about Congress stresses the divisions within it, the difficulties members have in reaching agreement on salient issues, and the obstacles to the president's legislative success. Because the internal policymaking processes of Congress are complex, slow moving, undramatic, and often unpredictable, the news media describe Congress as struggling within and against itself, as well as with the president. Is it any wonder that the public continues to have such negative perceptions of Congress and the job it is doing?

In addition to being harsh on Congress as an institution, the national news networks are tough on individual members, when they receive any coverage at all. Their personal foibles and questionable behaviors, such as abuse of the perquisites of their office, periodic charges of sexual harassment, and investigations into relationships with special interest lobbyists, command the most attention.

How the news media report on Congress and what they report affects the behavior of representatives and senators in several ways. Members of Congress consciously position themselves to be newsmakers, granting interviews to reporters, attending committee hearings that the news media are likely to cover, using their staffs to issue press releases about their positions and policy initiatives, and keeping the press, particularly the local media, informed about their activities. Most of them take advantage of radio and television studios in Congress to record programs for the folks back home. In the words of one media-oriented student of Congress, "making news has become a crucial component of making laws."[49]

In contrast to the critical and largely negative coverage by the national media, the local news media present a different and more positive picture. They report less on the institution as a whole and more on their local representatives, especially when members of Congress return home to their districts. Local coverage tends to be of the "soft," human-interest variety—a speech to the chamber of commerce, a tour of the state fair, a ceremony at a high school graduation, a ribbon cutting at a senior center for which the member was instrumental in obtaining federal funds, or a protest over the closing of a federal facility in their districts, such as a veterans' hospital or military base, by an executive department.

Coverage of the Judiciary

The third branch of government, the judiciary, is often a stranger to the national media, except for major trials; controversies over presidential judicial nominations, such as the confirmations of John Roberts and Samuel Alito Jr. to the

Supreme Court; or when the Court issues a landmark decision.[50] The Supreme Court receives only a fraction of the attention received by the president and Congress, and only a few news organizations assign full-time reporters to it.

There are several reasons for this lack of coverage. The Supreme Court does not welcome attention: justices rarely give interviews or discuss their decisions. Besides, many judicial decisions are simply too complex for reporters who lack legal training to understand, much less evaluate. Only a few major newspapers, networks, and magazines can afford to hire journalists with such knowledge of the law. Therefore, the initial reports of Supreme Court decisions are often brief descriptions of the majority and minority opinions, the justices who voted on each side, and the implications of the decision for those directly affected it. Information is often presented in terms of whose interests were benefited or hurt.

Reporters who cover the lower courts tend not to be lawyers. Their focus is often on sensational cases rather than on far-reaching legal issues and trends. Trials for murder, rape, child molestation, and embezzlement make front-page news in Washington and other parts of the country, but speeches by Supreme Court justices on legal trends and constitutional interpretation do not.

At the state level, coverage of the judiciary is more common because many judges are elected rather than appointed. And some state courts now permit radio and television coverage of trials, some of which appear on the cable court channel. Moreover, highly publicized events involving alleged criminal activity, such as the O. J. Simpson and Scott Peterson murder trials, the beating of Rodney King by several Los Angeles policemen, and the child molestation charges against Michael Jackson. Recently, there has also been considerable attention devoted to people accused of white-collar crime and the trials that convicted or acquitted them.

The Effect of the News Media on People and Their Government

Some people believe the press is too powerful. They question the news media's motives, the fairness of news reporting, and especially, the assessments implicit in the stories. The public is concerned about the critical evaluation of government in time of crisis. The issue of the patriotism of the press or government critics is often raised as a response to bad news in period in which there are threats to the country's national security. In general, Republicans tend to be more critical than Democrats and much more critical than Independents.[51] Nevertheless, on balance, the public likes the mainstream news media, believe that most of their reports are accurate and true, and regularly turn to them for information about current events.

News coverage of government naturally affects the public's evaluation of government. According to S. Robert Lichter, the president's public opinion ratings follow news coverage. Lichter found that monthly variations in President Clinton's good press/bad press ratio were reflected in subsequent Gallup polls.[52] With respect to Congress, public approval follows media coverage.

In addition to affecting the public's assessment of how government is working, news coverage influences the content of policy and the behavior of public officials. It does so in three ways: it helps shape priorities by the attention it devotes to certain issues; it shortens time frames for government decisions and actions; and it limits options to those within the mainstream of public opinion.

The news media help set the agenda for government. For example, in 1979–1980, through their extensive daily coverage of the Iranian hostage crisis, when diplomats at the American embassy in Tehran were taken hostage by paramilitary guards loyal to the Iranian government, the news media kept the problem before the public and thereby heightened the demand for a satisfactory solution. Coverage of the hostage crisis also raised expectations for a quick solution, effectively shortening the response time available to the Carter administration. The daily television coverage began by noting the number of days the hostages had been in captivity and thus reminded the public not only of the problem but also of the administration's inability to deal with it.

Media hype can also force a government's hand. Pictures of burning oil wells in Kuwait, starving children in Somalia or a civil war in Sudan, ethnic Albanians fleeing their homes in Kosovo, and the twin towers collapsing, and armed resistance to the U.S. occupation in Iraq create pressures for the government to do something. Inaction, for the most part, is the only unacceptable

© EPA/Landov

An image of an Iraqi prisoner, in Abu Ghraib prison in Baghdad, allegedly standing on a box with his head covered by a hood and electrical wires attached to his hands. The photo was first seen on the CBS television program *Sixty Minutes II,* which aired April 28, 2004. Several U.S. soldiers have been reprimanded and President George W. Bush stated May 5 in an Arabic-language television interview, "that what took place in that prison does not represent the America that I know."

response. On the other hand, the absence of coverage, as in the cases of the civil war in Rwanda, the sweatshops of Asia, the failure for many years to report on the magnitude of the AIDS epidemic in Africa, and the child sex trade in Asia, makes it possible for the government to avoid issues.

Finally, and over the long haul, news media coverage of politics and government shape public perceptions and expectations. They condition beliefs about what government should do and how and when it should do it. In this way, the news media provide public officials with broad policy guidelines, a time frame in which to respond, and evaluative criteria by which their performance in office will be judged.

Review Questions

1. The principal focus of the news media's attention on television is on which institution?

   A. The presidency
   B. The executive bureaucracy
   C. Congress
   D. The Supreme Court

2. Which of the following is the main source of information about government today?

   A. The Freedom of Information Act
   B. Anonymous leaks
   C. Formal news conferences by public officials
   D. Sunday morning interview shows

3. The news media's ongoing ability to influence politics and government lies in its ability to

   A. Focus attention on salient issues
   B. Change public attitudes on salient issues
   C. Fool the American people on salient issues
   D. Point to the discrepancies between what public officials say and do on salient issues

4. Compared with the national news networks, local news coverage of national issues is

   A. More extensive
   B. More favorable
   C. More manipulable
   D. More dependent on investigative reporting

Answers:

   1. A
   2. B
   3. A
   4. B

continued

Conflict and Consensus in Review

The American people agree that the press should be a watchdog. In theory, they support the norm of objectivity in performing this critical democratic role; in practice, however, they perceive the news media as increasingly biased along partisan lines. Those who are most critical tend to be the partisans whose party controls the government or at least that part of it that the press is scrutinizing most closely.

In the past, the only option for those who perceived and objected to such a bias was to tune out or complain. Today with the proliferation of news networks on cable, there is a third option, change networks to the one that most closely coincides with one's own views. For those in government, the objects of critical media scrutiny, the task is different. The options are to exercise more control over information government reveals and place greater emphasis on public relations. The goal is to shape the news media's agenda before that agenda forces the government's hand. Such a media strategy by those in power can work in the short run but over the long haul it is usually overtaken by events and by revelations by those who do not like what is going on.

Politics in Action

Private Behavior and the Public Interest

A society that values individual liberty naturally values personal privacy. The Supreme Court has ruled that the right to privacy is protected by the Constitution even though it is not explicitly set forth in the First Amendment. On the other hand, openness is essential for a democracy. How can the public make informed judgments about voting without information about candidates running for office or public officials in office? But what type of information does the public need to make an informed judgment? Should individuals lose their right to privacy when they seek or occupy public office?

There is both a distinction and an overlap between private behavior and performance in office. Private behavior may reflect on public performance, especially when that behavior breaks a law or conflicts with community norms. If an official who has sworn to uphold the law violates that

law, then that official should be subject to the same penalty as others who violate it.

Another issue is relevance. There is some private behavior that may not be relevant to public performance. Is how an individual interacts with his or her family relevant? Is whether a person has been married before or has extramarital affairs relevant? Is whether a candidate tells the truth about such personal information, especially that which occurred a long time ago, relevant? When the news media report on behavior that occurred decades ago or even in more recent times, are they performing a public service or a diversion from issues that matter to society as a whole? Moreover, does the practice of publicizing private behavior discourage otherwise qualified people from seeking elective and even appointive office or making sure that scoundrels and other undesirables are not elected?

continued

Politics in Action *continued*

Take the case of former Senator Gary Hart. In the early summer of 1987, Hart seemed to be at the peak of his political career. The two-term senator from Colorado was ahead in the polls for the Democratic nomination for president. To many in the press, however, Hart was an enigma. Strange aspects of his life were beginning to surface, raising questions about his character: He had changed his last name from Hartpence without informing the public; he had misreported his age by one year on official documents; and he had changed the style of his signature several times during his career. Rumors of infidelity also plagued him in public office, but he refused to discuss these matters with the press.

On May 3, 1987, E. J. Dionne, then a political correspondent for the *New York Times,* wrote a long feature on Hart in the paper's Sunday magazine. Dionne recounted Hart's life from childhood. In his biographical presentation, the New York Times reporter also raised questions about Hart's fidelity to his wife. When asked about these questions later, Hart not only denied them but challenged the media to check the facts. "Follow me around. I don't care," Hart said. "I'm serious. If anybody wants to put a tail on me, go ahead. They'd be very bored."[53]

The press accepted his challenge. The same morning that the *New York Times* feature was published, the *Miami Herald* printed a front-page article that claimed Hart had spent the night with an unidentified woman from Miami in his Washington, D.C. townhouse. Acting on a tip that the senator had been romantically involved with Donna Rice, a model from Miami, the newspaper had arranged for several of its reporters to stake out Hart's house.[54] When the story was published, Hart denied any improprieties, although he did acknowledge that he knew Rice and had called her several times during his presidential campaign.

The battle lines were drawn. Campaign spokespeople for the senator blasted the *Miami Herald* for "character assassination" and for "hiding in bushes, peeking in windows and personal harassment." A *Herald* editor responded that the investigation was justified, that the fidelity issue raised legitimate questions concerning the

candidate's judgment and integrity, and that the public had a right to know. "That's why we reported on this story," he said.[55] Other newspapers agreed with the *Herald*. An editorial in the *Washington Post* stated that Hart himself made "his veracity on this question a kind of test of his general truthfulness [by] inviting reporters to examine the evidence."[56]

Hart, however, remained defiant. As his campaign tried to distract the public with questions about the *Herald's* tactics and the accuracy of its reporting, Hart and Rice denied any sexual liaison. Hart even involved his wife in his defense. In a news conference, Mrs. Hart stated, "When Gary says nothing happened, nothing happened. … In the 28 years we have lived together I have always trusted him."[57]

But the press refused to let up. The *Washington Post* published another story that rumored Hart had engaged in another extramarital affair, this one with the wife of an ex-senator. Hart's poll numbers began to tumble. His financial backers lost their enthusiasm for his candidacy. With his campaign in debt, his honesty questioned, and his support rapidly dwindling, Hart returned to Colorado and ended his presidential campaign.

In five days, Gary Hart went from being the leading contender for the Democratic presidential nomination to a politician with no political future. That whirlwind descent was brought about by an investigative media that focused on a controversial issue: character. Did the public have a right to know about the senator's personal relationships? Were they relevant?

The other candidates who were running at the time had mixed reactions. Of the group, only Pat Robertson said that the scandal was a relevant issue. It was later reveled by the press that Robertson's wife had been pregnant before they were married. Jesse Jackson said that the scandal was not relevant. Years later, he, too, admitted to having had an extramarital affair. Vice President George H. W. Bush, who was a candidate for the Republican nomination, said, "We move with great caution and respect for privacy before we enact a new, broader journalistic test of candidate fitness

continued

Politics in Action *continued*

based upon unseemly inquiries into private behavior."[58] Four years later, the Bush campaign targeted his two opponents in the general election, Democrat Bill Clinton and Independent H. Ross Perot, for their character failings.

The character issue has reappeared in every campaign since 1988. In 1992, it was Clinton's reputation for infidelity, draft dodging, and pot smoking that raised questions about his character; in the same election, Perot accused Republicans of trying to sabotage his daughter's wedding and of planting untrue stories about his professional ethics and personal relationships. Rumors of womanizing continued to plague Clinton in 1996 and burst into the open two years later, when his affair with a White House intern became known. His initial denial, "I did not have sex with that woman," added fuel to the public reaction and ultimately led to the impeachment proceedings against him.

In 2000, character issues were more pronounced than ever: George W. Bush's mediocre academic record in high school and college, his binge drinking and carousing as a young man, allegations that he had used drugs, and his verbal slips, which the press presented as a communications deficiency, and Al Gore's penchant for exaggerating his own importance (including the claim on a television show that he had invented the Internet) and embellishing

stories about his life and his difficulties in interacting with everyday people also became subjects of press scrutiny.

In 2004, it was more of the same. John Kerry's personal integrity was challenged in a series of hard-hitting ads. CBS News purported to have memoranda that indicated George W. Bush has shirked his duties as a member of the Alabama National Guard; these turned out to be fraudulent.

Character issues may or may not be relevant. Take the case of John F. Kennedy. In a 1975 Senate inquiry into the CIA, it was discovered that Kennedy had had a long-running affair with Judith Campbell, who had been introduced to Kennedy by Frank Sinatra in 1960. Sinatra had also introduced Campbell to Mafia boss Sam Giancana. It appears that Campbell had affairs with both Kennedy and Giancana during the same period, and apparently both men knew it. In fact, there were allegations that Campbell served as a go-between who obtained political donations for Kennedy from Mafia bosses—as well as their help in mobilizing "grassroots" support in Chicago, just enough to give him a close win in Illinois. Campbell may also have coordinated a CIA plot to engage the Mafia to assassinate Cuban dictator Fidel Castro.[59]

The Campbell connection was known but not reported at the time. In those days, the private affairs of politicians were off limits to reporters eager to ingratiate themselves with the Washington elites. Should they have been?

What Do You Think?

1. Did Kennedy's alleged affair with Campbell pose greater risks to the country and the presidency than Clinton's? Was Gary Hart's alleged affair a legitimate issue in the press, or was media coverage of the affair irresponsible?

2. In what areas of a politician's life does he or she have a right to privacy?

3. Does today's press scrutiny help the public by weeding out bad candidates, or does it hurt the public by deterring good candidates from running for office?

4. Should the government regulate what the press can publish, or should candidates be able to sue media for inaccurate and libelous reporting?

5. What publication guidelines would you propose for the press?

Summary

We began this chapter by noting the public's ambiguity about the news media. Americans believe in a free press and support the First Amendment's protection of that fundamental democratic principle. Yet in practice there is considerable disagreement on what constraints, if any, should be imposed on the media, when, and by whom. People also disagree over how the news media can and should perform its watchdog role. Similarly, they enjoy keeping up with the news but are doing so less than in the past. They value objectivity in reporting the news, but are increasingly prone to turn to those media outlets that are most sympathetic to their own political orientations.

The news media have responded to these audience perceptions and preferences by offering more choices, more critical commentary, more investigative journalism, and more of the type of news that their particular audience desires. Moreover, whatever that news, it is presented in an entertaining format designed to hold the audience's attention. As a consequence of these developments, news coverage is perceived as more biased with the public evidencing less confidence in its truth and reliability.

Criticism of the press is not new. It has existed from the beginnings of the republic. A free press, by definition, is always controversial. Those who are subjects of unflattering stories and their supporters are naturally going to be upset with the message such stories convey and direct much of their anger to the messenger, particularly if that messenger is associated with a political party, interest group, or set of beliefs that differ from their own.

The history of the news media in the United States is also marked by professional change, economic competition, and technological advances. Newspapers were the principal source of news for most people until the 1940s, when they were replaced first by radio and then by television. Today, advances in communications technology have supplemented radio and television as satellites, fiber optics, and new online technologies have opened additional channels for communicating quickly. For television, the major change has been the growth of cable and satellite networks.

Twenty-four–hour news networks can report news as it happens almost anywhere in the world, and public-service cable channels provide in-depth coverage of some official proceedings of government and discussion of public issues. Moreover, the Internet is rapidly becoming a major vehicle through which information is conveyed and public opinion is expressed. Politicians and government officials are using it to reach out to younger Americans, those raised in the computer age.

The primary orientation of the news media is to report on newsworthy happenings and events. They do so by creating or employing a dominant story line that helps explain the "what" and "why" of the particular snapshot of reality they are reporting. During election campaigns or when there is disagreement among those inside and outside of government, they often use the game format as a framing and explanatory tool. Divisions over issues are portrayed as arguments among two or more sides and congressional votes as victories or defeats for the president, congressional leadership, or the Democratic or Republican parties. The news media also tend to be critical when evaluating the performance of candidates or government officials. They justify their hard-nosed outlook on the basis of their watchdog role in society.

The press affects politics and government in several ways: through the selection of the issues they choose to cover, the information they choose to present, the manner in which they present it, and the analyses they offer. Those decisions influence the agenda of electoral campaigns, perceptions of the candidates, and public evaluations of their suitability for office. They also affect the government's agenda, especially its priorities; they shorten time frames for policy decisions; and they help define the scope and parameters of policy options and political decisions. Finally, news media coverage shapes the public's evaluation of events and the performance of government. Some people believe that the news media's increasingly critical evaluations of politics and government have contributed to lower public esteem for the political system and how it works, but that view is not universally accepted.

Key Terms

whistleblower
yellow journalism
newsworthy

story line
news spin
sound bite

feeding frenzy

Discussion Questions

1. What do you think would happen if the First Amendment protection of freedom of the press were removed?
2. How does the private ownership of most of the news media in American affect the scope and content of the news reported to the American people?
3. What are the principal ways in which the news media coverage of elections and government contribute to or detract from the politics of American democracy?
4. Does the news media in the United States affect public opinion and political beliefs? If so, how? If not, why not?
5. What have been the principal changes in the way Americans acquire their news in the last several decades? Have these changes made Americans more informed? Have they made them more current?
6. Do the news media in the United States usually provide the public with sufficient information to make an informed judgment on elections and on government performance?

Topics for Debate

Debate each side of the following propositions:

1. A free press cannot be fair and balanced.
2. The news media should be required to provide its audience with in-depth coverage of the most salient issues so that people can make informed judgments and communicate those judgments to elected officials.
3. No information should be communicated by the news media until it is confirmed by at least two reliable sources.
4. Sources of information leaked to the media should be identified by name.
5. The press should never communicate information that is critical of the government in time of war.

Where on the Web?

Center for Media and Public Affairs
www.cmpa.com

Federal Communications Commission
www.fcc.gov

Freedom Forum **www.freedomforum.org**

Pew Research Center for the People and the Press
www.people-press.org

Reporters Committee for Freedom of the Press
www.rcfp.org

Go to **www.thomsonedu.com/thomsonnow** to learn about a powerful online study tool. You will get a personalized study plan based on your responses to a diagnostic Pre-Test. Once you have mastered the materials with the help of interactive learning tools, activities, timelines, video case studies, simulations, and an integrated E-Book, you can take a Post-Test to confirm you are ready to move to the next chapter.

Selected Readings

Ansolabehere, Stephen, and Shanto Iyengar. *Going Negative: How Political Advertisements Shrink and Polarize the Electorate.* New York: Free Press, 1995.

Baum, Matthew. *Soft News Goes to War* Princeton, NJ.: Princeton University Press, 2003.

Cook, Timothy. *Governing with the News: The News Media as a Political Institution.* Chicago: University of Chicago Press, 1997.

Davis, Richard, and Diana Owen. *New Media and American Politics.* New York: Oxford University Press, 1998.

Fallows, James M. *Breaking the News: How the Media Undermine American Democracy.* New York: Pantheon, 1996.

Farnsworth, Stephen J., and S. Robert Lichter. *The Nightly News Nightmare: Network Television's Coverage of U.S. Presidential Elections, 1988–2000.* Lanham, Md.: Rowman & Littlefield, 2003.

Hamilton, James. *All the News That's Fit to Sell.* Princeton, NJ.: Princeton University Press, 2004. Jamieson, Kathleen

Hall and Paul Waldman. *The Press Effect.* New York: Oxford University Press, 2002.

Kalb, Marvin. *One Scandalous Story: Clinton, Lewinsky and Thirteen Days that Tarnished American Journalism.* New York: Free Press, 2001.

Kurtz, Howard. *Spin Cycle.* New York: Free Press, 1998.

Leighley, Jan E. *Mass Media and Politics: A Social Science Perspective.* Boston: Houghton Mifflin, 2004.

Patterson, Thomas E. *Out of Order.* New York: Random House Publishers, 1994.

Sparrow, Bartholomew H. *Uncertain Guardians.* Baltimore: Johns Hopkins University Press, 1999.

West, Darrell M. *Air Wars: Television Advertising in Election Campaigns, 1952–2004,* 4th ed. Washington, D.C.: Congressional Quarterly, 2004.

Woodward, Bob, and Carl Bernstein. *All the President's Men.* New York: Simon and Schuster, 1987.

Notes

[1]"The Media Go to War: TV News Coverage of the War in Iraq," *Media Monitor* (July/August 2003): 1–3.

[2]Ibid, 2–3.

[3]"War Coverage Praised, but Public Hungry for Other News," Pew Research Center for the People and the Press, April 9, 2003, question 6.

[4]"Topics and Trends: Presidential Ratings: Job Approval," Gallup Poll, http://www.gallup.com; "Topics and Trends:

Iraq," Gallup Poll, http://www.gallup.com (accessed June 1, 2005).

[5]"TV News Turned Sour on Bush After Iraq War Ended," Center for Media and Public Affairs, press release, December 17, 2003, http://www.cmpa.com/pressReleases/TVNewsTurnedSour.htm (accessed June 1, 2004).

[6]"Support for U.S. Troops in Iraq Rebounds," Gallup Poll, December 12, 2003.

[7]George W. Bush, October 6, 2002, quoted in "Media Advisory: Is Media Bias Filtering Out Good News from Iraq?" Fairness and Accuracy in Reporting, press release, October 28, 2003, http://www.fair.org/index.php?page=1840 (accessed January 21, 2004).

[8]George W. Bush, "Interview with Sir David Frost," BBC-TV, November 12, 2003, http://www.whitehouse.gov/news/releases/2003/11/20031117-1.html (accessed January 21, 2004).

[9]"Public More Critical of Press, but Goodwill Persists," Pew Research Center for the People and the Press, June 26, 2005, http://people-press.org/reports/display.php3?ReportID=248 (accessed June 28, 2005).

[10]"State of the First Amendment 2005." Survey conducted May 13–25, 2005, for the First Amendment Center, http://www.firstamendmentcenter.org/sofa_reports/index.aspx (accessed August 11, 2005).

[11]If a valid request for information has been made but the government believes that release of this information would be improper or harmful to the security or operation of the government, it must provide reasons for denying the request. The denial can be appealed and ultimately taken to court. The appeals process can take time, however, and going to court can be expensive.

[12]*Cheney v. United States Dist. Court for D.C.,* 542 U.S. 367 (2004).

[13]Before the war in Iraq, Plame's husband, Joseph Wilson, a former foreign service officer, was sent to Africa by the State Department to investigate the allegation that Saddam Hussein was trying to purchase uranium for nuclear weapons. He found no support for these allegations and so advised the department. Nonetheless, the president in his 2003 State of the Union address repeated the accusation, although he claimed that it came from British intelligence sources. In an op-ed piece following the State of the Union Address, Ambasssador Wilson criticized the president's statement as untrue. The White House was not pleased with Wilson's criticism—hence the retribution in the form a leak that identified his wife, a CIA employee, as the person who initially recommended that he take the trip. Because Plame was a covert operative, the revelation of her name was a federal crime.

[14]Ironically, Miller did not even write a story about the matter, but she did learn about it from her source(s) at the White House.

[15]A recent poll conducted by the Pew Research Center for the People and the Press found that 44 percent of respondents thought that "it was OK for news organizations to use unnamed sources to find out important news they otherwise would not get" and 52 percent believed that dependence on unnamed sources was simply "too risky." "Public More Critical of Press," question 15.

[16]The Federal Communications Commission (FCC), the government body charged with overseeing and regulating public communications, has issued a series of rules designed to ensure fairness in the discussion of important issues, equal time for candidates to present their views to the electorate, and the right of rebuttal for candidates attacked on the air. These rules, however, have discouraged the major television broadcast networks from becoming a forum on which candidates could present their views. Free time costs money, which the predominantly private and profit-oriented American media are reluctant to provide.

[17]According to the 2005 edition of the annual *Editor & Publisher International Year Book,* which lists all publications in the United States, there were 1,457 daily newspapers as of September 30, 2004. Of these, thirty were published in cities with populations of more than 1 million. *Editor and Publisher International Yearbook 2005.* New York: Editor and Publisher Co., 1959-present.

[18]*Editor & Publisher International Year Book: 2005,* vol. 1, sec. 2, p. 5. Ibid.

[19]A concentration of news organizations is evident in the television industry as well, with the three major commercial networks (ABC, CBS, and NBC) and the twenty-four–hour cable news networks (CNN, Fox, and MSNBC) dominating national news. There are independent local stations and a few small independent networks, but the resources they have devoted to national news have been limited. With relatively few reporters, camera crews, and producers, these and other stations are forced to follow the lead of the major cable and broadcast networks for national news. Not surprisingly, there is a tendency toward "pack journalism" as reporters focus on the same events, often in the same way.

[20]They also contend that the news media give more favorable treatment to those sympathetic to their pro-business orientation, especially those who provide the advertising dollars. Special treatment, if given to advertisers, undercuts the equality principle because it is the news media's responsibility to be as objective and accurate as possible.

[21]Before to the development of the penny press, news was rarely "new" or exciting; many stories were weeks old before they appeared in newspapers and were simply rewritten or reprinted from other newspapers.

[22]"Trends 2005," Pew Research Center for the People and the Press, 2005, 47. http://people-press.org/reports/ReportID=6 (February 21, 2006).

[23]"Newspaper readership among young people continues to be relatively limited. Among those under age 30, just 23% report having read a newspaper yesterday. This . . . stands in marked contrast to the 60% of older Americans who say they read a newspaper yesterday. "Public More Critical of Press," Pew Research Center http://www.pewresearch.org.

[24]Ibid.

[25]*Statistical Abstract of the United States: 2004–2005,* United States Census Bureau, November 2004, 717, Table 1120.

[26]Ibid.

[27]"Trends 2005," 42.

[28]Woodward and Bernstein were helped by an anonymous source they referred to as "Deep Throat." In 2005, thirty-two years after the Watergate break-in, the identity of the source was revealed in an article in *Vanity Fair.* W. Mark Felt, the number two person in the Federal Bureau of Investigation (FBI), was the source. Felt, who was passed over by the administration to be its director after the death of J. Edgar Hoover, was alleged to be upset at the way the administration was using the FBI.

[29]*Statistical Abstract: 2004–2005,* 716.

[30]"Cable and Internet Loom Large in Fragmented Political News Universe," Pew Research Center for the People and the Press, January 11, 2004.

[31]Ibid.

[32]"Trends 2005," 48.

[33]Ibid, 58.

[34]Ibid, 68.

[35]Every major news organization has their own website and people use these sites to keep up with the latest news. A recent survey conducted by the Pew Research Center for the People and the Press found that 89 percent of those going online for news get it from the websites of one of the major news organizations. Ibid, 60.

[36]Ibid, 68.

[37]Not only does the government make information available on the Internet, but public officials increasingly are using it to communicate to and gain information from their constituents and the public. A survey based on interviews with Washington-based officials found that 42 percent of members of Congress, 68 percent of presidential appointees, and 74 percent of senior civil servants regularly or sometimes go online, compared with 28 percent of the general population. "Washington Leaders Wary of Public Opinion," Pew Research Center for the People and the Press, April 17, 1998, 9.

[38]"Trends 2005," 58 and 68.

[39]Ibid, 68.

[40]Thomas E. Patterson, *Out of Order* (New York: Alfred A. Knopf, 1993), 106.

[41]Robert Lichter, Stanley Rothman, and Linda S. Lichter, *The Media Elite* (Bethesda, Md.: Adler and Adler, 1986), 294.

[42]"Trends 2005," 49.

[43]L. Patrick Devlin, "Contrasts in Presidential Campaign Commercials of 1992," *American Behavioral Scientist* 37 (November 1993): 288; Lynda Lee Kaid and Anne Johnston, "Negative Versus Positive Television Advertising in U.S. Presidential Campaigns, 1960–1988," *Journal of Communications* 41 (Summer 1991): 54; L. Patrick Devlin, "Contrasts in Presidential Campaign Commercials of 2000," *American Behavioral Scientist* 44 (August 2001): 2,338, 2,367–2,368; L. Patrick Devlin, "Contrasts in Presidential Campaign Commercials of 2004," *American Behavioral Scientist,* 49 (October 2005): 279–313.

[44]Martin Wattenberg and Craig Brians, "Negative Campaign Advertising; Demobilizer or Mobilizer?" *American Political Science Review,* 93 (December 1999): 891–899.

[45]By the end of the campaign, 25 percent of the electorate knew who Willie Horton was, what he had done, and who had furloughed him; 49 percent thought Dukakis was soft on crime. Edwin Diamond and Adrain Marin, "Spots," *American Behavioral Scientist* 32 (March/April 1989): 386.

[46]One blatant example was the case of Representative Gary Condit of California and a missing intern from his office with whom he admitted having had an affair in the summer of 2001. In a period of only two months, the *Washington Post* carried 205 stories on the matter, the three broadcast networks in their morning and evening news had 382 stories, and CNN and Fox News had 216. "The Missing Intern Mystery," *Media Monitor* (July/August 2001): 2.

[47]"No Second Term Media Honeymoon for Bush," Center for Media and Public Affairs, News Release, July 11, 2005.

[48]Most coverage on the major broadcast networks is not live, however. Rather, the networks report snippets of what Congress does or does not do and how representatives and senators behave. The major live coverage is on the three C-SPAN channels, which record the official proceedings taking place on the House and Senate floors and, along with CNN, cover selected committee hearings.

[49]Timothy E. Cook, *Making News and Making Laws* (Washington, D.C.: Brookings Institution, 1989), 7.

[50]"Judging Judge Roberts—Part I" *Media Monitor* 19 (July/August 2005).

[51]"Public More Critical of Press," Pew Research Center, (accessed June 26, 2005)

[52]"The Invisible Man," *Media Monitor* (May/June 1995): 5.

[53]E. J. Dionne, "Gary Hart, the Elusive Front Runner," *New York Times Magazine,* May 3, 1987, 28ff.

[54]Tom Fiedler and Jim McGree, "Miami Woman Is Linked to Hart" *Miami Herald,* May 3, 1987, A1.

[55]James R. Dickenson and Paul Taylor, "Newspaper Stakeout Infuriates Hart; Report on Female House Guest Called 'Character Assassination.'" *Washington Post,* May 4, 1987, A1.

[56]Editorial, "The Gary Hart Dispute," *Washington Post,* May 5, 1987, A18.

[57]T. R. Reid, "Lee Hart Breaks Silence to Defend Her Husband," *Washington Post,* May 7, 1987, A23.

[58]George H. W. Bush as quoted in Phil Gailey, "Presidential Hopefuls Uneasy on Question of Adultery," *New York Times,* May 14, 1987, A1.

[59]Larry Sabato, *Feeding Frenzy* (New York: Lanahan Publishing, 2000): 23–25.

10

Congress

Introduction

He had talked of it often during the 2000 presidential campaign and, once in office President George W. Bush took little time in proposing what came to be known as his "faith-based initiative." The idea was simple enough: to provide federal funds to charitable organizations, many of them church related, that already had successful programs for helping poor families with child care, homelessness, food aid, and other basic social needs. Why create more government offices and bureaucracies, the president argued, when much of the infrastructure was already in place? Why not simply provide federal funds directly to those organizations that were already doing what the government wanted?

But no idea in politics is ever simple or uncomplicated, and this one was neither. The principal impediment was the First Amendment to the Constitution and its proscription that "Congress shall make no law respecting an establishment of religion." Would the provision of federal aid to faith-based groups be an "establishment of religion"? The president and his supporters argued that it was not, that his proposal would only support the social service activities of these groups, not their religious programs or beliefs. Any faith-based group, whatever its religious affiliation, could apply for federal funds as long as those funds would be used in its social service programs, not to support its religious activities.

When the president's proposal went to the House of Representatives, the Republican majority there embraced it and passed a bill in the summer of 2001 that contained most of the president's plan. But in the Senate, the plot thickened. A switch in party affiliation by Senator Jim Jeffords of Vermont in the spring of 2001 had shifted the delicate balance in the Senate from a Republican to a Democratic majority. The Democrats took control of all Senate committees, and among Democrats there was deep concern about President Bush's proposal. Many Democrats worried that federally funded programs that took place in a church, synagogue, or mosque would appear to be federal support for that religious organization or that religion.

So the Senate began to peck away at the president's proposal. A compromise bill was proposed by Senators Joseph Lieberman (D-Connecticut) and Rick Santorum (R-Pennsylvania) that would permit religious organizations to compete with other nonreligious organizations for federal funds, but it would require all groups that received federal funds to abide by federal nondiscrimination laws. If, for example, a church opposed equality among the sexes, it could not receive federal funds under the compromise proposal. The Senate Finance Committee approved a bill that shifted the focus to charitable donations instead of direct federal grants, allowing Americans who did not itemize their tax deductions to deduct their charitable contributions to those organizations.

But as the 107th Congress came to an end, the two houses—one controlled by Republicans, the other by Democrats—could not agree on a compromise. No bill passed. President Bush then used executive orders to implement some of the proposals in the failed legislation. In 2005, he called on Congress to codify those executive orders into law. But, even with Republicans firmly in charge, no legislation emerged. Congress had played a familiar role as a graveyard for presidential proposals.

Congress is the place where Americans agree to disagree.

They agree that a law making body representing the people is a vital cog in the U.S. constitutional system. They also agree with the principles upon which such a body is based: that it be representative of the country; that it resolve policy disputes through legislation; and that it prevent the other branches from exceeding their authority—the president's appointment and treaty-making powers, the executive branch's implementation of legislation, and the judiciary's capacity to reverse law through constitutional interpretation.

Americans disagree, however, over how representative Congress really is, how well it resolves policy differences, whether the nation's interest is served or special interests within that nation benefited by policy decisions, and whether Congress simply checks the executive and judicial branches or actually interferes with their exercise of prescribed constitutional powers. Moreover, Americans are impatient when Congress deliberates, resistant to the legislature's public educational efforts—be it in the form of hearings, reports, or speeches—and cynical about the motives of its members, the political contributions they seek, the access they provide, and the votes they take. The attention the press gives to the foibles, gaffes, and self-interested behavior of members adds to the public suspicion of an institution that people believe, at least in theory, is the heart and soul of democratic government.

Herein lies the dilemma of Congress as a democratic institution. More often than its designers hoped or history demonstrated, the modern Congress is paralyzed by conflict and unable to generate the consensus required for effective lawmaking.

This chapter examines the role of Congress in the politics of American democracy, the type of institution it is, and its players and their interaction within the current political environment. It describes the principal responsibilities of Congress—representation, legislative policymaking, and administrative oversight—and how it exercises those responsibilities today. The ways in which political parties and interest groups affect the legislative process are also explored. The chapter concludes with a discussion of congressional reform and its effect on how American democracy works today.

Questions to Ponder

- What do you believe is the most important role Congress performs today? How well does the legislature perform that role? What are the principal criteria by which we should evaluate Congress today?
- How do the roles of its individual members differ from the role of Congress as an institution? Why do Americans tend to like their representative and senators more than they like Congress as a whole?
- Should partisan politics exercise the greatest influence over legislative policy judgments?
- A long time ago a political scientist said, "Congress can represent public opinion or it can pass laws, it just can't do both at the same time." Do you agree with this statement? Do you think it is applicable today?
- One of the common ways in which presidential initiatives fail in Congress is that one or both of the houses simply do not vote on them. Should presidential proposals always be brought to a vote in Congress?
- Is it proper for Congress to defend the language of the Constitution from presidential proposals that challenge it, or should that be the responsibility of the Supreme Court?

The Institution of Congress

The U.S. Congress is a **bicameral legislature**—that is, it is composed of two legislative bodies. The larger is the House of Representatives, which has 435 voting members plus 5 other delegates who represent the District of Columbia and the U.S. territories and possessions; these delegates have a vote on committees and subcommittees but do not vote on the passage of bills in the full House. Each member of the House represents a congressional district with a population of about 690,000. The districts are distributed among the states according to population, with each state having at least one and California having the largest number (fifty-three). All House members serve terms of two years.

The smaller legislative chamber is the Senate. It has 100 members, two from each state. Senators serve six-year terms, but the terms are staggered so that every two years approximately one-third of the seats in the Senate are up for election.

Elections to Congress occur in November in even-numbered years. The new Congress convenes in the following January. Each Congress lasts two years and is numbered; thus the 1st Congress convened in 1789 and the 109th convened in 2005. The first year of a Congress is called the first session, and the second year is called the second session. The first session of the 109th Congress met in 2005, and the second session in 2006.

bicameral legislature
A legislature composed of two houses, such as the U.S. Congress.

Vice President Dick Cheney, left, and Speaker of the House Dennis Hastert, R-Ill., right, look on as President Bush delivers his State of the Union address before Congress in Washington, Jan. 31, 2006.

© Ap/World Wide Photos

The Members of Congress

The Constitution establishes minimum requirements for service in Congress. To serve in the House, representatives must have reached the age of twenty-five, have been a U.S. citizen for seven years, and be a resident of the state (but not necessarily the district) from which they are elected. Senators must also be residents of the state from which they are elected, and they must be at least thirty years old and have been a U.S. citizen for nine years at the time they begin their service.

Although all members of Congress have those simple qualifications in common, they differ widely in other ways. In their speech, ideas, and values they mirror the regional and religious diversity of the American people. Despite their varied backgrounds, members cannot be accurately described as a cross section of the American people. As a group they rank relatively high in socioeconomic status. Few blue-collar workers serve in Congress, and not one of its members is poor. The percentages of women and of members of ethnic minorities are also smaller than their percentages of the whole population.

In short, Congress provides representation for America but is not representative of America. Those at the lower end of the socioeconomic scale, which includes disproportionately more African Americans and Latinos, are underrepresented, and white, male, better educated, higher-income Americans are overrepresented. This skewed representation affects how Congress works and what it does; it detracts from its democratic character.

The Work Environment

In recent decades, service in Congress has become difficult and demanding. The demands on a member's time are enormous and constant. Hundreds of thousands of people view the member as their personal representative in the federal government. When they have problems such as a lost Social Security check or when they need help obtaining a small-business loan or a passport, they expect their representative to assist them. They also expect their representative to be a source of information about what is going on in Washington and around the world.

Members are also legislators. Each year they must vote on hundreds of issues, many of which are too complex to be grasped in the short time available before the vote. Each member also serves on several congressional committees and subcommittees, where members are expected to involve themselves deeply in the development of new legislation and in reviewing the implementation of legislation passed by previous Congresses. Furthermore, they must attend meetings of party caucuses and other specialized groups that members form to help advance their legislative priorities.

In addition, most members of Congress are candidates for reelection. The election campaign requires frequent meetings with the leaders of various interest groups in the home state or district, regular travel to meet with constituents, and contact with political action committees and other funding sources to ensure the availability of campaign funds.

As a consequence, members live frenetic and fragmented lives. Few have the time to develop real expertise on more than a handful of the issues that come

Above: Rep. Mark Foley (on left) listens to John Walsh (center) of *America's Most Wanted* talk about legislation on Capitol Hill on May 18, 2005. On right is Senator Orrin Hatch (R-UT).

Right: U.S. Speaker of the House J. Dennis Hastert (R-IL) speaks during a news conference outside his office in Batavia, Illinois, Thursday, October 5, 2006. Hastert accepted responsibility for the Mark Foley sex scandal while saying he won't resign.

before Congress. In casting the hundreds of votes they confront each year, members must rely for information and guidance on their party leaders, their colleagues, their constituents, and others.

To help them deal with their workloads, senators and representatives are surrounded by thousands of congressional employees whose principal responsibility is to provide various kinds of support. One form of support is provided by personal staff. Each member has the authority to hire staff employees to work for him or her alone. In recent years House members have typically had about twenty people on their personal staffs. Senators have larger staffs; those from the largest states employ as many as sixty people. The personal staff is divided between the member's Washington office and the offices that most members operate in their district.

Personal staff aides handle a range of chores: word processing, greeting visitors, writing speeches, answering the mail, photocopying. They handle **casework,** the individual problems that constituents bring to the member's attention for assistance or solution.[1] They work closely on issues that come up in the committees on which their employers serve, and they monitor issues as they develop in other committees, especially legislation that may be of concern to constituents.

casework
The individual problems that constituents bring to the attention of a member of Congress for assistance or solution.

Members also receive support from the staff members of each committee and subcommittee on which they serve and from the three specialized support agencies in the legislative branch: the Congressional Research Service of the Library of Congress, the Congressional Budget Office, and the Government Accountability Office.

The number of people employed in congressional staff support functions has risen sharply over the last few decades. This rapid expansion has several causes. The federal budget increased tenfold from the mid-1970s to the mid-1990s and hundreds of new government programs were initiated. Public dissatisfaction with the presidencies of Lyndon Johnson and Richard Nixon created a demand for greater congressional effectiveness and more vigilant oversight of executive actions.

There is a more political reason as well: the widespread perception that staff aides help members do things that contribute directly to reelection. The more legislation members can be involved in, the more publicity their offices can generate, and the more efficiently and successfully they can respond to constituents' requests for help, the more likely they are to succeed at election time. To the intensely political people who serve in Congress, the prospect of reelection has been a powerful motive for the steady enlargement of congressional staff and support agencies—yet another way in which politics helps determine the shape of American government.

10.1 In Theory . . .

Congress

The legislature is the keystone in any democracy, the place where disparate people and interests come together to make laws under which all will agree to live. Successful legislatures develop rules and procedures that permit the open expression of opinion, the building of consensus, and the brokering of compromise.

But democratic legislatures are always challenged by inherent conflicts. First among those is conflict among constituencies. Some regions of a country or some special interests will want things different from others.

States that produce natural gas will want policies that permit it to be sold at a free market price without regulation. States that rely on natural gas for home heating will want price and production regulations.

Competing constituency demands also come from the two levels of representation inherent in every legislature: the collective versus the individual and the local versus the national. What is good for an individual state or district may not be in the best interest of the country. Legislators must constantly restrike the balance between their

collective national constituency and the individual constituencies they are elected to represent.

Legislatures must also work with other governing institutions: executives, courts, and bureaucracies. Each will have its own culture, its own political and ideological priorities, and its own jurisdiction to advocate and defend. In democratic systems like the United States, where power is divided and shared among institutions, tensions along institutional boundary lines—and the need to resolve them—are constants of daily life.

Legislatures also face challenges in their internal operations. How do they maintain a balance between the right of every representative to be treated equally, which serves the goal of

continued

10.1 In Theory . . . *continued*

procedural democracy, and the need for leadership and necessary concentrations of authority, which serve the goal of efficiency? How powerful should leaders be, and how independent should individual members be?

These are questions with which legislatures wrestle constantly. The quality of democracy is deeply affected by the way they are resolved.

Review Questions

1. Which of the following best describes a typical congressional district?

 A. It has a surface area of 100 square miles.
 B. It has a population of about 690,000.
 C. It has one-tenth the population of the state in which it is located.
 D. It has about 150 Wal-Marts.

2. All members of the House of Representatives must possess all of the following qualifications:

 A. Must be at least fifty years old, with a Harvard Ph.D., an IQ of 150, fluency in three languages, and at least 2.4 children
 B. Must be at least twenty-five years old, a U.S. citizen for at least seven years, and a resident of the congressional district that they represent
 C. Must be at least thirty years old, a U.S. citizen for at least nine years, and a resident of the state that they represent
 D. Must be at least twenty-five years old, a U.S. citizen for at least seven years, and a resident of the state that they represent

3. Which of the following would *not* be a part of the job description of a congressional staff member?

 A. Write speeches for a member of Congress
 B. Research specific issues coming before congressional committees
 C. Organize activities for a Congress members' reelection campaign
 D. Handle casework involving the concerns of individual constituents

Answers:

 1. B
 2. D
 3. C

continued

Conflict and Consensus in Review

Americans agree that Congress should be a representative body, but disagree over how representative Congress actually is. Similarly, members of Congress agree on their basic roles but attach different priorities to them. They also agree on the need for expert staff but disagree over how much power to give to that staff, often referred to as unelected representatives, in a democratic government.

The Organization of Congress

The way Congress organizes itself reveals a great deal about the allocation of legislative power, and that allocation of power tells us much about the politics of public policymaking. Congressional organization is not just operational detail; it is about power.

The internal structure of Congress has changed and grown over time, as each generation of legislators has shaped Congress to fit its needs. Early in the nation's history, parties emerged to organize the business of the initial Congresses, and party caucuses hammered out important policy decisions. For a few decades after the Civil War, committees began to play a more dominant role in lawmaking. By the last decade of the nineteenth century, however, party leaders in Congress, particularly the Speaker of the House and the majority leader of the Senate, had become the principal powers.

But the party leaders of the time, notably Speaker Joseph G. Cannon (R-Illinois) and Speaker Thomas Brackett Reed (R-Maine), became so dominant that the rank-and-file members of Congress staged a revolt at the end of the first decade of the twentieth century. The authority of the party leaders was reduced, and for most of the next seventy years committees were again the power centers in Congress. A **seniority system** ensured that the member of the majority party with the longest consecutive service on each committee would automatically be named chairperson of the committee for as long as he or she remained in Congress. Seniority permitted the committee chairpeople, many of whom were elderly men, to assume powerful roles in the legislative process. But another revolt, this time against the dominance of the committee chairpeople, unfolded in the 1970s and produced another restructuring of congressional power.[2]

Throughout these decades of change, two principles have remained at the core of congressional organization: (1) control of the legislative agenda and the legislative machinery ought to be in the hands of the majority party; and (2) for purposes of efficiency and enhanced expertise, most day-to-day details of legislative work ought to be handled by small groups of legislators meeting as committees. Indeed, since the early decades of the nineteenth century the party system and the committee system have been the dominant elements in every congressional organization.

seniority system
The former system under which the member of the majority party with the longest consecutive service on each congressional committee was automatically its chairperson for as long as he or she remained in Congress.

Congressional Parties

The single most distinctive feature of political parties in Congress is their limited control over their own members, particularly over the way their members vote. In both the House and the Senate, leaders have little direct control over the members of their own party and therefore have few ways either to force them to vote for the party's position on a bill or to punish them if they do not. They cannot prevent party members from running for reelection; they have little influence on the outcome of elections; and, without the support of the majority of their party, they cannot even affect committee assignments. To better understand the relationship between party leaders and rank-and-file party members, it is useful to look separately at party organization in the House and the Senate.

Parties in the House Because the House is larger than the Senate, parties play a more important role there in organizing the legislative agenda and building legislative majorities. The majority party has the principal responsibility for both tasks. It controls the selection of the Speaker of the House, and its members compose a majority on nearly all committees and subcommittees.

The **Speaker of the House** is almost always the most important figure in the lower house of Congress. Technically, the Speaker is the presiding officer, but little of the Speaker's time is spent in the chair. Political leadership of the majority party is the Speaker's dominant concern. Working with other party leaders—especially those designated as **whips,** who work closely with rank-and-file members to determine party positions and form legislative coalitions—the Speaker helps determine the issues that will be given top priority in the House.[3]

Among the Speaker's other duties are participating in scheduling debates, mediating among members of the majority party who disagree on important legislation, working with the White House to coordinate measures important to the president, representing the majority party to the public, and assisting members of the majority party in such matters as receiving the committee assignments they want and retaining their seats at election time.[4]

Although the Speaker's leadership is based more on persuasion and political skill than on any real authority over individual House members, an astute Speaker can have a substantial effect on the kinds of policy issues that come before the House and the way they are decided. Strong Speakers make full use of the tools of authority available to them: parliamentary direction of floor debate and assignment of bills to committee, control over the flow of information within the House, scheduling of legislative action, power of appointment, and personal prestige and influence with other political actors in Washington. For example, a member who consistently supports the Speaker can expect assignment to preferred committees, assistance in securing campaign funds from political action committees, and help from the leadership in gaining passage of legislation introduced by that member.

Speaker of the House
The elected leader of the majority party in the House of Representatives, who serves as the presiding officer of the House.

whips
Members of each party's leadership structure in the House and the Senate who work closely with rank-and-file members to determine party positions and form legislative coalitions.

When Newt Gingrich was elected Speaker by the new House Republican majority in the 104th Congress, he quickly asserted himself as one of the most potent legislative leaders of his time. He dominated the House agenda, selected all committee and some subcommittee chairpeople, and became the leading public spokesman for Republican policies. But this was more power than many of his Republican colleagues wanted in a Speaker; Gingrich's influenced waned sharply after 1995, and the role of the Speaker reverted close to the late twentieth century norm.

The Speaker does not act alone in attempting to guide the operations of the House. The Speaker is supported by, and works through, a variety of committees and networks that enhance internal communication in the party, aid in the formation of party positions on policy issues, and help improve the chances of the party's candidates for seats in the House. In recent years, Republican Speakers were buttressed by the efforts of Texas Representative Tom DeLay. Occupying the positions of majority whip and then majority leader, he used a forceful personality and no-holds-barred legislative strategies to sustain the voting unity and ideological coherence of House Republicans and his skills as a fund-raiser to sustain the political support of GOP members of Congress.

The minority party in the House has its own elected leaders and a structure that mirrors, on a reduced scale, the organization of the majority party. There are, of course, fewer members to organize in the minority party, and the minority party has less responsibility for managing the House agenda. The leader of the minority party is the minority leader who is assisted by the minority whip. Both are elected by the minority party caucus, made up of all minority party members.

Parties in the Senate   Because the Senate is smaller and individual senators are able to deal with each other directly on most matters, parties play a less important role there than in the House. Most leadership functions in the Senate are concentrated in the hands of the elected party leaders. The majority party elects a majority leader and a majority whip; the minority party elects a minority leader and a minority whip. Each party also has a structure of leadership committees, but these committees have less influence on party operations than do their counterparts in the House.[5]

The primary job of the party leaders, especially the majority leader, is to organize the business of the Senate: to nudge legislation through the legislative process, to schedule debate, and to oversee most aspects of day-to-day administration. Party leaders also help the proponents of legislation round up the votes necessary for a majority, meet regularly with the president to discuss policy and legislative strategy, and serve as public spokespeople for their party on important policy matters.

Despite the extent of their duties and their public visibility, party leaders in the Senate are severely constrained in their ability to influence the outcome of policy debates. This constraint is a product of Senate rules and tradition that gives individual senators considerable independent authority. The party leadership is even weaker than that of their House counterparts. In the Senate, therefore, leadership is even more dependent on persuasion and political sensitivities than it is in the House. Senator Mike Mansfield (D-Montana), who served as majority leader in the Senate longer than anyone else in the twentieth century, once said:

> What power do the leaders have to force these committees, to twist their arms, to wheel and deal, and so forth and so on, to get them to rush things up or to speed their procedure? The leaders in the Senate, at least, have no power delegated to them except on the basis of courtesy, accommodation, and a sense of responsibility.[6]

Recent Senate majority leaders have defined their roles more in administrative than in policy terms. They have concentrated on organizing the business of the Senate to fit the needs of individual members and have spent less time trying to define positions on issues. Since 1961, when Lyndon Johnson left the Senate to become vice president, the formal party structure in the Senate has ceased to play a major role in the development of public policy.

Party Politics in Congress

The proponents of each bill introduced in Congress must form a coalition in support of that bill. These coalitions, which may include members of the opposition party, vanish as quickly as they appear; their composition changes from bill to bill and from day to day. Politics in Congress focuses on the task of building these shifting alliances. Bargaining and negotiation among individual members, rather than edicts from party leaders, are the principal techniques used in the formation of coalitions. Party leaders often play an important role, but the role is that of lead negotiator, not commanding officer.[7]

In recent years some individual legislators, often called **policy entrepreneurs,** have tended to specialize in particular substantive matters and to seek support among their colleagues for policies dealing with those matters. In the House, policy entrepreneurs are often subcommittee chairpeople; in the Senate, entrepreneurship is widely dispersed and bears little relation to formal institutional roles. Senator Kay Bailey Hutchison (R-Texas) was a leader in the battle to save the National Endowment for the Arts (NEA) in the late 1990s, usually in opposition to other conservatives. She often spoke of her personal belief that the NEA plays a valuable role in funding ballet, opera, and theater. In the intense debate on campaign finance reform in the 107th Congress, Senators John McCain (R-Arizona) and Russ Feingold (D-Wisconsin) and Representatives Christopher Shays (R-Connecticut) and Martin Meehan (D-Massachusetts) played critical roles in making the case for reform and building the legislative majorities necessary for passage. Senator Gordon Smith, a conservative Republican from Oregon, persuaded Senate colleagues of both parties to reject President George W. Bush's proposed cut of $9 million from the federal Medicaid payment. And Senator Smith's determination to help teenagers at risk stemmed from a tragedy in his own family.

policy entrepreneurs
Members of Congress who take a special interest in a substantive issue and seek to influence the shape of public policy on that issue.

Figure 10.1 Party Unity Voting in Congress, 1961–2004*

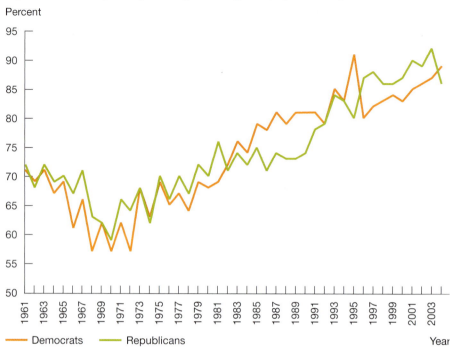

Percent

— Democrats   — Republicans   Year

*Party Unity scores are calculated each year by *Congressional Quarterly*. They are an average of all members' party unity scores. A party unity score is the percentage of the time that each member votes with a majority of his or her own party on those votes on which a majority of one party opposes a majority of the other party.
Source: Congressional Quarterly Almanacs and Weekly Reports.

A powerful tendency toward increased and often hostile partisanship has emerged in Congress in the past two decades. Party unity in voting is on the rise, as Figure 10.1 indicates. Republicans are more likely to vote with their party colleagues and Democrats with theirs when the two parties differ on legislation. Republicans have grown more consistently conservative, Democrats more consistently liberal. And as the parties have divided more sharply ideologically and in their legislative votes, personal animosities have followed and civility has suffered.

As a consequence, it is often difficult to build majority coalitions across party lines today. When controversial bills pass, it is often with the near unanimous support of the majority party and the near unanimous opposition of the minority. But a few defections from the majority party in closely divided Congresses may be enough to prevent important legislation from passing at all, as evidenced by the decreasing number of laws Congress has enacted in recent years (see Figure 10.2).

Figure 10.2 Average Number of Public Laws Enacted per Congress, by Decade, 1950–2004

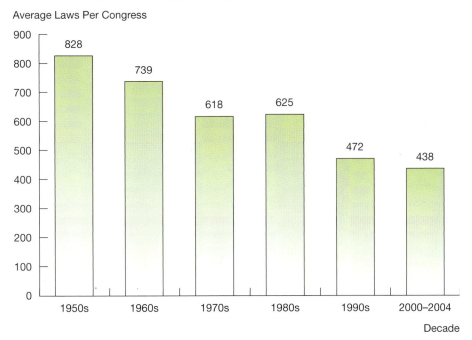

Average Laws Per Congress

Decade

Source: Data from Norman Ornstein et al., *Vital Statistics on Congress, 2001–2002* (Washington, D.C.: AEI Press, 2002), 146–149; http://thomas.loc.gov/bss/d109/d109laws.html.

The Committee System

Most of the work of Congress is done in committees, which serve several important functions. Committees prepare legislation for consideration on the floors of the House and Senate, but they also delete from the legislative agenda matters that are not important, urgent, or politically viable. Only a small percentage of the bills referred to a committee survive its scrutiny.

Committees also hold public hearings at which experts, leaders of interest groups, and other supporters and opponents of bills are permitted to express their views. In addition, they initiate studies, conduct investigations, and publish information. Each year, for example, the State Department is required by law to submit a report to Congress on the human rights policies of all the world's countries. The House International Relations Committee's Subcommittee on International Terrorism, Nonproliferation and Human Rights holds hearings at which it reviews that report and receives comments on it from government officials, interest groups, and private citizens. The subcommittee publishes those hearings, which are used by other committees in their annual decisions on American foreign aid.

Another important function of committees is **administrative oversight.** Committees monitor the work of the executive agencies in their areas of

administrative oversight
The review and control by congressional committees of the work conducted by the executive branch of the federal government.

jurisdiction, review budget requests, and pass judgment on the qualifications of presidential appointees. They are the principal contact points between the executive and the legislative branches.

Committees, however, are also the primary source of creativity and policy leadership in Congress. The most knowledgeable military specialists in Congress are members of the House and Senate Armed Services Committees. Those most familiar with farm issues are on the agriculture committees. Because the senior members of most congressional committees have been dealing for several decades with policy issues that fall within their committee's area of jurisdiction, they are usually well informed about those issues and have the support of specialists on the committee staffs. It is not surprising, therefore, that committees initiate much of the legislation that makes its way to the floors of the House and Senate.[8]

Most committees are divided into subcommittees, which hold most of the hearings and conduct the initial review of most legislation. Full committees rarely convene to consider a piece of legislation until after it has been carefully reviewed by the appropriate subcommittee. As the legislative workload has grown in size and complexity, experience and specialized knowledge have made the subcommittees increasingly important. The committees of the 109th Congress are listed in Table 10.1.

Table 10.1 Committees of the House and Senate, 109th Congress

House	Senate
Agriculture	Agriculture, Nutrition, & Forestry
Appropriations	Appropriations
Armed Services	Armed Services
Financial Services	Banking, Housing, & Urban Affairs
Budget	Budget
Energy & Commerce	Commerce, Science, & Transportation
Education & Workforce	Health, Education, Labor, & Pensions
Government Reform	Homeland Security & Governmental Affairs
House Administration	Rules & Administration
International Relations	Foreign Relations
Judiciary	Judiciary
Permanent Select Intelligence	Select, Intelligence
Resources	Energy & Natural Resources
Rules	Special, Aging
Science	Indian Affairs
Small Business	Small Business
Standards of Official Conduct	Select Ethics
Transportation & Infrastructure	Environment & Public Works
Veterans' Affairs	Veterans' Affairs
Ways & Means	Finance
Homeland Security	

A few committees, the **joint committees,** are composed of members of both houses of Congress. Some of them are permanent groups with no authority to initiate legislation; the most important of these is the Joint Economic Committee, which reviews the president's annual Economic Report and conducts studies of the national economy. In addition, scores of temporary joint committees known as **joint conference committees** are formed during each Congress. Their principal function is to resolve the differences that occur when the House and the Senate pass varying forms of the same bill. In the 105th Congress, for example, House and Senate conferences wrangled at length over different versions of the Balanced Budget Act of 1997. It was here that members finally worked out their disagreements over the proper mix of spending restraints and tax changes.

joint committees
Committees composed of members of both houses of Congress. They are permanent study committees with no authority to initiate legislation.

joint conference committees
Temporary joint committees whose principal function is to resolve the differences between forms of the same bill passed by the House and the Senate.

Review Questions

1. According to tradition, each committee chair is normally given to the committee member from the majority party who

   A. Has served for the longest consecutive amount of time on the committee
   B. Has served for the longest consecutive amount of time in Congress
   C. Is most knowledgeable about the committee's area of focus
   D. Is the most powerful party leader on the committee

2. The person mainly responsible for persuading majority party members of Congress to vote along party lines is called the

   A. Party boss
   B. Sergeant-at-arms
   C. Majority whip
   D. Majority organizing secretary

3. Which of the following statements is *true* about the role of political parties in Congress?

   A. With rising partisanship in Congress, the power of congressional party leaders is greater than it was fifty years ago
   B. The most effective tool available to congressional party leaders is persuasion, rather than coercion
   C. Many members of Congress are neither Republican nor Democrat
   D. In some instances, the chairperson of a congressional subcommittee may be a member of the minority party

Answers:

   1. A
   2. C
   3. B

continued

Conflict and Consensus in Review

The organization of Congress, especially the selection of committee chairpeople and party leaders, is a frequent source of conflict. Members of Congress, in theory, want the Congress to work smoothly. But they also want people who hold the positions of power to share their views on policy issues and they want opportunities to take their own places among the powerful. Consensus is often hard to achieve in Congress because the leaders who must forge it are often chosen in a process that is full of conflict.

The Functions of Congress

Because the framers of the Constitution viewed the legislative branch as the safest and most reliable arbiter of the disagreements likely to arise among a democratic people, they assigned several important functions to Congress. Those functions have expanded in number and complexity as the scope of the federal government's responsibilities has grown. Historically, the two most significant congressional responsibilities were legislation and representation. In this century, the expansion of presidential power and the growth of a large federal bureaucracy have added a third major function—administrative oversight—to the legislature's responsibilities.

Legislation

People who are not familiar with Congress tend to regard it as a kind of factory where laws are made. In reality, Congress makes few public laws, a couple of hundred at most, even in its most productive years. And many of those laws are of minor consequence—for example, the recent laws to proclaim October 16–24 as National Character Counts Week (PL 103–301) or to designate the facility of the United States Postal Service located at 3698 Inner Perimeter Road in Valdosta, Georgia, as the "Major Lyn McIntosh Post Office Building" (PL 107–160).

legislation
The making of laws, one of the major functions of Congress.

Legislation, or lawmaking, is accomplished through deliberation and partisan adjustment, a process that involves information gathering, prolonged discussion, complex and often tedious negotiation, bargaining, and compromise. Most of the time the result of this process is nothing. In fact, 90 percent of the bills introduced in a typical Congress never become law, and enactment of the few that survive may require years, even decades. A long gestation period is common for significant legislation. For example, Congress debated tax reform for more than five years before it passed the Tax Reform Act of 1986. Federally funded health care for the elderly, a proposal first introduced during the Truman administration, was not enacted (as Medicare) until 1965. The line-item veto bill passed by both houses of the 104th Congress (but later struck down by the Supreme Court) had been debated repeatedly over the entire history of the United States.

In recent decades the impediments to legislation have been greatly increased by the proliferation and growing sophistication of political interest groups, which affect lawmaking at every stage. Many members of Congress feel indebted to groups that support their campaigns, or at least feel obligated to listen when representatives of those groups present their positions on legislation.[9]

The pervasiveness of political maneuvering and bargaining among interest groups results in most legislative decisions being compromises, and compromise usually weakens the effect of legislation. Yet the openness of congressional lawmaking to politics can also be viewed as one of its strengths. Politics flourishes in Congress because the setting provides a forum for a broad spectrum of voices and opinions and because the legislative process provides many opportunities for individuals and groups to express the substance and the intensity of their concerns.

This feature of the lawmaking process also has the advantage of legitimating public policy decisions, or making them seem fair and acceptable even to those who disagree with them. Everyone has opportunities to speak out about legislation and to try to influence its ultimate shape. Few laws are abhorrent to any group because all groups are able to achieve at least some protection for the interests they value most. And groups can always try to enact new laws to undo the harm they perceive in existing ones.

The Lawmaking Process It is no simple matter to enact a law in the United States. A bill becomes a law only after it has successfully passed several hurdles, traps, and pitfalls. It can die in subcommittee, in full committee, on the floor of either house, in conference committee, or by presidential veto. It must pass all these obstacles to become law; defeat at any one of them will likely be a death knell. Figure 10.3 indicates the complexity of the congressional lawmaking process.

The process begins when an individual member of the House or Senate introduces a bill. A **bill** is a proposal, drafted in the form of a law, that a member would like his or her colleagues to consider. A bill may be introduced in either house of Congress by any member of that house. Often, to give the appearance of broad political support, members solicit their colleagues to cosponsor a bill. When a bill is introduced, it is assigned a number by the clerk and referred to a committee by the presiding officer. Many bills go no farther; they die because the committee lacks the time or interest to deal with them.

For bills that do not die, the next step is examination by the committee.[10] Subcommittees conduct the initial examination of most legislative proposals, holding hearings at which they gather written and oral testimony from witnesses who have knowledge of, or interest in, the bill. At hearings on the regulation of cable television, for example, members of Congress heard testimony from local cable company owners and from the National Cable Television Association in opposition to federal control. They also heard from local mayors, the National League of Cities, and the Consumer Federation of America about the need for more consistent and effective federal regulation.

At the conclusion of the hearings, the subcommittee votes on the bill. Usually the voting occurs after a **mark-up session** in which all members of the subcommittee participate in revising the bill to put it into a form acceptable to a

bill
A proposal, drafted in the form of a law, that a member of Congress would like the other members to consider. A bill may be introduced into either house of Congress by any member of that house.

mark-up session
A meeting at which all members of a congressional subcommittee or committee participate in revising a bill to put it into a form acceptable to a majority of them.

Figure 10.3 How a Bill Becomes a Law

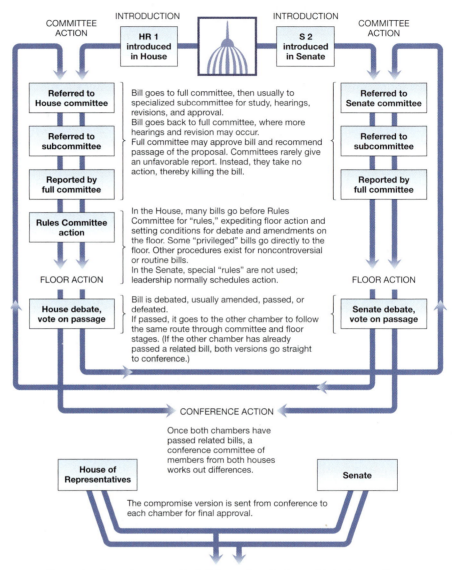

COMMITTEE ACTION | INTRODUCTION | INTRODUCTION | COMMITTEE ACTION

HR 1 introduced in House

S 2 introduced in Senate

Referred to House committee

Referred to Senate committee

Bill goes to full committee, then usually to specialized subcommittee for study, hearings, revisions, and approval.
Bill goes back to full committee, where more hearings and revision may occur.
Full committee may approve bill and recommend passage of the proposal. Committees rarely give an unfavorable report. Instead, they take no action, thereby killing the bill.

Referred to subcommittee

Referred to subcommittee

Reported by full committee

Reported by full committee

Rules Committee action

In the House, many bills go before Rules Committee for "rules," expediting floor action and setting conditions for debate and amendments on the floor. Some "privileged" bills go directly to the floor. Other procedures exist for noncontroversial or routine bills.
In the Senate, special "rules" are not used; leadership normally schedules action.

FLOOR ACTION

FLOOR ACTION

House debate, vote on passage

Bill is debated, usually amended, passed, or defeated.
If passed, it goes to the other chamber to follow the same route through committee and floor stages. (If the other chamber has already passed a related bill, both versions go straight to conference.)

Senate debate, vote on passage

CONFERENCE ACTION

Once both chambers have passed related bills, a conference committee of members from both houses works out differences.

House of Representatives

Senate

The compromise version is sent from conference to each chamber for final approval.

The compromise version approved by both houses is sent to the president, who can either sign it into law or veto it and return it to Congress.
Congress may override a regular veto by a two-thirds majority vote in both houses. When this happens, the bill then becomes law without the president's signature.

HR 1 *Veto*   S 2 Signed

Source: *Guide to Congress* (Washington, D.C.: Congressional Quarterly, 1976), 345, updated by the authors. Reprinted by permission.

majority of them. If the subcommittee supports the bill it is returned to the full committee, where another mark-up may take place, followed by a vote of the full committee. Mark-up sessions are a key battleground for all political forces that seek to shape the text—and thus the effect—of a bill. In 1997, for example, Congress worked on the most significant changes in federal tax law in a decade. The mark-up in the House Ways and Means Committee occurred in a room full of lobbyists who communicated with members and staff throughout the process, often haggling over the tiniest details. In a tax bill, of course, a tiny detail can be worth hundreds of thousands of dollars to individual taxpayers.

If a majority of the full committee supports the bill, it is reported to the full House or Senate. The committee normally issues a written report in which it explains the contents of the bill, justifies committee support for it, and explains the arguments of dissenting committee members. The House's procedure at this point differs from the Senate's. Bills reported out of committee in the Senate go directly to the floor, where debate is scheduled by the party leaders.

The House, because of its larger size, has a Rules Committee that determines when a bill will be debated, how long the debate will last, and what kinds of amendments (if any) may be introduced during debate. Because the rules that govern a bill's consideration on the floor often have a significant effect on its final shape, the Rules Committee sometimes wields significant power in the House legislative process. For example, the committee that reports a bill often wants it to go to the House floor with few or no amendments permitted, whereas opponents of the bill want free rein to amend so that they can cripple it or water it down. The Rules Committee must referee these disputes.

Once a bill has been reported to the floor, it is placed on a legislative calendar. In the House, debate is usually limited to a few hours or less, depending on how important or controversial a bill is. Senate floor rules are less rigid, and debate there may last several hours or days—in some cases, weeks. In each house, debate is usually controlled by members designated as floor managers for the bill. The floor manager for the proponents (typically a committee or subcommittee chairperson who has worked on the bill) and the floor manager for the opposition (usually, but not always, a member of the minority party) organize the debate and allot time to other members who share their views on the bill.[11]

During the debate individual members may introduce amendments that change the substance of the bill in some way. The House has more rigid rules about amendments than the Senate. Unless the rule on the bill specifically permits otherwise, amendments offered in the House must be directly related, or germane, to the substance of the bill. In the Senate there are few restrictions on amendments, and senators are more prone to attaching nongermane amendments to any bill that happens to be under consideration. A common political tactic in the Senate, for example, is to attach a controversial unrelated provision to an essential or popular piece of legislation. Such additions are called **riders** because they "ride" through the legislative process on the backs of other bills when they might not have survived on their own. In 1990, for example, proponents attached to a widely supported bill creating new federal judgeships a proposal that would permit the copyrighting of architectural designs of buildings.

riders
Controversial provisions attached to a piece of legislation. Proposals that might have difficulty surviving on their own are thereby permitted to "ride through" the legislative process on the backs of other bills.

The amendment bore no relation to the content of the judgeship bill; the bill was simply a convenient vehicle for the amendment to "ride."

Amendments are voted on as they are introduced. Those that receive the support of a majority are integrated into the bill. When debate is completed and all amendments have been considered, a final vote on the bill occurs. Today this is almost always a recorded vote—that is, the position of each member is noted and recorded in the *Congressional Record,* the official journal of House and Senate proceedings. Senators vote orally when their names are called by the clerk. In the House, voting is done electronically. Members insert a plastic card in one of the teller machines on the House floor and push a button to indicate a vote of yea, nay, or present. Each member's vote is then indicated on a large tote board on the wall at the front of the chamber.

How do members decide their position on a bill or an amendment? For most members, the answer involves a complex personal calculus. Although the position taken by the party leaders often has a significant effect, Congress does not have the kind of party discipline that requires members to vote the party line on every issue. Some issues are highly relevant to particular members' constituents, and on such votes these members are strongly inclined to take a position that best serves the

© AP/Wide World Photos

It looks like chaos but this was the scene when Members of the U.S House of Representatives voted on a resolution supporting President Bush and his use of military force against Iraq on March 21, 2003.

interests of the people they represent. On other issues, members' personal views may determine how they vote. Some votes come in response to heavy lobbying by the president or by interest groups.[12] On many legislative votes most or all of these pressures are at work, often tugging members in different directions. Most studies suggest that in such situations constituency interests and party loyalty weigh most heavily. But there is no simple, consistent explanation of individual voting behavior.

Even if a majority of the members present vote in favor of a bill, to become law it also requires approval by the other house, which must go through the same process. It often happens that when a bill passes in the second house, it differs from the version passed in the first house. To resolve the differences, the leaders in each house appoint a joint conference committee. Its sole purpose is to construct from the differing versions a single bill that can win the approval of both houses. When the conference committee has completed its work (usually by forging a compromise), it reports back to each house, and another floor vote is taken in each. If both houses agree to the conference committee's version of the bill, it is sent to the president for signature.

The president has several options. One is to sign the bill, at which point it becomes law. Another is to allow the bill to become law without a signature; this will occur ten working days after the bill is received if Congress is still in session. The president may also veto the bill by declining to sign it and returning it within ten days to the house where it originated, accompanied by a message stating the reasons for the veto. Congress then has an opportunity to override the president's veto. An override, however, requires a two-thirds majority in each house and has occurred on fewer than 20 percent of all bills vetoed in the past half-century (see Table 10.2).

Table 10.2 **Presidential Vetoes of Congressional Bills, 1933–2005**

Period	President	Regular Vetoes	Pocket Vetoes	Total Vetoes	Vetoes Overridden
1933–1945	Roosevelt	372	263	635	9
1945–1953	Truman	180	70	250	12
1953–1961	Eisenhower	73	108	181	2
1961–1963	Kennedy	12	9	21	0
1963–1969	Johnson	16	14	30	0
1969–1974	Nixon	24	18	42	6
1974–1977	Ford	53	19	72	12
1977–1981	Carter	13	18	31	2
1981–1989	Reagan	39	39	78	9
1989–1993	G. H. W. Bush	31	15	46	1
1993–2001	Clinton	37	1	38	2
2001–2006	G. W. Bush	1	0	1	0

Source: Data from *Congressional Quarterly Weekly Report*, December 19, 1992, 3925–3926, and the website of the Clerk of the U.S. House of Representatives, http://clerk.house.gov/histHigh/Congressional_History/vetoes.html (accessed February 12, 2006); updated by authors.

pocket veto

A presidential veto of a bill that occurs when a congressional session concludes within ten days of the bill's passage and without the president having signed it. Because Congress is not in session, the president does not return the bill, nor is there any possibility of a congressional override.

If the annual session of Congress ends within ten days of the passage of a bill, the president may exercise another option, the **pocket veto,** simply by declining to sign the bill. Because Congress is not in session, the president does not return the bill, nor is there any possibility of a congressional override. Because many bills are passed in the legislative rush that comes at the end of a congressional session, opportunities for pocket vetoes occur with some frequency.

The veto power is an important source of political leverage in the struggle between the president and the Congress over the shape of legislation. For example, after the Chinese government's crackdown on dissident students in 1989, Congress passed a bill that would have allowed Chinese students to stay in the United States longer than their original visas permitted. This measure was intended to protect the students from prosecution when they returned to China. President George H. W. Bush vetoed the bill. He was concerned with the effect it would have on his efforts to reestablish relations with China, and he believed that protection of the Chinese students could be accomplished by other means. Bush's veto angered many members of Congress, where the bill had passed overwhelmingly. The House overrode the veto by a vote of 390–25. But Bush lobbied heavily in the Senate to retain support for his authority to lead the country in foreign affairs. The Senate voted 62–37 to override, a few votes short of the two-thirds majority needed. The veto stood.

© AP/Wide World Photos

President Bush meets with members of Congress about his trip to Europe in the Cabinet Room of the White House May 11, 2005. From left to right are: House Speaker Dennis Hastert, R-Ill., Bush, Senate Majority Leader Bill First, R-Tenn. and Senate Minority Leader Harry Reid, D-Nev.

Rules, Procedures, and Precedents The lawmaking process is governed by a highly developed set of rules and precedents. The first rules, written by Thomas Jefferson, still exist, although they have been altered considerably since Jefferson's time. Rules and precedents control such matters as parliamentary procedures in debate, the assignment of bills to committees, the operations of committees, and legislative record keeping. Because the rules shape political conflicts in Congress and play a large role in determining the strategies of political adversaries, some of their general effects on the operations and decisions of Congress are worth noting.[13]

First, the rules enforce a decentralization of legislative power in both houses of Congress. They require that legislation be considered and acted on at several points (committee, subcommittee, floor, and joint conference) before final passage. In effect, each of these stages is a veto point, because defeat at any one of them usually kills a bill. There are procedures in the House and Senate rules for bypassing some of these steps, but they are unwieldy and rarely employed. Hence, members who control the veto points in the legislative process—an especially strong and obdurate committee chairperson, for instance—have significant power in determining what will or will not become law.

Second, the rules favor the status quo by, in effect, biasing the legislative process against change. The proponents of a new piece of legislation must succeed at every stage in the process: their bill must win majorities in subcommittee, in full committee, on the floor, and so on. Opponents must win at only one of these stages: they can defeat the bill in subcommittee, in full committee, or wherever they can construct a majority in opposition to the bill. The cards thus are stacked against new legislation. In recent Congresses only about 5 percent of all bills and joint resolutions introduced have been enacted.

Third, the rules work to slow the pace of legislative consideration. Congress has occasionally shown an ability to legislate quickly, particularly when confronted with a national security crisis. In September 1983, for instance, Congress was able in just a few days to work out a compromise with President Ronald Reagan permitting American peacekeeping forces to remain in Lebanon. On September 18, 2001, Congress passed PL 107–40, authorizing President George W. Bush to use military force against those responsible for the terrorist attacks that had occurred only a week earlier. But quick action by Congress is the exception, not the norm. Most of the time, the legislative process grinds away slowly because so many participants at so many stages have to study, deliberate, and add their own ideas and projects to the legislation.

Fourth, the rules provide several mechanisms by which determined minorities can thwart the will of congressional majorities. In the Senate, for instance, much is accomplished through a procedure called **unanimous consent.** Action can be taken without debate when all members consent to that procedure, but only one dissenting senator can prevent action under unanimous consent and thus slow the progress of the Senate. For decades, former Senator Jesse Helms (R–North Carolina) used this tactic to force the Senate to pay attention to issues important to him personally. His objections to unanimous consent resolutions earned him the title "Senator No."

unanimous consent
A common device used for procedural efficiency in the Senate, in which action is taken without debate when all members consent to it.

Also in the Senate, which has a long tradition of unlimited debate, a small group of senators may delay or even prevent a vote on a bill, nomination, or treaty by carrying out a **filibuster.** They do this by gaining recognition to speak in debate and then not relinquishing the floor. A group of senators working together can hold the floor indefinitely. It now takes a vote by three fifths of the entire Senate (sixty senators) to invoke **cloture** and thereby end a filibuster. This means that if 41 percent or more of the senators are intensely opposed to a bill that has majority support, final action on the bill can be slowed or prevented. Even after cloture, loopholes in the Senate rules permit a single senator to prolong debate.

Finally, a bill can die when a majority of the members of a committee or subcommittee opposes it, even though a majority of the members of the house in which it was introduced favors it. In these and other ways, the rules permit the will of a determined minority to supersede that of a majority. Why?

We discussed this issue in Chapter 1. The framers desired to design a republican form of government. They were fearful that a group, be it a minority or a majority, could dominate the government and deny the people their basic rights and liberties.

The legislative process is decentralized, slow, and tedious, and it crushes most bills. For members of Congress who have legislative goals, it is a demanding consumer of time and effort and an unrelenting source of frustration. But it does ensure that in most cases new laws are carefully considered and solidly supported before they are enacted. The framers believed that deliberation improves legislation and makes it more acceptable to more people.

Representation

In the United States, participation in the national government occurs through the process of **representation**. The framers of the Constitution were most concerned about the quality of representation. To help ensure that members of Congress would be sensitive to the interests of the people they represent, the Constitution requires that they reside in the state from which they are elected. This requirement does not exist in most other countries. To ensure that the people know what the government is doing, the Constitution requires both houses of Congress to keep and publish a journal of their activities in which the yea and nay votes are recorded so that individual members can be held accountable. And to ensure that members of Congress keep faith with their constituents, the Constitution provides for regular and frequent elections.

Every member of Congress represents two groups of citizens. In that every member has some responsibility to the national interest, he or she represents the nation. The member also represents a **constituency,** the state or congressional district that elects him or her to Congress.

The interests of these two groups may be in conflict. Sometimes what is best for the district may not be best for the nation or even the state in which the district is located. Higher farm prices benefit individual farmers but not the nation's consumers. Federal subsidies for the construction of a dam in a particular district

---

filibuster

A technique for preventing a vote in the Senate in which senators gain recognition to speak in debate and then do not relinquish the floor. A filibuster can be ended only by a vote of cloture, and even then, loopholes in the Senate rules permit a single senator to prolong debate.

cloture

The limitation of debate on a measure before the Senate. It takes a vote by three fifths of the entire Senate (sixty senators) to invoke cloture and thereby end a filibuster.

representation

The processes through which members of Congress seek to determine, articulate, and act on the interests of residents of their state or district.

constituency

The residents of the state or district that elects a particular member of Congress.

will have local benefits but will increase everyone's taxes. Balancing the national interest with their constituency is a constant concern for members of Congress.

How do members of Congress keep in touch with their constituents? How do they know their constituents' opinions? How do they deal with disagreements within their constituency? Each member develops his or her own ways of doing these things.

Constituencies are not monolithic, single-minded groups of voters. They tend instead to be composed of people with varying attitudes, levels of information, interests, and partisan preferences. Richard Fenno, a political scientist who has studied relationships between members of Congress and their constituents, has indicated that most members view their constituencies in several ways, or as what he calls a "nest of concentric circles."[14] The outer and largest of these circles is the "geographic constituency," the whole district viewed from the standpoint of location and demographic characteristics. Is it a farm district or an inner-city district? What are its principal commercial products? What is the religious and ethnic composition of the people who live there? The largest circle represents the district in the broadest sense.

The next circle is the "reelection constituency," the people who vote for the member in the general election. The reelection constituency is more important than the geographic constituency in determining the member's positions on policy issues. Indeed, members often perceive communities and special interests in their district in terms of the political support they provide, saying things like "I never get many votes over on the west side" or "I can always count on the support of the Chamber of Commerce crowd." It is a fact of political life that members of Congress are more responsive to those who vote for them than to those who do not.

Members of Congress are even more responsive to people in the inner circle, the "primary constituency." These are the people who provide loyal support in primary elections, who not only vote for members but also work and spend for them. They form the core of the member's political support.

The fourth circle is the "personal constituency," people with whom the member has close personal ties. Although some may be active in politics and others not, this group includes the people who are most likely to advise the member on political and policy matters and whose advice the member is most likely to trust and follow. Like the primary constituency, they provide funds and help during campaigns.

Fenno's explanation of congressional constituencies sheds light on the politics of representation. Constituencies are quite complex, with overlapping and often conflicting interests. As a consequence, members must constantly interact with the "folks back home" to discern the direction and intensity of their constituents' opinions.

The Representative at Work Although many people think that representation is a one-way process, it is not and does not just react to "instructions" from constituents. Rarely do members receive anything resembling instructions from home. They do tend to hear a good deal from the people they represent, but studies of incoming congressional communications suggest that this type of communication has several limitations.

First, although members may receive hundreds of letters, faxes, and e-mail communications each week, most of their constituents never write or call. A flood of communications about some particular issue is likely to indicate a campaign "stimulated" by one or more interest groups. The communications that members receive on such occasions often look or sound exactly the same, and this diminishes their effect. Public opinion polls indicate that only about 15 percent of all adults have ever communicated with their representatives in Congress.[15]

Second, many of the communications that members receive have little to do with legislative issues. They are requests for help with specific problems such as expediting a passport, assisting with a grant application, or placing a disabled veteran into a veterans' hospital.

Third, many of the communications that a member receives contradict each other. Some constituents may recommend a vote for a bill, others a vote against it. On clean air legislation, for instance, environmentalists may want the member to vote for stringent regulations, but factory owners may want weaker regulations. Members hear a lot from constituents—veterans, farmers, schools, hospitals, and others—who want increases in the benefits they receive from the government. But they also hear frequently from people who want budget cuts and lower taxes.

Fourth, members hear nothing or next to nothing from their constituents about many issues, especially issues that have little direct bearing on the district. Members from inner-city districts hear little from their constituents about agricultural subsidies, for example; representatives from New England hear little from the folks at home about citrus subsidies.

To overcome deficiencies in the communications received from constituents, many members of Congress work hard to interact with the people they represent. They try to improve their understanding of constituent opinion, especially on complex issues important to the district. But they also want to build constituent support for their own views. For many issues on which the members' personal opinions are clearly formulated, constituents' opinions are ambiguous or contradictory. In these cases members have genuine opportunities to become opinion leaders in their district. Leadership of constituent opinion is an important, but often overlooked, component of the representative relationship.

franking privilege

The right of members of Congress to mail newsletters and questionnaires free of charge to every mailbox in their state or district.

Members of Congress have developed several successful techniques for reaching out to their district. A generous **franking privilege** enables them to mail newsletters and questionnaires to every postal box in their state or district, free of charge, and the congressional recording studios enable them to send video or audiotapes to television and radio stations back home. Members also receive ample funds for travel between Washington and their district. Most spend at least part of every month back home, aided by the typical monthly schedule of Congress: three weeks in session and one week for "district work periods." Many of those who live east of the Mississippi River try to return home every week. In addition to their Washington office, all members have one or more offices in their district with full-time staffs. Members also keep in touch by reading local newspapers, telephoning district leaders, and meeting with visitors from the district when they come to Washington.

But the relationship between members and their constituents is based on more than just the frequency and technology of communication. Most members have grown up in their district. Their political socialization took place there; they entered politics and achieved their first political successes there. As a result, they tend to share the economic and social values of the people they represent, not simply because it is politically expedient to do so but because those are their personal values. In reality, much of the relationship between members and their district is felt rather than communicated.

Members of Congress who run for reelection are extraordinarily successful. Here is an important part of the reason: in their voting behavior, Americans seem to be expressing considerable satisfaction with the way they are represented by their own member of Congress. Far from being easy or automatic, this satisfaction reflects the substantial effort that contemporary members of Congress apply to their responsibilities as representatives and the abundant array of resources available to them in carrying out those responsibilities. Recent studies of the House of Representatives, for example, show that on average House members now have more than a quarter of their allotted staff working on specific constituent problems.[16] For members of Congress, the clear electoral reward for responsive representation gives them a powerful incentive to concentrate a substantial portion of their energies on this aspect of their job.

Administrative Oversight

Administrative oversight is another essential congressional function. Because Congress is ill equipped to make every important public policy decision, in many areas it delegates responsibility to bureaucratic agencies, charging them with making expert decisions but subjecting those decisions to legislative review. When this process works as intended, it combines bureaucratic expertise and popular control. The policy experts in the executive branch of government make the day-to-day decisions on public policy, and the people's representatives in the legislative branch review them and, when necessary, attempt to alter them.

Techniques Congress performs its oversight function in many ways.[17] Most standing committees of Congress conduct **oversight hearings** as a regular part of their responsibilities. (Some have subcommittees to which they assign those hearings.) During an oversight hearing the activities of an executive agency or the management of a specific program is reviewed in depth. Often held when the authorized tenure of an agency or a program is nearing an end, the hearing is usually preceded by an investigation by the committee staff. At the hearing itself, executive branch officials are called on to explain their activities and to answer the committee's questions. The report produced by an oversight hearing may suggest changes in administrative procedures, reauthorization of the agency or program, or legislation to remedy its perceived defects.

oversight hearings
Regular in-depth reviews by congressional committees of the activities of executive agencies or the management of specific programs. Such a hearing is usually preceded by an investigation by the committee staff. At the hearing itself, executive branch officials are called to explain their activities and to answer the committee's questions. The product of an oversight hearing may be a report suggesting changes in administrative procedures, remedial legislation, or reauthorization of the agency or program.

special investigations

Special examinations by Congress of executive branch or presidential activities. Some are conducted by permanent committees and subcommittees with no special appropriations of funds or additions to committee staffs. More commonly, investigations differ from routine oversight hearings in the depth of their examinations, the vigor with which they are conducted, and the amount of funds and staff resources committed to them.

Committees are essentially free to conduct investigations of anything within their jurisdictions. After the financial failings of the Enron Corporation came to light in 2002, several committees undertook detailed investigations. In the aftermath of the terrorist attacks of September 11, 2001, committees in both houses investigated the FBI and the CIA to determine why adequate warnings of pending attacks had not been provided. When media personality Martha Stewart was accused of "insider trading" in selling her shares of ImClone Systems just before its price fell precipitously, a congressional committee conducted an investigation of that as well. Investigations occur in some cases, but not in others. The difference is often determined by politics, by the desire of some members to shed harsh light on political opponents or simply to shed light on themselves, as with the Martha Stewart investigation, by investigating celebrities.

In addition to oversight hearings, Congress conducts **special investigations.** Some of these investigations are virtually indistinguishable from oversight hearings. They are conducted by permanent committees and subcommittees with no special appropriations of funds or additions to committee staffs. More commonly, however, investigations differ from routine oversight hearings in the depth of their examinations, the vigor with which they are conducted, and the amount of funds and staff resources committed to them.

© Shawn Thew/epa/Corbis

Congress investigates the federal government's slow response to the hurricane victims in Louisiana and Mississippi. Here former FEMA Director Michael Brown testifies that it was not the fault of his agency, but that of dysfunctional state and local governments. In later testimony, he also blamed the organization and operation of the Department of Homeland Security and its Secretary, Michael Chertoff, as well as the White House.

Congress often establishes temporary committees to conduct major investigations. Each committee has its own staff (frequently headed by an attorney with a national reputation) and its own, often ample, budget. For example, to conduct the investigation of 1972 presidential campaign activities, which came to be known as the Watergate investigation, a separate committee headed by Senator Sam Ervin (D-North Carolina) was established. It lasted for a year and a half and had a budget of almost $2 million and a staff of more than sixty people. Similar investigations have been conducted in the past four decades on such matters as the assassination of President John F. Kennedy, the fate of soldiers missing in action in Vietnam, the diversion of funds by Reagan administration officials from Iranian arms sales to the contras in Nicaragua, and possible intelligence failures before the terrorist attacks on September 11, 2001.

Special investigations often raise tension between Congress and presidents, who say that such investigations are inspired by the opposition party to embarrass or weaken the administration. In the late 1940s, President Harry Truman, a Democrat, made the claim of partisanship against a young Republican representative named Richard Nixon for his role in the aggressive investigation of communist influence in Truman's administration. A quarter of a century later, Nixon, then the Republican president, made the same claim against the Democrats who led the Watergate investigations.

Employees of the executive branch also fall under congressional oversight through **personnel controls.** Those who serve at the top levels—cabinet secretaries, agency heads, regulatory commissioners—are presidential appointees whose appointments are subject to Senate confirmation. When the president nominates a candidate to fill one of these positions, the nomination must be reviewed and approved by majority vote in the Senate before it takes effect. The Senate can, and occasionally does, reject candidates proposed by the president. If opponents cannot defeat a nomination, they can at least try to delay or even prevent a vote on it by placing a hold or threatening to filibuster the nomination. Sixty votes are needed to stop debate and vote on the nomination.

In addition, Congress has control over the salaries and employment conditions of all federal employees, both career civil servants and presidential appointees. It sets pay scales, establishes "personnel ceilings" that limit the number of people who can work in a specified agency or office, creates general hiring qualifications, and approves routine personnel policies regarding annual leave, sick pay, dismissals, retirements, and pensions. This range of control gives Congress some discretion in determining who will work where in the executive branch and under what conditions. Congress sought to enlarge its political control over the activities of the inspector general of the CIA, for example, by enacting legislation making that position a presidential appointment subject to Senate confirmation.

Financial controls—the power of the purse—are the most important and effective of Congress's techniques for overseeing the work of the executive branch. The Constitution (Article I, Section 9) is quite specific on this point: "No money shall be drawn from the treasury, but in consequence of appropriations made by law." Before Congress appropriates funds to an agency or program, it

personnel controls
Congressional control over presidential appointments and over the number, qualifications, salaries, and employment conditions of all federal employees.

financial controls
The most important and effective of Congress's techniques for overseeing the work of the executive branch. Before it appropriates funds to an agency or a program, Congress assesses the manner in which previous appropriations have been used and examines the stated plans for use of the funds being requested.

assesses the manner in which previous appropriations have been used and it examines the stated plans for the use of the funds being requested. This work is usually conducted by the House and Senate Appropriations Committees, which hold annual hearings for virtually every program and agency in the government. At the hearings, executive branch officials must explain their past activities and defend their budget requests for the coming year.

In many cases Congress appropriates less money than executive agencies request. By shifting funds from one program to another, it may also change the priorities reflected in executive budget requests. In 1995, for example, the House slashed President Bill Clinton's request for antimissile defenses from $3 billion to $763 million, and instead appropriated $553 million to resume production of the B-2 bomber, which neither the president nor Pentagon leaders wanted. When Secretary of Defense Donald Rumsfeld, with the support of President George W. Bush, decided in 2002 to end the development of the Crusader, a large mobile artillery weapon, the administration ran into stiff opposition in Congress, especially from members in whose district components of the weapon were to be built.

Another tool of congressional oversight is the Government Accountability Office (GAO), the federal government's accounting arm. Located in the legislative branch, the GAO conducts audits of government programs to determine whether they have been well managed and whether their benefits justify their costs. GAO audit reports are submitted to Congress, which sometimes uses them to target inefficiency or malfeasance in the management of federal programs or in the use of federal funds.

impeachment

The power of Congress to remove from office any civil officer of the United States who has been found guilty, as stated in the Constitution, of "Treason, Bribery, or other high Crimes and Misdemeanors." The impeachment process begins with the introduction of a bill of impeachment in the House of Representatives. If the House approves the bill by majority vote, the impeached person is then tried in the Senate. Conviction requires the votes of two thirds of the senators present and voting.

Finally, should other means of oversight prove insufficient, **impeachment** constitutes the legislature's weapon of last resort. It is the power to remove from office the president, the vice president, or any other civil officer of the United States who has been found guilty of (in the words of Article II, Section 4, of the Constitution) "Treason, Bribery, or other high Crimes and Misdemeanors."

The impeachment process begins with the introduction of a bill of impeachment in the House of Representatives. This bill is referred to the Judiciary Committee, which may do nothing or may debate the bill and report it to the full House. In the latter case, the House debates the charges and then votes. If a plurality opposes the bill, the charges are dropped; if a plurality supports the bill, the person is impeached. The process then moves to the Senate for trial, with the members of the Senate serving, in effect, as the jury. When the impeached officer is the president, and only then, the Chief Justice of the United States presides over the Senate trial. Conviction by the Senate requires the assent of two thirds of the senators present and voting.

As this description suggests, the framers of the Constitution devised an impeachment procedure that is unwieldy and difficult to use.[18] They did not intend impeachment to be routinely used, and it has not been. Over the course of American history, impeachment proceedings have been initiated in the House more than sixty times, but as of the end of 2005 only sixteen federal officials had ever been impeached and only seven had been convicted. Most of them were federal judges, including three who were impeached and removed from office in the 1980s.

President Andrew Johnson was impeached in 1868, on grounds not of corruption but of personnel actions that offended his opponents in Congress. He was acquitted in 1868 and remained in office until the expiration of his term. President Richard Nixon's timely resignation in 1974—he decided to resign when support from members of his own party in Congress collapsed—prevented his near-certain impeachment and conviction. And in 1998 President Bill Clinton was impeached by the House of Representatives on charges relating to his testimony about relationships with Paula Jones and Monica Lewinsky. He was acquitted by the Senate and remained in office.

Divided Government Among the contemporary democracies of the world, America's is unique in permitting the possibility of "divided government." Divided government occurs when the presidency is controlled by one political party and at least one house of Congress is controlled by the other. In the parliamentary democracies, the executive is chosen by the dominant party in the legislature, but in America the president and members of Congress are separately elected by the people.

For most of American history, divided government was a rare occurrence, with voters choosing a president and congressional majorities of the same party. But in the last half-century, divided government has occurred more often than unified government. From 1900 through 1950, the government was divided only 16% of the time. But from 1951 through 2008, divided government occurred 59% of the time.

Some Americans favor divided government because they believe it keeps any person or any branch of government from becoming too powerful. Some who think government is too large or too expensive also support divided government, believing that it slows the creation of new programs or the imposition of new taxes.

But for most Americans, divided government is problematic. Few Americans cast their votes for presidential candidates of one party and congressional candidates of another. Most Americans want their government to work efficiently, want new programs to meet their needs, and want cooperation and consensus rather than constant conflict in Washington. But when control of the government is divided between the parties, none of that is easy.

On the other hand, people also want to hold their government accountable. Congress oversees the executive branch; it investigates the implementation of public policy. There is little incentive for a Congress of the same party as the president to investigate and potentially embarrass the executive, but there is incentive for one or both houses controlled by a different party to do so. In an age of party polarization, that incentive is magnified.

Review Questions

1. The rules of congressional procedure are designed to ensure that

    A. Good legislation will become law quickly
    B. Any bill supported by a majority of the American people will become law
    C. Most bills will become law only after a lengthy process of deliberation
    D. All members of Congress have equal influence in passing legislation

2. All of the following are differences between the legislative processes in the House and in the Senate *except* one:

    A. Bills approved by committee in the Senate go straight to the full Senate; in the House they must first go through the Rules Committee
    B. In the House, debate over bills usually only lasts a few hours; in the Senate, debate can take much longer
    C. Amendments to bills in the Senate must directly relate to the original legislation; in the House riders are often attached that have nothing to do with the original legislation
    D. Senators vote orally but members of the House vote electronically

3. Cloture on Senate debate can be achieved through

    A. The support of a simple majority of all senators
    B. An order by the Senate majority leader
    C. The support of two fifths of the senators present and voting
    D. The support of three fifths of all senators

4. When the Senate and House pass bills on the same issue that have significant differences, how are these differences resolved?

    A. Because the Senate is the upper house, its bill is sent to the president rather than the House bill
    B. The president chooses among the two bills and signs the one he prefers
    C. The Speaker of the House and the Senate majority leader hold a meeting to negotiate and resolve any differences between the two bills
    D. A joint conference committee is formed with members from both houses to resolve the differences and to produce a revised bill to be approved by both houses

5. Impeachment and conviction of the president or any other federal official requires

    A. Two-thirds majority votes by the House and Senate
    B. A two-thirds majority vote by the House and a simple majority vote by the Senate
    C. A simple majority vote by the House and a two-thirds majority vote by the Senate
    D. Simple majority votes by the House and Senate

Answers:

    1. C
    2. C

continued

3. D
4. D
5. C

Conflict and Consensus in Review

Consensus is the goal of most congressional activity: to construct majority coalitions for the passage of legislation and other collective activities. But the path to consensus is lined with conflict: between the parties, among committees with different views of bills, across geographical regions. The depth and ferocity of that conflict often overwhelms the capacity for consensus. When it does, legislation stalls, nominations fail, treaties remain unratified. In Congress, the capacity for consensus building is too often overwhelmed by the differences that divide the American people and their representatives.

10.2 Politics in the 21st Century
A Congress of the People

Imagine this. You're a member of the minority party in Congress and you've been unsuccessful in convincing the House to approve your proposal for federal subsidies for eye exams for poor children. Your bill has not even had hearings in the Subcommittee on Health. In frustration, you circulate a petition for a national electronic referendum on this issue. Eventually, 40 percent of the members sign the petition, the minimum percentage necessary to approve the referendum under the provisions of a new amendment to the Constitution, the so-called electronic democracy amendment.

Two months later, on the scheduled date, all Americans of voting age are able to cast their vote on the issue. A web page created for this purpose provides a clear statement of the proposal, background on the issue, and statements by the supporters and opponents of the proposal. A ballot on the web page allows citizens to vote on the issue. If a majority approve, the eye exam subsidies will go into effect six months later.

Sound far-fetched? No national referenda procedure, electronic or otherwise, currently exists. But more than half of the states already allow their citizens to vote in some sort of referenda, and several of those states have begun to contemplate the possibilities of electronic voting in those referenda. (See Chapter 8.) If some of those possibilities are successfully implemented, proposals for national electronic referenda will soon follow.

But would this be a good idea? Proponents argue that electronic referenda would cure the gridlock that has beset Congress in recent years. When there is national support for a change in policy, citizens could bypass Congress to make the change. This, in the view of the advocates, would be genuine popular democracy.

But opponents worry about the risk of a largely uninformed citizenry making important policy decisions without careful deliberation. And cynics see such electronic referenda as an invitation to manipulative and expensive media campaigns by self-interested groups seeking to change policy for their own benefit. Finally, there is the issue of the security of the vote. What if hackers break into the system, change the votes, and affect the outcome?

What do you think?

Congressional Reform and Its Effect on American Democracy

After 1968, Congress changed its rules and procedures in dramatic ways. To understand those changes, put yourself in the position of a new member who is trying to establish a legislative career. To establish a career, you need to accomplish two things: (1) get yourself reelected every time your term is over, and (2) make your influence felt in legislative policymaking. The former is essential to any legislative career; the latter is essential to achieving a measure of satisfaction and success. During the 1950s and early 1960s, however, a new legislator could not easily accomplish either goal. The electoral process was dominated by party leaders outside Congress to whom members were often beholden. The internal operations of Congress were dominated by the chairpeople of the powerful committees and by the party leaders, such as Senate Majority Leader Lyndon Johnson and House Speaker Sam Rayburn, who worked with them. Junior members had small staffs, meager allowances, little access to committee and subcommittee influence, and minimal effect on the policy agenda.

That situation began to change in the late 1960s under the impetus of an organization called the Democratic Study Group, formed by Democrats recently elected to the House. The study group sought to alter House rules so that members who lacked seniority could play a more significant role in legislative policymaking.

The first target of reform was the seniority system. For most of the twentieth century, committee chairs had automatically gone to the member of the majority party with the longest consecutive service on the committee. No meaningful provision existed for altering that selection process or for removing a committee chairperson who was unresponsive to party leaders or colleagues. Safe from the threat of removal, some chairpeople acted arbitrarily: putting on the committee agenda only the bills that they personally supported, granting subcommittee chairs to their friends and not to their adversaries, tightly controlling staff and other committee resources. In the heyday of the seniority system, Congress operated much like an oligarchy in which a score or so of committee chairpeople dominated.

In the 1970s the newer members of the House succeeded in loosening the hold of the seniority system. Although most committees continue to be chaired by the senior majority party member of the committee, the majority party caucus now elects committee chairpeople at the beginning of each Congress. Some senior members have been removed by this procedure, and those removals have had a chastening effect on the others. In addition, committee chairpeople have lost much of the control they once had over subcommittees and committee resources. Although they are still powerful figures in Congress, committee chairpeople are no longer an unassailable oligarchy.

During the 1970s junior members also started to obtain seats on the most prestigious committees. The number of subcommittees grew to the extent that virtually every member of the majority party could expect to be the chairperson of a subcommittee after just a few years in Congress, and the enlargement of subcommittee and personal staffs and the growth in support agencies like the Congressional Research Service made individual members less reliant on congressional leaders for information. All of these changes enhanced the ability of new members to develop legislation and conduct their own inquiries. As a result, legislative initiatives succeeded that might previously have been quashed at the whim of a party leader or committee chairperson.

The most far-reaching reform took place in the House, but similar efforts were under way in the Senate. In both houses individual members achieved greater and more effective involvement in the legislative process, and they acquired more autonomy than their counterparts had at any time in the previous century.

For the performance of Congress as an institution, this change had both advantages and disadvantages.[20] Although the openness and representative quality of the legislative process was expanded, Congress's capacity for coordination was weakened because the autonomy of members came at the expense of the authority of leaders. No individual or ruling elite could effectively provide a clear sense of direction, set priorities, or coordinate legislative activities.

In the early 1980s a reaction set in to this powerful wave of congressional reform, leading to what some scholars have referred to as the "post-reform Congress."[21] It is characterized principally by a resurgence in partisanship. Party leaders, especially in the House, have regained a significant portion of the influence they lost during the previous two decades. Their success has partly resulted from internal efforts to reinvigorate and institutionalize the party caucuses. Party leadership committees such as the Republican Policy Committees in the House and Senate have become important forums for the development of substantive party positions. The whip system in the House, an essential element of the party leadership structure, has grown so that now nearly a quarter of House Republicans have whip responsibilities.

Two other changes in the 1980s abetted the revitalization of congressional partisanship. One was the growing ideological homogeneity of the legislative parties. As politics in the South was changing, the southern Democrats in Congress came to resemble their northern colleagues more closely than at any time since World War II. At the same time, the liberal, or moderate, wing of the Republican Party was shrinking almost to the vanishing point. Beginning in the late 1970s, party unity in floor voting began to grow. Although the congressional Democrats and Republicans can hardly be compared to the tightly disciplined parliamentary parties of Western Europe, they did reach important new levels of internal unity and consistency in the post-reform period.

The momentum of party revitalization in Congress was accelerated by a period of divided government that lasted from 1981 through 1992. With Republicans firmly in control of the White House and Democrats equally firmly in control of the House of Representatives, partisan disagreements between the executive and the legislative branches reinforced party unity in Congress. Realizing that they had little chance for presidential support of their policy initiatives, Democrats in Congress turned increasingly to their own party leaders, to whom they began to grant the instruments of power and the deference they needed to construct and pursue a party program. Emboldened, successive Speakers of the House responded with increasingly vigorous leadership efforts.

When the Republicans took control of both houses of Congress after the 1994 elections, they wasted no time in taking policy initiatives in several areas. In the House especially, the new Speaker, Newt Gingrich, asserted firmer leadership over his party than had any Speaker in decades. He was highly successful in maintaining Republican cohesion in support of a lengthy agenda of legislative proposals.

Over the course of American history, the internal organization of Congress has swung back and forth between the desire for a legislative process that is truly democratic and participatory and the desire for legislative efficiency. These are contradictory goals. Efficiency requires centralization of authority; broad participation does not easily tolerate centralized authority. Efficiency contributes to consensus building; participation encourages conflict. Unable to accomplish both objectives simultaneously, Congress periodically reforms itself to adjust the balance between them. The legislative upheaval of the 1960s and 1970s maximized procedural democracy and broad participation in decision making at the expense of legislative efficiency, decentralizing conflict within the committee structure and between and within both major parties. To enact legislation under this arrangement, broad coalitions had to be built on an issue-by-issue basis and incentives given members to join the coalition.

The efforts of the recent post-reform period swung the balance in the other direction by empowering central leadership mechanisms, which when they work effectively make it easier to produce a consensus, particularly along party lines. In the process, however, the power of the minority party has been weakened. If history is a reliable guide, neither change will be permanent.

Politics in Action
The Case of the Killed Crusader

Imagine that you are a U.S. senator up for reelection this fall. You've nearly completed your first term in the Senate, where you've built a reputation as a hard-headed fiscal conservative. Sometimes you've even irritated other senators by opposing appropriations for projects that were important to their states but that, in your view, were of little value to the country.

Last month, for example, you offered an amendment on the Senate floor that would have stripped three construction projects from an education appropriations bill. These were for sports facilities on the campuses of three large universities. They were inserted in the bill by the senators from the three states in which those universities were located. In each case, the appropriation was technically for projects with names like "human development center" and "health and fitness study institute." Members of Congress often attach these provisions to spending bills. They are called "earmarks," and they require the relevant executive agency to spend money for the purpose specified.

This is a routine and significant part of the relationship between Congress and the executive bureaucracy. Congress appropriates funds, then it is the duty of executive agencies to spend them efficiently to achieve the goals identified in legislative authorizations. Congress performs various kinds of oversight to ensure that the agencies are following the will of Congress. To define that will more clearly, Congress often inserts detailed directives in legislation or in the committee reports that accompany it to the floor.

More important, these earmarks help members of Congress win reelection by demonstrating their ability to "bring home the bacon" or "deliver the pork" to their state and district. Incumbents love to point to all of the funds

continued

Politics in Action

they've directed to their home state when they run for reelection.

But you've avoided that approach. In fact, you've attacked it as a cause of much unnecessary federal spending. And although some people in your state wonder if it wouldn't be better for you to just play the game and obtain some projects for them, others admire your independence and integrity.

Now that you're running for reelection, however, there will be a clearer test of constituent response to your efforts. Your opponent has decided that your opposition to earmarks for your state is a major political vulnerability, and she has begun running TV ads showing how much the senators from neighboring states have done for the economies of their states and how little you've done for yours. The election is still months away, but your campaign advisers are worried about the potentially corrosive effect of these ads on your support.

As the election approaches, you find yourself facing one of the stiffest tests yet of your interpretation of the role of members of Congress in overseeing the decisions made by executive agencies. For several years, the Defense Department has been developing a new weapons system for the Army called the Crusader. The Crusader is the largest and most potent artillery weapon ever developed for the American armed forces. The Army described it this way:

> The Crusader artillery system was intended to provide enhanced survivability, lethality and mobility and be more easily deployable and sustainable than current systems. A battery of six Crusaders can deliver 15 tons of ammunition in less than 5 minutes.

> The Crusader consists of two vehicles, the XM2001 155-mm self-propelled howitzer and the XM2002 armored re-supply vehicle. The high level of automation means that the howitzer and re-supply vehicle each require only three men to operate. The gunners can control the entire loading and firing process from the safety of the computerized cockpit under armor and nuclear, biological and chemical warfare protection.

Crusader's 155-mm self-propelled howitzer, XM2001, has fully automated ammunition handling and firing that allows firing of the 48 on-board rounds at rates of up to 10 rounds per minute to ranges in excess of 40 km. The first rounds of a mission can be fired in 15 to 30 seconds. Crusader can deliver any type of round including high explosive, white phosphorus and smoke, DPICM, illumination, and SADARM rounds. The Crusader's engine and hydropneumatic suspension give a road speed of up to 67 km/hour and a cross-country speed of 48 km/hour.[22]

To many in the Army, the Crusader is a massive weapon that will allow American forces to control the battlefield. Army Secretary Thomas White said in congressional testimony in early 2002, "If we had it in Afghanistan today . . . we wouldn't have to worry about the mortars that have been causing casualties in the 10th Mountain and the 101st on that battlefield. It will be a tremendous counterfire capability. So I am foursquare behind Crusader."[23]

The problem in the battlefield is a rapidly changing concept of modern warfare. For most of human history, wars have been won or lost by armies directly confronting each other across front lines on a physical field of battle: at Waterloo or Gettysburg, along the Somme, or on the beaches at Normandy. In those situations, the Army with the biggest guns, which could propel their rounds at enemy targets while remaining out of the reach of enemy guns, had a great advantage. From your study as a senator, you've come to recognize that if the Crusader had been developed a century ago or even twenty years ago, it would be a project well worth your support, one that would genuinely increase strategic opportunities and protection for American troops.

But modern warfare no longer fits the old battlefield model, with great armies confronting each other across battle lines. Today, conflicts are fought with high-technology weapons and with small units engaging in quick strikes, often in urban areas. The demands are for sophisticated

continued

Politics in Action *continued*

smart weapons that can hit precisely defined targets, for mobility of equipment and troops, and for elite forces that can move quickly and deliver an effective blow in difficult environments. Big guns are hard to move from one place to another. They are inviting targets to enemy forces, and they have a limited mission. In your view, and the view of other critics, the Crusader is a weapon designed for an old style of warfare, and it ill fits contemporary needs.

By 2002 that had become the view of leading officials in the Pentagon as well. Development of the Crusader had begun many years earlier. Much of the research had been completed and it was almost time for the Crusader to go into production. This would require an appropriation of $9 billion. But every dollar spent on the Crusader was a dollar that could not be spent on other weapons systems or saved.

Shortly after becoming secretary of defense in 2001, Donald Rumsfeld engaged in a top-to-bottom review of American national security strategies and the weapons and forces needed to support defense plans. Part of that review yielded the conclusion that further spending on the Crusader was not justified, and in May 2002, he announced his decision to terminate the Crusader program.[24]

The decision to terminate the Crusader did not sit well in many places around the country or among many members of Congress. As with most defense projects, many companies were involved in developing the Crusader—prime contractors and subcontractors. The facilities of those companies were located in states around the country, and the Crusader project was an important source of income to the economies of many of those states. The decision to terminate the project, whatever its strategic justification, was therefore a severe economic blow to many local economies. And the representatives of those localities were not happy with the decision and sought to convince the administration to change its mind or even to introduce legislation forcing the Defense Department to continue the development of Crusader.

This is the dilemma you face. You've been an opponent of federal spending on unnecessary projects in the past. You share the view of the Defense Department that Crusader is an unnecessary project because it does not fit into contemporary military planning. But the project would have brought hundreds of millions of dollars into your state over the next decade in construction funds, and its termination will be a severe economic blow there. With an election at hand, your own political fate may be affected by the growing sense at home that you could have done more to help save the Crusader.

What Do You Think?

1. Should Congress include detailed spending directives in legislation to limit the discretion of executive agencies, or should the specialists in those agencies be free to make decisions about how best to accomplish the policy objectives Congress sets without such detailed interference?

2. How large a role should concerns about domestic economic consequences play in the decision that agencies make about spending projects? Was the Pentagon obligated to consider those consequences in making the Crusader decision?

3. If you were the senator in this case, how would you decide? Would you support the continuation of Crusader, or would you support the administration's decision to terminate it?

4. How would you explain your decision to your constituents at home?

5. Is it appropriate for a member of Congress always to be guided by broad principles, even if those may sometimes harm his or her constituents' economic interests?

Summary

We began this chapter by noting the consensus surrounding Congress's role as the central policy-making institution of American democracy. We then quickly described how social conflict finds its way into the congressional decision-making processes. Congress tries to channel and resolve that conflict through legislation, but consensus is often elusive. Congress's success in brokering competing regional and special interests, in balancing national versus local constituencies, in working constructively with the other branches of the national government, and in managing its own affairs efficiently and evenhandedly largely determines the quality of democracy in the United States.

As a bicameral legislature composed of two legislative bodies, the House of Representatives and the Senate, Congress represents the people of the United States. However, it represents them more effectively in legislative districts and the states than it does in the nation as a whole.

To aid them in this representative process, members of Congress typically have large staffs that perform clerical chores, write speeches, meet with lobbyists, and handle casework—the individual problems of constituents. Congressional committees also have staffs, which assist them in setting an agenda, scheduling hearings, developing legislation, and overseeing the work of executive agencies. A third group of congressional employees includes those who work for specialized support agencies: the Congressional Research Service, the Congressional Budget Office, and the GAO.

In the initial Congresses, party caucuses hammered out important policy decisions. Committees began to play a more dominant role after the Civil War, but by the end of the nineteenth century party leaders in Congress had become the principal powers. Within a decade they had become so powerful that a revolt occurred and the committees again became the power centers. The seniority system ensured that the member of the majority party with the longest consecutive service on a committee would automatically be its chairperson.

Political parties in Congress have limited control over their own members. In the House, the majority party controls the selection of the Speaker of the House. Working with other party leaders, especially whips, the Speaker helps determine the issues that will be given top priority. The Speaker's leadership is based less on real power than on persuasion and political skill. In the Senate, the primary job of the party leaders is to organize the business of the Senate.

The proponents of each bill introduced in Congress must form a coalition in support of that bill. Politics in Congress focuses on the task of building these shifting alliances. In recent years individual legislators known as policy entrepreneurs have tended to specialize in particular substantive matters and to seek support among their colleagues for policies dealing with those matters.

Most of the work of Congress is done in committees. Committees hold public hearings at which supporters and opponents of bills may express their views. They also engage in administrative oversight—monitoring the work of the executive agencies in their areas of jurisdiction, reviewing budget requests, and passing judgment on the qualifications of presidential appointees. Most are permanent committees that have full authority to recommend legislation and are divided into subcommittees. Others deal with a specific set of issues and have limited functions and authority. A few are joint committees, composed of members of both houses of Congress, like the joint conference committees that try to resolve the differences in legislation on the same topic that passes the House and the Senate.

The lawmaking process begins when a member of the House or Senate introduces a bill, or proposal, for consideration. The bill is then assigned to a committee, which may decide not to consider it. If the bill is considered, it is initially examined by a subcommittee, which holds hearings, may mark up the legislation, and returns it to the full committee with a recommendation to approve or reject.

If the full committee supports the bill, it is reported to the House or Senate, where it is placed on a legislative calendar and sent to the floor for debate. In the House, a Rules Committee determines the rules for debate, the amount of time for consideration, and whether amendments may be permitted. Senate rules provide for unlimited debate and nongermane amendments. Terminating debate requires a consensus among senators or the imposition of cloture, which itself requires the support of sixty senators. If the two houses pass different versions of the bill, it is sent to a conference committee to work out the differences. Both houses must agree to the conference committee's version of the legislation for the bill to be passed and sent to the president who has ten days (excluding Sunday) to sign or veto the measure.

The congressional decision-making process is highly decentralized. There are several points in that process at which legislation can be stopped. The rules thus favor proponents of the status quo, work to slow the pace of legislation, and enable determined minorities to thwart the will of majorities.

During the 1970s several reforms were made in congressional rules and procedures. In the House, the majority party now elects committee chairpeople at the beginning of each Congress. Junior members may obtain seats on prestigious committees and may chair subcommittees. In both houses of Congress, individual members have more effective involvement in the legislative process and more autonomy than their counterparts of earlier decades had.

| Key Terms |

bicameral legislature
casework
seniority system
Speaker of the House
whips
policy entrepreneurs
administrative oversight
joint committees
joint conference committees

legislation
bill
mark-up session
riders
pocket veto
unanimous consent
filibuster
cloture
representation

constituency
franking privilege
oversight hearings
special investigations
personnel controls
financial controls
impeachment

| Discussion Questions |

1. Are the two houses of Congress equal in every way, or is one more powerful than the other?
2. What are the principal factors that members of Congress consider when they cast votes on legislative proposals?
3. Should a representative seek to mirror public opinion in his or her district, or should representatives rely on their own judgment in determining their positions on issues?

4. What powers do party leaders in Congress have in trying to convince other members to vote a particular way on a bill?
5. Why do so few of the bills introduced in Congress become laws?
6. What are the major changes that have occurred in Congress in the past few decades? In what ways have they improved or weakened Congress as a legislative body?

Topics for Debate

Debate each side of the following propositions:

1. The term of members of the House of Representatives should be lengthened to four years and all House members should be elected in the same year that presidents are elected.
2. Members of Congress should be limited to no more than twelve consecutive years of service before they must leave Congress.
3. To minimize internal political conflict, all committee chairpeople should be chosen by strict adherence to the rule of seniority.
4. Congress should be more thorough and comprehensive in its oversight of the executive branch.
5. Filibusters should be prohibited in the Senate.

Where on the Web?

Official Congress website **thomas.loc.gov/**

Information about Congress **www.congress.org/**

Finance in Congressional elections **www.opensecrets.org/**

C-SPAN **www.c-span.org/**

Go to **www.thomsonedu.com/thomsonnow** to learn about a powerful online study tool. You will get a personalized study plan based on your responses to a diagnostic Pre-Test. Once you have mastered the materials with the help of interactive learning tools, activities, timelines, video case studies, simulations, and an integrated E-Book, you can take a Post-Test to confirm you are ready to move to the next chapter.

Selected Readings

Congressional Quarterly. *Guide to Congress,* 5th ed. Washington, D.C.: Congressional Quarterly, 1999.

Gingrich, Newt. *Lessons Learned the Hard Way.* New York: HarperCollins Publishers, 1998.

Hamilton, Lee H. *How Congress Works and Why You Should Care.* Bloomington: Indiana University Press, 2004.

Jacobson, Gary C. *The Politics of Congressional Elections.* Boston: Addison-Wesley, 2000.

Jones, Charles O. *Separate but Equal Branches: Congress and the Presidency.* Washington, D.C.: CQ Press, 1999.

Mayhew, David. *America's Congress: Actions in the Public Sphere, James Madison through Newt Gingrich.* New Haven, Conn.: Yale University Press, 2000.

Oleszek, Walter J. *Congressional Procedures and the Policy Process.* Washington, D.C.: CQ Press, 2003.

Patterson, Richard North. *Protect and Defend.* New York: Balantine Books, 2001.

Schickler, Eric. *Disjointed Pluralism: Institutional Innovation and Development of the U.S. Congress.* Princeton, N.J.: Princeton University Press, 2001.

Sinclair, Barbara. *Unorthodox Lawmaking: New Legislative Processes in the U.S. Congress.* Washington, D.C.: CQ Press, 2000.

Notes

[1]John R. Johannes, *To Serve the People: Congress and Constituency Service* (Lincoln: University of Nebraska Press, 1984).

[2]For an overview of congressional reform, see David W. Brady, Joseph Cooper, and Patricia A. Hurley, "The Decline of Party in the U.S. House of Representatives, 1887–1968," *Legislative Studies Quarterly* 4 (1979): 381–407.

[3]The term *whip* derives from a participant in English fox hunts, the "whipper-in," whose task was to keep the hounds from leaving the pack.

[4]Barbara Sinclair, "House Majority Party Leadership in the Late 1980s," in *Congress Reconsidered,* eds. Lawrence C. Dodd and Bruce I. Oppenheimer (Washington, D.C.: CQ Press, 1989).

[5]Frank H. Mackaman, ed., *Understanding Congressional Leadership* (Washington, D.C.: Congressional Quarterly, 1981).

[6]Quoted in Robert L. Peabody, *Leadership in Congress* (Boston: Little, Brown & Co., 1976), 339–340.

[7]Samuel C. Patterson and Gregory A. Caldeira, "Party Voting in the United States Congress." *British Journal of Political Science* 18 (1988): 111–131.

[8]Richard L. Hall, "Participation and Purpose in Committee Decision Making," *American Political Science Review* 81 (1987): 105–127.

[9]Gary C. Jacobson, *The Politics of Congressional Elections,* 2nd ed. (Boston: Little, Brown & Co., 1987).

[10]Steven S. Smith and Christopher J. Deering, *Committees in Congress* (Washington, D.C.: Congressional Quarterly, 1984).

[11]Steven S. Smith, *Call to Order: Floor Politics in the House and Senate* (Washington, D.C.: Brookings Institution, 1989).

[12]John W. Kingdon, *Congressmen's Voting Decisions,* 3rd ed. (Ann Arbor: University of Michigan Press, 1989).

[13]Walter J. Oleszek, *Congressional Procedures and Policy Process,* 3rd ed. (Washington, D.C.: Congressional Quarterly, 1989).

[14]Richard F. Fenno, Jr., *Homestyle: House Members in their Districts* (New York: Longman, 2002, 1).

[15]U.S. Congress, House Commission on Administrative Review, *Final Report,* 95th Cong., 1st sess., 1977, 830.

[16]Johannes, *To Serve the People,* 64.

[17]See, for example, Morris S. Ogul, *Congress Oversees the Bureaucracy* (Pittsburgh: University of Pittsburgh Press, 1976).

[18]Raoul Berger, *Impeachment* (Cambridge, Mass.: Harvard University Press, 1973).

[19]Quoted in "Oversight Congress," *Congressional Quarterly Weekly Report,* December 22, 1979, 2880.

[20]Burton D. Sheppard, *Rethinking Congressional Reform* (Cambridge, Mass.: Schenkman Books, 1985).

[21]See, for example, David W. Rohde, *Parties and Leaders in the Postreform House* (Chicago: University of Chicago Press, 1991).

[22]Adapted from "Crusader 155-mm Self-Propelled Howitzer, USA," http://www.army-technology.com/projects/crusader (accessed April 29, 2004).

[23]Quoted in Jim Unterseher, "Crusader Howitzer Will Give U.S. Army an Edge," May 28, 2002, http://www.teamcrusader.com/(accessed April 29, 2004).

[24]Adapted from testimony by Secretary of Defense Donald H. Rumsfeld on Crusader Artillery System before Senate Armed Services Committee, Washington, D.C., May 16, 2002, http://usinfo.state.gov/regional/nea/sasia/afghan/text/0519rmfd.htm (accessed April 29, 2004).

11

The Presidency

Introduction

PRESIDENTS ARE EXPECTED to make foreign policy, yet the Constitution requires Senate consent to all treaties and alliances. Legislation implementing international agreements must be enacted by both houses of Congress. These requirements for joint institutional action place the president in a difficult negotiating position because leaders of other countries may be reluctant to make their best offer to U.S. negotiators if they fear that Congress will want additional concessions.

The negotiating issue, in which rival institutions compete to exercise their constitutional powers, has plagued presidents as they have tried to fulfill their roles as head of state and chief foreign policy initiator. To help them rectify this problem, Congress enacted fast-track authority in 1973, which gives the president the power to negotiate international agreements and then present them to Congress. No amendments may be added; Congress conducts an up-or-down vote.

Fast-track authority lapsed in 1994, the last year in which the Democrats controlled the White House and both houses of Congress. It lapsed because the Democrats objected to treaties, especially to free-trade agreements negotiated by both Republican and Democratic presidents that they believed had an adverse environmental impact, reduced product safety, and resulted in a loss of American jobs. Their concerns, echoed by environmental and consumer groups and by labor unions, made it difficult for President Bill Clinton, himself a free trader, to convince enough of his fellow Democrats to reauthorize fast-track legislation during his presidency. Clinton's failure forced the next president, George W. Bush, to place the reauthorization of fast-track authority high on the list of his legislative priorities.

Turning first to the Republican-controlled House of Representatives, Bush urged its leadership to support the legislation. Opposition, however, quickly developed among those members of Congress, both Republican and Democrat, who were leery of the expansion of presidential power at Congress's expense. It was not until President Bush's meteoric rise in popularity in the aftermath of the terrorist attacks of September 11, 2001, that the House leadership moved the bill to the floor for a vote. Their narrow, four-vote victory (with only twenty-one Democrats supporting the legislation) indicated how divisive the issue had become and the hurdles it would have to overcome in the Democratic-controlled Senate. Although Senate Democrats were more favorably disposed to giving the president this authority, they still needed to insist on labor protections and wage and health benefits for displaced workers before they could obtain sufficient political support to enact the measure.

Senate passage of fast-track authority did not end the partisan and institutional bickering, however. The rival House and Senate bills had to be reconciled in conference. It was at this point that the president's lobbyists went into action and, simultaneously, the White House launched a public relations offensive with help from multinational corporations, the telecommunications industry, agricultural exporters, and the defense industry to pressure the conferees to reach an agreement.

The combined internal and external campaigns worked, a conference agreement was reached, and the legislation was enacted by both houses of Congress. The president had won the battle, which he touted as one of his major legislative achievements, but the fight had also demonstrated the limits of presidential persuasiveness and the perennial clash with Congress over the scope of presidential power. Even in foreign affairs, a popular president had to go all out to win.

The story of fast-track authority, of Clinton's failure and Bush's success, illustrates the institutional rivalry between the president and the Congress that is built into the American system of government. It shows how partisanship can affect that rivalry, either to reinforce it or to help overcome it. The battle over fast-track authority also reveals how those outside the government—in this case, multinational corporations, trade associations with international interests, labor unions, and environmental groups—become involved in the politics of policymaking and thereby influence the outcome of the final product. Most important, the president's desire for fast-track authority points to the gap between the public's expectations that the president decide on the country's foreign policy and the president's ability to do so in a constitutional system that divides rather than accumulates powers.

Fast-track authority also illustrates the ambiguity that most Americans feel about presidential power. They want strong and assertive leadership in the White House, but they fear that such leadership can be exercised in an irresponsible and dangerous manner with harmful results. They want a president who stands out yet is a person with whom they can identify and feel comfortable. They want someone they respect, who in turn respects and empathizes with them— an individual who can figure out the problems, devise workable solutions, and persuade others, not someone who thinks simplistically, reacts on the basis of some general beliefs, and uses demagoguery, exaggeration, or false information to gain public support. The public wants a loyal servant, a person who thinks and acts in terms of national interest, not on the basis of some personal or partisan interest.

In theory, people desire as strong a president as necessary, but they disagree over how strong that should be. In times of crisis, there is greater support for assertive and decisive presidential leadership than in a politics-as-usual environment. As the crisis fades, however, support begins to

decline and public differences emerge over priorities, policies, and strategies and tactics that presidents employ to meet the challenges of their presidency.

This chapter will examine the president's power dilemma and how recent chief executives have tried to overcome it. The first section of the chapter will discuss the formal powers of the presidency as enunciated in the Constitution, codified by statute, and expanded by precedent. It will then examine the contemporary president's informal powers: persuasiveness, partisanship, and public relations. The second section deals with the structure of the office—the Executive Office of the President and its two principal components, the Office of Management and Budget and the White House Office—plus those people in a unique position to influence the president, the vice president, and the spouse of the president. In the third section, the personal dimension of the office will be analyzed: the physical health, personal character, and management styles of the president. The final section turns to the operation of the presidency in the policymaking process: agenda setting, congressional influence, and implementation in the executive branch.

Questions to Ponder

- Why do presidents have such a difficult time leading?
- What are their principal instruments of power?
- What are the major constraints they have to overcome?
- How does the personality of the president (character, style, and cognition) affect presidential decision making?
- How do presidents make and shape public policy?

11.1 In Theory . . .

Presidential Leadership Within a Democratic Government

The theoretical issue is straightforward: Presidents are weak, given all that we expect them to do. Their weakness stems from a constitutional system that divides powers, a representative system that consists of multiple, distinct, and overlapping constituencies whose officials are chosen in different election cycles and for different periods or terms of office, and a party system that reflects diversity better than it builds a public consensus.

To exercise leadership within such a political system, presidents must beg, bargain, and bamboozle those whose support they need to achieve their political and policy goals. It is not easy. It takes time and political savvy. Yet their own popularity, reelectability, and ongoing perceptions of success depend on exercise of these personal skills.

Professor Richard Neustadt, who wrote about this problem more than forty years ago in his classic study, *Presidential Power,* contends that the key to overcoming this dilemma is for presidents to weigh the situation carefully before they decide to pursue an objective. Then if they decide to pursue it, they must persuade others that it is in their interests to support the president. Appealing to the public is another way for presidents to enhance their persuasive skills. Resorting to the executive's command authority is a third option, but one that can backfire if it circumvents others in the policy-making process.

Presidents who achieve their policy goals also face opposition from those who object to the policies or actions or to the means by which presidents try to accomplish them. Accusations of manipulating public opinion, using heavy-handed tactics, and relying excessively on executive powers are among the criticisms typically voiced against leaders who seem out of sync with public opinion or trying to increase their power at the expense of others.

The Powers of the Presidency

The ambiguity with which the American people view the president is reflected in the ebb and flow of the president's powers. From the perspective of the president, the powers are deficit in view of the demands placed on the office; there is a gap between public expectations and presidential performance that needs to be bridged by a combination of formal authority, informal influence, and rhetorical skills. If presidents are successful, their popularity will increase; if they are unsuccessful, it will decrease.

From the perspective of the public, the persistence of a gap indicates dissatisfaction with the president's performance, a political danger sign for the White House. In those rarer cases in which presidents achieve most of their objectives without much opposition for an extended period, then the constitutional balance may be upset and allegations that the president has come to dominate the system may be heard.

Constitutional Authority

The constitutional framers were concerned about both situations; the president having too much or too little power. To guard against the first of these situations, which had beset the colonists under British rule—recall the accusations against King George III in the Declaration of Independence—the delegates at the Philadelphia meeting placed the executive branch within a separation of powers system that was internally checked and balanced. They purposefully limited those executive powers that they alleged had been most abused during the colonial period: war and peace, treaty making, appointments, and the veto. In each case they left the initiative with the president but gave one or both houses of Congress the last word. And if all else failed, the president would be subject to impeachment for "Treason, Bribery, or other high Crimes and Misdemeanors."

Within these constraints, the president was given the traditional executive authority and charged with faithfully executing the law. He has the power to appoint those not otherwise provided for, exercise a qualified veto, and be a court of last resort for those convicted of a federal crime. Moreover, because of the president's continuous tenure in office, he was given emergency power to call Congress into special session, to provide that institution information it needed on the state of the union, and to recommend necessary and expedient legislation.

Article II of the Constitution lacks the specificity of Article I. Much remained for later generations to interpret. Having left executive powers vague, the framers ensured that these powers would be sufficiently elastic to adjust to changing circumstances. But that elasticity also ensured that political controversy over these powers would persist, and it has.

The Evolution of Presidential Authority

Over the years Congress and the president have clashed repeatedly over the scope of their respective powers. If the framers were alive today, they would not be surprised. The constitutional structure they established was based on the assumption that institutional rivalry would limit the excesses and abuses of power.

But the rivalry between the Congress and the presidency has also made governing difficult, particularly when partisan control of these institutions is divided. And today the role of government is much larger than it was in the eighteenth century, when the Constitution was written.

The Executive Power It was assumed that the president would not perform the executive function alone. But how many subordinates there would be, how they would be organized, and if need be, how they could be removed from office were issues left to the first Congress to resolve. Thus, the president was placed in the unenviable position of directing a branch of government for which Congress established the organization, authorized the mission, set up the personnel system, and appropriated the money to run it. Only the appointment process to federal office was specified by the Constitution. The president nominated people for the executive branch and the judiciary, subject to the advice and consent of the Senate.

Almost immediately the Senate exercised its discretion. In 1789, Georgia's two senators opposed George Washington's nomination of Benjamin Fishbourn to be naval officer of the port of Savannah and persuaded their colleagues to reject him.

To minimize the likelihood of others being rejected, Washington began to consult informally with the senators from the same state as the prospective nominee before placing a name in nomination. This practice, known as senatorial courtesy, has become standard operating procedure, but it has not eliminated Senate opposition to presidential nominations, particularly to the Supreme Court. Not only can the Senate still defeat a nomination, but its rules also allow individual senators to delay or filibuster a nominee, which prevents an up-or-down vote from being taken.

The minority party has used this tactic in recent years to prevent nominees whom they considered to have extreme policy views from being confirmed. Presidents have occasionally responded to this tactic by making recess appointments when the Senate is not in session. Such appointees serve until the end of the Congress. President George W. Bush appointed two appellate court judges in his first term and the U.S. ambassador to the United Nations in his second term in this manner. Outright rejection of presidential nominees is rare, however, because presidents can usually see the writing on the wall and withdraw the nomination rather than having it formally rejected.

Although the Constitution divides the appointment power, it is less clear about removal from office. Those who abuse their authority by committing, as the Constitution states, "Treason, Bribery, or other high Crimes and Misdemeanors" are subject to impeachment, but what about those who do not commit an impeachable offense yet are seen as incompetent, insubordinate, or in other ways inappropriate?

The First Congress dealt with this issue in 1789, when it vested the removal power in the president alone.[1] All political appointees who serve in executive positions do so at the pleasure of the president.[2] Those appointed to independent regulatory agencies, such as the Securities and Exchange Commission, the Federal Trade Commission, and the Federal Election Commission, however, serve for a specific term of office.

Even though presidents have the power to remove most political appointees, such actions can be politically costly. At the very least, they indicate that the president exercised poor judgment in proposing the appointment. Nevertheless, Richard Nixon, Jimmy Carter, Ronald Reagan, George H. W. Bush, Bill Clinton, and George W. Bush each had to ask for the resignations of at least one of their cabinet secretaries, as well as some of their top political aides.

The power to hire and fire can foster but not guarantee political loyalty. Executive officials still exercise considerable discretion in their jobs. Technically, presidents can order their subordinates to perform a task in a certain way, but constrained by time and expertise, they usually cannot supervise executive branch activities on a day-to-day basis.

executive orders
Directives by the president to his subordinates on how they should be organized, on how they should function, or on the policy they should implement and the way they should do it. Executive orders have the force of law so long as they do not violate existing statutes or the Constitution.

Presidents do have the authority to issue **executive orders** and have done so since the administration of George Washington. Since 1908, when orders began to be consecutively numbered, more than 13,000 have been issued. Although most of these orders have been specific, occasionally they can have broad policy implications. Presidents also have used executive orders to restructure the executive branch within the context of legislatively granted powers. President Franklin Roosevelt created the Executive Office of the President by executive order; Richard Nixon used an executive order to set up the Environmental Protection Agency, and President George W. Bush originally designated an office of homeland security in the White House by executive order.

Presidents have also made social policy using executive orders. Examples include John F. Kennedy's order declaring segregated housing off-limits to military personnel, Ronald Reagan's order requiring all executive departments and agencies to assess the costs of any new regulation before promulgating it, and George W. Bush's order preventing U.S. foreign aid from being given to international population groups that promote abortion.[3]

Executive orders have the force of law although Congress can override them with legislation. In the controversy over lifting the ban on homosexuals in the armed forces Clinton did not issue an order to the military to accept people regardless of their sexual orientation for fear that Congress would overturn such an order.

Professor Kenneth Mayer has categorized all executive orders issued between 1936 and 1999. His findings are listed in Table 11.1.

Table 11.1 Executive Orders, 1936–1999

Subject	Percentage
Executive Administration	25.5
Civil Service	19.6
Public Lands	15.6
Defense and Military	11.9
Foreign Affairs	11.3
War and Emergency Powers	7.1
Labor Policy	5.4
Domestic Policy	3.8

Source: Kenneth Mayer, *With the Stroke of a Pen* (Princeton, N.J.: Princeton University Press, 2001), 81.

Although the number of executive orders has declined in recent years, the number of significant orders, ones that deal with foreign and domestic policy and executive branch organization and operations, have increased.[4]

Mayer attributes the increase to the political environment in which contemporary presidents must function. In situations in which persuasion becomes more difficult, presidents issue orders to achieve their policy and governing objectives. They tend to issue more at the end of their terms, when they run for reelection, and when their popularity lags in the polls.[5]

Another device that presidents have used with increasing frequency has been presidential directives in the form of proclamations. Perhaps the most famous proclamation was Lincoln's Emancipation Proclamation, issued January 1, 1863, which freed slaves in the areas of civil insurrection. William McKinley's proclamation to institute a blockade of Cuba led to the outbreak of the Spanish-American War. More recently, but no less controversially, Clinton, in his last nine months in office, issued twenty-one monument proclamations protecting millions of acres of federal land from economic development. Environmentalists applauded his actions, but the fossil fuel industry, ranchers who graze their cattle on government land, and western states that would profit from economic development were furious. Clinton's proclamations, taken in accordance with the Antiquities Act of 1906, illustrate how much discretion presidents can have interpreting legislation. But they also testify to the controversy that presidents can stimulate through their exercise of unilateral executive powers.

Clinton's actions also point to another aspect of the presidency's power dilemma: the increasing use of executive powers by presidents in their final year in office, the so-called **lame duck period,** when they are not eligible for reelection, their political power has declined, and their incentive to placate Congress has been reduced. During this period, they do whatever they can using their executive authority.

The other time when executive powers are used extensively is during crises, particularly those that threaten the nation's security. Abraham Lincoln, Woodrow Wilson, Franklin Roosevelt, Harry Truman, Lyndon Johnson, Richard Nixon, George H. W. Bush, and George W. Bush extended the scope and usage of their authority as commander in chief. In the aftermath of the terrorist attacks on the World Trade Center and the Pentagon in 2001, President George W. Bush, in addition to visiting ground zero, ordered the Justice Department to hunt down suspected terrorists in the United States and gave the department broad authority in interpreting and enforcing the USA Patriot Act, which Congress enacted soon after the attack. Bush ordered the secretary of defense to draft regulations for military tribunals for non citizens accused of terrorist activities, and he ordered the secretary of the treasury to freeze the assets of any group that provided direct or indirect aid to terrorist organizations. He also ordered intelligence authorities to monitor telephone calls from suspected terrorists living abroad to people living in the United States without first obtaining a warrant to do so. When news of this order became public, more than three years after the policy went into effect, many members of Congress and the public objected, alleging that the president had exceeded his constitutional and statutory authority.

lame duck period
The last years of a presidency when the president is not eligible for reelection; political power usually decreases during this period.

© AP/Wide World Photos

President Bush at ground zero talking to workers right after the terrorist attacks on September 11, 2001.

presidential pardon
The ability of the president to pardon people convicted of a federal crime; the president cannot use this power to prevent the impeachment of a government official.

clemency
The ability of the president to reduce or terminate the prison sentence imposed on a person convicted of committing a federal crime.

amnesty
A general pardon given to a class of people; Jimmy Carter granted amnesty to Americans who had dodged the draft to avoid military service in the Vietnam War.

Over time, as a crisis atmosphere dissipates, the public becomes less tolerant of these unilateral presidential actions; the groups that have suffered the most from them and their civil libertarian allies complain; Congress, particularly when one or both of its houses is controlled by the opposition party, balks and demands an end to the crisis mentality; and the courts begin to intervene.

A democratic government can suspend some of its normal procedures and processes during a crisis, but only if that crisis is temporary. Attempts to prolong a crisis so that presidents can continue to exercise expanded executive powers without the constraints imposed by a checks-and-balances system will almost always be met by increasing partisan criticism and public opposition, both of which are likely to be magnified by the news media.

In other words, disagreement over policy is the norm. That disagreement can be muted or silenced temporarily by a crisis. However, as the crisis fades or when it ends, political disagreement will reemerge.

The Judicial Power Derived from the king's traditional status as the court of last resort, the president's judicial powers include issuing a **presidential pardon,** granting **clemency,** and proclaiming **amnesty.** Although the scope of these powers has not been subject to much controversy, their exercise certainly has been. President Gerald Ford's pardon of his predecessor, Richard Nixon, in 1974 is a case in point. Issued before any judicial proceedings could determine Nixon's innocence or guilt in the Watergate affair, the pardon, which subverted the legal process, was criticized as ill timed and politically inspired. Ford's authority to issue it, however, was not in dispute. Similarly, President Carter's proclamation of amnesty for Vietnam War-era draft resisters in 1977 was criticized by veterans' groups and members of Congress, yet there was little these critics could do to prevent the amnesty from taking effect.

One of the most controversial exercises of presidential pardons occurred at the end of the Clinton administration. On his final day in office, Clinton issued 140 pardons, almost 40 percent of all the pardons he granted in his eight years in office. Some of these pardons seemed to be motivated by partisan politics. The pardon of financier Marc Rich is an example. Convicted of tax evasion, Rich had given up his U.S. citizenship and was living abroad in exile. His ex-wife, Denise, who communicated with the president on Rich's behalf, had been a major contributor to the Democratic Party and the Clinton presidential library. The president denied any impropriety in his issuance of the pardon, although he did claim that he was unaware of all circumstances surrounding the Rich case. Normally, the pardoning process includes an extensive background investigation by the Justice Department.

Presidents can exercise judicial power in other ways. They can influence the composition of the federal judiciary through their nominations of judges—subject to Senate approval (for an extended discussion of judicial appointments, see Chapter 13). In addition, they and their political appointees in the Justice Department can determine the government's position on controversial legal matters, deciding which cases the department will prosecute and whether to appeal adverse decisions to a higher court. Similarly, in cases in which the government is not directly involved but has an interest, the Justice Department can try to influence the thinking of the court by filing a brief in which the administration presents arguments on how it believes the case should be decided. There is little that presidents can do, however, if the final judgment of the court goes against their position.

The independence of the judiciary in determining matters of law limits the extent to which presidents can directly influence judicial judgments, including those of their own appointees. Clinton discovered this when the two Supreme Court justices he nominated, Ruth Bader Ginsburg and Stephen G. Breyer, voted in the case of *Clinton v. Jones* against his contention that a sitting president could not be subject to a civil suit.[6]

The Treaty-Making Power The framers of the Constitution anticipated that the power to enter into treaties and alliances would be shared between the president and the Senate. They conceived of the Senate as the president's principal foreign-policy advisory body. However, almost from the outset, the Senate has had difficulty in performing its advisory role, partly because presidents want to act on their own more quickly, more secretly, and more independently than Senate deliberation would permit. As a consequence, presidents go to the Senate when they have to—to have a treaty ratified—not by choice.

And they have tried to make their negotiating task easier by getting Congress to grant them **fast-track authority** as we illustrated in the opening case study.

fast-track authority
Legislation that authorizes the president to negotiate treaties on behalf of the United States, subject to an up-or-down vote of Congress.

executive agreement
An agreement between the heads of two countries that establishes policy between them; it may not require Senate concurrence or action by the House of Representatives.

And to the extent that they can skirt the treaty-making function entirely through the use of an **executive agreement,** they do so. Executive agreements are compacts made with the heads of other governments; they remain in effect as long as those governments consider them to be in their country's best interests.

To be ratified, treaties require the vote of two-thirds of the Senate; to terminate them, presidents may act alone. Thus, in pursuing the development of an antimissile shield, President George W. Bush announced that a treaty to which the United States was a party, the Anti-Ballistic Missile Treaty, which prohibited such a defensive system, had become obsolete and, hence, no longer binding on the United States. Similarly, Bush announced that his administration would not be a party to the Kyoto accords on global warming, even though the Clinton administration had helped negotiate them.

There are many more executive agreements than treaties, as Table 11.2 indicates, because they are easier to conclude and do not require Senate or congressional approval.

The Constitution gives the president the authority to receive ambassadors, ministers, and other public officials. Presidents have used this power to recognize the governments of other countries, as Jimmy Carter did when he acknowledged the People's Republic as the legitimate government of China and terminated official U.S. relations with the Chinese Nationalists on the island of Taiwan. Presidents have also cited their constitutional duties as chief of state and commander in chief when ordering military forces into troubled areas to protect American interests. Recent examples include the U.S. military and peacekeeping

Table 11.2 Treaties and Executive Agreements, 1933–2004

Year	Number of Treaties	Number of Executive Agreements
1933–1944 (Roosevelt)	131	369
1945–1952 (Truman)	132	1,324
1953–1960 (Eisenhower)	89	1,834
1961–1963 (Kennedy)	36	813
1964–1968 (Johnson)	67	1,083
1969–1974 (Nixon)	93	1,317
1975–1976 (Ford)	26	666
1977–1980 (Carter)	79	1,476
1981–1988 (Reagan)	125	2,840
1989–1992 (G. H. W. Bush)	67	1,371
1993–2000 (Clinton)	209	2,048
2001–2004 (G. W. Bush)	72	274

Note: Varying definitions of what comprises an executive agreement and its entry-into-force date make the above numbers approximate.
Source: Harold W. Stanley and Richard G. Niemi, *Vital Statistics on American Politics: 2005–2006* (Washington, D.C.: Congressional Quarterly, 2006), p. 339.

actions in Haiti, Bosnia, and Kosovo during the Clinton administration and in Afghanistan and Iraq during the Bush administration—although in the case of Bush, Congress enacted resolutions supporting the president's use of military force, if necessary.

Even though Congress has generally accepted the principle of presidential leadership in foreign and military affairs, it has not always approved of what presidents have done. In some cases, Congress has criticized and formally condemned presidents, as it did after James K. Polk sent troops into territory claimed by Mexico in 1846. In other instances, it has used its appropriations power to thwart presidential policy, as Congress did in the 1970s when it refused to appropriate additional money to fund bombing operations in Cambodia. Congress has also used its oversight authority to investigate the conduct of national security and foreign policy, such as the abuses of prisoners held at U.S. facilities in Iraq and Guantanamo, Cuba.

The struggle between the Congress and the presidency concerns all aspects of policy, but Congress is disadvantaged when the issues involve national security. Despite the enactment of the **War Powers Resolution** in 1973, which requires the president to consult with Congress and gain its approval when ordering armed forces into hostile situations without a declaration of war, Congress has been unable to exercise its statutory authority effectively in times of crisis. One reason is that the country rallies behind the president, not Congress, when there is a perceived threat to national security. With less information and expertise at its disposal, Congress is at a competitive disadvantage and often has to accept the president's appraisal of the situation. Thus, when President George W. Bush claimed that Iraq had weapons of mass destruction, there were few in Congress willing to dispute his claim. Similarly, When President Lyndon Johnson asserted that North Vietnam gunboats had attacked U.S. vessels in the Bay of Tonkin, Congress had little option but to believe him. Both claims subsequently turned out to be false.

Nonetheless, Congress has become more involved in noncrisis, foreign policymaking, particularly since the end of the Vietnam War in the early 1970s. The absence of public consensus on many foreign policy issues, the growth of political interest groups concerned with the effect of foreign policy on domestic politics, and the increasing economic interdependence of the United States and the rest of the world have encouraged that involvement. Presidential leadership in foreign affairs is still expected, but congressional approval can no longer be taken for granted. Politics no longer stops at the water's edge.

The Legislative Power The Constitution did not anticipate a major domestic policymaking role for the president, but it did give the president the authority to summon Congress into special session. Beginning with the Civil War and continuing until the enactment of the Twentieth Amendment to the Constitution, newly elected presidents regularly exercised their discretion to have their cabinet confirmed and to address the principal issues of the day. Following the ratification of the Twentieth Amendment, which begins the new Congress on the day its members take their oath of office in early January, and the adoption of a year-long legislative calendar, there has been little time and need for special sessions.

War Powers Resolution
Enacted in 1973 over President Richard Nixon's veto, the War Powers Resolution requires the president to inform and consult with Congress before putting American military forces in a hostile situation.

The president also has the power to adjourn Congress if both legislative bodies disagree on an adjournment date, but that power has never been exercised.

Presidents regularly communicate with Congress throughout the legislative session. They write letters to the congressional leadership; have their White House liaison aides and other executive officials brief committee chairpeople and rank-and-file members, often behind closed doors; send White House aides, including the vice president, to party caucuses; and talk with members individually or in groups.

Since the administration of George Washington, presidents have also given or distributed an annual **State of the Union address.** In its modern form, the address provides Congress with the president's agenda for legislative action. The first two presidents to provide Congress with comprehensive legislative programs were Theodore Roosevelt and Woodrow Wilson. Franklin Roosevelt continued and extended the president's legislative agenda-setting role with his economic and social initiatives during the Depression and later with his administration's proposals to direct America's actions during World War II. By the end of the Roosevelt era, presidential agenda setting had become established practice.

In addition to proposing policy, the president can prevent an enactment of Congress from becoming law by exercising a veto. Overturning a veto requires a two-thirds vote in both legislative branches. The first six presidents exercised a total of eight vetoes on bills, mostly ones that they believed were unconstitutional. Andrew Jackson extended the use of the veto to bills that he did not like. Jackson was also the first president to threaten a veto to force Congress to modify bills in the legislative pipeline. Because only around 4 percent of all presidential vetoes have been overridden, the threat of a veto must be taken seriously by legislators who support the bill in question. Clinton used the veto threat extensively; George W. Bush has not done so as much.

Vetoes are not rare occurrences. A total of 2,552 (1,484 regular vetoes and 1,068 pocket vetoes), have been exercised through 2004; of them, only 107 have been overridden.[7] In his study of the veto as an instrument of presidential power from 1945 to 1992, Charles M. Cameron found that a majority of vetoes were exercised when government was divided.[8] The reason that more vetoes occur under conditions of divided government is that presidents have less political influence. As a consequence they "routinely and successfully use vetoes to extract policy concessions."[9] A president whose party controls Congress has less need and incentive to veto legislation. In fact, veto threats under conditions of unified government suggest that the president lacks influence and is unable to lead his congressional party.

Political Power

How can presidents achieve their domestic policy goals in the absence of sufficient constitutional and statutory authority? This was the question posed by Professor Richard E. Neustadt in his book *Presidential Power,* which was first published in 1960. Neustadt, who worked in the Roosevelt and Truman

State of the Union address

An annual speech to Congress and the American people, usually given in January, in which the president cites the accomplishments of his administration and provides a legislative agenda for the year.

administrations, saw the principal task of presidents as convincing others to follow their lead in the absence of the power to force them to do so.[10]

Neustadt argued that in a system of "separate institutions sharing powers," persuasion is essential. Presidents bargain, not command, most of the time. To be successful, they must first assess their power to do something before they commit to doing it. Then they need to use their political reputations, public prestige, and persuasive abilities to get their way.

In the give and take of bargaining, presidents have certain advantages. Their office is highly respected. Others look to them for guidance. Moreover, they control some valued commodities, such as publicity, nominations, and even social invitations, as well as the support they can give to policies that benefit particular groups and constituencies. They can also withhold favors or even impose sanctions, but they usually do so only as a last resort because they want to avoid alienating those whose support they may need on other issues.

Political scientists have found empirical evidence to support Neustadt's sage advice that the legislative influence of presidents increases as their popularity, measured in terms of their public approval, increases. Professor George C. Edwards III, who has analyzed the results of Gallup polls and congressional voting patterns over several decades, has found that the more popular presidents are, the more congressional support they receive, regardless of their partisan affiliation.[11] But he also found that presidents need to cultivate their popularity and have only limited ability to do so. They can rarely affect public opinion for extended periods.[12]

Going Public

For presidents to gain influence from their public standing, there must be a relationship between the basis of the president's popularity and the issue before Congress. George H. W. Bush found this out the hard way during the budget deficit debate of 1990. Despite the president's high approval ratings following the Persian Gulf War, his plea to Republican members of Congress to support the compromise fell on deaf ears. George W. Bush had more success in converting his popularity in the aftermath of the terrorist attacks into support for crisis-related legislature, a second tax cut, and eventually Medicare reform.

Presidents "go public" to call attention to an issue, raise public awareness about White House priorities and activities, or mobilize public support for their policy position. When Cindy Sheehan, a mother whose soldier son was killed in Iraq, camped outside the president's home in Crawford, Texas, and demanded a meeting with George W. Bush, the White House orchestrated a public relations campaign to counter the negative publicity the president was receiving. As part of that campaign, the president spoke to military families about the sacrifices their loved ones were making.

Speaking before responsive groups, making sure that critics are kept at a distance, and planting questions the president wants to answer are tactics used to enhance the president's image and build backing for his initiatives. The backdrop of the White House gives status to the president's remarks. Carefully crafted and emotionally laden words and phrases, often derived from focus group discussions, are designed to evoke a favorable response. Yet, with all the theatrics, presidential speeches have limited effect. They can inform, but they rarely change opinions.[13] The major effect of speeches is to help the president mobilize his base, turning on those already relatively inclined to support him. Demonstrations of such support increase a president's leverage with his fellow partisans, but they rarely convince the opposition.

Franklin Roosevelt and Ronald Reagan were extremely successful at building and maintaining loyal followings through direct public appeals. Roosevelt's "fireside chats" calmed a jittery nation during the Great Depression and World War II; similarly, Reagan's presidential addresses, particularly during his first term in office, buoyed the spirits of a people upset by a stagnant and inflated economy.[14]

going public

The process by which the president makes a public appeal to build support for himself, his administration, or his policies.

Going public is essential for a president today. But there are dangers in relying too heavily on a public forum. As noted in previous chapters, people are not well informed and do not follow issues closely. They may find arguments for or against a particular policy equally persuasive. Even if presidents are initially successful in making a case for a particular policy or course of action, they can run into difficulty later if their claims turn out to be incorrect or exaggerated. George W. Bush's credibility was seriously damaged when his allegations that Iraq was trying to purchase uranium in Africa for nuclear weapons proved to be erroneous and when weapons of mass destruction were not found in Iraq. Presidents often face another problem when they go public: They raise expectations, sometimes to unrealistic heights. Wary of these high expectations, George W. Bush and members of his administration warned the American public against anticipating an easy or quick victory in their war against terrorism.

Failure to meet expectations results in disappointment and damages a president's reputation, making it more difficult to generate support for other proposals. The priority that President Bill Clinton gave to health-care reform early in his administration is a classic example. By emphasizing this issue and his plans for dealing with it, and by putting his wife in charge of it, Clinton heightened public awareness of the problem and expectations that his administration could and would deal with it. When Congress failed to support his efforts, the president's prestige and that of his wife's fell accordingly.[15]

Similarly, President Bush created great expectations when he announced in a nationally televised address from New Orleans after Hurricane Katrina that the federal government would provide the help necessary to rebuild the city.

The Clinton and Bush examples illustrate the necessity and hazards of going public. Although public approval may contribute to political power in the short run, it raises the stakes and may hurt a president's ability to lead in the long run. In an age dominated by television, however, presidents believe that they have little alternative but to take the public route. Besides, it is easy and natural for politicians who have achieved office by working the crowds to continue to do so when in office, especially with the help they get from White House aides skilled in public relations. Their constant campaign has become part of the politics of American democracy.

President Bush addresses the nation from New Orleans several weeks after Hurricane Katrina.

Review Questions

1. The ambiguity with which the framers dealt with presidential powers is best reflected in which phrase of the Constitution?

   A. "The executive Power shall be vested in a President of the United States of America."
   B. "The President shall be Commander in Chief of the Army and Navy of the United States."
   C. "The President shall have Power to fill up all Vacancies that may happen during the Recess of the Senate, by granting Commissions which shall expire at the End of their next Session."
   D. "Every Order, Resolution, or Vote to which the Concurrence of the Senate and House of Representatives may be necessary . . . shall be presented to the President of the United States; and before the Same shall take Effect, shall be approved by him, or being disapproved by him, shall be repassed by two thirds of the Senate and House of Representations."

continued

2. What is the president's power dilemma?

  A. Public expectations often exceed the legal and political powers a president has to achieve them
  B. Presidents make foreign policy but lack the authority to make war
  C. Presidents can negotiate treaties, but the Senate can reject them
  D. Congress can override a presidential veto

3. In which policy area has the president's authority been most expanded by Congress?

  A. Executive
  B. Legislative
  C. Judicial
  D. Treaty making

4. Executive orders have been used in the twentieth and twenty-first centuries to do all of the following except

  A. Declare war
  B. Establish policy for the federal government
  C. Instruct subordinates how to execute a law
  D. Create an organization within the Executive Office of the President

Answers:

  1. A
  2. A
  3. D
  4. A

Conflict and Consensus in Review

There is a public consensus on the need for a strong presidency today, especially during crises. But there is also agreement on the merits of a constitutional system that divides powers and on the need to constrain a chief executive that abuses the institution's authority. Herein lies a dilemma for the public and presidents alike.

For the public the dilemma is how to judge when the exercise of presidential powers is appropriate and when it is not. For the president, the dilemma is how to exercise sufficient power to lead without commanding all or most of the time. The resolution to that quandary lies in the persuasive powers of the office. That persuasive task is enhanced by partisanship in a unified government and by public appeals that hit a responsive cord. Conflict is minimized when the president is successful and maximized when he is not.

The Institutional Presidency

Given the leadership dilemma presidents face, they need all the help they can get. This conclusion was reached by the Brownlow Committee on Administrative Management in 1937, when it recommended the establishment of an Executive Office of the President. Although the Constitution anticipated that the president would have advisers, it did not establish a formal advisory body. So presidents, beginning with George Washington, turned to their top executive branch officials for advice.

In 1792, President Washington began to meet frequently with the heads of the three executive departments in existence at that time—State, War, and Treasury—plus the attorney general, who initially did not head an executive department. These meetings became more frequent and eventually evolved into an informal advisory system. Known as the **cabinet,** it assumed a partisan coloration in 1794 after Thomas Jefferson resigned as secretary of state to protest the administration's economic and foreign policies.

For more than 160 years the cabinet, composed of the heads of the various executive departments plus the vice president, functioned as the president's principal advisory body. (Figure 11.1 depicts the growth of the cabinet over the years.)

cabinet

The principal advisory body for most presidents from Washington's administration to Eisenhower's; it consists of the heads of the executive departments, the vice president, and other invited executive officials.

Figure 11.1 The development of the president's cabinet

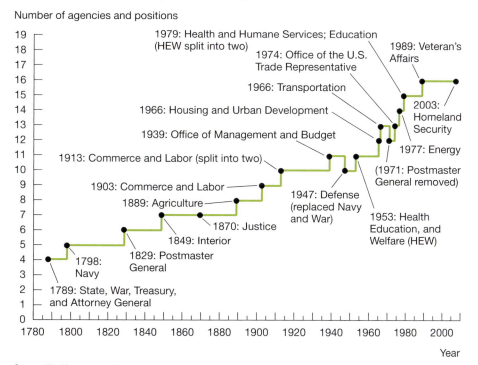

Number of agencies and positions

Year

Administration positions on controversial proposals were often thrashed out in cabinet meetings. Department secretaries also lent their prestige to the president, helping the administration maintain its political support in the president's party, Congress, and the country.

Although presidents have continued to consult with department heads individually or in small groups, they have turned increasingly to smaller, more cohesive staffs for policy advice and coordination rather than their cabinet. President Reagan and his successor, George H. W. Bush, created cabinet councils, organized on the basis of broad policy areas, to debate policy, develop recommendations, and help implement key presidential priorities. Presidents Clinton and George W. Bush have used a variation of this approach: three principal policy councils (economic, domestic, and national security) and several minor ones (space and technology, environmental policy, and an advisory council on homeland security) as advisory and coordinating bodies.

The Executive Office of the President

With the cabinet declining in importance, the roles, influence, and visibility of senior presidential aides have increased. Before 1939, the White House staff was small. It was not until 1857 that Congress authorized the president to hire a secretary. Whatever help presidents had before then, they paid for themselves. They also performed much of the day-to-day administrative work themselves. George Washington maintained custody of public papers; Abraham Lincoln wrote his own speeches; Grover Cleveland often answered the White House phone; and Woodrow Wilson typed the final drafts of his principal addresses.

Executive Office of the President (EOP)
Established in 1939, this is the formal structure of the presidency; it consists of ten offices, two residences, and several presidential councils and task forces today.

When the inadequacy of presidential staffing became apparent during the 1930s, Congress gave President Roosevelt the authority to create an **Executive Office of the President (EOP).** Over the years that office has grown in size, responsibility, and power. Today it consists of five councils, ten offices, two boards, and two executive residences and has around 1,800 employees and a budget of approximately $331 (see Figure 11.2). The largest and most powerful of these offices are the Office of Management and Budget and the White House.

The Office of Management and Budget The Budget and Accounting Act of 1921 created a Bureau of the Budget to help the president prepare an annual budget to be submitted to Congress. Initially housed in the Department of the Treasury, the bureau was moved into the newly created EOP in 1939. This move converted the Budget Bureau into an important presidential agency, extending the president's reach first to the budgetary process and later to executive branch policymaking and implementation.[16]

As presidential roles expanded, so did the bureau's functions as a coordinating and policing agent for the president over executive branch departments and agencies. In the mid-1940s, the Budget Bureau began to operate as a central clearinghouse, monitoring what the executive departments and agencies were doing.

Figure 11.2 **Executive Office of the President at Its Inception and Today**

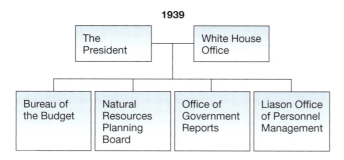

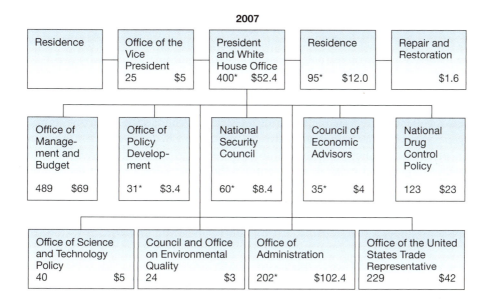

Note: Total personnel estimated in FY 2007 budget is 1,826. Dollar amount (in millions) indicate proposed budget authority for FY 2007. There are separate budget lines in the FY 2007 budget for the unanticipated emergency response fund ($6 million), unanticipated needs ($1 million), unanticipated natural disasters ($12 million), and Iraq Relief and Reconstruction Funds ($2.0 billion). Total amount for the Executive Office is $330.8.

*Numbers are from FY 2002 budget. FY 2007 budget specifies an overall number of 906 for the White House. Included are the White House Office and Residence, the Office of Policy Development, the National Security Council, the Council of Economic Advisers, the Office of Administration, and the Privacy and Civil Liberties Oversight Board.

Source: Budget of the United States, Fiscal Year 2007, http://www.whitehouse.gov/omb/budget/fy2007

All their proposals for new legislation, positions on existing legislation, and testimony before congressional committees had to be cleared by the budget office to make certain they were in accord with the president's objectives. This coordination is referred to as the **legislative clearance process.**

legislative clearance process
An internal review process in which the Office of Management and Budget ensures that executive departments and agencies' positions, testimony, and legislative requests are in accordance with or at least do not conflict with the president's program.

Office of Management and Budget (OMB)
An office in the Executive Office of the President charged with overseeing and improving the management and operation of the government; it coordinates the executive branch's budget, legislative, and regulatory review activities on behalf of the president.

Statement of administration policy
A statement prepared by the OMB of the president's position on pending legislation.

enrolled bill process
An internal review process in which the Office of Management and Budget solicits department and agency advice on whether the president should approve or disapprove legislation enacted by Congress.

regulatory review
An internal review process in which the Office of Management and Budget reviews pending regulations of the departments and agencies to make sure that they are necessary, cost-effective, and consistent with the president's program.

White House Office
The president's top staff aides and their assistants; there are approximately 400 full-time employees on the White House budget.

While Congress is considering the legislation, the budget office, which was restructured in 1971 and given a new title, the **Office of Management and Budget (OMB),** issues a **statement of administration policy (SAP)**. The SAP conveys the president's position on legislation as it moves from committees to the floors of the House and the Senate. Occasionally, the SAP will contain a threat of a presidential veto unless parts of the legislation are changed in accordance with the president's wishes.

Finally, at the end of the process when legislation has been enacted by Congress, the OMB coordinates executive branch recommendations to the president to approve or disapprove the legislation; this is known as the **enrolled bill process.** All departments that may be involved in the implementation of the legislation if it becomes law are included in this process so that the president has the advice of those most expert in the matter.

Since the 1980s, the OMB has reviewed all significant regulations proposed by departments and agencies to implement legislation to make sure that they are necessary, cost-effective, and consistent with administration policy; this is known as the **regulatory review** process.

The OMB functions as the funnel through which all executive departments and agencies must pass before they can take new policy positions and propose new regulations to implement existing legislation. Whereas the departments and agencies serve their clientele and advocate more parochial views, the OMB serves the presidency and imposes discipline on the executive branch. Its bottom line is to save money and make government as efficient as possible. Both feared and powerful, the OMB enjoys the reputation as the office that says "no." In this capacity, the OMB protects the presidency. Its clout stems from the president's desire to make sure that the executive branch acts in accordance with the policy of his administration.

The White House Office   Whereas the OMB serves the presidency, the **White House Office** serves the president. It, too, has increased in size and especially in power. Initially, the White House Office consisted of a handful of administrative aides who helped the president perform assignments dictated by specific needs, such as writing a speech, planning a trip, proposing an appointment, answering correspondence, or collecting information. During the 1950s, an official liaison with Congress was established. During the 1960s, a policymaking capacity in national security and domestic affairs was created. During the 1970s and 1980s, regular links with the president's principal constituencies—interest groups, state and local governments, and political parties—were set up. By the 1990s, an economic policy council was added, as well as directorships for key presidential programs. Today there are about 400 people on the White House staff, with another 100–150 borrowed from executive departments and agencies and sent to the White House on specific assignments.

In theory, most White Houses have had similar organizational hierarchies and decision-making processes. There is a formalized structure with a chief of staff who directs operations,[17] a staff secretary who oversees the flow of paper into and out of the Oval Office, presidential assistants who coordinate priority policymaking, public relations operatives who promote policies, and traditional staffing units that help the president meet day-to-day responsibilities and link him to his principal political constituencies (see Figure 11.3).

As the White House Office has expanded in functions and responsibilities, the influence of the department and agency heads as presidential policy advisers and even as spokespeople has declined. Power has been centralized in the White House, enhancing the status, visibility, and influence of the president's principal aides. Proximity to the president's Oval Office (illustrated in Figure 11.4) growing policymaking responsibilities, and large support staffs have placed White House aides in a better position than other executive branch officials to shape administration goals and coordinate strategies to achieve them.

Figure 11.3 The George W. Bush White House

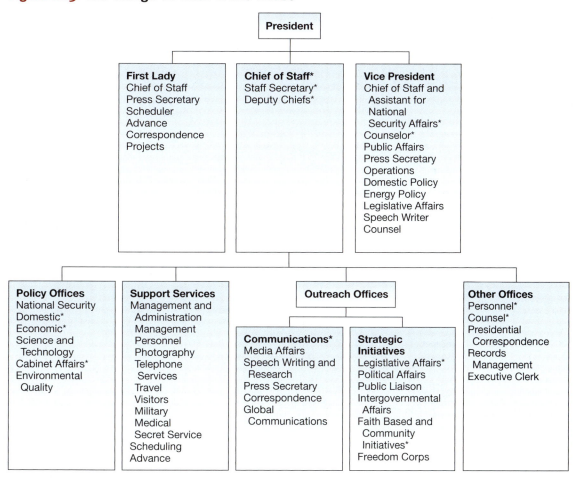

*Indicates senior staff

Source: *The Government Manual,* 2001–2002, http://frwebgate6.access.gpo.gov/cgi-bin/; updated by authors.

Figure 11.4 The West Wing of the White House

1. Personal aide
2. Personal secretary
3. Press secretary
4. Vacant
5. Assistant press secretary
6. Deputy national security adviser
7. National security adviser
8. Vice president
9. Assistant to the president for policy and strategic planning
10. Assistant to the senior adviser; Special assistant to the president for operations
11. Deputy chief of staff
12. Deputy chief of staff/senior adviser
13. Chief of staff
14. Counselor
15. Assistant to the president for communications
16. Legislative director
17. Deputy legislative director
18. National Economic Council director
19. National Economic Council deputy director
20. Chief speechwriter
21. Personnel director
22. Deputy White House counsel
23. Domestic policy adviser
24. Deputy domestic policy adviser
25. Adviser to the chief of staff
26. White House counsel

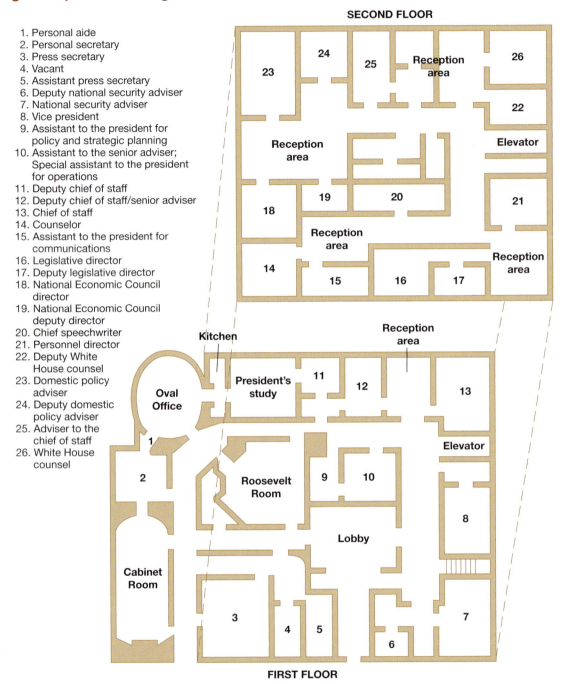

Source: "Inside the Real West Wing," *Washington Post,* at http://www.washingtonpost.com. Copyright ©2005 *The Washington Post.* Reprinted by permission.

By providing a cadre of politically loyal strategists and technicians, the White House has enhanced presidential discretion and influence, but it has done so at a cost. Presidents have become more dependent on their staffs and exercise less personal control over them. As a consequence, they are more likely to be tainted by the agendas and actions of ambitious aides. "Kiss and tell" accounts by disgruntled assistants have also become a recurring problem.[18] Most White Houses try to exercise information control. Their objective is to convince everyone to sing from the same hymn book and do so in unison, because the press will highlight dissident voices and discordant information. On the other hand, within the White House it is important to create an atmosphere in which frank discussions can occur and unpopular political ideas can be debated. That is why presidents of all political persuasions have sought to protect the confidentiality of internal communications with the claim of executive privilege.

The George W. Bush administration has been particularly concerned with maintaining the privacy of internal communications. Vice President Dick Cheney refused to reveal the names of the people with whom he met to discuss energy policy, and the courts held that he did not have to identify the people he turned to for advice. For a time, the Bush White House opposed the creation of a cabinet department on homeland security on the ground that the president did not want to have its director testify before Congress.

The Clinton administration was also concerned with the dissemination of unfavorable information, but it was not nearly as successful in squashing it. During the investigation of the Monica Lewinsky affair, Kenneth Starr, the independent counsel who headed the investigation, called several top presidential assistants to testify before a grand jury that was hearing evidence. Two of these aides, Sidney Blumenthal and Bruce Lindsay, refused to answer certain questions, citing executive privilege. Starr took the issue to the Supreme Court to compel their testimony and won.[19]

Another related confidentiality issue concerns e-mail, which top officials use to communicate with one another (see Box 11.2).

11.2 Politics in the 21st Century
Electronic Communications

The White House began to use e-mail in 1982. Within three years, members of the president's national security staff were communicating with one another via computers. Fast, mobile, and seemingly secure, e-mail became the preferred means by which junior staffers kept their seniors informed and by which seniors could oversee and coordinate their subordinates. In the planning and execution of the secret sale of U.S. weapons to Iran and the use of the profits from this sale to support opposition to the Marxist government of Nicaragua, Oliver North, a Marine officer detailed to the president's national security staff and given the responsibility for this operation, regularly corresponded with the head of the staff, Admiral John Poindexter, by e-mail. When the Iran-contra affair became public, North and Poindexter deleted their correspondence, trying to cover up their involvement.

Although backup files of national security correspondence were made

continued

by civil servants, those files were routinely reused after two weeks, thereby erasing the older data on them. Unbeknownst to North and Poindexter, however, the tapes of their messages on the backup files were not destroyed but were kept by an alert public official in case they might be needed by the special counsel that Congress established to investigate the Iran-contra affair and by the Tower Commission, to which the president had given a similar assignment.

A staff aide who had previously worked in the White House discovered the existence of the backup files and gave them to the Tower Commission, which published them in its report. The e-mail correspondence clearly showed the involvement of these two White House aides in an illegal operation. But the story of White House e-mail does not end here.

As the Reagan administration was leaving office, a consultant for a public interest group, the National Security Archive, found out that the White House was planning to destroy all of its computer hard drives to clear the system for the new administration. "Normal housekeeping" was the term an administration spokesman used to defend its action. Fearing the loss of valuable information, the public interest group went to court to prevent the destruction of the computer drives, which it contended were protected by the Freedom of Information Act and the Presidential Records Act. The public's right to know, the need to hold government officials accountable, and the importance of maintaining an accurate historical record were the principal arguments advanced for keeping the electronic files.

The White House, however, saw things differently. It feared that making e-mail correspondence public would inhibit communication among the president's advisers and thus deny the president the information and advice needed to make sound policy decisions. In hearings that extended over a five-year period, both the Bush and Clinton administrations sided with the Reagan White House, but to no avail. In 1993 a federal judge ruled that e-mail was like written correspondence and, as such, had to be maintained as part of the public record. A unanimous Court of Appeals in the District of Columbia upheld the lower court's ruling. As a result, the e-mail correspondence of presidential aides can be examined in presidential libraries five years after a president leaves office unless the correspondence is classified, in which case it can be withheld from public view for up to twenty-five years.

Do you think the court made the right decision? Is such information essential for a free and open democracy? And what about the negative consequences of keeping such information as part of the public record? Do you think presidential advisers will be less candid and more careful in their recommendations? Would you be, if you were a presidential aide? Do you think presidential judgments will be impaired by the decision?

Significant Others

The Vice Presidency The vice president's role has been enlarged and enhanced as well. Today the vice presidency is considered prestigious in its own right and is a steppingstone to the party's presidential nomination. That was not always the case.

Throughout much of American history, the position of vice president was not well regarded even by those who served in it. The nation's first vice president, John Adams, once complained, "My country has in its wisdom contrived for me the most insignificant office that ever the invention of man contrived or his imagination conceived."[20] Thomas Jefferson, the second person to hold the office, was not quite as critical. Describing his job as "honorable and easy," he added, "I am unable to decide whether I would rather have it or not have it."[21]

Until the middle of the twentieth century, vice presidents performed limited functions.[22] It was only after Roosevelt's sudden death in 1945, Eisenhower's illnesses in the 1950s, and Kennedy's assassination in 1963 that the position became an issue of public concern and presidential succession became a subject for congressional hearings and eventually an amendment to the Constitution. The Twenty-Fifth Amendment, ratified in 1967, permits the president to fill the office of vice president if it becomes vacant by nominating a candidate who must be approved by majorities in both houses of Congress. Two vice presidents, Gerald Ford and Nelson Rockefeller, have been selected in this manner.

Since the end of World War II, presidents have also given their vice presidents more responsibilities. Vice Presidents Nelson Rockefeller and Walter Mondale regularly advised their presidents, Gerald Ford and Jimmy Carter, respectively, on policy issues, particularly in the domestic sphere, and acted as their liaison with Congress, interest groups, and the president's political party. Symbolically, Carter moved Mondale into the West Wing of the White House, making him the first vice president to have an office in the White House. Carter's precedent is now firmly established, with the vice president's office near the president's.

Vice Presidents George H. W. Bush and Dan Quayle attended policy meetings, participated in political strategy sessions, and traveled on the president's behalf at home and abroad. Vice Presidents Al Gore and Dick Cheney regularly participated in their administration's decision-making process. Gore headed the Clinton administration's effort to "reinvent government," oversaw the coordination of regulatory priorities and agendas, and operated as a key legislative lobbyist, a foreign policy ambassador, and a spokesman on technology, science, and environmental issues. Cheney presided over the Bush transition, coordinated the administration's energy task force, and negotiated with congressional Republicans to resolve differences over the White House's legislative policies. Cheney has also been an influential presidential counselor and sometimes spokesperson on the administration's antiterrorist activities and defense policy and actions. Except for his occasional appearances on behalf of the administration, making a speech, appearing on a news show, or visiting a foreign country, Cheney has tried to stay out of public view, but he has not always been successful.

Unlike the relationship between the president and the cabinet or between presidential staff and executive departments and agencies, the relationship between the vice president and the president cannot tolerate any tension. Elected on the same ticket, the president and the vice president are expected to work together, with the president calling the shots. A vice president that hopes to maintain influence within an administration, be chosen as a running mate for a second term, or gain the president's support for a future presidential campaign cannot disagree publicly with the "boss," take attention from him, or appear eager to have the number one job. Thus, after President Ronald Reagan was shot in 1981, Vice President George H. W. Bush, who was in Texas at the time of the assassination attempt, had his helicopter land at the vice president's residence in Washington, D.C., rather than at the White House, so as not to appear too eager to take over.

© David Bohrer / Reuters

U.S. Vice President Cheney hunting pheasant in South Dakota on November 5, 2002. In February 2006, Cheney accidentally shot and injured a fellow hunter and friend.

The President's Spouse The role of the president's spouse has changed significantly over the years. Although the Constitution does not acknowledge a spousal responsibility, presidential spouses have performed social and ceremonial functions from the time the government began to operate. Initially, and throughout the nineteenth century, the first ladies, as they were called, avoided involvement in policy matters and, to a slightly lesser extent, in politics. Even though they were expected to stay out of the limelight, some became controversial, such as Rachel Jackson and Mary Todd Lincoln, both of whom became objects of ridicule by their husband's political opponents.

In the twentieth century, and with the development of a White House press corps, presidential spouses became more visible at ceremonial affairs with or without the president. As a consequence they became public figures with public responsibilities. They were not necessarily more influential in matters of state.

© AP/Wide World Photos

Presidents have to spend considerable time representing the country to the rest of the world. Here President and Mrs. Clinton greet Pope John Paul II upon his arrival in the United States.

The earliest exception to this limited role was Edith Wilson, who allegedly made decisions in Woodrow Wilson's name and shielded him from Washington politicians, the press, and the public after he was felled by a serious stroke in 1919.

Eleanor Roosevelt and Hillary Rodham Clinton also had an impact on presidential decision making. Eleanor Roosevelt traveled across the country, monitored public opinion, and reported its mood to the president.

Hillary Clinton was the first spouse to be given an office in the West Wing of the White House with the rest of the president's principal policy advisers. She designed, coordinated, and promoted the administration's health-care reform plan. Her activities, however, engendered considerable criticism from those who opposed her policy and others who complained that her unique relationship to the president immunized her from the usual constraints on presidential advisers—that is, she could not be fired—and placed her in a position to impose her own views on the staff and even on the president.[23]

The role of a president's spouse can only be advisory. By law, members of the president's immediate family may not hold paid appointed positions with the federal government, although they may hold private-sector jobs.

Review Questions

1. Richard Neustadt believes that presidents are

   A. Too strong
   B. Too weak
   C. Too persuasive
   D. Too partisan

2. The Executive Office of the President consists of

   A. The principal units that design, coordinate, and sell the president's program
   B. The president's cabinet
   C. All executive departments and agencies
   D. All political appointees of the president

3. The Office of Management and Budget does all of the following except

   A. Coordinate the budget review process in the executive branch
   B. Balance the books by ensuring that revenue equal expenditures
   C. Coordinate the legislative input of departments and agencies
   D. Oversee the regulatory review process

4. The contemporary duties of the vice president are

   A. Enumerated in the Constitution
   B. Defined by statute
   C. Determined by the president
   D. Prescribed by the Twenty-Fifth Amendment

Answers:

   1. B
   2. A
   3. B
   4. C

Conflict and Consensus in Review

Americans expect the president to be an active Chief Executive. Although people may not be aware of all or most of the president's policy priorities and oversight activities, they do hold him accountable for the overall operation of the executive branch. When something goes wrong, such as the government's slow initial response to Hurricane Katrina, the president takes much of the heat.

continued

Those who work in the executive branch also look to the president for policy guidance, management initiatives, and political judgments. However, the interests of the departments and agencies they serve may differ from those of the White House. Conflict within an administration, as well as between it and its clientele, results from this clash of interests. Executive branch agencies also compete for limited resources, a competition most evident in the budgetary process. It is up to the president and his EOP staff to resolve these conflicts, coordinate executive branch activities, and ensure that the polices of the departments and agencies coincide with those of the administration. It is a tough job because the executive branch reflects and responds to the country's economic and social diversity.

The Personal Dimension

Presidents need advice, but they also have discretion in making decisions and relating to others. How skilled and smart they are, what they believe, how quickly they absorb information and take action, how they view their roles and tasks, and how they feel on a particular day all affect their perceptions, their evaluations, and ultimately their behavior in office.

Physical Health

Despite the importance of good health, public information about the diagnosis and treatment of presidential illnesses has usually been vague and incomplete, particularly at the onset of a problem. In an effort to prevent precipitous reactions and maintain continuity, White House spokespeople have tended to downplay the president's medical problems and not fully inform the public about them. Thus, it was not until weeks after Ronald Reagan left the hospital following the 1981 attempt on his life that the public learned how close to death he actually had come. Similarly, Grover Cleveland's two cancer operations in 1893, Woodrow Wilson's incapacity after a stroke in 1919, Franklin Roosevelt's worsening health during the 1940s, and John F. Kennedy's affliction with Addison's disease were not publicized during their tenure in office.[24] When George W. Bush choked on a pretzel and briefly passed out, the episode quickly came to national attention because the president's bruised face was readily apparent to White House reporters.

The effects of illness, injury, and mental stress on presidential performance vary. Some presidents are better able than others to cope with them. In general, the more serious the medical problem and the longer the recovery period, the more removed presidents have become from the day-to-day functioning of their office, with critical decisions delayed or delegated to others.

What is more difficult to discern is how decision making is affected when presidents are not feeling up to par or when their judgment is affected by medications they may take or pain they may feel. Consider these potential trouble signs: Ronald Reagan's forgetfulness, George H. W. Bush's hyperactivity, Bill Clinton's distraction by the personal scandals in which he was involved, and

George W. Bush's inability or refusal to acknowledge his mistakes or errors in judgment in his decision to go to war in Iraq.

Character

Common sense suggests that personality affects behavior in some way, but it is hard to identify, much less measure, its effect on job performance. It must be inferred from rhetoric and behavior. How much did George H. W. Bush's reaction to press stories that he was weak and indecisive in the failed Panamanian coup attempt in 1989 influence his later decisions to use overwhelming military force to invade Panama and remove dictator Manuel Noriega from power and to forcibly repel Iraq's invasion of Kuwait? How much did George W. Bush's need to prove himself as president, especially to his father, affect his judgment about the need to remove Saddam Hussein from power in Iraq and maintain the course despite the continued resistance to America's military presence in that country?

According to Stanley A. Renshon, a political scientist and psychoanalyst, three character dimensions are particularly relevant for assessing presidential leadership: personal ambition, political integrity, and social relatedness.[25] Personal ambition is a drive to pursue and accomplish objectives and values. Without it, the motivation for being involved in the political world would be lacking. Too much of it, however, can be dangerous because it can warp perceptions, obscure reality, interfere with judgment, and tend toward rationalization rather than a rational thought process. Overly ambitious people will stop at nothing to succeed. Johnson, Nixon, and Clinton are three examples of contemporary presidents whose uncontrolled ambition marred their personal judgment and allowed their private needs to adversely affect their public performance.[26]

A second component is political integrity, the capacity to remain true to ideals and beliefs, standing for something and acting on the basis of it. Integrity provides an ethical framework that makes it possible for people to see and understand themselves within greater society. According to Renshon, ambition in the pursuit of ideals contributes to a strong sense of self; but ambition in the pursuit of self-interest does not. Rather it reinforces self-perceived inadequacies and personal needs.[27]

Social relatedness—how a person interacts with others—is a third aspect of character that is highly relevant for people in positions of power. Bill Clinton was particularly skilled at public relations. He mastered the art of identifying and empathizing with his audience. Democrats saw this behavior as natural, one of his principal political strengths; Republicans saw it as purposeful and manipulative.

George W. Bush also seems to get along with most people. He connects on a personal level. His disarming charm, conversationalist style, and "good guy" image, which his White House staff has worked hard to project, have served him well. In a more intellectual environment in which detailed policy is dissected and nuanced decisions debated, Bush does not appear as comfortable or as patient.

In the presidency, personal relationships and policy judgments go hand in hand. Presidents who do not trust others, who have difficulty coping with differences of opinion, and who purposefully surround themselves with like-minded people are more likely to make quick and ill-considered judgments, the consequences of which may not have been thought out in advance. John F. Kennedy's decision to allow Cuban refugees in the United States to invade their homeland, the so-called Bay of Pigs invasion, Lyndon Johnson's pursuit of the Vietnam War, Richard Nixon's responses to the Watergate burglary, and George W. Bush's path to war in Iraq are examples of decisions affected by the relatively narrow group of advisers on whom these presidents depended.

Character stands out especially when a president makes a difficult decision, particularly one that responds to an unexpected event. Routine decisions are less a product of personal character and more one affected by internal processes and standard operating decisions. But when presidents have their backs against the wall, when much rides on their decisions, when they personalize policy judgments, then character is more apt to affect their judgment.

Managerial Style

Character also affects style, which is a way of doing things. How presidents make decisions, interact with their aides, and think about problems are three important stylistic aspects of the presidency.

A president's managerial style affects the way the White House works. In the George W. Bush White House, the key staff attributes have been loyalty and teamwork. Control proceeds from the top down. Professionalism, punctuality, and proper dress are expected of everyone. Straying off message is discouraged. The Bush White House tries to maintain tight control over information.

Cognition

Belief systems are also shaped by the ways in which individuals view themselves and others. Beliefs about how the world works provide a frame of reference for presidents, who must filter information, evaluate options, and choose a course of action consistent with their policy goals.[28]

The mindset with which a president approaches a problem is important. About a month before the commencement of hostilities in the Persian Gulf in 1991, George H. W. Bush told an interviewer, "I've got it boiled down very clearly to good and evil. And it helps if you can be that clear in your own mind."[29] His son used similar language in justifying the U.S. attack against the Taliban-controlled government in Afghanistan and its search for Osama bin Laden and other "evil" men in the Al Qaeda network. He referred to an "axis of evil" and the need to contain and counter the support provided by the governments of Iraq and Iran to international terrorists and the aggressive and repressive policies of North Korea.[30]

Review Questions

1. Which of the following is not a component of presidential character?

   A. Physical health
   B. Personal ambition
   C. Political integrity
   D. Social relatedness

2. The president's character influences all of the following except

   A. The way the White House is managed
   B. The way the president thinks
   C. How the president relates to his staff
   D. What the president does on a daily basis

3. Presidential character is apt to be most important in which of the following decisional situations?

   A. A decision to approve or disapprove of legislation
   B. A decision to issue disaster relief
   C. A decision to respond to an unanticipated threat from abroad
   D. A decision to grant a freedom award to a prominent American

4. Which of the stylistic attributes best describes the way in which the White House of George W. Bush operates?

   A. Deferential to Congress and the Cabinet
   B. Decentralized and reactive
   C. Centrally-managed and highly-controlled
   D. Loose and flexible

Answers:

   1. A
   2. D
   3. C
   4. C

Conflict and Consensus in Review

The president personifies the government, thereby making the president's personality a relevant component of the office. Personality is important in another respect. A president's cognition, beliefs, style, empathy, and understanding follow from his character.

There is a consensus on the attributes that Americans expect from their president: strength and vision, courage and decisiveness, intelligence and emotional maturity, empathy and caring. The priorities placed on these attributes will change, however, with the times and particular circumstances a president faces. Americans also hold the president to a high standard of personal behavior. They expect the president to be a role model, to set a good example.

Presidential Policymaking

The increasing number of presidential decisions with major national and international consequences not only has inflated the importance of the president's character, managerial style, and beliefs but also has directed attention to the president's expanding policy role. As noted at the beginning of the chapter, public expectations of presidential performance often exceed the president's ability to meet them. To avoid public disappointment, presidents try to define and limit their goals when they set their agendas, maneuver their legislative proposals through Congress, and finally, oversee the implementation of their policy goals.

Setting the Agenda

Presidents are expected to set the country's agenda with a comprehensive legislative program. Roosevelt's New Deal, Truman's Fair Deal, Kennedy's New Frontier, Johnson's Great Society, Nixon's New Federalism, and George W. Bush's Ownership Society are examples of such programs. Beginning in the 1980s policy agendas have been constrained by scarce resources, budget deficits, and competing needs. As a consequence, presidents have been forced to limit the scope, cost, and content of their policy proposals. They must establish clear but definable priorities.

Limiting priorities has several advantages for presidents. It not only enables them to focus their administration's effort on the issues most important to them but also gives them leverage over the news media's agenda. The disadvantage of concentrating on a few policy proposals, on the other hand, is that issues a sizable portion of the public believes are important may be issues another sizable portion of the public believe may be ignored. And if the few designated priorities are not converted into public policy, as occurred during Clinton's first two years in office, the president's reputation may be damaged more than it would otherwise have been with a mixed record of successes and failures.

Timing is another strategic concern. Presidential influence tends to decrease over the course of an administration. As members of Congress position themselves for the next election, as bureaucrats begin to press their claims on political appointees, and as the opposition party coalesces against the incumbent, it becomes more difficult to achieve domestic policy goals. This problem often becomes acute before and after a midterm election if the president's party loses seats in Congress.

Declining political influence requires presidents to take advantage of their initial position of strength and move as quickly as possible after inauguration to achieve their most important goals. Jimmy Carter and Bill Clinton learned this lesson the hard way. They used the early months of their administrations to develop their principal priorities. By the time those priorities had been converted into legislative policy proposals, both presidents had lost much of their momentum and the political clout that follows from it. In contrast, Ronald Reagan and George W. Bush moved quickly and successfully to achieve key components of their legislative agendas: tax cuts, military reform, and budget restructuring.

Getting It Enacted into Legislation

Presidents have to work hard at influencing Congress. Key to their success is the capacity to plan the administration's efforts on Capitol Hill. During Reagan's first term, the White House assembled a legislative strategy group to accomplish this task. Subsequent administrations have operated in a more informal manner.

Regardless of their strategic approach, presidents must be personally involved in lobbying. The extent of their involvement is often taken as a sign of how much importance they attach to a particular issue. There are a variety of ways to become involved, ranging from personally requesting support to twisting arms to making deals. Lyndon Johnson, who was legendary for browbeating members of Congress, used persuasion supplemented by promises and threats to get his way.

Johnson had one major advantage over contemporary presidents. In his day, Congress operated largely behind closed doors. Now it is more open to public view, and partisan divisions are stronger. Exercising influence within the public arena under a media spotlight is more difficult.

How effective can presidents become? According to political scientist George Edwards, they can influence Congress only at the margins.[31] Within a closely divided legislature, however, affecting the votes of only a few members of Congress can be crucial. Presidential support increases when the president's party controls both houses of Congress. But partisan control is not a guarantee of legislative success.

Although presidential influence varies with the issue, presidents generally have had more success on foreign policy issues than on domestic ones. This success, which was particularly evident in the period from the end of World War II to the Vietnam War, led some political scientists to conclude that there were actually two presidencies: one in foreign affairs and one in domestic policy.[32]

Today the distinction between foreign and domestic policies is less clear-cut. Foreign policy issues have a greater effect on domestic policy than they did in earlier decades, and as we have noted previously, Congress has become more interested and involved in them. Presidents can no longer be assured that their foreign policy initiatives will always prevail. They must mobilize support for them, as George W. Bush did to gain fast-track authority in 2002 and a resolution to use force against Iraq in 2003.

Implementing Policy in the Executive Branch

Implementation is the final stage in the policy process. Here the president must deal primarily with officials in the executive branch. Traditionally, presidents have not become deeply involved in the details of implementation because of the size of the bureaucracy, their own time constraints, and their limited resources for affecting executive branch decisions. However, with the increased attention given to management issues today—such as costs, regulations, and enforcement—the efficient operation of government has become a key concern for contemporary presidents.

The easiest and most direct way for presidents to exercise control over policy implementation is to have White House aides communicate their wishes to those responsible for implementation. In most cases, a telephone call or White House meeting will suffice. Occasionally, to emphasize or oversee a presidential policy, an executive order may be necessary.

A significant part of the president's managerial problems is rooted in politics. The sharing of powers creates multiple allegiances for executive branch agencies, which must be sensitive to the interests of their clientele and to those of Congress and the administration. Part of the difficulty also stems from a civil service system based on merit rather than partisanship. Finally, the development of an outside clientele for the departments and agencies has also eroded the president's influence. Even political appointees must be sensitive to the interests and needs of their department's constituency. When those interests and needs are at odds with the president's, political appointees face a dilemma. If they are to maintain credibility with the clients they serve, they must be advocates for them; but over time this advocacy may strain their relationship with the president. John Ehrlichman, Richard Nixon's chief domestic adviser, once observed that after the initial attention newly appointed cabinet members received from the president, "We only see them at the annual White House Christmas party; they go off and marry the natives."[33] (We discuss these issues in Chapter 12.)

In summary, the problems that presidents encounter in their efforts to formulate policy are the consequences of multiple pressures that affect all aspects of presidential decision making. In a pluralistic society, politics occurs within and among institutions of government, making it hard for any one of them to dominate the policymaking process.

Presidents have become the prime agents for initiating policy. As such, they shoulder the burden of building support for their policies. It is a continuous task, one that requires a **constant campaign** to win the hearts and minds of the people. And one that requires a lot of help from their staff, their party, their public constituency, and occasionally from their family, friends, and even ex-presidents.

In a politics-as-usual environment, the president is the chief consensus builder. Conflict among partisans, over issues, within and among institutions is standard fare once the election is over and governing begins. The institutional resources of the presidency, the bully pulpit, and the initial goodwill given to an administration when it begins a new term provide an initial advantage to the president in this consensus-building task. Setting priorities, moving on them quickly, going public, and lobbying Congress are the strategic imperatives necessary to this task. A narrow election victory will make the process more critical and also more difficult. A large victory or a crisis will make it easier. The bottom line, however, is that presidents who wish to fulfill their campaign promises and achieve their policy goals have no other option but to coalesce competing and often disparate groups into a majority coalition in order to govern effectively.

constant campaign
The ongoing public relations effort by the president and his staff to appeal directly to the American people.

President Bush asks former President George H.W. Bush, right, and former President Bill Clinton, left, in September 2005 to lead a private fund-raising campaign for victims of Hurricane Katrina. The previous year, he asked them to raise money for the victims of the Asian tsunami.

Politics in Action

Presidential Decision Making on Iraq: Which Bush Was Right?

In 1990 Iraqi forces invaded the neighboring country of Kuwait. With the words, "this will not stand," President George H. W. Bush indicated his determination to oust the invaders. The government of Iraq, under the dictatorship of Saddam Hussein, refused to withdraw, citing a historical claim to the land. The U.S. president then organized an international coalition, mobilized an international military force, and mounted a successful attack against the Iraqi invaders. Once the goal of liberating Kuwait was achieved and Iraq's military was in retreat, the president ordered an end to the fighting, thereby allowing Hussein's government to remain in power.

Some of the president's advisers were upset. They thought that the president had prematurely terminated the military action. They wanted U.S. forces to move into the country, go to Baghdad, and remove Saddam Hussein and

continued

Politics in Action *continued*

his regime from power. But the president thought otherwise. He did not want to extend the United Nations' mandate under which the U.S. and its coalition partners were operating; he did not want to enlarge the mission beyond its original goal of removing Iraqi troops from Kuwait; he feared that Arab states would desert the coalition if American forces entered Iraq; he saw no viable exit strategy for the United States if the war continued into Iraq; and he feared world condemnation if coalition forces continued the fight against the retreating and defenseless Iraqi army. Bush was also keenly aware of the human and political costs of continuing the military action. In a book coauthored with his national security adviser, Brent Scowcroft, after his presidency, Bush stated his administration's position prophetically:

> Had we gone the invasion route, the United States could conceivably still be an occupying power in a bitterly hostile land. It would have been a dramatically different—and perhaps barren—outcome.[34]

Bush thought that Hussein would be overthrown. However, uprisings in the northern and southern parts of Iraq, encouraged by the CIA, were ruthlessly put down by forces loyal to the Iraqi dictator. Moreover, Hussein defied the terms of the peace accord that ended hostilities by using helicopters, which the Iraqis claimed they needed for internal communications, as gunships. He also initially refused to allow United Nations inspectors into Iraq to search for weapons of mass destruction (WMDs), impeding inspectors' searches after they were allowed in, and finally, kicking them out of the country. In 1995 Hussein sent agents into Kuwait in an attempt to kill ex-president Bush, who was visiting the country, but the plot was discovered and the perpetrators were captured.

Fast forward to the terrorist attacks of September 11, 2001, and the subsequent hard line taken by the administration of George W. Bush against terrorists, nations that continue to harbor them, and nations pursuing anti-American policies. The very presence of Hussein in power, his verbal and financial support for suicide bombings in Israel, his flagrant violation of human rights in his own country, his refusal to abide by UN resolutions, and his alleged possession of weapons of mass destruction led George W. Bush

and his advisers to conclude that Hussein was an evil person who had to be removed from office, by force if necessary.

Over the next year and a half, Bush convinced a majority of the American people that preemptive action was necessary to remove the threat that Saddam Hussein allegedly posed to U.S. national security. Stunned by the terrorist attacks and fearful of others to come, Americans were inclined to believe their president that Iraq had WMDs and that these weapons could get into the hands of the terrorist group Al Qaeda and threaten the United States. The president's strong approval ratings reflected satisfaction with the manner in which his administration had responded to the terrorist attacks; and his successful military action against the Taliban in Afghanistan also contributed to the domestic public support that the his plan received. Both houses of Congress enacted resolutions giving the president the authority to use military force if he believed it was necessary. Most congressional Democrats, reluctant to attack a popular president and fearful of appearing "soft" in an election year, voted in favor of the resolutions.

Bush had more difficulty convincing the world community, however. Already suspicious of American unilateralism, especially the doctrine of preemption; desirous of maintaining their ties, and especially oil contracts, with Iraq; and sensitive to their populations' aversion to war, France, Germany, and Russia opposed U.S. military action, arguing that Iraq did not pose a threat to the rest of the world at the time. They wished diplomacy to run its course. Britain, Spain, and some countries in Eastern Europe, under pressure from the United States, backed the American effort.

Despite the division among America's allies and the reluctance of most Arab countries to join the American-led coalition, President Bush moved ahead. With 235,000 U.S. and British forces in place, aware that his administration's credibility was on the line, and wanting to send a clear message to other countries included in his "axis of evil," notably Iran and North Korea, the president ordered coalition forces to begin the invasion of Iraq on March 19, 2003.

Military operations went well. Using precision weapons, conducting a rapid strike, and exercising total air superiority, coalition forces easily overran Iraqi defenses. After several Iraqi divisions were defeated, the rest took flight, oppo-

continued

Politics in Action *continued*

sition melted away into the native population, and by May 1, forty-two days after hostilities began, the president announced the end of the military phase of Operation Iraqi Freedom as he stood on the flight deck of the aircraft carrier USS *Abraham Lincoln.* It was after this victory proclamation that the president's troubles began.

Maintaining domestic security, providing essential services, rebuilding Iraq's infrastructure, and energizing its economic base proved much more difficult than the administration anticipated. Moreover, the United States and its coalition allies seemed unprepared for the turmoil and sectarian violence that followed the military success; the resistance of Iraqi citizens to the occupation; and the explosion of anti-American feelings on the Arab streets, in most of Europe, and around the world that continued after the initial hostilities ended. Nor were weapons of mass destruction found in Iraq. Saddam Hussein was finally captured, but the situation remained shaky. With news headlines report-

ing the continuing loss of American lives, the high costs of the occupation to U.S. taxpayers, and continued political instability within Iraq, public support for the president's policy began to decline. By January 2005 a plurality of Americans (50 percent) believed the war was a mistake. As news reports of increased sectarian violence and loss of American lives persisted, that viewpoint has continued to grow (see Table 11.3).[35] The administration had landed in a quagmire from which it could not extricate itself. The president lost credibility, political capital, and the confidence of the American people; his leadership was increasingly questioned by Democrats and even many Republicans that objected to the postwar policy and the manner in which it had been carried out. The president was forced to modify his rhetoric as the 2006 midterm elections approached. The phrase "stay the course" was replaced with statements that Iraq would be expected to provide for its own security and should set timetables for doing so.

Table 11.3 Public Support for the War in Iraq

"In view of the developments since we first sent our troops to Iraq, do you think the United States made a mistake in sending troops to Iraq, or not?"

Date of Survey	Yes (%)	No (%)	No Opinion (%)
2006 NOV 2–5	55	40	5
2006 OCT 6–8	56	40	4
2006 SEPT 15–17	49	49	2
2006 JULY 21–23	56	41	2
2006 JUNE 9–11	51	46	2
2006 APRIL 7–9	57	42	1
2006 MAR 10–12	57	42	1
2006 FEB. 9–12	55	42	3
2006 JAN.6–8	50	47	3
2005 DEC. 9–11	48	50	2
2005 NOV. 11–13	54	45	1
2005 OCT. 21–23	49	49	2
2005 SEPT. 8–11	53	46	1
2005 AUG 5–7*	54	44	2
2005 JUL 22–24	46	53	1
2005 JUN 24–26	53	46	1
2005 APR 29–MAY 1*	49	48	3

continued

Table 11.3 *continued*

Date of Survey	Yes (%)	No (%)	No Opinion (%)
2005 MAR 18–20*	46	51	3
2005 FEB 25–27	47	51	2
2005 FEB 4–6	45	55	—
2005 JAN 14–16	52	47	1
2005 JAN 7–9	50	48	2
2004 NOV 19–21	47	51	2
2004 OCT 29–31*	44	52	4
2004 OCT 22–24	47	51	2
2004 OCT 14–16	47	52	2
2004 OCT 9–10*	46	53	1
2004 OCT 1–3	48	51	1
2004 SEP 24–26	42	55	3
2004 SEP 3–5*	38	57	5
2004 AUG 23–25*	48	50	2
2004 JUL 30–AUG 1	47	51	2
2004 JUL 19–21	50	47	3
2004 JUL 8–11	54	45	1
2004 JUN 21–23	54	44	2
2004 JUN 3–6	41	58	1
2004 MAY 7–9	44	54	2
2004 APR 16–18	42	57	1
2004 JAN 12–15	42	56	2
2003 NOV 3–5	39	60	1
2003 OCT 6–8	40	59	1
2003 JUL 7–9	27	72	1
2003 MAR 24–25	23	75	1

*Asked of a half sample.
Source: Gallup Poll, "Topics and Trends: Iraq." http://www.gallup.com/defaultaspx?ci=1633 (accessed November 6, 2006). Used by permission.

What Do You Think?

1. In retrospect, which president, George H. W. Bush or George W. Bush, pursued the wiser course?
2. Did George H. W. Bush's decision not to remove Saddam Hussein from power force George W. Bush's hand, encouraging him to do what his father was unable or unwilling to do, or should the younger Bush have followed his father's example?
3. Do you believe that the president's anger toward Hussein for trying to kill his father, for violating human rights in Iraq, and for his anti-American policies blinded him to the realities of the Iraqi situation in 2003? Did the international environment following the terrorist attacks in the U.S. change the calculus sufficiently to justify a new national security strategy? Did it justify a preemptive, even preventive war?
4. What are the principal lessons in designing and implementing a national security strategy for the United States that should be drawn from the actions of these two presidents?
5. Is it more dangerous for a president to exercise too little or too much power today?

Summary

We began this chapter by emphasizing the ambiguity with which most Americans view the president's power. They want a strong presidency but fear one whose policy goals differ from theirs. They want the president to lead the country but want the president to take public opinion into account when doing so. They are willing to defer to the president in times of crisis but become impatient and more critical if that crisis is not resolved satisfactorily and within a reasonable period.

Public ambiguity with respect to presidential powers is not new. The delegates at the Constitutional Convention had concerns about the executive branch being too weak or too strong. They resolved these concerns by giving the president a broad grant of executive authority, constrained by a constitutional framework that divided powers and checked and balanced them so that no branch of government would become dominant. The good news is that this constitutional framework has worked and is still intact. The bad news is that it inhibits presidential leadership much of the time.

Even though the president's formal powers have been extended by acts of Congress, their extension has not been sufficient to meet expanded roles, responsibilities, and demands placed on the office. The gap between public expectations and presidential performance has widened. How to overcome this leadership dilemma is the principal challenge that presidents face.

Presidents operate within a political environment that complicates their task, an environment in which competing desires and public pressures, dispersed and often inadequate resources, and complex policy problems—spotlighted and magnified by the news media—raise the stakes, shorten the time frame, and make coalition building more difficult. To be successful within such an environment, presidents must carefully weigh the pros and cons of taking on a problem, and if they decide to go ahead, they must use their persuasive skills to convince others to follow their lead. Key to their success is the reputation they have within the government and the prestige they have outside it.

Advances in communications technology have created incentives to "go public." The White House performs public relations designed to enhance a president's persuasive skills and the odds of achieving the administration's political and policy goals.

The magnitude of a president's tasks requires considerable staff support. This requirement has made contemporary presidents increasingly dependent on the EOP for extending their reach, maximizing the information available to them, and exerting their influence. The OMB is the principal office that performs these functions with the executive departments and agencies, and the White House does so with Congress and the general public.

How well presidents lead also depends on their own skills and personal qualities, which in turn are affected by their health and personality. Character, style, and world views are attributes that presidents bring to the office and that affect their performance in that office. There is no set formula for personal success. Much depends on how they react to the ever-changing situations in which they find themselves and over which they have only limited control.

Although their problems extend across policy areas, international and institutional boundaries, and partisan lines, presidents seem to have more influence and success in setting and conducting foreign and national security policy than they do in achieving their domestic policy goals. Their constitutional position as head of state and commander in chief, the expectation that it is the president's job to deal with the rest of the world on behalf of the United States, the statutory power that Congress has given the chief executive in negotiating with other countries, and the increasing need for speed, secrecy, and consistency in this arena of policymaking have all increased the time, expertise, and energy that presidents must devote to foreign affairs. By the same token, the increasing effect of foreign policy on domestic matters has encouraged Congress to play a more active role.

Presidents usually encounter more difficulty in achieving their domestic policy goals. They can usually prevent legislation they oppose from becoming law, but getting their own initiatives enacted into law is another story. The problem stems from the constitutional system of separate institutions with overlapping powers, particularly when that system is reinforced by divided partisan control of government, political diversity within the country, and the absence of a consensus on many policy issues. To meet this challenge, presidents must state their priorities clearly, focus their administration's resources, conduct a public relations campaign, and put pressure on Congress to get their way. The task is not easy; it takes time, energy, and skillful political leadership.

Exercising presidential leadership in normal times has prompted presidents to emphasize foreign policy or create or calm crises as a means of enhancing their political capital. The war on terrorism is the latest example of a battle carried on in the name of the national interest. But using a crisis to persuade Congress and the public to follow the president's lead or to justify the exercise of unilateral executive powers is not and cannot be a permanent feature of a democratic government. It is only a short-term solution to a longer term problem: exercising strong leadership in a system designed to constrain such leadership most of the time.

In the short run, crises help the president build a public consensus; in the long run, however, if the crisis is not satisfactorily resolved within a reasonable period of time, it will generate additional conflict within the country and could become an albatross that weighs heavily on the president's leadership abilities for the remainder of the administration.

Key Terms

fast-track authority
executive orders
lame duck period
presidential pardon
clemency
amnesty
executive agreement
War Powers Resolution

State of the Union address
going public
cabinet
Executive Office of the President (EOP)
legislative clearance process
Office of Management and Budget (OMB)

statement of administration policy (SAP)
enrolled bill process
regulatory review
White House Office
constant campaign

Discussion Questions

1. What is the president's power dilemma? Is it a problem that all presidents have had, or is more applicable for contemporary presidents?

2. Today does the presidency's constitutional authority exceed its political powers or does the political power of presidents exceed their constitutional authority? Cite examples to support your answer.

3. What are the most effective tools that presidents can use to enhance their prospects for legislative success? Are these tools applicable for exerting influence within the judiciary as well?

4. Has the growth of the Executive Office of the President strengthened or weakened the president's personal influence?

5. What are some of the ways in which presidential character affects performance in office? Do you think that President George W. Bush's character had any effect on his decision to go to war with Iraq or on his domestic priorities? How has Bush's character affected his management style?

6. At what stages of the policymaking process do presidents tend to be most influential? What are the principal constraints on their ability to shape public policy?

Topics for Debate

Debate each side of the following propositions:

1. Strong presidential leadership in the American constitutional system is a contradiction in terms.
2. If presidents promise more than they can deliver during election campaigns or while in office, it is their own fault.
3. Going public hurts presidents more than it helps them.
4. The key to presidential effectiveness today is partisanship.
5. Politics not character drives presidential decision making.

Where on the Web?

American Presidency Project
www.presidency.ucsb.edu

National Archives and Records Administration (You can access the presidential libraries from this website.) **www.archives.gov**

Office of Management and Budget **www.whitehouse.gov/omb**

Miller Center Presidential Oral Histories
www.millercenter.virginia.edu

White House **www.whitehouse.gov.**

Go to **www.thomsonedu.com/thomsonnow** to learn about a powerful online study tool. You will get a personalized study plan based on your responses to a diagnostic Pre-Test. Once you have mastered the materials with the help of interactive learning tools, activities, timelines, video case studies, simulations, and an integrated E-Book, you can take a Post-Test to confirm you are ready to move to the next chapter.

Selected Readings

Cameron, Charles M. *Veto Bargaining: Presidents and the Politics of Negative Power.* Cambridge, U.K.: Cambridge University Press, 2000.

Edwards, George C. III. *On Deaf Ears.* New Haven, Conn.: Yale University Press, 2003.

Edwards, George C. III, and Stephen J. Wayne. *Presidential Leadership,* 7th ed. New York: Thomson/Wadsworth, 2006.

Greenstein, Fred I. *The Presidential Difference.* New York: Free Press, 2000.

Greenstein, Fred I., ed. *The George W. Bush Presidency: An Early Assessment.* Baltimore: Johns Hopkins University Press, 2003.

Kernell, Samuel. *Going Public,* 3rd ed. Washington, D.C.: Congressional Quarterly, 1997.

Mayer, Kenneth. *With the Stroke of a Pen.* Princeton, N.J.: Princeton University Press, 2001.

Neustadt, Richard E. *Presidential Power and the Modern Presidents.* New York: Free Press, 1990.

Rudalevige, Andrew. *Managing the President's Program.* Princeton, N.J.: Princeton University Press, 2002.

Skowronek, Stephen. *The Politics Presidents Make.* Cambridge, Mass.: Belknap Press, 1993.

Woodward, Bob. *Plan of Attack.* New York: Simon and Schuster, 2004.

Woodward, Bob, and Carl Bernstein. *The Final Days.* New York: Simon and Schuster, 1989.

Notes

[1]The other options were to establish a procedure similar to appointments, that is, removal initiated by the president with the advice and consent of the Senate; to resolve the issue individually by the statute that created the department; or, of course, by impeachment.

[2]A 1926 Supreme Court decision, *Myers v. United States,* 272 U.S. 52 (1926), written by Chief Justice and former President William Howard Taft, upheld this broad interpretation of executive authority.

[3]Presidents can issue memoranda as well to their subordinates. Memoranda can take the form of presidential determinations, which usually concern foreign policy; disapproval, which often focuses on legislation; and simply announcements or proclamations. Unlike executive orders, memoranda do not have to be published in the *Federal Register.* Although they receive less attention then do executive orders, they often have the same effect.

[4]For an extended discussion of how presidents have used executive orders, see Kenneth R. Mayer, *With the Stroke of a Pen* (Princeton, N.J.: Princeton University Press, 2001), 79–87.

[5]Ibid, 96–102.

[6]*Clinton v. Jones* 520 US 681 (1997)

[7]In his study of contemporary vetoes, Charles M. Cameron notes that only 2.3 percent of the 17,428 public bills enacted between 1945 and 1992 have been vetoed. Charles M. Cameron, *Veto Bargaining: Presidents and the Politics of Negative Power* (Cambridge, U.K.: Cambridge University Press, 2000), 46.

[8]Ibid, 49.

[9]Ibid, 68.

[10]Richard E. Neustadt, *Presidential Power and the Modern Presidents* (New York: Free Press, 1990).

[11]George C. Edwards III, *At the Margins* (New Haven, Conn.: Yale University Press, 1989).

[12]George C. Edwards III, *On Deaf Ears* (New Haven, Conn.: Yale University Press, 2003).

[13]Ibid.

[14]Roosevelt's and Reagan's success stemmed from their communication skills. Roosevelt had a reassuring tone well suited to radio; Reagan, an experienced actor, used tough language but spoke in a calm and earnest manner to convince television viewers of the merits of his policy proposals. John F. Kennedy's quick wit and pleasant appearance also projected a favorable image. In contrast, Jimmy Carter's low, monotonous singsong, Gerald Ford's and George H. W. Bush's inarticulateness, and Lyndon Johnson's and Richard Nixon's unease, particularly before a television camera, adversely affected their public persuasive skills. Unlike his father, George W. Bush has used the public forum effectively in "connecting" with his base.

[15]The electoral process also tends to inflate public hopes. In his quest for the presidency, Jimmy Carter talked in unequivocal terms about the strong, honest, purposeful leadership he would provide as president. His inability to project that type

of leadership or to make good on many of the 125 promises he had made during the campaign contributed to the sharp decline in his popularity over the course of his presidency. All presidents are judged to some extent by the promises they make, which are duly recorded by the news media, remembered by their partisan opponents, and used as criteria for evaluating performance in office.

[16]For an excellent institutional history of the Office of Management and Budget, see Shelley Lynne Tomkin, *Inside OMB: Politics and Process in the President's Budget Office* (New York: M. E. Sharpe, 1998).

[17]The chief of staff has four important responsibilities: (1) to act as an honest broker, ensuring that the president has a range of information and advice; (2) to offer recommendations to the president about decisions that need to be made and actions that need to be taken; (3) to serve as the president's political antenna and lightning rod for criticism; and (4) to exercise operational control over the White House.

[18]Take the comment of John DiIulio, the first head of George W. Bush's office for faith-based initiatives:

> There is no precedent in any modern White House for what is going on in this one: a complete lack of a policy apparatus . . . what you've got is everything—and I mean everything—being run by the political arm. It's the reign of the Mayberry Machiavellis.

> John DiIulio, as quoted in Ron Suskind, "Why Are These Men Laughing?" *Esquire* (January 2003), http:// www.ronsuskind.com/newsite/articles/archives/000032.html (accessed February 1, 2003).

Paul O'Neill, who was asked to resign as treasury secretary, was even more critical, telling author Ron Suskind that he never heard George W. Bush ". . . analyze a complex issue, parse opposing positions, and settle on a judicious path." O'Neill describes the president in meetings as silent and expressionless, uninformed and unengaged: "The only way I can describe it is that, well, the President is like a blind man in a room of deaf people." Ron Suskind, *The Price of Loyalty* (New York; Simon and Schuster, 2004), 114, 149.

[19]The administration then decided to invoke lawyer–client privilege to prevent Lindsay from testifying. Although Lindsay was an attorney he was not acting in the capacity of a lawyer in the president's defense. Again the Court rejected the claim, arguing that the privilege extended only to lawyers defending the president against a specific charge, not to government lawyers in general.

[20]John Adams, *The Works of John Adams,* vol. 1, ed. C. F. Adams (Boston: Little, Brown & Co., 1850), 289.

[21]Thomas Jefferson, *The Writings of Thomas Jefferson,* vol. 1, ed. P. L. Ford (New York: Putnam, 1896), 98–99.

[22]Why would the framers create such an ignominious position? The answer is that they wanted to ensure that the second most qualified person would be in line to succeed to the presidency if the president died or could not perform the duties of the office. Originally, the candidate with the second-highest number of Electoral College votes was to become the vice president.

In 1800, however, the presidential election ended in a tie in the Electoral College. Because the electors could not designate which position, president or vice president, they wished Jefferson and Burr to have, both candidates received the same number of votes and the House of Representatives had to determine the winner. To prevent this situation from happening again, Congress proposed and the states ratified the Twelfth Amendment to the Constitution, which requires separate Electoral College ballots for president and vice president. This modification in voting upset the logic of the framers' reasoning, because the political parties began to choose their vice presidential nominees for reasons of partisanship rather than solely on merit.

[23]After the defeat of the administration's health-care proposals, Hillary Clinton played a less visible policymaking role in her husband's administration but continued her speaking, writing, and traveling—acting as an administration spokesperson. When allegations surfaced that the president had a sexual encounter with a White House intern, she vigorously defended her husband, accusing his critics of conspiratorial behavior. Her defense elevated her stature with those who opposed the president's impeachment.

[24]Robert E. Gilbert, *The Mortal Presidency: Illness and Anguish in the White House* (New York: Fordham University Press, 1993).

[25]Stanley A. Renshon, *The Psychological Assessment of Presidential Candidates* (New York: Routledge, 1998).

[26]Ibid, 186–188.

[27]Ibid, 188–190.

[28]John P. Burke and Fred I. Greenstein, *How Presidents Test Reality* (New York: Russell Sage Foundation, 1991).

[29]Quoted in Kenneth T. Walsh, "Commander in Chief," *U.S. News and World Report* (December 31, 1990–January 7, 1991): 24.

[30]George Bush, "Press Conference," October 9, 2001, http:// www.whitehouse.gov/news/releases/2001/09/20010916-2.html; George W. Bush, "Press Conference with Italian Prime Minister," October 15, 2001, http://www.whitehouse.gov/news/releases/2001/10/20011015-3.html; George W. Bush,

"State of the Union address," January 29, 2002, http://www.whitehouse.gov/news/releases/2002/01/20020129-11.html (accessed February 3, 2002).

[31]Edwards, *At the Margins,* 213–214.

[32]The theory of the two presidencies was first proposed by Aaron Wildavsky in "The Two Presidencies," *Trans-Action,* 4 (December 1966): 7–11. It has subsequently engendered considerable debate. Much of that debate appears in Steven A. Shull, ed., *The Two Presidencies: A Quarter Century Assessment* (Chicago: Nelson-Hall, 1991).

[33]Richard P. Nathan, *The Plot That Failed* (New York: John Wiley, 1975), 40.

[34]George Bush and Brent Scowcroft, *A World Transformed* (New York: Vintage Books, 1998), 489.

[35]Gallup Poll, "Topics and Trends: Iraq," www.gallup.com./default.aspx?ci=1633 (accessed October 30, 2006).

12

The Federal Bureaucracy

Introduction

It almost seemed like "embattled" was Harvey Pitt's first name, so often had he been described that way in press reports. But anyone else in his job as chairperson of the Securities and Exchange Commission (SEC) probably would have borne the same description in the months that followed the collapse of Enron and WorldCom and the spectacular decline of public faith in the nation's financial auditing system.

Like that of many leaders in the executive branch, Pitt's professional life included stints in public service mixed with work in the private sector. After law school, he joined the staff of the SEC, the federal agency responsible for regulating the country's financial markets. He rose quickly to the position of general counsel for the agency. After highly regarded service in that position, he left for the private sector, where he practiced securities law and represented several companies regulated by the SEC. The expertise he had gained from his public service enhanced his value to clients in the private sector—a common reward for former government officials.

When President George W. Bush nominated Pitt to become the new chairperson of the SEC in 2001, it was widely hailed as an excellent appointment of a man who had experience at the agency and knew its business as well as anyone. But the bloom was quickly off the rose. Critics worried that Pitt, having been an attorney for companies regulated by the SEC, would find it hard to be a vigilant and evenhanded regulator. The worries multiplied after it became known that Pitt had held private meetings at the SEC with some of his former clients. He was forced to negotiate an elaborate ethics agreement in which he removed himself during his first year in government from decisions affecting former clients.

Then came the Enron collapse and revelations that a major auditing firm had deceived Enron investors and the financial markets. Similar revelations involving other companies soon followed. The stock market went into one of its biggest declines ever, losing trillions of dollars in value in a matter of weeks. Suddenly the SEC, invisible to most Americans since its creation during the Great Depression, was at the

center of a storm of public concern. And most eyes focused on its chairperson, Harvey Pitt. When a series of controversial decisions embroiled the agency in turmoil and reflected badly on the president who had appointed him, Pitt resigned.

This is a regular feature of bureaucratic life in America. Federal agencies perform their jobs competently in normal times, and Americans pay little attention. But when a crisis or controversy arises, a bright light shines on them. We learn the names of public servants and acquire a quick education in what their agencies do. Although the executive branch of government is the branch with which Americans have the most contact—in using the post office, obtaining student loan guarantees, renewing their passports, or paying their taxes—it rarely attracts much direct attention until bad things happen. Then people like Harvey Pitt become central figures in public life.

The federal bureaucracy is the part of government that implements decisions made by the president, Congress, and the federal courts. Many people believe that bureaucracies are complex, apolitical, and controlled by stringent rules and procedures. That is only partially true. The federal bureaucracy is certainly complex, and its activities are guided by a mystifying array of rules, but it is anything but apolitical.

Administrative offices and the people who staff them are important political actors. Having their own policy preferences and prejudices, they fight to protect and expand their vision of what is best for the country. They are not merely neutral implementers of decisions made elsewhere in the political process; they are at the center of that process, involved in the struggles among individuals, interest groups, and government institutions to affect policy decisions. One cannot understand the administration of public policy without acknowledging the fundamental political character of policy implementation. Conflict is as common an occurrence

and as profound a force in the halls and offices of federal agencies as it is anywhere else in government. The search for consensus is as challenging and elusive there as in the White House, Congress, or the courts.

When you hear the word *bureaucrat,* what images come to mind? An overweight middle-aged man sitting at a desk shuffling papers from one pile to another, or an air traffic controller bringing planes in through an ice storm? A curt woman peering out through a barred window to announce that the deadline for your application was yesterday, or a young microbiologist doing AIDS research? An anonymous person with an ink pad and stamp who sends you the wrong tax forms, or a diplomat held hostage in a small African nation?

The word bureaucrat is loosely used to describe career government employees. It often brings to mind a bored and rigid person interested only

in collecting a paycheck and putting in enough time to receive a lucrative pension. Nothing could be further from the truth. Among the millions of career government employees, many have demanding, important, and interesting jobs; most enjoy their work; and the vast majority of civil servants are expert in what they do and skillful in doing it.

This chapter looks at American public servants, the work they do, and the political environment in which they do it. The discussion begins with the complex structure of the contemporary executive branch and how that branch is staffed. Then the chapter examines the various roles that bureaucratic agencies play in the implementation of public policy. It concludes by probing the issue of bureaucratic accountability, the ability of the American people to ensure that this set of hierarchical institutions operates democratically.

Questions to Ponder

- How should the president be held accountable when one of his appointees fails?
- Should the administration of public policy be separated from partisan politics? Can it be?
- Would you want to be a presidential appointee? What are the rewards and costs of service in those positions?

The Organization of the Federal Bureaucracy

Bureaucracy is a system for carrying on the business of an organization through a clear hierarchy of authority and an emphasis on fixed routines. **Bureaucrats** are the people who perform this function. Bureaucracies have jurisdictions established by law or administrative rules, and their employees are specialists who are trained to perform the specific tasks assigned to them and who maintain written records of their decisions and activities. The purpose of bureaucracies is to achieve objectivity, precision, efficiency, continuity, consistency, and fairness.

Except for the Post Office Department, the administrative agencies of the U.S. government were few in number and small in size until the second half of the nineteenth century. Their growth began to accelerate after the Civil War as the population grew and the range of federal government activities expanded. Nevertheless, the federal bureaucracy remained a relatively small enterprise until the onset of the Great Depression and World War II. Today the executive branch is the largest component of the federal government. Its civilian employees number 2.7 million (including the Postal Service, the government-owned corporation that replaced the cabinet-level Post Office Department); its active-duty military employees come to more than 1 million; and there are more than 100 separate organizational units. Federal employees include not only clerks, soldiers, and letter carriers but also physicians, attorneys, physicists, historians, economists, accountants, and pharmacists. In size and complexity the federal executive branch is an entity without peer in American society.

Types of Organizational Structures

The federal bureaucracy is composed of many kinds of organizations. Because the labels attached to particular units do not always precisely define their functions or levels of authority, its structure is a little difficult to comprehend at first. Sometimes an "agency," a "bureau," and an "office" are indistinguishable from one another. Some agencies are subunits of cabinet departments, and others are independent from those departments. A bureau may be a small, barely visible unit like the Bureau of Justice Statistics in the Department of Justice, or it may be relatively large and highly visible, like the FBI.

Politics is responsible for this apparent confusion, because the creation of bureaucratic organizations is itself a political process. What a unit is called, where it is placed, the degree of authority it is granted, and the qualifications established for its leaders are all political decisions, usually resulting from conflict and compromise in the legislative process. These decisions reflect the balance of political forces existing at the time the unit was created. Because the balance of political forces changes over time, units created in one period often differ from units created in another.

Figure 12.1 shows the organizational structure of the entire federal government. Figure 12.2 shows the structure of a single cabinet department, the Department of Agriculture.

bureaucracy

An organization of activity based on hierarchies of authority and fixed routines. Bureaucracies have jurisdictions established by law or administrative rules. Their employees are specialists, and they maintain written records of their decisions and activities. Bureaucracies are created to achieve objectivity, precision, efficiency, continuity, consistency, and fairness.

bureaucrat

A government employee who works in one of the agencies or offices of the executive branch. Many bureaucrats in the federal government are part of the civil service.

Figure 12.1 Organization Chart of the Federal Government

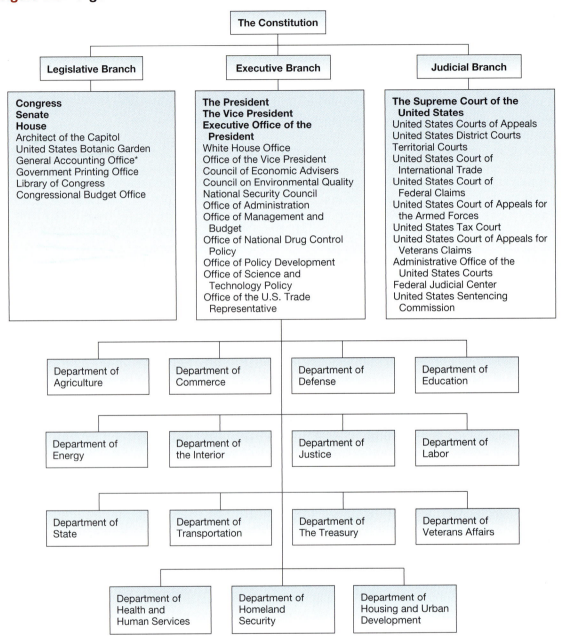

*Officially renamed Government Accountability Office, effective July 7, 2004.

Source: *U.S. Government Manual, 2004–2005 edition,* http://www.gpoaccess.gov/gmanual/browse-gm-04.html.

Figure 12.1 *continued*

Independent Establishments and Government Corporations

African Development Foundation	Federal Mine Safety and Health Review Commission	Nuclear Regulatory Commission
Central Intelligence Agency	Federal Reserve System	Occupational Safety and Health Review Commission
Commodity Futures Trading Commission	Federal Retirement Thrift Investment Board	Office of Government Ethics
Consumer Product Safety Commission	Federal Trade Commission	Office of Personnel Management
Corporation for National and Community Service	General Services Administration	Office of Special Counsel
Defense Nuclear Facilities Safety Board	Inter-American Foundation	Overseas Private Investment Corporation
Environmental Protection Agency	Merit Systems Protection Board	Peace Corps
Equal Employment Opportunity Commission	National Aeronautics and Space Administration	Pension Benefit Guaranty Corporation
Export-Import Bank of the U.S.	National Archives and Records Administration	Postal Rate Commission
Farm Credit Administration	National Capital Planning Commission	Railroad Retirement Board
Federal Communications Commission	National Credit Union Administration	Securities and Exchange Commission
Federal Deposit Insurance Corporation	National Foundation on the Arts and the Humanities	Selective Service System
Federal Election Commission	National Labor Relations Board	Small Business Administration
Federal Housing Finance Board	National Mediation Board	Social Security Administration
Federal Labor Relations Authority	National Railroad Passenger Corporation (Amtrak)	Tennessee Valley Authority
Federal Maritime Commission	National Science Foundation	Trade and Development Agency
Federal Mediation and Conciliation Service	National Transportation Safety Board	U.S. Agency for International Development
		U.S. Commission on Civil Rights
		U.S. International Trade Commission
		U.S. Postal Service

*Officially renamed Government Accountability Office, effective July 7, 2004.

Departments The major operating units of the federal government are **departments.** There are fifteen of them, each an aggregate of many related functions. The head of a department—the secretary or, in the case of the Justice Department, the attorney general—is a member of the president's cabinet. The number of departments is not fixed. In the late 1970s two new ones were added: the Department of Education and the Department of Energy. In 1988 the Veterans Administration, an independent agency, became the Department of Veterans Affairs. And in 2002, a major government reorganization created a new Department of Homeland Security.

Agencies In general, **agencies** are responsible for a narrower set of functions than departments. Some agencies exist within departments, and some are independent. The Food and Drug Administration (FDA) is part of the Department of Health and Human Services. The Federal Bureau of Investigation (FBI), another agency, is located in the Department of Justice. (Notice that agencies do not necessarily have the word *agency* in their names.) The General Services Administration and the Social Security Administration are independent agencies; they are not components of any department.

departments
The major operating units of the federal government and of the president's cabinet.

agencies
Units of the federal government with responsibility for a set of functions generally narrower than those of departments. Some agencies are independent; others exist within departments.

Figure 12.2 Organization Chart of the U.S. Department of Agriculture

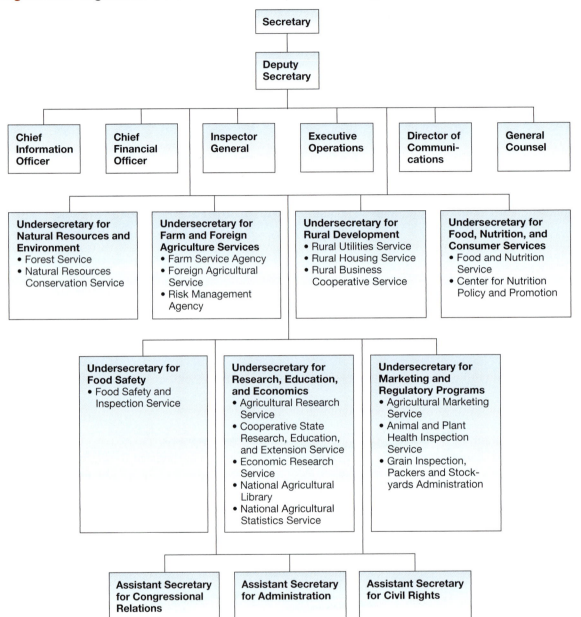

Although an agency's jurisdiction is likely to be narrower than a department's, some agencies spend more money and employ more people than some departments do. For example, the National Aeronautics and Space Administration is an independent agency that had discretionary budget authority of $16.1 billion for fiscal year 2005. The State Department had $11.3 billion in discretionary budget authority for the same fiscal year.

Bureaus, Offices, Administrations, and Services The subunits of agencies and departments have a variety of names, none denoting a set of consistent, distinguishable characteristics. In the Department of Agriculture, for instance, the Food and Nutrition Service, the Grain Inspection, Packers and Stockyards Administration, and the Office of Community Development are all located at roughly the same level of the hierarchy. The differences in their titles do not indicate significant differences in their authority or functions.

Bureaus and other subunits are the specialized operating units of the government. Their jurisdictions are defined by the programs Congress has assigned to them and tend to be quite specific. Although many of these units may exist within the same department, they do not necessarily work closely together. Often they engage in intense competition for larger budgets and more influence over policies that affect the groups they serve. The Army and the Marine Corps, for example, have often been at odds over which of them ought to have jurisdiction over land warfare, each wanting a larger share of responsibility and resources. Bureaucratic conflict is a common feature of contemporary government.

Independent Regulatory Commissions Separate from the departments and to some extent independent of the president are the **independent regulatory commissions.** Run by a group of commissioners, the commissions have both quasi-legislative and quasi-judicial authority—that is, they can issue rules and regulations and can adjudicate disputes and issue rulings. The principal purpose of a regulatory commission is to regulate commerce and trade in an assigned area of jurisdiction. For example, the SEC regulates the stock markets, and the Federal Communications Commission (FCC) regulates telephones and the use of the public airwaves for radio and television broadcasting.

Currently there are about a dozen independent regulatory commissions. Each has at least five commissioners, who serve for fixed but staggered terms. Presidents designate the chairperson of each commission but may otherwise make appointments only as vacancies occur. Thus, a president does not have the same degree of control over personnel in these units as over employees in the agencies and departments.

Government Corporations The federal government owns, wholly or partly, a variety of economic enterprises. Most of these are operated as **government corporations,** a form of ownership that is supposed to protect the enterprises against political meddling and encourage them to use businesslike and efficient methods of operation. Most government corporations have a board of directors

independent regulatory commissions
Units of the federal government whose principal purpose is to regulate commerce and trade in an assigned area of jurisdiction. Commissions are independent of any department and, to some extent, of presidential control. All are run by a group of commissioners rather than a single executive.

government corporations
Economic enterprises owned wholly or partly by the federal government; examples are the Tennessee Valley Authority and the Federal Deposit Insurance Corporation.

© AP/Wide World Photos

Local officials in Alabama prepare to meet with the U.S. Nuclear Regulatory Commission to discuss their city's interest in pursuing a license for a very small nuclear reactor.

whose members are appointed by the president, usually for long and staggered terms that make it difficult for any single president to radically change the board's composition. Nevertheless, politics sometimes influences the selection of directors of government corporations, as well as the corporations' decisions and activities. For example, President George W. Bush appointed several people with strong conservative views to the board of the Corporation for Public Broadcasting.

Most of these corporations can operate their own personnel systems, borrow money, sell stock, and even operate at a profit. Some, like the Federal Deposit Insurance Corporation and the Tennessee Valley Authority (TVA), are totally independent. Others fall within a department's jurisdiction; an example is the Commodity Credit Corporation in the Department of Agriculture.

Boards, Committees, Commissions, and Advisory Committees In addition to the major structural entities already identified, the federal government contains many units of lesser significance. Some, like the Committee for the Implementation of Textile Agreements, have narrow functions; others, like the Secretary of Energy Advisory Board, provide advice to specific officials or agencies. Few of these advisory committees have any significant effect on public policy. Rather, many of them serve primarily as places where presidents can make appointments to reward individuals for their political support. Hundreds of advisory committees are located throughout the federal government. Most people who serve on them work for the federal government only a few days each year and regard their appointments as honorific.

12.1 In Theory . . .

The Bureaucracy

Equality and justice are important democratic goals, and in any democracy the executive bureaucracy plays a critical role in accomplishing them. Equality means that all citizens are treated equally; justice means that citizens are treated fairly. Bureaucracies are charged with developing processes and rules to guarantee fair and equal treatment of citizens.

When we pay our income taxes, for example, we must fill out extensive forms that some Americans find daunting. But their purpose is to ensure that one person's tax liability is calculated in exactly the same way as another's so that two people earning similar incomes from similar sources will pay similar taxes. Federal law also requires that citizens must pay Social Security taxes for a fixed period before they qualify for Social Security benefits. The Social Security Administration, a federal agency, keeps track of everyone's contributions to be sure that all who have earned Social Security benefits receive them and that no one receives them without first earning them.

All this requires extensive and sometimes tedious record keeping. Some people call this "red tape." But would we rather live in a society where the distribution of benefits and the enforcement of regulations was inconsistent, whimsical, or—more likely—corrupt? Bureaucratic rules and the burdens they impose are among the prices democratic citizens pay for fair and equal treatment by their government.

Staffing the Bureaucracy

Before 1883, nonelective positions in the federal bureaucracy were filled by **patronage**—the distribution of jobs by winning candidates to those who had worked for their political campaign and supported their party. "To the victor go the spoils" was the rallying cry of the day, and the spoils of election victory were usually jobs in government. This use of patronage in federal employment was known as the **spoils system.**

By the latter part of the nineteenth century the spoils system had fallen into disrepute: The administration was too often in the hands of political hacks; corruption was common; and fending off job seekers was a major burden for successful politicians. In 1881 a disappointed applicant for a federal job shot and killed President James Garfield, an event that strengthened cries for reform of the federal personnel system. In 1883 Congress responded by passing the Pendleton Act, which established the **civil service system.**

The civil service system requires that two important criteria be met in hiring people for government jobs. First, jobs must be open to any citizen regardless of political preference; everyone must have an opportunity to compete. Second, civil servants must be chosen on the basis of some objective measure of their abilities—that is, on their merits. Historically the second criterion has meant qualification based on open, competitive examinations.

patronage
The distribution of government jobs as a reward for working on a winning candidate's campaign or providing other services to a party or political machine.

spoils system
The distribution of federal jobs to supporters of the victorious presidential candidate. It was the primary way of staffing the federal bureaucracy before the creation of the civil service system.

civil service system
The system for filling most federal government jobs that was established by the 1883 Pendleton Act, whereby jobs must be open to any citizen and merit must be the basis for choosing employees.

civil service
The career employees of federal departments and major agencies whose salaries and fringe benefits are determined by Congress and implemented by the Office of Personnel Management.

Senior Executive Service (SES)
The highest-ranking group of federal civil service employees, created in 1979 to provide agencies with greater flexibility in deploying, compensating, and, if necessary, removing their senior managers and technical specialists. There are now about 7,000 SES members, of whom at least 90 percent must always be career federal employees.

The Civil Service System At first the civil service system covered only a small percentage of federal employees. Gradually its coverage grew, until today it includes more than 90 percent of all federal civilian employees. About two-thirds of civil service employees are in what is known as the regular **civil service,** a group that includes most career employees of the departments and the major agencies. Regardless of where they work, their salaries and fringe benefits are determined by Congress and implemented by the Office of Personnel Management, an independent agency in the executive branch. All civil service positions are graded according to the character of the work to be done, and a pay range is assigned to each grade level.

In 1979 the **Senior Executive Service (SES)** was created to provide departments and agencies with greater flexibility in deploying, compensating, and if necessary removing senior managers and technical specialists. There are now about 7,000 SES members, of whom at least 90 percent must always be career federal employees. Although they are entitled, and sometimes encouraged, to move from one agency to another where their skills and experience are needed, most spend their entire careers in a single agency. SES members have their own pay grades, and they are eligible each year for merit pay raises and special performance and incentive bonuses.

About one third of the federal government's civilian career employees work in agencies that have merit systems similar to but distinct from the regular civil service. These agencies include the TVA, the FBI, the Public Health Service, the Foreign Service, and the Postal Service. In addition, members of the uniformed armed services are part of an entirely separate career system with its own ranks and rules. In most cases, the reasons for the existence of the separate merit systems have to do with politics and tradition. The agency merit systems work in much the same way as the regular civil service, but they have different terminology and are run by the agencies themselves, not by the Office of Personnel Management.

Once federal employees are installed in one of the government's career personnel systems, they are relatively secure in their jobs. This security is intended to protect them from inappropriate political pressures and from removal when there is a change of administration. Although career employees can be removed for inadequate performance, it is difficult for managers to prove that performance is inadequate. Because of an elaborate appeals procedure, firing a civil servant may take two years or more; as a consequence, it rarely happens.

Among the 10 percent of federal employees who are not part of the career merit system are a variety of people whose jobs are incompatible with systematic personnel procedures or competitive selection techniques. These include presidential appointees to the top positions in the government, some attorneys, faculty members at the military service academies, undercover drug enforcement agents, foreign nationals who work at U.S. installations overseas, and employees who hold short-term or summer jobs.

Political Appointees Nearly all top-level positions in the executive branch are held by political appointees. Typically, these appointees are individuals from the private sector who serve in the government for only a short time (about two years on average). Included in this group are cabinet secretaries and senior officers in each of the cabinet departments, heads of the independent agencies, and members of the federal regulatory commissions, all of whom are appointed by the president and confirmed by the Senate.

Some appointees, such as regulatory commissioners, have fixed terms of service. Most, however, serve at the pleasure of the president: They can be removed by a president who is unhappy with their performance or loyalty. In 1994, for example, Bill Clinton fired Joycelyn Elders, the surgeon general he had appointed, after she made remarks that were politically embarrassing to him.

The system of drawing the highest-ranking executive branch officials from the private sector is uniquely American. No other country relies so heavily on leaders who are not career government employees. The American approach has several advantages. It ensures a constant infusion of new creative energy and fosters responsiveness to the popular will. Moreover, the dual tests of presidential nomination and Senate confirmation promote care and judiciousness in the choice of people to fill important government offices.

But there are disadvantages as well. For one thing, leaders often lack experience or technical competence in the complex policy areas over which they have jurisdiction. Many members of regulatory commissions, for example, receive their appointments as rewards for previous support of the president. In addition, the short tenure of most appointees leads to inconsistency in administration and policy direction. Many appointees are more concerned with making an impact in a brief time than with developing management or program initiatives that may take a while to bear fruit.

In recent years the appointment and confirmation processes have become major policy battlefields. Presidents nominate individuals with the opinions and skills necessary to redirect the flow of public policy. Senators often oppose those nominations because they disagree with the policy preferences of the president or the nominees. As the battles play out, confirmation is often delayed and sometimes denied. This has made the prospect of enduring the appointment process less attractive to talented Americans. And it has made it more difficult for presidents to use the appointment power to further their policy goals.

The Executive Bureaucracy in Perspective

The bureaucracy has been developing over two centuries of practice and experimentation; it is not the product of a single blueprint. Although administrative units have been added and eliminated, merged and subdivided, the structure and location of those that currently exist reflect the political battles surrounding their origins rather than any consistent administrative theory. The personnel system shows the same inconsistencies. The head of one bureau is a career civil servant; the head of another is a presidential appointee. One must look to the political history of each bureau to explain such inconsistencies, because the process of constructing a government is no less political than the process of operating one.

In 1979, for example, Congress created a new cabinet department, the Department of Education. Among the principal proponents of this change in the structure of government was the National Education Association (NEA), a powerful organization of elementary and secondary school teachers. Opponents of the new department included another teachers' organization, the American Federation of Teachers (AFT). Whereas the NEA sought to increase its political advantage by reshaping the administration of education programs, the AFT sought to retain relationships it had already developed within the existing educational bureaucracy. After Congress had approved the creation of the new department, both organizations lobbied President Jimmy Carter to appoint a secretary who would be responsive to their individual interests. To prevent the appearance of favoring one group or one educational interest over another, Carter decided to appoint Shirley Hufstedler, a federal judge with no direct experience in educational matters.

When legislators create a new agency, their decisions about where to locate it, what to call it, and what to include in it are strongly influenced by the search for political advantage. Conflict is common to these debates; consensus is often elusive. When presidents appoint the leaders of such an agency, they too are deeply affected by the political situation of the moment. Legislators and presidents are politicians, and they are less concerned with symmetry and consistency than with policy outcomes. At their core, questions about bureaucratic organization and personnel focus on power—who has it and how it is used—not efficiency or logic.

Review Questions

1. Which of the following people could *not* be described as a federal bureaucrat?

   A. A ranger in Acadia National Park
   B. A U.S. Army lieutenant colonel in Baghdad
   C. A legislative assistant answering mail for a congressman
   D. A lawyer assessing claims for the Department of Veterans Affairs

2. The president's degree of control is lowest over which units of the federal bureaucracy?

   A. Departments
   B. Regulatory commissions
   C. Bureaus
   D. Agencies

3. What problem was the civil service created primarily to solve?

   A. The scarcity of federal jobs
   B. The lack of flexibility of the federal bureaucracy in policy implementation
   C. The poor compensation of federal employees
   D. The tendency of powerful politicians to pack the bureaucracy with friends and supporters

4. Which of the following categories of personnel are *not* found in most federal government agencies?

   A. Civil servants
   B. Presidential appointees

continued

C. Members of the Secret Service
D. Members of the Senior Executive Service

5. The first independent regulatory commission, established in 1887, was the

A. Federal Trade Commission
B. Interstate Commerce Commission
C. Federal Communications Commission
D. Securities and Exchange Commission

Answers:

1. C
2. B
3. D
4. C
5. B

Conflict and Consensus in Review

Ambiguity characterizes Americans' feelings about government. On one hand, people see the need for government; they have come to rely on its services and turn to it when problems develop that cannot or will not be resolved adequately by the private sector be it Avian flu, port security, race relations, prescription drugs, or pensions for senior citizens. Simultaneously, however, people criticize the red tape they must go through to avail themselves of government services and bemoan the inefficiency of the government's workforce and the complexity of its bureaucractic structure.

Much of the public's criticism has been directed against executive branch departments and agencies. Since 1980, and especially during periods of Republican control, there has been an antigovernment undercurrent that has pervaded the government and affected its decisions and actions. Paralleling that undercurrent, however, have been political feuds among president, Congress, and the bureaucracy, and within the bureaucracy itself over how government resources should be distributed. This conflict takes the form of fights over budgets, turfs, and implementation policies.

Thus, there is a consensus on the need for some form of government activity in most issue areas, but conflict over policy outcomes in those areas, over "who gets what, when, and how." As we have said before, that consensus and conflict is the essence of politics.

Functions of the Executive Bureaucracy

Many people assume that the executive bureaucracy merely executes policy decisions made by Congress and the president. In fact, the administrative agencies of the federal government are important participants in policymaking and implementation. Almost every public policy is shaped in some way by the characteristics and actions of the agencies that oversee its implementation.

Implementation

The principal responsibility of most public agencies is action. They are the delivery end of the policymaking process, the government's agents in dealing directly with the people (hence the name *agency*). Their task is to translate the policy objectives determined in the legislative process into goods and services that will help accomplish those objectives. They do this in several ways, including regulation, rule making, adjudication, compliance enforcement, and allocation of funds. The example that opened this chapter noted the important role played by the SEC in ensuring the honesty of corporate behavior.

Regulation   In regulating economic and social activity, agencies are guided by two primary objectives: (1) to maintain the stability of the free-market system and its openness to competition, and (2) to protect the health, safety, and welfare of the American people. The first agency designed solely to perform regulatory activities was the Interstate Commerce Commission, established in 1887 and terminated in 1995. Others have been added since. There are now few economic functions that do not fall under the regulatory jurisdiction of one or more federal agencies in what has become a heavily regulated American economy.

Contemporary regulation takes two broad forms: economic regulation and social regulation. **Economic regulation** aims to control prices, market entry, and conditions of service in specific industries. The principal objective of economic regulation is to promote competition within a single industry and protect the competitive position of individual companies. When the Antitrust Division of the federal Justice Department sued the Microsoft Corporation in 1998, for example, it was seeking to protect competition in the computer software market, not undermine it.

Social regulation aims to control the social and physical effects of a range of economic activities. It includes such objectives as protecting the environment, eliminating employment discrimination, and enhancing consumer safety. In the 1960s, public interest groups, spearheaded by the efforts of consumer activist Ralph Nader, put political pressure on Congress and the administrative agencies for greater protection of consumer welfare in such areas as automobile safety, truth in advertising, and truth in lending. Each of these initiatives found important support among the American people and yielded a stream of new regulatory legislation.

Since the late 1960s, however, there has been a significant movement toward **deregulation**—freeing some industries from the broad government control of earlier years. In the 1970s the president and Congress moved to deregulate the airline industry to stimulate competition. The principal regulatory agency, the Civil Aeronautics Board, went out of existence; price competition intensified; new airlines sprouted up; and several mergers occurred. But in the years that followed, many airlines experienced financial problems; the cost of some air travel escalated; concern about safety grew; and some people called for reregulation of the industry by the federal government.

Rule Making   Most agencies, operating within the jurisdiction granted them by Congress, have the authority to issue rules. **Rules** are best described as elaborations of the law. If the law says that you cannot fly an airplane without a pilot's

---

economic regulation
Government regulation of particular industries to correct what economists call market failures, such as natural monopolies.

social regulation
Government regulation of certain economic functions common to many or most industries to ensure that specific objectives are pursued. Typically, the process involves setting standards deemed to be in the national interest, applying those standards to all industries, and enforcing them.

deregulation
An effort begun in the late 1960s to reform the federal regulatory process by reducing or eliminating regulations that seemed to stifle competition.

rules
Edicts issued by a federal agency, after study and comment, that implement laws.

license, rules will describe in detail the steps you must take to obtain a license and the penalties you will incur if you fly without one. Rules have the force of law.

In making rules, agencies must follow procedures laid out in the Administrative Procedures Act of 1946 and its amendments. Several steps must be completed before a new rule can take effect. For example, the draft of a new rule must be published in the *Federal Register* at least thirty days before the rule is to go into effect. When the draft of the rule is published, the agency must invite public comment on it. After the comments have been reviewed (a task that may take months or even years) and any changes have been made, the rule is issued officially by being published in final form in the *Federal Register* and codified in a volume called the *Code of Federal Regulations.*

As the scope of government activity expanded in the twentieth century, so did the number of administrative rules. One measure of rule-making activity is the number of pages in the *Federal Register.* In 1960 there were 14,479 pages in the *Federal Register;* by 1979 the number was up to 71,191.[1] As a result of deregulation during the administration of Ronald Reagan, the number of *Federal Register* pages declined to 50,997 in 1984, but by 2002 it had crept back up to 74,528, the most ever.

The Reagan administration added another step to the rule-making process when it came to power in 1981. Because of the president's suspicion that government rules were interfering with private economic activity, the administration added another step to rule-making procedures. All significant rules, defined as a major policy change or having a cumulative effect of $100 million or more on the economy, had to obtain the approval of the Office of Management and Budget (OMB) before issuance. A new office, the Office of Information and Regulatory Affairs (OIRA) was established in the OMB to review proposed agency rules to make certain that they were necessary, cost-effective, and consistent with the president's program. Since its inception during the Regan presidency, this office has expanded its scope to include rules already on the books. OIRA now prompts agencies to perform a quantitative, cost-benefit analysis of existing rules to determine whether they still necessary and effective.

Adjudication No matter how diligently executive agencies strive to remove ambiguity from the rules they issue, they are never completely successful. There are always some areas of uncertainty about the application of a specific law or rule to a particular circumstance. An agency may interpret a rule to mean one thing; a corporation may interpret it to mean another. When such differences of opinion occur, the agency is often asked to hold a hearing at which the affected party appeals what it perceives as an inappropriate or unfair interpretation.

The hearings are often run like legal proceedings. Attorneys are usually present for both sides. Sometimes a hearing is presided over by an **administrative law judge,** an independent third party whose rulings are binding on both the agency and the complainant, although either side may appeal a ruling in the federal courts. Many of the rulings are published in the *Federal Register* so that other interested parties can develop a clearer picture of the application of rules and laws to specific cases.

Federal Register
A daily publication of the federal government that communicates the activities and the proposed and actual decisions of federal agencies to the American people.

administrative law judge
A quasi-independent employee of a federal agency who supervises hearings at which disputes between the agency and a regulated party are resolved. The judge's rulings are binding on both the agency and the complainant, although either side may appeal a ruling in the federal courts.

A Department of Homeland Security official assists a Mexican national as he scans his fingerprint as part of a new exit process for foreign visitors. Visitors must now record their fingerprints, have their pictures taken, and have their passport digitally recorded at their airport departure gates.

Compliance Enforcement   Ensuring that laws and rules are obeyed is one of the important tasks of executive agencies. For some—the FBI and the Bureau of Alcohol, Tobacco, and Firearms, for instance—it is the dominant concern, but virtually all agencies spend some of their efforts on compliance enforcement.

Some agencies conduct regular, scheduled inspections to ensure that agency guidelines are followed. For example, the Department of Agriculture routinely inspects food-processing facilities; the tag "USDA inspected" on food products indicates that they were processed under conditions that satisfied federal government standards. Other agencies prefer to make unscheduled inspections. The Coast Guard, for instance, stops private boats without prior notice to inspect their life-saving equipment. In addition, many government agencies employ accountants to examine the financial records of individuals, corporations, or groups to ensure that they are complying with applicable laws and rules. The Internal Revenue Service audits individual and corporate tax returns for this purpose, and the Comptroller of the Currency audits the financial records of national banks.

The imposition of reporting requirements is another way in which compliance enforcement is carried out. Institutions and corporations are required to file periodic reports on their activities. Employers must file regular reports on the number of workers they employ, the amounts they have withheld from paychecks for taxes, and other matters relevant to specific businesses. Federal contractors must file reports indicating that their employment practices are nondiscriminatory. When businesspeople complain about the "red tape" they have to endure as a result of government regulation, they often identify these reports as the principal culprits.

One other important way in which agencies oversee compliance with laws and rules is by responding to complaints. Noncompliance often harms someone, and the harmed party may bring a complaint to the government agency that has jurisdiction. If a factory is dumping more pollutants into a stream than the law permits, people who enjoy fishing in that stream may bring a complaint to the Environmental Protection Agency (EPA). If the EPA finds that the factory is indeed violating the law, it can take steps to bring the factory into compliance.

If those harmed cannot obtain satisfaction within the government, they can take their complaints to their allies on Capitol Hill, go public, or both. One of the first steps on the public route is to alert the news media to the problem. From the perspective of achieving objectivity, groups would rather have the press reveal the problem than do it themselves.

Allocation of Funds In one way or another, almost all government agencies allocate funds to purchase the goods and services necessary to implement federal programs. The awarding of contracts is one of the principal ways in which they do this. Federal contractors include construction companies that build veterans' hospitals, corporations that supply ships for the Navy, organizations that do economic research for the Treasury Department, museums that present exhibits sponsored by the National Endowment for the Arts and a variety of other individuals and organizations. and even service providers in time of war, such as the Halliburton Corporation, a major food, fuel, and security provider for the U.S. government's occupation forces in Iraq.

Policymaking

That agencies play an important role in making public policy is not surprising; agency employees are usually experts in a particular policy area. Because their day-to-day activities provide a unique vantage point for observing the strengths and weaknesses of particular programs, it is only natural for them to suggest policy changes. Soldiers who find that their rifles jam in wet weather may suggest changes in weapon design. Tax auditors who see that much revenue is being lost because of a loophole in the tax laws may recommend changes to close the loophole.

More important, agency employees have ideas of their own. Their training, their experience, and the values prevailing in their work environment shape their perceptions of the form policies should take. Agency staffs may care deeply about the policies they are responsible for, and they play an active role in trying to define and perfect them. Often they become vigorous advocates of their own views, negotiating with their superiors in the bureaucracy, with members and staff in Congress, and with their political constituencies to try to bring policies into line with their ideas. In the late 1990s, for example, statistical experts in the Census Bureau wanted the 2000 census to include "sampling" of communities that had traditionally suffered from underreporting in census counts. This approach, however, was opposed by some Republicans in Congress, who feared that sampling would lead to a larger count, and thus greater representation, of people who traditionally voted Democratic. Congressional opponents and employees of the agency negotiated for many months before agreeing on a compromise in which both sampling and traditional enumeration would be conducted and compared. The compromise was eventually scrapped by a Supreme Court decision that stipulated an actual head count was necessary for determining legislative representation and by the new secretary of the Commerce Department, who rejected the survey proposal.

Bureaucratic agencies share some of the characteristics of other institutions that participate in policymaking. Despite efforts to isolate them from partisan politics, bureaucracies are intensely political organizations. They are concerned about their own interests; they seek to enlarge their resources and protect their turf; they develop mutually beneficial long-term relationships with other political actors; and they engage in bargaining and negotiation to accomplish their objectives. The political character of the American policymaking process shapes the bureaucracy as thoroughly as it shapes Congress, the courts, the presidency, and interest group activity. But bureaucratic agencies are distinct from other kinds of government decision makers in some important ways: their hierarchical organization, their character and culture, their professionalization, and their organizational pathologies. In the rest of this section we take a closer look at each of these characteristics.

Character and Culture Bureaucratic agencies are not empty vessels into which new programs are poured. Every agency has its own character and culture, and over time it acquires certain orientations in how it implements the kinds of programs it is asked to administer, the contacts it has with the interest groups it serves, and the operating procedures it employs.

standard operating procedures (SOPs) Predetermined ways of responding to a particular problem or set of circumstances. SOPs simplify bureaucratic decisions and contribute to their consistency, but they also channel bureaucratic activity into rigid patterns and make agencies less adaptable to change.

The Labor Department is a case in point. Initially created to protect the health and safety of American workers, it quickly came to be perceived as an advocate for workers in the policymaking process. Its relationship with labor unions was symbiotic: Organized labor and the Labor Department supported each other. Thus, people opposed to the labor movement found a hostile reception at the Labor Department and either did not seek or were not offered employment there. When President George W. Bush nominated Linda Chavez to be Secretary of Labor in 2001, for example, her appointment was quickly opposed by many labor unions who thought her views were detrimental to their interests.

One of the important ways in which agencies institutionalize their biases is by reducing their work to a routine. They develop **standard operating procedures (SOPs):** predetermined ways of responding to a particular problem or set of circumstances. For example, the State Department has SOPs for dealing with foreign citizens who enter American embassies seeking political asylum. The Navy has SOPs for responding to contacts with foreign vessels in international waters. The Internal Revenue Service has SOPs for determining whether a tax return will be audited. Although SOPs simplify bureaucratic decisions and contribute to their consistency, they also channel bureaucratic activity into rigid patterns and thus make agencies less adaptable to change, especially change imposed from outside—by Congress or the president.

During the Cuban missile crisis in 1962, for example, Secretary of Defense Robert McNamara was worried about the way in which the Navy intended to carry out President John F. Kennedy's orders to blockade all shipping to and from Cuba. He posed a series of hard questions to Admiral George Anderson, the chief of naval operations, about procedures for managing a blockade at sea. Anderson waved the *Manual of Naval Regulations* in McNamara's face and said, "It's all in there." McNamara replied, "I don't give a damn what John Paul Jones would have done. I want to know what you are going to do now." Anderson ended the exchange by saying, "Mr. Secretary, if you and your deputy will go back to your offices, the Navy will run the blockade."[2]

Professionalization In recent years decision making by the executive bureaucracy has become increasingly professionalized because of the technical complexity of modern public policy. To deal with this complexity, agencies hire experts. For example, in recent years the federal government employed 150,000 architects and engineers, 10,000 physicians, 14,000 scientists, and more than 30,000 attorneys.[3] Because of their command of specific and detailed information, such experts have steadily enlarged their role in bureaucratic policymaking and widened the path into and out of government.

Striking a balance between professional advice and political realities is a constant struggle for executive branch officials. When health policy officials in the Reagan administration planned a national survey of Americans' sexual habits to assist in formulating a program to combat the spread of AIDS, political appointees at the OMB quashed the survey because they found some of its questions too controversial. Those who intervened were responding to the moral qualms of congressional conservatives on whom the administration relied heavily for support. The expenditure of taxpayer money to conduct public opinion polls is another example of professional desires for more information competing with political pressures not to spend money on inappropriate services.

Bureaucratic Pathologies The natural characteristics of bureaucratic agencies often produce certain pathologies, unhealthy conditions that adversely affect the way they approach policy decisions. These reduce the efficiency and effectiveness of some agencies and are a principal source of the criticism directed at the federal bureaucracy.

Among these is persistence, the tendency of agencies to endure long after their reason for existence has passed. Resistance to change is another bureaucratic characteristic. As noted earlier, agencies become set in their ways and tend to resist new ideas or new techniques that threaten to disrupt business as usual. Expansionism is yet another bureaucratic trait. Growth in their own budgets, workforce, and responsibilities are the changes that nearly all agencies seem to welcome because they create new opportunities for promotion, prestige, power, and policy impact—all matters of importance to bureaucrats.

Capture, the tendency of an agency to develop a symbiotic relationship with the special interests that it oversees and thus to protect rather than regulate those interests, is another potentially troublesome pattern of bureaucratic behavior. So, too, is **territorial imperative,** the irresistible urge of an agency to jealously guard its territory or turf. Indeed, the most furious conflicts that agencies wage are those with other agencies that seem to be encroaching on their area of jurisdiction. Turf clashes within the intelligence community are one reason the 9/11 Commission proposed and Congress enacted a national intelligence director to referee and minimize these turf-related issues.

Every agency suffers, at least occasionally, from some of these pathologies. They are a common part of administrative life. They add new dimensions to the political struggles within the executive branch and between executive agencies and other political actors. And they help account not only for the difficulties in imposing a rational pattern of organization on the federal executive branch but also for the problems that presidents encounter in their efforts to use the executive branch for their own purposes.

Determinants of Bureaucratic Influence

Agencies vary in their ability to affect public policy. Some, like the Marine Corps, are potent and respected. Others, like the Occupational Safety and Health Administration, are weak and maligned. Still others, like the Energy Department, are influential in some periods and less influential in others.

Many scholars have tried to identify factors that help certain agencies play a substantial role in shaping public policy. Francis E. Rourke has identified four such factors: expertise, political support, organizational vitality, and leadership. To a significant extent, the ways in which these variables combine determine an agency's impact. They are not all easily controlled, however. Sometimes agencies are under presidential orders to pursue policies that are unpopular with their political constituencies. Leadership selection is an imperfect art, and old agencies are hard to shake out of their familiar habits. Thus, it is not surprising that agencies differ—often widely—in their ability to shape public policy. In this section we look more closely at each of the key factors in an agency's ability to influence policy.

Expertise Specialized knowledge has long been regarded as bureaucracy's principal contribution to the process of government. But some kinds of expertise are more valuable than others. The more technical and specialized an agency's expertise, the greater the agency's opportunity to dominate policymaking in its area of concern. If an agency has technical capabilities that few people possess or understand, challenges to its judgment will be rare. For many years the space program was in this position. Because most of the country's experts on space

capture
the tendency of federal agencies to develop symbiotic relationships with the special interests that they oversee and thus to become protectors rather than regulators of those interests. This has been a special problem with regulatory commissions.

territorial imperative
The tendency of federal agencies to guard their area of jurisdiction against other agencies that seem to be trespassing on it.

and rocketry worked for the government, there was little opportunity for serious technical criticism of the program. Once the political decision to explore space was made, policy decisions on how to go about it were left largely to the National Aeronautics and Space Administration.

Conversely, the more widely expertise is available outside an agency, the less valuable it is likely to be as a source of agency influence on public policy. The federal agencies that specialize in economic policy, for instance, have no corner on the market of economic expertise. Their recommendations are routinely challenged by other experts, both inside and outside of government.

Political Support The more widespread and intense an agency's support in Congress, in the White House, among interest groups, and in the public mind, the greater its ability to affect policymaking in its area of jurisdiction. Agencies therefore work hard to cultivate external support. For example, they cooperate closely with the congressional committees that oversee their programs and their budgets, doing everything in their power to curry the favor of committee members. They also try to develop strongly supportive clienteles among the groups that benefit from their programs, hoping that those clienteles will generate political pressure for the continuation and growth of those programs.

During the forty-eight years that J. Edgar Hoover was its director, the FBI was remarkably successful in cultivating external support. It assisted in the production of radio programs and films that glorified its accomplishments, and it created the "Ten Most Wanted" list to dramatize its crime-busting efforts. Hoover himself devoted considerable attention to relations with his congressional overseers. As a result, FBI budget requests were rarely cut and FBI recommendations regarding crime policies were usually heeded.

Today, it is different. The FBI no longer enjoys the reputation it had in the Hoover days. Instead, the agency's bureaucratic structure, its internal operating procedures, its antiquated computer network, and its failure to anticipate the terrorist attacks of September 11, 2001, by following through on the tips it received from its own agents in the field have relegated the FBI to just one of the many federal law enforcement bodies.

The close relationships that often develop among executive agencies, special interest groups, and congressional subcommittees are called **iron triangles** or **subgovernments.** All across the government, in almost every policy area, these mutually supportive relationships exist. Some of the most powerful participants in each triangle endure year after year: the subcommittee's ranking members and staff, the agency bureaucrats, and the leaders of the special interest groups. They come to know one another well, and over time they develop understandings and procedures that allow all three points on the triangle to serve the interests of the affected constituents.

Recent changes in American political life have caused some analysts to suggest a revision of the iron triangle metaphor. Noting the growing prominence of experts in health, transportation, welfare, and many other areas of public policy, they argue that political power increasingly resides in issue networks. An **issue network** consists of specialists in a particular subject working in bureaucratic agencies at all levels of government, along with experts employed by legislative

iron triangles or subgovernments
Close, mutually supportive relationships that often develop in a particular policy area among executive agencies, special interest groups, and congressional subcommittees.

issue network
An interconnected group of specialists in a particular subject area working in bureaucratic agencies at all levels of government, along with experts employed by legislative committee staffs, interest groups, think tanks, and universities. Issue networks play an important role in developing the national policy agenda, shaping consensus about preferred policies, and directing political leaders to develop and implement new policy proposals.

Figure 12.3 **The Iron Triangle of Merchant Shipping Policy**

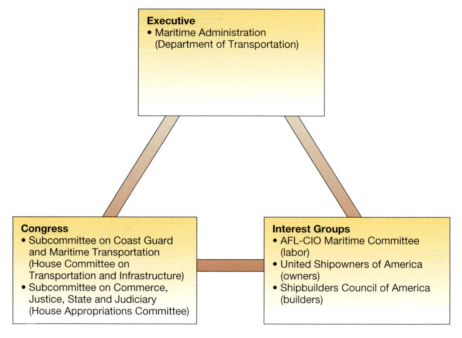

committee staffs, interest groups, think tanks, and universities. Such networks play an important role in developing the national policy agenda, shaping consensus about preferred policies, and directing political leaders to develop and implement new proposals.

To take just one example, as government struggled to address the terrifying threat of the AIDS epidemic, an issue network quickly developed. As knowledge about AIDS grew, it was widely shared among experts in and out of government. They worked together in a variety of ways to develop a sense of direction for public policy and then to put pressure on public agencies to implement that agenda. Few issues have risen to prominence as quickly as AIDS did in the 1980s.

Organizational Vitality   Like people, organizations have the capacity to stir the emotions. Such organizational vitality is most likely in an agency that is new and fresh. The agency bursts onto the scene, full of enthusiasm and staffed by bright, aggressive people carrying out a popular mission. Many of the New Deal agencies did this in the 1930s. The Peace Corps did it in the early 1960s, and so did the Army's Green Berets a few years later. A high level of vitality facilitates the recruitment of talented people and opens the budget floodgates. The president is happy to be associated with such a popular enterprise, and people are likely to defer to the agency's judgment.

The revitalizing of the Federal Emergency Management Agency (FEMA) during the Clinton presidency under the direction of James Lee Witt is another example of an agency that had been highly criticized restructuring itself and improving its capacity to deal with natural disasters. But those positive changes were later undermined when FEMA was incorporated into the new Department of Homeland Security after the terrorist attacks on September 11, 2001. Stripped of its independence and led by appointees who lacked Witt's skills and political vigor, the agency went into a decline that was starkly revealed in its ineffective responses to Hurricane Katrina in 2005.

Unfortunately, organizational vitality is difficult to sustain. The enthusiasm of an agency's youth rarely lasts. As an agency ages, it makes enemies. Its routines harden, slowing the decision-making process. The enthusiasts who ran the agency in its early days go on to other pursuits, and the quality of its performance declines. Before long the agency begins to drop back into the pack. As its vitality decreases, so, too, does its influence on policymaking.

Leadership The way an agency is run can make a difference in the way it is perceived and in the attention given to its recommendations. To improve an agency's effectiveness, leaders can boost internal morale. By providing a sense of excitement and improving the work environment, they can enhance performance. Good leaders can also be persuasive and effective in dealing with the agency's constituencies, especially the interest groups and congressional committees most concerned with the agency's programs. For example, in a study of the congressional appropriations process, political scientist Richard Fenno discovered that appropriations subcommittees were more likely to support an agency's budget request when they had confidence in its leader.[4]

During the Clinton administration, Dr. David Kessler served as head of the federal FDA. A physician who deeply believed that tobacco use was one of the country's most severe yet most correctable health hazards, Kessler led his agency in vigorous efforts to establish the link between tobacco use and illness. His office put constant pressure on tobacco companies, especially to convince them to back away from their efforts to market tobacco products to young people. In these activities, the actions of the FDA were a reflection of the intense concerns of its leader.[5]

Review Questions

1. Which of the following is *not* a characteristic of the federal rule-making process?

   A. Proposed rules must be published in the *Federal Register* at least thirty days before they go into effect

   B. Any citizen or group may comment on a proposed rule

   C. Congress has to enact legislation making a rule into a law

   D. At the end of each year, all new rules are codified in the *Code of Federal Regulations*

continued

2. A standard operating procedure is

A. A federal regulation imposed on hospitals
B. A predefined way in which government agencies handle routine or anticipated tasks
C. An injunction against regulated industries
D. The way the president fills vacancies in senior positions in the executive branch

3. Among the common characteristics of bureaucracies that sometimes lead to performance failures are

A. Persistence
B. Capture
C. Turf guarding
D. All of the above

4. If a federal regulatory commission declares a product unsafe and bans its sale, the most common recourse for the corporation that manufactures the product would be to

A. Appeal the decision in a federal court
B. Demand that another agency consider the case
C. Ask its representatives in Congress to introduce legislation reversing the commission's decision in this matter
D. Ask the president to fire the chairperson of the commission

Answers:

1. C
2. B
3. D
4. A

Conflict and Consensus in Review

Theorists of bureaucracy often maintain that government agencies and their employees should seek "neutral competence," that they should avoid politics or be above politics. In reality, that goal is rarely achieved and only infrequently pursued. Conflict is common in bureacratic decision making as it is throughout the governing process. There are clientele to be served, civil servants and poitical appointees to serve them, but competing needs and demands that government must address. Sometimes, the policy solution will produce a consensus. Most often, it does not. It will temporarily resolve the issue but not end the conflict over the allocation and cost of resources the government provides. In short, federal agencies are often as much a political venue as the Congress or the White House.

12.2 Politics in the 21st Century

E-Government

E-government. Get used to it. It's already here, and there's a lot more coming.

E-government is a term that broadly defines hundreds of initiatives under way in the federal bureaucracy to use electronic means to replace traditional ways of providing services to the American people. Examples of e-government innovations already developed include the use of electronic "smart cards" to provide identification for airport security screeners, the ability of citizens to calculate their Social Security benefits or file their income taxes online, and the convenience of making reservations at all national park campsites on a single website. It also involves internal communication within the government by officials in various agencies. For example, today most of the work of the OMB in clearing legislation and regulations is done electronically. Federal officials do not have to leave their offices to conduct the business of government. Soon they may not have to leave their homes either. Congress has enacted legislation to encourage federal officials to telecommute from their homes or telecommuting centers around the country.

Soon, many of the routine functions of the federal bureaucracy will be performed electronically. One study noted some of the possibilities:

- Exporters could fill out just one electronic form that is automatically routed to all government agencies involved in export issues.
- Individuals could bid on government surplus items online.
- Companies could file environmental compliance forms online.
- Businesses could query a computerized "expert system" to find out what regulatory requirements their particular facility faces.
- Individuals could store and access their medical information on a smart card.
- Individuals could search for federal employees through a centralized and integrated online database.
- Government officials could purchase goods using electronic catalogs.[6]

This is just the beginning. As electronic technologies mature, more opportunities for their use in government will arise. And as more Americans become familiar with the use of electronic communications, the demand for even more electronic services from government will grow.

What problems do you see with this trend? Will electronic government be better government than currently exists? What are the risks that the federal government faces as it moves to greater use of electronic technologies? And how can policymakers ensure that those risks are minimized as the transition unfolds?

Problems of Performance and Accountability

Although bureaucrats are not elected, many of them spend their entire careers in government, often in the same agency. Although they make critical decisions about the economy, human welfare, protection of the environment, and war and peace, only the most important, the most misguided, or the most blatantly corrupt of those decisions attract much public attention. Although bureaucrats operate in a political environment, they are often isolated from direct public scrutiny and public review.

That isolation is a significant concern in a democracy where public policy is supposed to serve the public interest. What can be done to ensure that bureaucratic choices will give due priority to the public interest and that bureaucrats will be held accountable for their actions? How can the checks and balances that are so essential to curb the excesses of authority be imposed on agencies and individuals whose work is so often out of public view? Chapter 11 discussed what efforts presidents undertake to control and direct the work of the executive branch. Several other approaches have been used to accomplish these objectives, including legal controls, legislative checks, press scrutiny, and finally participation by groups that comprise the agency's clientele.

Legal Controls

Bureaucratic decisions are subject to judicial review—that is, they may be challenged in the federal courts. Most legal challenges are based on one of two grounds. The first is that the agency has acted outside its legal authority or jurisdiction. The second is that the agency's decision-making process has violated one or more of the legal rights and protections guaranteed by the Constitution. If a court finds that such a challenge is valid, it can respond in several ways. It can issue a declaratory judgment against the agency, restricting its actions in specified ways. Or it can grant an **injunction**—an order that usually prohibits the agency from taking further action against the aggrieved party until certain conditions, such as another hearing, are satisfied. If the plaintiff has sued for damages, the court may also order an agency to pay a sum of money as compensation for those damages.

injunction
A prohibitory court order, such as one that prevents a federal agency from taking further action against an aggrieved party until certain conditions—a rehearing, for example—have been met.

At any given time, thousands of lawsuits are pending against federal agencies. They serve as an important control technique, but a difficult and inconsistent one. Often such suits take many years to wend their way through the courts, and the high cost of litigation deters the filing of suits by many people who have a genuine grievance. Even those who file suits are rarely satisfied, because agencies win most cases in which they are involved. That some of these suits may be frivolous complicates the problem and adds to the costs of using the judiciary to circumvention administration decisions. Legal controls thus provide an imperfect guarantee of bureaucratic accountability.

Legislative Checks

Because administrative oversight is conducted by Congress, the popularly elected branch of the government, it provides the most important guarantee of agency responsiveness to the public interest. Chapter 10 identified some of the ways in which Congress performs its oversight function. The most important of these are its review of personnel policy and presidential appointments and its ultimate control over agency budgets. Congress also exercises oversight through its central role in determining the organizational structure and location of administrative agencies. Congress determines the maximum number of people an agency may employ. It also determines the qualifications that certain executive branch officials must possess. Statutes require, for example, that the head of the Federal Aviation Administration be a civilian and that one of the members of the Federal Coal Mine Safety Board of Review be a "graduate engineer with experience in the coal mining industry."

Congress determines which positions are subject to Senate confirmation, and it has tended to expand that requirement when it has been in conflict with the executive branch. During the administration of Richard Nixon, for instance, the Senate confirmation requirement was imposed on appointments of the director and the deputy director of the OMB and the director of the FBI. In the case of most senior, noncareer appointments in the executive branch, the Senate exercises direct oversight through the confirmation power.

Congress determines the location and level of new agencies and sometimes alters these aspects of existing agencies. When it approved the establishment of the EPA as an independent agency, it did so to keep the EPA from falling under the control of one of the existing cabinet departments. Independent status was the structure preferred by most environmentalists who worked for the EPA's creation. Similarly, Congress responded to pressure from veterans' groups by elevating the Veterans Administration to cabinet status as the Department of Veterans Affairs. Organizational decisions of this sort are one of the ways in which Congress imposes its political preferences on the executive branch.

Federal Register / Vol. 70, No. 3 / Wednesday, January 5, 2005 / Rules and Regulations   1045

Section 219.8—Application of a New Plan, Plan Amendment, or Plan Revision

This provision, found in § 219.10 in the 2002 proposed rule, has been redesignated at § 219.8 as part of the overall reorganization of the final rule. This section of the final rule describes how and when new plans, plan amendments, or plan revisions are applied to new or ongoing projects or activities. The general outline and intent of this section in the final rule is similar to the corresponding section of the 2002 proposed rule. However, § 219.10(e) of the proposed rule addressing testing and research projects was removed from the final rule because the acknowledgement that these projects are subject to all applicable laws is not necessary. While the 2002 proposed rule required project or activity consistency with standards, the final rule requires consistency with the applicable plan.

Comment: Valid existing rights. Respondents were both for and against the 2002 proposed rule provision that new plan direction is subject to valid existing rights. Those in favor supported respecting these rights. Those against said that protection of ecological conditions should take precedence.

Response: The final rule at § 219.8(a)(2) is consistent with NFMA (16 U.S.C. 1604(i)) which specifies that any revision in present or future permits, contracts, and other instruments made pursuant to the act shall be subject to valid existing rights.

Comment: Consistency with the desired conditions. Several respondents commented that under the 2002 proposed rule, projects do not need to be consistent with standards; they only have to disclose the project's relationship with desired conditions. Some said that NFMA requires all projects to be consistent with the plan and said that if desired conditions are in the plan, projects need to be consistent with them. They also said the public will be disappointed to find out that plans have no "teeth." Others were concerned that the 2002 proposed rule emphasizes desired conditions and objectives, which by definition may never be attained.

Response: NFMA (16 U.S.C. 1604(i)) requires that resource plans, permits, contracts, and other instruments for use and occupancy of NFS lands be consistent with land management plans. In response to public comment, § 219.8(b) was added to the final rule to describe how projects or activities developed after approval of the plan must be consistent with applicable plan components. The Department removed

two provisions: (1) the provision limiting consistency to standards and (2) the provision requiring disclosure of the project's relationship to desired conditions.

In the final rule, if an existing or proposed project or activity is not consistent with the applicable plan, the Responsible Official must take one of the following actions: (1) Modify the existing or proposed project; (2) reject the proposal or terminate the existing project; or (3) amend the plan. The Department changed the final rule so the wording conforms to 16 U.S.C. 1604(i).

Comment: Consistency with standards. Several respondents commented on the requirements that projects or activities not consistent with standards be either modified or rejected, or the plan be amended. Some said projects should not be exempted from standards, while others said that the final rule should specify that changes must be considered within the context of NEPA.

Response: The Department changed the final rule so that projects or activities must be consistent with the applicable plan. A project or activity-specific amendment does not "exempt" a project from the plan, but rather, the amendment changes the plan for that project. If a plan amendment is necessary as part of a project or activity decision, that decision will be considered in accordance with project NEPA procedures.

Section 219.9—Public Participation, Collaboration, and Notification

This section of the final rule consolidates 2002 proposed rule provisions for public notifications and comment periods found in §§ 219.7, Amending a plan; 219.8, Revising a plan; 219.12, Collaboration, cooperation, and consultation; and 219.21, Notice of plan decisions and effective dates. A discussion of public involvement is found in the "Overview of the Final 2004 Rule" section of the preamble.

General comments: Some respondents expressed the belief that the 2002 proposed rule excludes the public from participation in the planning process, and they wanted clarification of what the public's role would be under the final rule. Some were concerned that the 2002 proposed rule no longer requires landscape goals be developed collaboratively. Additionally, some wanted a uniform process for public involvement. One person suggested the agency allow e-mail and other nontraditional forms of public participation and notification. One

respondent said the Forest Service should not allow any public participation in planning. Many supported the 2002 proposed rule requirements for public involvement. Some respondents stressed the need for open and vigorous public participation. One Tribal group supported the requirement for consultation with federally recognized Indian Tribes. Others supported a broader range of media than is currently being used for public notification. Another felt the final rule should be specific about where plans are made available and about local public meetings. Some felt that a Notice of Intent should be placed in the Federal Register for all revisions.

Response: The Department strongly supports public involvement in planning. Public participation, collaboration, and notification requirements found in §§ 219.7, 219.8, and 219.12 of the 2002 proposed rule have been moved to § 219.9 in the final rule to improve clarity and readability. The final rule states that the Responsible Official shall use a collaborative and participatory approach to land management planning. The final rule does not exclude the public from participation in the planning process. There is a wide variety of methods for public involvement. For example, where practical, Responsible Officials may give extended notice of public meetings, including the use of unit Internet web sites. It is virtually impossible at the national level to specify details for each type of public involvement used during a planning process; however, the Forest Service is developing techniques that will improve public notification and participation in the planning process. Because planners are constantly improving these techniques, other forms of direction, such as the Forest Service directives, are more appropriate ways to prescribe the "how to" details of public notification.

Neither the 2002 proposed rule nor the final rule used the cooperative development of landscape goals, because this specific activity should not be a requirement of all planning efforts. It may not always be achievable and may often be unachievable with participating groups. The Department also believes that one standard process for public involvement would not be effective for every unit in the NFS. The size and scope of issues, the interest level of the public, and the resources vary across the country. Therefore, the final rule requires the Responsible Official to involve the public, but allows discretion for the particular type of public involvement process used.

© The Federal Register

The Federal Register.

The Government Accountability Office (GAO), an arm of Congress, plays an important role in legislative efforts to control the bureaucracy. The GAO was first created in 1921 to perform financial audits of agency accounts. Over the years its functions have expanded, and now congressional committees often ask it to investigate agencies' management practices and the effectiveness of specific programs. GAO reports cover a range of subjects and often lead to congressional oversight hearings and to changes in the way agencies do business.

The most important form of legislative control is the power of the purse—the control that Congress exercises over agency budgets. Each year, agencies must appear before congressional appropriations subcommittees to present and defend their budgets. Those subcommittees then make recommendations that find their way into budget and appropriations bills.

Subcommittee decisions rarely follow the agency presentations precisely. Sometimes the subcommittees add funds for certain programs; more often they reduce funding. The subcommittee or the full Congress often shifts funds from one program to another, replacing agency and presidential preferences with those that have gained political support in the subcommittee or in Congress. One of Jimmy Carter's first initiatives on becoming president was to cut funding for nineteen dams, reservoirs, and other water development projects in different areas of the country. Because these projects were important to the representatives from those areas, however, they were able to build coalitions to support them. As a result, the projects were included in the budget that was finally enacted.

Press Scrutiny

As the watchdog of government, the news media can blow the whistle on an agency that is not performing its mission appropriately, is beset by internal tensions, may not be using its funds wisely, or is granting special favors or status to certain groups. The press often will be alerted to a problem by a source within the agency who requests anonymity. The attention that the news media bring to the issue forces the agency to correct the problem or deny that it exists. Examples of press scrutiny that have resulted in correcting past behavior or current decisions include revelations about the Air Force contract with the Boeing Company to lease planes, breeches in national security at the Los Alamos National Laboratory in New Mexico, and fraud, waste, and abuse in the Medicare system. By pointing out the tensions and difficult working relationships among the CIA, FBI, and Department of Defense in the intelligence arena, the news media contributed to the changes that resulted in a national intelligence director overseeing and coordinating the nation's intelligence agencies.

Popular Participation

The opportunity of the American people to know about, participate in, and respond to bureaucratic decisions is greater now than it has ever been. Part of the reason for this increase in popular participation is the constantly expanding access to employment in federal agencies. Most federal jobs are now filled through competitive procedures open to all citizens, and equal opportunity and affirmative action programs are designed to ensure the inclusion of female and minority employees in every agency. Moreover, the dispersion of agency staffs into local and regional offices around the country has enhanced geographic representation among federal employees.

Agencies also take steps to encourage public comment on the issues they confront. Often they hold hearings in Washington and elsewhere before making preliminary decisions on new rules or regulations. The Administrative Procedures Act requires that proposed rules be published to permit public comment; so-called **sunshine laws** require that important agency meetings and hearings be open to the public; and the Freedom of Information Act of 1967 permits public access to all but the most sensitive government documents.

sunshine laws
Laws requiring important meetings and hearings of federal agencies to be open to the public.

When agencies take actions that threaten the public interest, they are often called to account by groups representing the public. There is a network of public interest groups—such as Common Cause, environmental groups, and the organizations founded by consumer advocate Ralph Nader—that monitor agency decisions and are quick to criticize those that seem to favor special interests at a high cost or danger to the public. Other groups with special interests that may be adversely affected by bureaucratic actions also launch public relations campaigns aimed at increasing bureaucratic accountability and convincing the bureaucracy to change its ways.

Reform

The federal bureaucracy is constantly changing. Agencies and departments reorganize their operations when their missions change or evolve or as new leaders arrive. New systems for assessing the performance of bureaucrats and new approaches to compensating them and managing their careers are constantly discussed and occasionally implemented. And once every generation or so, a major reform of the bureaucracy is undertaken.

After World War II, the first and second Hoover Commissions, named after former President Herbert Hoover who served as their chairperson, recommended several changes in the way the federal bureaucracy was organized and operated. In 1978, President Jimmy Carter proposed and Congress passed another major reorganization of the civil service. President Bill Clinton sought improved performance in the executive branch, and at his initiative the Congress passed the Government Performance and Results Act of 1993.

Initiatives of this sort usually seek to make bureaucratic operations more efficient and less costly, give managers more authority to deploy their resources in the most effective ways to solve the problems they face, and tie the compensation of government employees to their performance.

But reform of the bureaucracy is never easy, and most reform efforts fall short of their goals. Government employees often resist change because they fear that it will diminish their authority or interfere with traditional practices and procedures. Members of Congress often resist reforms that threaten their jurisdictions over certain agencies or programs. The powerful labor unions that represent federal employees oppose changes that would give managers more freedom to set pay levels for or punish their subordinates. And presidents, in view of all this, are often unwilling to invest the time and energy necessary to accomplish bureaucratic reforms that are unlikely to have much short-term effect on their administration's priorities.

Nonetheless, during the Clinton presidency, a major initiative, headed by the vice president, was established to "reinvent government." Referred to as the National Performance Review, one of its principal objectives was to increase the discretion that agencies had in performing their functions. President George W. Bush also proposed a program, modeled on practices in the private sector, to increase the efficiency of government.

The Adequacy of Controls

As the U.S. government's reliance on bureaucracies grows and the complexity and power of bureaucracies increase, the need for effective control mechanisms becomes more acute. Bureaucracies are crucial to efficient management of the national government because of their expertise and their ability to simplify complex tasks and make them routine. To obtain those benefits, however, Congress and the president have to delegate considerable authority and discretion to bureaucratic agencies. Delegation creates the problem of ensuring that authority and discretion are used in the public interest.

That is no easy task. Effective checks and balances, ever difficult to create and sustain, are especially elusive in the web of relationships that enmesh the bureaucratic agencies of the executive branch. The executive bureaucracy is huge; many of its functions are technically complex; and some of its functions must be conducted in secret. Moreover, the routine and repetitive nature of much government work encourages bureaucrats and other political actors to develop and maintain enduring and mutually beneficial relationships. The desire to sustain these relationships and the shared rewards they produce often inhibits efforts to control bureaucratic activity.

Review Questions

1. The federal agency that performs financial audits of other government agencies is the

    A. IGA
    B. FAA
    C. GAO
    D. AGFA

2. Which of the following approaches is never used by Congress to control the performance of executive agencies?

    A. Confirming the appointments of agency leaders
    B. Setting agency budgets

continued

   C. Having agency heads placed under arrest
   D. Requiring periodic reports on agency activities

3. Sunshine laws

   A. Require the federal weather bureau to report their forecasts to radio and television stations
   B. Determine when daylight saving time will start and end
   C. Set environmental conditions for workers in federal offices
   D. Provide opportunities for citizens to obtain information about government

Answers:

   1. C
   2. C
   3. D

Conflict and Consensus in Review

People agree on the need for government to be efficient and effective, but achieving both is a difficult and, often, elusive undertaking. It is hard to strike the proper balance between giving bureaucracies the freedom and encouragement they need to be effective and retain sufficient control to redirect them when they go astray. And those who seek change in bureaucratic structures and processes or in the outcomes of bureacratic decision making often encounter intense poltical conflict from those who benefit from the status quo. There is no right way to reform the bureaucracy; structural and process changes have costs and consequences that the news media, special interest groups, and the public calculate differently depending on their needs and interests. Organizational stability or change is always subject to a political calculus.

Politics in Action

Why Is Smokey the Bear Crying?

It was the summer of 2002 and the West was burning. Or so it seemed. Day after day, forest fires burned out of control, first in Colorado, then in New Mexico and California. The news brought pictures of flames leaping from tree to tree, of smoke billowing into the clouds, of exhausted firefighters, exasperated governors, and—most of all—terrified people watching the fires creeping down mountainsides toward their homes.

Forest fires, or wildland fires as they are called by the experts, are a fact of life in heavily wooded areas. They are a special concern in the American West, where forests are abundant, rainfall is slight, and increasing numbers of Americans have built homes in and around areas of natural beauty.

Wildland fires are also an important matter of public policy, both in Washington and in state capitals. Fires threaten citizens' lives. They destroy valuable timber crops. They cost money. For all those reasons, federal and state governments have wildland fire policies. And wherever policy

continued

Politics in Action *continued*

Fire rages through a wooded area as the Biscuit Fire burns near O'Brien, Ore., August 4, 2002.

is made in America, there is conflict—conflict among the varied interests affected by such policy.

In wildland fire policy, the range of concerned interests is broad. It includes the federal agencies that manage most of the forest land; the timber companies that seek to make a profit by harvesting from that land; the people employed by those companies, whose livelihood depends on the forests; the backpackers, campers, and others who enjoy the natural beauty of the forests and mountains; the homeowners in areas surrounding and in forest land; the governors and members of Congress who represent the states where fires are most common; and the environmental groups that cherish wilderness and species preservation. All of them are vitally interested in wildland fire policy. And they disagree.

Many federal agencies have jurisdiction over the lands on which fires occur most often. The U.S. Department of Interior includes the Bureau of Land Management, which has jurisdiction over millions of acres of western land owned by the federal government. It implements policies established by law for the management of that land, trying to balance protection of the resources there with encouragement of prudent exploitation of those resources.

The National Park Service is also part of the Interior Department. It has jurisdiction over land that has been designated as national parks. One of the worst wildland fires of recent years occurred in Yellowstone National Park in Wyoming in 1988; 800,000 acres were burned.

Other Interior Department agencies, such as the Fish and Wildlife Service and the Bureau of Indian Affairs, also have responsibilities that directly engage them in wildland fire policy. But the most important agency in setting wildland fire policy, the U.S. Forest Service, is part of the Agriculture Department, not the Interior Department. The Forest Service was created in 1905 during the administration of Theodore Roosevelt. Roosevelt had lived in the West and was deeply interested in its development and its protection. The mission of the Forest Service was to protect the forests from timber companies by imposing rational forest management plans. That the Forest Service ended up in the Agriculture Department reflects the prevailing view at the

continued

Politics in Action *continued*

time that timber was a crop and should be managed like other crops.

But over the years the relationship between the Forest Service and the timber companies grew closer. Instead of closely regulating the practices of the timber companies, the Forest Service came to support the companies, often with subsidies worth hundreds of millions of dollars, especially in the form of road construction that gave the companies greater access to the forests. The Forest Service received ample political support for this policy from members of Congress representing states and communities where wood-related businesses such as timber, plywood, pulp, and paper were staples of the local economy.

In 1945 the Forest Service started a national advertising campaign using the figure of Smokey the Bear as its symbol. Smokey reminded us to be careful in the forest and that "Only you can prevent forest fires." Smokey became a national icon, and the benign symbolism contributed to an image of the Forest Service as a public-spirited agency.

But as the environmental movement emerged and expanded over the last three decades of the twentieth century, the policies of the Forest Service became a subject of much debate. Was the Forest Service dedicated to protecting the national forests and sustaining them for the long term? Or was the agency so closely connected to the timber industry that its policies were really designed to help that industry maximize profits even if that caused long-term harm to the value of the forests?

This larger debate was the context for much of the focused debate over wildland fire policy. In its early decades, the Forest Service followed a policy of fire suppression. Whenever forest fires erupted, the Forest Service would devote its resources to putting them out. This was widely regarded as a policy that benefited the timber products industry because it prevented the destruction of unharvested wood. And to most people who lived near forest tracts or enjoyed hiking or camping in them, the policy seemed sensible enough. For most Americans, the normal response to fire is to try to suppress it.

But scientific studies began to challenge this policy after World War II. Fire is natural to forests, the studies argued. In the life cycle of a forest, fire plays an important part.

Forests need to be thinned so that sunlight can reach the ground and aid new growth. Fire destroys pests, and the ashes from fire provide important nutrients for soil. Some plants even depend on fire to germinate their seeds.

Responding to the combination of scientific argument and pressure from environmental groups, the Forest Service began to reexamine and alter some of its policies. By the end of the twentieth century, a new doctrine had emerged: fire was good for the forest. But the problem then was how to control fire so that it did not explode out of control and devastate forests or threaten human lives and communities.

In 1996, an interagency task force representing all relevant federal agencies issued a new federal fire policy based on the key principles of firefighter and public safety, fire management plans, and resource management plans and implementation.[7]

A new centerpiece of Forest Service policy was the use of "prescribed fires," fires that are planned and set by the Forest Service. As part of a forest management plan, the Forest Service designates areas that may have accumulated a "fuel load" of dead trees and underbrush and are thus vulnerable to natural fires that could easily burn out of control. By setting prescribed fires, the Forest Service hoped to reduce the vulnerability by burning in a controlled way.

That's the theory. But it has plenty of critics. Some objected to the policy out of the fear that prescribed fires can get out of control. One of the worst wildland fires of recent years, for example, was a prescribed fire started in New Mexico in 2000 that spread to more than 50,000 acres and destroyed more than 200 homes. Others, including many in the timber industry, argued that timber harvesting is a better way than prescribed burning to manage the forests. But those advocates are, in turn, criticized by environmentalists, who point to scientific evidence that devastating fires occur more often in forests that have been harvested than in those left in a natural state.

Environmental groups, although active in this debate, are not unanimous in their opinions about fire policy. Most, however, generally support planned burning as an alternative to logging.

State governors want a wildland fire policy that protects the resources of their states. Timber companies want

continued

Politics in Action *continued*

minimal government interference with their access to forests and the practices they employ there. Citizens who live in vulnerable areas want their homes and their lives protected. Environmental groups want preservation and sustainability and protection of species habitat. And caught in the middle of these conflicting interests are the U.S. Forest Service and other federal agencies that bear responsibility for developing rational forest management policies. It's task that would make even Smokey the Bear cry.

What Do You Think?

1. Should management of the national forests be the responsibility of the Department of Interior or the Department of Agriculture?
2. Should federal policy encourage timber harvesting in the national forests to strengthen local economies and provide jobs? Or should it limit timber harvesting to preserve the forests in a natural state and protect the species that live there?
3. If you were the head of the Forest Service, what wildland fire approach would you adopt?
4. What role, if any, should state governors have in setting wildland fire policy?
5. What obligations should the federal government have to protect the homes and lives of citizens who build in areas they know to be highly vulnerable to forest fires? Should the Forest Service be required to pay the costs of protecting those homes from wildland fires? Should permission from the Forest Service be required before people build homes in areas prone to fires?

Summary

We began this chapter by stating the obvious. Government needs to implement policy in a fair and equitable manner; on this point there is consensus. But the implementation of policy is fraught with political conflict. The conflict is between the beneficiaries of these policies and those who shoulder the costs. After presenting the struggle inherent in the politics of implementation, we turned to the structures and procedures that the executive branch uses to achieve efficient and effective administration of public policy: 15 departments and more than 150 executive and independent agencies, commissions, boards, corporations, and other units that comprise the executive branch and employ about 3 million people.

Before 1883, nonelective positions in the federal bureaucracy were filled by patronage. People who had supported winning candidates received government jobs in what was known as the spoils system. Calls for reform led to the establishment of the civil service system, in which federal employment is based on merit rather than on political considerations. The regular civil service now includes most career employees of the departments and the major agencies. All civil service positions are graded according to the character of the work to be done, and a pay range is assigned to each grade level. The positions of senior managers and technical specialists are covered by the Senior Executive Service, which has its own pay grades.

Nearly all top-level positions in the executive branch are held by political appointees. Most of them can be removed by a president who is unhappy with their performance or loyalty.

The primary task of federal agencies is to interpret and implement the public policies that emerge from the legislative process. They do this in several ways, one of which is regulation. Economic regulation aims to control prices, market entry, and conditions of service in specific industries. In recent decades there has been a movement toward deregulation of some industries. Social regulation is concerned with such matters as environmental protection, equal employment opportunity, and product safety. The emphasis on social regulation in recent decades has greatly expanded the scope of federal regulatory activity. Most agencies have the authority to issue rules, or elaborations of laws. The draft of a new rule must be published in the *Federal Register* at least thirty days before it is to go into effect. The agency invites and reviews public comment on the rule and then publishes the rule in its final form. Executive agencies perform quasi-judicial functions when they hold hearings to resolve conflicting interpretations of a rule. Bureaucratic policymaking is influenced by the distinctive characteristics of bureaucracy. The character and culture of an agency affect the policies it generates, and the biases of an agency may become institutionalized in its standard operating procedures. In recent years, decision making by the executive agencies has become increasingly professionalized. As a result, striking a balance between professional advice and political realities is a constant struggle for the hearts and minds of executive branch officials as is overcoming certain pathologies, or unhealthy characteristics that are the product of large bureaucratic organizations. Among these are persistence, resistance to change, expansionism, capture, and territorial imperative.

Several factors determine an agency's ability to affect public policy; they include expertise, political support, organizational vitality, and leadership. The more technical and specialized an agency's expertise, the greater its opportunity to dominate policymaking in its area of concern. Similarly, the more widespread and intense an agency's external political support, the greater its ability to affect policymaking. Agencies try to develop supportive clienteles among the groups that benefit from their programs. The resulting close relationships among agencies, interest groups, and congressional committees are called iron triangles or subgovernments. However, recent changes in American political life suggest that political power increasingly resides in issue networks consisting of specialists in a variety of public and private agencies. The bottom line, however, is that public and private sectors overlap and interact in the policy implementation stage much as they do in policymaking. People move into government from the private sector and out of government to the private sector, a movement we refer to as revolving-door politics.

Several approaches have been used to make bureaucratic agencies more accountable to the public. Bureaucratic decisions are subject to judicial review, and courts can issue a declaratory judgment against an agency, grant an injunction that prevents it from taking certain actions, or order it to compensate a plaintiff for damages. Legislative checks on the bureaucracy include congressional review of personnel policy and presidential appointments, control of the structure of administrative agencies, and control over agency budgets. Sunshine laws require important agency meetings and hearings to be open to the public. Other sources of pressure for accountability are the activities of public interest groups, investigative journalism, and whistleblowers within the government.

Key Terms

bureaucrat	civil service system	standard operating procedures
bureaucracy	civil service	(SOPs)
departments	Senior Executive Service (SES)	capture
agencies	economic regulation	territorial imperative
independent regulatory	social regulation	iron triangles or
commissions	deregulation	subgovernments
government corporations	rules	issue network
patronage	*Federal Register*	injunction
spoils system	administrative law judge	sunshine laws

Discussion Questions

1. What image comes to your mind when you hear the term *bureaucrat?* What is the source of that image?
2. With which federal and state government bureaucracies do you have the most contact? How well do those agencies perform in your opinion?
3. How has the federal government grown since World War II, and what have been the most important causes of that growth?
4. What are the advantages and disadvantages of a civil service? Why did the United States make the change from a "spoils system" to a civil service at the end of the nineteenth century?
5. What are the qualities a president should look for in choosing political appointees to staff the top positions in an administration?
6. Is the American economy overregulated by government, is it not regulated enough, or is the current pattern of regulation about right?

Topics for Debate

Debate each side of the following propositions:

1. Many of the top positions in government should be filled by career civil servants rather than presidential appointees, as is now the case.
2. Filibusters should not be permitted for presidential nominations to the executive branch.
3. To avoid conflict of interest, no regulatory commission should include commissioners who ever worked in the industry they are regulating.
4. Congress should not be permitted to provide any funding for an agency in amounts larger than the president requests in his annual budget.
5. Congress should have the power, by majority vote of both houses, to force the removal of any executive branch employee with whose performance it is dissatisfied.

Where on the Web?

Federal Register **www.gpoaccess.gov/fr/index.html**

Statistical Abstract of the United States
www.census.gov/statab/www

U.S. Government Manual **www.gpoaccess.gov/gmanual/index.html**

Go to **www.thomsonedu.com/thomsonnow** to learn about a powerful online study tool. You will get a personalized study plan based on your responses to a diagnostic Pre-Test. Once you have mastered the materials with the help of interactive learning tools, activities, timelines, video case studies, simulations, and an integrated E-Book, you can take a Post-Test to confirm you are ready to move to the next chapter.

Selected Readings

Dickson, Paul. *The New Official Rules.* Reading, Mass: Addison-Wesley, 1989.

Donahue, John. *Making Washington Work: Tales of Innovation in the Federal Government.* Washington, D.C.: Brookings Institution, 1999.

Goodsell, Charles. *The Case for Bureaucracy: A Public Administration Polemic.* Washington, D.C.: CQ Press, 2003.

Ingraham, Patricia Wallace. *The Foundation of Merit: Public Service in American Democracy.* Baltimore: Johns Hopkins University Press, 1995.

Kettl, Donald F. *The Transformation of Governance: Public Administration for Twenty-First Century America.* Baltimore: Johns Hopkins University Press, 2002.

Khademian, Anne M. *Working with Culture: The Way the Job Gets Done in Public Programs.* Washington, D.C.: CQ Press, 2002.

Light, Paul C. *The Tides of Reform: Making Government Work, 1945–1995.* New Haven, Conn.: Yale University Press, 1997.

Reich, Robert B. *Locked in the Cabinet.* New York: Random House Publishers, 1998.

Shafritz, Jay M., and Albert C. Hyde, eds. *Classics of Public Administration,* 4th ed. Belmont, Calif.: Wadsworth Publishing, 1996.

Wilson, James Q. *Bureaucracy: What Government Agencies Do and Why They Do It.* New York: Basic Books, 1991.

Notes

[1]George J. Gordon, *Public Administration in America,* 2nd ed. (New York: St. Martin's, 1982), 494.

[2]Reported in Graham T. Allison, *Essence of Decision: Explaining the Cuban Missile Crisis* (Boston: Little, Brown & Co., 1971), 131–132.

[3]Kenneth J. Meier, *Politics and the Bureaucracy: Policymaking in the Fourth Branch of Government* (Monterey, Calif.: Brooks/Cole, 1987), 65.

[4]Richard F. Fenno Jr., *The Power of the Purse: Appropriations Politics in Congress* (Boston: Little, Brown & Co., 1966), 288, 337.

[5]See David A. Kessler, *A Question of Intent: A Great American Battle with a Deadly Industry* (New York: PublicAffairs Books, 2001).

[6]Robert D. Atkinson, "Digital Government: The Next Step to Reengineering the Federal Government," http://www.netcaucus.org/books/egov2001/pdf/digigov.pdf (accessed February 17, 2005).

[7]U.S. Department of Agriculture, Forest Service, *Federal Wildland Fire Policy,* 1996, www.fs.fed.us/land/wdfire3.htm (accessed February 17, 2005).

13

The Judiciary

Introduction

Few symbols evoke more powerful responses among Americans than a burning cross—especially in the South, where a torched cross was long a symbol of racial oppression and hatred.

As the civil rights revolution unfolded across the South, some jurisdictions took legal steps to banish this deeply evocative reminder of an unhappy history. The State of Virginia was one of the first to do so; more than a half-century ago, the Virginia legislature enacted a statute that made it a crime to burn a cross "with the intent of intimidating any person or group of persons."

When several separate incidents of cross burning brought this law under judicial scrutiny, it raised a powerful constitutional question: Did Virginia's effort to prohibit cross burning trespass on the First Amendment's protection of freedom of speech? That is, is cross burning a constitutionally protected form of free expression?

Several defendants, who had been convicted in Virginia state courts of violating the law by burning crosses, appealed their convictions to the Virginia Supreme Court. That court consolidated the cases to focus on the central issue of free expression. Guided by a precedent set by the U.S. Supreme Court, the Virginia court overturned the convictions and found the statute unconstitutional because "it discriminates on the basis of content and viewpoint since it selectively chooses only cross burning because of its distinctive message; and [thus] chills the expression of protected speech."

The State of Virginia, seeking to protect one its laws, appealed this decision to the U.S. Supreme Court in the case of *Virginia v. Black*.[1] The nation's highest court ruled in April 2003, reversing the decision of the Virginia court on the central issue and upholding the constitutionality of the Virginia statute.

But as is common these days, the Supreme Court split narrowly. A slim majority of five of the nine justices believed that Virginia did not violate the First Amendment in prohibiting cross burning. The other four justices disagreed with the majority's conclusions or logic. Hence, by a single vote a Virginia statute survived judicial review and the meaning of the First Amendment's free speech guarantees was newly refined.

Justice Sandra Day O'Connor wrote the majority opinion; in it she noted that

> The protections the First Amendment affords speech and expressive conduct are not absolute. This Court has long recognized that the government may regulate certain categories of expression consistent with the Constitution. . . . [A] prohibition on true threats protects individuals from the fear of violence and the disruption that fear engenders, as well as from the possibility that the threatened violence will occur . . . . Resp-ondents do not contest that some cross burnings fit within this meaning of intimidating speech, and rightly so. As the history of cross burning in this country shows, that act is often intimidating, intended to create a pervasive fear in victims that they are a target of violence.[2]

The First Amendment, like most of the Constitution, has been the supreme law of the land for more than two centuries. But its meaning is constantly evolving as new issues arise and new interpretations are required.

With reverence is how Americans regard their Constitution in general and the protection of their basic rights in particular. Ask Americans whether the

Constitution should be modified and the protections of the Bill of Rights qualified, and most will look at you unbelievingly and say "no." Ask them if they would abolish the federal judiciary, limit the Supreme Court's power to interpret the Constitution, or reduce the lower courts' discretion in rendering judgments within the framework of precedence, and you will receive a similar reaction. Americans overwhelmingly approve of their Constitution, the federal judiciary's role in interpreting it, and the Supreme Court's position as the final judicial decision maker. The Constitution's adaptability to changing times is cited as a strength, as is the judiciary's resistance to making decisions on the basis of political factors, reinforced by partisan pressures.

Where Americans disagree is over the courts' decisions themselves. They disagree over the scope of judicial authority, especially when it impinges the judgments of elected officials. And Americans disagree over the extent to which people should use the courts to circumvent legislative and executive policy decisions.

Moreover, anger at particular judges for their verdicts and sentences is not uncommon. After all, courts are human institutions. Their members have personal histories, political views, and ideologies. They differ in how they interpret precedent and apply it to contemporary conflicts that find their way into the judicial arena. These interpretations are part and parcel of the politics of judicial decision making. Although unique in form, it is as much

a part of the democratic process in America as electoral, legislative, or executive politics.

This chapter begins by focusing on the organization and operation of courts and the politics of judicial federalism. It looks at the power of judicial review, the politics of selecting and appointing judges, the judicial process, and the Supreme Court. Finally, it examines the politics of judicial decision making and explores the interaction between courts and other political institutions. In all these areas, courts are common areas of democratic conflict and the judges who lead them are in constant, although sometimes unsuccessful, pursuit of democratic consensus.

Questions to Ponder

- Why does the federal Constitution supercede state laws when the two are in conflict?
- Why does the burning of a cross raise First Amendment issues? Why would the Court overturn a ban on flag burning but uphold a ban on cross burning?
- In making a decision like the one in this cross burning case, the Supreme Court is making public policy. Is it also usurping legislative authority?
- Should individuals and groups be able to use the judicial system to resolve disputes over policy issues? Where should the lines be drawn between the court's power to render legal judgments and the legislature and executive's power to decide political questions and render policy judgments?
- Who needs the judiciary more, those in the majority or those in the minority?

New technologies now play an important role in criminal prosecutions and in court proceedings.

Judicial Federalism

In most countries there is a single, unitary system of courts, but in the United States judicial power is decentralized and divided between two separate sets of judicial systems. Alongside the federal judiciary, each of the fifty states has an independent judiciary. Within both the federal and the state systems, judicial power is further divided between trial courts (and other lesser courts such as traffic courts) and one or two levels of appellate courts, which hear appeals from the lower courts. (The organization of the federal judicial system is shown in Figure 13.1.)

In this dual system, called **judicial federalism,** the federal courts largely consider disputes over national law and state courts consider only disputes arising under state law. If there is a conflict between national and state laws, the matter is settled by the federal courts and ultimately by the Supreme Court. This is so because the Constitution and federal law are supreme over state law.

Federal Courts

Article III of the Constitution vests judicial power "in one Supreme Court, and in such inferior courts as Congress may from time to time ordain and establish." Courts created under Article III are called **constitutional courts.** In addition, under Article I Congress may create **legislative courts** to carry out its own powers. The U.S. Court of Military Appeals, which applies military law, is one such court;

judicial federalism
The dual judicial system in the United States, consisting of a system of federal courts and separate judicial systems in each of the fifty states.

constitutional courts
The U.S. Supreme Court and other federal courts created under Article III of the U.S. Constitution, which gives Congress the power to establish "inferior courts" below the Supreme Court. Federal district courts and courts of appeals are constitutional courts and have general jurisdiction over virtually all matters of federal law.

legislative courts
The courts created by Congress under Article I of the U.S. Constitution and having jurisdiction or authority over particular areas of law. The U.S. Court of Military Appeals, which applies military law, is one such court.

federal bankruptcy courts are another type of legislative court. These courts have more specialized jurisdiction than those created under Article III, and their judges do not hold lifetime appointments.

In 1789 Congress divided the country into thirteen districts (one in each state) and created a federal district court for each. **District courts** are the trial courts of the federal system. In addition, the Judiciary Act of 1789 created three federal **courts of appeals** to hear appeals from decisions of district or state courts. But Congress did not provide for any appellate court judges. Instead, these courts were staffed by two Supreme Court justices who twice a year sat with a district court judge to hear cases. The federal courts of appeals were not staffed by full-time appellate judges for another 100 years.

As the country grew, so did the number of district courts, along with the number of appeals of their rulings to the Supreme Court. Eventually the workload of the Supreme Court became too large for the justices to handle. Congress responded in 1891 by creating the circuit courts of appeals, which now hear most of the appeals coming from the federal district courts or from state courts. Today, aside from legislative courts, the federal judiciary consists of ninety-four district courts, thirteen courts of appeals, and the Supreme Court.

district courts
The trial courts of the federal judicial system. There are ninety-four federal district courts, at least one in each state.

courts of appeals
The courts within the federal judicial system that hear appeals of decisions of lower courts, state courts, or administrative agencies. There are thirteen courts of appeals.

Figure 13.1 The Organization of the Federal Judicial System

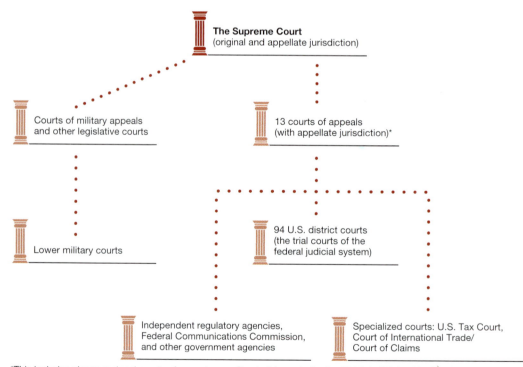

The Supreme Court
(original and appellate jurisdiction)

Courts of military appeals and other legislative courts

13 courts of appeals
(with appellate jurisdiction)*

Lower military courts

94 U.S. district courts
(the trial courts of the federal judicial system)

Independent regulatory agencies, Federal Communications Commission, and other government agencies

Specialized courts: U.S. Tax Court, Court of International Trade/ Court of Claims

*This includes eleven regional courts of appeals, one Court of Appeals for the District of Columbia Circuit, and one Court of Appeals for the Federal Circuit.

District Courts

There is at least one federal district court in each state and at least one judge is assigned to each court; the number of courts depends on the state's population, and the number of judges on the size of the court's workload. In 2004, there were 679 district judges in all. Every judge has the assistance of one law clerk, one or two secretaries, and additional research and clerical staff if needed. In criminal cases, district courts may also use a grand jury (a jury consisting of more than twelve jurors) to determine whether to indict individuals and a petit jury (a twelve-member jury) to try individuals who are indicted (see Chapter 4).

District judges preside over cases alone; they hear oral arguments at trial, decide cases if a jury is not involved, and impose sentences. They handle the bulk of all litigation in the federal system. Each year, more than 350,000 civil cases and more than 75,000 criminal cases are filed in federal district courts.[3] The cases generally involve federal law, but district judges may also decide disputes between citizens of different states and, when authorized by legislation, apply state law.

In most cases, a district court is the court of first and last resort in the federal judicial system—the place where a case begins and ends. A substantial number of federal criminal defendants do not even go to trial because they plead guilty, often as a result of plea bargaining. Of the criminal cases that do go to trial, less than 15 percent are later appealed. Thus, most of what district judges do is never reviewed by a higher court. Most of the time, their judgment is the first and final one.

Appellate Courts

In contrast with the individual decision making of district judges, appellate court judges decide cases in a collegial manner. In 2004, there were 167 appellate judges on the thirteen federal courts of appeals, sitting in rotating panels of three and deciding most cases solely on the basis of written **briefs** filed by attorneys for both sides in a dispute. These documents discuss the facts of the case and relevant laws and precedents (prior rulings by the Supreme Court or federal circuit courts). Occasionally the entire appellate court sits as a panel, or **en banc.** As the number of judges on appellate courts has increased from three to twenty or more, some judges complain that they function more like a legislative body, dividing into groups and being forced to seek compromises when deciding cases.

State Courts

State courts are by no means inferior to the federal judiciary, even though their decisions may be appealed to the federal courts and to the Supreme Court if they involve the application of federal law or issues governed by the federal Constitution. State courts play a crucial role in the administration of justice. When interpreting state constitutions and bills of rights, they have great freedom to pursue their own directions in policymaking rather than simply following the direction of the Supreme Court.

briefs
Written legal arguments filed by each side in cases or controversies before a court.

en banc
As a panel; with all judges participating. Cases in federal courts of appeals are usually heard and decided by three-judge panels, but in especially important cases the entire court will sit en banc.

State courts handle by far the greatest volume of litigation. More than 90 percent of all lawsuits filed each year are in state courts. The business of state courts also tends to diverge from that in federal courts. Apart from criminal cases, the largest portion of state supreme court litigation involves economic issues. State courts face, for instance, many cases involving zoning ordinances, minor business disputes, and government regulation of public utilities, as well as controversies over labor relations and the use of natural resources.

They have also been the favorite for trial lawyers initiating class-action lawsuits. Such lawsuits are brought on behalf of a group of people who believe that they have been hurt by the illegal decisions or actions of a company, industry, union, or other type of group. Victims of deceptive practices by credit card companies; smokers who acquire a debilitating, smoking-related illness; and automobile owners who get into accidents because of a faulty part of their vehicle are examples of classes of people who band together to sue those who they believe are responsible for their particular plight. The litigators like the state courts because they tend to receive more favorable verdicts and, when they do, larger financial judgments.

Naturally, the group being sued, more often than not a large corporation or an institution, dislikes these courts for the same reason. These large companies and their business allies have been putting pressure on Congress to move such lawsuits into federal courts. In 2005, Congress did so with legislation supported by the Republican majorities in both houses and signed by the president.

The Supreme Court intervenes in the work of state courts only in a narrow class of litigation: cases in which state courts deal with **federal questions.** A federal question involves a disagreement over the interpretation or application of the Constitution, the Bill of Rights, or other federal laws; such a question rarely emerges from the cases that normally come to the state courts. If a state court case is decided on **independent state grounds**—such as a state constitution or bill of rights—the Supreme Court will not overturn the decision out of respect for the **principle of comity** between federal and state courts. In other words, the Court defers out of courtesy to the decisions of state supreme courts that are based on state constitutions, not the U.S. Constitution.

Despite the principle of comity, tensions do exist in relations between state and federal courts. These tensions reflect the politics of a changing federal judiciary. In the 1950s and 1960s, for example, the Supreme Court applied the guarantees of the federal Bill of Rights to the states. Many state judges opposed these liberal rulings and attacked the Supreme Court for intruding on the autonomy of state courts. By contrast, during the 1970s, 1980s, and 1990s, under more conservative chief justices, the Supreme Court tended to take a more limited view of the role of the federal judiciary in protecting and expanding civil liberties and civil rights. As a result, some liberal state court judges are now going in the opposite direction of the Supreme Court, extending greater protection for civil rights and liberties under their state constitutions. Since 1969, in hundreds of cases state supreme courts have interpreted their state constitutions and bills of rights to provide greater protection and to afford rights that the U.S. Supreme Court has refused to recognize under the federal Constitution and Bill of Rights.[4] For

federal questions
Issues concerning the interpretation and application of federal as opposed to state law.

independent state grounds
A state constitution or state law used as the basis for a decision by a state court instead of a federal law or a federal court's interpretation of the U.S. Constitution and Bill of Rights.

principle of comity
The principle by which the U.S. Supreme Court will not hear an appeal of a state court case if the case was decided on the basis of a state constitution or a state bill of rights.

example, some courts have recognized a right to education, a right to die, and broader rights to privacy on the basis of their state constitutions.

Review Questions

1. Decisions of the federal district courts are normally appealed directly to the

   A. Supreme court
   B. State court
   C. Circuit court of appeals
   D. Legislative court

2. State court decisions can only be appealed to the U.S. Supreme Court if

   A. There is evidence that they were unfairly decided at the state level
   B. They involve a crime of a particularly serious or controversial nature
   C. They are first appealed to the federal circuit courts
   D. They involve a disagreement over how the Constitution, Bill of Rights, or other federal law should be interpreted

3. Which of the following does *not* contribute to someone's standing to sue in court?

   A. A person is suffering or is in danger of suffering significant personal damages
   B. A person is engaged in a dispute that cannot be resolved outside the court system
   C. A person is under the age of twenty-one
   D. The dispute in question remains unsettled

4. The concept of judicial review means that

   A. Nominees to federal courts must be reviewed and approved by the U.S. Senate
   B. The Supreme Court has the right to declare unconstitutional any state or federal law or government action
   C. Federal courts have the right to review any decision made by a state or district court
   D. The Supreme Court may reconsider and overturn any previous Supreme Court decision

5. Which of the following behaviors by a judge fits the common defenition of "judicial activism?" An "activist" judge i

   A. Takes a clear stand on a legal issue before the court
   B. Exercises regularly to be able to serve on the court into old age
   C. Appears regularly on television
   D. Makes decisions based on personal views or beliefs rather than the Constitution or other federal laws

Answers:

   1. C
   2. D

continued

jurisdiction
The authority of a court to decide particular cases. The jurisdiction of federal courts is provided for in Article III of the U.S. Constitution and by Congress in statutes.

original jurisdiction
The authority of a court to have a case originate in it. Article III of the U.S. Constitution specifies the "cases or controversies" over which the Supreme Court has original jurisdiction.

appellate jurisdiction
The authority of courts to review decisions of lower courts and administrative agencies. Under Article III of the U.S. Constitution, Congress has the power to provide for the appellate jurisdiction of the Supreme Court and courts of appeals.

standing to sue
The right or legal status to initiate a lawsuit or judicial proceedings. To have standing to sue, parties must show that they are suffering or in danger of suffering an immediate and substantial personal injury.

3. C
4. B
5. D

Conflict and Consensus in Review

Conflict like this is common in the complex American judicial process although there is a consensus on the need for a fair and just judicial system. The pursuit of consensus in courts is often as difficult as in the more overtly political institutions. Judicial decisions produce winners and losers; participants fight constantly to be among the former rather than the latter.

The Power of Judicial Review

Unlike other political institutions, courts are passive and reactive. They are not, as Justice Benjamin Cardozo once observed, "knights-errant" or "roving commissions." Rather than initiating policy, they must await the arrival of disputes in the form of a lawsuit—that is, an actual "case or controversy."

Article III of the Constitution, along with legislation, specifies the **jurisdiction** of federal courts—that is, the kinds of cases and controversies that courts may decide. Under Article III the Supreme Court has **original jurisdiction** in all cases involving disputes between two or more states and in cases brought against the United States by ambassadors of foreign countries. Original jurisdiction means that the case originates in the Supreme Court rather than in a lower court, but in practice the Court appoints a "special master" to hear the case and recommend a decision. Out of the more than 6,000 cases that come to the Court each year, only 2 or 3 involve matters of original jurisdiction. The rest arrive under the Court's **appellate jurisdiction,** as established by legislation. Under its appellate jurisdiction, the Court hears appeals from lower federal courts and state courts.

Federal legislation also defines the jurisdiction of the lower federal courts, and state constitutions and legislation define the jurisdiction of state courts. Courts have jurisdiction only over disputes involving adverse interests and real controversies. They will not take "friendly lawsuits" brought by two parties who simply want to have some legal question settled. The parties must have **standing to sue;** they must show that they are suffering or are in danger of suffering an immediate and substantial personal injury.

Traditionally, individuals could challenge government action only if they could demonstrate a personal and monetary injury. But since the 1960s Congress and the courts have altered the doctrine of standing in cases like *Griswold v. Connecticut*,[5] in which the right to privacy was acknowledged by the Court and extended to everyone, not simply the parties that brought the case. The principal result is that more individuals and interest groups may now gain access to the courts, and they may raise a wider range of disputes.

Figure 13.2 Avenues of Appeal to the Supreme Court

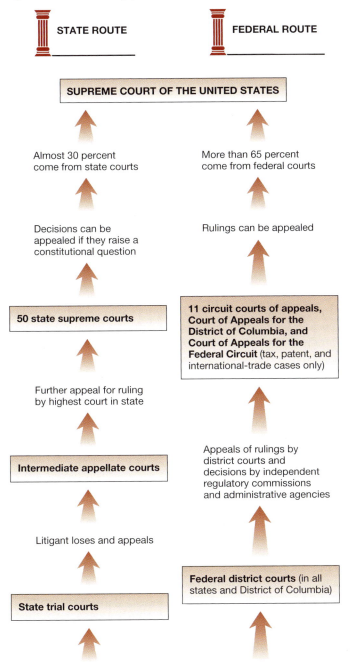

STATE ROUTE

FEDERAL ROUTE

SUPREME COURT OF THE UNITED STATES

Almost 30 percent come from state courts

More than 65 percent come from federal courts

Decisions can be appealed if they raise a constitutional question

Rulings can be appealed

50 state supreme courts

11 circuit courts of appeals, Court of Appeals for the District of Columbia, and Court of Appeals for the Federal Circuit (tax, patent, and international-trade cases only)

Further appeal for ruling by highest court in state

Intermediate appellate courts

Appeals of rulings by district courts and decisions by independent regulatory commissions and administrative agencies

Litigant loses and appeals

Federal district courts (in all states and District of Columbia)

State trial courts

Cases involving state law

Cases Involving federal law

Source: *Storm Center: The Supreme Court in American Politics*, 4th ed. by David M. O'Brien, p. 197. Copyright © 1996, 1993, 1990, 1986 by David M. O'Brien. Reprinted by permission of W.W. Norton and Company, Inc.

Box 13.1 Requirements for Gaining Standing

A personal injury must be claimed. For example, an individual must have been denied some right under federal or state law.

The dispute must not be hypothetical. Real adverse interests must be at stake.

A case must be brought before a court authorized to bear such dis- *putes.* Cases must be within the court's jurisdiction.

A case must be ripe for judicial resolution. Other remedies must have been exhausted. For example, the litigants must have exhausted administrative appeals and appeals in other lower courts.

The dispute must not be moot. Circumstances since filing the lawsuit must not have changed to end the dispute or make it hypothetical.

The dispute must be capable of judicial resolution. The dispute must not involve a political question that should be decided by another branch of government.

Today lawsuits may also involve nonmonetary interests such as aesthetic and environmental well-being. For example, in *United States v. Students Challenging Regulatory Agency Procedures (SCRAP)* (1973), the Court granted standing to a group of law students attacking a proposed surcharge on railroad freight. The students contended that the surcharge would discourage the recycling of bottles and cans and thus contribute to environmental pollution. In granting SCRAP standing to bring its lawsuit, the Court made the following observation: "Aesthetic and environmental well-being, like economic well-being, are important ingredients of the quality of life in our society, and the fact that particular environmental interests are shared by the many rather than the few does not make them less deserving of legal protection through the judicial process."[6]

Political Questions

After a lawsuit has been filed, judges may still refuse to decide a dispute. For example, they will not decide hypothetical disputes or give "advisory opinions" on possible future conflicts. Courts also avoid deciding **political questions**— issues that judges think should be resolved by other branches of government, either because of the separation of powers or because the judiciary is not in a position to provide a remedy. Thus, courts generally avoid disputes involving foreign policy and international relations. But this does not make the judiciary less political. Deciding what is a "political question" is itself a political decision and an exercise of judicial review.

For many decades, for instance, courts applied the political question doctrine to avoid entering the "political thicket" of state elections and representation.[7] But under these conditions urban voters were often denied equal voting rights. The Court finally responded to this injustice in *Baker v. Carr* (1962),[8] holding

political questions
Issues that judges decide would be more appropriately resolved by other branches of government.

that such disputes were within its jurisdiction and were **justiciable disputes**—that is, open to judicial resolution and a judicial remedy. After abandoning the political question doctrine in this area, the Court forced state and local governments to provide equal voting rights and established the principle of one person, one vote. (See Chapter 4, pages 125–126.)

justiciable disputes
Disagreements or conflicts appropriate for resolution by a court.

Judicial Review and Political Influence

In the United States, the judiciary, particularly the Supreme Court, exercises great political power because its members have the authority to interpret the Constitution and the laws of the nation. This power of judicial review gives the courts the power to strike down any law enacted by Congress or by the states and to declare official government actions unconstitutional (see Chapter 2).

Judicial review has remained controversial ever since Chief Justice John Marshall asserted that power for the Court in the landmark case of *Marbury v. Madison* (1803).[9] By striking down acts of Congress or state legislatures, the Court thwarts the democratic process and majority rule as expressed by elected representatives. This is so even when the Court uses its power to promote the democratic

John Marshall, (1755–1835) was Supreme Court Chief Justice
from 1801–1833. Portrait by T. Hamilton Crawford.

© Bettmann/CORBIS

Chisholm v. Georgia (1793), holding that citizens of one state could sue another state in federal court, was reversed by the Eleventh Amendment, which guaranteed sovereign immunity for states from lawsuits by citizens of another state.

Dred Scott v. Sanford (1857), ruling that blacks were not citizens under the Constitution, was technically overturned by the Thirteenth and Fourteenth Amendments, which abolished slavery and made blacks citizens of the United States.

Pollock v. Farmer's Loan and Trust Co. (1895), invalidating a federal income tax, was reversed in 1913 with the ratification of the Sixteenth Amendment.

Oregon v. Mitchell (1970), in which a bare majority of the Court held that Congress could not lower the voting age for state and local elections, was reversed in less than a year by the Twenty-Sixth Amendment, which extended the franchise to eighteen year olds in all elections.

---

process, as it does when it enforces the First Amendment guarantees of freedom of speech and press and when it strikes down barriers to the electoral process.

The political influence of the judiciary has grown dramatically since the nation's founding. No longer is the judiciary, as Alexander Hamilton claimed in *The Federalist,* No. 78, "the least dangerous branch" of the government. Instead, it has become a truly coequal branch. The Supreme Court increasingly asserts its power in striking down congressional legislation, state laws, and municipal ordinances. Likewise, lower courts no longer serve simply as tribunals for resolving private disputes but more often serve as problem solvers and policymakers.

In some instances, Congress has encouraged this trend: It has given the courts a role in the implementation of public policies by extending their jurisdiction and giving them the power to hear lawsuits brought under legislation. The National Environmental Policy Act, for example, provides that citizens may file lawsuits in federal courts to challenge the decisions of the Environmental Protection Agency and even to force that agency to promulgate regulations to protect the environment.

Judicial Activism Versus Self-Restraint

Do courts exercise too much power? Have they usurped the power of other branches of government? The power of judicial review has been criticized, at different times, by both liberals and conservatives. In the 1920s and 1930s, liberals attacked the Supreme Court for its **judicial activism** in striking down progressive economic legislation such as minimum-wage laws. (Judicial activism is the use of judicial review to invalidate state and federal laws.) Criticizing the Court for substituting its conservative economic views for the more progressive views of Congress and state legislatures, liberals urged the

judicial activism
The use of judicial review to invalidate a law or other official action.

Court to exercise **judicial self-restraint** and defer to legislative authority. (Judicial self-restraint is the practice of deferring to the executive and legislative branches, rather than asserting the Court's view.)

By contrast, the Court's activism in defending civil liberties and civil rights in the 1960s and 1970s led conservatives to charge that the Court was usurping the power of other political institutions and thwarting the will of the majority. Presidents Richard Nixon, Ronald Reagan, George H. W. Bush, and George W. Bush all called for the appointment of judges who would exercise judicial self-restraint.

The extent of the courts' political role is only partially explained by judicial definitions of the scope of judicial review. Courts sometimes must confront new problems created by technological advances and political and social changes. For instance, the federal judiciary played a minor role in environmental protection until the 1970s, when Congress passed legislation such as the Clean Air and Clean Water Acts and the National Environmental Policy Act. Then the courts had to resolve conflicts over the implementation of that legislation by federal agencies.

Other social trends have been no less significant in increasing and changing the business of courts. Even before the 1920s and 1930s, railroads and other businesses relied on the judiciary to protect property rights and strike down progressive economic legislation enacted under the influence of the labor and populist movements beginning in the late nineteenth century. The civil rights movement of the 1950s and 1960s brought lawsuits challenging racial discrimination in schools, employment, and public accommodations, including the most famous of those, *Brown v. Topeka, Kansas Board of Education,* in 1954.[10] A long and hard-fought lawsuit between the U.S. Justice Department and the Microsoft Corporation played a significant role in redefining the concept of monopoly as the electronic communications era unfolded early in the twenty-first century.

The pace of litigation is also influenced by economic cycles. Increased economic activity gives rise to new issues involving property rights and disputes over government regulations affecting labor-management relations; health, safety, and environmental matters; and other economic issues.

It is no less important that American society is exceedingly litigious—so much so that the United States is sometimes called an adversarial democracy. As the astute French commentator Alexis de Tocqueville observed in the 1830s, "Scarcely any political question arises in the United States that is not resolved, sooner or later, into a judicial question."[11] In 2004, for instance, more than 400,000 cases were filed in the federal courts and state courts were handling more than 25 million cases a year. Another measure of the increasing litigiousness of the United States is the rather dramatic increase in the number of lawyers and judges since the end of World War II. At the beginning of the twenty-first century, there was one lawyer for every 296 American citizens.

Although Americans agree in theory on the principle of judicial review, on judges interpreting the Constitution, they frequently disagree in practice with a particular judicial interpation. One of the primary institutional and political

judicial self-restraint
Deference by courts to the decisions of other branches of government.

13.3 In Theory . . .
Judicial Review

Every democracy has to face a central and fundamental question: Who protects the Constitution from laws? If a legislature passes a law or a government agency acts in a way that violates constitutional protections, how are those protections enforced?

Suppose, for example, that Congress passed a law extending the term of members of the House of Representatives from two years to four. The Constitution says the term should be two years; the law says it is four years. What prevails?

For Americans, the answer is determined by judicial review. Citizens can challenge laws or government actions in court and judges have the authority to determine whether the Constitution has been violated. When they believe it has, they can strike down a law or cause an agency to stop engaging in an unconstitutional practice. Judges have assumed responsibility for protecting the Constitution from the laws.

But who holds judges accountable for their actions? Federal judges in America are not elected, nor do they serve fixed terms. They are appointed for life. So how can citizens be protected from judges who use their powers of judicial review to overturn laws that a majority of the citizens want and support? Who protects the citizens (and democracy) from judges?

The answers to this second pair of questions are more complex. An intricate network of practices and procedures, ranging from presidential appointment and legislative oversight to impeachment and constitutional amendment, help hold judges accountable for their actions. But none of them is perfect, and judicial accountability, like judicial review, is a constant concern, not only of democratic theory but of modern governance as well.

conflicts in American politics occurs between the courts and the legislators, and sometimes executives, whose policies or actions are overturned. Every time the Supreme Court declares a state or congressional statute unconstitutional, that conflict flares anew, pitting two overlapping adversarial groups against each other: those who support or oppose the substantive result of Court's decision and those who believe the Court should protect the rights of minorities (judicial activists) and those who believe that the Court should not intrude itself into the political sphere and impose its policy judgment (judicial self-restraint) on the representatives of the people.

How Judges Are Chosen

A hallmark of the federal judiciary is the relative isolation of judges from political pressures such as the direct lobbying faced by senators, representatives, and other elected officials. Under the Constitution, federal judges are given lifetime appointments and Congress is barred from decreasing their salaries. Still, judges are appointed largely for political reasons, become involved in political controversies, and make judgments that affect the rules that govern politics. In American democracy today, no actions are more political than the selection and confirmation of federal judges.

Article II of the Constitution gives the president the power to appoint all federal judges, with the advice and consent of the Senate. Because federal judgeships provide lifetime tenure, these appointments are a prized form of political patronage. Presidents try to "pack" the federal courts in the hope of influencing the direction of public law and policy long after they have left the Oval Office.

In the 1980s and early 1990s, for instance, Republican Presidents Ronald Reagan and George H. W. Bush promised to appoint judges opposed to abortion. Political scientists studying the decisions of federal judges appointed by recent presidents have found that "Reagan appointees were much more resistant to abortion rights than were the appointees of his predecessors, including the appointees of fellow Republican Richard Nixon. Likewise, President Carter's appointees were much more supportive of abortion claims than were the appointees of other presidents."[12]

Despite their constitutional authority, however, presidents must often compete with the Senate and other political bodies in appointing judges. The traditional practice of **senatorial courtesy** also encourages presidents to consult with senators of their party in the state in which the judge will serve before making a formal nomination. Recently, the minority party in the Senate has used the filibuster to prevent the Senate from voting on some appellate court nominees and the threat of a filibuster to convince the president to nominate judges whom the minority perceives as centrists rather than ideologically extreme.

senatorial courtesy
Consultation by the president with senators before making a formal nomination that requires Senate confirmation. Begun during the administration of George Washington, this practice gives senators influence over potential presidential nominations, but it also enhances the prospects of nominees who have received prior clearance.

© AP/Wide World Photos

John Roberts prepares to begin confirmation hearings on his nomination to be Chief Justice of the United States in 2005.

The filibuster issue came to a head at the beginning of George W. Bush's second term. Frustrated by the inability to vote on the president's nominations, Senate Majority Leader Bill Frist threatened to change the rule on judicial nominations to preclude filibusters and thereby prevent Democrats from holding up the nomination of seven appellate court nominees. In the end a compromise was reached in which the Democrats promised to use the filibuster only in "extraordinary" situations and the Republicans left the rule intact.

Indeed, at the lowest level of the federal judicial structure, the district courts, "it's senatorial appointment with the advice and consent of the president," in the words of former Attorney General Robert Kennedy.[13] The president has greater discretion at the circuit court level. Because the jurisdiction of these courts spans several states, the president may play senators off one another by claiming the need for representation of different political parties, geographic regions, religions, races, and so forth, within a given circuit.

Appointment of Supreme Court Justices

Unlike other federal judgeships, appointments to the Supreme Court have traditionally been considered a prerogative of the president. As President Herbert Hoover's attorney general, William Mitchell, observed, "with the whole country to choose from, the senators from one state or another are in no position, even if they were so inclined, to attempt a controlling influence."[14] Although the Senate as a whole has the power to defeat a nominee, in the twentieth century only seven were blocked: Four were defeated, two were withdrawn, and no action was taken on one.

All presidents try to fill vacancies on the Supreme Court with political associates and individuals who share their ideological views. They make little or no effort to balance the Court by crossing party lines.

Most presidents delegate the responsibility for selecting candidates to their attorney general and other close advisers. The assistant attorney general in charge of the Office of Legal Policy in the Department of Justice usually compiles a list of candidates from recommendations by White House staff, members of Congress, governors, and state and local bar associations. When the president is ready to make the final choice, an exhaustive FBI investigation of the candidate or candidates is initiated. Once these reports have been reviewed by the attorney general and White House counsel, a recommendation is sent to the president. If he approves, the nomination is formally submitted to the Senate. The Senate Judiciary Committee then holds a **confirmation hearing** and recommends approval or rejection of the nominee by a vote of the entire Senate.

Packing the Court

How successful are presidents in packing the Court? Most succeed to some degree. Others fail, and some completely misjudge their appointees.

Democratic President Franklin Roosevelt succeeded more than most. He made eight new appointments and elevated Justice Harlan Stone to the position of chief justice. Having bitterly attacked the Court for invalidating most of

confirmation hearing
A hearing held by a legislative body before approving the appointment of a government official. Under the U.S. Constitution, the president nominates federal judges and other high officials in the executive branch, but they must be confirmed by the Senate.

Table 13.1 Supreme Court Nominations Rejected, Postponed, or Withdrawn Because of Senate Opposition

Nominee	Year Nominated	Nominated By	Actions[*]
William Paterson[†]	1793	Washington	Withdrawn
John Rutledge[‡]	1795	Washington	Rejected
Alexander Wolcott	1811	Madison	Rejected
John J. Crittenden	1828	J. Q. Adams	Postponed, 1829
Roger B. Taney[§]	1835	Jackson	Postponed
John C. Spencer	1844	Tyler	Rejected
Reuben H. Walworth	1844	Tyler	Withdrawn
Edward King	1844	Tyler	Postponed
Edward King[^]	1844	Tyler	Withdrawn, 1845
John M. Read	1845	Tyler	No action
George W. Woodward	1845	Polk	Rejected, 1846
Edward A. Bradford	1852	Fillmore	No action
George E. Badger	1853	Fillmore	Postponed
William C. Micou	1853	Fillmore	No action
Jeremiah S. Black	1861	Buchanan	Rejected
Henry Stanbery	1866	Johnson	No action
Ebenezer R. Hoar	1869	Grant	Rejected, 1870
George H. Williams[‡]	1873	Grant	Withdrawn, 1874
Caleb Cushing[‡]	1874	Grant	Withdrawn
Stanley Matthews[†]	1881	Hayes	No action
William B. Hornblower	1893	Cleveland	Rejected, 1894
Wheeler H. Peckham	1894	Cleveland	Rejected
John J. Parker	1930	Hoover	Rejected
Abe Fortas[¶]	1968	Johnson	Withdrawn
Homer Thornberry	1968	Johnson	No action
Clement F. Haynsworth	1969	Nixon	Rejected
G. Harrold Carswell	1970	Nixon	Rejected
Robert H. Bork	1987	Reagan	Rejected
Douglas H. Ginsburg	1987	Reagan	Withdrawn
Harriet Miers	2005	Bush	Withdrawn

[*]A year is given if different from the year of nomination.
[†]Reappointed and confirmed.
[‡]Nominated for chief justice.
[§]Taney was reappointed and confirmed as chief justice.
[^]Second appointment.
[¶]Associate justice nominated for chief justice.
Source: *Storm Center: The Supreme Court in American Politics*, 4th ed. by David M. O'Brien, p. 165. Copyright © 1996, 1993, 1990, 1986 by David M. O'Brien. Reprinted by permission of W.W. Norton and Company, Inc. Updated by authors.

his early New Deal program, in 1937 Roosevelt went so far as to propose expanding the size of the Court from nine to fifteen justices so that he could appoint justices who supported his economic policies. The Senate defeated this Court-packing plan. Later, however, when vacancies occurred on the Court, Roosevelt succeeded in appointing his supporters and thereby turning a conservative Court into a more liberal one.

Almost thirty years later, Republican President Richard Nixon achieved some success in remolding the Court in his image. Whereas Roosevelt had attacked the conservative Court in the 1930s, Nixon vehemently opposed the "liberal jurisprudence" of the Court as expressed in its rulings on school desegregation and criminal procedures. However, Nixon's appointments of Chief Justice Warren Burger and Justices Harry Blackmun, Lewis Powell, and William Rehnquist failed to turn the Court completely around. Under Chief Justice Burger the Court was increasingly fragmented, with votes often divided 6–3 or 5–4, and it was pulled in different directions by either its most liberal or its most conservative members.

In his 1980 and 1984 presidential campaigns, Ronald Reagan promised to appoint only justices opposed to abortion and to the judicial activism that had characterized the Court under Burger and his predecessor, Earl Warren. No other president since Roosevelt has had as great an effect on the federal judiciary. Before leaving the Oval Office in 1989, Reagan had appointed close to half of all lower-court judges and elevated William H. Rehnquist to chief justice, as well as appointing three other justices to the Supreme Court. Although he was hugely successful in appointing lower-court judges, Reagan failed to win a majority of the Court to his positions on abortion, affirmative action, and other hotly contested issues until Justice Lewis Powell stepped down in 1987. Powell held the pivotal vote; during his last two years on the Court, the justices split 5–4 in eighty-one cases, with Powell having the deciding vote more than 75 percent of the time. Several of these votes came in cases rejecting the Reagan administration's positions on abortion, affirmative action, and other social-policy issues.

With Powell's departure, Reagan had a chance to move the Court in a more conservative direction. His first nominee for Powell's seat, Judge Robert Bork, was defeated after a bitter confirmation battle. His second, Judge Douglas H. Ginsburg, was forced to withdraw after revelations about his personal affairs turned Republican senators against him. However, his third nominee, Judge Anthony M. Kennedy, won easy confirmation. Although Kennedy was not the kind of justice that officials in the Justice Department had hoped would "lock in the Reagan Revolution," there is no doubt that he and Reagan's other appointees brought a new conservatism to the Court. George H. W. Bush appointed two more justices, David H. Souter and Clarence Thomas. Souter has often sided with the more liberal faction on the court, and Thomas has become a reliable member of the conservative contingent.

In 1993, when Justice Byron White retired, Bill Clinton became the first Democratic president in more than twenty-five years to fill a vacancy on the Court. He chose Ruth Bader Ginsburg, a federal appellate court judge who had established a reputation as a moderate jurist and a consensus builder. Clinton's second appointee was Stephen G. Breyer. Both have proven to be moderately left of center and vote most often with Justices John Paul Stevens (appointed by President Gerald Ford) and Souter.

The Supreme Court

The Supreme Court is perhaps the least understood government institution in the United States. Although the public may attend oral arguments and the Court's rulings are handed down in the form of published opinions, a tradition of secrecy surrounds the justices' decision making. The Court stands as a temple of law, an arbiter of political disputes and an expression of the ideal of "a government of laws, and not of men." But it remains a fundamentally political institution. Behind the marble facade, the justices compete for influence.

The Court's annual term (or work year) begins on the first Monday in October and runs until the end of June. For most of this time, the justices are hidden from public view. They hear oral arguments only fourteen weeks a year—on Mondays, Tuesdays, and Wednesdays of every other two-week period from October through April. On Wednesday afternoons and again on most Fridays, they hold private conferences to decide which cases they will review and to make decisions on cases for which they have heard oral arguments. The rest of the time they work alone in their chambers with their law clerks, writing opinions and studying drafts of opinions circulated by other justices.

The Court's Caseload

The Court actually reviews and decides by written opinion only about 100 cases each year, about 1 percent of the more than 7,000 cases filed and placed on the Court's annual **docket.** The vast majority of these cases are denied review, leaving the lower-court rulings untouched.

The Court's caseload has grown and changed throughout its history. In the nineteenth century almost all cases came to the Court as mandatory appeals, which the justices had to decide. But as the caseload grew, Congress eliminated most provisions granting rights of appeal and substituted a **writ of certiorari** (a petition requesting a court to order a review of the ruling of a lower court), which the Court may simply deny. Congress thus permitted the justices to determine which cases they would review. Figure 13.2 presents the main avenues of appeal to the Supreme Court.

The Court now exercises virtually absolute control over its caseload. The power to turn away cases enables it not only to limit the number of cases it reviews but also to pick what issues it wants to decide and when. In this sense the modern Supreme Court functions like a legislative body, setting its own agenda for adjudication and policymaking. Even in this ostensibly administrative procedure, the justices often disagree, reflecting their conflicting political views and their varied understandings of the role of the courts in American democracy.

docket
The list of filings or cases that come before a court. The U.S. Supreme Court, for example, has an annual docket of more than 7,000 cases.

writ of certiorari
A formal order issued by the U.S. Supreme Court to a lower federal court or state court requesting the record of the decision in a case that the Supreme Court has accepted for review. Four of the Court's nine justices must agree to grant a writ of certiorari for a case to be reviewed.

Deciding What to Decide

When the justices meet in conference, they vote on which cases to review. The chief justice presides over conferences, as well as over oral arguments and all of the Court's other public functions. At a conference, he usually begins by summarizing each case and indicating why he thinks it should be accepted or denied. Discussion then passes from one justice to another in order of their seniority on the bench.

Although the Court decides all other matters by majority rule, review of a case can be granted on the vote of only four justices—the informal **rule of four.** However, only a small number of the cases granted review are actually accepted on this basis. For more than 70 percent of the cases accepted for review, a majority of the justices agree on the importance of the issues presented.

Because of the Court's heavy docket, it does not accept cases to decide questions of fact, such as a person's guilt or innocence, or simply to correct mistakes made in lower courts. Instead, it takes cases that involve questions of law on which lower courts have disagreed. The Court thus tends to decide only cases that have national scope and involve significant controversies over public law and policy.

rule of four
The informal rule that for a case to be accepted for review by the U.S. Supreme Court at least four of the justices must vote to take it.

13.4 **Politics in the 21st Century**
Electronic Justice

The modern courtroom is a far cry from what John Marshall or Abraham Lincoln knew. Large-screen televisions, laptop computers, headphones, and laser pointers are just some of the tools used in legal practice as courts keep pace with modern electronic and communications technologies.

In many jurisdictions today, judges may preside over hearings in which one or both of the parties are not actually present in court but appear there on television screens. Some criminals are arraigned in proceedings in which the criminal goes no farther than a small TV studio in the local jail. Lawyers can go online during a case to draw cases and precedents from huge legal databases.

When trials occur, attorneys may recreate crime scenes electronically or even virtually in computer-generated renderings that provide visual images for the jury. Police cruisers are increasingly equipped with video cameras, so the judge doesn't have to take the cop's word that a driver was swerving dangerously or was inebriated. The judge can review the videotape.

Modern forensics has been overtaken by a similar technological revolution. Tiny fibers of hair or clothing can place a defendant at a crime scene. Cell phone records can sustain an alibi. DNA tests now provide nearly irrefutable forms of

identity and evidence of contact between victim and criminal.

Lawyers and judges still play important roles in court cases, of course, but forensics experts, computer animators, and lab technicians have become highly important participants in the judicial process.

Think about some of the consequences of these changes. Courtrooms and court proceedings are more expensive when the costs of all this technology are added. What effect will that have on the number of cases brought to trial? Are defendants more likely to be convicted or acquitted in a modern court? What effect will all this technology have on juries? Does the average juror have the analytical skills necessary to cope with the new kinds of evidence that these technologies will bring? Does all this enhance the quality of American justice?

Hearing and Discussing Cases

Each case is allowed only one hour for oral argument—thirty minutes for each side. The Court hears four cases on each oral-argument day, which is virtually the only time the public may see the justices. Seating in the courtroom is limited to about 250 spectators, most of whom hear only three to four minutes of oral arguments before they are ushered out. Only by special request may members of the public hear entire arguments in a case. The press may hear all arguments, but no cameras are allowed in the courtroom when the Court is in session.

Within a day or two after oral arguments have been presented, the justices meet in secret conference to discuss and vote on the cases. The chief justice opens the discussion, which moves to each of the other justices in order of seniority. For much of the Court's history, the justices voted in reverse order of seniority, the junior ones voting first so as not to be swayed by the votes of their senior colleagues. But that practice has been abandoned. Because of the heavier caseload, each justice has only about three minutes to express his or her views and vote on each case. As a result, conferences involve less collective deliberation than was generally true in the past.

The justices' votes at conference are always tentative. Until the day the final decision comes down, justices may use their votes in strategic ways to influence the disposition of a case, offering or threatening to switch sides depending on whether or not their conditions are met. Before and during conference as well, justices bargain and negotiate over the treatment of issues and the language of opinions.

Writing Opinions

After every three-day oral-argument session, one of the justices is assigned to write the **opinion** for the Court on each case. This is a crucial aspect of the work of the Court because how an opinion is written—the legal reasoning used to justify the decision—is just as important as the decision itself. The justice selected must be one who voted with the majority during conference; if the chief justice did so, he assigns the opinion, either to himself or to another justice. By tradition, if the chief justice did not vote with the majority, the senior associate justice in the majority makes the assignment.

opinion
The written explanation or justification of a court's or an individual judge's decision.

The power to assign opinions presents significant opportunities for the chief justice to influence the final outcome of cases. In unanimous and landmark cases, chief justices often write opinions themselves. Chief Justice Earl Warren wrote the opinion striking down segregated schools in *Brown v. Board of Education* (1954). Chief Justice Warren Burger likewise delivered the opinion in *United States v. Nixon* (1974), rejecting President Nixon's claim of executive privilege to withhold tape recordings made in the Oval Office during the Watergate crisis.[15]

Chief justices usually try to see that all justices are assigned about the same number of opinions (thirteen to fifteen per year), so as to distribute the workload evenly and avoid angering their colleagues. They may make assignments on the basis of a justice's background and particular expertise or in anticipation of public reactions to a ruling. For example, Chief Justice Warren Burger chose Justice Harry Blackmun to write the majority opinion in the 1973 abortion case

U.S. SUPREME COURT JUSTICES

STEPHEN
BREYER

JOHN
ROBERTS

RUTH BADER
GINSBURG

ANTHONY
KENNEDY

SAMUEL
ALITO

ANTONIN
SCALIA

DAVID
SOUTER

JOHN PAUL
STEVENS

CLARENCE
THOMAS

The Justices of the Supreme Court in 2006.

institutional opinion
An official explanation or justification of a decision by a court with multiple judges or justices.

concurring opinion
A document submitted by one or more justices or judges of a court that agrees with the decision reached in a case but not with all of the reasoning or explanations offered in the institutional opinion. It explains how the same result would have been reached by different reasoning.

Roe v. Wade[16]; Blackmun had been counsel to the Mayo Clinic in private practice before serving on the Court, and his extensive medical knowledge was relevant to the issues in the case. In addition, chief justices will sometimes ask the justice whose opinion is closest to the views of the dissenting justices to write the majority opinion in the hope that other justices will switch their votes and thereby bolster the authority of the Court's decision.

Opinions announcing the decision of the Court are not statements of the author's particular views of jurisprudence. Rather, they are negotiated documents forged from ideological and political divisions within the Court. The justice writing the Court's opinion must avoid pride of authorship and attempt to reach a compromise that will secure a majority and an **institutional opinion** for the Court's decision. If a justice fails to achieve this goal, the opinion is reassigned.

What makes writing an opinion for the Court so difficult is that all other justices are free to write individual opinions. They may write a **concurring opinion**—an opinion agreeing with the result reached by the majority but disagreeing with its reasons or legal analysis. Justices differ on the propriety of such an opinion, which reflects failure or unwillingness to compromise. Some think that it is a sign of "institutional disobedience"; others believe that it is a valuable record of the justices' differing views. In any event, every justice now writes several concurring opinions each term.

Justices who disagree with the majority opinion usually write a **dissenting opinion.** In the words of Chief Justice Charles Hughes, dissenting opinions appeal "to the brooding spirit of the law, to the intelligence of a future day, when a later decision may possibly correct the error into which the dissenting judge believes the Court to have been betrayed."[17] Because dissenting opinions undercut the Court's decision, justices may use them as threats when trying to persuade the majority to narrow the scope of its ruling or tone down its language. Some justices write more dissents than others, but as a group they average about ten each term. Behind the doors of the Court's chambers, persuasive efforts are constantly under way to try to build and broaden support for majority opinions.

Litigants, lawyers, the media, and the public finally learn the outcome of the justices' votes on opinion days, the days when the Court hands down its final published opinions. The Court once announced opinions only on "Decision Mondays," but now it may do so on any day of the week. By tradition, there is no prior announcement as to when cases will be handed down. Instead of reading their opinions from the bench, as was formerly done, the justices simply announce them in two to four minutes, merely stating the result in each case.

dissenting opinion
a document submitted by one or more justices or judges of a court that disagrees with the majority's reasoning and decision in a case.

Review Questions

1. The isolation of the federal judiciary from political pressures is best explained by the fact that

   A. Presidents tend to appoint impartial judges willing to set their political beliefs aside when deciding cases
   B. Federal judges enjoy lifetime tenure
   C. Federal judges cannot be impeached
   D. Lobbying of federal judges is outlawed

2. One example of a Supreme Court justice whose appointment by a U.S. president failed to advance that president's judicial ideology is

   A. Ruth Bader Ginsburg
   B. William Rehnquist
   C. Clarence Thomas
   D. David Souter

3. A writ of certiorari is

   A. A dissenting opinion by an individual justice on a Supreme Court decision
   B. A petition asking a justice to recuse himself or herself from deciding on a case in which he or she may have a personal stake
   C. A petition to have a case heard by the Supreme Court
   D. A lawyer's brief summarizing his or her argument on one side of a Supreme Court case

continued

4. By Supreme Court tradition, how many justices need to give their approval before a case is heard by the Court?

   A. One
   B. Four
   C. Five
   D. Nine

Answers:

   1. B
   2. D
   3. C
   4. B

Conflict and Consensus in Review

Politics intrudes itself into the selection of judges; to some extent, it also affects the cases that are initiated and heard, and the legal judgment that is made. Judges are naturally affected by the society in which they live and work, their perception of the legal issues and how those issues have been resolved by previous courts, and their judicial philosophy as it applies to their understanding of the Constitution. Within the Supreme Court, decision making is a political process of give and take, argument and counterargument, not unlike the political efforts that occur in a legislature as majorities take shape. Although the terms and tone may differ, such majority building is the essence of American democracy, whether in court or in Congress. In American politics, consensus is almost always built, not born, but it is also framed by the democratic values and beliefs that most Americans share.

The Politics of Judicial Policymaking

The Court is an independent arbiter of political conflicts. Through its decisions it legitimates one set of government policies or another, and in so doing it invites political controversy. Much of the Court's work involves disputes over the interpretation and enforcement of statutes, and it is essential that those disputes be settled in one way or another. Moreover, relatively few of the many controversies over domestic and foreign policy that arise in government actually reach the Court. Yet those few cases are almost always difficult cases involving controversial matters such as abortion, affirmative action, and religious liberty.

Although the Court depends on lower courts to enforce its rulings, compliance is invariably uneven because the ambiguity of judicial opinions allows lower courts to pursue their own policy goals. Crucial language in an opinion may be treated like dicta—language that is not binding in other cases. Or differences between the facts on which the Supreme Court ruled and the circumstances in a later case may be emphasized by a lower court to reach a result opposite to that reached by the Supreme Court. For example, lower courts interpreted *Abington School District v. Schempp* (1963), which struck down a law requiring the reciting of the Lord's Prayer in public schools, as permitting voluntary and nondenominational prayer in public schools.[18] Likewise, state courts in Texas refused to extend the Court's ruling in *Norris v. Alabama* (1935) forbidding racial discrimination against blacks in the selection of juries.[19] They continued to allow the exclusion of Mexican Americans from juries until the Court finally ruled, in *Hernandez v. Texas* (1954), that all kinds of racial discrimination in jury selection violate the Fourteenth Amendment's equal protection clause.[20] In summary, open defiance is infrequent but not unprecedented. When it occurs, it reflects the differing policy preferences of state and federal judges.

On major issues of public policy, Congress is likely to prevail or at least to temper the effect of the Court's rulings. Congress may pressure the Court in several ways. The Senate may try to influence future judicial appointments, and the House may even try to impeach justices. More often, Congress uses institutional and jurisdictional changes as weapons against the Court.

© AP/Wide World Photos

Cases before the Supreme Court involving controversial issues like abortion often inspire demonstrations by the opposing interests.

Under Article III of the Constitution, Congress has the power to "make exceptions" to the appellate jurisdiction of the federal courts. That authorization has been viewed as a way of denying courts the power to review certain kinds of cases. During the Reagan administration, for instance, there were numerous unsuccessful proposals to deny courts the power to decide cases involving school prayer and abortion. But only once has Congress succeeded in cutting back on the Supreme Court's jurisdiction; this occurred in 1868 with the repeal of the Court's jurisdiction over writs of habeas corpus.

Congress has had slightly greater success in reversing the Court through a constitutional amendment, which three-fourths of the states must ratify. The process is cumbersome, and thousands of amendments designed to overrule the Court have failed. But four Court decisions have been overturned by constitutional amendments (see Box 13.2).

More successful has been congressional enactment or rewriting of legislation in response to the Court's rulings. In *Zurcher v. The Stanford Daily* (1978), for example, the Court held that there is no constitutional prohibition against police searching newsrooms without a warrant for "mere evidence" of a crime, such as photographs.[21] Two years later, however, Congress essentially reversed that ruling by passing the Privacy Protection Act of 1980, which prohibits unannounced searches of newsrooms and requires that police obtain a subpoena ordering writers to turn over the desired evidence. So, too, Congress overrode more than a dozen rulings of the conservative Rehnquist Court when it enacted the Civil Rights Act of 1991.

But Congress is not always successful in reversing the Court's decisions through legislation. In response to the Court's ruling in *Texas v. Johnson* (1989), which held that a state law prohibiting desecration of the American flag violated the First Amendment's guarantee of freedom of speech, Congress enacted the Flag Protection Act of 1989, which also forbade desecration of the flag.[22] But when that law was challenged, the Court again defended the First Amendment and struck down the act in *United States v. Eichman* (1990).[23]

Although Congress cannot always overturn the Court's rulings, it can often thwart their implementation. For example, Congress delayed implementation of the school desegregation decision in *Brown v. Board of Education* (1954) by not authorizing the executive branch to enforce the ruling until the passage of the Civil Rights Act of 1964. Later, by cutting back on appropriations for the Department of Justice and the Department of Health, Education, and Welfare during the Nixon and Ford administrations, Congress registered its opposition to busing and further attempts to integrate public schools.

When it threatens to go too far or too fast in its policymaking, the Court is ultimately curbed by public opinion. Public opinion toward the Supreme Court tends to fluctuate with public reactions to government as a whole. Issues such as school desegregation, school prayer, and abortion focus public attention and mobilize political interest groups in support of or in opposition to the Court. But those issues are also the ones most likely to sharply divide public opinion and fuel political struggles at all levels of government. Thus, in the late 1960s, public confidence in the Court declined when it was widely criticized for handing down rulings guaranteeing the rights of individuals accused of crimes. But in the early 1970s the Court's standing improved, largely because its rulings helped resolve a "crisis in confidence" in the presidency that had resulted from the Nixon administration's involvement in the Watergate episode and its attempts to cover up other illegal activities. A backlash of criticism against the Supreme Court in its *Bush v. Gore* decision that decided the outcome of the 2000 presidential election also occurred but did not continue for long.[24]

A fundamental principle of American democracy is that political actions should be rooted in the consent of the governed. That principle applies to courts as well as to legislatures and executives. Federal judges are not elected, and they serve life terms. Some Court watchers warn of an "imperial judiciary" and a "government by the judiciary." They point out that judicial review is antidemocratic because it enables the Court to overturn laws enacted by popularly elected legislatures. But the Court's duty is to interpret the Constitution, and compliance with and enforcement of the Court's rulings depend on the cooperation of other political institutions, as well as on public acceptance. Major confrontations over public policy are determined as much by what is possible in a pluralistic society with a system of free government as by what the Court says about the meaning of the Constitution. That is the essence of politics in a constitutional democracy.

Review Questions

1. Congress may use all of the following tactics to provide a check on judicial power except for

    A. Amending the Constitution to overturn court rulings on particular issues
    B. Moving to impeach judges
    C. Failing to authorize the implementation of court rulings
    D. Voting to suspend or cancel court rulings on individual cases

2. Which of the following is among the ways that Congress may thwart judicial policymaking?

    A. Congress can indict a judge by vote of the Senate Judiciary Committee
    B. The Senate can limit future judicial confirmations to nominees whom it believes will change the direction of court decisions
    C. Congress can force the retirement of judges who are older than sixty-five
    D. Congress has no power to thwart judicial policymaking

Answers:

   1. D
   2. B

continued

Conflict and Consensus in Review

The Supreme Court resolves constitutional conflict. Its decisions guide lower courts on their interpretation of the Constitution and its applicability to the issue that is being litigated. It also establishes the legal and constitutional framework within which legislatures must formulate public policy. Over time, a body of Supreme Court decisions lead to a consensus on the meaning of the Constitution. For those who object to that meaning, their principal options are to initiate political pressure for a constitutional amendment or reinitiate test cases, particularly if the composition of the Supreme Court has changed.

The ultimate check on judicial interpretation is public opinion. In a democracy no court can sustain its legitimacy for long if it constantly acts in ways that fail to gain the implicit consent of the governed. For judges as for legislators, public tolerance and support are vital concepts that shape and constrain much of judicial decision making.

Politics in Action

The Case of the Unconfirmed Judge

Politics is where many of the country's social forces and historical trends collide. So it was with the nomination of Judge Charles Pickering.

Pickering, who is white, was born in 1937 in Jones County, Mississippi. At that time, most of the American South was in the grip of policies of racial separation known as Jim Crow laws. Black citizens were relegated to separate restaurants and hotels, separate sections of railroad cars and public buses, separate schools and neighborhoods. Most blacks could not vote or hold public office.

The society in which Charles Pickering was born evolved over his lifetime. Federal laws and court decisions demolished Jim Crow practices and the legal foundation of racial separation. But full equality was slow in coming. Centuries of slavery and discrimination had left a legacy that was tough to overcome. And that legacy became a central issue when President George W. Bush nominated Pickering to serve on the Fifth Circuit Court of Appeals.

Pickering had earned a B.A. from the University of Mississippi in 1959 and a degree from the university's law school in 1961. For the next thirty years he practiced law in Jones County, serving also as a local judge, a prosecutor,

and a state senator. His involvement in state Republican politics and his friendship with Mississippi's representatives in Congress led to his appointment by the first President Bush to the U.S. District Court for the Southern District of Mississippi in 1990. He was confirmed to that position by the Senate and was serving there in May 2001 when President Bush nominated Pickering for a seat on the federal appellate court with jurisdiction over Louisiana, Mississippi, and Texas.

Under the Constitution, the Senate must confirm the appointments of all federal judges. This requires a majority vote. For most of U.S. history, this was a routine process. Occasionally the Senate would object to a judicial nominee—usually because the candidate lacked appropriate qualifications or judicial temperament. But in the vast majority of cases the Senate's review was perfunctory and the nomination was confirmed shortly after it was received. Questions about a nominee's ideology or personal views on legal issues were rare. The common assumption was that the president was entitled to pick judges, and as long as there was no objection from either of the senators from the judge's home state, the Senate would confirm the president's appointment.

continued

Politics in Action *continued*

But that long-standing practice began to dissolve in the 1980s. President Reagan, more than any other chief executive in modern times, sought judicial candidates who shared his political views. He especially wanted judges who were opposed to abortion and took a strict or literal view of the language of the Constitution. He set up a team in his administration to identify and recruit such candidates. The Senate reacted by inquiring more deeply than before into the ideology and opinions of judicial candidates. Just as presidents became more focused on the substantive views of their nominees, senators developed a similar focus in their confirmation proceedings.

Abetting this change was another: the growing involvement of special interest groups in the judicial appointment process. For most of American history, interest groups played little or no part in this process. They didn't communicate their views to the president or the Senate; they didn't testify at confirmation hearings; they didn't put political pressure on the decision makers. But by the late 1980s that, too, had changed. When Robert Bork was nominated to the Supreme Court in 1987, scores of interest groups—some conservative, some liberal—weighed in for or against his nomination. Bork was rejected by the Senate, and the lesson drawn by many interest groups was that they could be influential players in judicial selection. They have been ever since.

One other change has also contributed to the new politics of judicial appointments: the growing role of the federal courts in the policymaking process. Over the years since World War II, courts have become more accessible to a range of political interests and have willingly entered into political disputes in many areas where they had not often ventured before: environmental protection, civil rights, voting procedures, public education, mental health, and so on. As courts have come to play a larger role in making some of the country's most important policy decisions, it has come to matter more who sits on those courts. So the judicial appointment process has become a major battleground in American politics, the place where the policy direction of courts is shaped by decisions about who will sit on those courts.

During the years that Charles Pickering served as a district court judge, he developed a record and a reputation. Both, however, were in dispute. Some thought him a fair and tolerant judge whose court was open to all views, one in which litigants were treated equally. But others thought he was not evenhanded in his treatment of litigants and was sometimes disparaging toward female or African American attorneys and their clients. Pickering was also criticized for his conservative views on several issues and for using his judicial opinions to question or undermine established law.

When the nomination arrived at the Senate, it was instantly contentious. On one side were Pickering's supporters: the president and the Justice Department; Senator Trent Lott of Mississippi, an old friend of Pickering's and then the Republican leader in the Senate; Clay Pickering, the judge's son and a Republican representative from Mississippi; many other Republican senators; and a host of conservative interest groups.

"I have known Judge Pickering for many years, and I know he will certainly be an excellent nominee for this important post in our national judicial system," Lott said. "Throughout his distinguished career, Judge Pickering has shown himself to be a man of both professional and personal integrity."[25]

Opposing the Pickering appointment was a long list of civil rights, women's, and other more liberal interest groups. Although most of President Bush's judicial nominees were more conservative than these groups would have wished, they targeted a few as the focus of their opposition, and Pickering was one of those. In the Senate, there was also significant opposition from Democrats, especially some of those who sat on the Senate Judiciary Committee, which holds hearings on and has jurisdiction over court nominees.

Democrats argued that Pickering had opposed school desegregation in Mississippi and made special provisions in his court for a defendant charged with cross burning, but Senator Mitch McConnell (R-Kentucky) argued that he had displayed "moral courage" on the civil rights issue and had not pushed for more progress to avoid inciting violence in Mississippi.

continued

Politics in Action *continued*

When the time came for the committee to vote in March 2002—almost ten months after it received Pickering's nomination—it divided along party lines. Ten Democrats voted to defeat the nomination, nine Republicans voted to recommend Pickering's confirmation. Under Senate practice, the failure of a nomination to win majority support in committee is usually the end of the process; no vote takes place in the full Senate.

There was no Senate floor vote on Pickering's nomination in the 107th Congress, which ended in 2002. But in the 2002 congressional elections the Republicans gained a slim majority in the Senate and took control of all its committees. Conservative Senator Orrin Hatch (R-Utah) became the chair of the Judiciary Committee and promised swift action on President Bush's judicial nominations. Emboldened by this, President Bush again nominated Charles Pickering and several others whose judicial nominations had not been confirmed in the 107th Congress.

In 2003, the Judiciary Committee, still split along party lines but with the Republicans now in the majority, voted to recommend Pickering's confirmation and his nomination was sent to the Senate floor for a vote. But opponents employed a filibuster to prevent a vote on Pickering's confirmation. Although Pickering's nomination appeared to have the support of more than half of the Senate, the Republican leadership could not muster the sixty votes needed to end the filibuster. Even in the minority, opponents of the Pickering nomination were able to prevent its confirmation.

Then in January 2004, President Bush employed a rarely used constitutional authority to give Pickering a recess appointment to the Fifth Circuit. Recess appointments do not require Senate confirmation but only last until the end of the Congress then sitting. Pickering retired from the Appeals Court shortly before his recess appointment would have ended in January 2005.

What Do You Think?

1. Is it appropriate for one party to use delaying tactics simply because the other party used them previously? Should there be a time limit on confirmation decisions—for example, requiring the Senate to vote on a nomination within three months of receiving it from the president?

2. Should presidents use their judicial appointment power to try to nominate judges who share their ideology and policy views? Does their victory in an election entitle them to "stack the courts"?

3. Should the Senate deny confirmation to a judicial nominee because a majority of its members disagree with the nominee's ideological or policy views, even if the nominee is intelligent and experienced?

4. Had you been a member of the Senate Judiciary Committee, would you have supported the appointment of Judge Charles Pickering to the Court of Appeals? What arguments would you have used to defend your action?

5. Would it be better to staff federal judgeships by popular election rather than presidential appointment? What are the costs and benefits of each approach?

Summary

We began this chapter by noting the beliefs that most Americans share about the judiciary: the Constitution is sacred; the courts should interpret it in the light of precedent and changing times; and the Supreme Court's decision on the meaning of the Constitution is the final one. Most Americans believe that judicial decision making should not be subject to the same partisan politics that affect Congress and the presidency in the normal course of their policymaking and implementation responsibilities.

Nevertheless, the judiciary is a political institution and must often rule on some of the most divisive social issues of the day. Courts provide forums in which individuals and interest groups can obtain hearings of their disputes and legal claims. Courts and judges thus are integral players in the politics of American democracy.

The United States has two separate sets of judicial systems, federal and state, an arrangement referred to as judicial federalism. If there is a conflict between national and state laws, the matter is settled by the federal courts and ultimately by the Supreme Court. Federal law takes precedence over state law.

In 1789 Congress divided the country into thirteen districts and created a federal district court for each. Today there are ninety-four district courts; there are thirteen appeals courts that review cases appealed to them from the district courts; and there is one Supreme Court, the final judge and jury in the federal system. The Supreme Court hears cases from state courts only if the cases deal with federal questions—that is, issues involving the interpretation of the Constitution or other federal laws. Under the principle of comity, the Court does not review cases decided on independent state grounds, such as a state constitution.

The Supreme Court has original jurisdiction in cases involving disputes between two or more states and cases brought against the United States by foreign ambassadors; such cases originate in the Supreme Court. However, the majority of the cases that come to the Court arrive under its appellate jurisdiction: they are appealed from lower federal courts and from state courts.

Courts have jurisdiction only over disputes involving adverse interests and a real controversy. The parties must have standing to sue, meaning that they must show that they are suffering or are in danger of suffering an immediate and substantial personal injury. Courts avoid deciding political questions that the judges think should be resolved by other branches of government. Disputes open to judicial resolution are referred to as justiciable. The definition of justiciable issues has broadened over the years and now involves the Court in many political disputes, such as the resolution of the 2000 presidential election and the determination of whether legislative districts conform to the dictates of the Constitution.

The power of judicial review gives the courts the ability to strike down any law enacted by Congress or by the states and to declare official government actions unconstitutional. Although judicial review is controversial because it enables the Supreme Court to thwart the democratic process, the Court has nonetheless increasingly asserted this power. As a result, it has been criticized for its judicial activism and urged to exercise judicial self-restraint—to defer to Congress and state legislatures.

Federal judges are appointed by the president with the advice and consent of the Senate. Senators exercise considerable influence over lower-court appointments, and the president often encounters considerable senatorial opposition to his nominees for the Supreme Court, who usually share his political views. Some presidents have been more successful than others in "packing" the Court. Franklin Roosevelt was unable to change the size of the Court, but he succeeded in appointing enough of his supporters to turn a conservative Court into a liberal one. Presidents Nixon, Reagan, and George H. W. Bush each appointed several conservative justices, thereby shifting the Court from the "liberal jurisprudence" of earlier decades.

The Supreme Court decides less than 1 percent of the cases placed on its docket each year. Most cases come to the Court through petitions for a writ of certiorari, which requests the Court to review the ruling of a lower court; it may deny such a petition.

The grant of review requires the vote of four justices (the so-called rule of four), but usually a majority of the justices vote for the grant. The Court takes only cases that involve questions of law on which lower courts have disagreed. Litigants then submit briefs on the merits—the questions to be decided.

The Court hears oral arguments in only about 100 cases a year. Each side in a case has thirty minutes to present its arguments. Within a day or two after oral arguments, the justices meet in secret conference to discuss and vote on the case. One of the justices in the majority is assigned to write an opinion for the Court. The justice writing the opinion must attempt to reach a compromise that will serve as an institutional opinion stating the reasons for the Court's decision. The other justices are free to write concurring opinions, which agree with the decision but for different reasons, or dissenting opinions.

The Court decides conflicts by bringing them within the language, structure, and spirit of the Constitution. In this way it determines public policy. The reactions of other institutions of government and the public may enhance or thwart the implementation of the Court's rulings. Congress can temper the effect of a ruling through jurisdictional changes, through a constitutional amendment, or by rewriting legislation. The president can undercut the Court by issuing contradictory directives to federal agencies, assigning low priority to enforcement, or publicly disagreeing with its rulings. Ultimately, however, the Court is constrained by public opinion and its desire to create public confidence in its judicial judgments.

Key Terms

judicial federalism
constitutional courts
legislative courts
district courts
courts of appeals
briefs
en banc
federal questions
independent state grounds

principle of comity
jurisdiction
original jurisdiction
appellate jurisdiction
standing to sue
political questions
justiciable disputes
judicial activism
judicial self-restraint

senatorial courtesy
confirmation hearing
docket
writ of certiorari
rule of four
opinion
institutional opinion
concurring opinion
dissenting opinion

Discussion Questions

1. What kinds of court cases are most likely to be reviewed by the U.S. Supreme Court? What happens to other cases that the Supreme Court declines to review?
2. Why is it important for courts to follow precedent in making their decisions?
3. In a democracy, should the Supreme Court have the power to overturn legislation or administrative judgments made by elected officials?

4. If you were an American president faced with the task of filling a vacancy on the Supreme Court, what characteristics would you seek in a nominee? Did President George W. Bush seek those characteristics in his nomination of John Roberts?
5. Should the Supreme Court be attentive to public opinion in its decision making? If so, in what way? If not, why not?

Topics for Debate

Debate each side of the following propositions:

1. U.S. District Court judges should be elected by the citizens of the state in which they will have jurisdiction.
2. Supreme Court justices should be forced to retire at the age of seventy.
3. All federal court proceedings, including oral arguments before the Supreme Court, should be televised by C-SPAN.

4. No one should be appointed to the Supreme Court without prior judicial experience in the state or federal courts.
5. To help Congress avoid the enactment of unconstitutional laws, the Supreme Court should provide advisory opinions on pending legislation when such legislation is under consideration.

Where on the Web?

U.S. Supreme Court **www.supremecourtus.gov/**

U.S. Federal Courts **www.uscourts.gov/**

Historic Collection of Supreme Court Opinions **supct.law.cornell.edu/supct/**

Audio recordings of oral arguments in the Supreme Court **www.oyez.org**

Go to **www.thomsonedu.com/thomsonnow** to learn about a powerful online study tool. You will get a personalized study plan based on your responses to a diagnostic Pre-Test. Once you have mastered the materials with the help of interactive learning tools, activities, timelines, video case studies, simulations, and an integrated E-Book, you can take a Post-Test to confirm you are ready to move to the next chapter.

Selected Readings

Abramson, Jeffrey. *We, the Jury: The Jury System and the Ideal of Democracy.* New York: Basic Books, 2000.

Clayton, Cornell W., and Howard Gillman, eds. *Supreme Court Decision Making: New Institutionalist Approaches.* Chicago: University of Chicago Press, 1999.

Congressional Quarterly. *Guide to the United States Supreme Court.* Washington, D.C.: Congressional Quarterly, 2004.

Friedman, Lawrence M. *A History of American Law.* New York: Touchstone Books, 2005.

Goldman, Sheldon. *Picking Federal Judges.* New Haven, Conn.: Yale University Press, 1999.

Hall, Kermit L., James W. Ely, and Joel B. Grossman, eds. *The Oxford Companion to the Supreme Court of the United States.* New York: Oxford University Press, 2005.

Lazarus, Edward. *Closed Chambers: The First Eyewitness Account of the Epic Struggles Inside the Supreme Court.* New York: Crown Publishing Group, 1998.

Lewis, Anthony. *Gideon's Trumpet.* New York: Random House Publishers, 1964.

O'Connor, Sandra Day. *The Majesty of the Law: Reflections of a Supreme Court Justice.* New York: Random House Publishers, 2003.

Rosenberg, Gerald. *The Hollow Hope: Can Courts Bring About Social Change?* Chicago: University of Chicago Press, 1993.

Scalia, Antonin. *A Matter of Interpretation: Federal Courts and the Law.* Princeton, N.J.: Princeton University Press, 1998.

Notes

[1] *Virginia v. Black* 358 US 343 (2003).

[2] Ibid.

[3] Judicial Conference of the United States,www.uscourts.gov/cgi-bin/cmsd2004.pl.

[4] See Ronald Collins and Peter Galie, "Models of Post-Incorporation Judicial Review," *University of Cincinnati Law Review* 55 (1986): 317.

[5] *Griswold v. Connecticut* 381 US 479 (1965).

[6] *United States v. Students Challenging Regulatory Agency Procedures,* 412 U.S. 669 (1973).

[7] *Colegrove v. Green,* 328 U.S. 549 (1946).

[8] *Baker v. Carr 369 US 186 (1962).*

[9] Marlbury v. Madison 5 US 137 (1803).

[10] *Brown v. Board of Education* 34 US 483 (1954).

[11] Alexis de Tocqueville, *Democracy in America,* ed. Philip Bradley (New York: Doubleday, 1945), 151.

[12] Steven Alumbaugh and C. K. Rowland, "The Links Between Platform-Based Appointment Criteria and Trial Judges' Abortion Judgments," *Judicature* 74 (1990): 153.

[13] Quoted in David M. O'Brien, *Storm Center: The Supreme Court in American Politics,* 6th ed. (New York: W. W. Norton & Co., 2002), 74; Kennedy oral history interview.

[14] Ibid.

[15] *United States v. Nixon,* 418 U.S. 683 (1974).

[16] *Roe v. Wade* 410 US 113 (1973).

[17] Charles E. Hughes, *The Supreme Court of the United States* (New York: Columbia University Press, 1928), 68.

[18] *Abington School District v. Schempp,* 374 U.S. 203 (1963).

[19] *Norris v. Alabama,* 294 U.S. 587 (1935).

[20] *Hernandez v. Texas,* 347 U.S. 475 (1954).

[21] *Zurcher v. The Stanford Daily,* 436 U.S. 547 (1978).

[22] *Texas v. Johnson,* 491 U.S. 397 (1989).

[23] *United States v. Eichman,* 496 U.S. 310 (1990).

[24] *Bush v. Gore,* 531 US 98 (2000).

[25] "Cochran, "Lott Recommend Judge Charles Pickering For U.S. Court Of Appeals," January 31, 2001, www.senate.gov/~cochran/press/pr013101.html (accessed June 28, 2001).

14

Domestic Policy

Introduction

WE SAID IN CHAPTER 1 THAT the output of government takes the form of public policy. Simply stated, public policy is what government does (or does not do). In Chapter 1 we also noted the imperfect relationship that often exists between what people want and what government does. Public opinion in a particular issue area may provide policymakers with incomplete or even conflicting directives. Although public opinion polls often reveal a broad consensus on identifying general policy issues or goals, these same polls usually indicate considerable conflict over specific policy approaches to achieving those goals. For example, virtually all Americans believe that improving public education should be a high national priority; how to achieve that objective is another question. Some people favor encouraging more independent, charter schools; some favor more extensive national testing of students; some favor providing parents with vouchers that would give them the choice of sending their children either to public or to private schools; some favor reducing federal spending to school districts in which students fail to improve on standardized tests; and others do not favor any of these. The list of disagreement exceeds in number the areas of agreement.

American democracy does not always require a direct relationship between the public's attitude on some issue and the policy developed by government to respond to that issue. Charles E. Lindblom, a distinguished scholar and observer of American government and politics, recognized this when he observed that "no straightforward relation holds between what citizens want and the policies they get. How elected officials will make policy depends on the structure of rules, authority relations, procedures, and organizations mediating between an elected official and the effect he or she exerts on policy." "The rules of democracy," Lindblom reminds us, "throw important powers and liberties into the citizen's hands, but confer only a loose control over policy."[1]

The making of public policy, then, often appears to be a "zigzag" process. There is a relationship between what the public wants and what government does. But the path from one to the other often appears disjointed.

Typically, the journey is excruciatingly slow. And although there may appear to be consensus on goals or ends, considerable conflict often exists over specific approaches or the means to achieve those goals.

For years, public opinion polls have shown the cost of prescription drugs to be a major concern for many Americans, particularly for senior citizens. Since the enactment of Medicare in 1965, the cost of prescription drugs has been rising at nearly three times that of inflation. Those seniors in the lower income group often have had to choose between food and drugs.

Recognizing this issue, President George W. Bush made prescription drug coverage a priority policy issue early in his administration. In 2001, he advanced a prescription drug card proposal in which pharmacies would be asked to provide bulk prescription discounts to seniors. But the president's proposal was derailed by a lawsuit filed by the National Association of Chain Drug Stores. In his 2002 State of the Union address, President Bush returned to the prescription drug issue, asking Congress "to join me this year to . . . give seniors a sound and modern Medicare system that includes coverage for prescription drugs."[2]

Soon thereafter, numerous prescription drug options were proposed by House and Senate members, Democrats and Republicans alike. Debates between Republican and Democratic lawmakers were especially pointed, bitter, and partisan. Arguing that private insurance companies can give seniors more choices and lower cost, Republicans generally looked to the private sector and competition in the marketplace to solve the problem. Democrats were more skeptical of such coverage, demanding that a prescription drug benefit be added to the Medicare system. Republicans countered that such a proposal would be too costly. The debate continued.

Representatives of the drug and health industry and insurance companies, as well as lobbyists for senior citizens, supported different options. The pharmaceutical industry was dubious of government-run programs; it maintained that such programs control prices, stifle research, discourage the development of new drugs, and lower profits. Insurance companies,

wary of an approach that would increase premium rates, also were leery of government efforts. In contrast, consumer groups and labor unions generally supported the more comprehensive government-funded programs, as did the AARP (the influential lobby for older Americans). In this controversy, the AARP threw its weight behind the GOP proposal precisely because it had a prescription drug plan.

After several alternative prescription drug bills were considered in the House and Senate, Congress approved a proposal in November 2003 that added a prescription drug plan to the Medicare program. Called the biggest change in Medicare since the program was created in 1965, the prescription drug plan will pay $1,500 (not including annual premium costs) of the first $5,100 worth of medicine in a year and will cover 95 percent of the cost of each prescription after the patient has spent $3,600.

President Bush was quick to take credit for the bill. The day after Senate passage, the president declared that "For the sake of our seniors, we got something done." Democrats remained skeptical, however.

The struggle for passage of a prescription drug bill illustrates several aspects of the consensus and conflict that underlie policymaking in America. Although most people and their elected representative agree on the nature of the problem, Americans disagreed on the solution. Politics, which involves give and take, finally led members of Congress to find a solution that would be acceptable to most people they represent. But every policy has an effect that benefits some and hurts others; the new Medicare bill was no exception. It was projected to increase the national debt; there were gaps in the drug coverage. Doctors and the pharmaceutical community were unhappy, claiming that it would raise their costs, require considerable paperwork, and not reduce the problem. And the grumbling has continued—that's politics. That the Medicare system will have to continue to be adjusted also indicates that the political struggle is likely to continue and may have an effect down the road. For now, the people have spoken, the policymakers have acted, and the policy is being implemented. Only time will tell if it is successful.

Questions to Ponder

- How do issues like the cost of prescription drugs for seniors become part of the national political agenda and viewed as important enough to warrant public attention and consideration by Congress?
- Why and how is government persuaded to act on public issues?
- Are compromises among vastly different views and approaches easy to work out?
- What is the relationship between public opinion in various policy areas and actual decisions reached through the policy process?

14.1 In Theory . . .
Making Policy

In a democratic political system, everyone is entitled to voice their opinions. The opinion favored by the most people generally prevails. In applying democratic principles to policy options, however, these principles can lead to a situation in which no option emerges as the optimum choice. Articulated by Kenney Arrow—and known as "Arrow's paradox"—the paradox shows that in aggregating preferences among various groups a situation may arise in which no option emerges as the preferred choice; democracy may lead to "gridlock."

Arrow's paradox also shows that the more complicated the policy issue, the more likely "gridlock" is to result. Followed strictly, democratic principles may lead to contradictory, incoherent, or deadlocked policymaking.

The solution to the paradox lies in the realm of politics, not necessarily that of public opinion.

Thus, policymaking in a democracy is not simply the application of the principle that numbers rule, that the side with the greater number should prevail. Rather, it is the result of coalition building, negotiating, compromising, bargaining, and persuading; often the art of the "possible," not merely the "desirable" or even the result, is most consistent with democratic values. Thus, sometimes a consensus is reached and policy is formulated despite citizen preferences rather than because of them.

Kenneth Arrow, *Individual Values and Social Choice* (Cambridge, Mass.: Harvard University Press, 1953); Charles E. Lindblom, *The Policy-Making Process* (Englewood Cliffs, N.J.: Prentice-Hall, 1980); and Charles Bonser, Eugene McGregor, and Clinton Oster, *American Public Policy Problems* (Upper Saddle River, N.J.: Prentice-Hall, 2000).

Types of Policy

If public policy is what the government does or does not do, then it can also be thought of as "a goal-directed or purposive course of action [taken by government] to deal with a public problem."[3] Whether the policy succeeds or fails is the principal criterion used to evaluate it.

Public policies may be classified in several ways: in terms of costs, who pays and how much; in terms of benefits, who gains and how much; and in terms of issue and impact, whether it effectively addresses the problem and what consequences it produces.

During the 1960s and early 1970s, civil rights and foreign and defense issues (particularly the Vietnam War) were dominant policy concerns. During the 1970s, energy was a major issue, and in the 1980s, especially during Ronald Reagan's presidency, government organization and economic recovery received much attention. In the 1990s, health care, environmental degradation, crime, and welfare received considerable attention. Today, issues such as homeland security, medical coverage for older Americans, corporate accountability, retirement security, and immigration, both legal and illegal, are considered major problem areas.

Impact-Based Classification

Theodore Lowi suggested that policy be classified in terms of its impact on society. His basic categories were distributive, regulatory, or redistributive.[4]

distributive policies
Policies that distribute goods and services to citizens (for example, Social Security).

Distributive policies are those that distribute goods and services to citizens. Policies that provide recreational, public safety, transportation, and educational services are examples. Distributive policies direct their benefits to different population groups: subsidies to farmers, Social Security payments to retirees, money to states for highway construction, grants to scientists for research, grants-in-aid to cities and states, tax deductions to mortgage holders and people who contribute to charities.

Although some group or groups gain from a distributive policy, the costs associated with the policy are viewed as minimal because they are shared by the public. Even national defense is sometimes regarded as a distributive policy, because lucrative defense contracts are distributed among the districts of many members of Congress.

In distributive policymaking, everyone seems to win; no one appears to lose, or at least not much. The politics of distributive policymaking is often described as pork-barrel politics—there is something for everyone, and individual legislators support one another's particular programs. Although such programs may cost billions of dollars, they generate surprisingly little controversy.

regulatory policies
Policies that restrict or regulate certain types of behavior (for example, child labor laws).

Regulatory policies are those by which government constricts certain types of behavior. Developed in response to practices deemed harmful or destructive, these policies include laws that regulate child labor, automobile emissions, minimum wages, harmful gas or food additives, and dumping of industrial wastes in streams and rivers. Regulatory policymaking usually involves costs and benefits that have the opposite effect than those of distributive policy. Certain groups will be constrained in their activities for the protection and benefit of society. The "Do Not Call List" is a good example of a regulatory policy. Telemarketers lose potential customers from this restriction, but the portion of the public that have indicated they do not want to be bothered by such telephone calls benefits. Regulatory politics often involve compromise as the cost and benefits to the policy are weighed.

Redistributive policies are those perceived to take benefits (wealth, property, or other values) from some groups and give them to others. Examples include welfare programs that help the poor, tax credits for those who earn under a certain amount, and affirmative action programs designed to help certain minority groups in education and the marketplace. Because redistributive policy involves costs to some and benefits to others, it may be least amenable to compromise. Usually there are clearly identifiable interests that compete with one another for the most desirable outcome.

redistributive policies
Policies that take benefits from some group and give them to others (for example, welfare).

Stages of Policy Development

Policymaking can best be thought of as a process that involves five principal stages: problem recognition, policy formulation and adoption, policy implementation, policy evaluation, and policy reconsideration or termination.

Problem Recognition

Problem recognition is probably the most important stage in the policymaking process. Before Congress considers an issue, before an agency of the executive branch administers a program, and before the courts consider any disputes, the issue must first be recognized as a problem requiring government attention and possible action. Not every problem requires attention, particularly at the national level. Many issues are resolved privately without government intervention. Many more are dealt with by local and state authorities. Only a small portion rise to the level of national importance.

problem recognition
The initial stage of the policy process, at which issues are first recognized as problems requiring government action.

Public awareness is critical for an issue to receive serious consideration. Dramatic social and economic events often trigger that awareness. The Great Depression of the 1930s is a classic example of an event that forced the country to pay attention to the need for significant public action in welfare, employment, housing, and social policy. The terrorist attacks in September 2001 prompted President George W. Bush and Congress to propose a series of policy initiatives, including the creation of a new Department of Homeland Security.

For the public to recognize a national problem and believe that it requires government action, it must affect large numbers of people. Widespread declines in student scores on standardized achievement tests, high and persistent levels of unemployment, upward surge in the cost of imported oil, dramatic declines in the nation's economic health, and sudden and long-lasting increases in levels of crime, poverty, or serious illness are examples of problems that elicit widespread public concern, which, in turn, encourages the government to address them.

Sometimes a small issue can provide the spark that ignites a large conflict. Take the plight of the northern spotted owl, which environmentalists highlighted in the 1980s. This small, two-pound bird, whose habitat is fir and spruce forests in Washington, Oregon, and California, was threatened by logging. Concerned environments succeeded in having the bird placed on the endangered-species list and forcing at least a temporary reduction in logging activities. Loggers were not particularly happy with the result.

The resulting battle between the environmentalists and the timber industry was the most intense ever generated by the Endangered Species Act. Environmentalists pointed out that the entire ecosystem of the forest was in decline and that more than 100 species of plants and animals, including the spotted owl, were threatened with extinction. The timber industry countered that the forest provided employment for thousands of families, as well as lumber for millions of homes. Undeterred, environmentalists filed lawsuits claiming that the Interior Department and the U.S. Forest Service, the two federal agencies managing the forests, were violating the Endangered Species Act. By 1992, former President George H. W. Bush grudgingly concurred and approved a plan to restrict logging on 5.4 million acres of Pacific Northwest forest where the spotted owl lives.

The spotted owl controversy continued to be a catalyst for policy change in the administration of Bill Clinton. Secretary of the Interior Bruce Babbitt announced that, henceforth, his department would focus on entire ecosystems rather than on individual plants and animals. Babbitt's proposal provided for intervention before any crises arose and individual species were endangered. But the battle was not over. After the Republicans took control of Congress in 1995, they enacted legislation that permitted the resumption of logging across vast sections of public land. Despite his threat to veto the legislation, President Clinton ultimately signed it into law. And in April 2001 the George W. Bush administration asked Congress to approve a one-year moratorium on the provision of the Endangered Species Act that permits citizens to bring legal action to force the Fish and Wildlife Service to declare a species endangered, such as with the spotted owl.

Public awareness is not enough to ensure that an issue will be placed on the policy agenda. Skillful advocacy by interest groups is also critical. Political interest groups see to it that issues of concern to them are brought to the public's attention and make their way to the agenda-setting stage of the policy process. In the case of the northern spotted owl, environmental groups such as the Wilderness Society and the Environmental Defense Fund were instrumental in this process.

Policy Formulation and Adoption: Iron Triangles and Issue Networks

policy formulation
The stage of the policy process at which effective and feasible solutions are developed.

Once a problem has been placed on the government's agenda, an effective and feasible solution must be found. In this **policy formulation** stage, there are many possible courses of action. For example, the perceived problem of declining test scores among college-bound high school seniors might be addressed by policies to encourage better-trained teachers, smaller classes, curriculum modification, or some combination of these. From the variety of options that exist, policymakers must identify a solution or set of solutions that will be effective in addressing the problem, acceptable to the parties concerned, and affordable.

Many actors and organizations may be involved in the actual formulation of policy. Legislators and their staffs, the president and the White House staff, government bureaucrats and agencies, specially appointed commissions, and "think tanks" (such as the Brookings Institution, the American Enterprise Institute, the Heritage Foundation, and the CATO Institute) may all be involved in the drafting of policy alternatives.

Moreover, policy is rarely formulated without the active involvement of the interest groups most likely to be affected. An interesting example of this occurred in 1995, when Republican Senator Slade Gorton of Washington introduced a bill that would have scrapped major provisions of the Endangered Species Act, first passed in 1973. The bill was largely drafted by groups that had been most negatively affected by the act: timber, mining, ranching, and utility interests. When asked by reporters if he believed that groups with such a direct stake in the outcome of policy should be involved in formulating legislation, the senator replied, "I don't think that's how good public policy should be made, but I'm perfectly willing to get the free services of good lawyers in drafting my views."[5] Although Gorton's bill was not enacted, Congress did impose a thirteen-month moratorium on adding new species to the list.

Policy formulation does not always result in a new law or administrative action. Policymakers often may decide not to act. That an issue has made it to the agenda-setting stage does not automatically mean that action will be taken.[6]

Marshaling the support needed to win official approval of a specific course of action is called **policy adoption.** At this stage, lobbying, bargaining, negotiating, and compromising may be needed. Seldom does any policy emerge from the process in the form in which it was initially proposed. To be adopted—that is, to gain sufficient political support to be adopted—policies typically must be modified significantly.

Often the activities that take place during the formulation and adoption stages occur among a cluster of actors and institutions. The special relationship that sometimes develops among executive agencies, interest groups, and congressional committees, which we describe in Chapter 12 as an iron triangle, occurs in distinct issue areas or networks.

Figure 14.1 is a diagram of the energy issue network. Similar networks exist in education, employment and labor, health, urban affairs, agriculture, transportation, national security, and other issue areas. In such networks, influential individuals and groups move freely in and out of the policy arena. In many cases, it appears that no single group is "in control" of policymaking. Issue networks supplement the iron triangle with a host of other policy professionals and experts.

Health policy, for example, is characterized by many sets of people knowledgeable about various aspects of this complex issue: physicians and other health-care professionals, hospitals and clinics, mental health centers, nursing homes, pharmaceutical companies, insurance companies, patients, senior citizens, and so forth. Health policy cannot possibly be made in isolation from these and many other groups. Hugh Heclo, who first advanced the idea of issue networks, argues that they have added a new and complicating dimension to policy formation and

policy adoption
The state of the policy process at which official courses of action are approved and adopted.

Figure 14.1 The Energy Issue Network

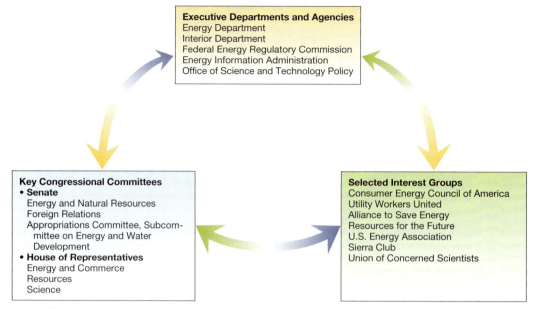

Source: *Washington Information Directory,* 2004–2005 (Washington, D.C.: Congressional Quarterly, 2004).

adoption. Issue networks, he says, "overlay the once stable political reference points with new forces that complicate calculations, decrease predictability, and impose considerable strains on those charged with government leadership."[7]

Moreover, revolving-door politics, discussed in Chapter 6, allow individuals to move freely among private and public institutions, as the illustrations through this book indicate.

Policy Implementation

Policies that have been adopted must be administered. The process of putting policies into place is termed **policy implementation.** In a few cases, policy decisions may be self-executing; for example, the decision to extend formal diplomatic recognition to a new foreign government is a policy that is essentially in place as soon as it is adopted, although the country must first establish an embassy and designate an ambassador. Most laws and policy decisions, however, are not implemented automatically.

Policy implementation is not a simple, routine process. The administration of policy can be highly political, sometimes involving struggles as intense as those occur during the policy adoption process, be it environmental policy, labor–management disputes, or community action programs by faith-based groups.

Administrators and bureaucrats in any agency often have wide latitude in the implementation and administration of policy. By choosing to apply laws rigorously or leniently, bureaucrats may shape the effect of policies and thus

policy implementation
The stage of the policy process at which adopted policies are put into place.

incur the wrath of Congress, the president, and outside groups. These struggles can produce a cycle of frustrating policymaking, implementation, and public reaction. Reporter Rochelle Stanfield describes one such struggle in the area of environmental politics. "In air pollution control, solid waste disposal, and other environmental protection programs, Congress passes laws, EPA implements them in ways displeasing to Congress, Congress passes more specific laws, EPA again carries them out to the dissatisfaction of Congress, and Congress threatens to enact even more specific legislation."[8]

The courts, too, may be important in shaping policy during the implementation phase. Judicial rulings often establish the precise direction a policy will take. In public education, for example, court decisions have required the busing of schoolchildren to achieve racial balance, limited the power of local school boards to set student dress codes, forced local authorities to provide more educational options for disabled and other disadvantaged children, and altered the methods of state school financing to achieve greater equality among local school districts.

Policy Evaluation

A policy that has been formulated, adopted, and implemented is ready to be evaluated. **Policy evaluation** consists of a set of activities designed to determine whether a policy is working as intended. Does an energy policy reduce wasteful use of energy? Did the Patriot missile perform effectively under combat conditions? Does an environmental policy result in a less polluted environment? Does a child nutrition policy lead to healthier children? Does an educational program for disadvantaged children result give better education to those children? Does an antipoverty policy reduce poverty? And what is the cost of each of these programs? For many policies, cost must be measured not only directly, in terms of federal dollars expended on a program, but also indirectly, in terms of the cost of compliance with the policy's requirements to state and local governments, as well as private firms and individuals.

Not only intended consequences but also unanticipated ones need to be evaluated. A highway construction program, for example, may relieve traffic congestion as hoped but may also stimulate commercial growth and development in areas unprepared for such growth. Moreover, it may generate unexpectedly higher levels of pollution or reduce ridership on mass transit.

Policy evaluation may be conducted in two ways. The first is an informal or "seat of the pants" evaluation.[9] For example, if the residents and administrators of a housing project express satisfaction with the program, there is at least an informal indication that the program is working. The problem with such impressionistic evaluations is that the evaluators may not be disinterested parties. If they have been advocates of the program, have a stake in its success, or depend for their information on those who do, this can affect their judgments.

To avoid this problem, evaluators try to measure the effect of policy in more rigorous ways by collecting information from a variety of sources, using sophisticated statistical analyses, and following accepted social–scientific research methods.

policy evaluation
The stage of the policy process at which adopted and implemented policies are evaluated for effectiveness.

When this is done, others can check the results and analysts can determine whether the policy is having the desired effect. This leads to the last stage in the policy process.

Policy Reconsideration or Termination

policy termination
The process by which policies that are not meeting their objectives are overhauled or terminated.

Programs that are not meeting their objectives or have outlived the problem for which they were created may be overhauled or undergo **policy termination.** As one team of policy analysts has noted, "Policies get old, they wear out, or they keep solving problems that have long since been resolved or replaced by more pressing social priorities. . . . Releasing dollars and other resources invested in outdated programs makes them available for deployment against new problems."[10] President Bush made much of the fact that his 2007 budget called for the elimination of many programs that he considered poorly performing or duplicative, including 42 education programs totaling more than $3 billion.

Periodically, the public's dissatisfaction with government and government policies reaches a point at which fundamental changes are considered. In 1993, Congress, bowing to pressure to cut spending, terminated support for the $11 billion Superconducting Super Collider project being built in Texas. And in 1995, citing the need to set an example for cost savings in government, Congress abolished its Office of Technology Assessment, an agency that for twenty-three years had provided members with advice on technical issues such as nuclear proliferation, medical research, and telecommunications policy.

But there are many obstacles to program termination, and halting an ongoing project can be difficult. Employees of the agency created to administer a program will fight to hold on to their jobs. Agency employees typically seek ways to demonstrate their value and publicize the negative consequences of terminating the program. The agency's clients—those served by the program—will also rally around continuation of the program, as may legislators responding to pressure from potential voters or government contractors. Despite such difficulties, however, program terminations and modifications occur; they are part of the policymaking process.

Politics and the Policy Process

The making of public policy is a process that moves and is never complete. What, then, are the implications of the continually changing and incomplete nature of domestic policy?

Incrementalism

Policymaking is often extremely slow; and even when changes are made in a policy, they are likely to be small departures from the status quo. In the areas of health, housing, welfare, education, and the environment a span of years typically separates problem recognition from the adoption of meaningful policy. In national defense policy, a decade or more is usually needed to develop a new weapons system.

Incrementalism is a salient characteristic of policymaking in the United States. Often policymakers seem to take two steps forward and one step back. Many factors account for the slow pace: Social problems often are complex, simple solutions are rarely possible, and funds are almost always limited. The most important factor, however, is the fragmentation of political power.

Responsibility for any policy area is shared by a host of congressional committees and subcommittees; numerous executive departments, commissions, and agencies; and the already overloaded and overburdened court system. Moreover, the fragmentation found at the national level is magnified many times over at the state and local levels. **Fragmented power** means that interested groups and individuals have numerous opportunities to block or alter suggested policy changes, and an extraordinary amount of coalition building is necessary to bring about any significant change. Coalition building not only takes time but also necessitates a considerable amount of bargaining and compromising to satisfy the concerns of numerous groups and organizations.

Major Policy Shifts

Major changes in policy sometimes occur. Examples include the social-welfare programs initiated during the 1930s and the Elementary and Secondary Education Act of 1965, both of which are discussed later in the chapter. In 1996, significant changes occurred in the nation's approach to welfare policy, as a major federal antipoverty program was replaced with lump-sum payments to the states, giving them broad discretion to run their own welfare programs. President George W. Bush's "No Child Left Behind" education reform bill of 2002, and the Medicare reform measures that—beginning in 2006—included a benefit for prescription drugs, are two recent examples. Professors Frank Baumgartner and Bryan Jones use the term **punctuated equilibrium** to describe those periods in which, in a short, rapid time frame, major policy change occurs. Any study of American politics, they say, "must be able to account for both long periods of stability and short, violent periods of change."[11]

In the American system, large-scale, fundamental policy shifts are often associated with major social, economic, or international upheavals, such the Great Depression of the 1930s, the emergence of the Soviet Union as a superpower after World War II, or the terrorist attacks of September 11, 2001. Such events create a sense of urgency. Suddenly everyone agrees that something must be done, and it is possible to overcome some of the resistance inherent in American politics.

Major policy changes are also often associated with strong and persistent pressure from the White House. Presidents Lyndon Johnson's and George W. Bush's extraordinary interest in education played a major role in their enactment of major education reforms during their administrations. Similarly, President Ronald Reagan's philosophy of new federalism was the catalyst for the large grant consolidation programs enacted early in his administration.

Finally, the chances of major policy shifts are usually enhanced when the same political party controls Congress and the presidency. President Johnson was greatly

incrementalism
Policymaking in the United States at times seems to be extremely slow and to result in only minor or marginal change from the status quo.

fragmented power
Because governmental power and authority in the United States is so fragmented, interest groups and individuals have numerous opportunities to block or alter policy changes.

punctuated equilibrium
Periods when in a short, rapid time frame major policy change takes place.

assisted in his campaign for passage of education reform, as well as other parts of his Great Society program, by the presence of large Democratic majorities in both the House and the Senate who were sympathetic to his proposals. President Reagan was aided by a Republican majority in the Senate and a strong Republican unity in the House during the first years of his administration. Republican majorities in the House and Senate undoubtedly contributed to the approval of the prescription drug plan supported by President George W. Bush in 2003. On the other hand, in 1994 President Clinton failed to convince the Democratic-controlled Congress to pass his health-care reform proposals; and the 1996 welfare reform bill that he signed was enacted by a Republican-dominated Congress.

Mixed Results

Does public policy have much effect on the problems it is designed to solve? Successful policy initiatives include the Social Security system, the Peace Corps, the Head Start program for preschool children, the school lunch program for those who cannot afford adequate meals, and the federal job training program, which has provided numerous people with the education and skills necessary for steady employment.

But, some problems persist despite massive efforts to wipe them out. Billions of dollars have been spent to combat poverty, but there are still large numbers of poor people in the United States. Billions of dollars have been spent to clean up the environment, but there are still many polluted lakes and streams. Billions of dollars have been spent on housing, but there are still large numbers of homeless people.

Why are some problems solved, and others progress with some improvement, but some just seem to defy solutions? One reason is the complexity of the problems. Poverty, for example, has multiple causes, and experts often disagree about which of them are most important. Another reason is that the costs of a proposed solution may be greater than what society is willing to pay. Cleaning up the environment to a degree that would satisfy the most ardent environmentalists might consume funds that most people would prefer to spend on other programs.

The high cost of solving problems, or even significantly altering them, brings its own set of policy questions. Proposals for solving a particular problem almost always raise the question of how to pay for it. Should the funds be generated by raising taxes, be taken from programs, or simply be borrowed from the Treasury?

Politicians naturally want to avoid answering painful questions as long as possible. Consider, for instance, former President George H. W. Bush's response to a reporter's question about how he intended to finance his "war on drugs":

> Q: Mr. President, you've told us you're going to expand vastly the fight against drugs. Are you willing to raise taxes to pay for that?
>
> A: We're not going to have to, but we are going to expand federal expenditures.
>
> Q: Follow up on that. Mr. President, if you're not gong to raise revenues to fight the drug war, where are you going to get this money? Could you be specific?
>
> A: Stay tuned, and we will show you [later] how we're going to allocate the resources for this.[12]

Some problems are not solved because there is disagreement about what the problem really is. In the area of housing, for example, public policy has had a split focus. At some times, the emphasis has been on the construction of large public housing projects. At other times, the goal has been to clean up urban blight. At still other times, policies have been designed to provide subsidies for homeowners and renters.

What exactly is the problem? How are programs going to be paid for? Which groups are going to benefit, and which ones are going to lose? These are the sorts of political questions that policymakers must resolve. When the groups most directly involved in making policy decisions—Congress and its various committees, the president, agency administrators, interest groups, and political parties—can reach an agreement about the nature of the problem, and about the measure required to resolve it, solutions tend to be reached fairly quickly.

At the core of policymaking in the United States lies politics, the struggle among people with differing goals, objectives, and resources. The adoption of public policy is often a slow, complex process that involves a considerable amount of bargaining, negotiating, and compromise among all groups that make up the issue network concerned with any particular policy area. Those who seek changes in public policy—especially major changes—can rarely take a position on the extreme left or the extreme right of the given issue. To capture the support of all individuals and groups needed to pass and implement a new policy, the initiators usually must stake out and defend a more centrist position. But on some complex issues the "middle ground" is hard to find, and the search for that position may alienate friends, as well as foes. In the following sections we illustrate all of these points as we examine the nation's approach to education, welfare, housing, and environmental policy.

Review Questions

1. Policies characterized as those through which the government establishes rules and standards and thereby regulates or controls the behavior of individuals, groups, businesses, or other entities are known as

   A. Regulatory policies
   B. Democratic policies
   C. Distributive policies
   D. Redistributive policies

2. Probably the most important state in the process of making public policy is

   A. Problem recognition
   B. Policy formation

continued

   C. Policy adoption
   D. Policy implementation
   E. Policy termination

3. The term used to characterize policymaking in the United States, which often seems to be slow and marginal, is

   A. Zigzag
   B. Issue networks
   C. Interest group dominated
   D. Incrementalism
   E. Partisan politics

4. In public policy formation, the special relationship that sometimes develops among executive agencies, interest groups, and congressional committees is known as the

   A. Committee system
   B. Iron triangle
   C. Interest group system
   D. Process of competing elites
   E. Political party system

Answers:

   1. A
   2. A
   3. D
   4. B

Conflict and Consensus in Review

Americans often share a consensus on broad policy goals and objectives (like "quality education for all children," independence from foreign sources of oil," "elimination of poverty," and so forth), yet frequently disagree on the specifics of achieving those policy goals. Issues, such as distributive policies like Social Security, generate comparatively little conflict. Policies like these benefit everyone, and no one appears to lose much. On the other hand, issues like welfare and universal health care tend to be very controversial because they are perceived as taking resources from some groups and shifting them to others—there seems to be clear "winners" and "losers." Nevertheless, for issues to be resolved and for progress to be made, these conflicts must be overcome. Yet most change comes slowly although a crisis can precipitate policy change more quickly. How overcoming conflicts over public policy and building and maintaining a policy consensus is much of what politics in America is all about.

© Yellow Dog Productions/Getty Images

Today, approximately 30 million school children participate in the National School Lunch Program, a program providing free or reduced-price meals for eligible children at an annual cost of about $7 billion.

| Education Policy |

The federal government spends about $25 billion annually on elementary and secondary education and about $10 billion on higher education, amounts that represent less than 10 percent of all spending on public education in the United States. The percentage is small because historically education has been left largely to state and local governments. As recently as 1974, the U.S. Supreme Court stated that "no single tradition in public education is more deeply rooted [in the United States] than local control over the operations of schools."[13] Nevertheless, federal involvement in education policy is growing. Indeed, in the 1988 presidential election campaign George H. W. Bush declared that he would like to be known as the "education president," and in 2000 his son, George W. Bush, made education reform a centerpiece of his own campaign for the presidency.

Education in America: An Overview

National education policy is partly distributive and partly redistributive. For most of the country's history, the federal government's major policy concern in the educational arena has been to ensure equal access to educational opportunities.

Federal courts have invalidated laws that denied equal access to schools and colleges, and Congress has designed legislation to reduce racial and income disparities in educational opportunity.

Before 1965, the federal program with the greatest effect on education was the Serviceman's Readjustment Act of 1944 (the so-called GI bill), which provided assistance to millions of veterans who wished to complete their education. At the elementary and secondary levels, the major federal programs in education were the school lunch and milk program, the "impact" aid program (which made federal aid available to areas affected by federal activities), and programs that provided funds for vocational rehabilitation education. In addition, the National Defense Education Act, passed in 1958, was designed to upgrade science, math, and foreign-language facilities in the public schools.

The level of federal involvement in education changed significantly with the passage of the Elementary and Secondary Education Act in 1965. This legislation, originally designed to distribute federal aid to school districts on the basis of the proportion of low-income children in those districts, virtually doubled the amount of federal aid allocated to public education. When signing the act, President Johnson proclaimed the measure "the greatest breakthrough in the advance of education since the Constitution was written." The Elementary and Secondary Education Act has been renewed and modified numerous times, most recently in 2001, and remains the centerpiece of the national government's education policy. In 1979, another major event occurred when Congress created a cabinet-level Department of Education and gave it responsibility for the implementation of federal education policy. (The education issue network is illustrated in Figure 14.2.)

Education Policy in the 1980s and 1990s

In his 1980 campaign for the presidency, Ronald Reagan opposed the new Department of Education and called for its abolition. As president, he did not dismantle the department, but he did ask Congress to fold many of the federal government's education programs into a single large block grant. Such a measure, he argued, would give state and local officials more control over the allocation of federal education funds. Although the president also proposed significant reductions in levels of federal aid to education, he argued that the savings achieved through the use of a block grant would offset any losses to particular school districts.

Civil rights groups and groups representing disabled children and the poor opposed Reagan's proposal. These organizations feared that without federal guidelines on how education funds were spent, the groups they represented would not fare as well under the block grant philosophy. On the other hand, many state officials and educators supported the block grant proposal. Although they opposed reductions in education funding, these groups believed that the president's proposal would provide them greater flexibility in the expenditure of

Figure 14.2 The Education Issue Network

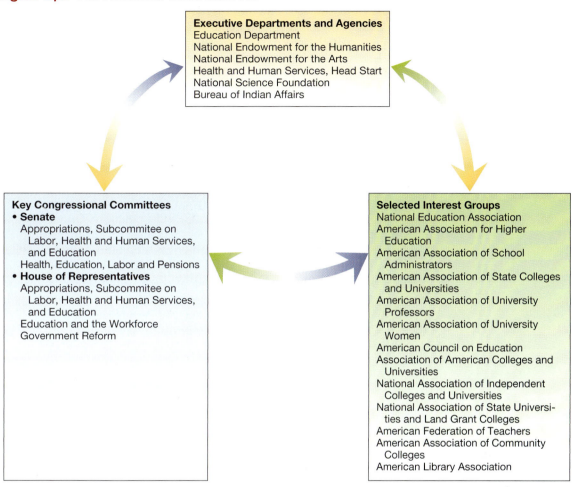

Executive Departments and Agencies
Education Department
National Endowment for the Humanities
National Endowment for the Arts
Health and Human Services, Head Start
National Science Foundation
Bureau of Indian Affairs

Key Congressional Committees
• **Senate**
Appropriations, Subcommitee on
   Labor, Health and Human Services,
   and Education
Health, Education, Labor and Pensions
• **House of Representatives**
Appropriations, Subcommitee on
   Labor, Health and Human Services,
   and Education
Education and the Workforce
Government Reform

Selected Interest Groups
National Education Association
American Association for Higher
   Education
American Association of School
   Administrators
American Association of State Colleges
   and Universities
American Association of University
   Professors
American Association of University
   Women
American Council on Education
Association of American Colleges and
   Universities
National Association of Independent
   Colleges and Universities
National Association of State Universi-
   ties and Land Grant Colleges
American Federation of Teachers
American Association of Community
   Colleges
American Library Association

education funds and would reduce the amount of paperwork and bureaucratic red tape required of local school officials.

In 1981, Congress sided with the president and passed an education block grant, known as the Education Consolidation and Improvement Act. Funds allocated under the block grant went to state education agencies, which then distributed the bulk of the money to local school districts.

Upon becoming president in 1988, George H. W. Bush graded the nation's schools "merely average" and pointed to the large number of dropouts, disappointing test scores, and low levels of state and local spending on education. Speaking for the administration, Education Secretary Lauro Cavazos called the nation's educational situation "a disaster that we must turn around."[14] In 1991 he outlined his education proposals, which called for additional spending of $670 million, most of it to enable parents to choose the schools their children would attend and to provide seed money for the establishment of 535 innovative schools, at least 1 in each congressional district. The administration also called for a system of national testing and challenged business leaders to raise about $200 million to help fund the innovative schools.

Overall, through certain highly publicized activities such as calling for the 1989 education summit conference and appointing a National Education Goals Panel, the president attempted to use his persuasive powers to shape national educational priorities, but his administration was reluctant to commit much new federal spending to the effort. As a result, the educational legislation passed by Congress during Bush's term, known as Goals 2000, was limited largely to outlining broad objectives and standards.

In April 1993, President Clinton proposed a "national service program" (commonly known as AmeriCorps) designed to make a college education available to all students, regardless of their financial situation. Under his proposal, students could receive college loans and pay them off through automatic deductions from their future earnings or by performing community service jobs—as teachers, police officers, or social workers, for example—after graduation. In September 1993, Congress passed and sent to the White House the National Service Bill, which provides education grants to each volunteer who completes a community service job. Although the Republican Congress elected the next year tried to eliminate the program, it survived, albeit in a scaled-back form.

Education Policy in the Twenty-First Century

George W. Bush made education reform a centerpiece of his campaign for the presidency. In January 2001, just three days after taking office, the president sent to Congress the outlines of his "No Child Left Behind" plan, calling for comprehensive education reform. Less than a year later, in December 2001, Congress—in its reauthorization of the 1965 Elementary and Secondary Education Act—passed the so-called No Child Left Behind Act, the most extensive federal involvement in elementary and secondary education since passage of the 1965 act. The act, signed by President Bush on January 8, 2002, allocates approximately $25 billion per year in education dollars, an increase of approximately $6 billion over previous annual allocations. Although Bush's proposal for support of school vouchers was not approved, the bill requires schools to comply with new federal requirements for testing students, hire "highly qualified" teachers, give parents progress reports, and develop alternatives for failing schools. The most controversial of these requirements is the annual testing of student performance in reading and math for every child in third through eighth grades, beginning with the 2005–2006 school year. The act requires schools to raise the percentage of students proficient in reading and math, reaching 100 percent within twelve years. If scores fail to improve, low-income students can receive money for tutoring or may transfer to another public school. A school in which scores fail to improve over six years could be required to hire new staff.

When signing the bill, President Bush commented, "Today begins a new era, a new time for public education in our country. Our schools will have higher expectations—we believe every child can learn. From this day forward, all students will have a better chance to learn, to excel, and to live out their dreams." At the signing ceremony, Representative John Boehner (R-Ohio), chairperson of the House committee that considered the legislation, said, "Today we witnessed the signing of the most important piece of legislation most of us will ever work on. This bill gives new freedom, new flexibility, and new resources to local school officials."[15]

But the bill had its critics. Michele Forman, to whom Bush had awarded the National Teacher of the Year distinction in 2001, disapproved of the testing portion of the new act, saying, "The type of test that I have no use for as a teacher is one that ranks students and ranks schools." Under the new law, both students and schools would be ranked, with rewards for the best-performing schools and penalties for the worst. Bob Chase, president of the National Education Association, called the bill a major disappointment. "While the bill sets out noble goals to raise student achievement and increase accountability, it fails to deliver the support required to help children achieve higher standards."[16]

State education officials, too, soon complained that the act was underfunded and its requirements unrealistic. In 2004, fourteen states petitioned the Bush administration for permission to use alternative methods for showing academic gains. The Education Department did announce that year that certain groups of students—such as those with grave injuries or medical conditions—could be exempt from the required standardized exams. Despite criticism, however, President Bush continued his strong endorsement of the education law, proclaiming in a speech delivered in May 2004 that "we're not backing down."[17] Indeed, a study from the National Assessment of Educational Progress released in 2005 showed significant improvements among white, black, and Hispanic nine year olds and modest gains registered by thirteen year olds in math and reading during the 2003–2004 school year compared with results from five years earlier. Administration officials were quick to cite the report as evidence that the president's "No Child Left Behind" policy was working. Education Secretary Margaret Spellings said of the study, "It shows that 'No Child Left Behind' is working . . . that as a country we're headed in the right direction."[18] Others, however, were more cautious, pointing out that the study was conducted in the early stages of implementation and that narrowing of the achievement gap for white, black, and Hispanic students can be traced to a period before Bush took office. For most people the jury is still out.

Health and Social Welfare Policy

Although by many standards the United States is the richest country in the world, the distribution of wealth and income among its citizens is among the most unequal of any industrialized nation. Similarly, despite having the world's most technologically advanced system of medical care, the United States is the only major industrialized country without a national health insurance system; and about 47 million Americans are uninsured or underinsured. Thus, many Americans live in a state of chronic economic insecurity, made worse by the fear of incurring medical expenses that in recent decades have been rising far faster than the general rate of inflation.

The federal government attempts to alleviate this insecurity through a variety of health and social-welfare programs. For example, in the past several decades the government has spent billions of dollars on programs designed to combat poverty. In 1965, federal spending on poverty programs totaled about $8 billion. Although this amount increased to more than $100 billion by 2000, large numbers of Americans continue to live in poverty. The government's definition of "poor" is based on household size and income. For example, in 2005 the definition applied to a family of four (two adults and two children) living on an annual cash income of less than $19,971. According to federal standards, in 2005 approximately 37 million Americans (or 12.6 percent) were poor. The proportion of Americans living in poverty varies greatly by race, ethnicity, age, and geographic region (see Figures 14.3 through 14.5).

Since 1965, the income gap between poor and rich Americans has increased, as has the poverty rate among children and among households headed by women. Today it is estimated that close to 20 percent of all children under the age of eighteen live in poor households.[19]

Figure 14.3 Percentage of People Living Below the Poverty Level, by Race and Ethnicity

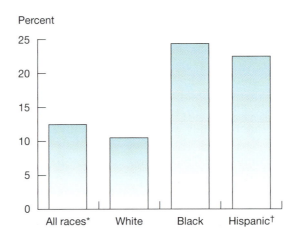

*Includes other races not shown separately.
†Hispanic persons may be of any race.

Source: *Statistical Abstract of the United States,* U.S. Department of Commerce, Bureau of the Census, 2006.

Figure 14.4 **Percentage of People Living Below the Poverty Level, by Age**

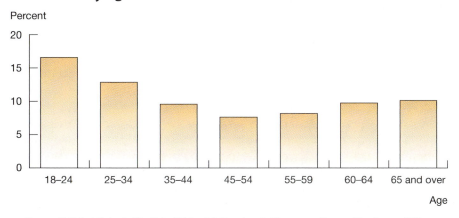

Source: *Statistical Abstract of the United States,* U.S. Department of Commerce, Bureau of the Census, 2006.

Figure 14.5 **Percentage of People Living Below the Poverty Level, by Region**

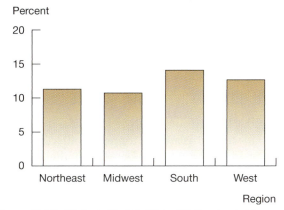

Source: *Statistical Abstract of the United States,* U.S. Department of Commerce, Bureau of the Census, 2006.

Social Welfare Programs: An Overview

Although "welfare" is commonly thought of as a redistributive policy, many of the nation's social-welfare programs are actually distributive. Nationally funded programs for retirement, health, housing, and college loans provide benefits to the public at large and enjoy widespread public support.

Before the 1930s, the United States had virtually no national social-welfare policy. Problems of hunger, unemployment, poverty, old age, and disability were handled by families, private charities, and state and local governments. The

© Brooks Kraft/Corbis

President Bush campaigning for his Social Security reform proposal before an audience gathered at the Kentucky Center for the Performing Arts in Louisville, Ky., March 10, 2005.

Great Depression of the 1930s dramatically revealed the inadequacies of the old system and the need for federal assistance for people affected by harsh economic and social conditions. In response to the Depression, the Social Security Act of 1935 established the framework for federally funded social-welfare programs in the United States.

Broadly speaking, there are two types of social-welfare programs. Social insurance requires employees and employers to contribute to a national insurance fund. Public assistance provides money and other forms of support directly to needy people. Public assistance programs are means tested; that is, they require a certain level of poverty for eligibility. They are paid for out of general revenues and are what the public commonly thinks of as "welfare programs." The issue network of these entitlement programs is pictured in Figure 14.6.

Social Insurance

The basic social insurance programs in operation in the United States are old-age, survivors, and disability insurance, commonly known as Social Security, Medicare, and unemployment insurance. The largest of these programs,

Figure 14.6 The Social Welfare Issue Network

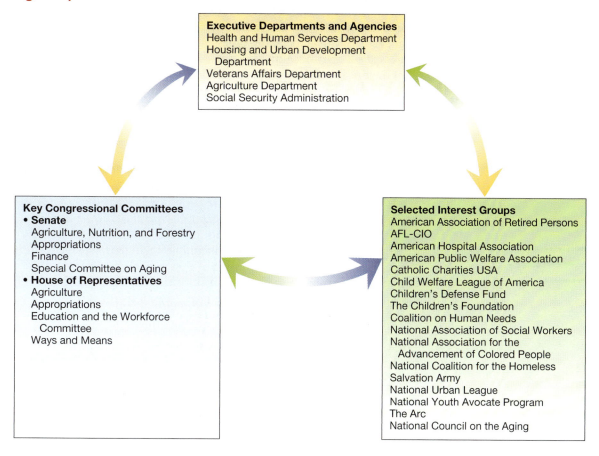

Executive Departments and Agencies
Health and Human Services Department
Housing and Urban Development
   Department
Veterans Affairs Department
Agriculture Department
Social Security Administration

Key Congressional Committees
- **Senate**
   Agriculture, Nutrition, and Forestry
   Appropriations
   Finance
   Special Committee on Aging
- **House of Representatives**
   Agriculture
   Appropriations
   Education and the Workforce
      Committee
   Ways and Means

Selected Interest Groups
American Association of Retired Persons
AFL-CIO
American Hospital Association
American Public Welfare Association
Catholic Charities USA
Child Welfare League of America
Children's Defense Fund
The Children's Foundation
Coalition on Human Needs
National Association of Social Workers
National Association for the
   Advancement of Colored People
National Coalition for the Homeless
Salvation Army
National Urban League
National Youth Avocate Program
The Arc
National Council on the Aging

Social Security, provides monthly payments to retired and disabled workers and to survivors of workers covered by the program. Contributions to the program are made through a tax levied on employees and employers. Each employee and employer pays 6.2 percent of the employee's income, up to an annual level of $90,000, into the Social Security trust fund. (Self-employed people must pay both the employer's and the employee's share, or 12.4 percent.)

As the program is currently operated, workers who retire at the age of sixty-two qualify for partial Social Security payments if they worked for about ten years. Workers may receive full benefits beginning at the age of sixty-five, but over the next few years this age requirement will rise to sixty-eight. The actual amount that an individual receives depends on several factors, including age of retirement, category of recipient (employee or survivor), and average income over a period of years. In 2006, more than 45 million Americans received Social Security benefits, with an average monthly payment of $874 for retired workers.

Social Security
The federal social insurance program that provides monthly payments to retired and disabled workers and to survivors of workers eligible for the benefits.

Largely because of the increasing aged population in the United States, many analysts predict that the Social Security fund as presently established will not be able to provide full benefits to all retirees by 2042. Arguing that as early as 2018 Social Security will start taking in less in payroll tax revenue than it pays out in benefits, President Bush in 2005 proposed significant changes to the system. Part of the president's proposals called for individuals to have the option of setting up personal accounts that would be theirs and could be left to whomever they wished. However, individuals who established these accounts would receive less from the Social Security trust fund than those who chose not to do so. The president also suggested people with higher incomes should receive less money than those with lower incomes. Opposition to the president's plan developed almost immediately from Democrats and others who opposed the personal accounts and feared that taxpayers would have to make up any revenue loss to the system.

In 1965, the **Medicare** health insurance program was added to the Social Security package as part of President Johnson's Great Society proposals. Medicare pays part of the costs of hospital bills and (for those who choose to pay extra for this coverage) part of physicians' fees for retired people age sixty-five and older. It is also financed by a payroll tax to which employees and employers contribute 2.9 percent of earned wages. As of 2002, approximately 40 million people were enrolled in the Medicare program at an annual cost of more than $200 billion.

The 1988 amendments to the Medicare program present an interesting case study in the politics of American democracy. In that year, Congress, with much fanfare, expanded the program to provide protection against the costs of catastrophic illness. This change represented the greatest expansion of Medicare benefits since the program's inception in 1965. In signing the 1988 act into law, President Reagan proudly proclaimed that it "will remove a terrible threat from the lives of elderly and disabled Americans."[20]

Less than eighteen months later, however, Congress repealed the new legislation as a result of a tremendous lobbying effort by older Americans and organizations representing them, who objected to the way the act was funded. Under the law, Medicare enrollees themselves paid for the cost of expanded benefits. But only some older Americans—those who owed more than $150 in federal income taxes, or about 40 percent of all enrollees—had to pay the surtax for the new benefit. Congress was bombarded with complaints by people in this income group. By wide margins both the House and the Senate responded to this pressure by voting to repeal this legislation.

Unemployment Insurance

A program enacted as part of the 1935 Social Security Act, **unemployment insurance** is designed to pay benefits to people who lose their jobs. It is financed jointly by the federal government and the states through taxes paid by employers and in some cases by employees as well. States have considerable discretion in determining the amount of benefits and the duration of coverage.

Medicare
The federal health insurance program for people older than sixty-five, added to the Social Security system in 1965.

unemployment insurance
A federal program, created as part of the 1935 Social Security Act, that pays benefits to people who lose their jobs.

Public Assistance

The 1935 Social Security Act established three public-assistance programs: old-age assistance, aid to the blind, and a program eventually called Aid to Families with Dependent Children. Over time, this package of programs was supplemented with other legislation designed to provide assistance for various categories of needy people. In 1950, aid to the permanently and totally disabled was enacted. In 1964, Congress established the food stamp program. In 1965, Medicaid was approved. In 1974, Congress passed the Supplemental Security Income program, which was designed to establish uniform federal benefits for people receiving assistance under the aged, blind, and disabled programs.

Aid to Families with Dependent Children The most controversial public-assistance program was always the **Aid to Families with Dependent Children (AFDC)** program. In 1935, the program was seen as a way to provide some income assistance to widows while their children were maturing. Over the years, however, because of increases in rates of divorce, desertion, and teenage pregnancy, both the number of recipients and the costs of the program rose substantially (see Figure 14.7). In 1988, Congress undertook a major overhaul of the program by requiring states to establish job training programs for most AFDC recipients and to guarantee child care, transportation, and medical coverage to participants. But well into the 1990s about half of AFDC recipients were long-term recipients; about 25 percent had been receiving benefits for ten years or more. Moreover, critics charged that the program indirectly encouraged people to have children in order to obtain AFDC payments. In 1996, Congress abolished the AFDC program and replaced it with a system of lump-sum federal payments to the states for welfare assistance; at the same time, national limits were imposed on the length of time people can receive welfare, and work obligations were imposed.

Food Stamps Another major public-assistance program is **food stamps,** government-issued coupons that can be used to purchase food. The amount of food stamps people receive is determined by their family's size and income level. Under the program as it was initially passed in 1964, low-income families could purchase food stamps at some fraction of their actual value and redeem them for food. In 1977, Congress eliminated the provision that recipients must pay a portion of the value of the stamps; in 2004, the Bush administration eliminated paper coupons and replaced them with electronically issued benefits and debit cards. When this change was implemented, approximately 24 million Americans were receiving food stamp benefits each month, at an annual cost in excess of $25 billion.

Medicaid In 1965 Congress established **Medicaid,** a program designed to help low-income people pay hospital, doctor, and other medical bills. Today almost 43 million people receive Medicaid benefits, at a total annual cost in excess of $150 billion.

Aid to Families with Dependent Children (AFDC)
A federal social-welfare program that made monthly payments to any family with children and an income below a certain level. This program was ended by Congress in 1996.

food stamps
Government-issued coupons that can be used to purchase food.

Medicaid
A federal program established in 1965 to help people with low incomes pay for hospital, doctor, and other medical bills.

The Politics of Social Welfare

Political parties, interest groups, the president, and numerous departments and agencies of the state and federal governments all have a significant interest in the social-welfare agenda (see Figure 14.6). Much of the policy formation and agenda setting that occurs in the welfare arena, however, takes place directly on the floor of Congress or in its various committees. Congress probably is a more significant actor in welfare policy than in almost any other area of domestic social policy because of the high public visibility of welfare issues, the sophisticated organization and legislative skills of interest groups in this arena, and the large amount of money appropriated for welfare programs each year. Legislators see welfare policy as an opportunity for significant resource distribution: most want to obtain as large a share of benefits as possible for their districts and their constituents.

Key Actors A host of committees and subcommittees in Congress are responsible for the various aspects of the welfare program. The Finance Committee in the Senate and the Ways and Means Committee in the House are important because they are responsible for the legislation that raises the money to pay for federal programs. Two subcommittees of the Finance Committee—the one on Medicaid and health care for low-income families and the one on Social Security and family policy—are key in the Senate, and the health and Social Security subcommittees of the Ways and Means Committee are key in the House.

But power is exercised by other committees as well. The Senate has subcommittees on aging, children and family, alcoholism, and disability—all of which are concerned with aspects of the welfare program; its Agriculture, Nutrition, and Forestry Committee is responsible for oversight of the food stamp program. In the House, the Economic and Educational Opportunities Committee is a key actor in welfare policy and the Agriculture Committee is concerned with the food stamp program.

Numerous interest groups also are active in the welfare arena. The American Federation of Labor and Congress of Industrial Organizations, the National Association of Chambers of Commerce, the National Association for the Advancement of Colored People, and others usually want to testify before any congressional committee or subcommittee considering alterations in the welfare system. Other interested parties include groups of state and local officials, such as the National Governors' Association, the National League of Cities, and the American Public Welfare Association (representing state welfare officials). In addition, experts from universities, religious groups, and think tanks may play an active role in the problem recognition and policy formulation stages of welfare policy.

Some interest groups focus on particular aspects of welfare policy. For example, AARP and the National Council of Senior Citizens are most concerned with the problems of the aged, whereas the American Hospital Association and the American Medical Association are concerned with health-care costs. The Children's Defense Fund and the Child Welfare League of America focus on programs dealing with children, youth, and families.

Figure 14.7 Numbers of Recipients of AFDC Payments

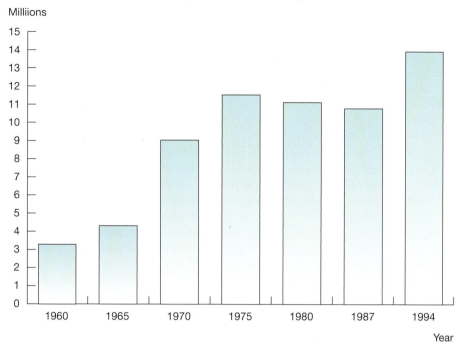

Statistical Abstract of the United States, U.S. Department of Commerce, Bureau of the Census, for the years shown.

The political parties take stands on these and other issues. Historically, the Democratic Party has tended to advocate an active role for government in establishing welfare programs and expanding benefits. The Republican Party generally opposes expansion of welfare programs and, at times, favors a ceiling on costs and rollbacks in program activities. It emphasizes work incentives and private-sector action to help those unable to work.

Welfare Reform Welfare reform was a major domestic policy issue throughout the 1990s. Both liberals and conservatives endorsed sweeping reform proposals; the Republican and Democratic Parties each made welfare reform a central feature of their party and campaign platforms. In his 1992 presidential campaign, Bill Clinton promised to "end welfare as we know it." Two years later, President Clinton unveiled a $9.3 billion plan that would have expanded job training programs and required those on welfare rolls to join a work program after two years or risk losing benefits.

Clinton's plan was pushed out of the spotlight by his proposal to reform the health-care system, but the welfare issue returned to center stage when the Republicans took over Congress in 1995. As part of their Contract with America, the GOP proposed that welfare spending be capped at 1994 levels, that government subsidies for the poor children be ended and replaced with a few broad-based block grants to the states, and that a work requirement be instituted for people on welfare for two years or more.

The block grant aspect of the proposal, which would have the effect of shifting major areas of welfare responsibility to the states, was most controversial, but reforming welfare was not. The Republicans enacted their proposal in the fall of 1995, but President Clinton vetoed it and a subsequent GOP plan. However, with Republicans threatening to make the president's welfare vetoes an issue in the 1996 election, Clinton approved a third, more moderate version in the summer of 1996, which effectively dismantled the federal welfare program begun in the New Deal. It was replaced with a plan that gave each state a lump-sum payment (now called Temporary Assistance to Needy Families) and vast new authority to run its own welfare and work programs. Furthermore, the bill established a lifetime limit of five years for welfare payments to any family (states may establish stricter time limits, and certain hardship exemptions are available for 20 percent of families), and it required states to enroll 30 percent of their recipients in work programs. The head of most families on welfare were required to work within two years or lose benefits; states were permitted to provide payments to unmarried teenage mothers only if they stay in school and live with an adult. Funding for food stamps was also reduced considerably.

Soon after passage of the legislation, Congress restored some of the cuts it had made in immigrant programs. The legislation has reduced the number of families on welfare. Deemed successful, the welfare bill was reauthorized by Congress in 2005.

The Cabrini-Green housing project in Chicago, where at one time 15,000 residents were concentrated in 22 high-rise buildings. Today, housing policy is designed to provide low income families with more dispersed housing options.

Housing Policy

Federal subsidies for housing have also decreased, and federal programs have changed a great deal since they were initiated during the presidency of Franklin Roosevelt. Early housing programs generally adopted an intergovernmental approach, one in which the federal government was largely responsible for establishing, funding, and evaluating such programs and state and local governments were primarily responsible for implementing them. The nation's first significant housing act, passed in 1937, provided housing assistance for people who had been displaced by the harsh economic conditions of the Depression. Under the act, the federal government assumed most of the cost of constructing public housing, and local governments were responsible for developing and managing project sites.

The original program was not aimed at the poorest Americans, nor was it intended to provide permanent shelter for homeless families. Rather, it was designed to assist the working poor, people who could pay enough rent to cover the units' operating costs and would leave public housing when their economic situation improved. Over the years, public housing increasingly served people permanently trapped in poverty, many of whom were members of racial and ethnic minorities.

In 1949, the new approach was initiated. Known as **urban renewal,** it was directed toward clearing deteriorating areas and replacing them with commercial and residential establishments in which people could live and work. Under this program, cities were to create local agencies that would identify and purchase the land to be cleared, relocate residents and commercial establishments, tear down deteriorated structures, reinstall public facilities such as water and sewer services, and sell the land to developers at favorable prices. The federal government would pay much of the cost of land acquisition, demolition, and new construction.

The policy was a compromise between those who saw deteriorating economic conditions as a prime cause of urban poverty and the crime that went with it and liberals who wanted to provide adequate living conditions for everyone, regardless of their ability to pay. The new urban renewal program, enacted in 1949, authorized the construction of more than 800,000 government-subsidized "low rent" housing units during the next six years, but it also authorized the demolition of many dilapidated buildings, thereby displacing more than 240,000 people from their homes. Many of those displaced people were forced to pay higher rents in their new locations—if they were able to find new accommodations. A 1954 amendment required local agencies to provide relocation assistance, but to those being displaced such assistance often seemed inadequate.[21]

Liberals and conservatives continued to spar over the program and its deficiencies. Community activists and minority groups saw government housing as a device to remove minorities from inner-city business districts; liberals saw it as a "federally financed gimmick" to provide cheap land for developers.

urban renewal
An approach to federal housing policy, established in 1949 and terminated in 1974, that was designed to clear blighted and deteriorating areas of inner cities and replace them with new commercial and residential establishments.

Conservatives, for their part, were disappointed with the program's inability to reverse, or even slow, the decline of inner cities. The program was abolished in 1974 even as proponents and opponents of new federally financed housing took the issue to court.

The courts did not resolve the issue. In 1976 the Supreme Court indicated that the federal government might be forced to locate public housing in predominantly white suburbs, not just in the inner cities. The following year, it modified its judgment by holding that suburban communities could not be forced to change their zoning laws to provide affordable housing for low-income families unless it could be shown that the intent of the existing zoning laws was to keep out certain minority groups.[22]

Urban renewal was terminated when Congress passed the Housing and Community Development Act of 1974, which established the Community Development Block Grant (CDBG) program. In this new effort, the federal government consolidated money that had previously been allocated through urban renewal and several other housing programs into block grants and made them available to local governments, which could use the grants for street paving, lighting, attracting commercial development, industrial parks, and numerous related activities, in addition to urban renewal and public housing. During the Reagan administration the amount of money allocated through the CDBG program was reduced significantly, but local governments were given greater flexibility in spending the funds.

The 1974 legislation also established an assistance program for poor families: a rent supplement program and a long-term subsidy program. The rent supplement was designed to provide freedom of choice to low-income families and incentives for landlords to rehabilitate and repair rental units; the subsidies were designed to lower the risk to developers of having unoccupied units in hopes that it would encourage them to construct new low-cost apartment complexes. The Department of Housing and Urban Development (HUD) also was authorized to insure many of the construction loans.

Housing Policy in the 1980s and 1990s

As homeless people became increasingly numerous and visible during the 1980s and early 1990s, the major controversy in the area of public housing was whether the nation's policy should be designed to increase the supply of public housing (as advocated by liberals, Democrats, and some urban Republicans) or to provide rent vouchers or subsidies to poor families (as favored by conservatives and many Republicans). Put simply, was the nation's housing problem one of availability or one of affordability?

Arguing that there was an adequate supply of rental housing units across the nation, the Reagan administration favored a plan in which eligible families received vouchers to pay rent on units of their choosing. Although critics pointed out that most available vacant units were too expensive or not located in the urban markets, where they were needed most, the production of new subsidized housing units declined sharply in the 1980s as a result of the administration's approach.

Following Reagan, President George H. W. Bush focused on enabling tenants in housing projects to purchase their units. Democrats were skeptical. As the party that controlled Congress during the four years of the Bush administration, they refused to support the president's initiative. Deadlock resulted.

One of President Bill Clinton's earliest policy initiatives on housing and neighborhood renewal was the establishment of **urban empowerment zones,** defined as areas with substantial concentrations of poverty that would benefit from substantial tax incentives and regulatory relief. In 1993, Congress enacted legislation to create a process by which six urban and three rural empowerment zones could receive approval to issue tax-exempt bonds, receive social-service block grants, obtain special consideration for various federal programs, and grant wage credits to employers for hiring residents of the empowerment zone. The act permitted another sixty cities and thirty-five rural areas to receive less intensive support.

Housing in the Twenty-First Century

In 2002, President George W. Bush proposed a budget in which he targeted $200 million for low-income families to make down payments on their first home. His budget also provided for the renewal of all expiring low-income subsidies and the addition of 34,000 vouchers to help low-income families find housing. On the other hand, Bush's budget called for significant cuts in HUD's public housing program. Two years later, the president announced and Congress enacted the American Dream Down Payment Act to help low-income families purchase their own homes by providing an average of $5,000 in government assistance. However, the administration changed the formula for financing the nation's approximately 3,100 public housing agencies, which would increase money available to many small, rural places in the South but decrease that available for the large urban areas in the Northeast and Midwest.

Historically, housing has been an area in which the lines of division have been sharply drawn, one in which partisan politics rules, Congress and the president have often clashed, and a national consensus concerning a solution has been slow to emerge. But at the dawn of the twenty-first century it appeared that the partisan conflict and sharp political debate are beginning to subside. Politicians, as well as the American public, seemed increasingly aware of the dominant role that housing plays in the well-being of elderly Americans, in the educational attainment of children, in the maintenance of the economic and social stability of working-class families, and in the ability of welfare recipients to find and keep jobs. As a result, all parties seemed more willing to find permanent and effective solutions.

The issue network for housing is depicted in Figure 14.8.

urban empowerment zones
Housing policy established during the Clinton administration by which urban areas are defined as those with substantial concentrations of poverty would benefit from tax incentives and regulatory relief.

Figure 14.8 **The Housing Issue Network**

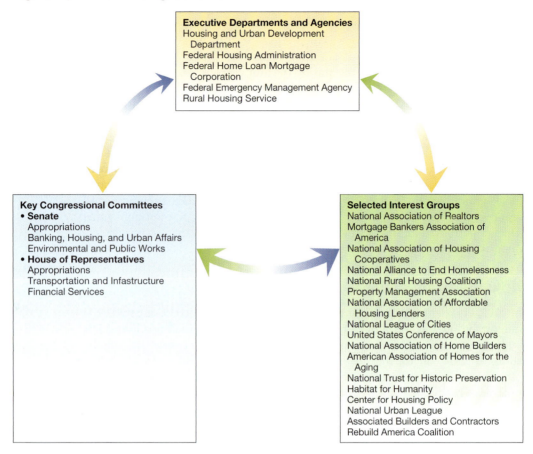

Executive Departments and Agencies
Housing and Urban Development
  Department
Federal Housing Administration
Federal Home Loan Mortgage
  Corporation
Federal Emergency Management Agency
Rural Housing Service

Key Congressional Committees
• **Senate**
  Appropriations
  Banking, Housing, and Urban Affairs
  Environmental and Public Works
• **House of Representatives**
  Appropriations
  Transportation and Infastructure
  Financial Services

Selected Interest Groups
National Association of Realtors
Mortgage Bankers Association of
  America
National Association of Housing
  Cooperatives
National Alliance to End Homelessness
National Rural Housing Coalition
Property Management Association
National Association of Affordable
  Housing Lenders
National League of Cities
United States Conference of Mayors
National Association of Home Builders
American Association of Homes for the
  Aging
National Trust for Historic Preservation
Habitat for Humanity
Center for Housing Policy
National Urban League
Associated Builders and Contractors
Rebuild America Coalition

Environmental and Energy Policy

The policy areas discussed so far—education, housing, and welfare—are all matters of long-standing concern in the United States. In contrast, public concern with environmental and energy issues developed relatively recently. For most of the nation's history, Americans have thought of their natural resources as almost inexhaustible free goods. But dramatic events of recent decades—including severe energy shortages, electrical blackouts, nuclear plant disasters, oil spills, toxic chemical leaks, and significant increases in environmentally related diseases and deaths—have directed the public's attention to environmental and energy issues.

Today it is widely recognized that the nation's resources are limited and that serious, even life-threatening consequences result from unwise use of them. Americans also realize that human activities can cause fundamental changes in the earth's ecosystem. Increasingly, scientists warn of the potentially catastrophic consequences of the greenhouse effect—the trend toward global warming—that

Figure 14.9 The Environment Issue Network

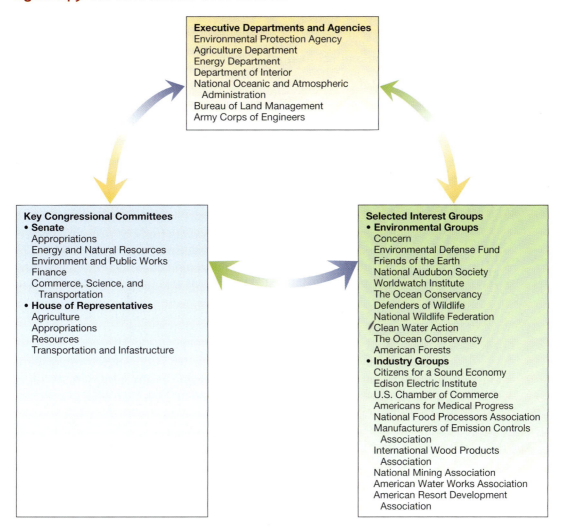

Executive Departments and Agencies
Environmental Protection Agency
Agriculture Department
Energy Department
Department of Interior
National Oceanic and Atmospheric
  Administration
Bureau of Land Management
Army Corps of Engineers

Key Congressional Committees
• **Senate**
  Appropriations
  Energy and Natural Resources
  Environment and Public Works
  Finance
  Commerce, Science, and
    Transportation
• **House of Representatives**
  Agriculture
  Appropriations
  Resources
  Transportation and Infastructure

Selected Interest Groups
• **Environmental Groups**
  Concern
  Environmental Defense Fund
  Friends of the Earth
  National Audubon Society
  Worldwatch Institute
  The Ocean Conservancy
  Defenders of Wildlife
  National Wildlife Federation
  Clean Water Action
  The Ocean Conservancy
  American Forests
• **Industry Groups**
  Citizens for a Sound Economy
  Edison Electric Institute
  U.S. Chamber of Commerce
  Americans for Medical Progress
  National Food Processors Association
  Manufacturers of Emission Controls
    Association
  International Wood Products
    Association
  National Mining Association
  American Water Works Association
  American Resort Development
    Association

results from the unlimited emissions of carbon dioxide, methane, nitrous oxides, and various other chemicals into the earth's atmosphere. And Americans are increasingly aware of their special role in addressing this problem. The United States is the world's leading emitter of carbon dioxide—one-quarter of the worldwide total.

Environmental and energy policy is largely an example of regulatory policy that began in the 1970s when Congress passed several environmental laws and President Richard Nixon created the Environmental Protection Agency (EPA) by executive order. The EPA is the administrative agency responsible for enforcing environmental legislation. (The environment issue network is illustrated in Figure 14.9.)

Because of the high cost of environmental protection, the EPA has often come under attack by regulated industry, as well as by state and local governments. In recent years, these critics have found receptive ears in Congress, especially among Republicans. As noted in Chapter 6, Congress considered (but rejected) legislation that would have sharply cut the EPA's budget in the 1990s. The Republican-controlled legislature was also constrained from imposing more demanding cost–benefit analyses and risk assessments on the EPA by threatened vetoes by Clinton. Nonetheless, the EPA shifted from issuing heavily prescriptive regulations to using more flexible and market-oriented mechanisms for achieving environmental goals.[23] To illustrate controversies in environmental policymaking, we turn to the Clear Water and Air Acts and their implementation over the last 50 years.

Clean Water

Congressional action to limit water pollution dates from 1956, when Congress approved major amendments to the Water Pollution Control Act of 1948. The 1956 amendments authorized the federal government to convene conferences, which would be open to all interested individuals and groups, to study the problems of streams and lakes—that is, to stimulate public participation and tie congressional responses more closely to public opinion. Although much discussion ensued, only one injunction against a polluter was issued.[24]

The Water Quality Act of 1965 represented the first attempt to establish standards for water quality. It permitted each state to develop its own standards and submit them to the federal government for approval. However, because many state officials were reluctant to do anything that might deter businesses from locating in their states, the standards established in response to this legislation were minimal.[25]

Seven years later, however, Congress enacted the Clean Water Act, designed to establish more uniform and rigorous national standards for water. The goal of this legislation was the complete elimination of discharges of pollutants into the nation's waterways by 1985. The EPA was authorized to set quality standards for interstate streams, as well as for intrastate waters if states refused to do so, and funds totaling $18 billion were authorized to help states pay for the construction of sewage treatment facilities.

In 1977, the 1965 and 1972 acts were amended to extend some of the deadlines set in 1972 and strengthen the EPA's control over the discharge of certain toxic substances. Overriding President Reagan's veto in 1987, Congress reauthorized the legislation, pledging $18 billion over the next ten years for continued assistance to states and localities for the construction of sewage plants. Although Congress could not agree on a major overhaul of the Clean Water Act, President Clinton issued regulations in 1997 that tightened limits on real estate developments in wetlands.

Early in his administration, President George W. Bush proposed modifying drinking water regulations to raise the restriction on arsenic levels from 10 to 50 parts per billion. Mining and chemical companies applauded Bush's proposal;

conservationists, and many Democrats, sharply criticized them. Representative Henry Waxman (D-California) called the proposal "another example of a special interest payback" to chemical and mining companies.[26] Public opposition forced the president to withdraw the proposal.

Early in 2003 the Bush administration issued guidelines that would have removed federal protection from many streams, wetlands, and natural ponds covered by the Clean Water Act. However, facing considerable opposition, including a letter of protest signed by 218 members of the House of Representatives, this proposal also was eventually withdrawn.

Clean Air

The Clean Air Act of 1963 was intended to develop a role for the federal government in reducing air pollution, much like the role envisioned in the area of water pollution by the 1956 amendments. The government was to convene conferences and hearings, and court action would be taken only after polluters had been given ample opportunity to correct offending situations. Only eleven conferences were held in the first seven years of the act's existence, however, and only once did the federal government actively attempt to stop the actions of a polluting company.

The 1970 amendments to the Clean Air Act set strict national air-quality standards for local governments and industry, including controls on automobile emissions, and provided heavy fines for violators. Subsequent amendments extended the deadlines for compliance. In 1982, President Reagan endorsed amendments that would have weakened the Clean Air Act, which business leaders claimed was costing them billions of dollars. Although those amendments were never passed, the Reagan administration blocked any serious attempt to strengthen existing laws.[27]

President George H. W. Bush, in contrast, voiced a strong commitment to clean air, and in 1990 he signed into law new amendments to the Clean Air Act that set strict federal limits on automobile exhaust, urban smog, toxic air pollution, and acid rain. During the Clinton presidency, the focus of attention shifted to the greenhouse effect and global warming. In 1993, President Clinton proposed reducing U.S. emissions of so-called greenhouse gases to 1990 levels by 2000. However, his proposal provided for voluntary goals and incentives and avoided issuing new industrial mandates and regulations. President Clinton also proposed tightening standards for ozone emissions as well as for soot produced by such sources as coal-fired power plants and diesel engines.

In his 2003 State of the Union address, President George W. Bush proposed an overhaul of the Clean Air Act designed to slowly phase in (over a fifteen-year period) mandatory power plant cuts for three emissions: sulfur dioxide, nitrogen oxide, and mercury. Environmentalists and many Democrats, however, were pressing for stricter and timely caps on power plant emissions in these areas and challenged the failure of business to adhere to existing standards. In a significant ruling in 2005, a federal appeals court sided with the Bush administration's contention that power plants, refineries, and factories could modernize without installing expensive new pollution control equipment.[28]

As the price of oil soared in recent years, so also has the per-gallon price of gasoline. In response, President Bush in his 2006 State of the Union Address declared America to be "addicted to oil," and called for a national commitment to the development and use of alternative energy sources.

Energy Policy

By the 1990s, the United States, with only about 5 percent of the world's population, was consuming more than 25 percent of the world's energy supplies.[29] America's dependence on foreign oil was particularly worrisome. Before World War II, virtually all oil consumed in the United States was domestically produced. By the mid-1990s, however, more than 50 percent was imported; and by 2005 almost 50 percent of the imports came from nations belonging to the Organization of Petroleum Exporting Countries (OPEC).[30]

America's heavy and precarious dependence on foreign sources of energy was driven home in 1973 and 1974, when OPEC imposed an embargo on shipments of oil to the United States. The resulting gasoline shortages forced motorists to wait in long lines for a turn at the gas pump. Throughout the rest of the 1970s and into the 1980s, the escalating cost of fuel to heat and cool homes, run automobiles, and power factories made energy an important political issue.

Concern over the nation's dependence on foreign oil led to a search for other sources of energy. One was nuclear energy, which was highly controversial because of the danger of radioactive leakages. Perhaps no single event more dramatically focused the public's attention on these issues than the 1979 accident at the Three Mile Island nuclear power plant in Pennsylvania, the worst nuclear accident in the nation's history. Although a meltdown (in which the nuclear core melts through its steel-and-concrete casing) did not occur, some radioactivity did escape. This incident, along with a more serious accident in 1986 at a nuclear plant at Chernobyl in the Soviet Union, greatly intensified the debate between proponents and opponents of this type of energy.

The debate extended to alternative sources and has extended over a long period. In 1977, President Jimmy Carter described the nation's energy crisis as "the moral equivalent of war" and proposed new programs to conserve energy and develop new energy sources. He recommended, and Congress enacted, laws creating a Department of Energy and a Synthetic Fuels Corporation. The latter provided subsidies for the production of fuels from sources other than oil, fuel such as coal, wind, garbage, and plants. However, the corporation received only token support from the Reagan administration and was abolished in 1986 with limited tangible results.

Early in 1991, President George H. W. Bush submitted energy-related legislation to Congress. Emphasizing production over conservation, the proposal called for opening new oil and natural-gas fields in the Arctic National Wildlife Refuge and on the outer continental shelf and for speeding up the process of federal licensing of nuclear power plants. Democrats opposed easing restrictions on the nuclear energy industry and opening the wildlife refuge to oil and gas exploration. Many Republicans also questioned some aspects of the legislation, especially those requiring an increase in gas mileage for new cars. Environmentalists opposed virtually the whole package. In 1992, Congress passed and the president signed the Energy Policy Act, a bill that aimed to decrease American dependence on foreign oil by promoting conservation and supporting domestic production. The bill as passed did not, however, include references to drilling in the Arctic National Wildlife Refuge, nor did it attempt to force U.S. automakers to build more fuel-efficient automobiles.

The return to more "normal" and affordable fuel prices in the 1990s lessened the public's interest in the pursuit of a comprehensive energy policy. To many Americans, President Carter's call for a "war" on energy problems seemed distant and largely irrelevant. In 1993, President Clinton proposed an energy tax (specifically, a tax on the energy output of oil, gas, coal, and other fuels) as part of his deficit-reduction plan. In the president's view, the new tax would both raise revenue and promote energy conservation. But in the face of great opposition from energy-intensive industries (petrochemicals, steel, cement) and from House and Senate members in energy-producing states, Clinton backed off. He settled for an increase in the federal excise tax on gasoline, as well as other sources of revenue.

After his election victory in 2000, President George W. Bush proposed opening for oil and gas drilling some 1.5 million acres of the Arctic National Wildlife Refuge. Although the House passed the measure, strong opposition in the Senate killed it for the duration of the president's first term. Instead, the Senate focused on energy conservation. No comprehensive energy legislation was enacted until 2005, when an increase in the GOP composition of Congress, the president's reelection, spiraling gas and oil prices, and increasing dependence of the United States on Middle East oil combined to give impetus to energy legislation, a key legislative priority for the Bush administration. The legislation provided tax incentives for increased exploration of fossil-based fuel, a doubling of ethanol production (which is made from corn), and incentives for renewable energy sources, new nuclear power plants, and conservation measures.

Predictably, supporters and opponents offered contrasting interpretations of the bill's merits. Representative Joe Barton (R-Texas), chairperson of the House Energy and Commerce Committee, called the measure "a darn good bill, and it's going to help the country." Representative Edward Markey (D-Massachusetts), on the other hand, said, "This is a huge giveaway for the oil and gas industry. The bill just tips the American consumer and taxpayer upside down and shakes money out of their pockets. This bill is an historic failure."[31]

With the country facing rapidly escalating oil prices and increasing dependency on unpredictable sources in the Middle East, President Bush in his 2006 State of the Union Address declared the nation to be "addicted to oil." In that address, the President challenged the nation to reduce its dependence on Mideast oil imports by 75 percent by the year 2025 and to increase its consumption of alternative sources, such as that supplied by ethanol, solar technology, wind power, and nuclear energy. Critics, though, were quick to point out that the country is years away from developing truly viable and cost-effective alternatives to oil and that a reduction of Mideast oil would still leave the country vulnerable to even larger foreign suppliers like Canada, Mexico, and Venezuela.

Another major environmental issue of the twenty-first century has been the nation's policy toward nuclear waste. How do we deal with the radioactive and highly dangerous waste produced by the nation's nuclear power plants? This topic is the subject of the case study at the end of this chapter.

Review Questions

1. A major feature of the education measure supported by President George W. Bush, known as "No Child Left Behind" and signed into law by him in 2002, is

   A. The requirement that all students learn at least one foreign language
   B. The requirement for annual testing of student performance in reading and math
   C. A gradual reduction in federal support of higher education
   D. The elimination of affirmative action as a criterion for admission to colleges and universities

continued

2. The welfare reform law passed by Congress and signed by President Bill Clinton in 1996 had as one of its major provisions

   A. The elimination of the Aid to Families with Dependent Children program
   B. The elimination of the nation's food stamp program
   C. The elimination of Social Security
   D. The elimination of the Medicaid and Medicare programs

3. The approach to housing policy initially adopted in 1949 and designed to clear deteriorating areas of inner cities and replace them with new commercial and residential establishments was know as

   A. Community development
   B. Neighborhood restoration
   C. Section 8 housing
   D. Urban renewal

4. The agency of the federal government responsible for enforcing the nation's environmental and energy policies is known as the

   A. National Institute of Health
   B. National Science Foundation
   C. Environmental Protection Agency
   D. National Regulatory Agency

Answers:

   1. B
   2. A
   3. D
   4. C

Conflict and Consensus in Review

In each of the policy areas examined, conflict has been temporarily resolved only to erupt again. When consensus has been achieved, it hasn't lasted for long. The nature of the problem and the impact it has affects the political pressure directed at government officials to find policy solutions.

Policy change is a product of the economic and social environment as well as political leadership. Large-scale change is frequently associated with major social or economic upheavals—like the Great Depression of the 1930s or the terrorist attacks of 2001. Strong presidential leadership is also essential today. Although such leadership does not guarantee a successful policy outcome, as Clinton's failure to gain major health care reform and Bush's failure to achieve an overhaul of the Social Security system attest, the absence of a strong administration initiative and presence slows and reduces policy change. The politics in action case study illustrates the need for continued presidential involvement in national policy making.

14.2 Politics in the 21st Century

Privatization

The line separating those policies and services that should be provided by the public sector (government) and those that should be provided by the private sector is becoming increasingly blurred and hard to define. "Privatization," the transfer of service functions from the public sector to the private or not-for-profit sector, has been occurring at the state and local levels at a fairly rapid rate over the past couple of decades. Advocates of privatization argue that in many areas the private sector can provide better services more cheaply and effectively than can the public sector.

Privatization at the state and local level has become a fairly common practice. Today virtually all state and local governments "contract out" for at least some of their services. It is not unusual to find private companies providing prisons, refuse collection, education, health care, mental health services, nursing homes, day care centers, drug abuse clinics, public transportation, and many other services previously provided by government.

At the federal level, privatization in some form has been supported by every president from Ronald Reagan through George W. Bush. In 1988, the President's Commission on Privatization identified several areas (including air traffic control, prisons, and housing) that could effectively be turned over to the private sector, and in 1992 David Osborne and Ted Gaebler popularized this notion in their widely read book, *Reinventing Government*.[32] Indeed, one of the most controversial aspects of the prescription drug plan approved by Congress in 2003 was the huge new role it gave to insurance companies and private health plans in the Medicare program.

Despite the increasing government–private partnership, privatization has advanced more slowly at the federal level than at the state and local level. It has done so because the beneficiaries of federal programs are fearful of changing them. Those helped by government social programs are suspicious that the private sector could not be counted on to provide equivalent services and benefits at or near the same cost they had been provided by government.

Nevertheless, the shift to privatization has advanced in the twenty-first century because of the convergence of politics and beliefs. The electoral success of congressional Republicans and the policies of the Bush administration have spurred an increasing role for the private sector in providing many services and products previously made available by government. There is more competition between the government and the private sector, more pressure to reduce the overall size of the government, and more emphasis on individual initiative and responsibility. Today, the key terminology that those in government use is downsizing, competitive sourcing, and self-reliance.

Consider the policy issues examined in this chapter—education, health and social welfare, housing, environment, and energy:

1. Which, if any, of these areas do you believe could be turned over to the private sector?
2. What factors should be considered in "privatizing" public services such as these?
3. What might be the costs and what might be the benefits of such privatization?
4. Do you expect increased political pressure for privatizing public services at the federal level in the near future? Why or why not?

Politics in Action

Where Do We Put Nuclear Waste?

In 2002 Energy Secretary Spencer Abraham announced his recommendation that Yucca Mountain in Nevada be selected to receive the nation's thousands of tons of nuclear waste. Abraham called the site "scientifically sound and suitable" as a repository for the used radioactive fuel kept at commercial reactors in other states. The announcement came after forty years and the expenditure of more than $8 billion on scientific study and research.

For years the question of where and how to store radioactive waste materials has been one of the country's most vexing and politically charged issues. Although concern about radioactive waste management dates to the 1950s, contemporary policy debates began in 1982 when Congress passed the Nuclear Waste Policy Act. That act established the Office of Civilian Radioactive Waste Management within the Department of Energy. The act also directed the department to issue guidelines for selecting sites for waste disposal and for the secretary of energy to recommend disposal sites to the president. The law stipulated that if the president accepted the secretary's recommendation, he had to submit the recommendation to Congress for its approval. Following Congress' positive action, the waste disposal site would become effective after sixty days unless the governor and legislature of the state in which the site was located objected, in which case additional congressional concurrence would be necessary. These elaborate procedures were designed to ensure that the selection of a site would be based purely on science and safety, not politics.

In 1983, the department selected nine sites for deposit, and by the late 1980s it had narrowed its search for a permanent site to three western states: Nevada, Texas, and Washington. At that time, both Texas and Washington were represented in Congress by prominent and powerful representatives, Speaker Jim Wright from Texas and Majority Leader Thomas Foley from Washington. Nevada, on the other hand, lacked such influence and had only one representative in the House. As a consequence, Congress directed the Energy Department to study just a single site: the one at Yucca Mountain in Nevada. Nevada's congressional delegation was able to stall the project for many years but not prevent it once the Bush administration and Republican leaders decided that the time had come. So fourteen years later, after spending an additional $4.5 billion on study, Energy Secretary Abraham announced January 11, 2002, his selection of the Yucca Mountain site, a decision Abraham said was based on "sound science and compelling national interests.[33]

But the controversy has not ended. The issue of shipping the spent fuel to Nevada, the fear of leakage, and concerns about accidents or terrorists attacking the trains and trucks that carry the fuel still remain. Besides, it is estimated that it will take at least a decade to dig deep into the mountain, build a road, and construct the fortified walls necessary to store the nuclear waste until it is no longer a lethal threat, plenty of time for more political battles to be fought and for a different set of policymakers to reverse, reaffirm, or delay the judgment of those who preceded them in office. Stay tuned!

What Do You Think?

1. Participants in the decision to select a site for disposal of the nation's nuclear waste claimed throughout the process that their decisions were based on sound scientific evidence, not politics. Do you think this is the case?
2. Can politics ever be eliminated from the process of policymaking in the American democratic system? Why or why not?

3. Do you think politics should be eliminated? Why or why not?
4. How does this case illustrate the role of special interest groups in the formulation, implementation, and oversight of public policy? Can the influence of such groups be minimized or eliminated. Should it be?

Summary

We began this chapter by discussing public consensus and controversy over the type of policy that government makes, the content of that policy, and the process by which it is formulated, implemented, and evaluated. Since the 1930s, the U.S. government has emphasized distributive policies, those that distribute goods and services to citizens. These policies have tended to be the most popular because the benefits that groups of people receive from these policies tend to outweigh the burden to society. Costs are spread out, and benefits are concentrated. Regulatory policies are more controversial. They restrict certain types of activities, thereby evoking the hostility of those who actions are constrained by the government. Redistributive policies are also controversial because they take from one group and give to another. Moreover, the groups that they take from tend to be the most advantaged and politically active.

Regardless of the type of policy, the process of making and implementing it goes through five distinct stages. The first and most important is problem recognition. An issue must be recognized before those in government place it on the agenda. Public awareness is essential for an issue to receive serious consideration. Such awareness is usually the consequence of media coverage, group advocacy, and social concern.

Once a problem has been recognized as a salient issue, a feasible solution must be found. This is the stage of policy formulation. In most cases, there are many potential courses of action. It is the job of those in government to agree on one of them or, if they cannot do so, not act. Agreement involves marshaling the support needed among interested groups. To achieve this support, lobbying, bargaining, negotiating, and compromising are usually necessary.

Often these processes occur within a cluster of actors and institutions that has been described as an issue network. Participants in that network interact with one another to agree on acceptable policies. The networks are fungible in the sense that people move back and forth between the public and the private sectors.

Policies that have been adopted must be administered; putting them into practice is known as implementation. Few policy decisions are self-implementing, and many require a complex implementation structure. Officials in executive agencies typically have wide latitude in their administration of policy, which, in turn, can shape its effect on society. Judicial rulings may also establish the precise direction a policy will take.

Policy evaluation consists of determining whether a policy is working as intended. Not only intended consequences but also unanticipated effects need to be assessed. The final stage of the policymaking process is policy reconsideration or termination. There are many political obstacles to program termination. Agency employees want to keep their jobs; clients served by a program want it to continue; voters place pressure on legislators to preserve the program. Nevertheless, programs are terminated or overhauled when they have outlived their usefulness, cost too much, or lose their political support.

The policymaking process is usually slow. It also tends to be incremental, achieving what is feasible and not necessarily optimal. Major policy changes can occur, but they usually do so in times of crises and during periods of unified government when partisanship unites what the U.S. constitutional system divides.

Finally, it is usually easier to identify and overcome technical problems than to solve problems that are more political in nature. Complex social issues are by definition difficult to solve because there is less agreement and more confusion among those who interests are directly affected. There is likely to be more conflict among the parties. The costs may also be more than society is willing to pay.

Key Terms

distributive policies
regulatory policies
redistributive policies
problem recognition
policy formulation
policy adoption
policy implementation

policy evaluation
policy termination
incrementalism
fragmented power
punctuated equilibrium
Social Security
Medicare

unemployment insurance
Aid to Families with Dependent
 Children (AFDC)
food stamps
Medicaid
urban renewal
urban empowerment zones

Discussion Questions

1. Policymaking in the United States often is slow, and change when it occurs tends to be incremental. Yet sudden and major change sometimes does occur. Discuss those factors associated with major policy change in the United States. Which political, social, and economic conditions contribute to large-scale policy change, and which ones inhibit it?

2. Why have distributive policies been easier to enact than regulatory or redistributive policies? Do distributive policies contribute to or detract from the economic vitality of the country as much as redistributive policies do? What about regulatory policies?

3. Discuss the major stages in the process of policymaking in the United States. Are any of these more critical than others? Why is this so?

4. What is meant by the term *iron triangle?* What is meant by the term *issue networks?* (See Chapter 12 for more information.) Evaluate the roles these play in the process of policymaking in the United States. Is their effect positive, negative, or both?

5. Select one policy area discussed in the chapter. How you think that policy will develop over the next ten to twenty-five years? Do you think that development inevitable?

| Topics for Debate |

Debate each side of the following propositions:

1. Government officials should defer to policy experts in their formulation and implementation of public policy decisions.
2. To speed up the policy process, the number of people in government who can affect that policy should be reduced.
3. Energy and environmental policies will always conflict.
4. Redistributive policies are un-American in that they conflict with a basic democratic premise, the value of individualism and personal freedom.
5. Public policies can never permanently solve major problems among contending groups.

| Where on the Web? |

National Center for Policy Analysis
www.ncpa.org/

Electronic Policy Network
www.movingideas.org/

Brookings Institution **www.brookings.edu/**

Urban Institute **www.urban.org/**

Go to **www.thomsonedu.com/thomsonnow** to learn about a powerful online study tool. You will get a personalized study plan based on your responses to a diagnostic Pre-Test. Once you have mastered the materials with the help of interactive learning tools, activities, timelines, video case studies, simulations, and an integrated E-Book, you can take a Post-Test to confirm you are ready to move to the next chapter.

| Selected Readings |

Anderson, James E. *Public Policy Making.* Boston: Houghton Mifflin, 1997.

Birkland, Thomas A. *An Introduction to the Policy Process.* New York: M. E. Sharpe, 2001.

Bonser, Charles F., Eugene McGregor, and Clinton Oster. *American Public Policy Problems.* Upper Saddle River, N.J.: Prentice-Hall, 2000.

Cochran, Clarke, Lawrence Mayer, T. R. Carr, and N. Joseph Cayer. *American Public Policy.* New York: Worth Publishers, 1999.

Kraft, Michael E., and Scott R. Furlong. *Public Policy.* Washington, D.C.: CQ Press, 2004.

Kuletz, Valerie L. *The Tainted Desert: Environmental and Social Ruin in the American West.* New York: Routledge, 1998.

Lester, James, and Joseph Stewart. *Public Policy: An Evolutionary Approach.* Belmont, Calif.: Wadsworth, 2000.

Lomborg, Bjorn. *The Skeptical Environmentalist: Measuring the Real State of the World.* New York: Cambridge University Press, 2001.

Peters, B. Guy. *American Public Policy: Promise and Performance.* Washington, D.C.: CQ Press, 2004.

Peterson, Thomas V., and Steve Myers. *Linked Arms: A Rural Community Resists Nuclear Waste.* Albany: State University of New York Press, 2001.

Rifkin, Jeremy, and Carol Gruenwald Rifkin. *Voting Green: Your Complete Environmental Guide to Making Political Choices in the '90s.* New York: Doubleday, 1992.

Rushefsky, Mark E. *Public Policy in the United States.* New York: M. E. Sharpe, 2002.

Notes

[1]Charles E. Lindblom, *The Policy-Making Process* (Englewood Cliffs, N.J.: Prentice-Hall, 1980), 62–63.

[2]President George W. Bush, *State of the Union Address,* January 29, 2002.

[3]James E. Anderson, David W. Brady, and Charles Bullock, *Public Policy and Politics in America* (North Scituate, Mass.: Duxbury Press, 1978), 5.

[4]Theodore J. Lowi, "American Business, Public Policy Case Studies, and Political Theory," *World Politics* 16 (July 1964): 677–715. In later works Lowi added a fourth policy type, constituent policies, which are administrative in nature and are of little concern to the public. For a critique of the Lowi theory see Hugh H. Heclo, "Review Article. Policy Analysis," *British Journal of Political Science* 2 (1972): 83–108.

[5]Quoted in Timothy Egan, "Industry Reshapes Endangered Species Act," *New York Times,* April 13, 1995, A9.

[6]See James E. Anderson, *Public Policy Making* (New York: Houghton Mifflin, 1997), 106–109, for a discussion of this point.

[7]Hugh Heclo, "Issue Networks and the Executive Establishment," in *The New American Political System,* ed. Anthony King (Washington, D.C.: American Enterprise Institute, 1978), 105.

[8]Rochelle L. Stanfield, "Stewing over Superfund," *National Journal* (August 8, 1987): 2,031.

[9]"Seat of the pants" is a term used by Anderson, Brady, and Bullock in *Public Policy and Politics in America,* 11.

[10]Gary D. Brewer and Peter deLeon, *The Foundations of Policy Analysis* (Homewood, Ill., Dorsey Press, 1983), 387.

[11]Frank R. Baumgartner and Bryan D. Jones, *Agendas and Instability in American Politics* (Chicago: University of Chicago Press, 1994), 4.

[12]President Bush's news conference August 15, 1989, *Weekly Compilation of Presidential Documents,* vol. 25, no. 26 (Washington, D.C.: Office of the Federal Register, National Archives and Records Administration), 1,241–1,248.

[13]Advisory Commission on Intergovernmental Relations, *Intergovernmentalizing the Classroom: Federal Involvement in Elementary and Secondary Education* (Washington, D.C.: ACIR, 1981), 1.

[14]Quoted in the *New York Times,* May 4, 1989.

[15]Both cited at "President Bush Signs Landmark Education Reforms into Law," http://edworkforce.house.gov/press/press107/hr1signing1082.htm, January 8, 2002 (accessed September 15, 2002).

[16]Both cited at: David Nather, "Student-Testing Drive Marks an Attitude Shift for Congress," *Congressional Quarterly Weekly* (June 30, 2001): 1560.

[17]David Sanger and Jim Rutenberg, "Education Law Will Stand, Bush Tells Its Detractors," New York Times, May 12, 2004 (accessed May 13, 2004).

[18]Sam Dillon, "Younger Students Show Gains in Math and Reading," *New York Times,* July 14, 2005, http://www.nytimes.com/ (accessed July 15, 2005).

[19]U.S. Census Bureau, "U.S. Census Bureau News," August 26, 2004, http://www.census.gov/Press-Release/ (accessed February 24, 2006).

[20]Julie Rovner, "The Catastrophic-Costs Law: A Massive Miscalculation," *Congressional Quarterly Weekly,* October 14, 1989, 2,712.

[21]Herbert Gans, "The Failure of Urban Renewal: A Critique and Some Proposals," *Commentary* 39, No. 4 (April 1965): 29–37.

[22]*Hills v. Gautreaux,* 425 U.S. 284 (1976); *Village of Arlington Heights v. Metropolitan Development Corporation,* 429 U.S. 252 (1977).

[23]Michael E. Kraft, *Environmental Policy and Politics* (New York: HarperCollins Publishers, 1996).

[24]Anderson, Brady, and Bullock, *Public Policy and Politics in America,* 76.

[25]Ibid.

[26]Cited by Rebecca Adams in "Bush Attack on Regulations for Arsenic, Surface Mining has Democrats Vowing Action," *Congressional Quarterly Weekly* 59, no. 12 (2001).

[27]For background, see "Clean Air Act Rewritten, Tightened," *Congressional Quarterly Almanac, 1990,* 229–247.

[28]Michael Janofsky, "U.S. Court Backs Bush's Changes on Clean Air Act," *New York Times,* June 25, 2005, A1, http://www.nytimes.com/ (accessed June 27, 2005).

[29]*Statistical Abstract of the United States: 1992,* United States Census Bureau, 515.

[30]*Statistical Abstract of the United States: 2004,* United States Census Bureau, 580.

[31]Justin Blum, "Negotiators Agree on Tax Breaks in Energy Bill," *Washington Post,* July 27, 2005, A4, http://www.washingtonpost.com (accessed July 27, 2005).

[32]David Osborne and Ted Gaebler, Reinventing Government (New York: Addison Wesley, 1992).

[33]"Nevada Picked for Nuclear Waste," New York Times, January 10, 2002 (accessed, January 10, 2002).

15

International and National Security Policy

Introduction

THE NUCLEAR AGE BEGAN WITH a terrible explosion over the Japanese city of Hiroshima on August 6, 1945. President Harry Truman had ordered an atomic bomb dropped, hoping that it would force a surrender and end World War II. It didn't. Three days later, he ordered another atomic bomb dropped on the city of Nagasaki. Six days later, Japan surrendered. More than 150,000 people ultimately died from the two attacks. Nuclear weapons redefined warfare and all of international relations. For the first time in history, nations had the capacity to annihilate their enemies with nuclear weapons. For more than 40 years during the Cold War, the United States and the Soviet Union pointed their nuclear weapons at each other. In 1962, they narrowly avoided hostilities over the Soviet placement of nuclear weapons in Cuba, 90 miles from Florida.

In the years that followed the development of atomic weapons, the number of countries possessing nuclear capabilities slowly grew. The Soviet Union acquired nuclear weapons in 1949. Since then Great Britain, France, China, India, and Pakistan have joined the "nuclear club." Israel is also believed by most analysts to have nuclear weapons.

Nuclear weapons are a threat in two ways primarily. One is the danger that dominated during the Cold War—that one powerful country would launch a nuclear strike against another using missiles and long-range bombers to deliver warheads against multiple targets. Though such possibilities still exist in the contemporary world, that threat was minimized by the end of the Cold War.

The greater fear today is nuclear terrorism by a rogue country or a terrorist organization. The detonation of a nuclear device on the streets of New York or London or Mumbai would potentially kill hundreds of thousands of people and yield radioactive fallout that would be a fatal menace for years thereafter.

Nuclear proliferation—the spread of nuclear weapons to countries that do not currently possess them and the sale of nuclear technology to those countries or to non-state actors—has been a concern of the international community for decades. In 1968, the major nuclear powers agreed to a Nuclear Non-Proliferation Treaty, which by the end of the twentieth century, 185 nations had signed. (Among the countries that have not signed the treaty are India, Pakistan, and Israel.) The treaty's provisions include the creation of the International Atomic Energy Agency (IAEA) to monitor compliance of all signatory nations.

American diplomats and military planners have additional concerns about possible dangers from nuclear weapons. One concern is the existence of thousands of nuclear warheads in Russia. Today there is little assurance that the warheads are carefully controlled and protected from theft or sale to irresponsible clients outside Russia, the "loose nukes" problem. A second concern is that the non-proliferation provisions put in place in the 1960s may now be outdated and no longer fully effective in a world full of small states that believe that possession of nuclear weapons is an effective shield against external attacks from larger countries. One of the lessons of the war in Iraq to many international strategists is that the United States and its allies would have been much more reluctant to attack Iraq if it had possessed nuclear weapons in 2003.

A third concern is Iran and North Korea, two countries ruled by unpredictable leaders that appear determined to develop nuclear weapons despite the disapproval of the international community. North Korea claimed that it tested a nuclear device in October 2006, much to the consternation of the international community. Iran seems determined to continue its nuclear enrichment program despite the opposition of much of Europe and the United States. Both countries have been vociferously anti-American in their public statements and highly resistant to diplomatic pressure to curb their weapons development programs.

Protecting national security has always been a prime responsibility of American leaders. But their task is complicated by the ever-evolving character of the threats to which they must respond and by political disagreement at home about how to deal with the problem: pay more attention to "loose nukes," aggressively confront North Korea and Iran, engage in patient diplomacy, or rely more on international organizations. These debates will continue as part of the search for consensus amid the normal conflicting political forces in the national security policy environment.

This chapter focuses on the politics of national security policymaking. We first examine the principal participants, giving special attention to the president's influence on that process. Then we turn to the substance of recent American foreign and defense policies, placing particular emphasis on the changes wrought by international terrorism. In our discussion we note the continuing effect of these policy judgments on the constitutional character and political climate in the United States.

South Koreans at a railway station in Seoul watch a television broadcasting file footage on Monday, October 9, 2006, of a previous nuclear test . North Korea said Monday it has performed its first-ever nuclear weapons test, which would confirm that the country has a working atomic bomb as it has long claimed. The writing on the screen read: "North Korea has performed its first-ever nuclear weapons test."

Questions to Ponder

- What was the original constitutional design for making foreign and national security policy? Did that design make sense in 1787? Does it still make sense today?
- What factors within the internal and external environment affect and are affected by U.S. policy toward other countries?
- Should the power to make war be vested exclusively or primarily in a single institution? If so, which institution? If not, why not?
- As the United States has moved into a dominant leadership position within the world community, should the process by which it exercises that leadership be altered? If so, how?
- How does the continuing threat of international terrorism affect the politics of American democracy? Has it produced greater consensus or conflict with the population?

Foreign and Defense Policymaking

The United States ranks third among the world's countries in size and population. It has the world's most productive economy and is the world's largest producer of food. It is a military superpower. There is little that happens in the United States that doesn't affect other parts of the world. The election of a new president, changes in the value of the dollar, a severe drought in the Midwest, the development of new commercial products—all of these have international consequences. But the relationship works in both directions; happenings abroad can have significant effects at home. No country is an island in the modern world.

The United States may exert more influence than other countries because of its size, wealth, technology, military, and democratic tradition, but it is still one country among many. All nations desire to pursue what they consider to be their national interests and to determine their policies as free and independent countries. International bodies need to recognize this desire for autonomy at the same time as they calibrate the differing capacities of countries to exercise influence within the world community. Struggles within the international community are as constant and compelling as they are within the domestic policy arena except that the stakes may be higher.

The Conflict–Consensus Quandary in National Security Policy

Throughout this book we have pointed to the conflict and consensus that underlie the politics of American democracy. Within the foreign and national security policy arena, the consensus is clear. Americans agree that the country must maintain means of defending itself, which requires at the least that the geographic integrity of the borders be protected; that the constitutional system of government be preserved; that the free-enterprise, private ownership economy be maintained; and that the country's social structure, as modified by the enhanced opportunities and rights given women and minorities, be supported and strengthened. Threats to any one of these critical components of the American democratic system must be addressed by government. That is what the framers intended when they wrote in the preamble to the Constitution that the role of government was "to establish Justice, insure domestic Tranquility, provide for the common defense, promote general Welfare, and secure the Blessings of Liberty."[2]

Americans expect their government not only to protect them from threats emanating from abroad but also to look out for their interests within the international community. Nevertheless, people disagree about which interests should take precedence and to what extent the United States should go to protect them. As in the domestic policy sphere, internal politics has a major effect on foreign and national security policy.

The environment conditions public demands and the government's response to them. Times of crisis help generate a political consensus and the unity that consensus produces. The more threatened people feel, the more likely they are to defer to government and to look to it, especially to the president, for leadership. An examination of President George W. Bush's job approval ratings before (51 percent) and after the terrorist attacks of September 11, 2001 (86 percent), attest to how crisis becomes a consensus-building and action-forcing mechanism for the president.[3]

When the crisis atmosphere diminishes, however, the opposite effect occurs. Presidential popularity declines as new issues command attention, new political forces are unleashed, constitutional balance is reestablished, and politics as usual returns. Such is the nature of the politics of American democracy.

Foreign and National Security Policymakers

International relations proceed through multiple channels: economic, diplomatic, and military. The primary task for foreign and defense policymakers is to see that those channels flow in the same direction, that all contribute to a coherent purpose. But this is not a simple task. The range of institutional participants in foreign policymaking is wide and varied. Each group sees the world in different colorations. Each has its own information sources and its own internal processes for analysis and decision making. In addition, each spins in its own political orbit, drawing popular support from distinct and traditional sources and interacting routinely with a unique set of special interest groups and congressional committees. Most important, each participant has its own special—and constantly changing—relationship with others in the foreign and national security policy network, especially with the president.

The President As we noted in Chapter 11, the president has been the dominant participant in foreign policymaking throughout the nation's history. Although presidential authority in this area is not unlimited and is sometimes successfully challenged, the American political system and tradition afford great advantages to presidents in their efforts to shape national security policy.

Little in the language of the Constitution suggests that its framers intended the executive to dominate foreign policy.[4] In fact, the Constitution is relatively silent on matters of foreign policy except for the powers we discussed in the chapter on the presidency: the authority to receive ambassadors, to appoint (with the advice and consent of the Senate) American ambassadors abroad, to serve as commander in chief of the armed forces, and to negotiate treaties with foreign nations (subject to the consent of two-thirds of the Senate). These threads of authority do not constitute "the power to conduct foreign affairs," nor has presidential dominance in foreign policy been based solely on the enumeration of constitutional authority. It has also been based on the Constitution's peripheral language and, especially, its silences—that is, on implied or inherent powers (see Chapter 2). Wherever authority to conduct foreign affairs is not specifically granted to some other branch of the government, presidents have claimed it for themselves.

For example, the Constitution states that the president will be commander in chief of the armed forces.[5] Presidents have successfully argued that they have broad authority, implied by that power, to move American troops around the globe whenever they think American lives are endangered or American security is jeopardized. When Thomas Jefferson sent the Navy to protect American shipping from the Barbary pirates and when Ronald Reagan sent Marines to help keep peace in Lebanon, they both acted under the implied power of the commander in chief clause.

Because of the imprecision of the Constitution, presidential authority to conduct foreign affairs has often been subject to legal challenges. With few exceptions, the federal courts have sided with the president, adopting the position that the president is the sole organ of the nation in matters of foreign affairs. In case after case the courts have upheld broad interpretations of presidential authority for the conduct of foreign affairs and the protection of national security.[6]

Contemporary presidents have multiple sources of information and advice upon which to draw. Of these various advisers, the staff of the **National Security Council (NSC)** has assumed the dominant role. Created in 1947 to assist the president in coordinating national security policy, the formal membership of the NSC includes the president, the vice president, the secretary of state, and the secretary of defense. The director of national intelligence and the chairperson of the Joint Chiefs of Staff are statutory advisers. Beginning in the 1960s, the NSC also has had its own staff in the Executive Office of the President. The head of that staff, the assistant to the president for national security affairs, has direct, daily access to the president and thus often becomes the president's principal adviser on national security issues.[7]

National Security Council (NSC)
The principal advisory body to the president on national security issues. It was created in 1947 and is composed of the president, vice president, and secretaries of state and defense.

President George W. Bush meets with his National Security Council in the White House situation room Tuesday, October 2, 2001. Clockwise, from center are, White House Chief of Staff Andrew Card, Vice President Dick Cheney, President Bush, Secretary of State Colin Powell, Defense Secretary Donald H. Rumsfeld, and National Security Adviser Condoleezza Rice.

Indeed, some recent presidents have sought a national security adviser who could play that role precisely because they feared that the secretaries of defense and state and other important agency heads would become "captives" of the narrow and biased viewpoints of their own agencies. The national security adviser, on the other hand, was beholden only to the president and, therefore, was likely to offer more balanced judgments. Many prominent people skilled in international politics have served as the assistant to the president for national security. They include Dr. Henry Kissinger (Richard Nixon), Dr. Zbigniew Brzezinski (Jimmy Carter), General Brent Scowcroft (George H. W. Bush), and Dr. Condoleezza Rice (George W. Bush).[8]

Although the structure of the NSC and its staff has remained relatively constant, the manner in which presidents have sought advice has varied with their decision-making style. Some presidents, such as Dwight Eisenhower and Gerald Ford, have relied heavily on a single adviser; John F. Kennedy preferred a collective approach. During the Cuban missile crisis, he brought together a group of advisers that included the secretaries of defense and state but also some "old Washington hands" who held no formal position in the government. The main criterion for their selection was Kennedy's trust in their judgment.[9]

In the first term of President George W. Bush, Secretary of State Colin Powell and Secretary of Defense Donald Rumsfeld often took different positions on major issues, especially on how to deal with the terrorist threat. The two departments and their secretaries engaged in regular political conflict—sometimes in the Oval Office, sometimes at meetings of the NSC, sometimes in "leaks" reported in the news media.[10] Condoleezza Rice was the "neutral" arbiter and primary link to the president.

When all is said and done, the opportunities contained in the Constitution, the support of federal courts, the enlargement of the institutionalized presidency and the executive branch, and the nature of public expectations have put the president in the vanguard of foreign policymaking. These are inherent advantages that every president possesses, but what a president makes of those advantages is heavily dependent on his political skills. Truly effective leadership in foreign affairs can result only from the political arts of persuasion, coordination, and compromise, and as we noted at the outset, strong leadership is often only possible during crises that threaten the national security of the country.

15.1 In Theory . . .

Can Terrorism Be Confronted Democratically?

Alexis de Tocqueville noted in 1835, "Foreign politics demand scarcely any of those qualities which are peculiar to democracy; they require on the contrary, the perfect use of almost all those in which it is deficient."[11]

National security policy has always been resistant to democratic management, but never more so than now.

How would you answer the following questions?

If you were president, would you willingly share with Congress intelligence information on the whereabouts of Osama bin Laden? Democratic

continued

15.1 **In Theory . . .** *continued*

theory holds that Congress should have all information necessary to properly oversee the activities of the executive branch. But there have also been occasions when members of Congress have revealed or leaked secret information for political purposes.

If you were director of the Federal Bureau of Investigation and you believed that a captured terrorist had direct information about a bombing plot about to unfold in an American city, would you authorize torture of the captive to force him to reveal the information that might save thousands of

American lives? Torture is a violation of the Geneva Convention, many American laws, and a long American tradition. But would you authorize it despite those constraints if you thought there was no other way to discover potentially lifesaving information?

After September 11, 2001, Congress passed the USA Patriot Act to improve the quality of intelligence gathering about terrorism. One of the provisions of the act permitted government agencies to require libraries to provide the book-borrowing records of their patrons. If you were a librarian,

would you comply with such a request? Americans have long believed that what they read, think, or say is protected by a broad blanket of freedom. But what if that blanket seems to block a legitimate government investigation into terrorists reading books on bomb making at the library? Should individual rights always stand in the way of effective pursuit of dangerous enemies?

In an age of terrorism, there are many hard questions like these. Democratic theory and tradition is sometimes in conflict with the immediate needs of national security. How those conflicts are resolved will play a major role in our time in defining the meaning of democracy and liberty.

Congress Congress is a potent but inconsistent participant in foreign and national security policy decisions. Its members are often overmatched and out-maneuvered by the president when they disagree with the president's initiatives. Although it often plays a significant role in shaping the details of policy implementation, Congress has rarely demonstrated much aptitude for defining broad foreign policy directions. Its effect is more often felt when it reacts to or alters presidential proposals.

There have been some exceptions to this general pattern, especially in the period after 1968, when Congress and the presidency were often controlled by different political parties. In 1986, for example, Congress initiated sanctions against the government of South Africa that were more severe than those President Ronald Reagan wanted. And after the Tiananmen Square uprising in 1989, it responded to violence against student protesters in China by moving more assertively than President George H. W. Bush to extend the visas of Chinese students studying in the United States. President Bill Clinton had intense battles with Congress when he sought approval of several major trade agreements, as did George W. Bush with the Central American Free Trade Agreement (CAFTA).

Congressional participation in national security policymaking is usually led by members of committees with jurisdiction in this area, especially the Foreign Relations Committee in the Senate, the International Relations Committee in the House, the House and Senate Armed Services Committees, and the appropriations subcommittees in each house that oversee the military and foreign aid budgets. A determined committee majority or a powerful chairperson can occasionally affect the shape of national security policy, but most of the time Congress reacts to presidential initiatives. It reviews presidential proposals, perhaps altering them somewhat, but usually it acquiesces to presidential leadership.

Congressional deference to the president has resulted partly from the recognition and tradition that the rational conduct of foreign affairs requires the president to serve as an authoritative point of contact with other nations. Congressional deference has also resulted, however, from the popular support that usually accompanies national security actions initiated by the president. Congress is rarely willing to tangle with a president who commands popular support. And on most foreign policy issues, public opinion initially supports the president. This is a potent deterrent to congressional opposition.

Even when it opposes the president, however, Congress has great difficulty thwarting presidential initiatives because it has only limited "handles" for controlling national security decisions. Many important actions in this sphere are nonstatutory and not dependent on congressional action. The president can recognize the legitimacy of a foreign government, negotiate with foreign leaders, enter into executive agreements, issue communiqués, and even blockade a foreign country's ports without asking Congress for permission to do so.

In addition, the president can initiate many foreign policy actions without special appropriations. The "power of the purse" has long been Congress's most effective control over presidential behavior. But when the president negotiates a grain sale with another country, recognizes the new state of Israel, or cuts off purchases of oil from Iran, no appropriations are needed and Congress cannot use this "handle" to control executive action.

During and after the Vietnam War, Congress took several steps designed to strengthen its role in national security policymaking. New laws and resolutions were enacted to ensure that commitments of troops, agreements with foreign countries, sales of weapons, and covert operations would receive closer scrutiny and prior approval by Congress. New committees and subcommittees were established to expand congressional participation in national security decisions, and those committees became more aggressive in questioning officials of the executive branch and more assertive and creative in developing policy alternatives.

These efforts were driven partly by intensified conflict among special interest groups—such as farmers selling grain in overseas markets, Greek Americans concerned with the dispute over the island of Cypress between Greece and Turkey, and human rights activists concerned with the political freedoms and economic benefits given to those in the less developed world. Bipartisanship, a guiding principal in foreign policymaking in the immediate aftermath of World War II, deteriorated, and congressional deference to the president declined. But the latter change was not a total break from the past, nor is it set in stone for the future. Although the president is still the leader on most foreign and defense policy matters, Congress follows that lead less than it did in the past.

Diplomacy Governments talk to one another. Sometimes they do this in public, in the forums provided by international organizations like the United Nations. Sometimes they do it through public statements released to the news media;

sometimes they do so in private, in face-to-face meetings or direct correspondence among national leaders or ministers of foreign affairs; and sometimes they do it in secret, in contacts among designated emissaries. All of these activities constitute **diplomacy,** the conduct of relations among nations, which are seen as rational actors trying to maximize their power and direct it toward their country's self-interest. In this section, we briefly describe the key elements of American diplomacy.

The State Department   The principal diplomatic agency of the United States is the State Department. One of the original cabinet offices created by the First Congress in 1789, the State Department manages much of the day-to-day activity involved in conducting relations with foreign governments. The secretary of state heads the department and is normally regarded as the country's principal foreign minister. The senior levels of the department are composed of several deputy secretaries, undersecretaries, and assistant secretaries who manage specific aspects of American foreign policy.

The secretary of state usually serves as the government's most visible foreign policy spokesperson. The State Department maintains and manages American embassies and consulates in virtually all foreign countries and is the primary but not exclusive channel for routine communications between the United States and

diplomacy
The conduct of relations among nations, depending heavily on mutual communication conducted by professional diplomats.

U.S. Secretary of State Condoleezza Rice prepares to testify before the U.S. Senate Foreign Relations Committee on Capitol Hill, February 16, 2005.

foreign governments. In Washington, D.C., the State Department is organized into a series of regional and country desks, which interpret information and make policy recommendations. Each of these is staffed by people who are knowledgeable about, and usually have served in, the countries for which they have responsibility. Although it has always had a central role in foreign policymaking, the State Department has often been criticized by presidents and their White House aides for lack of creativity in its policy recommendations, for tardiness in carrying out presidential directives, and for its "overemphasis" on rhetorical and other diplomatic solutions.

Within the State Department, conflict on policy matters is a way of life. On no matter of national concern is there a monolithic view. In recent years, for example, political appointees at the senior positions have often been more supportive of Israel's actions in the Middle East than have career foreign service officers. Determining the State Department's position on any issue is a complex juggling act among competing political factions within the department and public pressures acting on the department; its policy positions often take longer to unfold than presidential patience can tolerate.

Bilateral Relations **Bilateral relations** are the one-to-one dealings between the United States and a foreign government. Routine interactions between American diplomats and foreign officials are the most common form of bilateral relations. Much of this interaction involves the mundane details of processing visas, passports, customs claims, and the like. The U.S. government is represented in most foreign countries, except for those that have not yet been officially recognized or with which diplomatic relations have been severed as a result of some unresolved issue. For example, no American ambassador served in the People's Republic of China from 1949 until 1979, first because the government of the United States declined to give formal recognition to the revolutionary regime of Mao Zedong and later because the Chinese were reluctant to reestablish full diplomatic relations as long as the United States continued to grant recognition to the government of Taiwan. Similarly, in 1979 diplomatic relations between the United States and Iran were severed after the overthrow of the Shah of Iran and the seizure of American hostages by a new regime headed by the Ayatollah Khomeini.

The American **embassy** is usually located in the capital city of the country. In some larger countries, there may also be American **consulates** in cities outside the capital. The embassy and the consulates are staffed by State Department employees. In most countries the leader of the delegation is the American **ambassador.**[12]

Ambassadors fall within the organizational structure of the State Department, but all of them are nominated by the president and must be confirmed by a majority of the Senate. Normally, about 75 percent of the ambassadors are members of the Foreign Service, America's professional diplomatic corps, and the other 25 percent are private citizens, most of whom have been personal or political allies of the president.[13] Some of America's most effective and most esteemed ambassadors have come from the latter group, but so, too, have some who turned out to be embarrassments because they lacked the knowledge, skills, or sensitivity needed to operate effectively in a foreign country.

bilateral relations
The direct relations between two countries, involving diplomacy, trade, foreign aid, and military interaction.

embassy
The primary office representing American interests in a foreign country. It is located in the capital city of the foreign country and headed by a chief of mission called an ambassador.

consulates
Offices representing the interests of the United States in a foreign country. In countries with which America has full diplomatic relations, consulates are located in cities other than the capital.

ambassador
The highest ranking U.S. representative to a foreign government. The majority are senior career foreign service officers.

Other departments of the federal government also have overseas representatives, and they often work at American embassies and consulates. Most embassies have military attachés from the U.S. armed forces, and many have trade, cultural, scientific, and agricultural representatives. Embassies and consulates may also be part—usually a covert and unacknowledged part—of American intelligence operations in a foreign country. In addition, some American government employees overseas, such as members of the Peace Corps and the U.S. Agency for International Development, are scattered about the countryside and not attached to embassies or consulates.

Personal Diplomacy and Summit Meetings

Bilateral relations may also occur on a higher level. On some occasions another nation's foreign minister or national leader meets directly with the president, the secretary of state, or some other high-ranking federal government official. These may be ceremonial or courtesy visits or important official discussions of matters of high importance to both countries. Often these meetings are as valuable for allowing national leaders to develop personal relationships as for their substantive, diplomatic accomplishments.

At the grandest scale, bilateral relations might take the form of a **summit meeting** between the American president and an important foreign leader. Between World War II and the demise of the Soviet Union in 1991, every American president met with his Soviet counterpart at least once. Summit meetings serve several purposes. They allow leaders of the most powerful and dangerous countries in the world to get to know one another in a personal way. Richard Nixon noted that his two summit meetings with Soviet Premier Leonid Brezhnev

summit meeting
A meeting between the leaders of two or more countries at which matters of mutual interest are discussed and sometimes resolved.

> gave me an opportunity to get to know [Brezhnev] better and to try to take his measure as a leader and as a man. I had spent forty-two hours with him in 1972, and now thirty-five hours with him in 1973. However superficial this kind of personal contact may be, it can still provide important insights. . . .
>
> Despite the shortness of [Brezhnev's] visit, I felt that he had seen a diversity of American life for which no briefing books and studies could possibly have prepared him. I know that he returned home with a far better understanding of America and Americans than he had before he came.[14]

Ronald Reagan's and George H. W. Bush's meetings with Soviet leader Mikhail Gorbachev served a similar purpose, allowing the men to overcome personal and ideological biases and to better understand one another. After George W. Bush's first meeting with Vladimir Putin of Russia, the American president stated, "I looked the man in the eye. I was able to get a sense of his soul."[15] The quote, although seemingly naïve, was meant by Bush to imply that Putin was a man with whom he could deal and, to some extent, empathize.

On some occasions, summit meetings have been the last stage in a long series of negotiations between representatives of the two countries, a stage at which painstakingly negotiated agreements are finalized and signed. In 1961, for example, President John F. Kennedy and Soviet Premier Nikita Khrushchev met in

Vienna to discuss differences over the future of Berlin. In 1975, President Gerald Ford and Soviet Premier Leonid Brezhnev met in Helsinki to sign an agreement supporting human rights and freer movement of citizens between nations. But summit meetings can also be risky, generating unmet expectations or jeopardizing the reputations of one or both of the leaders involved. President Ronald Reagan and Soviet leader Mikhail Gorbachev failed to reach an agreement on the limitation of nuclear missiles at their summit in Reykjavik in 1986, and Reagan was criticized in the American press for having been poorly prepared for the meeting.[16]

The character of high-level communication among national leaders has begun to change in recent years as a partial consequence of advances in technology. The time frame becomes shorter and the contact more direct. George H. W. Bush, for example, often communicated on the telephone with his counterparts in other countries. This form of **rolodex diplomacy** was especially notable as Bush sought to construct a coalition of countries to oppose the Iraqi invasion of Kuwait in 1990. His successors have often undertaken similar personal contacts. Television satellites and the emergence of international, twenty-four-hour, seven days per week networks like CNN, Fox, and MSNBC, as well as news services, permit leaders to communicate using television. After the coup against Soviet leader Mikhail Gorbachev in 1991, American leaders acquired important information about the status of authority in the Soviet Union by watching television coverage of the coup and its aftermath. Employing a combination of these new technologies, President George H. W. Bush held a press conference to inform the world that he had talked with Boris Yeltsin by telephone and Yeltsin had informed him that the coup was unraveling.

rolodex diplomacy
A term used to describe the recent pattern of direct telephone communications between the president of the United States and foreign leaders.

15.2 Politics in the 21st Century

Direct Diplomacy

Imagine what diplomacy was like before the steam engine was invented. Countries sent their diplomats to other countries then relied almost entirely on their skills and judgment in conducting international relations. An American diplomat in Europe with a question for the government in Washington would have to wait months for the answer. Most questions couldn't wait that long, so the diplomat would have to take responsibility for the answer. Not

surprisingly, in the early days of the republic, America called on some of its most important citizens—Thomas Jefferson, John Adams, Benjamin Franklin, and others—to be its ambassadors abroad.

Before the twentieth century, American presidents played a limited role in direct relations with other countries. Although they were significant in shaping broad American foreign policies at home, they never played a direct role

in implementing those policies nor in conducting negotiations with other countries. Foreign leaders never came to the White House, and American presidents never traveled across the oceans. Woodrow Wilson was the first American president to go to Europe while in office. He spent eleven weeks out of the country helping negotiate the Versailles Treaty at the end of World War I, traveling each way on a Navy ship. Franklin Roosevelt left the country on only one important trip during his first eight years in office, traveling to Buenos Aires for a naval conference.

All that has now changed. Modern transportation and communications

continued

15.2 **Politics in the 21st Century** *continued*

technology permits presidents, secretaries of state and defense, and national security advisers to stay in constant and immediate contact with American diplomats, soldiers, and spies abroad. Recent presidents have used the telephone for conversations with their foreign counterparts whenever an issue demands presidential attention. *Air Force One* is a flying communications center. The president can travel anywhere in the world at high speed yet still be able to contact anyone anywhere. Diplomats can bring their questions directly to their superiors in

Washington and receive instantaneous answers. Commanders in the field are never out of touch with the Pentagon.

One effect of these changes is a centralization of national security policymaking. American representatives abroad are no longer isolated from their government at home. Their independent judgment is relied upon less than it was when communication was difficult. Washington leaders can oversee diplomacy, war, and surveillance more directly and effectively than ever before. They are more powerful and influential as a result.

We may never again have American diplomats as important as Jefferson or Adams, nor generals as influential as John Pershing or Douglas MacArthur. The limits of technology freed them from many of the tethers of Washington. But those limits have largely evaporated. Modern communications and transportation technology tie American representatives abroad more tightly to their leaders in Washington than ever before. And they have enlarged as never before the president's role as America's chief diplomat.

Treaties and Executive Agreements

A common result of bilateral relations is the establishment of formal agreements among nations. These may take the form of treaties or executive agreements.

A **treaty** is an official, written set of accords in which the parties agree to certain specific actions. When the United States enters into a treaty with a foreign government, it is negotiated by American diplomatic officials, sometimes including officials from the Executive Office of the President and even the president. The Senate's role in treaty making can be important because it takes the votes of only one-third plus one of the members of the Senate to defeat one. Hence, in treaty making, the political negotiations between the president and the opposition in the Senate are often as telling as the diplomatic negotiations between the United States and a foreign government.

The Panama Canal Treaties of 1978 is a case in point. In the summer of 1977 President Jimmy Carter completed lengthy negotiations with the government of Panama. Carter and General Omar Torrijos Herrera of Panama signed two treaties, returning control of the canal to the Panamanian government after 1999 and guaranteeing the political neutrality and accessibility of the canal to all nations.

The Senate discussed and debated the treaties for six months, during which the opponents used every available political and legislative means to prevent ratification: a massive public opinion and mail campaign, heavy pressure on senators who were undecided or uncommitted, threats to make the treaties the dominant issue in the upcoming congressional campaigns, and proposed amendments to

treaty
A formal agreement between two or more countries. In the United States, treaties require the ratification, by a two-thirds majority, of the Senate.

the treaty that would push it through the Senate in a form unacceptable to Panama. Ultimately the Senate discussed and voted on 145 amendments, 26 "reservations," 18 "understandings," and 3 "declarations." Following discussions between the Senate and the administration that were as intricate as the negotiations between the United States and Panama, the two treaties were ratified in March and April 1978 by identical votes of 68–32.[17]

Executive agreements often have the same legal effect as treaties, but they differ from treaties in an important respect: they do not have to be approved by the Senate (see Chapter 11). They are negotiated and finalized between the president (or his deputies) and the representatives of foreign countries. Not only can presidents conclude such agreements on their own, but before 1972 there also was no requirement that they be made public. When Congress discovered secret agreements that Presidents Lyndon Johnson and Richard Nixon had made during the Vietnam War, it enacted legislation to prevent this from happening again. The legislation, named after its sponsor, Senator Clifford Case (R-New Jersey), requires the executive branch to reveal all international agreements to Congress within sixty days of their execution. A provision of the Case Act, however, permits the administration to submit any such agreement to the Senate Foreign Relations and House International Relations Committees in secret if it determines that disclosure of the agreement would jeopardize national security.

Participation in International Organizations

international organizations

Organizations like the United Nations and the Organization of American States in which countries come together to seek peaceful resolution of their disagreements and to work jointly in pursuit of mutual goals.

Relations between the United States and other countries also unfold in a variety of **international organizations.** These are formal institutions that have been established to provide member nations with a place and a set of procedures for resolving their differences and for working together on problems of mutual concern.

The best known of these international organizations is the United Nations (UN), which was created in 1945 and is currently headquartered in New York City. Nearly 160 nations are represented in the membership of the UN—all but a few of the countries of the world. Many other international organizations are part of the UN, including the International Labor Organization, the United Nations Educational, Cultural, and Scientific Organization, the World Health Organization, and the United Nations Children's Fund.

Most international organizations are federations: They provide forums in which nations may meet and discuss international issues, but they have little real authority to direct or constrain the actions of member nations. In 1980, for example, the International Court of Justice declared that Iran had acted unlawfully in seizing American hostages and ordered their release. However, the court was powerless to force Iran to free those hostages. In 1984, the court held that the government of the United States had violated international law by providing military support to rebels opposing the Sandinista government in Nicaragua, including mining the harbors of that country. But the United States argued that the world court was not an appropriate forum for the resolution of complex political issues in Central America and refused to abide by the court's findings.

International organizations have been especially helpful in organizing international efforts in matters of world health, agricultural development, and commerce. However, those organizations have been unable to substitute for direct discussions among nations, particularly on matters on which the countries disagree deeply. After George W. Bush became president, for example, American concerns over North Korea's expanding nuclear program have been principally addressed in six-party talks in Asia, not through the more formal mechanism of the UN. In general, the more important an international dispute and the wider the division among the contesting nations, the greater the likelihood that critical negotiations will not be relegated to the formal procedures of an international organization.

Intelligence, Spying, and Covert Operations

In the uncertainties of contemporary world politics, national security policymakers hunger for accurate and relevant information critical to wise decisions, but this information is often difficult to collect and verify. Hence, all large governments now have their own intelligence agencies, charged with using every available means to find out about real and potential adversaries—and often about allies.

The Cuban missile crisis of 1962 demonstrated the importance of such information. The discovery of nuclear missile installations under construction in Cuba resulted from aerial photographs taken during routine intelligence overflights. The interpretation of these photos by intelligence agencies determined that the missile bases were being constructed by the Soviet Union, that the missiles had long-range nuclear capability, and that construction was nearing completion. President Kennedy thus was provided with relatively reliable information about the nature and imminence of the threat.

Espionage and intelligence gathering have long been part of national security policymaking in the United States. The intelligence establishment was modernized in 1947 when, as part of a broad reorganization of the national security apparatus, the Central Intelligence Agency was created. More than forty other agencies of the government collect and analyze intelligence information. They include the State Department's Bureau of Intelligence and Research, the Defense Intelligence Agency, the National Security Agency, and the Federal Bureau of Investigation. In response to the recommendations of a commission studying the 2001 terrorist attacks on the World Trade Center in New York, Congress in 2004 further restructured the intelligence network by creating the new position of director of national intelligence to improve coordination among the various intelligence agencies and an interagency terrorist integration center to analyze the intelligence.

The techniques of modern intelligence gathering are amazingly sophisticated. In some areas of activity—determining troop strength, monitoring military movements, and detecting nuclear tests, for example—the United States can use satellite and other aerial reconnaissance to know a great deal about what its adversaries and allies are up to. Other areas are more difficult to penetrate, especially those involving the development of new weapons technologies, strategies for negotiation, and military activity. Information about the latter is often best derived through **espionage**—that is, through the deployment of human agents

espionage
The use of spying techniques to collect intelligence information.

who spy on foreign governments or terrorist organizations. Human espionage remains a critical ingredient of the American intelligence operations, but one important lesson of the current era is that terrorist networks like Al Qaeda are extremely difficult to penetrate with human operatives. Reliance on sophisticated spying technology, such as capturing cell phone conversations, is therefore more important than ever before.

Gathering and properly using intelligence is not a simple matter in any country. It is an especially difficult task in a democracy in which inherent secrecy and dependence on stealth activities may violate important democratic principles.[18] Congress, for example, has long had difficulty overseeing the intelligence agencies, which sometimes involves reviewing and approving programs that would become ineffective if their existence were to become known. In the 1970s, after several intelligence agencies abused the freedom of action they had traditionally been accorded, Congress sought to tighten its control over intelligence activities. Both the Senate and the House created select committees on intelligence and began more thorough reviews of their intelligence budgets and programs. In 2004, Congress agreed on legislation that established a National Intelligence Director to oversee all U.S. intelligence operations and the intelligence budget, most of which is not made public.

Despite these measures, there remains considerable tension between the legislative and the executive branches with regard to intelligence gathering and analysis. Congress often feels that it has been denied the information it needs to carry out its constitutional responsibilities. But the president and his advisers often worry about congressional meddling in intelligence activities and the consequent risk of leaks of sensitive information.

Armed Forces and National Security

At the beginning of the twenty-first century, the United States loomed as the world's great military superpower. Rarely, if ever, in human history have one country's military capabilities so exceeded those of any other country. In 2004, America spent more money on defense than all of the other countries of the world combined.[19] Figure 15.1 indicates the comparison between American military spending and that of the other nine countries among the top ten military spenders.

The size, cost, and strength of American military forces present opportunities and challenges for foreign and national security policymakers. The opportunities are to extend U.S. values and policy interests; the challenges are to do so without becoming an imperial power or an international police force. In other words, the task is how to use military force as an instrument of diplomacy, not in place of it.

The historic tradition of civilian control of the armed forces requires the Department of Defense to be led by a civilian secretary and civilian deputies who work closely with their counterparts in the military. The highest-ranking uniformed officer in each of the armed services also serves as a member of a body called the **Joint Chiefs of Staff.** The chairperson of this group is an officer from one of the services appointed by the president for a two-year term. The Joint

Joint Chiefs of Staff
Military advisers to the president composed of the highest ranking officers of each of the armed services.

Figure 15.1 American Defense Spending Compared to the Other Nine Largest Spending Countries

IISS Military Balance, 2003–2004, current year 2002 dollars

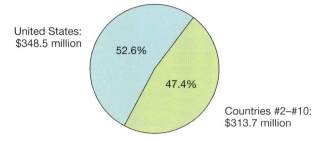

United States: $348.5 million — 52.6%

Countries #2–#10: $313.7 million — 47.4%

Source: Congressional Research Service, *Comparisons of U.S. and Foreign Military Spending: Data from Selected Public Sources,* January 28, 2004.

Chiefs of Staff are important advisers to the president on military matters and work to coordinate the input of the individual armed services in operations, strategy, and even research and development.

One of the largest departments of government, the Department of Defense has a budget that is approximately half of the discretionary budget. In 2006, President Bush requested $504.9 billion for the department. During periods of armed conflict, such as the war in Iraq, that budget is supplemented with additional appropriations. In February 2005, for example, President Bush requested

The Pentagon has been the headquarters of the Department of Defense since its creation in the 1940s.

an additional $74.9 billion for the Defense Department. Table 15.1 indicates recent patterns in defense spending and personnel.

Because it is so large and complex, the department is difficult to manage and the coordination of military policy is an enormous administrative challenge. Political infighting is a common occurrence. The different service branches have their own traditions and cultures, and they are often at odds with one another about military strategy and the choice of new weapons systems. A new airplane design that might be entirely suitable for the Air Force, in which all planes are launched from the ground, may not be suitable for the Navy, in which planes are often launched from aircraft carriers at sea. Similarly, a strategy that calls for heavy artillery support from Navy ships may please the Navy but displease the Army, which has its own artillery units. These interservice rivalries and tensions are constant, and civilian leaders must resolve them.

In foreign affairs, diplomatic and military initiatives usually occur simultaneously. But diplomacy is a difficult process that may drag on for long periods without producing satisfactory results. Diplomatic undertakings, which depend on persuasion and mutual accommodation, may not succeed in convincing foreign nations to agree with one another or to act in accordance with American national interests. Military initiatives are often more promising, or so they may appear to American policymakers. The leaders of the administration of George W. Bush grew increasingly frustrated with the efforts of the UN to curb what they believed were efforts by Saddam Hussein in Iraq to develop weapons of mass destruction. So in 2003, America and a small number of allied forces launched a military strike that removed Hussein from power. The administration's objective was to succeed through the use of military force where it had failed diplomatically.

Table 15.1 **Defense Expenditures and Active Duty Personnel Levels, 1960–2003**

Year	Active Duty Personnel (in millions)	Defense and Veterans Expenditures (in billions)
1960	2.475	$53.5
1965	2.654	56.3
1970	3.065	90.4
1975	2.128	103.1
1980	2.051	155.1
1985	2.151	279.0
1990	2.044	328.4
1995	1.518	310.0
2000	1.384	341.6
2003	1.434	461.9

Source: *Statistical Abstract of the United States: 2004–2005.* United States Department of Commerce, Census Bureau, http://www.census.gov/prod/www/statistical-abstract.html.

Part of the appeal of military over diplomatic approaches is the common perception among American presidents that the Defense Department is more responsive than the State Department or other diplomatic agencies to presidential wishes. John F. Kennedy, for example, once called the State Department a "bowl of jelly."[20] This perception may be misleading because there are also many examples of military resistance to presidential leadership, such as the Army leadership's contention in 2002 that a military invasion and occupation in Iraq would require 300,000 troops, far more than the defense secretary and president were prepared to use. Nonetheless, most presidents have felt that military approaches promised quicker and surer responses than diplomacy and that they often generate greater public support at home.

On national security issues, as in all aspects of policymaking, the president may be engaged in political struggles even with his highest-ranking and closest advisers. For example, after sixty-six American hostages were seized in Iran in 1979, intense debate occurred within the top levels of the Carter administration over how to respond.[21] Some of Carter's advisers, especially National Security Adviser Zbigniew Brzezinski and Defense Secretary Harold Brown, felt that bold action, perhaps even military intervention, was necessary. Others, including Secretary of State Cyrus Vance, believed that the military risks were too high and that the best hope for avoiding injury to the hostages lay in patient diplomacy. When public support for Carter's handling of the hostage crisis diminished—and with the presidential election of 1980 looming on the horizon—Carter began to side with those who urged bolder action. Against the strong counsel of Secretary of State Vance, Carter ordered a military rescue mission. The mission failed when a helicopter and an airplane collided before reaching their objective. Vance, feeling that his effectiveness as an adviser to the president had been compromised, resigned in protest.

Review Questions

1. The overall effect on U.S. foreign policy of decisions made by the Supreme Court has been that they have

   A. Decreased presidential authority over foreign affairs
   B. Increased presidential authority over foreign affairs
   C. Increased congressional authority over foreign affairs
   D. Decreased congressional authority over foreign affairs

2. In which of the following foreign policy areas has Congress historically been most effective?

   A. Outlining broad foreign policy strategies and doctrines
   B. Choosing leaders of major military commands
   C. Deciding when and where the United States will apply military force
   D. Determining and modifying the manner in which foreign policy initiatives will be implemented

continued

3. Presidents often prefer executive agreements to formal treaties because

   A. They are less binding than treaties
   B. There is no requirement that they be made public, even to Congress
   C. They do not require Senate approval
   D. They end automatically after five years

Answers:

   1. B
   2. D
   3. C

Conflict and Consensus in Review

A decision by the president to pursue a particular policy course is no guarantee that all other participants will agree with the policy goals, the strategy to achieve them, or the personnel necessary to carry them out. The president must struggle not only with the legislative branch in defining policy but also with the elements of the executive branch for implementing it. The constancy of conflict and the relentless pursuit of consensus are enduring features of national security policymaking. And as we noted, consensus is more likely to apply to the goals of the policy and the values that underlie them, whereas conflict occurs over the details, the strategies to achieve those goals.

The Evolution of National Security Policy

The two atomic bombs that American planes dropped on Japanese cities in 1945 marked the beginning of contemporary American international policy. Rarely has a historical turning point been more clearly—and more dramatically—marked. On those two August days a new era in world affairs began, one dominated by the availability and the fear of a single terrifying weapon.

Before World War II, the history of American foreign policy had been characterized by almost continual **isolationism:** disengagement from the affairs of foreign countries except when they intersected directly with our own. The isolation was occasionally broken by wars—wars with Britain and Spain and World War I. But each of those wars was followed by rapid demobilization and a return to isolationism.

After World War II, however, the historical pattern of American isolationism was broken, probably irrevocably. The decades following the war were markedly different from the prewar world. Two superpowers—the United States and the Soviet Union—loomed over it, "super" in terms of natural resources, military might, and international objectives.

isolationism
A characteristic of American foreign policy for much of the period before World War II. Many Americans believed that the United States should not be directly engaged in the affairs or the wars of European or other foreign countries.

© Bettmann/CORBIS

President Franklin D. Roosevelt appears before Congress on December 8, 1941 to ask for a declaration of war against Japan.

The two superpowers had different concepts of the proper economic and political organization of a society and different visions of the future. Their differences bred suspicion and distrust between them and among the countries caught in the middle. The United States and the Soviet Union quickly came to focus on each other as adversaries, and the result was what came to be called the **Cold War,** a period of intense and often hostile competition between the United States and the Soviet Union. All of this required—and caused—some critical changes in American foreign policy.

The Cold War

In the years following World War II, American policymakers began to develop responses to the changes that had taken place in the international environment. By the end of the 1940s, several new and fundamental principles of American national security policy had emerged.[22]

The first of these held that America must play an active and continuing role in world affairs. Isolationism was rejected. American interests were not limited to the continental United States but extended all over the globe. The lesson drawn

Cold War

A term used to describe the hostile relationship between the United States and the Soviet Union in the decades that followed World War II.

from the two world wars was that America could never again afford to withdraw from world affairs. As a superpower it had a responsibility to deter aggression and to prevent local hostilities from ballooning into worldwide conflicts.

Second, American policy strategists identified communism as the greatest danger confronting the United States. In the early postwar years, communism was widely regarded as a monolithic movement based on Marxist ideology and directed insidiously from the Soviet Union, a view that dominated American policymaking for almost two decades. By the late 1960s a more sophisticated perception began to emerge, one that recognized distinctions among communist governments.

Third, the objective of American national security policy would be **containment** of the influence of the Soviet Union. The Soviet Union was regarded as the driving force in the world communist movement, and it therefore became the principal focus of American policymakers, who devised a policy of containment to prevent the spread of Soviet influence into noncommunist countries.[23]

Containment of Soviet expansionism remained the dominant focus of American national security policy, but it inspired plenty of political debate. Some political and opinion leaders thought the communist threat was imminent and that it could be effectively opposed only by using military force. They supported large peacetime military expenditures and military responses to acts of communist aggression. But others believed that the threat was most likely to be felt in the smaller industrialized nations and in the less developed countries. The best response to the spread of communism, in their view, was to use America's wealth and ideological commitment to freedom and human rights—not its armed forces—to win support in those countries. They supported policies to encourage foreign trade, increase foreign aid, and help foreign political leaders most likely to pursue democratic goals. What came out of the post-World War II debate over foreign policy was a mixture of diplomatic, economic, and military initiatives.

Nuclear Deterrence

For most of the postwar period, American policy strategists regarded nuclear weapons as primarily defensive in purpose, preventing wars, especially among the superpowers. They believed that peace could best be accomplished through strength, and that nuclear weapons were the best deterrent against attacks.

For nuclear deterrence to be effective, the United States had to convince the Soviet Union and other potential adversaries that the United States possessed the capability to inflict significant damage in a nuclear attack, even if that attack came as a retaliatory response to a nuclear attack on the United States. In the jargon of nuclear policymakers, this was labeled **mutual assured destruction (MAD).** It implied that a nuclear attack on the United States would be suicidal for the country that launched it. Yet the fear of devastation that such an attack and counterattack would produce prompted critics to denounce nuclear war, oppose nuclear proliferation, and reject the basic foundation upon which a MAD strategy was built—arguing that the nuclear war was so awful to consider that it could and should never be considered a possibility.

---

containment
The policy developed after World War II to prevent the spread of communism through the use of strong alliances, foreign aid, nuclear deterrence, and military assistance. Containment was the centerpiece of American foreign policy in those years.

mutual assured destruction (MAD)
A policy of nuclear deterrence in which America sought to convince its adversaries in the Cold War that any nuclear attack on the United States would result in the assured destruction of the attacker.

Foreign Economic and Military Aid

Many of the European nations devastated by World War II experienced great difficulty in reestablishing their economies after the war. As a consequence, many of them experienced periods of worrisome political instability that made them vulnerable to external threats and internal revolt. In 1947, America responded with an emergency program known as the **Marshall Plan** (for George C. Marshall, the secretary of state who announced it) to provide economic aid to many war-torn countries of Europe. This established a pattern and a precedent for a major new component of American national security policy: the annual distribution of American economic assistance—and, later, other forms of assistance—to countries all over the world (see Figure 15.2).

Today most foreign economic aid programs are administered by the U.S. Agency for International Development. Increasingly in recent years, however, foreign aid programs have taken the form of military rather than simply economic aid. Instead of giving cash and subsidies to foreign countries, the United States has given or sold arms or provided direct military assistance in the forms of American advisers or training.

Marshall Plan

A policy introduced after World War II to provide financial aid to European countries that had been devastated by the war. Named after Secretary of State George C. Marshall, it became the precursor to decades of American foreign assistance.

Figure 15.2 United States Economic and Military Aid, 1980–2000

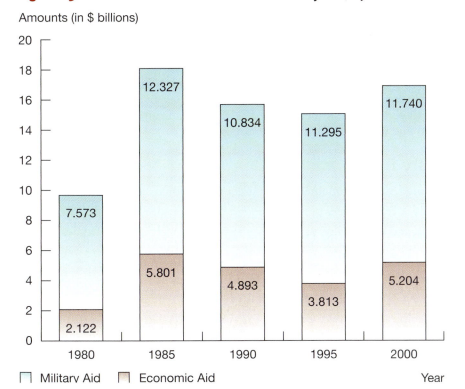

Amounts (in $ billions)

Source: United States Department of Commerce, *Statistical Abstract of the United States: 2004–2005* (Washington, D.C.: Government Printing Office, 2004), 809.

The strong bipartisan congressional support for the foreign aid program that existed at the time of its establishment has dissipated. Many members of Congress now question the benefits produced by the billions of dollars spent every year on foreign aid. As a consequence, the American foreign aid program has become controversial, and passage of the foreign aid bill each year has grown politically more complex and difficult—a constant source of tension between the president and Congress.[24]

Alliances

The policy of containment also produced a flurry of American alliance building in the years following World War II. The North Atlantic Treaty Organization (NATO), the Central Treaty Organization, the Southeast Asian Treaty Organization, and the Organization of American States were all formed during that period.

What is remarkable about this spate of alliance building is how profoundly it reversed America's historical aversion to such activity. In his farewell address, President George Washington had declared it "our true policy to steer clear of permanent alliances with any portion of the foreign world."[25] Avoidance of entangling alliances was a characteristic of American foreign policy through the 1930s. But the changed environment of the postwar world brought about a significant shift in American strategy.

In reality, these alliances were employed to define the frontiers of American influence and to draw the lines behind which Soviet expansion was to be contained. The borders of the nations to which the United States had pledged its protection marked the boundaries between the communist and noncommunist worlds. In essence, the treaties were a statement to the Soviet Union that crossing any of these lines would be regarded as a direct affront to American national interests and would invoke a forceful response.

Military Force

The United States maintained much larger armed forces after World War II than it had after previous wars. Several million Americans remained in uniform and were stationed at posts around the world. Their principal role was to indicate to the Soviet Union that the United States was prepared and willing to respond to communist aggression.

This was not an idle threat. Twice since 1945—in Korea and in Vietnam—American forces engaged in lengthy "frontier wars" to defend U.S. allies against the perceived threat of communist aggression. On several other occasions—in the Dominican Republic, Grenada, Panama, the Persian Gulf, Bosnia, Kosovo, and most recently in Afghanistan and Iraq, for example—American troops intervened to protect American political and economic interests, to export American values of freedom and human rights, and to ensure the stability or control of regimes friendly to the United States.

Postcommunism and the Era of Uncertainty

The deterioration of Soviet alliances in Eastern Europe and the disintegration of the Soviet Union itself in the early 1990s forced the United States to begin a broad review of its national security policies. This generated widespread political debate about America's military needs and objectives in a rapidly changing world. President George H. W. Bush began to talk in general terms about a "new world order," in which America would seek to encourage peaceful, diplomatic resolution of world tensions but would maintain potent, mobile armed forces to deter aggression.

Some elements of—and some uncertainty about—the meaning of this new approach emerged in the aftermath of Iraq's invasion of Kuwait in 1990. The George H. W. Bush administration undertook unprecedented efforts to engage the UN in condemning and imposing economic sanctions against Iraq. At the same time, the president initiated the placement of a large, multinational force in Saudi Arabia and in January 1991 launched a formidable military assault that quickly evicted the occupying Iraqi troops from Kuwait.

When the United States emerged from the Cold War as the world's only military superpower, pressures began to build—at home and abroad— for it to play a new role: peacekeeper. Wherever democratic flames were snuffed by rebellion, as in Haiti; ethnic strife resulted in genocide, as in Bosnia; government failure caused intense human suffering, as in Somalia; or one country invaded another, as Iraq did to Kuwait, those in trouble looked to the United States for help. In many of these cases, the UN became the forum for multinational action. But the UN rarely acted militarily without the acquiescence of the United States. UN peacekeeping missions were usually dominated by American military forces and equipment.

With the Cold War over, however, and the United States the only remaining superpower, the rationale for American intervention became less clear and popular and congressional support for the use of American forces abroad diminished. In 1993, for example, when American soldiers began to die in what had been described as a humanitarian engagement in Somalia, a growing chorus in Congress and the country called for withdrawal. When a military dictator in Haiti expelled a democratically elected president and Haitians began to pour into the United States illegally, America participated in a naval blockade as part of a UN economic embargo. But there was little support at home for the use of American ground troops in Haiti because of the absence of a direct threat to the United States.

International relations in this increasingly complex environment have a highly dynamic quality. Change is normal and constant as countries seek to serve their own self-interests by establishing more favorable economic, political, and military relationships with other nations. Among the most significant changes in the last two decades are the fading of communism, the emergence of nationalism and movements for cultural independence, growing economic interdependence, and worldwide terrorism.

The Fading of Communism

The major premise of U.S. foreign policy was that communism posed a direct and significant threat to the political and economic values of the United States and had to be contained by U.S. military might and economic muscle, combined with alliances of friendly countries in Europe and Asia. Events in the 1980s and 1990s challenged this premise. Many of the world's communist governments initiated significant changes that moved them from the collectivist economic and repressive political policies that seemed to characterize communism after World War II. The government and the Communist Party in the Soviet Union were racked by powerful centrifugal forces and came apart. And the Soviet military threat—the central impetus of American foreign policy for forty-five years—no longer seemed imminent. The Russian government was even willing to dismantle some of its nuclear weapons and, with American help, try to recover others that remained in the newly independent states of the former Soviet Union.

In China, the other great communist power of the twentieth century, a broad governmental effort brought about unprecedented economic growth by introducing some elements of private ownership and market competition. The Communist Party continued to dominate China's government, but it ceased to appear to be a direct or significant security threat to the United States. Relations between the two countries improved to the point of China becoming a major trading partner of the United States and a principal source of financing for the borrowing necessitated by large American budget deficits.

The Fracturing of Nation–States

The geopolitical character of the world changed remarkably over the course of the twentieth century. The edifice of relatively large, heterogeneous nation–states that existed at mid-century steadily broke down, first through decolonization then through a process that some analysts call "ethnolinguistic fractionalization."

The colonial empires that were in place at the beginning of the century broke up under the force of nationalism: in India, Africa, the Far East, and elsewhere. Now even those newly independent nations—and many older nations as well—are struggling to hold together in the face of internal conflicts among different ethnic, religious, and language groups. Tibetans seek their independence in China, Quebec pursues its own French-language identity in Canada, Kurds struggle for freedom in Iraq and Turkey, and Basque separatists continue to be a force in Spain. No continent on the globe is free of these vigorous efforts by groups of people seeking to govern themselves in their own language and in the tradition of their own culture.[26]

For American policymakers, weaned on notions of superpower competition and the threat of communist expansionism, the growing influence of ethnic, linguistic, and other cultural movements is another complicating factor in the policymaking process. The foreign policy agenda is now in constant flux; defense priorities are increasingly difficult to calculate. The value of foreign aid in general, and the apportionment of it in particular, are debated more intensely than ever.

Economic Interdependence

In recent decades politics in many countries has been influenced by a growing scarcity of critical resources. Many nations must now search beyond their borders for essential products like food, minerals, technology, and energy. Even the United States, long blessed with an abundance of natural resources and enormous productive capacity, has found itself deeply entrenched in the world marketplace as both a buyer and a seller.[27] The United States buys a considerable portion of the fuel it consumes from foreign countries. It also buys coffee from Colombia, automobiles from Japan, shoes from Italy, and countless consumer goods, from clothes to toys, from China. Since the mid-1970s, as Figure 15.3 indicates, the United States has spent more to purchase foreign goods than it has earned from the sale of its own goods abroad. This difference between imports and exports is called the **balance of trade.**

America's economic hegemony has been especially undermined in two economic areas: energy and technology. The United States has long been the world's major consumer of energy. Although its citizens make up only 5 percent of the world's population, they account for about 30 percent of its annual energy consumption. In the 1970s the international oil cartel, the Organization of Petroleum Exporting Countries (OPEC), initiated a steady increase in the price of oil, from less than $2 a barrel to more than $30 a barrel at its peak. At the same time,

balance of trade
The difference between a country's imports and exports. A country that imports more than it exports has a negative balance of trade.

Figure 15.3 **United States Exports and Imports, 1960–2004**

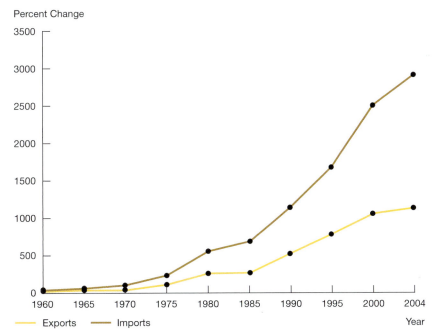

Source: United States Commerce Department data, http://ita.doc.gov/td/industry/otea/usfth/aggregate/H04t01.html.

American oil imports almost doubled. This created a substantial transfer of wealth from the United States to the oil-exporting countries.

Control over technology also dispersed broadly in this period. America stayed on the cutting edge in the development of many new technologies—indeed, America's technological creativity is still one of the wonders of our time. But other countries, especially in the Far East, made significant advances in their ability to convert those new technologies into industrial and consumer products that competed aggressively and effectively with American products. In automobiles, consumer electronics, textiles, steel, and a host of other commodities, the American market share has diminished as a result.

The trend to interdependence accelerated in the 1990s. The European Community formed its own cooperative economic unit. The former communist nations of Eastern Europe turned to capitalism and sought to become partners in the world market. The nations of the Pacific Rim, many of them industrializing rapidly, became increasingly aggressive and successful participants in the world marketplace. China's economic growth has been especially rapid. Most economists assume that China will surpass America as the world's largest economy sometime in the twenty-first century.

A consequence of these changes is that the lines between American domestic and foreign policies are increasingly blurred. The failure of a steel company in Pittsburgh is as likely to result from competition in Korea as in Alabama. The market price of a commercial product at Wal-Mart may well be determined in Shanghai, not New York. The welder on an auto assembly line in Tennessee may receive her paycheck from a company with headquarters in Tokyo.

International economics has helped create several new world powers whose international role is not based on military strength. China is the most notable of these. But Japan, Germany, the oil-rich members of OPEC, and the high-capacity manufacturing countries of East Asia have also risen to prominence on the strength of their economic advantages. American foreign policy can no longer rest on economic superiority any more than it can on military dominance. The world's wealth is no longer concentrated in a few countries, and successful trade relations have become an increasingly critical component of effective foreign policy.

In recent decades, increased international trade has often been used as a wedge to open and strengthen relations between the United States and other countries, even those that were once adversaries. Sales of grain and technology to the Soviet Union, which began in earnest in the 1970s, helped provide food for Soviet citizens and cash for American farmers. But in broader terms they contributed a degree of interdependence to American–Soviet relations that had not existed previously. Similarly, a significant expansion of trade with the People's Republic of China has been an important part of improved American relations with that country.

Review Questions

1. Which of the following was a common characteristic of U.S. foreign policy before World War II?

   A. Frequent participation in international alliances and organizations to maintain global security
   B. Acquisition of natural resources through imperial expansion
   C. Disengagement from foreign affairs except when significant U.S. interests were threatened
   D. Projection of military power abroad through the use of a large standing army

2. Which of the following was *not* a guiding principle of U.S. policy during the Cold War?

   A. Communism was the most important threat to the United States
   B. Engaging in foreign trade with communist countries was the primary strategy for combating the spread of communism
   C. Containment of Soviet influence was the main objective of national security policy
   D. Active and consistent involvement by the United States in international affairs as imperative

3. After World War II, the United States aided the reconstruction of war-torn countries as functioning democracies through all of the following policies *except*

   A. Providing direct economic aid to those countries
   B. Establishing U.S. military bases in Western Europe to limit the spread of Soviet influence
   C. Assisting political reform in postwar Germany and Japan through the drafting of democratic constitutions
   D. Recruiting large numbers of federal marshals to root out communist infiltration

4. Which of the following is *not* a likely outcome of China's rising power in the next fifty years?

   A. China will become the world's largest economy
   B. China will continue to be a principal financier of America's budget deficits
   C. China's importance as a trading partner for the United States will increase
   D. China will overtake the United States as the world's greatest military power

Answers:

1. C
2. B
3. D
4. D

Conflict and Consensus in Review

The complexities of the world economy make this a difficult area of international policymaking. That difficulty is compounded by the American tradition of a free market economy in which

continued

individual corporations, labor unions, farmers, and banks have economic self-interests, not national interest, as their highest priority. The character and success of international economic policy thus is determined to a substantial extent by the ability of political leaders to build and maintain a consensus within the government and in the public arena from this diverse set of economic and political interests.

Terrorism and the New Demands of National Security Policy

terrorism

The use of violence to disrupt the routines of international activity and to demoralize and frighten a country's population or regime. Assassinations of political leaders, kidnappings of diplomats, and bombings of public buildings or transportation are all examples of terrorism.

The diversity and decentralization of the modern world have had many effects on international relations. None is more troublesome, however, nor more resistant to solution, than the spread of terrorism. **Terrorism** is the use of violence to disrupt the routines of international activity and to demoralize and frighten a country's population or regime. Assassinations of political leaders, kidnappings of diplomats, and bombings of public buildings or transportation are all examples of terrorism. Terrorists have the advantage of stealth and surprise, and their actions are difficult to prevent, especially when the bombers are willing to sacrifice their lives to accomplish their objectives. Their activities have become an increasingly common factor in world politics.[28]

Contributing to the spread of terrorism has been the emergence of nonstate organizations like the Irish Republican Army, the Islamic Jihad, and Al Qaeda. These organizations have been unable to achieve their objectives by attaining political power in any country—although often they don't seek political power.

The 2001 terrorist attack on the World Trade Center in New York cost the lives of nearly 3,000 people. Like the attack on Pearl Harbor sixty years earlier, it caused the American people and their government to rethink entirely the concept of national security. In the years after World War II, national security policies focused on the threats posed by militarily powerful nations like the Soviet Union and China. Now the focus is on elusive groups and dangerous international criminals. Traditional armed forces and effective international diplomacy do not afford the protection against terrorism that they once did against nation–state adversaries. The intensity, invisibility and ingenuity of this new enemy impose great burdens on the policymakers who now share responsibility for national security in the United States.

The New York attacks led to what some scholars have called a revolution in American foreign policy.[29] Some of George W. Bush's principal national security advisers have long thought that America needed to take a new approach in dealing with the changed international landscape. They have come to believe that the time was ripe for a vast expansion of political democracy in parts of the world where repressive governments still reigned. They also believe that because American military power so exceeds that of any other nation it should be used as an instrument for confronting dictatorship and expanding democracy. They even argue that the American tradition of using military force only in response to an attack or perceived threat should be replaced with a new doctrine of preemption—that military force should be used to remove an adversary even before a direct threat to America (see Chapter 3). Some of them have also come to believe that the America's postwar adherence to alliances is undermining America's ability to act in its best interest in international affairs, that America should do what it thinks best even if its allies disagree.

The most dramatic application of these new approaches came early in 2003 when the United States launched a military assault on Iraq. Although Great Britain contributed substantial forces to this assault and other countries contributed smaller numbers, many traditional allies like Germany, France, and Turkey, strongly opposed the invasion of Iraq. The Iraqi armed forces were quickly defeated and the Iraqi leader, Saddam Hussein, was removed from power and later captured and tried. A new government emerged in Iraq with the charge of conducting free elections and writing a democratic constitution in which the various religious and ethnic groups would receive representation. But a violent insurgency and persistent difficulties in finding political solutions to the ancient enmities among religious groups in Iraq have made the effective establishment of the new government an undertaking of ongoing complexity and uncertainty.

Review Questions

1. The decision to invade Iraq in 2003 was deeply influenced by the George W. Bush administration's belief that

   A. The United States should actively defend its interests through the use of military force, even if its allies fail to offer their support
   B. Preemptive military action should be used against hostile states before they develop the capacity to harm U.S. security, even if this means attacking first
   C. The United States should use its military superiority to expand democracy and roll back tyranny
   D. All of the above

Answers:

   1. D

Conflict and Consensus in Review

These new foreign policy approaches continue to be a topic of broad debate in partisan politics. The doctrine of preemption, the apparent disregard for important allies, and the aggressive and expensive use of American military forces were significant issues in the 2004 presidential election and continue to be concerns for many Americans. Of special concern is the relationship between the new foreign policy directions and the central objective of combating terrorism. President George W. Bush argued that the use of military forces in Iraq and

continued

Afghanistan has played a critical role in weakening terrorists. His political opponents do not agree. As the twenty-first century unfolds, terrorism will continue to be the primary threat to American national security. To this threat, there is no disagreement. How to confront it, however, is another story, one upon which Americans will continue to debate hotly.

Politics in Action

To Intervene or Not: The Cases of Bosnia and Rwanda

For much of American history, a dominant strain in conventional thinking about foreign policy was that America ought to keep its nose out of other people's business. George Washington warned in his farewell address about the dangers of entangling foreign alliances. America entered World War I only in its final stages and only after a presidential campaign in which Woodrow Wilson's slogan was "He kept us out of war." Isolationism prevailed after that war, and even as Franklin Roosevelt saw the growing necessity of an active American role in World War II, he moved cautiously in the face of broad popular reluctance to become involved. A week before the election in 1940, after war had been raging in Europe for more than a year, Roosevelt said in a speech, "I have said this before, but I shall say it again and again and again: Your boys are not going to be sent into any foreign wars. They are going into training to form a force so strong that, by its very existence, it will keep the threat of war far away from our shores. The purpose of our defense is defense."[30]

All that seems like ancient history now. In the years after World War II, America has been constantly engaged all over the world. American soldiers are on post in Asia and Europe. American naval ships sail all seas. American satellites and spy planes subject to surveillance every continent. The most common question now is not whether Americans will ever intervene in the affairs of other countries but rather which situations are appropriate for American involvement.

During the Cold War, the threat of communist expansion was used to justify long and costly military interventions in Korea and Vietnam. Briefer engagements occurred in many places. When the Cold War ended, the justifications became more complex. Sometimes America intervened when American citizens or the holdings of American companies were at risk. Sometimes it intervened for humanitarian reasons, to help ward off famine or to respond to natural disaster. Sometimes it intervened when a country's government failed and anarchy threatened the lives of innocent citizens. And sometimes it intervened to prevent genocide, the slaughter of some of a country's citizens by its own leaders.

The difficulty American leaders face in deciding when and how to intervene in foreign matters is illustrated by two different situations they faced in the 1990s. One occurred in the Balkans in eastern Europe in territory that had once been part of the country known as Yugoslavia. Yugoslavia ceased to exist in the 1990s, and ethnic conflict soon broke out between Serbian and Croatian forces seeking to dominate the succession. Complicating the struggle was the presence in Bosnia, another former Yugoslav republic, of a large Muslim population called Bosniaks.

Faced with a spreading genocide of Serbs against Bosniaks, America and its allies in NATO decided to intervene, to stop the killing and to create an enforced peace in which the conflict could be resolved through negotiation. NATO forces shot down Serbian aircraft and bombed Serbian positions on the ground until a truce occurred. Under American guidance, a longer term set of agreements was negotiated between the warring parties in meetings held in Dayton, Ohio, in 1995. The genocide ended. Thousands died, but many thousands more would have had it not been for NATO intervention.

continued

Politics in Action *continued*

Another genocide happened in the 1990s in the African country of Rwanda. In a period of just a few months in 1994, a rampage by the dominant Hutu tribe killed nearly 800,000 members of the Tutsi tribe, as well as some moderate Hutus. The violence was devastating, persistent, and widely reported. But America did not intervene, nor did any other western power.

The reasons for nonintervention are complex. President Clinton received daily briefings on the events in Rwanda from the State Department; some of those briefings described the events there as a genocide. But Rwanda was a country of no strategic or commercial importance to the United States and Clinton had been criticized for an unsuccessful American intervention in Somalia in 1993. Many of his advisers warned him that intervening in Rwanda would be even more difficult. Besides, the civil strife in Rwanda was not front-page news in the United States as the ethnic cleaning in Bosnia and Kosovo had been. With no public outcry at home, and no strategic interests or American military presence in that part of Africa, the president decided not to intervene. In retrospect, however, the slaughter of thousands of ethnic Tutsis might have been prevented had the world community taken notice and become involved.

On a visit to Rwanda in 1998, Clinton apologized but also noted that "all over the world there were people like me sitting in offices, day after day after day, who did not fully appreciate the depth and speed with which you were being engulfed by this unimaginable terror."[31]

The modern world is complicated and challenging to national security policymakers in the United States. Although the United States has vast military, economic, and diplomatic resources, there can never be much certainty about when and how those resources should be deployed. And history's lessons are often hard to discern.

Summary

We began this chapter by noting the consensus that Americans share that government must preserve, protect, and defend the Constitution, the geography, the culture, and the political tradition against threats from home and abroad. But we also noted that sharp disagreement exists over the strategy and tactics the government may pursue in performing its critical national security role. That disagreement is sometimes muted by a crisis, but it reemerges once that crisis has been resolved.

Presidents are expected to take the lead in shaping the country's policy, more so in the foreign and national security spheres than with domestic concerns. Congress plays a more reactionary but still critical function in checking presidential initiatives and in overseeing how those initiatives are implemented. The judiciary may also become involved, although it tends to defer to the president in the exercise of powers in this policy area.

Over the years, the distinction among domestic, foreign, and national security has become less clear. There is more overlap, so it would stand to reason that political struggles that occur within one sphere will carry over into the others. The news media plays a role by informing the public of the domestic effect of foreign and national security issues.

In thinking about foreign and national security policymaking, it is useful to envision a set of concentric circles. At the center is the president and his cadre of policy advisers. Control over information sources, direct access to levers of authority in the armed forces, and traditionally broad interpretations of constitutional authority provide the presidency with potent advantages in the constant political debates that swirl around national security policymaking.

The outer circles are composed of those on the outside of government: the American people and their opinions, special interest groups, and the news media. They are the background against which important policy struggles are played out. On some issues and on certain broad directions, they set the boundaries of policy debate. But on many national security issues the public opinion is amorphous or uncertain and the informed opinions of interest groups and journalists are divided. Thus, although public opinion is a persistent factor in national security decisions, only on rare occasions does it provide clear cues to national leaders. On most issues of international policy, decision makers have broad latitude to define their course and then to persuade the American people of its propriety.

Moving inward in the concentric circles are other institutions, groups, and political actors seeking to influence national security decisions. They include a host of agencies and departments in the executive branch—the State and Defense Departments, the Treasury and other economic agencies, and the intelligence networks. Although technically all are part of the president's team, each brings its own traditions, perspectives, objectives, and the interests of its own clientele to the ongoing struggle to shape national security policy. They often disagree with one another and seek to muster whatever political support they can, in Congress and the country, to influence the president's policy choices.

Congress itself is in one of these circles of influence. Presidents and their advisers consult with Congress, although not as often as Congress might desire. The president mainly takes the initiative and Congress responds to it—sometimes tempering or altering the details, on occasion refusing to accept them, but on balance giving the president substantial latitude to set the contours of national security policy. Although it has undertaken significant efforts in the past two decades to enlarge its role in national security policymaking, Congress continues to have difficulty competing day in and day out with presidential advantages in this area.

The circle with the president at the center is the most difficult to define because it is composed informally of the president's closest advisers. Presidents learn to draw advice selectively from people in and out of government in whose judgment they have faith. In each administration, the makeup of that group of close advisers evolves constantly. But when they face critical and difficult decisions, presidents will rely most heavily on that small circle of close advisers whose opinions have been tested and have come trusted over time.

The contentious nature of national security policymaking is evident in all stages of policy evolution since the end of World War II. The Cold War yielded a policy called containment, aimed preventing the spread of communism. Adherence to that policy produced lengthy wars in Korea and Vietnam that became unpopular with sizable segments of the American population. When the Soviet Union dissolved, America searched, not always successfully, for a new set of fundamental policy principles. Then after the terrorist attacks September 11, 2001, the administration of George W. Bush significantly reframed national security policy to include an enlarged focus on the use of American military power, sometimes in preemptive strikes against potentially dangerous adversaries. Heated debate accompanied all of these changes, and that debate continues, driven by many of the same political considerations and beliefs that affect policymaking in other areas. It could not be otherwise in a democratic political system.

Key Terms

National Security Council
  (NSC)
diplomacy
bilateral relations
embassy
consulates
ambassador

summit meeting
rolodex diplomacy
treaty
international organizations
espionage
Joint Chiefs of Staff
isolationism

Cold War
containment
mutual assured destruction
  (MAD)
Marshall Plan
balance of trade
terrorism

Discussion Questions

1. In what important ways is national security policymaking different from other policy areas?
2. What accounts for the unique role the president plays in making national security policy? Was this the intent of the framers of the Constitution?
3. What are the costs and benefits of the large role that presidents play in shaping national security policy?
4. What considerations should be most important when American leaders make decisions about intervening in other countries? Had you been president in 1994, would you have ordered American forces to intervene in Rwanda?
5. Now that the Cold War is over, what are the greatest threats to national security in the United States? How should America respond to those threats?
6. How is the threat posed by international terrorism different from the perceived threat posed by international communism after World War II?

Topics for Debate

1. The United States should act as the world's police force, using its vast military power to suppress hostilities and keep the peace around the world.
2. Congress should play a larger role in national security policy decision making.
3. In retrospect, the Cold War was an overreaction to a communist threat that was not as dangerous as it may have appeared at the time.
4. The current size and cost of America's military forces are too great and should be significantly reduced.
5. America spends too little on economic aid to other countries, particularly those countries beset by poverty or disease.

Where on the Web?

U.S. Department of State **www.state.gov/**

U.S. Department of Defense **www.defense.gov/**

Rand Corporation **www.rand.org/research_areas/ national_security/**

Go to **www.thomsonedu.com/thomsonnow** to learn about a powerful online study tool. You will get a personalized study plan based on your responses to a diagnostic Pre-Test. Once you have mastered the materials with the help of interactive learning tools, activities, timelines, video case studies, simulations, and an integrated E-Book, you can take a Post-Test to confirm you are ready to move to the next chapter.

Selected Readings

Albright, Madeleine. *Madam Secretary: A Memoir.* New York: Miramax Books, 2003.

Barnett, Thomas P. M. *The Pentagon's New Map.* New York: G. P. Putnam's Sons, 2004.

Daalder, Ivo H., and James M. Lindsay. *America Unbound: The Bush Revolution in Foreign Policy.* Washington, D.C.: Brookings Institution, 2003.

Ferguson, Niall. *Colossus: The Price of America's Empire.* New York: Penguin Books, 2004.

Friedman, Thomas L. *The World Is Flat: A Brief History of the Twenty-First Century.* New York: Farrar, Straus and Giroux Publishers, 2005.

Gaddis, John Lewis. *Surprise, Security, and the American Experience.* Cambridge, Mass.: Harvard University Press, 2004.

Haass, Richard N. *The Opportunity: America's Moment to Alter History's Course.* New York: Public Affairs Press, 2005.

Holzgrefe, J. L., and Robert O. Keohane, eds. *Humanitarian Intervention: Ethical, Legal and Political Dilemmas.* New York: Cambridge University Press, 2003.

Jervis, Robert. *American Foreign Policy in a New Era.* New York: Routledge, 2005.

Mann, James. *Rise of the Vulcans: The History of Bush's War Cabinet.* New York: Viking Press, 2004.

Nye, Joseph S. Jr. *The Paradox of American Power: Why the World's Only Superpower Can't Go It Alone.* New York: Oxford University Press, 2002.

Woodward, Bob. *Plan of Attack.* New York: Simon and Schuster, 2004.

Notes

[1] A Gallup poll fielded March 24–25, 2003, indicated that 68 percent of the American people thought it was worth going to war in Iraq. Gallup Poll, http://www.gallup.com (accessed August 22, 2005).

[2] From the Preamble to the Constitution of the United States.

[3] Gallup Poll, http://www.pollingreport.com/BushJob1.htm (accessed February 22, 2006).

[4] Edward S. Corwin, *The President: Office and Powers, 1787–1984,* 5th rev. ed. (New York: New York University Press, 1984).

[5] For an example of presidential use of this power, see Eric Larrabee, *Commander in Chief: Franklin Delano Roosevelt, His Lieutenants and Their War* (New York: Harper and Row, 1987).

[6] See, for example, *Ware v. Hylton,* 3 Dall. 199 (1796); *Williams v. Suffolk Insurance Company,* 13 Pet. 415 (1839); and *U.S. v. Curtiss-Wright Corporation,* 299 U.S. 304 (1936).

[7] On the operation and procedures of the National Security Council, see Karl F. Inderfurth and Loch K. Johnson, eds.,

Fateful Decisions: Inside the National Security Council (New York: Oxford University Press, 2004).

[8] On presidential interaction with the National Security Council, see David J. Rothkopf, *Running The World: The Inside Story of the National Security Council and the Architects of American Power* (New York: Public Affairs Press, 2005).

[9] The process is described by Robert F. Kennedy in *Thirteen Days: A Memoir of the Cuban Missile Crisis* (New York: W. W. Norton & Co., 1969).

[10] For a discussion of the differing views of George W. Bush's principal foreign policy advisers, see James Mann, *The Rise of the Vulcans: The History of Bush's War Cabinet* (New York: Penguin Books, 2004).

[11] Alexis de Tocqueville, *Democracy in America* (New York: Alfred A. Knopf, 1948), 234.

[12] The embassies also employ foreign nationals who provide much of knowledge diplomats need to get around and make contacts.

[13]Shawn Dorman, *Inside a U.S. Embassy: How the Foreign Service Works for America* (Washington, D.C.: American Foreign Service Association, 2003).

[14]Richard M. Nixon, *RN: The Memoirs of Richard Nixon,* vol. 2 (New York: Warner Books, 1978), 432–433.

[15]"Bush and Putin: Best of Friends," http://news.bbc.co.uk/1/hi/world/europe/1392791.stm (accessed February 22, 2006).

[16]Subsequently, however, the two countries agreed to a treaty to limit intermediate-range ballistic missiles.

[17]For more on the Panama Canal Treaties, see George D. Moffett, *The Limits of Victory: The Ratification of the Panama Canal Treaties* (Ithaca, N.Y.: Cornell University Press, 1985).

[18]Loch K. Johnson, *America's Secret Power: The CIA in a Democratic Society* (New York: Oxford University Press, 1989).

[19]Central Intelligence Agency, *World Factbook: 2004,* http://www.photius.com/rankings/military/military_expenditures_dollar_figure_2004_0.html (accessed February 22, 2006).

[20]Quoted in Arthur M. Schlesinger Jr., *A Thousand Days* (New York: Fawcett, 1965), 377.

[21]For a discussion of these debates, see Hamilton Jordan, *Crisis: The Last Year of the Carter Presidency* (New York, G. P. Putnam's Sons, 1982).

[22]For a more elaborate discussion of postwar changes, see Charles W. Kegley, James M. Scott, and Eugene R. Wittkopf, *American Foreign Policy* (New York: Wadsworth, 2002).

[23]The primary author of that policy was a State Department official named George Kennan. He described the approach in 1947:

> It is clear that the main element of any U.S. policy toward the Soviet Union must be that of a long-term, patient but firm and vigilant containment of Russian expansive tendencies . . . .
>
> It is clear that the United States cannot expect in the foreseeable future to enjoy political intimacy with the Soviet regime. It must continue to regard the Soviet Union as a rival, not a partner, in the political arena. It must continue to expect that Soviet policies will reflect no abstract love of peace and stability, no real faith in the possibility of a permanent happy coexistence of the Socialist and capitalist worlds, but rather a cautious, persistent pressure toward the disruption and weakening of all rival influence and rival power. . . .
>
> This would itself warrant the United States entering with reasonable confidence upon a policy of firm containment, designed to confront the Russians with unalterable counterforce at every point where they show signs of encroaching upon the interests of a peaceful and stable world. Kennan's argument appeared in a famous but anonymous article called "The Sources of Soviet Conduct," published in *Foreign Affairs* magazine in July 1947.

[24]Carol Lancaster and Ann Van Dusen, *Organizing U. S. Foreign Aid: Confronting the Challenges of the 21st Century* (Washington, D.C.: Brookings Institution, 2005).

[25]George Washington, "Farewell Address," in Robert A. Goldwin and Harry M. Clor, *Readings in American Foreign Policy,* 2nd ed. (New York: Oxford University Press, 1971), 127.

[26]Michael E. Brown, ed., *Nationalism and Ethnic Conflict* (Cambridge, Mass.: MIT Press, 2001).

[27]C. Fred Bergsten, *The United States and the World Economy* (Washington, D.C.: Institute for International Economics, 2005).

[28]Paul R. Pillar, *Terrorism and U.S. Foreign Policy* (Washington, D.C.: Brookings Institution, 2004).

[29]See, for example, Ivo H. Daalder and James M. Lindsay, *America Unbound: The Bush Revolution in Foreign Policy* (Washington, D.C.: Brookings Institution, 2003).

[30] Speech on October 30, 1940, *Public Papers and Addresses of President Franklin D. Roosevelt,* Volume IX, p. 514.

[31]Rory Carroll, "U.S. Chose to Ignore Rwandan Genocide," *Guardian,* March 31, 2004, http://www.guardian.co.uk/rwanda/story/0,14451,1183889,00.html.

The Declaration of Independence

When in the Course of human Events, it becomes necessary for one people to dissolve the political bands which have connected them with another, and to assume among the Powers of the earth, the separate and equal station to which the Laws of Nature and of Nature's God entitle them, a decent respect to the opinions of mankind requires that they should declare the causes which impel them to the separation.

We hold these truths to be self-evident, that all men are created equal, that they are endowed by their Creator with certain unalienable Rights, that among these are Life, Liberty, and the pursuit of Happiness. That to secure these rights, Governments are instituted among Men, deriving their just powers from the consent of the governed, that whenever any Form of Government becomes destructive of these ends, it is the Right of the People to alter or to abolish it, and to institute new Government, laying its foundation on such principles, and organizing its powers in such form, as to them shall seem most likely to effect their Safety and Happiness. Prudence, indeed, will dictate that Governments long established should not be changed for light and transient Causes; and accordingly all Experience hath shewn, that mankind are more disposed to suffer, while evils are sufferable, than to right themselves by abolishing the forms to which they are accustomed. But when a long train of abuses and usurpations, pursuing invariably the same Object, evinces a design to reduce them under absolute Despotism, it is their right, it is their duty, to throw off such Government, and to provide new Guards for their future security.

Such has been the patient sufferance of these Colonies; and such is now the necessity which constrains them to alter their former Systems of Government. The history of the present King of Great Britain is a history of repeated injuries and usurpations, all having in direct object the establishment of an absolute Tyranny over these States. To prove this, let Facts be submitted to a candid world.

He has refused his Assent to Laws, the most wholesome and necessary for the public good.

He has forbidden his Governors to pass Laws of immediate and pressing importance, unless suspended in their operation till his Assent should be obtained; and when so suspended, he has utterly neglected to attend to them.

He has refused to pass other Laws for the accommodation of large districts of people, unless those people would relinquish the right of Representation in the Legislature, a right inestimable to them, and formidable to tyrants only.

He has called together legislative bodies at places unusual, uncomfortable, and distant from the depository of their public Records, for the sole purpose of fatiguing them into compliance with his measures.

He has dissolved Representative Houses repeatedly, for opposing with manly firmness his invasions on the rights of the people.

He has refused for a long time, after such dissolutions, to cause others to be elected; whereby the Legislative Powers, incapable of Annihilation, have returned to the People at large for their exercise; the State remaining in the mean time exposed to all the dangers of invasion from without, and convulsions within.

He has endeavoured to prevent the population of these States; for that purpose obstructing the Laws for Naturalization of Foreigners; refusing to pass others to encourage their migrations hither, and raising the conditions of new Appropriations of Lands.

He has obstructed the Administration of Justice, by refusing his Assent to Laws for establishing Judiciary powers.

He has made Judges dependent on his Will alone, for the tenure of their offices, and the amount and payment of their salaries.

He has erected a multitude of New Offices, and sent hither swarms of Officers to harrass our People, and eat out their substance.

He has kept among us, in times of peace, Standing Armies, without the Consent of our legislatures.

He has affected to render the Military independent of and superior to the Civil power.

He has combined with others to subject us to a jurisdiction foreign to our constitution, and unacknowledged by our laws; giving his Assent to their acts of pretended Legislation:

For quartering large bodies of armed troops among us:

For protecting them, by a mock Trial, from punishment for any Murders which they should commit on the inhabitants of these States:

For cutting off our Trade with all parts of the world:

For imposing taxes on us without our Consent:

For depriving us in many cases, of the benefits of Trial by Jury:

For transporting us beyond Seas to be tried for pretended offences:

For abolishing the free System of English Laws in a neighbouring Province, establishing therein an Arbitrary government, and enlarging its Boundaries, so as to render it at once an example and fit instrument for introducing the same absolute rule into these Colonies:

For taking away our Charters, abolishing our most valuable Laws, and altering fundamentally the Forms of our Governments:

For suspending our own Legislatures, and declaring themselves invested with Power to legislate for us in all cases whatsoever.

He has abdicated Government here, by declaring us out of his Protection and waging War against us.

He has plundered our seas, ravaged our Coasts, burnt our towns, and destroyed the lives of our people.

He is at this time transporting large Armies of foreign Mercenaries to compleat the works of death, desolation, and tyranny, already begun with circumstances of Cruelty and perfidy scarcely paralleled in the most barbarous ages, and totally unworthy the Head of a civilized nation.

He has constrained our fellow Citizens taken Captive on the high Seas to bear Arms against their Country, to become the executioners of their friends and Brethren, or to fall themselves by their Hands.

He has excited domestic insurrections amongst us, and has endeavoured to bring on the inhabitants of our frontiers, the merciless Indian Savages, whose known rule of warfare, is an undistinguished destruction, of all ages, sexes and conditions.

In every stage of these Oppressions We have Petitioned for Redress in the most humble terms: Our repeated Petitions have been answered only by repeated injury. A Prince, whose character is thus marked by every act which may define a Tyrant, is unfit to be the ruler of a free People.

Nor have We been wanting in attentions to our British brethren. We have warned them from time to time of attempts by their legislature to extend an unwarrantable jurisdiction over us. We have reminded them of the circumstances of our emigration and settlement here. We have appealed to their native justice and magnanimity, and we have conjured them by the ties of our common kindred to disavow these usurpations, which, would inevitably interrupt our connections and correspondence. They too have been deaf to the voice of justice and of consanguinity. We must, therefore, acquiesce in the necessity, which denounces our Separation, and hold them, as we hold the rest of mankind, Enemies in War, in Peace Friends.

We, therefore, the Representatives of the United States of America, in General Congress, Assembled, appealing to the Supreme Judge of the world for the rectitude of our intentions, do, in the Name, and by Authority of the good People of these Colonies, solemnly publish and declare, That these United Colonies, are, and of right ought to be, Free and Independent States; that they are Absolved from all Allegiance to the British Crown, and that all political connection between them and the State of Great Britain, is and ought to be totally dissolved; and that as Free and Independent States, they have full Power to levy War, conclude Peace, contract Alliances, establish Commerce, and to do all other Acts and Things which Independent States may of right do. And for the support of this Declaration, with a firm reliance on the protection of divine Providence, we mutually pledge to each other our Lives, our Fortunes, and our sacred Honor.

The Constitution of the United States of America

We the People of the United States, in Order to form a more perfect Union, establish Justice, insure domestic Tranquility, provide for the common defence, promote the general Welfare, and secure the Blessings of Liberty to ourselves and our Posterity, do ordain and establish this Constitution for the United States of America.

[Three Branches of Government]

[The legislative branch]

| Article I |

[Power vested]

Section 1 All legislative Powers herein granted shall be vested in a Congress of the United States, which shall consist of a Senate and House of Representatives.

[House of Representatives]

Section 2 The House of Representatives shall be composed of Members chosen every second Year by the People of the several States, and the Electors in each State shall have the Qualifications requisite for Electors of the most numerous Branch of the State Legislature.

No Person shall be a Representative who shall not have attained to the Age of twenty-five Years, and been seven Years a Citizen of the United States, and who shall not, when elected, be an Inhabitant of that State in which he shall be chosen.

[Representatives and direct Taxes shall be apportioned among the several States which may be included within this Union, according to their respective Numbers, which shall be determined by adding to the whole Number of free Persons, including those bound to Service for a Term of Years, and excluding Indians not taxed, three fifths of all other Persons.][1] The actual Enumeration shall be made within three Years after the first Meeting of the Congress of the United States, and within every subsequent Term of ten Years, in such Manner as they shall by Law direct. The Number of Representatives shall not exceed one for every thirty Thousand, but each State shall have at Least one Representative; and until such enumeration shall be made, the State of New Hampshire shall be entitled to chuse three, Massachusetts eight, Rhode-Island and Providence Plantations one, Connecticut five, New-York six, New Jersey four, Pennsylvania eight, Delaware one, Maryland six, Virginia ten, North Carolina five, South Carolina five, and Georgia three.

When vacancies happen in the Representation from any State, the Executive Authority thereof shall issue Writs of Election to fill such Vacancies.

The House of Representatives shall chuse their Speaker and other Officers; and shall have the sole Power of Impeachment.

[The Senate]

Section 3 The Senate of the United States shall be composed of two Senators from each State, [chosen by the Legislature thereof],[2] for six Years; and each Senator shall have one Vote.

Immediately after they shall be assembled in Consequence of the first Election, they shall be divided as equally as may be into three Classes. The Seats of the Senators of the first Class shall be vacated at the Expiration of the second Year, of the second Class at the Expiration of the fourth Year, and of the third Class at the Expiration of the sixth Year, so that one third may be chosen every second year; [and if Vacancies happen by Resignation, or otherwise, during the Recess of the Legislature of any State, the Executive thereof may make temporary Appointments until the next Meeting of the Legislature, which shall then fill such Vacancies].[3]

No Person shall be a Senator who shall not have attained to the Age of thirty Years, and been nine Years a Citizen of the United States, and who shall not, when elected, be an Inhabitant of that State for which he shall be chosen.

The Vice President of the United States shall be President of the Senate, but shall have no Vote, unless they be equally divided.

The Senate shall chuse their other Officers, and also a President pro tempore, in the absence of the Vice President, or when he shall exercise the Office of the President of the United States.

The Senate shall have the sole Power to try all Impeachments. When sitting for that Purpose, they shall be on Oath or Affirmation. When the President of the United States is tried, the Chief Justice shall preside: And no Person shall be convicted without the Concurrence of two thirds of the Members present.

Judgment in Cases of Impeachment shall not extend further than to removal from Office, and disqualification to hold and enjoy any Office of honor, Trust, or Profit under the United States: but the Party convicted shall nevertheless be liable and subject to Indictment, Trial, Judgment, and Punishment, according to Law.

[Elections]

Section 4 The Times, Places and Manner of holding Elections for Senators and Representatives, shall be prescribed in each state by the Legislature thereof; but the Congress may at any time by Law make or alter such Regulations, except as to the Places of chusing Senators.

The Congress shall assemble at least once in every Year, and such Meeting shall [be on the first Monday in December,][4] unless they shall by Law appoint a different Day.

[Powers, duties, procedure both bodies]

Section 5 Each House shall be the Judge of the Elections, Returns and Qualifications of its own Members, and a Majority of each shall constitute a Quorum to do Business; but a smaller number may adjourn from day to day, and may be authorized to compel the Attendance of absent Members, in such Manner, and under such Penalties as each House may provide.

Each House may determine the Rules of its Proceedings, punish its Members for disorderly Behavior, and, with the Concurrence of two thirds, expel a Member.

Each House shall keep a Journal of its Proceedings, and from time to time publish the same, excepting such Parts as may in their Judgment require Secrecy; and the Yeas and Nays of the Members of either House on any question shall, at the Desire of one fifth of those Present, be entered on the journal.

Neither House, during the Session of Congress, shall, without the Consent of the other, adjourn for more than three days, nor to any other Place than that in which the two Houses shall be sitting.

[Compensation, privileges, limits on other government service]

Section 6 The Senators and Representatives shall receive a Compensation for their Services, to be ascertained by Law, and paid out of the Treasury of the United States. They shall in all Cases, except Treason, Felony, and Breach of the Peace, be privileged from Arrest during their Attendance at the Session of their respective Houses, and in going to and returning from the same; and for any Speech or Debate in either House, they shall not be questioned in any other place.

No Senator or Representative shall, during the Time for which he was elected, be appointed to any civil Office under the Authority of the United States, which shall have been created, or the Emoluments whereof shall have been encreased, during such time; and no Person holding any Office under the United States, shall be a Member of either House during his Continuance in Office.

[Origin of revenue bills; presidential approval or disapproval of legislation, overriding the veto]

Section 7 All Bills for raising Revenue shall originate in the House of Representatives; but the Senate may propose or concur with Amendments as on other Bills.

Every Bill which shall have passed the House of Representatives and the Senate, shall, before it become a Law, be presented to the President of the United States; If he approve he shall sign it, but if not he shall return it, with his Objections, to that House in which it shall have originated, who shall enter the Objections at large on their Journal, and proceed to reconsider it. If after such Reconsideration two thirds of that House shall agree to pass the Bill, it shall be sent, together with the Objections, to the other House, by which it shall likewise be reconsidered, and if approved by two thirds of that House, it shall become a Law. But in all such Cases the Votes of both Houses shall be determined by Yeas and Nays, and the Names of the Persons voting for and against the Bill shall be entered on the Journal of each House respectively. If any Bill shall not be returned by the President within ten Days (Sundays excepted) after it shall have been presented to him, the Same shall be a Law, in like Manner as if he had signed it, unless the Congress by their Adjournment prevent its Return, in which Case it shall not be a Law.

Every Order, Resolution, or Vote to which the Concurrence of the Senate and House of Representatives may be necessary (except on a question of Adjournment) shall be presented to the President of the United States; and before the Same shall take Effect, shall be approved by him, or being disapproved by him, shall be repassed by two thirds of the Senate and House of Representatives, according to the Rules and Limitations prescribed in the Case of a Bill.

[Powers granted to Congress]

Section 8 The Congress shall have Power To lay and collect Taxes, Duties, Imposts and Excises, to pay the Debts and provide for the common Defence and general Welfare of the United States; but all Duties, Imposts and Excises shall be uniform throughout the United States;

To borrow money on the credit of the United States;

To regulate Commerce with foreign Nations, and among the several States, and with the Indian Tribes;

To establish an uniform Rule of Naturalization, and uniform Laws on the subject of Bankruptcies throughout the United States;

To coin Money, regulate the Value thereof, and of foreign Coin, and fix the Standard of Weights and Measures;

To provide for the Punishment of counterfeiting the Securities and current Coin of the United States;

To establish Post Offices and Post Roads;

To promote the Progress of Science and useful Arts, by securing for limited Times to Authors and Inventors the exclusive Right to their respective Writings and Discoveries;

To constitute Tribunals inferior to the Supreme Court;

To define and punish Piracies and Felonies committed on the high Seas, and Offenses against the Law of Nations;

To declare War, grant Letters of Marque and Reprisal, and make Rules concerning Captures on Land and Water;

To raise and support Armies, but no Appropriation of Money to that Use shall be for a longer Term than two Years;

To provide and maintain a Navy;

To make Rules for the Government and Regulation of the land and naval forces;

To provide for calling forth the Militia to execute the Laws of the Union, suppress Insurrections and repel Invasions;

To provide for organizing, arming, and disciplining the Militia, and for governing such Part of them as may be employed in the Service of the United States, reserving to the States respectively, the Appointment of the Officers, and the Authority of training the Militia according to the discipline prescribed by Congress;

To exercise exclusive Legislation in all Cases whatsoever, over such District (not exceeding ten Miles square) as may, by Cession of particular States, and the acceptance of Congress, become the Seat of the Government of the United States, and to exercise like Authority over all places purchased by the Consent of the Legislature of the State in which the Same shall be, for the Erection of Forts, Magazines, Arsenals, dock-Yards, and other needful Buildings;—And

[Elastic Clause]

To make all Laws which shall be necessary and proper for carrying into Execution the foregoing Powers, and all other Powers vested by this Constitution in the Government of the United States, or in any Department or Officer thereof.

[Powers denied to Congress]

Section 9 The Migration or Importation of Such Persons as any of the States now existing shall think proper to admit, shall not be prohibited by the Congress prior to the Year one thousand eight hundred and eight, but a tax or duty may be imposed on such Importation, not exceeding ten dollars for each Person.

The privilege of the Writ of Habeas Corpus shall not be suspended, unless when in Cases of Rebellion or Invasion the public Safety may require it.

No Bill of Attainder or ex post facto Law shall be passed.

[No capitation, or other direct, Tax shall be laid unless in Proportion to the Census or Enumeration herein before directed to be taken.][5]

No Tax or Duty shall be laid on Articles exported from any State.

No preference shall be given by any Regulation of Commerce or Revenue to the Ports of one State over those of another: nor shall Vessels bound to, or from, one State, be obliged to enter, clear, or pay Duties in another.

No Money shall be drawn from the Treasury, but in Consequence of Appropriations made by Law; and a regular Statement and Account of the Receipts and Expenditures of all public Money shall be published from time to time.

No Title of Nobility shall be granted by the United States: And no Person holding any Office of Profit or Trust under them, shall, without the Consent of the Congress, accept of any present, Emolument, Office, or Title, of any kind whatever, from any King, Prince, or foreign State.

[Powers denied to State]

Section 10 No State shall enter into any Treaty, Alliance, or Confederation; grant Letters of Marque and Reprisal; coin Money; emit Bills of Credit; make any Thing but gold and silver Coin a Tender in Payment of Debts; pass any Bill of Attainder, ex post facto Law, or Law impairing the Obligation of Contracts, or grant any Title of Nobility.

No State shall, without the Consent of the Congress, lay any Imposts or Duties on Imports or Exports, except what may be absolutely necessary for executing its inspection Laws: and the net Produce of all Duties and Imposts, laid by any State on Imports or Exports, shall be for the Use of the Treasury of the United States; and all such Laws shall be subject to the Revision and Control of the Congress.

No State shall, without the Consent of Congress, lay any duty of Tonnage, keep Troops, or Ships of War in time of peace, enter into any Agreement or Compact with another State, or with a foreign Power, or engage in War, unless actually invaded, or in such imminent Danger as will not admit of delay.

[The executive branch]

Article II

[Presidential term, choice by electors, qualifications, payment, succession, path of office]

Section 1 The executive Power shall be vested in a President of the United States of America. He shall hold his Office during the Term of four Years, and, together with the Vice President, chosen for the same Term, be elected, as follows:

Each State shall appoint, in such Manner as the Legislature thereof may direct, a Number of Electors, equal to the whole Number of Senators and Representatives to which the State may be entitled in the Congress: but no Senator or Representative, or Person holding an Office of Trust or Profit under the United States, shall be appointed an Elector.

[The Electors shall meet in their respective States, and vote by Ballot for two persons, of whom one at least shall not be an Inhabitant of the same State with themselves. And they shall make a List of all the Persons voted for, and of the Number of Votes for each; which List they shall sign and certify, and transmit sealed to the Seat of the Government of the United States, directed to the President of the Senate. The President of the Senate shall, in the Presence of the Senate and House of Representatives, open all the Certificates, and the Votes shall then be counted. The person having the greatest Number of Votes shall be the President, if such Number be a Majority of the whole Number of Electors appointed; and if there be more than one who have such Majority, and have an equal Number of Votes, then the House of Representatives shall immediately chuse by Ballot one of them for president; and if no Person have a Majority, then from the five highest on the List the said House shall in like Manner chuse the President. But in chusing the President, the Votes shall be taken by States, the Representation from each State having one Vote; A quorum for this Purpose shall consist of a Member or Members from two thirds of the States, and a Majority of all the States shall be necessary to a Choice. In every Case, after the Choice of the President, the Person having the greatest Number of Votes of the Electors shall be the Vice President. But if there should remain two or more who have equal votes, the Senate shall chuse from them by Ballot the Vice President.][6]

The Congress may determine the Time of chusing the Electors, and the Day on which they shall give their Votes; which Day shall be the same throughout the United States.

No person except a natural born Citizen, or a Citizen of the United States, at the time of the Adoption of this Constitution, shall be eligible to the Office of President; neither shall any Person be eligible to that Office who shall not have attained to the Age of thirty-five Years, and been fourteen Years a Resident within the United States.

[In case of the removal of the President from Office, or of his Death, Resignation, or Inability to discharge the Powers and Duties of the said Office, the same shall devolve on the Vice President, and the Congress may by Law provide for the Case of Removal, Death, Resignation, or Inability, both of the President and Vice President, declaring what Officer shall then act as President, and such Officer shall act accordingly, until the disability be removed, or a President shall be elected.][7]

The President shall, at stated Times, receive for his Services a Compensation, which shall neither be increased nor diminished during the period for which he shall have been elected, and he shall not receive within that Period any other Emolument from the United States, or any of them.

Before he enter on the execution of his Office, he shall take the following Oath or Affirmation:—"I do solemnly swear (or affirm) that I will faithfully execute the Office of President of the United States, and will to the best of my Ability, preserve, protect and defend the Constitution of the United States."

[Powers to command the military and executive departments, to grant pardons, to make treaties, to appoint government officers]

Section 2 The President shall be Commander in Chief of the Army and Navy of the United States, and of the Militia of the several States, when called into the actual Service of the United States; he may require the Opinion, in writing, of the principal Officer in each of the executive Departments, upon any subject relating to the Duties of their respective Offices, and he shall have Power to grant Reprieves and Pardons for Offenses against the United States, except in Cases of Impeachment.

He shall have Power, by and with the Advice and Consent of the Senate, to make Treaties, provided two thirds of the Senators present concur; and he shall nominate, and by and with the Advice and Consent of the Senate, shall appoint Ambassadors, other public Ministers and Consuls, Judges of the Supreme Court, and all other Officers of the United States, whose Appointments are not herein otherwise provided for, and which shall be established by Law: but the Congress may by Law vest the Appointment of such inferior Officers, as they think proper, in the President alone, in the Courts of Law, or in the Heads of Departments.

The President shall have Power to fill up all Vacancies that may happen during the Recess of the Senate, by granting Commissions which shall expire at the End of their next Session.

[Formal duties]

Section 3 He shall from time to time give to the Congress Information of the State of the Union, and recommend to their Consideration such Measures as he shall judge necessary and expedient; he may, on extraordinary Occasions, convene both Houses, or either of them, and in

Case of Disagreement between them, with respect to the Time of Adjournment, he may adjourn them to such Time as he shall think proper; he shall receive Ambassadors and other public Ministers; he shall take Care that the Laws be faithfully executed, and shall Commission all the Officers of the United States.

[Conditions for removal]

Section 4 The President, Vice President and all civil Officers of the United States, shall be removed from Office on Impeachment for, and Conviction of, Treason, Bribery, or other high Crimes and Misdemeanors.

[The judicial branch]

Article III

[Courts and judges]

Section 1 The judicial Power of the United States, shall be vested in one supreme Court, and in such inferior Courts as the Congress may from time to time ordain and establish. The Judges, both of the supreme and inferior Courts, shall hold their Offices during good Behaviour, and shall, at stated Times, receive for their Services, a Compensation, which shall not be diminished during their Continuance in Office.

[Jurisdictions and jury trials]

Section 2 The judicial Power shall extend to all Cases, in Law and Equity, arising under this Constitution, the Laws of the United States, and Treaties made, or which shall be made, under their Authority;—to all Cases affecting ambassadors, other public Ministers and Consuls;—to all Cases of admiralty and maritime Jurisdiction;—to Controversies to which the United States shall be a Party;—to Controversies between two or more States;—[between a State and Citizens of Another State;][8]—between Citizens of different States;—between Citizens of the same State claiming Lands under Grants of different States, and [between a State, or the Citizens thereof, and foreign States, Citizens or Subjects].[9]

In all Cases affecting Ambassadors, other public Ministers and Consuls, and those in which a State shall be Party, the supreme Court shall have original Jurisdiction. In all the other Cases before mentioned, the supreme Court shall have appellate Jurisdiction, both as to Law and Fact, with such Exceptions, and under such Regulations as the Congress shall make.

The trial of all Crimes, except in Cases of Impeachment, shall be by Jury; and such Trial shall be held in the State where the said Crimes shall have been committed; but when not committed within any State, the Trial shall be at such Place or Places as the Congress may by Law have directed.

[Treason and its punishment]

Section 3 Treason against the United States, shall consist only in levying War against them, or in adhering to their Enemies, giving them Aid and Comfort. No person shall be convicted of Treason unless on the Testimony of two Witnesses to the same overt Act, or on Confession in open Court.

The Congress shall have power to declare the Punishment of Treason, but no Attainder of Treason shall work Corruption of Blood, or Forfeiture except during the Life of the Person attainted.

[The Rest of the Federal System]

Article IV

[Relationships among and with States]

Section 1 Full Faith and Credit shall be given in each State to the public Acts, Records, and judicial Proceedings of every other State. And the Congress may by general Laws prescribe the Manner in which such Acts, Records and Proceedings shall be proved, and the Effect thereof.

[Privileges and immunities, extradition]

Section 2 The Citizens of each State shall be entitled to all Privileges and Immunities of Citizens in the several States.

A Person charged in any State with Treason, Felony, or other Crime, who shall flee from Justice, and be found in another State, shall on demand of the executive Authority of the State from which he fled, be delivered up, to be removed to the State having Jurisdiction of the crime.

[No person held to Service or Labour in one State, under the Laws thereof, escaping into another, shall, in Consequence of any Law or Regulation therein, be discharged from such Service or Labour, but shall be delivered up on Claim of the Party to whom such Service or Labour may be due.][10]

[New States]

Section 3 New States may be admitted by the Congress into this Union; but no new State shall be formed or erected within the Jurisdiction of any other State; nor any State be formed by the Junction of two or more States, or parts of States, without the Consent of the Legislatures of the States concerned as well as of the Congress.

The Congress shall have power to dispose of and make all needful Rules and Regulations respecting the

Territory or other property belonging to the United States; and nothing in this Constitution shall be so construed as to prejudice any Claims of the United States, or of any particular State.

[Obligations to States]

Section 4 The United States shall guarantee to every State in this Union a Republican Form of Government, and shall protect each of them against Invasion; and on Application of the Legislature, or of the Executive (when the Legislature cannot be convened) against domestic Violence.

[Mechanism for Change]

Article V

[Amending the Constitution]

The Congress, whenever two thirds of both Houses shall deem it necessary, shall propose Amendments to this Constitution, or, on the Application of the Legislatures of two thirds of the several States, shall call a Convention for proposing Amendments, which, in either Case, shall be valid to all Intents and Purposes, as part of this Constitution, when ratified by the Legislatures of three fourths of the several States, or by Conventions in three fourths thereof, as the one or the other Mode of Ratification may be proposed by the Congress; Provided that no Amendment which may be made prior to the Year One thousand eight hundred and eight shall in any Manner affect the first and fourth Clauses in the Ninth Section of the first Article; and that no State, without its Consent, shall be deprived of its equal Suffrage in the Senate.

[Federal Supremacy]

Article VI

All Debts contracted and Engagements entered into, before the Adoption of this Constitution, shall be as valid against the United States under this Constitution, as under the Confederation.

This Constitution, and the Laws of the United States which shall be made in Pursuance thereof; and all Treaties made, or which shall be made, under the Authority of the United States, shall be the supreme Law of the Land; and the Judges in every State shall be bound thereby, any Thing in the Constitution or Laws of any State to the Contrary notwithstanding.

The Senators and Representatives before mentioned, and the Members of the several State Legislatures, and all executive and judicial Officers, both of the United States

and of the several States, shall be bound by Oath or Affirmation to support this Constitution; but no religious Test shall ever be required as a Qualification to any Office or public Trust under the United States.

[Ratification]

Article VII

The Ratification of the Conventions of nine States shall be sufficient for the Establishment of this Constitution between the States so ratifying the same.

Done in Convention by the Unanimous Consent of the States present the Seventeenth Day of September in the Year of our Lord one thousand seven hundred and eighty seven and of the Independence of the United States of America the Twelfth. In witness whereof We have hereunto subscribed our Names.

[Bill of Rights and Other Amendments]

Articles in addition to, and amendment of, the Constitution of the United States of America, proposed by Congress, and ratified by the several States, pursuant to the fifth Article of the original Constitution.

Amendment I [1791][11]

[Freedoms of religion, speech, press, assembly]

Congress shall make no law respecting an establishment of religion, or prohibiting the free exercise thereof; or abridging the freedom of speech, or of the press; or the right of the people peaceably to assemble and to petition the Government for a redress of grievances.

Amendment II [1791]

[Right to bear arms]

A well regulated Militia, being necessary to the security of a free State, the right of the people to keep and bear Arms, shall not be infringed.

Amendment III [1791]

[Quartering of soldiers]

No Soldier shall, in time of peace be quartered in any house, without the consent of the Owner, nor in time of war, but in a manner to be prescribed by law.

Amendment IV [1791]

[Protection against search and seizure]

The right of the people to be secure in their persons, houses, papers, and effects, against unreasonable searches and seizures, shall not be violated, and no Warrants shall issue, but upon probable cause, supported by Oath or affirmation, and particularly describing the place to be searched, and the persons or things to be seized.

Amendment V [1791]

[Protection of citizens before the law]

No person shall be held to answer for a capital, or otherwise infamous crime, unless on a presentment or indictment of a Grand Jury, except in cases arising in the land or naval forces, or in the Militia, when in actual service in time of War or public danger; nor shall any person be subject for the same offence to be twice put in jeopardy of life or limb; nor shall be compelled in any criminal case to be a witness against himself, nor be deprived of life, liberty, or property, without due process of law; nor shall private property be taken for public use, without just compensation.

Amendment VI [1791]

[Rights of the accused in criminal cases]

In all criminal prosecutions, the accused shall enjoy the right to a speedy and public trial, by an impartial jury of the State and district wherein the crime shall have been committed, which district shall have been previously ascertained by law, and to be informed of the nature and cause of the accusation; to be confronted with the witnesses against him; to have compulsory process for obtaining witnesses in his favor, and to have the Assistance of Counsel for his defence.

Amendment VII [1791]

[Rights of complainants in civil cases]

In suits at common law, where the value in controversy shall exceed twenty dollars, the right of trial by jury shall be preserved, and no fact tried by a jury, shall be otherwise reexamined in any Court of the United States, than according to the rules of the common law.

Amendment VIII [1791]

[Constraints on punishments]

Excessive bail shall not be required, nor excessive fines imposed, nor cruel and unusual punishments inflicted.

Amendment IX [1791]

[Rights retained by the people]

The enumeration in the Constitution, of certain rights, shall not be construed to deny or disparage others retained by the people.

Amendment X [1791]

[Rights reserved to States]

The powers not delegated to the United States by the Constitution, nor prohibited by it to the States, are reserved to the States respectively, or to the people.

Amendment XI [1795][12]

[Restraints on judicial power]

The Judicial power of the United States shall not be construed to extend to any suit in law or equity, commenced or prosecuted against one of the United States by Citizens of another State, or by Citizens or Subjects of any Foreign State.

Amendment XII [1804]

[Mechanism for presidential elections]

The Electors shall meet in their respective States and vote by ballot for President and Vice-President, one of whom, at least, shall not be an inhabitant of the same state with themselves; they shall name in their ballots the person voted for as President, and in distinct ballots the person voted for as Vice-President, and they shall make distinct lists of all persons voted for as President, and of all persons voted for as Vice-President, and of the number of votes for each, which lists they shall sign and certify, and transmit sealed to the seat of the government of the United States, directed to the President of the Senate;—The President of the Senate shall, in the presence of the Senate and House of Representatives, open all the certificates and the votes shall then be counted;—The person having the greatest number of votes for President, shall be the President, if such number be a majority of the whole number of Electors appointed; and if no person have such majority, then from the persons having the highest numbers not exceeding three on the list of those voted for as President, the House of Representatives shall choose immediately, by ballot, the President. But in choosing the President, the votes shall be taken by states, the representation from each state having one vote; a quorum for this purpose shall consist of a member or members from two-thirds of the states, and a majority of all the states shall be necessary to a choice. [And if the House of Representatives shall not choose a President whenever the right of choice shall devolve upon them, before the fourth day of March next following, then the Vice-President shall act as President, as in the case of the death or other constitutional disability of the President.][13]—The person having the greatest number of votes as Vice-President, shall be the Vice-President, if such number be a majority of the whole number of Electors appointed, and if no person have a majority, then from the two highest numbers on the list, the Senate shall choose the Vice-President; a quorum for the purpose shall consist of two-thirds of the whole number of Senators, and a majority of the whole number shall be necessary to a choice. But no person constitutionally ineligible to the Office of President shall be eligible to that of Vice-President of the United States.

Amendment XIII [1865]

[Abolishment of Slavery]

Section 1 Neither slavery nor involuntary servitude, except as a punishment for crime whereof the party shall have been duly convicted, shall exist within the United States, or any place subject to their jurisdiction.

Section 2 Congress shall have power to enforce this article by appropriate legislation.

Amendment XIV [1868]

[Citizens' rights and immunities, due process, equal protection]

Section 1 All persons born or naturalized in the United States, and subject to the jurisdiction thereof, are citizens of the United States and of the State wherein they reside. No State shall make or enforce any law which shall abridge the privileges or immunities of citizens of the United States; nor shall any State deprive any person of life, liberty, or property,

without due process of law; nor deny to any person within its jurisdiction the equal protection of the laws.

[Basis of representation]

Section 2 Representatives shall be apportioned among the several States according to their respective numbers, counting the whole number of persons in each State, excluding Indians not taxed. But when the right to vote at any election for the choice of electors for President and Vice-President of the United States, Representatives in Congress, the Executive and Judicial officers of a State, or the members of the Legislature thereof, is denied to any of the male inhabitants of such State, being twenty-one years of age, and citizens of the United States, or in any way abridged, except for participation in rebellion, or other crime, the basis of representation therein shall be reduced in the proportion which the number of such male citizens shall bear to the whole number of male citizens twenty-one years of age in such State.

[Disqualification of confederates for office]

Section 3 No person shall be a senator or Representative in Congress, or elector of President and Vice-President, or hold any Office, civil or military, under the United States, or under any State, who, having previously taken an oath, as a member of Congress, or as an Officer of the United States, or as a member of any State legislature, or as an executive or judicial officer of any State, to support the Constitution of the United States, shall have engaged in insurrection or rebellion against the same, or given aid or comfort to the enemies thereof. But Congress may by a vote of two-thirds of each House, remove such disability.

[Public debt arising from insurrection or rebellion]

Section 4 The validity of the public debt of the United States, authorized by law, including debts incurred for payment of pensions and bounties for services in suppressing insurrection or rebellion, shall not be questioned. But neither the United States nor any State shall assume or pay any debt or obligation incurred in aid of insurrection or rebellion against the United States, or any claim for the loss or emancipation of any slave; but all such debts, obligations, and claims shall be held illegal and void.

Section 5 The Congress shall have the power to enforce, by appropriate legislation, the provisions of this article.

Amendment XV [1870]

[Explicit extension of right to vote]

Section 1 The right of citizens of the United States to vote shall not be denied or abridged by the United States or by any State on account of race, color, or previous condition of servitude—

Section 2 The Congress shall have power to enforce this article by appropriate legislation.

Amendment XVI [1913]

[Creation of income tax]

The Congress shall have power to lay and collect taxes on incomes, from whatever source derived, without apportionment among the several States, and without regard to any census or enumeration.

Amendment XVII [1913]

[Election of senators]

The Senate of the United States shall be composed of two Senators from each State, elected by the people thereof, for six years; and each Senator shall have one vote. The electors in each State shall have the qualifications requisite for electors of the most numerous branch of the State legislatures.

When vacancies happen in the representation of any State in the Senate, the executive authority of such State shall issue writs of election to fill such vacancies: *Provided,* That the legislature of any State may empower the executive thereof to make temporary appointments until the people fill the vacancies by election as the legislature may direct.

This amendment shall not be so construed as to affect the election or term of any Senator chosen before it becomes valid as part of the Constitution.

Amendment XVIII [1919]

[Prohibition of alcohol]

[**Section 1** After one year from the ratification of this article the manufacture, sale, or transportation of intoxicating liquors within, the importation thereof into, or the exportation thereof from the United States and all territory subject to the jurisdiction thereof for beverage purposes is hereby prohibited.

Section 2 The Congress and the several States shall have concurrent power to enforce this article by appropriate legislation.

Section 3 This article shall be inoperative unless it shall have been ratified as an amendment to the Constitution by the legislatures of the several States, as provided in the Constitution, within seven years from the date of the submission hereof to the States by the Congress.][14]

Amendment XIX [1920]

[Voting rights and gender]

The right of citizens of the United States to vote shall not be denied or abridged by the United States or by any State on account of sex.

Congress shall have power to enforce this article by appropriate legislation.

Amendment XX [1933]

[Terms of executives, assembly of Congress, presidential succession]

Section 1 The terms of the President and Vice President shall end at noon on the 20th day of January, and the terms of Senators and Representatives at noon on the 3d day of January, of the years in which such terms would have ended if this article had not been ratified; and the terms of their successors shall then begin.

Section 2 The Congress shall assemble at least once in every year, and such meeting shall begin at noon on the 3d day of January, unless they shall by law appoint a different day.

Section 3 If, at the time fixed for the beginning of the term of the President, the President elect shall have died, the Vice President elect shall become President. If a President shall not have been chosen before the time fixed for the beginning of his term, or if the President elect shall have failed to qualify, then the Vice President elect shall act as President until a President shall have qualified; and the Congress may by law provide for the case wherein neither a President elect nor a Vice President elect shall have qualified, declaring who shall then act as President, or the manner in which one who is to act shall be selected, and such person shall act accordingly until a President or Vice President shall have qualified.

Section 4 The Congress may by law provide for the case of the death of any of the persons from whom the House of Representatives may choose a President whenever the right of choice shall have devolved upon them, and for the case of the death of any of the persons from whom the Senate may choose a Vice President whenever the right of choice shall have devolved upon them.

Section 5 Sections 1 and 2 shall take effect on the 15th day of October following the ratification of this article.

Section 6 This article shall be inoperative unless it shall have been ratified as an amendment to the Constitution by the legislatures of three-fourths of the several States within seven years from the date of its submission.

Amendment XXI [1933]

[Repealing of Prohibition]

Section 1 The eighteenth article of amendment to the Constitution of the United States is hereby repealed.

Section 2 The transportation or importation into any State, Territory, or possession of the United States for delivery or use therein of intoxicating liquors, in violation of the laws thereof, is hereby prohibited.

Section 3 This article shall be inoperative unless it shall have been ratified as an amendment of the Constitution by conventions in the several States, as provided in the Constitution, within seven years from the date of the submission hereof to the States by the Congress.

Amendment XXII [1951]

[Limits on presidential term]

No person shall be elected to the office of the President more than twice, and no person who has held the office of President, or acted as President, for more than two years of a term to which some other person was elected President shall be elected to the office of the President more than once. But this Article shall not apply to any person holding the office of President when this Article was proposed by the Congress, and shall not prevent any person who may be holding the office of President, or acting as President, during the term within which this Article becomes operative from holding the office of President or acting as President during the remainder of such term.

Amendment XXIII [1961]

[Voting rights of District of Columbia]

Section 1 The District constituting the seat of Government of the United States shall appoint in such manner as the Congress may direct:

A number of electors of President and Vice President equal to the whole number of Senators and Representatives in Congress to which the District would be entitled if it were a State, but in no event more than the least populous State; they shall be in addition to those appointed by the States, but they shall be considered, for the purposes of the election of President and Vice President, to be electors appointed by a State; and they shall meet in the District and perform such duties as provided by the twelfth article of amendment.

Section 2 The Congress shall have power to enforce this article by appropriate legislation.

Amendment XXIV [1964]

[Prohibition of poll tax]

Section 1 The right of citizens of the United States to vote in any primary or other election for President or Vice President, for electors for President or Vice President, or for Senator or Representative in Congress, shall not be denied or abridged by the United States or any State by reason of failure to pay any poll tax or other tax.

Section 2 The Congress shall have power to enforce this article by appropriate legislation.

Amendment XXV [1967]

[Presidential disability and succession]

Section 1 In case of the removal of the President from office or of his death or resignation, the Vice President shall become President.

Section 2 Whenever there is a vacancy in the office of the Vice President, the President shall nominate a Vice President who shall take office upon confirmation by a majority vote of both houses of Congress.

Section 3 Whenever the President transmits to the President pro tempore of the Senate and the Speaker of the House of Representatives his written declaration that he is unable to discharge the powers and duties of his Office, and until he transmits to them a written declaration to the contrary, such powers and duties shall be discharged by the Vice President as Acting President.

Section 4 Whenever the Vice President and a majority of either the principal Officers of the executive departmentor of such other body as Congress may by law provide, transmit to the President pro tempore of the Senate and the Speaker of the House of Representatives their written declaration that the President is unable to discharge the powers and duties of his office, the Vice President shall immediately assume the powers and duties of the Office as Acting President.

Thereafter, when the President transmits to the President pro tempore of the Senate and the Speaker of the House of Representatives his written declaration that no inability exists, he shall resume the powers and duties of his office unless the Vice President and a majority of either the principal officers of the executive department or of such other body as Congress may by law provide, transmit within four days to the President pro tempore of the Senate and the Speaker of the House of Representatives their written declaration that the President is unable to discharge the powers and duties of his office. Thereupon Congress shall decide the issue, assembling within forty-eight hours for that purpose if not in session. If the Congress, within twenty-one days after receipt of the latter written declaration, or, if Congress is not in session, within twenty-one days after Congress is required to assemble, determines by two-thirds vote of both houses that the President is unable to discharge the powers and duties of his office, the Vice President shall continue to discharge the same as Acting President; otherwise, the President shall resume the powers and duties of his office.

Amendment XXVI [1971]

[Voting rights and age]

Section 1 The right of citizens of the United States, who are eighteen years of age or older, to vote shall not be denied or abridged by the United States or by any State on account of age.

Section 2 The Congress shall have power to enforce this article by appropriate legislation.

Amendment XXVII [1992]

[Congressional pay]

No law, varying the compensation for the services of the Senators and Representatives, shall take effect, until an election of representatives, shall have intervened.

[1]Modified by the Fourteenth and Sixteenth amendments.

[2]Superseded by the Seventeenth Amendment.

[3]Modified by the Seventeenth Amendment.

[4]Superseded by the Twentieth Amendment.

[5]Modified by the Sixteenth Amendment.

[6]Supereseded by the Twelfth Amendment.

[7]Modified by the Twenty-fifth Amendment.

[8]Modified by the Eleventh Amendment.

[9]Modified by Eleventh Amendment.

[10]Superseded by the Thirteenth Amendment.

[11]The first ten amendments were passed by Congress September 25, 1789. They were ratified by three-fourths of the states December 15, 1791.

[12]Date of ratification.

[13]Superseded by the Twentieth Amendment.

[14]Repealed by the Twenty-first Amendment.

From The Federalist Nos. 10 and 51

| FEDERALIST NO. 10 [1787] |

To the People of the State of New York: Among the numerous advantages promised by a well-constructed union, none deserves to be more accurately developed than its tendency to break and control the violence of faction. The friend of popular governments never finds himself so much alarmed for their character and fate, as when he contemplates their propensity to this dangerous vice. He will not fail, therefore, to set a due value on any plan which, without violating the principles to which he is attached, provides a proper cure for it. The instability, injustice, and confusion introduced into the public councils, have, in truth, been the mortal diseases under which popular governments have everywhere perished; as they continue to be the favorite and fruitful topics from which the adversaries to liberty derive their most specious declamations. The valuable improvements made by the American constitutions on the popular models, both ancient and modern, cannot certainly be too much admired; but it would be an unwarrantable partiality, to contend that they have as effectually obviated the danger on this side, as was wished and expected. Complaints are everywhere heard from our most considerate and virtuous citizens, equally the friends of public and private faith, and of public and personal liberty, that our governments are too unstable, that the public good is disregarded in the conflicts of rival parties, and that measures are too often decided, not according to the rules of justice and the rights of the minor party, but by the superior force of an interested and overbearing majority. However anxiously we may wish that these complaints had no foundation, the evidence of known facts will not permit us to deny that they are in some degree true. It will be found, indeed, on a candid review of our situation, that some of the distresses under which we labor have been erroneously charged on the operation of our governments; but it will be found, at the same time, that other causes will not alone account for many of our heaviest misfortunes; and, particularly, for that prevailing and increasing distrust of public engagements, and alarm for private rights, which are echoed from one end of the continent to the other. These must be chiefly, if not wholly, effects of the unsteadiness and injustice with which a factious spirit has tainted our public administrations.

By a faction, I understand a number of citizens, whether amounting to a majority or a minority of the whole, who are united and actuated by some common impulse of passion, or of interest, adverse to the rights of other citizens, or to the permanent and aggregate interests of the community.

There are two methods of curing the mischiefs of faction: the one, by removing its causes; the other, by controlling its effects.

There are again two methods of removing the causes of faction: the one, by destroying the liberty which is essential to its existence; the other, by giving to every citizen the same opinions, the same passions, and the same interests.

It could never be more truly said than of the first remedy, that it was worse than the disease. Liberty is to faction what air is to fire, an aliment without which it instantly expires. But it could not be less folly to abolish liberty, which is essential to political life, because it nourishes faction, than it would be to wish the annihilation of air, which is essential to animal life, because it imparts to fire its destructive agency.

The second expedient is as impracticable as the first would be unwise. As long as the reason of man continues fallible, and he is at liberty to exercise it, different opinions will be formed. As long as the connection subsists between his reason and his self-love, his opinions and his passions will have a reciprocal influence on each other; and the former will be objects to which the latter will attach themselves. The diversity in the faculties of men, from which the rights of property originate, is not less an insuperable obstacle to a uniformity of interests. The protection of these faculties is the first object of government. From the protection of different and unequal faculties of acquiring property, the possession of different degrees and kinds of property immediately results; and from the influence of these on the sentiments and views of the respective proprietors, ensues a division of the society into different interests and parties.

The latent causes of faction are thus sown in the nature of man; and we see them everywhere brought into different degrees of activity, according to the different circumstances of civil society. A zeal for different opinions concerning religion, concerning government, and many other points, as well of speculation as of practice; an attachment to different leaders ambitiously contending for preeminence and power; or to persons of other descriptions whose fortunes have been interesting to the human passions, have, in turn, divided mankind into parties, inflamed them with mutual animosity, and rendered them much more disposed to vex and oppress each other than to cooperate for their common good. So strong is this propensity of mankind to fall into mutual animosities, that where no substantial occasion presents itself, the most frivolous and fanciful distinctions have been sufficient to kindle their unfriendly passions and excite their most violent conflicts. But the most common and durable source of factions has been the various and unequal distribution of property. Those who hold and those who are without property have ever formed distinct interests in society. Those who are creditors, and those who are debtors, fall under a like discrimination. A landed interest, a manufacturing interest, a mercantile interest, a moneyed interest, with many lesser interests, grow up of necessity in civilized nations, and divide them into different classes, actuated by different sentiments and views. The regulation of these various and interfering interests forms the principal task of modern legislation, and involves the spirit of party and faction in the necessary and ordinary operations of the government.

No man is allowed to be a judge in his own cause, because his interest would certainly bias his judgment, and, not improbably, corrupt his integrity. With equal, nay with greater reason, a body of men are unfit to be both judges and parties at the same time; yet what are many of the most important acts of legislation, but so many judicial determinations, not indeed concerning the rights of single persons, but concerning the rights of large bodies of citizens? And what are the different classes of legislators but advocates and parties to the causes which they determine? Is a law proposed concerning private debts? It is a question to which the creditors are parties on one side and the debtors on the other. Justice ought to hold the balance between them. Yet the parties are, and must be, themselves the judges; and the most numerous party, or, in other words, the most powerful faction must be expected to prevail. Shall domestic manufactures be encouraged, and in what degree, by restrictions on foreign manufactures? These are questions which would be differently decided by the landed and the manufacturing classes, and probably by neither with a sole regard to justice and the public good. The apportionment of taxes on the various descriptions of property is an act which seems to require the most exact impartiality; yet there is, perhaps, no legislative act in which greater opportunity and temptation are given to a predominant party to trample on the rules of justice. Every shilling with which they overburden the inferior number, is a shilling saved to their own pockets.

It is in vain to say that enlightened statesmen will be able to adjust these clashing interests, and render them all subservient to the public good. Enlightened statesmen will not always be at the helm; nor, in many cases, can such an adjustment be made at all without taking into view indirect and remote considerations, which will rarely prevail over the immediate interest which one party may find in disregarding the rights of another or the good of the whole.

The inference to which we are brought is, that the *causes* of faction cannot be removed, and that relief is only to be sought in the means of controlling its *effects*.

If a faction consists of less than a majority, relief is supplied by the republican principle, which enables the majority to defeat its sinister views by regular vote. It may clog the administration, it may convulse the society; but it will be unable to execute and mask its violence under the forms of the constitution. When a majority is included in a faction, the form of popular government, on the other hand, enables it to sacrifice to its ruling passion or interest both the public good and the rights of other citizens. To secure the public good and private rights against the danger of such a faction, and at the same time to preserve the spirit and the form of popular government, is then the great object to which our inquiries are directed. Let me add that it is the great desideratum by which this form of government can be rescued from the opprobrium under which it has so long labored, and be recommended to the esteem and adoption of mankind.

By what means is this object attainable? Evidently by one of two only. Either the existence of the same passion or interest in a majority at the same time must be prevented, or the majority, having such coexistent passion or interest, must be rendered, by their number and local situation, unable to concert and carry into effect schemes of oppression. If the impulse and the opportunity be suffered to coincide, we well know that neither moral nor religious motives can be relied on as an adequate control. They are not found to be such on the injustice and violence of individuals, and lose their efficacy in proportion to the number combined together, that is, in proportion as their efficacy becomes needful.

From this view of the subject it may be concluded that a pure democracy, by which I mean a society consisting of a small number of citizens, who assemble and administer the government in person, can admit of no cure for the mischiefs of faction. A common passion or interest will, in almost every case, be felt by a majority of the whole; a communication and concert result from the form of government itself; and there is nothing to check the inducements to sacrifice the weaker party or an obnoxious individual. Hence it is that such democracies have ever been spectacles of turbulence and contention; have ever been found incompatible with personal security or the rights of property; and have in general been as short in their lives as they have been violent in their deaths. Theoretic politicians, who have patronized this species of government, have erroneously supposed that by reducing mankind to a perfect equality in their political rights, they would, at the same time, be perfectly equalized and assimilated in their possessions, their opinions, and their passions.

A republic, by which I mean a government in which the scheme of representation takes place, opens a different prospect, and promises the cure for which we are seeking.

Let us examine the points in which it varies from pure democracy, and we shall comprehend both the nature of the cure and the efficacy which it must derive from the union.

The two great points of difference between a democracy and a republic, are, first, the delegation of the government, in the latter, to a small number of citizens elected by the rest; secondly, the greater number of citizens, and greater sphere of country, over which the latter may be extended.

The effect of the first difference is, on the one hand, to refine and enlarge the public views, by passing them through the medium of a chosen body of citizens, whose wisdom may best discern the true interest of their country, and whose patriotism and love of justice will be least likely to sacrifice it to temporary or partial considerations. Under such a regulation, it may well happen that the public voice, pronounced by the representatives of the people, will be more consonant to the public good than if pronounced by the people themselves, convened for the purpose. On the other hand, the effect may be inverted. Men of factious tempers, of local prejudices, or of sinister designs, may, by intrigue, by corruption, or by other means, first obtain the suffrages, and then betray the interests, of the people. The question resulting is, whether small or extensive republics are more favorable to the election of proper guardians of the public weal; and it is clearly decided in favor of the latter by two obvious considerations:

In the first place, it is to be remarked that, however small the republic may be, the representatives must be raised to a certain number, in order to guard against the cabals of a few; and that, however large it may be, they must be limited to a certain number, in order to guard against the confusion of a multitude. Hence, the number of representatives in the two cases not being in proportion to that of the two constituents, and being proportionally greater in the small republic, it follows that, if the proportion of fit characters be not less in the large than in the small republic, the former will present a greater option, and consequently a greater probability of a fit choice.

In the next place, as each representative will be chosen by a greater number of citizens in the large than in the small republic, it will be more difficult for unworthy candidates to practice with success the vicious arts by which elections are too often carried; and the suffrages of the people being more free, will be more likely to centre in men who possess the most attractive merit and the most diffusive and established characters.

It must be confessed that in this, as in most other cases, there is a mean, on both sides of which inconveniences will be found to lie. By enlarging too much the number of electors, you render the representatives too little acquainted with all their local circumstances and lesser interests; as by reducing it too much, you render him unduly attached to these, and too little fit to comprehend and pursue great and national objects. The federal constitution forms a happy combination in this respect; the great and aggregate interests being referred to the national, the local and particular to the State legislatures.

The other point of difference is, the greater number of citizens and extent of territory which may be brought within the compass of republican than of democratic government; and it is this circumstance principally which renders factious combinations less to be dreaded in the former than in the latter. The smaller the society, the fewer probably will be the distinct parties and interests composing it; the fewer the distinct parties and interests, the more frequently will a majority be found of the same party; and the smaller the number of individuals composing a majority, and the smaller the compass within which they are placed, the more easily will they concert and execute their plans of oppression. Extend the sphere, and you take in a greater variety of parties and interests; you make it less probable that a majority of the whole will have a common motive to invade the rights of other citizens; or if such a common motive exists, it will be more difficult for all who feel it to discover their own strength, and to act in unison with each other. Besides other impediments, it may be remarked that, where there is a consciousness of unjust or dishonorable purposes, communication is always checked by distrust in proportion to the number whose concurrence is necessary.

Hence, it clearly appears, that the same advantage which a republic has over a democracy, in controlling the effects of faction, is enjoyed by a large over a small republic,—is enjoyed by the union over the states composing it. Does the advantage consist in the substitution of representatives whose enlightened views and virtuous sentiments render them superior to local prejudices and schemes of injustice? It will not be denied that the representation of the union will be most likely to possess these requisite endowments. Does it consist in the greater security afforded by a greater variety of parties, against the event of any one party being able to outnumber and oppress the rest? In an equal degree does the increased variety of parties comprised within the union, increase this security. Does it, in fine, consist in the greater obstacles opposed to the concert and accomplishment of the secret wishes of an unjust and interested majority? Here, again, the extent of the union gives it the most palpable advantage.

The influence of factious leaders may kindle a flame within their particular states, but will be unable to spread a general conflagration through the other states. A religious sect may degenerate into a political faction in a part of the Confederacy; but the variety of sects dispersed over the entire face of it must secure the national councils against any danger from that source. A rage for paper money, for an abolition of debts, for an equal division of property, or for any other improper or wicked project, will be less apt to pervade the whole body of the union than a particular member of it; in the same proportion as such a malady is more likely to taint a particular county or district, than an entire state.

In the extent and proper structure of the Union, therefore, we behold a republican remedy for the diseases most incident to republican government. And according to the degree of pleasure and pride we feel in being republicans, ought to be our zeal in cherishing the spirit and supporting the character of Federalists.

JAMES MADISON

FEDERALIST NO. 51 [1788]

To the People of the State of New York: To what expedient, then, shall we finally resort, for maintaining in practice the necessary partition of power among the several departments, as laid down in the constitution? The only answer that can be given is, that as all these exterior provisions are found to be inadequate, the defect must be supplied, by so contriving the interior structure of the government as that its several constituent parts may, by their mutual relations, be the means of keeping each other in their proper places. Without presuming to undertake a full development of this important idea, I will hazard a few general observations, which may perhaps place it in a clearer light, and enable us to form a more correct judgment of the principles and structure of the government planned by the convention.

In order to lay a due foundation for that separate and distinct exercise of the different powers of government, which to a certain extent is admitted on all hands to be essential to the preservation of liberty, it is evident that each department should have a will of its own; and consequently should be so constituted that the members of each should have as little agency as possible in the appointment of the members of the others. Were this principle rigorously adhered to, it would require that all the appointments for the supreme executive, legislative, and judiciary magistracies should be drawn from the same fountain of authority, the people, through channels having no communication whatever with one another. Perhaps such a plan of constructing the several departments would be less difficult in practice than it may in contemplation appear. Some difficulties, however, and some additional expense would attend the execution of it. Some deviations, therefore, from the principle must be admitted. In the constitution of the judiciary department in particular, it might be inexpedient to insist rigorously on the principle: first, because peculiar qualifications being essential in the members, the primary consideration ought to be to select that mode of choice which best secures these qualifications; secondly, because the permanent tenure by which the appointments are held in that department, must soon destroy all sense of dependence on the authority conferring them.

It is equally evident, that the members of each department should be as little dependent as possible on those of the others, for the emoluments annexed to their offices. Were the executive magistrate, or the judges, not independent of the legislature in this particular, their independence in every other would be merely nominal.

But the great security against a gradual concentration of the several powers in the same department, consists in giving to those who administer each department the necessary constitutional means and personal motives to resist encroachments of the others. The provision for defense must in this, as in all other cases, be made commensurate to the danger of attack. Ambition must be made to counteract ambition. The interest of the man must be connected with the constitutional rights of the place. It may be a reflection on human nature, that such devices should be necessary to control the abuses of government. But what is government itself, but the greatest of all reflections on human nature? If men were angels, no government would be necessary. If angels were to govern men, neither external nor internal controls on government would be necessary. In framing a government which is to be administered by men over men, the great difficulty lies in this: you must first enable the government to control the governed; and in the next place oblige it to control itself. A dependence on the people is, no doubt, the primary control on the government; but experience has taught mankind the necessity of auxiliary precautions.

This policy of supplying, by opposite and rival interests, the defect of better motives, might be traced through the whole system of human affairs, private as well as public. We see it particularly displayed in all the subordinate distributions of power, where the constant aim is to divide and arrange the several offices in such a manner as that each may be a check on the other—that the private interest of every individual may be a sentinel over the public rights. These inventions of prudence cannot be less requisite in the distribution of the supreme powers of the state.

But it is not possible to give to each department an equal power of self-defense. In republican government, the legislative authority necessarily predominates. The remedy for this incon-veniency is to divide the legislature into different branches; and to render them, by different modes of election and different principles of action, as little connected with each other as the nature of their common functions and their common dependence on the society will admit. It may even be necessary to guard against dangerous encroachments by still further precautions. As the weight of the legislative authority requires that it should be thus divided, the weakness of the executive may require, on the other hand, that it should be fortified. An absolute negative on the legislature appears, at first view, to be the natural defense with which the executive magistrate should be armed. But perhaps it would be neither altogether safe nor alone sufficient. On ordinary occasions it might not be exerted with the requisite firmness, and on extraordinary occasions it might be perfidiously abused. May not this defect of an absolute negative be supplied by some qualified connection between this weaker department and the weaker branch of the stronger department, by which the latter may be led to support the constitutional rights of the former, without being too much detached from the rights of its own department?

If the principles on which these observations are founded be just, as I persuade myself they are, and they be applied as a criterion to the several state constitutions, and to the federal constitution it will be found that if the latter does not perfectly correspond with them, the former are infinitely less able to bear such a test.

There are, moreover, two considerations particularly applicable to the federal system of America, which place that system in a very interesting point of view.

First. In a single republic, all the power surrendered by the people is submitted to the administration of a single government; and the usurpations are guarded against by a division of the government into distinct and separate departments. In the compound republic of America, the power surrendered by the people is first divided between two distinct governments, and then the portion allotted to each subdivided among distinct and separate departments. Hence a double security arises to the rights of the people. The different governments will control each other, at the same time that each will be controlled by itself.

Second. It is of great importance in a republic not only to guard the society against the oppression of its rulers, but to guard one part of the society against the injustice of the other part. Different interests necessarily exist in different classes of citizens. If a majority be united by a common interest, the rights of the minority will be insecure. There are but two methods of providing against this evil: the one by creating a will in the community independent of the majority that is, of the society itself; the other, by comprehending in the society so many separate descriptions of citizens as will render an unjust combination of a majority of the whole very improbable, if not impracticable. The first method prevails in all governments possessing an hereditary or self-appointed authority. This, at best, is but a precarious security; because a power independent of the society may as well espouse the unjust views of the major as the rightful interests of the minor party, and may possibly be turned against both parties. The second method will be exemplified in the federal republic of the United States. Whilst all authority in it will be derived from and dependent on the society, the society itself will be broken into so many parts, interests, and classes of citizens, that the rights of individuals, or of the minority, will be in little danger from interested combinations of the majority. In a free government the security for civil rights must be the same as that for religious rights. It consists in the one case in the multiplicity of interests, and in the other in the multiplicity of sects. The degree of security in both cases will depend on the number of interests and sects; and this may be presumed to depend on the extent of country and number of people comprehended under the same government. This view of the subject must particularly recommend a proper federal system to all the sincere and considerate friends of republican government, since it shows that in exact proportion as the territory of the union may be formed into more circumscribed confederacies, or states oppressive combinations of a majority will be facilitated: the best security, under the republican forms, for the rights of every class of citizens, will be diminished; and consequently the stability and independence of some member of the government, the only other security, must be proportionately increased. Justice is the end of government. It is the end of civil society. It ever has been and ever will be pursued until it be obtained, or until liberty be lost in the pursuit. In a society under the forms of which the stronger faction can readily unite and oppress the weaker, anarchy may as truly be said to reign as in a state of nature, where the weaker individual is not secured against the violence of the stronger; and as, in the latter state, even the stronger individuals are prompted, by the uncertainty of their condition, to submit to a government which may protect the weak as well as themselves; so, in the former state, will the more powerful factions or parties be gradually induced, by a like motive, to wish for a government which will protect all parties, the weaker as well as the more powerful. It can be little doubted that if the state of Rhode Island was separated from the confederacy and left to itself, the insecurity of rights under the popular form of government within such narrow limits would be displayed by such reiterated oppressions of factious majorities that some power altogether independent of the people would soon be called for by the voice of the very factions whose misrule had proved the necessity of it. In the extended republic of the United States, and among the great variety of interests, parties, and sects which it embraces, a coalition of a majority of the whole society could seldom take place on any other principles than those of justice and the general good; whilst there being thus less danger to a minor from the will of a major party, there must be less pretext, also, to provide for the security of the former, by introducing into the government a will not dependent on the latter, or, in other words, a will independent of the society itself. It is no less certain than it is important, notwithstanding the contrary opinions which have been entertained, that the larger the society, provided it lie within a practical sphere, the more duly capable it will be of self-government. And happily for the *republican cause,* the practicable sphere may be carried to a very great extent, by a judicious modification and mixture of the *federal principle.*

JAMES MADISON

APPENDIX D

Presidential Elections

CANDIDATES	PARTY	ELECTORAL VOTE
1789		
George Washington	Federalist	69
John Adams	Federalist	34
Others		35
1792		
George Washington	Federalist	132
John Adams	Federalist	77
George Clinton		50
Others		5
1796		
John Adams	Federalist	71
Thomas Jefferson	Democratic-Republican	68
Thomas Pinckney	Federalist	59
Aaron Burr	Democratic-Republican	30
Others		48
1800		
Thomas Jefferson[1]	Democratic-Republican	73
Aaron Burr	Democratic-Republican	73
John Adams	Federalist	65
Charles C. Pinckney		64
1804		
Thomas Jefferson	Democratic-Republican	162
Charles C. Pinckney	Federalist	14
1808		
James Madison	Democratic-Republican	122
Charles C. Pinckney	Federalist	47
George Clinton	Independent-Republican	6
1812		
James Madison	Democratic-Republican	122
DeWitt Clinton	Federalist	89
1816		
James Monroe	Democratic-Republican	183
Rufus King	Federalist	34

CANDIDATES	PARTY	ELECTORAL VOTE
1820		
James Monroe	Democratic-Republican	231
John Quincy Adams	Independent-Republican	1
1824		
John Quincy Adams[1]	Democratic-Republican	84
Andrew Jackson	Democratic-Republican	99
Henry Clay	Democratic-Republican	37
William H. Crawford	Democratic-Republican	41
1828		
Andrew Jackson	Democratic	178
John Quincy Adams	National-Republican	83
1832		
Andrew Jackson	Democratic	219
Henry Clay	National-Republican	49
William Wirt	Anti-Masonic	7
John Floyd	National-Republican	11
1836		
Martin Van Buren	Democratic	170
William H. Harrison	Whig	73
Hugh L. White	Whig	26
Daniel Webster	Whig	14
1840		
William H. Harrison[2]	Whig	234
(John Tyler)	Whig	
Martin Van Buren	Democratic	60
1844		
James K. Polk	Democratic	170
Henry Clay	Whig	105
James G. Birney	Liberty	
1848		
Zachary Taylor[2]	Whig	163
(Millard Fillmore)	Whig	
Lewis Cass	Democratic	127
Martin Van Buren	Free Soil	
1852		
Franklin Pierce	Democratic	254
Winfield Scott	Whig	42

CANDIDATES	PARTY	ELECTORAL VOTE
1856		
James Buchanan	Democratic	174
John C. Fremont	Republican	114
Millard Fillmore	American	8
1860		
Abraham Lincoln	Republican	180
Stephen A. Douglas	Democratic	12
John C. Breckinridge	Democratic	72
John Bell	Constitutional Union	39
1864		
Abraham Lincoln[2]	Republican	212
(Andrew Johnson)	Republican	
George B. McClellan	Democratic	21
1868		
Ulysses S. Grant	Republican	214
Horatio Seymour	Democratic	80
1872		
Ulysses S. Grant	Republican	286
Horace Greeley	Democratic	66
1876		
Rutherford B. Hayes	Republican	185
Samuel J. Tilden	Democratic	184
1880		
James A. Garfield[2]	Republican	214
(Chester A. Arthur)	Republican	
Winfield S. Hancock	Democratic	155
James B. Weaver	Greenback-Labor	
1884		
Grover Cleveland	Democratic	219
James G. Blaine	Republican	182
Benjamin F. Butler	Greenback-Labor	
1888		
Benjamin Harrison	Republican	233
Grover Cleveland	Democratic	168
1892		
Grover Cleveland	Democratic	277
Benjamin Harrison	Republican	145
James R. Weaver	People's	22

CANDIDATES	PARTY	ELECTORAL VOTE
1896		
William McKinley	Republican	271
William J. Bryan	Democratic, Populist	176
1900		
William McKinley[2]	Republican	292
(Theodore Roosevelt)	Republican	
William J. Bryan	Democratic, Populist	155
1904		
Theodore Roosevelt	Republican	336
Alton B. Parker	Democratic	140
Eugene V. Debs	Socialist	
1908		
William H. Taft	Republican	321
William J. Bryan	Democratic	162
Eugene V. Debs	Socialist	
1912		
Woodrow Wilson	Democratic	435
Theodore Roosevelt	Progressive	88
William H. Taft	Republican	8
Eugene V. Debs	Socialist	
1916		
Woodrow Wilson	Democratic	277
Charles E. Hughes	Republican	254
1920		
Warren G. Harding[2]	Republican	404
(Calvin Coolidge)	Republican	
James M. Cox	Democratic	127
Eugene V. Debs	Socialist	
1924		
Calvin Coolidge	Republican	382
John W. Davis	Democratic	136
Robert M. LaFollette	Progressive	13
1928		
Herbert C. Hoover	Republican	444
Alfred E. Smith	Democratic	87

CANDIDATES	PARTY	ELECTORAL VOTE
1932		
Franklin D. Roosevelt	Democratic	472
Herbert C. Hoover	Republican	59
Norman Thomas	Socialist	
1936		
Franklin D. Roosevelt	Democratic	523
Alfred M. Landon	Republican	8
William Lemke	Union	
1940		
Franklin D. Roosevelt	Democratic	449
Wendell L. Wilkie	Republican	82
1944		
Franklin D. Roosevelt[2]	Democratic	432
(Harry S Truman)	Democratic	
Thomas E. Dewey	Republican	99
1948		
Harry S Truman	Democratic	303
Thomas E. Dewey	Republican	189
J. Strom Thurmond	States' Rights	39
Henry A. Wallace	Progressive	
1952		
Dwight D. Eisenhower	Republican	442
Adlai E. Stevenson	Democratic	89
1956		
Dwight D. Eisenhower	Republican	457
Adlai E. Stevenson	Democratic	73
1960		
John F. Kennedy[2]	Democratic	303
(Lyndon B. Johnson)	Democratic	
Richard M. Nixon	Republican	219
1964		
Lyndon B. Johnson	Democratic	486
Barry M. Goldwater	Republican	52
1968		
Richard M. Nixon	Republican	301
Hubert H. Humphrey	Democratic	191
George C. Wallace	American Independent	46

CANDIDATES	PARTY	ELECTORAL VOTE
1972		
Richard M. Nixon[3]	Republican	520
(Gerald R. Ford)	Republican	
George S. McGovern	Democratic	17
1976		
Jimmy Carter	Democratic	297
Gerald R. Ford	Republican	240
1980		
Ronald Reagan	Republican	489
Jimmy Carter	Democratic	49
John Anderson	Independent	
1984		
Ronald Reagan	Republican	525
Walter Mondale	Democratic	13
1988		
George H. W. Bush	Republican	426
Michael Dukakis	Democratic	111
1992		
Bill Clinton	Democratic	370
George H. W. Bush	Republican	168
Ross Perot	Independent	
1996		
Bill Clinton	Democratic	379
Bob Dole	Republican	159
Ross Perot	Reform Party	
2000		
George W. Bush	Republican	271
Al Gore[4]	Democrat	266
Ralph Nader	Green	
2004		
George W. Bush	Republican	286
John Kerry[5]	Democrat	251

[1]Elected by the House of Representatives.
[2]Died while in office.
[3]Resigned from office.
[4]One Democratic elector from Washington D.C. cast a blank ballot as a protest against the district's lack of voting representation in Congress.
[5]One Democratic elector from Minnesota voted for John Edwards for president.

2004 Electoral and Popular Vote Summary

	Electoral Vote		Popular Vote			
STATE	BUSH (R)	KERRY (D)	BUSH (R)	KERRY (D)	ALL OTHERS	TOTAL
AL	9		1,176,394	693,933	13,122	1,883,449
AK	3		190,889	111,025	10,684	312,598
AZ	10		1,104,294	893,524	14,767	2,012,585
AR	6		572,898	469,953	12,094	1,054,945
CA		55	5,509,826	6,745,485	166,541	12,419,857
CO	9		1,101,255	1,001,732	27,343	2,130,330
CT		7	693,826	857,488	27,455	1,578,769
DE		3	171,660	200,152	3,378	375,190
DC		3	21,256	202,970	3,360	227,586
FL	27		3,964,522	3,583,544	61,744	7,609,810
GA	15		1,914,254	1,366,149	21,472	3,301,875
HI		4	194,191	231,708	3,114	429,013
ID	4		409,235	181,098	8,114	598,447
IL		21	2,345,946	2,891,550	36,826	5,274,322
IN	11		1,479,438	969,011	19,553	2,468,002
IA	7		751,957	741,898	13,053	1,506,908
KS	6		736,456	434,993	16,307	1,187,756
KY	8		1,069,439	712,733	13,710	1,795,860
LA	9		1,102,169	820,299	20,638	1,943,106
ME		4	330,201	396,842	13,709	740,752
MD		10	1,024,703	1,334,493	27,482	2,386,678
MA		12	1,071,109	1,803,800	37,479	2,912,388
MI		17	2,313,746	2,479,183	46,323	4,839,252
MN		9*	1,346,695	1,445,014	36,678	2,828,387
MS	6		684,981	458,094	9,070	1,139,824
MO	11		1,455,713	1,259,171	16,480	2,731,364
MT	3		266,063	173,710	10,672	450,434
NE	5		512,814	254,328	11,044	778,186
NV	5		418,690	397,190	13,707	829,587
NH		4	331,237	340,511	5,990	677,662
NJ		15	1,670,003	1,911,430	30,258	3,611,691
NM	5		376,930	370,942	8,432	756,304
NY		31	2,962,567	4,314,280	114,189	7,391,036
NC	15		1,961,166	1,525,849	13,992	3,501,007
ND	3		196,651	111,052	5,130	312,833
OH	20		2,859,768	2,741,167	26,973	5,627,908
OK	7		959,792	503,966	0	1,463,758
OR		7	866,831	943,163	26,788	1,836,782

	Electoral Vote		Popular Vote			
STATE	BUSH (R)	KERRY (D)	BUSH (R)	KERRY (D)	ALL OTHERS	TOTAL
PA		21	2,793,847	2,938,095	37,648	5,769,590
RI		4	169,046	259,765	8,323	437,134
SC	8		937,974	661,699	18,057	1,617,730
SD	3		232,584	149,244	6,387	388,215
TN	11		1,384,375	1,036,477	16,467	2,437,319
TX	34		4,526,917	2,832,704	51,144	7,410,765
UT	5		663,742	241,199	22,903	927,844
VT		3	121,180	184,067	7,062	312,309
VA	13		1,716,959	1,454,742	26,666	3,198,367
WA		11	1,304,894	1,510,201	43,989	2,859,084
WV	5		423,778	326,541	5,568	755,887
WI		10	1,478,120	1,489,504	29,383	2,997,007
WY	3		167,629	70,776	5,023	243,428
Total:	286	251	62,040,610	59,028,444	1,226,291	122,295,345
			50.73%	48.27%	1.00%	

Italics indicate Write-In Votes.
* MN has 10 Electoral Votes. One electoral vote was cast for John Edwards.
Total electoral votes: 538. Total Electoral Vote Needed to Elect: 270.
"Federal Elections, 2004: Election Results for the U.S. President, the U.S. Senate, and the U.S. House of Representatives, Federal Election Commission, http://www.fec.gov/pubrec/fe2004/federalelections 2004.shtml (accessed February 24, 2006).

APPENDIX E

Party Control of Congress, 1901–2006

	SENATE			HOUSE			
	DEM.	REP.	OTHER	DEM.	REP.	OTHER	PRESIDENT
57th Congress, 1901–1903	31	55	4	151	197	9	McKinley T. Roosevelt
58th Congress, 1903–1905	33	57	–	178	208	–	T. Roosevelt
59th Congress, 1905–1907	33	57	–	136	250	–	T. Roosevelt
60th Congress, 1907–1909	31	61	–	164	222	–	T. Roosevelt
61st Congress, 1909–1911	32	61	–	172	219	–	Taft
62nd Congress, 1911–1913	41	51	–	228	161	1	Taft
63rd Congress, 1913–1915	51	44	1	291	127	17	Wilson
64th Congress, 1915–1917	56	40	–	230	196	9	Wilson
65th Congress, 1917–1919	53	42	–	216	210	6	Wilson
66th Congress, 1919–1921	47	49	–	190	240	3	Wilson
67th Congress, 1921–1923	37	59	–	131	301	1	Harding
68th Congress, 1923–1925	43	51	2	205	225	5	Coolidge
69th Congress, 1925–1927	39	56	1	183	247	4	Coolidge
70th Congress, 1927–1929	46	49	1	195	237	3	Coolidge
71st Congress, 1929–1931	39	56	1	167	267	1	Hoover
72nd Congress, 1931–1933	47	48	1	220	214	1	Hoover
73rd Congress, 1933–1935	60	35	1	319	117	5	F. Roosevelt
74th Congress, 1935–1937	69	25	2	319	103	10	F. Roosevelt
75th Congress, 1937–1939	76	16	4	331	89	13	F. Roosevelt
76th Congress, 1939–1941	69	23	4	261	164	4	F. Roosevelt
77th Congress, 1941–1943	66	28	2	268	162	5	F. Roosevelt
78th Congress, 1943–1945	58	37	1	218	208	4	F. Roosevelt
79th Congress, 1945–1947	56	38	1	242	190	2	Truman
80th Congress, 1947–1949	45	51	–	188	245	1	Truman
81st Congress, 1949–1951	54	42	–	263	171	1	Truman
82nd Congress, 1951–1953	49	47	–	234	199	1	Truman
83rd Congress, 1953–1955	47	48	1	211	221	–	Eisenhower
84th Congress, 1955–1957	48	47	1	232	203	–	Eisenhower
85th Congress, 1957–1959	49	47	–	233	200	–	Eisenhower
86th Congress, 1959–1961	65	35	–	284	153	–	Eisenhower
87th Congress, 1961–1963	65	35	–	263	174	–	Kennedy
88th Congress, 1963–1965	67	33	–	258	177	–	Kennedy Johnson
89th Congress, 1965–1967	68	32	–	295	140	–	Johnson
90th Congress, 1967–1969	64	36	–	247	187	–	Johnson

	SENATE			HOUSE			
	DEM.	REP.	OTHER	DEM.	REP.	OTHER	PRESIDENT
91st Congress, 1969–1971	57	43	–	243	192	–	Nixon
92nd Congress, 1971–1973	54	44	2	254	180	–	Nixon
93rd Congress, 1973–1975	56	42	2	239	192	1	Nixon
							Ford
94th Congress, 1975–1977	60	37	2	291	144	–	Ford
95th Congress, 1977–1979	61	38	1	292	143	–	Carter
96th Congress, 1979–1981	58	41	1	276	157	–	Carter
97th Congress, 1981–1983	46	53	1	243	192	–	Reagan
98th Congress, 1983–1985	45	55	–	267	168	–	Reagan
99th Congress, 1985–1987	47	53	–	252	183	–	Reagan
100th Congress, 1987–1989	54	46	–	257	178	–	Reagan
101st Congress, 1989–1991	55	45	–	262	173	–	G. H. W. Bush
102nd Congress, 1991–1993	56	44	–	276	167	–	G. H. W. Bush
103rd Congress, 1993–1995	57	43	–	258	176	1	Clinton
104th Congress, 1995–1997	47	53	–	204	230	1	Clinton
105th Congress, 1997–1999	45	55	–	207	227	1	Clinton
106th Congress, 1999–2001	45	55	–	211	223	1	Clinton
107th Congress, 2001–2003	50	50	–	212	221	2	G. W. Bush
108th Congress, 2003–2005	48	51	1	204	229	2	G. W. Bush
109th Congress, 2005–2006	44	55	1	202	232	1	G. W. Bush

Numbers indicate initial composition of the Congress. The outcomes of several House races were subject to change because of recounts or runoffs.
Sources: Department of Commerce, Bureau of the Census, *Statistical Abstract of the United States* (Washington, D.C.: U.S. Government Printing Office); and *Members of Congress Since 1789*, 2nd ed. (Washington, D.C.: Congressional Quarterly Press, 1981), 176–177; updated by the authors.

APPENDIX F

United States Supreme Court Justices, 1789–2006

JUSTICE	PRESIDENT	YEARS OF SERVICE
John Jay	Washington	1789–1795
John Rutledge	Washington	(1789–1791)*
William Cushing	Washington	1789–1810
James Wilson	Washington	1789–1798
John Blair Jr.	Washington	1789–1796
James Iredell	Washington	1790–1799
Thomas Johnson	Washington	1791–1793
William Paterson	Washington	1793–1806
John Rutledge	Washington	(1795)*
Samuel Chase	Washington	1796–1811
Oliver Elsworth	Washington	1796–1800
Bushrod Washington	J. Adams	1798–1829
Alfred Moore	J. Adams	1799–1804
John Marshall	J. Adams	1801–1835
William Johnson	Jefferson	1804–1834
Henry B. Livingston	Jefferson	1806–1823
Thomas Todd	Jefferson	1807–1826
Gabriel Duval	Madison	1811–1835
Joseph Story	Madison	1811–1845
Smith Thompson	Monroe	1823–1843
Robert Trimble	J. Q. Adams	1826–1828
John McLean	Jackson	1829–1861
Henry Baldwin	Jackson	1830–1844
James M. Wayne	Jackson	1835–1867
Roger B. Taney	Jackson	1836–1864
Philip P. Barbour	Jackson	1836–1841
John Catron	Jackson	1837–1865
John McKinley	Van Buren	1837–1852
Peter V. Daniel	Van Buren	1841–1860
Samuel Nelson	Tyler	1845–1872
Levi Woodbury	Polk	1846–1851
Robert C. Grier	Polk	1846–1870
Benjamin R. Curtis	Fillmore	1851–1857
John A. Campbell	Pierce	1853–1861
Nathan Clifford	Buchanan	1858–1881
Noah H. Swayne	Lincoln	1862–1881
Samuel F. Miller	Lincoln	1862–1890
David Davis	Lincoln	1862–1877
Stephen J. Field	Lincoln	1863–1897

JUSTICE	PRESIDENT	YEARS OF SERVICE
Salmon P. Chase	Lincoln	1864–1873
William Strong	Grant	1870–1880
Joseph P. Bradley	Grant	1870–1892
Ward Hunt	Grant	1872–1882
Morrison R. Waite	Grant	1874–1888
John M. Harlan	Hayes	1877–1911
William B. Woods	Hayes	1880–1887
Stanley Matthews	Garfield	1881–1889
Horace Gray	Arthur	1881–1902
Samuel Blatchford	Arthur	1882–1893
Lucius Q.C. Lamar	Cleveland	1888–1893
Melville W. Fuller	Cleveland	1888–1910
David J. Brewer	Harrison	1889–1910
Henry B. Brown	Harrison	1890–1906
George Shiras Jr.	Harrison	1892–1903
Howell E. Jackson	Harrison	1893–1895
Edward D. White	Cleveland	1894–1910
Rufus W. Peckham	Cleveland	1895–1909
Joseph McKenna	McKinley	1898–1925
Oliver W. Holmes Jr.	T. Roosevelt	1902–1932
William R. Day	T. Roosevelt	1903–1922
William H. Moody	T. Roosevelt	1906–1910
Horace H. Lurton	Taft	1909–1914
Charles E. Hughes	Taft	1910–1916
Edward D. White	Taft	1910–1921
Willis Van Devanter	Taft	1910–1937
Joseph R. Lamar	Taft	1910–1916
Mahlon Pitney	Taft	1912–1922
James C. McReynolds	Wilson	1914–1941
Louis D. Brandeis	Wilson	1916–1939
John H. Clarke	Wilson	1916–1922
William H. Taft	Harding	1921–1930
George Sutherland	Harding	1922–1938
Pierce Butler	Harding	1922–1939
Edward T. Sanford	Harding	1923–1930
Harlan F. Stone	Coolidge	1925–1941
Charles E. Hughes	Hoover	1930–1941
Owen J. Roberts	Hoover	1930–1945
Benjamin N. Cardozo	Hoover	1932–1938
Hugo Black	F. Roosevelt	1937–1971
Stanley F. Reed	F. Roosevelt	1938–1957

JUSTICE	PRESIDENT	YEARS OF SERVICE
Felix Frankfurter	F. Roosevelt	1939–1962
William O. Douglas	F. Roosevelt	1939–1975
Frank Murphy	F. Roosevelt	1940–1949
James F. Byrnes	F. Roosevelt	1941–1942
Harlan F. Stone	F. Roosevelt	1941–1946
Robert H. Jackson	F. Roosevelt	1941–1954
Wiley B. Rutledge	F. Roosevelt	1943–1949
Harold H. Burton	Truman	1945–1958
Fred M. Vinson	Truman	1946–1953
Tom C. Clark	Truman	1949–1967
Sherman Minton	Truman	1949–1956
Earl Warren	Eisenhower	1953–1969
John M. Harlan	Eisenhower	1955–1971
William J. Brennan Jr.	Eisenhower	1956–1990
Charles E. Whittaker	Eisenhower	1957–1962
Potter Stewart	Eisenhower	1958–1981
Byron R. White	Kennedy	1962–1993
Arthur J. Goldberg	Kennedy	1962–1965
Abe Fortas	Johnson	1965–1969
Thurgood Marshall	Johnson	1967–1991
Warren E. Burger	Nixon	1969–1986
Harry A. Blackmun	Nixon	1970–1994
Lewis F. Powell Jr.	Nixon	1972–1988
William H. Rehnquist	Nixon	1972–1986
John Paul Stevens	Ford	1975 –
Sandra Day O'Connor	Reagan	1981–2005
William H. Rehnquist	Reagan	1986–2005
Antonin Scalia	Reagan	1986 –
Anthony M. Kennedy	Reagan	1988 –
David H. Souter	G. H. W. Bush	1990 –
Clarence Thomas	G. H. W. Bush	1991 –
Ruth Bader Ginsburg	Clinton	1993 –
Stephen Breyer	Clinton	1994 –
John G. Roberts	G. W. Bush	2005 –
Samuel A. Alito Jr.	G. W. Bush	2006 –

Bold type indicates chief justice.

* Rutledge resigned after his confirmation to become chief justice of South Carolina; in 1795 he served during a Court recess.

GLOSSARY

accommodationist or preferentialist approach The government may aid or extend benefits to religious groups for their nonreligious activities that benefit the community. President George W. Bush's faith-based initiative is based on such an approach.

administrative law judge A quasi-independent employee of a federal agency who supervises hearings at which disputes between the agency and a regulated party are resolved.

administrative oversight The review and control by congressional committees of the work conducted by the executive branch of the federal government.

affirmative action A program instituted to correct past discriminatory practices aimed at people identified as part of certain racial, ethnic, and gender-based groups. It provides hiring and promotion opportunities for members of these groups.

agencies Units of the federal government with responsibility for a set of functions generally narrower than those of departments. Some agencies are independent; others exist within departments.

agents of political socialization Factors that affect political socialization: family, school, peers, mass media, religion, party, and social groups.

Aid to Families with Dependent Children (AFDC) A federal social-welfare program that made monthly payments to any family with children and an income below a certain level. This program was ended by Congress in 1996.

ambassador The highest ranking representative to a foreign government. The majority of U.S. ambassadors are senior career foreign service officers.

amicus curiae brief A "friend of the court" legal argument, submitted in written form by a group or individual who has an interest in the outcome of a case but is not formally a party to the proceedings.

amnesty A general pardon given to a class of people; Jimmy Carter granted amnesty to Americans who had dodged the draft to avoid military service in the Vietnam War.

appellate jurisdiction The authority of courts to review decisions of lower courts and administrative agencies. Under Article III of the U.S. Constitution, Congress has the power to provide for the appellate jurisdiction of the Supreme Court and courts of appeals.

Articles of Confederation The first constitution of the United States, approved by the Second Continental Congress in 1777 but not ratified by all thirteen former colonies until 1781. It provided for a unicameral legislature, the Continental Congress, which had limited powers.

astroturfing A public relations campaign designed to give the impression of broad grass-roots support for a particular issue or candidate.

attentive public People who have a general knowledge; they tend to be more interested and involved than the general public.

authoritarian personality A personality type that requires a structured environment with clear rules of behavior; a person prone to doctrinaire views.

authoritative decisions Decisions made by public officials that have the force of law.

balance of trade The difference between a country's imports and exports. A country that imports more than it exports has a negative balance of trade.

bicameral legislature A legislature composed of two houses, such as the U.S. Congress.

bilateral relations The direct relations between two countries, involving diplomacy, trade, foreign aid, and military interaction.

bill A proposal, drafted in the form of a law, that a member of Congress would like to become public policy.

bill of information A document that specifies the charges and evidence against a criminal defendant; in some cases, such a document may be obtained by state prosecutors from a judge rather than a jury.

Bill of Rights The first ten amendments to the U.S. Constitution, which guarantee specific civil rights and liberties. Introduced in the First Congress, the amendments were ratified by the states in 1791.

block grants Grants-in-aid that state and local governments can spend as they wish within specified broad policy areas, such as housing, transportation, or job training.

briefs Written legal arguments filed by each side in cases or controversies before a court.

broad reading An approach to interpreting the U.S. Constitution that allows its general principles to be widely applied to different cases in light of changing circumstances.

bureaucracy An organization of activity based on hierarchies of authority and fixed routines. Bureaucracies have jurisdictions established by law or administrative rules. Their employees are specialists, and they maintain written records of their decisions and activities. Bureaucracies are created to achieve objectivity, precision, efficiency, continuity, consistency, and fairness.

bureaucrat A government employee who works in one of the agencies or offices of the executive branch. Many bureaucrats in the federal government are part of the civil service.

cabinet The principal advisory body for most presidents from Washington's administration to Eisenhower's; it consists of the heads of the executive departments, the vice president, and other invited executive officials.

candidate-oriented parties Parties organized to support a particular candidate and that candidate's major policy positions. The American Independent Party (George Wallace) and the Reform Party (H. Ross Perot) are examples.

capture The tendency of federal agencies to develop symbiotic relationships with the special interests that they oversee and thus to become protectors rather than regulators of those interests. This has been a special problem with regulatory commissions.

casework The individual problems that constituents bring to the attention of a member of Congress for assistance or solution.

categorical grants Grants-in-aid that can be used only for narrowly defined purposes, such as education for homeless children or prevention of drug abuse.

caucuses Meetings at the local level in which partisans conduct party business, including voting for candidates for president (or delegates pledged to them).

change of venue The practice of moving a trial from the area in which the crime was committed to another area in order to increase the chances for obtaining a fair trial and unbiased jury.

checks and balances An internal system of constraints on the exercise of power designed to prevent any one unit of government from becoming dominant.

citizen ballot initiatives Policy questions or constitutional amendments initiated by citizens, put on the ballot through a petition process, and voted on by the general electorate.

citizenship The responsibilities that people have by virtue of their birth or naturalization in a particular country.

civil service The career employees of federal departments and major agencies whose salaries and fringe benefits are determined by Congress and implemented by the Office of Personnel Management.

civil service system The system for filling most federal government jobs that was established by the 1883 Pendleton Act, whereby jobs must be open to any citizen and merit must be the basis for choosing employees.

clear and present danger doctrine A doctrine used by the Supreme Court to determine the bounds of speech protected by the First Amendment; it asserts that unless the speech presents "a clear and present danger" it is usually protected by the Constitution.

clemency The ability of the president to reduce or terminate the prison sentence imposed on a person convicted of committing a federal crime.

closed-ended questions Questions or responses selected from a list of items.

cloture The limitation of debate on a measure before the Senate. It takes a vote by three-fifths of the entire Senate (sixty senators) to invoke cloture and thereby end a filibuster.

coattails The political influence that a leading candidate (usually for the presidency) exerts to help others on that candidate's ticket get elected.

coercive federalism Term some apply to the period after the 1960s when the national government began forcing state and local government to conform with nationally set goals and objectives.

Cold War A term used to describe the hostile relationship between the United States and the Soviet Union in the decades that followed World War II.

commercial speech Advertising that is truthful and not deceptive may fall under the protections of the First Amendment.

common good That which benefits society as a whole.

community The collectivity of people living within a specified area; people who share a common history and culture.

concurrent powers Powers shared by both the national government and the state governments, such as the power to tax.

concurring opinion A document submitted by one or more justices or judges of a court that agrees with the decision reached in a case but not with all of the reasoning or explanations offered in the institutional opinion. It explains how the same result would have been reached by different reasoning.

confirmation hearing A hearing held by a legislative body before approving the appointment of a government official. Under the U.S. Constitution, the president nominates federal judges and other high officials in the executive branch, but they must be confirmed by the Senate.

conflict A disagreement over values, norms, and goals; results from struggle to pursue one's interests.

connected PACs Groups, active within the electoral arena, whose membership is connected by employment in a company, industry, or labor union.

consensus An agreement on values, norms, and goals; developed on the basis of shared background and experience.

conservatism An ideology that places the greatest value on economic freedom and social order; conservatives favor the use of government to maintain law and order, protect national security, and preserve and protect property.

constant campaign The ongoing public relations effort by the president and other elected officials to appeal directly to the people within their constituencies.

constituency The residents of the state or district that elects an individual member of Congress.

constitutional courts The U.S. Supreme Court and other federal courts created under Article III of the U.S. Constitution, which gives Congress the power to establish "inferior courts" below the Supreme Court. Federal district courts and courts of appeals are constitutional courts and have general jurisdiction over virtually all matters of federal law.

consulates Offices representing the interests of a country in another country. In countries with which America has full diplomatic relations, consulates are located in cities other than the capital.

containment The policy developed after World War II to prevent the spread of communism through the use of strong alliances, foreign aid, nuclear deterrence, and military assistance. Containment was the centerpiece of American foreign policy in the years from 1946 until the end of the cold war.

cooperative federalism A view of federalism held between the mid-1930s and the 1960s that stressed a partnership and sharing of government functions between the states and the national government.

courts of appeals The courts within the federal judicial system that hear appeals of decisions of lower courts, state courts, or administrative agencies. There are thirteen courts of appeals.

crosscutting requirements Conditions imposed on almost all grants-in-aid to further various social and economic objectives, such as nondiscrimination or environmental protection.

crossover sanctions Conditions imposed on grants-in-aid in one program area that are designed to influence state and local government policy in another area.

de facto segregation Segregation that exists as a consequence of living patterns, not because of law or official government policies.

de jure segregation Segregation that exists because of law or official government policies. The Supreme Court has declared that the Fourteenth Amendment to the Constitution forbids this type of segregation.

democracy A system of government in which the people rule directly or indirectly.

Democratic-Republicans (Republicans) The party, led by Thomas Jefferson, that was agrarian based; it became the first opposition party in the United States.

Democrats The faction of the Democratic-Republican Party led by Andrew Jackson that represented various economically disadvantaged groups and sought policies that would benefit these groups.

departments The major operating units of the federal government. Department secretaries are members of the president's cabinet.

deregulation An effort begun in the late 1960s to reform the federal regulatory process by reducing or eliminating regulations that seemed to stifle competition.

determinate sentencing The practice of specifying a mandatory length of imprisonment for an offense; it does not allow the sentencing judge to exercise discretion in determining the sentence.

devolution federalism A possible contemporary trend, beginning with the 1994 Republican congressional victories, in which many federal government responsibilities may be returned to state and local governments.

diplomacy The conduct of relations among nations, depending heavily on mutual communication conducted by professional diplomats.

direct democracy A system in which the people as a collectivity decide on public policy; examples include town meetings and ballot initiatives.

direct orders Legal measures adopted by the national government, and enforced by civil or criminal penalties, that require certain actions by state and local governments.

direction of public opinion The largest proportion of the population that holds a particular view.

dissenting opinion A document submitted by one or more justices or judges of a court that disagrees with the majority's reasoning and decision in a case.

distributive policies Policies that distribute goods and services to citizens (for example, Social Security).

district courts The trial courts of the federal judicial system. There are ninety-four federal district courts, at least one in each state.

docket The list of filings or cases that come before a court. The U.S. Supreme Court, for example, has an annual docket of more than 8,000 cases.

doctrine of nullification Doctrine of the claim, associated most closely with South Carolina Senator John C. Calhoun, that states could declare acts of Congress null and void within their borders.

double jeopardy The legal principle that a person cannot be tried twice for the same offense.

dual federalism A view of federalism held between the time of the Civil War and the mid-1930s that attempted to recognize and maintain separate spheres of authority for the national government and state governments.

economic liberty The freedom to purpose one's financial self-interests.

economic regulation Government regulation of particular industries to correct what economists call market failures, such as natural monopolies.

Electoral College The body that chooses the president and vice president. It consists of 538 electors chosen by states, and equal in number to the state's congressional representation.

electors Individuals nominated by their party and elected by the voters in states to cast the official votes for president and vice president.

embassy The primary office representing a country's interests in another country. It is usually located in the capital city of the foreign country and headed by a chief of mission called an ambassador.

en banc As a panel; with all judges participating. Cases in federal courts of appeals are usually heard and decided by three-judge panels, but in especially important cases the entire court will sit en banc.

enrolled bill process An internal review process in which the Office of Management and Budget solicits department and agency advice on whether the president should approve or disapprove legislation enacted by Congress.

equal protection of the laws The principle that all people are equal under law and must be protected equally by the law.

equality of opportunity The principle that all people should have an equal chance to pursue their goals and interests and to achieve them in the political, economic, and social systems.

equality of result Relates to the consequences of economic, social, or political activities—the results should be equal. The principle has limited applicability in a free enterprise, capitalistic system.

espionage The use of spying techniques to collect intelligence information.

establishment clause The separation of church and state; government may not establish religion, including prayer or other religious activities in public schools; it may, however, provide funds to religious organizations for nonreligious purposes.

executive agreement An agreement between the heads of two countries that establishes policy between them; it may not require Senate concurrence or action by the House of Representatives.

Executive Office of the President (EOP) Established in 1939, this is the formal structure of the presidency; it consists of ten offices, two residences, and several presidential councils and task forces.

executive orders Directives by the president to his subordinates on how they should be organized or function, or on the policy they should implement and the way they should do it. Executive orders have the force of law so long as they do not conflict with existing statutes or the Constitution.

expressed powers Powers enumerated in a constitution. Article I, Section 8, of the U.S. Constitution, for example, enumerates seventeen specific powers of Congress, including the powers to tax, coin money, regulate commerce, and provide for the national defense.

fast-track authority Legislation that authorizes the president to negotiate treaties on behalf of the United States, subject to an up-or-down vote of Congress.

federal questions Issues concerning the interpretation and application of federal as opposed to state law.

Federal Register A daily publication of the federal government that communicates the activities and the proposed and actual decisions of federal agencies to the American people.

federalism A system of government in which powers are shared between central or national government and state or regional governments. The U.S. Constitution establishes a federal system.

Federalists The party that supported the economic and foreign polities of the George Washington and John Adams administrations.

feeding frenzy The tendency of journalists to focus on the same person, issue, or event—particularly one that has broad public appeal, such as unethical behavior, criminal activity, or a sexual dimension.

filibuster A technique for preventing a vote in the Senate in which senators gain recognition to speak in debate and then do not relinquish the floor. A filibuster can be ended only by a vote of cloture, which requires the support of 60 senators.

financial controls The most important and effective of Congress's techniques for overseeing the work of the executive branch. Before it appropriates funds to an agency or a program, Congress assesses the manner in which previous appropriations have been used and examines the stated plans for use of the funds being requested.

food stamps Government-issued coupons that can be used to purchase food.

formula grants Grants-in-aid distributed on the basis of a formula applied to all eligible recipients.

fragmented power Divided and decentralized authority. The fragmentation of power in the United States gives interest groups and individuals numerous opportunities to block or alter policy changes.

franking privilege The right of members of Congress to mail newsletters and questionnaires free of charge to every mailbox in their state or district.

free enterprise system A competitive economic system in which people are encouraged to pursue material self-interests and the market determines their success or failure.

free exercise clause Individuals have the right to worship as they please; the government, however, may prevent people from engaging in those religious practices that are harmful to society.

freedom of association The right of individuals to organize and join groups; it also includes the right of groups to establish the criteria for membership.

front-loading The concentration of presidential primaries and caucuses at the beginning of the nomination process, normally in January, February, and early to mid-March of the election year.

general public Everyone in the society, both citizens and noncitizens. This tends to be the largest, least informed, and most apathetic population group.

general revenue sharing A federal program existing between 1972 and 1986 in which grants-in-aid were distributed to state and local governments with few strings attached.

general ticket system A method of voting that elects the entire slate (of electors) through the popular vote (for president).

gerrymandering The drawing of legislative district boundaries to achieve partisan advantage. Named for Elbridge Gerry, a governor of Massachusetts after the Constitution was ratified.

going public The process by which presidents make a public appeal to build support for themselves, their administration, or their policies.

government The formal institutions that have the authority to make, implement, and adjudicate public policy.

government corporations Economic enterprises owned wholly or partly by the federal government; examples are the Tennessee Valley Authority and the Federal Deposit Insurance Corporation.

grand jury A group of twelve to twenty-three people who decide whether the evidence presented is sufficient for an indictment.

Grand Old Party (GOP) Another name, coined during the last decades of the nineteenth century, for the Republican Party.

grant of immunity Protection given to people who have information that the government desires; in exchange for providing such information, the government agrees that none of it can be subsequently used in a criminal trial against the person who provided that information.

grants-in-aid Programs through which the national government shares its fiscal resources with state and local governments.

grantsmanship Efforts by state and local governments to maximize the federal aid they receive.

gravity of evil doctrine A doctrine to determine the bounds of protected speech; the doctrine asserts that speech is protected so long as the gravity of evil discounted by its improbability of occurrence is not at such a level as to threaten people individually or collectively and thereby justify constraints placed on that speech.

Green Party A party oriented toward a cleaner and safer environment; organizes on the local and national levels but has only received a small proportion of the national vote.

ideological parties Political parties whose members subscribe to a common belief system, such as socialism or communism.

impeachment The power of Congress to remove from office any civil officer of the United States who has committed "Treason, Bribery, and other High Crimes and Misdemeanors." The impeachment process begins with the introduction of a bill of impeachment in the House of Representatives; the trial takes place in the Senate. Conviction requires the votes of two-thirds of the senators present and voting.

implied powers Government powers inferred from the powers expressly enumerated in a written constitution. The "necessary and proper" clause of Article I, Section 8, of the U.S. Constitution has been interpreted to give Congress broad implied powers.

incrementalism Policymaking in the United States that results in only minor or marginal changes.

independent A voter who does not formally think of him or herself as a party partisan; the number of people who claim to be independent grew in the 1970s and early 1980s.

independent regulatory commissions Units of the federal government whose principal purpose is to regulate commerce and trade in an assigned area of jurisdiction. Commissions are independent of any department and, to some extent, of presidential control. All are run by a group of commissioners rather than a single executive.

independent state grounds A state constitution or state law used as the basis for a decision by a state court instead of federal law or federal courts' interpretation of the U.S. Constitution and Bill of Rights.

indictment A formal statement of charges brought against a criminal defendant by a prosecuting attorney.

informed judgment A decision made on the basis of knowledge of the choices and their consequences.

inherent powers Powers possessed by a national government that are not enumerated in a constitution. In the conduct of foreign affairs, presidents have often claimed that they possess inherent powers.

injunction A prohibitory court order that prevents some action from occurring.

institutional opinion An official explanation or justification of a decision by a court with multiple judges or justices.

intensity of public opinion The depth of feelings on an issue; the greater the intensity, the more likely a person will become politically involved.

intergovernmental lobby The group of state and local government organizations, such as the National League of Cities and the National Governors' Association, that lobbies the national government for legislation and decisions favorable to state and local governments.

international organizations Organizations like the United Nations and the Organization of American States in which countries come together to seek peaceful resolution of their disagreements and to work jointly in pursuit of mutual goals.

iron triangles or subgovernments Close, mutually supportive relationships that often develop in a particular policy area among executive agencies, special interest groups, and congressional subcommittees.

isolationism A characteristic of American foreign policy for much of the period before World War II. Many Americans believed that the United States should not be directly engaged in the affairs or the wars of European or other foreign countries.

issue advocacy Groups that advocate their own policy positions and support candidates with similar stands on their issues.

issue network An interconnected group of specialists in a particular subject area working in bureaucratic agencies at all levels of government, along with experts employed by legislative committee staffs, interest groups, think tanks, and universities.

issue parties Political parties whose members subscribe to a similar position on an issue that is important to them.

Jim Crow laws Laws enacted in many southern states after the Civil War to separate the races in public transportation, hotels, restaurants, and other places of public accommodation.

Joint Chiefs of Staff Military advisers to the president composed of the highest ranking officers of each of the armed services.

joint committees Committees composed of members of both houses of Congress. They do not have authority to initiate legislation.

joint conference committees Temporary joint committees whose principal function is to resolve the differences between forms of the same bill passed by the House and the Senate.

judicial activism The use of judicial review to invalidate a federal, state, or local law or other official action by government.

judicial federalism The dual judicial system in the United States, consisting of a system of federal courts and separate judicial systems in each of the fifty states.

judicial review Power and authority of a court to determine whether acts of a legislature or an executive violate a constitution. The U.S. Supreme Court has the power to strike down any congressional or state legislation, as well as any other official government action, that it deems to violate the U.S. Constitution.

judicial self-restraint Deference by courts to the decisions of other branches of government.

jurisdiction The authority of a court to decide particular cases. The jurisdiction of federal courts is provided for in Article III of the U.S. Constitution and by Congress in statutes.

justiciable disputes Disagreements or conflicts appropriate for resolution by a court.

lame duck period The last years of a presidency when the president is not eligible for reelection; political power usually decreases during this period.

Large State–Small State Compromise A compromise reached at the Constitutional Convention calling for a bicameral legislature in which representation in the House of Representatives would be based on population and representation in the Senate would be equal for every state.

leadership PAC A political action committee formed by a candidate or elected official; funds raised by the PAC are used to pay the costs of precampaign activities, give money to other candidates, and pursue a policy agenda.

legislation The making of laws, one of the major functions of Congress.

legislative clearance process An internal review process in which the Office of Management and Budget ensures that executive departments and agencies' positions, testimony, and legislative requests are in accordance with or at least do not conflict with the president's program.

legislative courts The courts created by Congress under Article I of the U.S. Constitution and having jurisdiction or authority over particular areas of law. The U.S. Court of Military Appeals, which applies military law, is one such court.

legislative referenda Policy questions or constitutional amendments put on the ballot by state legislatures for the approval or disapproval of the voters.

level of confidence The amount of certainty placed in the findings of a survey (within the range of sampling error).

libel A false statement about a person or defamation of a person's character by print or visual portrayal; for a "public" person, libel must be accompanied by evidence of actual malice to recover damages.

liberalism An ideology that places the greatest value on political freedom and social and economic equality; liberals tend to favor the use of government to redistribute resources from the wealthy to the poor and to provide a minimum standard of living for everyone.

limited government The idea that government powers are limited and specified or are traceable to enumerated powers in a written constitution.

literacy tests Tests formerly conducted by states, theoretically to determine whether a person had sufficient knowledge to make an informed voting decision but actually used to discriminate against poor, uneducated white and African American citizens. Today such tests are essentially banned by the Voting Rights Act of 1965 and its amendments.

lobby The practice of influencing public officials in their formulation and execution of public policy.

majority rule A principle based on the proposition that everyone is equal, all votes should be equal, and decisions should be made on the basis of the judgment of more than half of those involved.

mark-up session A meeting at which all members of a congressional subcommittee or committee participate in revising a bill to put it into a form acceptable to a majority of them.

Marshall Plan A policy introduced after World War II to provide financial aid to European countries that had been devastated by the war. Named after Secretary of State George C. Marshall, it became the precursor to decades of American foreign assistance.

meaningful choice An electoral decision in which voters have the ability to select from among alternative candidates, parties, and sometimes policy positions, generally within the political mainstream.

Medicaid A federal program established in 1965 to help people with low incomes pay for hospital, doctor, and other medical bills.

Medicare The federal health insurance program for people sixty-five and older, created in 1965 and restructured in 2003.

minimum scrutiny test The lowest standard that the Supreme Court uses to determine the constitutionality of state laws. According to this standard, laws must have a rational purpose to be valid.

Miranda warnings The warnings that police are usually required to give those whom they arrest on suspicion of having performed a crime; the warnings contain a list of the rights people have, including to remain silent and to have an attorney present during police interrogations.

multimember district A legislative district in which several people are elected, usually on the basis of the total proportion of the vote they or their party receive; more amenable to electing minority and third-party representation than a single-member district.

mutual assured destruction (MAD) A policy of nuclear deterrence in which America sought to convince its adversaries in the cold war that any nuclear attack on the United States would result in the assured destruction of the attacker.

National Security Council (NSC) The principal advisory body to the president on national security issues. It was created in 1947 and is composed of the president, vice president, and secretaries of state and defense.

nationalization of the Bill of Rights The interpretation of the Supreme Court over time that expanded the guarantees of the Bill of Rights to apply to states.

nation-centered federalism A view of federalism held in the pre–Civil War era that advocated an active and expanded role for the national government.

new federalism The view of federalism associated with Presidents Nixon and Reagan, which stressed greater flexibility in the use of grants-in-aid by the recipients and, in the Reagan years, reductions in the total amount of grants.

New Jersey Plan One of the main proposals for the overall structure of government presented at the Constitutional Convention in 1787, favored by the small states, it called for a unicameral legislature in which all states would be represented equally, a multimember executive with no power to veto legislation, and a supreme court.

news spin The interpretation that people in the news, including reporters and commentators, give to a speech, decision, action, or event.

newsworthy Items that are most likely to capture and hold public attention; items that are new, unexpected, surprising, or conflict oriented or that generate human interest.

nonconnected PACs Groups, active within the electoral process, that are not connected by employment or union membership.

North–South Compromise A compromise on slavery reached at the Constitutional Convention by which, for purposes of representation, slaves would be counted as "three-fifths of all other Persons."

obscenity Words or visual depictions that appeal to prurient interests, describe or show sexual behavior in an offensive way, and lack social value; obscene materials are not protected by the First Amendment to the Constitution.

Office of Management and Budget (OMB) An office in the Executive Office of the President charged with overseeing and improving the management and operation of the government; it coordinates the executive branch's budget, legislative, and regulatory review activities on behalf of the president.

open-ended questions Questions that have no predetermined answers; respondents can say whatever comes into their minds.

opinion (1) A judgment made about current issues, including feelings people have, positions they take, and conclusions they reach. (2) The written explanation or justification of a court's or an individual judge's decision.

opinion makers A small group of people in and out of government that inform and shape the views of others.

original jurisdiction The authority of a court to have a case originate in it. Article III of the U.S. Constitution specifies the "cases or controversies" over which the Supreme Court has original jurisdiction.

oversight hearings Regular in-depth reviews by congressional committees of the activities of executive agencies or the management of specific programs.

partial preemption The national government's establishment of minimum standards in a policy area and its requiring state and local governments to meet those standards or lose their authority in that area.

partisan identification The allegiances that people have toward political parties; these allegiances affect campaign participation and voting behavior.

partisans People who identify their political allegiances with a political party.

party bosses The elected political leaders of party organizations who hold considerable influence over their partisans within the locality in which their organization dominates.

party machines Tightly organized local parties that exercise control over nominations, job distribution, and other social benefits in certain counties or cities.

party platform A statement of the issue positions of the national party ratified by delegates at the party's national nominating convention.

patronage The distribution of government jobs as a reward for working on a winning candidate's campaign or providing other services to a party or political machine.

personal liberty The freedom to pursue one's values and interests; doing what one wants when one wants to.

personnel controls Congressional control over presidential appointments and over the number, qualifications, salaries, and employment conditions of all federal employees.

petit jury A jury usually consisting of twelve people selected from members of the community to sit in judgment during a trial.

plea bargaining The practice of allowing a person charged with a crime to plea guilty to a lesser offense; it is used when law enforcement officials need information or do not want to go through the process of a long and expensive trial.

plurality rule A decision made on the basis of the group that has the greatest number of people but not necessarily more than half of those participating.

pocket veto A presidential veto of a bill that occurs when a congressional session concludes within ten days of the bill's passage and without the president having signed it. Because Congress is not in session, the president does not return the bill, nor is there any possibility of a congressional override.

policy adoption The state of the policy process at which official courses of action are approved and adopted.

policy entrepreneurs Members of Congress who take a special interest in a substantive issue and seek to influence the shape of public policy on that issue.

policy evaluation The stage of the policy process at which adopted and implemented policies are evaluated for effectiveness.

policy formulation The process by which public policy is made.

policy implementation The process by which public policies are executed.

policy termination The process by which public policies are ended.

political action committees (PACs) Groups of employees, stockholders, and others associated on the basis of common beliefs or interests groups involved in election activity; they raise money and promote specific candidates and issue positions.

political belief system or ideology A set of beliefs that relate to one another and shape judgments about political issues.

political efficacy The perception that individuals can make a difference, that they can affect what government does and when and how it does it.

political elite A relatively small group interested, informed, and involved in politics; people who tend to exercise the greatest influence on government and its decisions.

political equality A principle based on the belief that everyone in society is of equal worth, should have equal voting power, and is equal under law.

political interest groups Organized groups of people with shared interests and goals who seek to influence public policy.

political parties Public organizations whose goals are to nominate and elect candidates for office, organize government, and affect public policy.

political questions Issues that judges decide would be more appropriately resolved by other branches of government.

political socialization The process by which people acquire the values, beliefs, and opinions that affect their involvement in the political system.

political tolerance A general acceptance of people with different lifestyles, beliefs, and opinions on public policy issues.

politically correct That which accords with the dominant view at the time; it pertains to words and actions.

politician A person who views the struggle for power within the political system as a profession or calling; one who seeks elective office.

politics A struggle by individuals and groups to achieve certain ends; "who gets what, when, and how."

poll taxes Fees formerly charged to individuals to pay the cost of conducting elections in states. Such taxes are now banned in federal elections.

popular sovereignty The idea that government is based on the consent of the people and is accountable to the people for its actions.

pork-barrel legislation Legislation that contains public works and other projects that provide specific benefits for congressional constituencies.

preempt The national government removes of an area of authority from state and local governments.

preferred freedom A Supreme Court doctrine that asserts free speech has a higher priority than other constitutional protections; therefore, any law that restricts speech will be viewed more closely and critically than laws that restrict the exercise of other freedoms and rights.

presidential pardon The ability of the president to pardon people convicted of a federal crime.

primary An election in which partisans choose candidates to run for specific offices on their party's label in the general election.

primary groups Family or a group of people with whom a person lives and associates regularly; such groups shape personalities and help provide an orientation toward life.

principle of comity The principle by which the U.S. Supreme Court will not hear an appeal of a state court case if the case was decided on the basis of a state constitution or a state bill of rights.

private property The right to own land and other commodities of value.

problem recognition The initial stage of the policy process, at which issues are first recognized as problems requiring government action.

procedural due process Concerned with the processes by which law is implemented and enforced; the enforcement must be fair and equitable for everyone.

project grants Grants-in-aid for which potential recipients must apply to a federal agency; such grants are usually awarded on a competitive basis.

proportional voting A voting rule for the Democratic Party's presidential nomination in which candidates receive delegate support in proportion to the popular vote they receive in a primary; in several democratic European countries, a proportional voting system is used to select legislative delegates or representatives.

prospective voting A judgment made primarily on the basis of the promises candidates make about the priorities and policies they will pursue if elected. People tend to vote for the candidate whose views and positions are closest to their own.

public policy The decisions and actions of government that establish rules for collecting and distributing economic costs and benefits and permitting and prohibiting certain behaviors in society.

punctuated equilibrium Periods when in a short, rapid time frame major policy change takes place.

random sample A sample in which every element in the populations has an equal chance of being included. The probability of accuracy can be calculated on the basis of the number of people included.

reapportionment The reallocation of state seats in the House of Representatives on the basis of population shifts, as indicated in the latest census.

redistributive policies Policies that take benefits from some group and give them to others (for example, welfare).

redistricting The process of redrafting legislative district boundaries within states. All legislative districts within a state must be approximately equal in population.

Reform Party A party organized and funded by Texas billionaire H. Ross Perot. The Reform Party has run candidates for the presidency since 1992.

regulatory policies Policies that restrict or regulate certain types of behavior (for example, child labor laws).

regulatory review An internal review process in which the Office of Management and Budget reviews pending regulations of the departments and agencies to make sure that they are necessary, cost-effective, and consistent with the president's program.

representation The processes through which members of Congress seek to determine, articulate, and act on the interests of their constituents.

representative democracy A system of government in which citizens choose others to represent them in the formulation and execution of public policy.

republic A government whose powers are exercised by elected representatives directly or indirectly accountable to the people governed.

Republican Party One of the two major parties in the U.S. today. It was founded in 1854. Abraham Lincoln was the nation's first Republican president, elected in 1860.

reserved powers Powers that have not been delegated to a government body are reserved to the states and the people, respectively, by virtue of the The Tenth Amendment to the U.S. Constitution.

responsible party government A model for governing in which the major parties take dissimilar policy positions during the campaign. The party that wins the election is expected to pursue its campaign agenda when governing. Such a model enhances public accountability of the party in power.

restrictive covenants Contracts in which the sellers of private property agree not to sell that property to members of certain religious, racial, or ethnic groups. Restrictive covenants have been deemed unconstitutional and, therefore, invalid since 1948.

retrospective voting A judgment made primarily on the basis of the past performance of the parties and their elected officials.

reverse discrimination Refers to discrimination of the majority that occurs when minorities or others are given additional advantages or opportunities.

revolving-door politics The practice of moving from the public to private sector and vice versa; individuals tend to work in the areas of their expertise, using their contacts to affect government decision making.

riders Controversial provisions attached to a piece of legislation. Proposals that might have difficulty surviving on their own are thereby permitted to "ride through" the legislative process on the backs of other bills.

right to privacy A right that may be inferred from the protections enunciated in the First, Third, Fourth, and Fifth Amendments and applied to the states through the Fourteenth.

rolodex diplomacy A term used to describe the recent pattern of direct telephone communications between the president of the United States and foreign leaders.

rule of four The informal rule that for a case to be accepted for review by the U.S. Supreme Court at least four of the justices must vote to take it.

rules Edicts issued by a federal agency to implement laws.

salience Refers to public policy issues that are considered important.

sampling error The difference between the results of the sample and the whole population, usually represented by $\pm$ the number. The difference tends to decrease as the size of the sample increases.

secondary groups Organizations and associations to which people belong that often help shape and reinforce their views.

secular regulation rule A Supreme Court rule that requires all laws to have a reasonable secular purpose and not discriminate on the basis of religion.

selective benefits Economic, social, or political benefits that result from group membership.

selective perception The tendency of people to see what they are looking for; information that accords with their existing beliefs.

self-incrimination The principle of being innocent until proven guilty includes the right not to testify or provide incriminating evidence against one's self.

senatorial courtesy Consultation by the president with senators before making a formal nomination that requires Senate confirmation.

Senior Executive Service (SES) the highest-ranking group of federal civil service employees, created in 1979 to provide agencies with greater flexibility in deploying, compensating, and, if necessary, removing their senior managers and technical specialists.

seniority system The former system under which the member of the majority party with the longest consecutive service on each congressional committee would automatically become its chairperson for as long as he or she remained in Congress and on that committee.

separate but equal doctrine The Supreme Court doctrine that upheld Louisiana's law requiring separate but equal facilities for the races in railroad cars and other forms of public transportation. In actuality, however, most facilities were not equal.

separation of powers The division of power and authority within a government among three branches, typically the legislature, the executive, and the judiciary.

single-member district A legislative district in which one candidate is elected to represent the people who live within that district; benefits the candidate of the dominant party in that district.

slander A false statement or defamation of character by speech.

social redeeming value That which is deemed to have merit and benefit for society.

social regulation Government regulation of certain economic functions common to many or most industries to ensure that specific objectives are pursued.

Social Security The federal social insurance program that provides monthly payments to retired and disabled workers and to survivors of workers eligible for the benefits.

socioeconomic status (SES) The social and economic standing of people relative to others in the society.

soft money Campaign contributions not subject to federal limits of $2,000 per candidate per election and $5,000 per nonparty group. Political parties can no longer accept soft money contributions.

sound bite A small part of a speech, interview, or conversation used to highlight an aspect of the communication.

Speaker of the House The elected leader of the majority party in the House of Representatives, who serves as the presiding officer of the House.

special investigations Special examinations by Congress of executive branch or presidential activities.

speech-plus-conduct The communication of ideas by marching, picketing, and demonstrations is protected provided that the conduct is not disruptive of public or private property.

spoils system The distribution of federal jobs to supporters of the victorious presidential candidate. It was the primary way of staffing the federal bureaucracy before the creation of the civil service system.

stability of public opinion The constancy of opinion; how much it changes over time.

standard operating procedures (SOPs) Predetermined ways of responding to a particular problem or set of circumstances. SOPs simplify bureaucratic decisions and contribute to their consistency, but they also channel bureaucratic activity into rigid patterns and make agencies less adaptable to change.

standing to sue The right or legal status to initiate a lawsuit or judicial proceedings. To have standing to sue, parties must show that they are suffering or in danger of suffering an immediate and substantial personal injury.

State of the Union address An annual speech to Congress and the American people, usually given in January, in which the president cites the accomplishments of his administration and provides a legislative agenda for the year.

state-centered federalism A view of federalism held in the pre–Civil War era that opposed increasing national power at the expense of the states.

statement of administration policy A statement issued by the Office of Management and Budget that describes the president's position on all major bills that have passed committee and are to be considered on the floor by either house of Congress.

story line The framework within which the news is fit to help explain it within a larger context.

strict construction The idea that the U.S. Constitution can and should be interpreted in a narrowly literal sense, as it was written and understood by its framers.

strict rationality or exacting scrutiny test A middle standard for determining the constitutionality of laws that involve nonracial discrimination such as gender, age or wealth; the laws must further some legitimate government interest in a reasonable way to be constitutional.

strict scrutiny test A higher standard for determining the constitutionality of federal or state laws; the state must demonstrate a "compelling interest" in laws that limit or deny people rights or that discriminate on the basis of race, national origin, or religion.

substantive due process Subjects laws to a standard of reasonableness; it has been used to limit what government may do in certain areas, such as privacy.

summit meeting A meeting between the leaders of two or more countries at which matters of mutual interest are discussed and sometimes resolved.

sunshine laws Laws requiring important meetings and hearings of federal agencies to be open to the public.

superdelegates Elected and appointed party officials who automatically serve as delegates at their party's nominating convention.

supremacy clause A clause of Article VI of the U.S. Constitution, providing that the Constitution and other national laws are "the supreme law of the land." National laws thus supersede state or local laws when there is a conflict between them.

symbolic speech Expressions of beliefs, such as wearing arm bands to protest a war or turning an American flag into a peace symbol, are a form of protected speech.

territorial imperative The tendency of federal agencies to guard their area of jurisdiction against other agencies that seem to be trespassing on it.

terrorism The use of violence to disrupt the routines of international activity and to demoralize and frighten a country's population or regime. Acts of terrorism include: assassinations of political leaders, kidnappings of diplomats, and bombings of public buildings or transportation.

treaty A formal agreement between two or more countries. In the United States, treaties require the ratification, by a two-thirds majority, of the Senate.

tyranny of the majority A term used to suggest that a majority of people can be as tyrannical as a few or one. Fear of the tyranny of the majority is one reason James Madison and others preferred a republican form of government to a direct democracy.

unalienable rights In the social theory of John Locke, certain natural rights of individuals that are believed to precede the creation of government and that government may not deny. The Declaration of Independence proclaimed that individuals have the unalienable right to "Life, Liberty, and the Pursuit of Happiness."

unanimous consent A common device used for procedural efficiency in the Senate, in which action is taken without debate when all members consent to it.

unemployment insurance A federal program, created as part of the 1935 Social Security Act, that pays benefits to people who lose their jobs.

universal suffrage The principle that every adult citizen should have the right to vote.

unreasonable searches and seizures Searches and seizures by enforcement officials that are arbitrary, unreasonable, or too general; these are usually prevented by requiring the enforcement officials to obtain a search warrant from a judge.

urban empowerment zones Housing policy established during the Clinton administration by which urban areas are defined as those with substantial concentrations of poverty would benefit from tax incentives and regulatory relief.

urban renewal An approach to federal housing policy, established in 1949 and terminated in 1974, that was designed to clear blighted and deteriorating areas of inner cities and replace them with new commercial and residential establishments.

Virginia Plan One of the main proposals for the overall structure of government presented at the Constitutional Convention in 1787, favored by the large states, called for a strong central government, including a bicameral legislature with representation of states based on their population, a chief executive chosen by the legislature, and a powerful judiciary.

War Powers Resolution Enacted in 1973 over President Richard Nixon's veto, the War Powers Resolution requires the president to inform and consult with Congress before putting American military forces in a hostile situation. Theoretically, Congress can prevent such action by not approving a resolution authorizing the president to use force; in practice, however, Congress has been unwilling and unable to exercise this power.

wards or precincts The smallest unit within the state in which elections occur.

Whigs A political party that opposed Jackson. The Whigs were composed of more prosperous farmers in the South and West, commercials interests in the East, and anti-slavery advocates.

whips Members of each party's leadership structure in the House and the Senate who work closely with rank-and-file members to determine party positions and form legislative coalitions.

whistleblower A person who alerts the public, usually through the news media, to improper or unethical decisions or actions occurring within an organization, frequently the national government.

White House Office The president's top staff aides and their assistants; there are approximately 400 full-time employees on the White House budget.

winner-take-all system A voting rule in which the candidate with the most popular votes wins all of the state's convention delegates or, in the case of the electoral college, all of the electoral votes. Such a system is permitted by the Republicans but not by the Democrats during the party primary.

writ of certiorari A formal order issued by the U.S. Supreme Court to a lower federal court or state court requesting the record of the decision in a case that the Supreme Court has accepted for review. Four of the Court's nine justices must agree to grant a writ of certiorari in order for a case to be reviewed.

yellow journalism News stories that emphasize the sensational or feature aggressive reporting and undercover investigations by the press.

INDEX

C

F

Q

R